From the libraey of
R C Couture

A COMPENDIUM

OF

CHRISTIAN THEOLOGY.

A

COMPENDIUM

OF

CHRISTIAN THEOLOGY:

BEING

ANALYTICAL OUTLINES OF A COURSE OF THEOLOGICAL STUDY,

BIBLICAL, DOGMATIC, HISTORICAL.

BY

WILLIAM BURT POPE, D.D.,

THEOLOGICAL TUTOR, DIDSBURY COLLEGE, MANCHESTER.

VOL. III.

SECOND EDITION, REVISED AND ENLARGED.

LONDON:
PUBLISHED FOR THE AUTHOR AT THE
WESLEYAN CONFERENCE OFFICE,
2, CASTLE STREET, CITY ROAD.
SOLD AT 66, PATERNOSTER ROW.
1879.

LONDON:

PRINTED BY BEVERIDGE AND CO.,

HOLBORN PRINTING WORKS, FULWOOD'S RENTS, W.C.

CONTENTS OF VOLUME THREE.

THE ADMINISTRATION OF REDEMPTION
(CONTINUED).

PAGE

CHRISTIAN SONSHIP . . . . 1—27

REGENERATION : Agent ; Nature and Definitions ; Means .   5—13

ADOPTION : The Term ; The Act of God ; Privilege Conferred on Man . . . .   13—16

PRIVILEGES OF CHRISTIAN SONSHIP : Access to God ; Liberty ;
Special Guidance of the Spirit ; Election ; Inheritance .   16—20

HISTORICAL : Judaism ; Early Fathers ; Sacramental Theo-
ries ; Theories of Co-operation or Divine and Human
Elements ; Baptismal Regeneration and Adoption ; Its
Order in Economy of Grace ; Relation of Christian Re-
generation to the Elements of Human Nature ; Various
Estimates of Regeneration . . . .   20—27

CHRISTIAN SANCTIFICATION . . . .   27—100

IN PRINCIPLE AND PROCESS : Purification, Consecration,
Holiness . . . .   29—35

PROGRESSIVE AND PERFECT : Progressive in Every Aspect .   35—44

ENTIRE SANCTIFICATION : Purification from Indwelling
Sin : Entire Consecration or Perfect Love ; Christian
Perfection . . . .   44—61

HISTORICAL : Theories of Christian Perfection ; The Early
Church ; Fanatical and Ascetic ; Pelagian ; Mystical ;
Romanist ; Calvinist ; Arminian ; Methodist . . . .   61—100

TENURE OF COVENANT BLESSINGS . . . .   100—147

PROBATION : Scriptural Doctrine ; Historical Review ; Test
of Religious Systems . . . .   100—112

ASSURANCE : Objective : Resurrection of Christ ; Means of
Grace. Subjective : The Spirit ; Plerophoria of Faith
and Hope and Understanding : Parrhesia : Witness of
the Spirit . . . .   112—122

VI

CONTENTS

PAGE

HISTORICAL REVIEW Sacramental, Mystical Calvinism
Methodism 122—130
PERSEVERANCE Grace and its Ground, Manifestation
Conditionality 130—137
CONTROVERSIAL Covenant of Redemption, Argument
from Scripture . 137—147

CHRISTIAN ETHICS 148—258

ETHICS OF REDEMPTION 118—192
The Christian Lawgiver The Relation of Gospel
Doctrine to Ethics, Christian Ethics and Moral
Philosophy, the Christian Law, Liberty, Love
and Law Biblical Methods of Teaching . 118—192
CHRISTIAN ETHICS SYSTEMATIC . 192—259
PERSONAL ETHICS of Conversion, of Intention of
the Conflict, of Service, of Devotion . 192—232
RELATIVE ETHICS of Man and Man of Family,
of Commerce of Politics, of the Church . . 232—258

THE CHURCH . 259—367

ITS HISTORICAL FOUNDATION Gospel Preparations,
Pentecostal Establishment . . . 259—266
ATTRIBUTES AND NOTES Unity One and Manifold
Holy and Mixed Visible and Invisible; Catholic
and Local, Indefectible and Mutable Militant
and Triumphant, Bearing of the Notes on Eccle-
siastical History 266—287
INSTITUTE FOR WORSHIP . 287—359
DIVINE SERVICE OR WORSHIP . 288—294
THE MEANS OF GRACE 294—334
THE WORD AND PRAYER . . 295—299
THE SACRAMENTS Ecclesiastical Theories as to the
Sign and Seal, Multiplication of Sacraments,
Under-valuation 299—310
BAPTISM Scripture: Historical and Controversial 310—324
EUCHARIST. Scripture Historical and Controversial 325—334
THE CHRISTIAN MINISTRY 335—359
THE UNIVERSAL PRIESTHOOD 335—337
OFFICES EXTRAORDINARY AND TRANSITIONAL 337—341
THE ORDINARY AND PERMANENT MINISTRY 341—350
THE PASTORAL OFFICE 342—347
THE DIACONATE . 347—348
VOCATION AND ORDINATION . 348—450
HISTORICAL Theories of the Ministry . 350—359
THE CHURCH AND THE WORLD 359—364

	PAGE
The Witness of Truth	359—361
The Missionary Institute	361—362
The Church and the Kingdom	362—364

ESCHATOLOGY.

Preliminaries	367—370
Death and the Kingdom of the Dead	371—376
Death and Immortality	371—376
The Intermediate State : Scripture and Ecclesiastical History	376—386
The Day of Christ	387—423
The Second Coming : Scriptural Doctrine and Historical Hypotheses	387—401
The Resurrection : Scriptural and Historical	401—411
The General Judgment : The Judge ; the Judged ; the Judgment, with its Standards and Results	412—423
The Consummation	424—454
End of Mediatorial Kingdom : Doctrine and Error	424—427
Salvation of the Human Race. Theories : Annihilation, Universalism, and Intermediate Tendencies	427—447
New Heavens and Earth	447—449
Eternal Life	449—454

THE ADMINISTRATION OF REDEMPTION

(CONTINUED).

———

THE STATE OF SALVATION (CONTINUED).
THE TENURE OF COVENANT BLESSINGS.
THE ETHICS OF REDEMPTION.
THE CHRISTIAN CHURCH.

THE STATE OF SALVATION

CHRISTIAN SONSHIP.

THE Christian privilege of Sonship is that of filial life restored to man in and through Christ. This blessing, connecting the Mediatorial Trinity, as the Father, the Son, and the Holy Spirit, in a special manner with the new relations of the believer, may be distinguished as the internal Regeneration and the external Adoption. But, however distinct, these two are to be united when we consider the peculiar Prerogatives of the children of God viewed as His children: they are the rights of adoption conferred on such as are made capable of them by their renewal, or, in another view, the rights of regeneration which in adoption are acknowledged and bestowed.

1. No terms are more strictly correlative than Regeneration and Adoption. They describe the same blessing under two aspects: the former referring to the filial character, the latter to the filial privilege. But they are not thus closely connected as cause and effect: they are co-ordinate, and the link between them is the common Sonship. The assurance of filial adoption does not produce the regenerate life; nor does the infusion of the perfect life of regeneration of itself invest the children of God with all the prerogatives of heirship. Moreover, they are as distinct from the other leading blessings in the economy of grace as they are themselves united. The justified state does not involve of necessity the special privileges of adoption; nor does regeneration as such imply the specific relation to God which sanctification signifies.

Regeneration and Adoption.

The two terms we now consider embrace in their unity an entirely distinct department of the Spirit's administration of the New Covenant; they lead us into the household of faith and the family of God. Touching at many points those other departments, they are nevertheless perfect and complete in themselves.

Connected with Trinity.

2. The privilege of Christian sonship connects the Holy Trinity in a peculiar manner with the administration of grace. If such a distinction may be allowed, it has a more direct connection than the other privileges of the covenant with the Son Incarnate. This specific blessing is in relation to justification and sanctification what the Son is in relation to the Father and the Holy Ghost.

John xx. 17.
Eph. iii. 15.

Among the last sayings of the Saviour were these : *I ascend unto My Father and your Father,* to that Father of whom *all paternity in heaven and earth is named.* He who is the Logos to the creation generally is the Son towards the filial creation. But this special relation to the Son extends to both aspects of sonship as adoption and regeneration. We are adopted into the relation which the Son occupies eternally : hence the term which expresses this prerogative is υἱοθεσία, where the υἱός is preserved as the solitary word that is ever used to signify the Son's relation to the Father. We are regenerated by the life of Christ imparted through the Spirit : hence it is παλιγγενεσία, and we are τέκνα, both terms as it were reproducing in time the eternal generation. Our regeneration answers to the eternally Begotten, our adoption to the eternally Beloved.

United.

3. There are some passages in the New Testament which unite the two ; and these may be introduced as the general preface to what follows. *But as many as received Him, to them gave He power to become the sons of God :* ἐξουσίαν τέκνα Θεοῦ γενέσθαι, authority or privilege to be made into children, because they believe on the name of the Son. This is precisely the same as what is afterwards called adoption. *Which were born, not of blood, nor of the will of the flesh, nor of the will of man, but of God :* here we have a most complete definition of regeneration. The two ideas run through the eighth chapter of the Romans ; though both there, and in the Galatian epistle, it is the adoption that is more conspicuous. In St. Peter we have both. *Which according to His abundant mercy hath begotten us again :* this is regeneration ; *to an inheritance incorruptible* denotes the adoption to which inheritance belongs as a

John i. 12, 13.

1 Pet. i. 3, 4.

privilege.   But best of all in St. John : Behold . . . *that we* SHOULD BE CALLED *and* WE ARE *the sons of God.*   In this however, as in all, our Lord Himself gave the word : *If the Son, therefore, shall make you free, ye shall be free indeed;* that is, by the possession of a place among the children, and the children's freedom.   *If God were your Father, ye would love Me:* here, as the context shows, regeneration or the possession of new life is meant.

1 Jno. iii.
1 : καὶ
ἐσμίν,
A.B.C.
Sin.
John viii.
36, 42.

REGENERATION.

Regeneration is the final and decisive work wrought in the spirit and moral nature of man when the perfect principle of spiritual life in Christ Jesus is imparted by the Holy Ghost.   Many and various descriptions of this fundamental change are given in Scripture : showing its relations to the several Persons of the Trinity, to the penitent faith of the recipient, to the means employed in effecting it. The best method of acquiring a clear view of the teaching of the word of God on this subject is simply to arrange and classify these descriptions.

I. The Divine Agent in the new life is the Holy Trinity, Whose agency is that of generation and creation : each of these terms being respectively the centre of a circle of phrases.

Divine.

1. The Persons of the Sacred Trinity are Severally Agents.   It is said of the Father : *Of His own will begat He us with the word of truth.   You hath He quickened.*   So God, generally, or God and the Father ; *Blessed be the God and Father of our Lord Jesus Christ . . . Who hath begotten us again!   The Son quickeneth whom He will. I am come that they might have life, and that they might have it more abundantly,* περίσσον : the higher, deeper, fuller life which is the result of Christian regeneration, in contradistinction to the preliminary life that precedes the new birth, as well as to the imperfect privilege of the older economy.   It is, however, the adoption of sonship which is more generally ascribed to the Son : *to them gave He power to become the sons of God* by privilege who were born *of God.*   But the Holy Ghost is the specific Agent : as

The
Trinity.
Jas. i. 18.
Eph. ii. 1.
1 Pet. i. 3.
John v.
21.
John x.
10.

Jno. i. 12,
13.

1 Cor. xv. 45. John iii. 6. the Administrator of redemption He is *a quickening Spirit. That which is born of the flesh is flesh, and that which is born of the Spirit is spirit.* There is no more exact translation of New-Testament thought into ecclesiastical phrase than that which gave the Holy Ghost the title : τὸ πνεῦμα τὸ ζωοποιόν, the Giver of life.

2. The Divine operation presents three general classes of terms.

Generation. 1 John v. 1. 1 Pet. i. 3. (1.) Some refer to generation. The simplest is that of begetting: *every one that loveth Him that begat, loveth him also that is begotten of Him,* τὸν γεννήσαντα. The idea is modified in St. Peter's *begotten us again,* ἀναγεννήσας. In one passage the mother's function is used in the original, though disguised in the translation :

James i. 15, 18. John v. 21. Eph. ii. 5 1 John iii. 9. *of His own will begat He us:* ἀπεκύησεν, as before in ver. 15 the same peculiar verb is employed, *bringeth forth death.* These are united in the general word quickening : *the Son quickeneth whom He will,* ζωοποιεῖ. This is modified again : *quickened us together with Christ.* St. John's is a remarkable variation on the thought : *whosoever is born of God doth not commit sin ; for His seed remaineth in him.* All these descriptions are very impressive as adopting and applying to Christians the sacred language first used of the

John i. 14. ONLY BEGOTTEN GOD.

Creation. James i. 18. (2.) Many others refer to creation. St. James unites this idea with the former : *begat He us . . . that we should be a kind of first-fruits of His creatures.* It is both creation, new creation, and the

2 Cor. v. 17. Eph. ii. 10. secondary creation of renewal. *If any man be in Christ he is a new creature :* κτίσις, creation or creature. He is *created in Christ Jesus unto good works.* It is however a secondary creation, or reduc-

Tit. iii. 5. tion of the soul to order out of its chaos : by the *renewing of the Holy Ghost,* ἀνακαινώσις. Here we must remember the analogy of the genesis of all things at the beginning : there was an absolute creation of matter, or calling that which was not into being ; and there was the subsequent fashioning of that matter into forms which constitute the habitable Cosmos. The latter is the creation on which the Scripture most dwells : whether it regards the physical or it regards the spiritual order. Just as the sleeper is

Eph. v. 14. dead and the dead is only asleep,—*awake thou that sleepest, and arise from the dead,*—so the creation is only a renewal, while the renewal

Col. iii. 10. is no less than a creation. The two sometimes are united. *And have put on the new man,* τὸν νέον, *which is renewed,* τὸν ἀνακαινούμενον.

And be renewed in the spirit of your mind, ἀνανεοῦσθαι; *and that ye* Eph. iv. *put on the new man,* τὸν καινὸν ἄνθρωπον, *which after God is created* 23, 24. *in righteousness and true holiness.* It is well to note, without pressing too far, the distinction between the two forms, νέος and καινός, and their combinations. The former refers to time: the new man is entirely different from his FORMER self. The latter refers to quality: the new man is different from his former SELF, and the idea of a great change is more marked. In these passages the creating act of God is regarded as a process issuing in the new character; as a process in which He uses the co-operation of man. But in another passage the creating idea is used rather of a definite act: *for we are His workmanship,* ποίημα, *created in Christ* Eph. ii. *Jesus unto good works.* We are saved apart from our own works, 10. through a new work of God, which prepares us for works which then are good: good because they spring from a renewed nature, are performed under the influence of the Holy Spirit, and for ever renounce all claim to goodness independent of His grace.

II. As wrought in man, regeneration is described in many Wrought ways: there is a greater variety of indirect and figurative defini- in Man. tions of this blessing than of any other in the covenant of grace.

1. The terms indicating the spiritual birth take the lead. NewBirth Christians are *born of God,* ἐκ τοῦ Θεοῦ; they are *children of God;* 1 John iii. they are *born again,* ἄνωθεν, which is the same as *from above:* indeed John iii. the expression has rather a local than a temporal meaning, and is 3. strictly from above, or from heaven, that is, *born of God,* according to St. John's interpretation in the epistle. As describing regeneration it must have the preeminence, being our Lord's own first and only formal word on the subject. When He adds: *the wind bloweth* John iii. *where it listeth, and thou hearest the sound thereof, but canst not tell* 8. *whence it cometh, and whither it goeth: so is every one that is born of the Spirit,* we are taught that the preliminary grace of the Holy Ghost has its mysterious issue in the new birth of him who *has been born* (ὁ γεγεννημένος, in the perfect, the completion of a process). It is, as we have defined it, the full filial life. The word distinguishes the new product from *that which is born of the* John iii. *flesh;* it is a παλιγγενεσία, and indicates the bestowment of a new 3, 6, 7. life according to the original idea of man in the Divine mind.

2. It is a resurrection from a state of death: from death, and Resurrection.

not merely a rising up generally from sin : *as those that are alive*

Rom. vi.
13.
Eph. ii. 1. *from the dead.* (1.) It is therefore the same man who was *dead in trespasses and sins ;* and the idea seems to be that the new man is raised up within the old : to be nourished and grow while the

John xii.
24. latter dies. This follows the analogy of our Lord's words : *except a corn of wheat fall into the ground and die, it abideth alone.* The old nature is mortified with Christ and the new rises from it. But the analogy in other respects fails. The true life of the spirit is life in death, and death unto life ; but it is not the dissolution of the new nature that feeds the new germ. (2.) Hence the stricter view of this interior new birth is that of a resurrection in

With
Christ. the fellowship of the risen Saviour, and connects it with the fellowship of His atoning death unto the condemnation of sin. In other words the new life is the counterpart of the death to the law.

Rom.vi. 4,
5, 7. *Therefore we are buried with Him by baptism into death that, like as Christ was raised up from the dead by the glory of the Father, even so we also should walk in newness of life. For if we have been planted together in the likeness of His death, we shall be also in the likeness of His resurrection.* He that is united to the Redeemer by faith, of which baptism is the sign, is *justified from sin ;* but this cannot be without a spiritual resurrection with Him, of which the rising out of the water is the symbol, as descending into it is the symbol of the former. In this passage regeneration is regarded rather as a process following the instantaneous death : *that the body of sin*

Rom. vi.
6, 11. *might be destroyed, that henceforth we should not serve sin.* Hence the expression, *Reckon ye also yourselves to be dead indeed unto sin, but alive unto God through Jesus Christ our Lord.* The same instantaneous life with Christ, followed by the same death in life of

Col. ii. 13;
iii. 5. spiritual mortification, is taught in the Colossian epistle. *And you, being dead in your sins and the uncircumcision of your flesh, hath He quickened together with Him, having forgiven you all trespasses.*

Spiritual
Circum-
cision. *. . . Mortify therefore your members which are upon the earth.* (3.) Spiritual Circumcision therefore with Christ is another aspect of the same truth. *The uncircumcision of your flesh* is spiritual death as contrasted with *dead in your sins* as the condemnation of the

Jer. iv. 4.
Rom. ii.
29. law. And in this fulfilment of the symbol, in the taking away *the foreskins of your heart,* that inward circumcision which *is that of the heart, in the spirit, and not in the letter,* we have the New-Testament antitype of a large series of Old-Testament types of the future regeneration.

3. It is the introduction into a new world. This follows from the former : the children of this resurrection are quickened or raised into *newness of life.* They have new tastes, appetites, dispositions, senses adapted to a new state of things. *If any man be in Christ he is a new creature, old things are passed away ; behold, all things are become new.* Of this change our Lord spoke when He said : *except a man be born of water and of the Spirit he cannot enter into the kingdom of God.* Christians, having ascended with Christ, sit *in the heavenly places ;* they are required therefore to set their *affection on things above.* This aspect of the new birth conjoins it with Illumination. It is *Let there be light !* in the soul. *For God who commanded the light to shine out of darkness hath shined in our hearts :* which connects the New-Testament spiritual genesis, or palingenesis, with the natural one of the Old Testament.

4. It is sharing in a deeper sense than any yet referred to the life of Christ. Our Lord at the outset of His teaching spoke of *that which is born of the Spirit :* at the close He represented regeneration as being union with Himself : *I am the Vine, ye are the branches. Because I live ye shall live also.* And, between these, He spoke of Himself, received by faith, as the life of the soul. *Except ye eat the flesh of the Son of Man and drink His blood ye have no life in you.* This is sometimes said to be *Christ in you,* and Christ *formed in* the nature. It is more than a federal fellowship in His death and life, such as results from faith in the common Redeemer, and exhibits regeneration in some sense as a corporate blessing. It is the mystical communication of a certain Divine-human virtue of the Saviour's being which cannot be defined in words. Thus we become *partakers of the Divine nature.* To this referred one of those profound sayings which our Saviour uttered, without interpretation, to be pondered by His people for ever : *I am come that they might have life, and that they might have it* MORE, περίσσον, *that, like as Christ was raised up from the dead by the glory of the Father, even so we also should walk in newness of life.*

5. It is a new law established in the heart ; according to the terms of the evangelical covenant : *I will put My laws into their hearts, and in their minds will I write them.* The law set up within

Margin notes:

A New World.
Rom. vi. 4.

2 Cor. v. 17.
State of Existence.
John iii. 5.

Eph. i. 20.
Col. iii. 2.
Illumination.
Gen. i. 3.
2 Cor. iv. 6.

Life of Christ Imparted.
John iii. 6.
John xv. 5.
John xiv. 19.
John vi. 53.
Col. i. 27.
Gal. iv. 19.

2 Peter i. 4.

John x. 10.
Rom. vi. 4.

Law within.
Heb. x. 16.

is a definition of the new birth which connects it with justification :

Rom. viii. 4.
that the righteousness of the law might be fulfilled in us. *Love is the*

Rom. xiii. 10.
fulfilling of the law. This also connects it with the Holy Spirit,

Rom. viii. 2.
not only with His agency, but with His indwelling : *the law of the Spirit of life in Christ Jesus.*

Divine Image.
Col. iii. 10, 11.
6. Lastly, regeneration is the renewal of man into the Divine image. This specific view of the doctrine is peculiar to St. Paul; but he gives it special prominence : *the new man which is renewed in knowledge after the image of Him that created him.* A careful study of these words yields much important truth. (1.) The standard of the renewal is the original image in which man was created. At the moment of the impartation of the new life that image was restored, as is more directly affirmed in the parallel

Eph. iv. 24.
passage, *which after God is created,* τὸν κατὰ Θεὸν κτισθέντα : the new man was once for all created anew; and the subsequent knowledge, and holiness of truth, are the end for which it was created. (2.) When St. Paul adds, *where there is neither Greek nor Jew . . . but Christ is all and in all,* he tells us that the new creation is specially related to Christ as the Archetype of this new image; which indeed was true of the original image that sin defaced, but is now more fully revealed. (3.) While the mysterious regenerating act was the restoration of that likeness, it is implied that the renewal, for this is the term, is a process ever going on towards completion. The pristine image was by one offence marred ; but by many successive stages is it entirely restored.

2 Cor. iii. 18.
We all with open face beholding (or *receiving*) *as in a glass the glory of the Lord are changed into the same image from glory to glory, even as by the Spirit of the Lord.* Thus the new image is gradually retrieved; the Holy Ghost is filling up and deepening the outline continually ; and the regenerate life, like righteousness and sanctification, has its issue in perfection. As the one regeneration leads to a continuous renewal, so the one image re-engraven leads to a

Rom. xii. 2.
continuous transformation : *be ye transformed by the renewing of your mind.* (4.) Once more, and this is of great moment, the object of this change, or the subject of this renewal, is the whole spiritual nature of man. Not his body ; for its regeneration will be its

Rom. viii. 10.
resurrection : *the body is* (and *remains*) *dead because of sin,* and must undergo its penalty. Doomed as it is to dissolution it must be pre-

sented in ceaseless oblation as the instrument of the spirit which *is life because of righteousness*, laid on the altar of service for the present and of hope for the future. But the spirit as the seat of reason, or the immortal principle in man, and the soul, as the same spirit linked with the phenomenal world by the body, are, in all their complex faculties which are a unity in diversity, brought under the regenerating power of the Holy Ghost. We read that *the natural man, ψυχικὸς ἄνθρωπος, receiveth not the things of the Spirit of God:* that is, the man whose spirit is subdued to the animal soul, *soulish, having not the Spirit.* But this does not signify that the soul itself, apart from the spirit, is the only defaulter: the spirit also is in the transgression; and the regenerate man becomes ὁ πνευματικός, *he that is spiritual*, only through his spirit being inhabited by the Spirit Divine. Neither is the soul without the spirit, nor the spirit without the soul, the seat of sin or the subject of regeneration. It is man who is renewed. (5.) Lastly, regeneration is therefore not the removal of anything infused by sin into the essence of the spirit or soul. It is not said that we receive a new nature: though no language is more common than this, it must be very carefully restricted and guarded. *Partakers of the Divine nature* we are; but as received into our own nature renewed. The heart is the man, the self; and the promise is, *a new heart also will I give you.*

1 Cor. ii. 14.

Jude 19.

1 Cor. ii. 15.

2 Peter i 4.
Ezek. xxxvi. 26.

7. We cannot review these various aspects of the new life without being impressed with the feeling that it is in some sense the central blessing of the Christian covenant. Justification is unto life, and this life is devoted to God in sanctification. But the life, as the life is in Jesus, is the unity of all. *I am the Way, the Truth, and* THE LIFE. The last book of the New Testament tells us that all its teaching concentres in *the Word of Life, περὶ τοῦ λόγου τῆς ζωῆς:* this testimony revolves again in its last accents: *this is the true God and eternal life*, words which closely follow St. John's last and most striking summary of the entire doctrine of the new birth. *Whosoever is born of God, ὁ γεγεννημένος ἐκ τοῦ Θεοῦ, is he that is begotten of God, ὁ γεννηθεὶς ἐκ τοῦ Θεοῦ; he sinneth not* but *keepeth himself: the whole world* around him *lieth in the Wicked One;* but he, or rather we, *are in Him that is true, even* IN HIS SON JESUS CHRIST. Thus the Bible closes with all the elements of the doc-

Central Blessing.

John xiv 6.

1 John i. 1.

1 John v. 18—20.

trine of Regeneration. It is the Divine begetting of the filial life of Christ in us: thus it is once for all. It is the progressive life which regarded in its perfected ideal cannot sin: thus it is the renewal into a finished birth. And it is that very eternal life which, begun on earth, will be consummated in heaven.

The Means.

III. Regeneration is described with reference to the means employed in the economy of grace. The Divine act is always represented in connection with instrumentality. God begets by the word of truth; our Lord gives His life, and not only sustains it, in the eating and drinking of Himself; the Holy Spirit instrumentally regenerates through the ordinance or sacrament of baptism. These points we need only now indicate briefly: they will be more fully discussed when we reach the Means of Grace and the Sacraments.

The Word.

1. The Word of God is the instrument and power of regeneration.

(1.) Not as the absolute authoritative voice which calls into new life, but as the truth which is applied to the understanding and to the feelings, and through them to the will. It is the word of conviction or reproof in the preliminary process: the reproof in the understanding which enforces on the sinner the Lord's

John iii. 7.

word *Ye must be born again,* which excites in the heart a profound sense of need and desire for the true life of the soul, and thus prepares the spirit, unregenerate as yet, but animated by the preliminary life of repentance, for the full power of regeneration. This influence of the truth is sometimes regarded as a fruit of the new birth: it is really a preparation for it.

(2.) It is the instrument, further, as it is the vehicle of the presentation of the Saviour Himself, the Truth, the supreme Object of trust. Embraced by the faith which is at once the last act of the unregenerate and the first act of the regenerate soul, He becomes the Life as well as the Truth. Of the word which offers

1 Pet. i. 23.

1 John iii. 9.

James i. 21.

and conveys the quickening Lord it is said by St. Peter that it is the *incorruptible seed,* and by St. John that it is the *seed* of God that *remaineth in* the human spirit. In St. James it·is the *engrafted word:* where we have a remarkable variation on the ordinary language of Scripture. Not we are engrafted into the Vine; but the Vine is engrafted into us: rather the Divine word with its doctrine is inserted into the nature for regeneration.

(3.) But, more generally still, it is the Word of God which is the instrument of every Divine operation in the human heart: *man shall not live by bread alone, but by every word that proceedeth out of the mouth of God.* The word is His sovereign and gracious will. As it is not the bread which sustains the life, but the Divine virtue of the bread, so it is not the preaching or the sacrament but the Divine virtue in both which imparts the life. Every energy of God from heaven at last goes back to His word.

Matt. iv. 4.

2. Baptism, also, as the sacrament of the new birth, or rather of the soul's entrance into Christ, gives regeneration both a special name and a special character. The baptism *with the Holy Ghost* is one of its definitions. The rite is *the washing of regeneration*, λουτρόν, the bath. It is the symbol of the putting away of sin, and in this is like its precursor, circumcision. This latter symbolised by the cutting off a portion of the natural body the destruction of *the body of sin.* Baptism, a gentler rite, symbolises the entrance into Christ, in His death and life: not the washing away of sin only, which refers to its relation to justification or forgiveness. It is the pledge of the gift of regeneration, abiding in the church: the symbolical laver which for ever assures of the invisible flowing of the *Fountain opened . . for sin and for uncleanness.* So long as the evangelical λουτρόν is in the Christian sanctuary, so long is there regeneration for all its members. It also seals it to the believer, whether as a gift already imparted, as given in conjunction with the rite, or to be fully given hereafter. Its close connection with the blessing of which it is the sacramental symbol is exhibited throughout the New Testament: from our Lord's words, *except a man be born of water and of the Spirit, he cannot enter into the kingdom of God,* which must not be emptied of their meaning, through the teaching and practice of the Acts of the Apostles, down to St. Paul's last words to Titus already quoted. The water in the doctrine of Christ becomes the laver in the Apostle's teaching.

Baptism.

Matt. iii. 11.
Titus iii. 5.

Rom. vi. 6.

Zech. xiii. 1.

John iii. 5.

ADOPTION.

Adoption is the term occasionally used to signify the Divine declaratory act by which those who are accepted in

Christ are reinstated in the privileges of forfeited sonship for the sake of the Incarnate Son. It is used also of the state to which these privileges belong.

The Term.

I. The term is used only by St. Paul. It was perhaps taken into the Christian vocabulary from the Roman law. Cum in alienam familiam inque liberorum locum extranei sumuntur, aut per prætorem fit, aut per populum. Quod per prætorem fit Aul. Gell. x. 19. ADOPTIO dicitur; quod per populum ARROGATIO. If the new son was received from under the authority of his natural parent the act was Adoption; if one who was his own master was adopted it was Arrogation. The Greek term, υἱοθεσία, is explained by Hesychius: οὐ φύσει ἀλλὰ θέσει. St. Paul uses it Rom. ix. 4. with three applications. First, of the Israelites, *to whom pertaineth* *the adoption,* that is, the special election among the nations. Gal. iii. 26. Gal. iv. 5. Eph. i. 5. Secondly, of *the children of God by faith in Christ Jesus: that we* *might receive the adoption of sons* unto which we were *predestinated.* Finally, of the full manifestation of the children of God in their Rom. viii. 23. Matt. xix. 28. perfect investiture with all their privileges: *waiting for the adop-* *tion.* This corresponds with the final *regeneration when the Son of* *Man shall sit in the throne of His glory:* a remarkable instance of the true relation between the terms regeneration and adoption. Both are used of the final restitution of all things, and both regard that restitution as being chiefly the restoration of man to his original and lost estate.

The Thing

II. As to the thing signified it may be regarded first as the act of God, and then as conferred on man: the Divine declaration and its human result.

Act of God. Eph. iii. 15.

1. Adoption is connected with the Triune God. (1.) It is the Father who adopts into His own household: *of Whom the whole* *family—all paternity* or *race relation—in heaven and earth is named.* (2.) But it has special reference to the Son: it is in union with Him, the Son, that we become sons; we are adopted into the Heb. iii. 6. John viii. 36. house by Christ, the *Son over His own house,* who imparts to us as His brethren a share in His own prerogative: *if the Son therefore* *shall make you free, ye shall be free indeed.* (3.) It is declared Rom. viii. 15. and attested by the Holy Ghost: *the Spirit of adoption.* It is administered to faith, as the common faith which saves but as having

in this case its specific object : the promise, that is, of the higher covenant, *I will be a Father unto you.* Not that the penitent sinner in coming to God regards every special blessing he needs as the object of trust. His faith is but one, and directed to one object ; nor does he at the first make any distinction ; afterwards, however, when he comes to understand his privileges, he learns to direct his confidence towards God under several aspects. And this, that He is a Father, is one that can never be forgotten. The seal of this faith is the testimony of the Spirit who *beareth witness with our spirit*—not to our spirit, but with it and through it—that *we are the children of God.* 2 Cor. vi. 18.
Rom. viii. 16.

2. As received by man, adoption defines the peculiarity of the filial relation as a sonship restored in respect to its privileges. Received by man.

(1.) It is not the sonship of creation which is signified. The angels are *the sons of God ;* as also those who bear authority among men : *I have said, ye are gods ; and all of you are children of the Most High.* The human race in its origin received this designation : *Adam, which was the son of God.* Hence the prodigal son is still a son. Even after the moral image departed the natural image remained ; the original prerogative can never be entirely taken away. *For this my son was dead and is alive again :* language put into the lips of an earthly father, but most assuredly only as the human echo of a Divine feeling. Job i. 6.
Ps. lxxxii. 6.
Luke iii. 38.
Luke xv. 24.

(2.) Nor is it the sonship of likeness : in the Hebrew idiom we read of the *children of light* and *children of this world,* and of the wicked our Lord said with that meaning only : *ye are of your father, the devil.* In the sense of conformity with His will, and followers of His example, Christ exhorts us to walk worthy of our filial relation : *that ye may be the children of your Father which is in heaven.* And we are predestinated *to be conformed to the image of His Son.* The relation of sons, however, precedes the conformity. Luke xvi. 8.
John viii. 44.
Matt. v. 45.
Rom. viii. 29.

(3.) But it is the restoration of prodigals to the household of God, and may be regarded in two lights : first, it is a simple reinstatement in the original position of children of the creating Father ; and, secondly, it is altogether a new prerogative, being an investiture with the special prerogatives of brethren of Jesus, *the Firstborn among many brethren.* This distinction, however, is not often to be observed. The new relation of sonship by adoption Rom. viii. 29.

has indeed revealed more fully the primary and inextinguishable Fatherhood of God, but that is scarcely remembered by reason of the new glory of His Fatherhood in Christ.

THE PRIVILEGES OF CHRISTIAN SONSHIP.

The privileges of entrance into the family of God by adoption—which as privileges are connected rather with adoption than regeneration—are distinctly exhibited in the New Testament. They are filial access in the confidence of devotion : freedom from all kinds of bondage ; the advantages of the election ; the assurance of a constant guidance and direction of the Holy Spirit ; and the enjoyment, first in earnest, and then finally, of the Christian inheritance. These all of course have relation to the other blessings of the new Covenant so far as these blessings are one in their diversity ; but they are specially connected with the Christian Sonship.

I. Access to God in filial confidence is the first prerogative. *Ye have received the Spirit of adoption whereby we cry, Abba, Father.* This is the secret of all Christian devotion and worship. The temple which our High Priest has consecrated is always the house of God : the house with a meaning unknown to the ancient economy, one in which the worshippers worship as children. After quoting the declaration, *I will be their God,* St. Paul adds another passage from another place, *and will be a Father unto you.* This addition is a very striking instance of the change which Christianity has introduced in the relations of His people to God. Of Solomon it had been said : *I will be his Father, and he shall be My son ;* and again, *I have chosen him to be My son, and I will be his Father.* The Apostle extends this special privilege to all believers in Christ ; an extension of which a distant hint had been given : *bring My sons from far and My daughters from the ends of the earth,* where St. Paul found the sanction of the inclusion of the daughters. *Our Father !* is the new invocation. This impresses its character on

Margin notes:
Rom. viii. 15.
Confidence in Devotion.
Ex. xxix. 45.
2 Cor. vi. 16, 18.
2 Sam. vii. 14.
1 Chron. xxviii. 6.
Isa. xliii. 6.
Matt. vi. 9.

worship, public and private; and on all the communion of the | Matt. vi.
soul with heaven. Christian fellowship with God is filial in and | 9.
through His Son. It is assured confidence in Him as a Father.

II. Whatsoever belongs to Liberty or Freedom, in the New- | Freedom.
Testament sense of the word, is linked with sonship. The
Saviour said, *the truth shall make you free*; and then declared that | John viii.
the sons in the house, made free by the Son, are *free indeed*, | 32, 36.
ὄντως ἐλεύθεροι: with an emphasis on the ὄντως which meant more
than the contrast with Jewish delusive freedom, the deep word
being left, like many others, to be interpreted by the Spirit and to be
understood by the meditation of faith. We are redeemed from *under* | Gal. iv. 5.
the law, that we might receive the adoption of sons. Between son-
ship and bondage there is no affinity. The law has become a *law* | James i.
of liberty. It is written in the heart, and obedience must spring | 25.
from filial love. The Christian privilege is thus contrasted with
that of the Jews, who were under the law and knew not the great
redemption: though the ancient people were one collective Son,
they were as such *under tutors and governors* in an estate of dis- | Gal. iv. 1,
cipline which *differeth nothing from a servant*, that is, *until the time* | 2.
appointed of the Father. In itself it is emancipation from every yoke:
we are *not under the law but under grace.* Grace is the new law, | Rom. vi.
working by faith through love an obedience which is acceptable | 14.
to God. Here justification and adoption join: the former is a
perpetual sentence of release from the condemning law, the latter
guarantees the strength of a new and better obedience. But, as
compared with the great future, there is still a bondage to corrup-
tion, so far as the body is concerned and its infirmities. *Waiting* | Rom. viii.
for the adoption, to wit, the redemption of our body: the resurrec- | 23.
tion will bring in perfected freedom.

III. The privileges of the Election of God belong to the filial | Election.
relation which is sealed by admission into the ark of the Christian
family. Israel was the chosen people, *to whom pertaineth the adoption*, | Rom. ix.
in St. Paul's eyes even yet untaken away; their election and their | 4.
adoption were one and the same prerogative. In Christianity the
election is still synonymous with adoption, but it is personal and
not national: rather it is both; for the elect are the foreknown
brethren of Christ and family of God glorified in eternity, even
as they are one by one gathered out of the world into the Divine

household through their obedience to the evangelical call. The
Eph. i. 5. Father has *predestinated us unto the adoption of children*, which is,
Rom. viii. being interpreted elsewhere, *to be conformed to the image of His Son.*
29. God's children as such are elected out of the world; they are,
1 Pet. ii. like their Elder Brother, and for His sake, *chosen of God and pre-*
4. *cious*, and are unspeakably dear to their heavenly Father, who
Rom. viii. orders everything for their welfare : *all things work together for good*
28. *to them that love God, to them who are the called according to His*
Eph. i. 6. *purpose.* Their highest prerogative as separated from the mass is
Phil. iii. 9. that they are *accepted in the Beloved* or *found in Him*, and regarded
Isa. xlii. with the same complacency which rests upon their Head : *Mine*
1. *Elect in whom My soul delighteth.* Jesus is our Election as well
Eph. i. 4. as our Righteousness and our Sanctification : The Father *hath*
chosen us in Him, and our election is no more and nothing less
than our union with the Redeemer.

The   IV. Another special prerogative of the adoption is the per-
Spirit's   sonal and never-failing direction and guidance of the Holy Spirit.
Guidance. *For as many as are led by the Spirit of God, they are the sons of*
Rom. viii. *God :* this may be regarded as meaning, conversely, they that are
14.   the sons of God are led by the Spirit. He who testifies within
them that they are children is given to them as a never-absent
Gal. v. 25. Guide : their religion is a life, a walk, a conversation *in the Spirit.*
Rom. viii. They *walk not after the flesh, but after the Spirit.* What the follow-
4.   ing of Christ is in the gospels, the following of the Holy Ghost is in
the epistles. He is at all points, under all circumstances, and in the
whole economy of life down to its minutest detail, the Monitor of
the children of God. And this He is to them as they are children.
Everywhere in the New Testament this special direction is pro-
1 Cor. ii. mised to Christians as the adopted sons of the Father. *The natural*
14. *man receiveth not the things of the Spirit of God ; but ye have an unction*
1 Jno. ii. *from the Holy One, and ye know all things.* St. John makes the
20, 18, promise to the Apostles extend to all the *little children :* submit-
28. ting to His teaching, with perfect renunciation of carnal wisdom,
John xvi. they are led *into all truth*, at least *as the truth is in Jesus.* It is of
13. the adopted children that St. Paul says : *the Spirit also helpeth*
Eph. iv. *our infirmities ; for we know not what we should pray for as we ought ;*
21. *but the Spirit itself maketh intercession for us . . . according to the will of*
Rom. viii. *God.* He is in us as the Spirit of regeneration ; our regenerate
26, 27.

nature itself cries unto God ; but it is the Spirit of our adoption Who *beareth witness with our spirit* of regeneration, in this sense also *the Spirit of your Father which speaketh in you.* It is impossible to exaggerate the blessedness of this interior and exterior guidance of the Holy Ghost given to the children of God. He is literally to them all and more than all the present Saviour was to His disciples. *He that is joined unto the Lord is one Spirit,* Who, common to Jesus and His brethren, is the everpresent Finger of God directing and Power of God defending the followers of Christ.

V. The inheritance to which Christians are called is the last privilege of their adoption. Of God's ancient children-people it was said : *I loved him, and called My son out of Egypt ;* that is, from the land of bondage. Moreover : *saying, unto thee will I give the land of Canaan, the lot of your inheritance.* And they were in all respects types : in their redemption from Egypt, in their journey to Canaan, and in their possession of the promised land.

1. The Christian inheritance belongs to the children of God in a twofold sense. *And if children, then heirs ; heirs of God, and joint-heirs with Christ.* (1.) Sin condemned and disinherited man : justification removes the condemnation, and adoption restores the inheritance. That inheritance is the abundance of the privileges of the covenant : it is the whole fulness of the promises ; but especially it is God Himself. The enjoyment of the Supreme Source of blessedness is the supreme good of the soul. (2.) Hence, that most sacred and eternal inheritance which the Son hath in the Father is in some as yet unknown sense shared by us. Our heirship in God is no other than our joint heirship of God with Christ. The only allusion to the eternal decree of man's salvation is that we are *predestinated to be conformed to the image of His Son.* This conformation, which is also transformation, is our eternal blessedness : it allows nothing beyond, for it is the perfection of man in the perfection of God. *Now are we the sons of God, and it doth not yet appear what we shall be : but we know that, when He shall appear, we shall be like Him, for we shall see Him as He is.* The utmost and highest hope of Christianity is derived from its privilege of sonship. *As for me, I will behold Thy face in righteousness. Blessed are the pure in heart, for they shall see God.* It is not however the justification of the former passage, nor the sanctifica-

Rom. viii 16. Matt. **x.** 20.

1 Cor. vi. 17.

Heirship.

Hosea **xi.** 1. Ps. cv. 11.

With Christ Rom. viii. 17.

Rom. viii. 29.

1 Jno. iii. 2.

Ps. xvii. 15. Matt. v. 8.

CHRISTIAN SONSHIP.

20

tion of the latter, but the adopted sonship which cries: *I shall be satisfied when I awake with Thy likeness!*

Earnest. 2. They enter into an heritage of which they have now only an earnest. The inheritance of Christians is in its deepest meaning *reserved in heaven.* Under whatever aspect it is viewed the Christian heritage is enjoyed only in its firstfruits. This is declared by St. Paul: *ye were sealed with that Holy Spirit of promise, which is the earnest of our inheritance until the redemption of the purchased possession.* When Christ shall claim us as His possession we shall claim Him as ours, *in Whom also we have become an inheritance.* It is after speaking of the Christian inheritance that the epistle to the Hebrews says: *for we are made partakers of Christ, if we hold the beginning of our confidence steadfast unto the end.*

Fulness. 3. That participation awaits the believer: we are *waiting for the adoption,* which will *change our body of humiliation, that it may be fashioned like unto His glorious body;* and will enable us in our integrity of body and spirit to *appear with Him in glory.* The *death of the Testator* has put us in possession of a portion of the goods that fall to us under His covenant-testament. But we must die ourselves to enter upon the vast remainder. Then will He at the last great distribution say to every one of His brethren: *all that I have is thine!* It is He who closes the New Testament with the promise of the filial inheritance: *he that overcometh shall inherit all things; and I will be his God and he shall be My son.* Thus does the new covenant echo at its close the final promise of the old: *and they shall be Mine, saith the Lord of hosts, in that day when I make up My jewels; and I will spare them as a man spareth his own son that serveth him.*

HISTORICAL.

Ecclesiastical Theories. The variations in opinion on this general subject may be classed under these heads: the various theories of the relation of the new birth to the sacrament of baptism; differences as to the measure of human co-operation admitted; its place in the Ordo Salutis, or plan of salvation; its effect upon the various constituent elements of human nature; and its value as a Divine gift in respect to the other blessings of the Christian covenant.

Margin references: Ps. xvii. 15. / Earnest. / 1 Peter i. 4. / Eph. i. 13, 14. / Eph. i. 11. / Heb. iii. 14. / Fulness. / Rom. viii. 23. / Phil. iii. 21. / Col. iii. 4. / Heb. ix. 16. / Luke xv. 31. / Rev. xxi. 7. / Mal. iii. 17. / Ecclesiastical Theories.

I. A certain theory of Baptismal Regeneration appears in the first ages of the Church, which seems in some measure to have merged the internal regeneration into the external adoption.

1. The first question will be considered again more fully when we reach the doctrine of the Sacraments; a brief statement, rather historical than polemic, is however necessary here also.

(1.) This was probably one out of many results of Jewish influence on Christian thought. During the interval between the Old and New Testaments the converts to Judaism were said to be born again: "a convert is like a newborn child." As to his new position he was called a Proselyte: either of the Gate, as admitted to civil privileges and a place in the Court of the Gentiles; or of Righteousness, as circumcised and baptized and bound to the whole law. The term therefore answered to the Christian Adoption. So Maimonides: "The Gentile that is made a proselyte, and the servant that is made free, behold, he is like a child new born. And, as to all those relations he had whilst either Gentile or servant, they now cease." But there was in Judaism no other regeneration than that of this external adoption.

(2.) Early Patristic literature similarly fell into a vague style of connecting the two. It represented the new birth as a translation into the Christian estate, an initiation by baptism into the Christian mysteries. The internal renewing process was faithfully taught; but was not connected always with the scriptural term: in fact, regeneration was equivalent to adoption simply. The new life was spoken of as renewal or renovation; and thus adoption, instead of being a concomitant of the new birth, was its precursor. The Regeneration was understood in the same broader meaning which our Saviour gave it when He spoke of the final restitution of all things; only that in their view this regeneration was simply the establishment of the new order of Christianity.

(3.) In this sense baptismal regeneration has been understood by very many advocates of infant baptism in every period. They use the term with a larger meaning than it generally bears: as the external estate out of which the new birth grows. Baptismal regeneration accordingly is, in the case of children, baptismal adoption, as baptism undeniably seals to the children of Christian parents their place in the family of God; it is also a seal or pledge

Sacramental Regeneration.

Early Church.

Rabbinical.

Regeneration in the broader sense.

of a regenerating grace awaiting all Christian children duly baptized, the pledge being the preliminary grace that rests upon them and prompts to personal dedication in due time when that pledge can be by themselves redeemed.

Confessions.

2. In a stricter sense the doctrine of baptismal regeneration is held by the larger part of Christendom : that, namely, which holds the sacraments to be the preeminent and proper Means of Grace. The Roman Catholic, Oriental, Lutheran, and Anglican communions, though in varying language, hold that regeneration is generally connected with baptism as its instrument. The Lutheran Augsburg Confession says : De baptismo docent, quod sit necessarius ad salutem. And what this necessity means is taught by Luther's Catechism : Baptismus operatur remissionem peccatorum, liberat a morte. The English Article xxvii. gives its sentiment thus : "But it is also a sign of regeneration or new birth, whereby, as by an instrument, they that receive baptism rightly are grafted into the church : the promises of forgiveness of sins, and of our adoption to be the sons of God, are visibly signed and sealed." Here it is obvious that a certain distinction is made between regeneration, of which baptism is the sign, and adoption, of which it is the instrument. The Westminster Confession declares the same ; with both a needful and a needless qualification . "Although it be a great sin to contemn or neglect this ordinance, yet grace and salvation are not so inseparably annexed unto it, as that no person can be regenerated or saved without it, or that all that are baptized are undoubtedly regenerated. The efficacy of baptism is not tied to that moment of time wherein it is administered ; yet, notwithstanding, by the right use of this ordinance, the grace promised is not only offered, but really exhibited and conferred by the Holy Ghost, to such (whether of age or infants) as that grace belongeth unto, according to the counsel of God's own will, in His appointed time." In these weighty words the regeneration of infants in baptism is clearly asserted to be possible, and, in the case of the elect, certain. But the addition of the words "not tied to that moment," and "in His own appointed time," may seem to allow that the full regeneration is reserved for the period when the infant shall be capable of receiving the gift.

3. By many the regeneration of the soul is regarded as sacramentally pledged and promised in virtue of the general grace bestowed upon mankind in redemption. Baptism is therefore a sign of the blessing into which preliminary grace is to mature ; and the seal of its bestowment if that preliminary grace is used aright. It should be remembered that in this theory regeneration stands connected with all the blessings of the Christian covenant, as in the sentences quoted from the formularies above. Baptism is not more intimately allied with the new birth than with remission of sins and sanctification to God. There is, according to the Nicene Confession, "one baptism for the remission of sins," that is, one baptism unto pardon, regeneration, sanctification, and all the benefits of our Lord's passion. Children baptized are externally pardoned, adopted, and made holy : the internal reality corresponding with these is sealed to them by the preliminary grace that belongs to the family of redeemed man, and especially to the children of the household of faith. Baptism in this doctrine, which carefully stated is irrefragable, is the sign and seal and instrument to adult believers of their pardon and renewal and sanctification. To the children of believers it is the sign and seal and instrument of imparting these blessings so far as they are capable of them : original guilt is removed, the bias to evil is counteracted by initial grace, and adoption into the household of faith is absolutely conferred. If what may be loosely called the germ of grace is regeneration in the infant, then it becomes new birth in the adult. Baptismal Adoption.

4. The strict systematic theory of the two mysteries which makes baptism the sacrament of birth, and the eucharist the sacrament of nourishment, may have some measure of truth in it so far as the word means the sacramental emblem. But it must not be forgotten that our Lord speaks of the sacramental eating and drinking of Himself as connected with regeneration. If the words of St. John's Gospel are referred to the Lord's Supper then we have a eucharistic regeneration as well as a baptismal : *Except ye eat the flesh of the Son of man and drink His blood, ye have no life in you:* it is not, *ye have no abiding life.* The two Sacraments one.

John vi. 53.

II. The measure of human co-operation has been much contested. Human Agency.

1. Extreme Calvinism holds that the life of regeneration is given by an act of as absolute sovereign power as that which

gave physical existence : therefore, as there are undeniably some stirrings of spiritual life in penitents, and the beginnings of tendency to life even before true repentance, these are all regarded as evidences of renewal, and regeneration is placed before all other blessings of the Spirit. Man in this theory is purely passive. This doctrine effaces preliminary grace, so far as that grace tends to spiritual activity : such grace is preliminary no longer, but the very regeneration itself. It forgets that wherever the human will is a factor, there can be no pure passivity ; and that the actual state of the soul in which it is passive under the regenerating power of the Spirit is itself produced by a self-surrendering faith of the penitent desire.

Pelagianism.

2. Pelagianism, at the opposite extreme, reduced the great change to an act of the human will: as it is always in man's power to choose, and act accordingly, he really may regenerate himself by fixing his purpose fully on the Good. Semi-Pelagianism admitted that the first conversion requires Divine power, but claimed that the human will in its freedom is that power itself ; and as to the regeneration of the soul it has always regarded that as the Divine blessing on human determination. But this theory in every form lowers grace to external teaching and inducements : nature itself is in a sense grace, and the operation of the Holy Ghost effects nothing that the human will does not under His influence itself accomplish. The error in every Semi-Pelagian theory is that of forgetting that the Holy Spirit always ends, even as He always begins, the work of goodness in man without human concurrence. He begins before co-operation joins Him ; and co-operation must cease at the crisis where He finishes the work.

Semi-Pelagianism

Synergism.

Arminian.

3. Synergism in the Lutheran church differed little from the latter ; but its theory of the sacramental blessing of baptism gave Divine grace its full honour in the case of baptized children. Arminianism in its doctrine of universal prevenient grace carries back the Synergism, or co-operation between God and man, to the nature behind and before baptism. In certain American schemes, which represent regeneration as the right ultimate choice of the soul, there are some errors to be noted. (1.) This choice is a conviction and desire before regeneration, and may be called conversion ; or, in its higher form of entire consecration of the will, it

is a fruit of renewal. It cannot be regeneration itself. (2.) The state of the soul before God is more than merely its present will and act or exercise : it has a disposition or character underlying this with which the new birth has most to do. (3.) Therefore, in common with almost all errors on this subject, these Semi-Pelagian rather than Arminian theories imply a failure to distinguish between the preliminary grace of life and the life of regeneration.

III. Regeneration is sometimes erroneously placed first in the order of the bestowment of Gospel privileges. The release of the sinner from condemnation must take precedence, his new life then begins in its fulness, and that life is consecrated to God in sanctification. But in many confessions regeneration takes the lead, and this doctrine is maintained in various forms by parties fundamentally differing as to the nature of the blessing itself.

Ordo
Salutis.

1. All advocates of sacramental regeneration ex opere operato hold this opinion, at least in the case of infants baptized. Generally, a distinction is established between the regeneration which confers at the outset a germ of spiritual life and the renewal which goes on, with varying and sometimes very irregular processes, to the end. Conversion, on that theory, is placed after regeneration, which is reduced in its significance to the infusion of a principle of grace neutralizing, or rather contending with, the vice of nature ; and, when fall from grace makes it needful, counteracting original sin as a principle of concupiscence.

2. The Latitudinarians who believe in the regeneration of mankind in Christ, and allow no subsequent regeneration as necessary, of course entertain the same notion. By some it is so far modified as to admit a difference, so to speak, between the regeneration that imparts to all the first germ of life, and the new birth or the full consummation of that life. The error of this system, in its best forms, is simply its effacing the distinction between the universal grace which is unto life and life itself. Its sufficient refutation is that one saying : *if any man be in Christ he is a new creature.*

2 Cor. v.
17.

3. This order is quite essential to Calvinism, which allows of no life in the soul of man other than regenerate life, and makes regeneration the precursor of conviction, repentance, faith, and conversion. The first spark of sovereign grace decides all: that once kindled introduces the rest, and can never be extinguished.

4. Calvinism and Sacramentarianism and Latitudinarianism strangely agree, therefore, in denying the possibility of the repetition of regeneration. It is certainly true that the New Testament speaks of one washing of the man who *needeth not save to wash his feet;* also that it declares the impossibility of renewal *unto repentance,* in the case of certain apostates, though not of renewal generally; also that it describes the extinction of the Spirit's life as very difficult. The renewal of regenerate life, however, is never absolutely denied. The theory of the Gospel as laid down by our Lord Himself indicates one regeneration and constant renewal unto its perfection as a full birth of God. But the infinite grace of the new covenant is not bound to that one theory : the high ideal is not to be rigorously pressed.

IV. It is important to notice the many views which are held by philosophic theologians as to the relation of the new birth to the constitution of human nature. This is literally an illimitable subject in itself, though limited in regard to the present question. The true principles of the question are simple.

1. Regeneration is the restored life of the whole nature of man : it is a new heart, the heart being the soul or self, including though distinct from the mind, the affections and the will. These three are one in human nature, and in regeneration, which, in its full meaning, is a new creation or a renewal of the inmost personality.

2. It is not a change in the substance of the soul, nor in its individual acts; but in the bias towards evil which is the character. That bias, however, is not destroyed though it is arrested and made subordinate. In perfect regeneration, which is equivalent in another region of thought to entire sanctification, that bias is utterly suppressed and destroyed.

3. Hence there is in regeneration no distinction between the spirit and the soul, between the πνεῦμα and the ψυχή. The regenerate is spiritual, inasmuch as the Holy Ghost reigns in his spirit : not because by the impartation of the Holy Ghost he has acquired that element, or even attained to the supremacy of the spirit in his nature. Both these are true in the popular and figurative speech of Scripture, which sometimes speaks as if the spirit in man is latent until possessed by the Divine Spirit, and as if the unregenerate spirit is no better than an animal soul.

Margin notes:

John xiii. 10.

Heb. vi. 6.

Human Nature.

But the development of this view into a theory of human nature as unrenewed and renewed leads to great confusion.

V. Lastly, divergences in regard to the value of regeneration as a principle of new life have been more or less anticipated.

Value of Regeneration.

1. The lowest degree is that assigned by those who regard it as the merely being born into a condition or constitution of things. Against this virtual annihilation of the specific gift of the new birth enough has already been said; too much, however, cannot be urged in opposition to a theory which limits the high estate of regeneration to a blessing unconsciously received. All men are born into the new constitution of grace; multitudes of Christian children are baptized into it. But regeneration is more than this universal blessing of redemption.

2. Next comes the theory of those who make it the mere infusion of a germ, so slight that (1) it can scarcely be distinguished from the universal preliminary life that is the gift of redemption, and (2) it is utterly inconsistent with the high views of the ascendency of the regenerate life which Scripture teaches. The lowest doctrine sanctioned by the Word of God includes freedom from the law of sin and death.

3. Some descriptions of this blessing pitch it in so high a strain as to be utterly inconsistent with the common facts of experience. St. John and St. Paul must be reconciled in the true doctrine of regeneration, even as St. Paul and St. James in the true doctrine of justification. St. Paul speaks of a conflict between the flesh and the Spirit, which are *contrary the one to the other* in the ordinary regenerate estate; St. John declares that the ideal and perfect new birth, or being *born of God*, is inconsistent with sin, it *cannot sin.* The one Apostle refers to regeneration in its earlier stages; the other to its perfection. But neither of them denies that a child of God may relapse into sin and need forgiveness. And St. John's sublime doctrine in this text must be harmonised with that of St. Paul, as well as with his own words: *if any man sin, we have an Advocate with the Father.*

Gal. v. 17.

1 John iii. 9.

1 John ii. 1.

CHRISTIAN SANCTIFICATION.

A very extensive class of terms—perhaps the most extensive—exhibits the Christian estate as one of consecration to God. This entire range of phraseology has been transferred from the ancient temple service to the use of the new temple or church. It embraces all aspects of the Christian privilege as one of dedication to God, whether the dedication be external or internal, effected by the Spirit or presented by the believer. But Sanctification is here viewed as a blessing bestowed freely under the covenant of grace; and we must therefore to some extent, though not altogether, omit its ethical relations. As a privilege of the covenant, its principle is twofold: purification from sin, consecration to God; holiness being the state resulting from these. As a gift of grace, it is declared to be perfect in the design of the Spirit; and full provision is made for the Entire Sanctification of the believer in the present life, even as full provision is made for his finished Righteousness and perfect Sonship.

Termi-
nology.
The terms which belong to this branch of Christian theology are abundant : they constitute the largest class of homogeneous phrases in the New Testament ; including almost every word pertaining to the Levitical economy. In their range they embrace the entire vocabulary of the Altar, its sacrifices, oblation, and priesthood, Divine and human; sanctification, dedication, presentation, hallowing, consecration; sprinkling, washing, and putting away sin; purity, sanctity, love and holiness, and the opposites of these, with all their shades; sealing, anointing, and therefore the very word Christian itself. The original terms form a wide and sacred assemblage for the department of Biblical theology; and the careful discrimination of their meanings, in

the light of the Old Testament and of classical Greek, is the best method of studying this whole subject. They may be distributed, however, into two groups : first, those which signify the process of sanctification, as it is negative and positive, that is, as purification from sin and consecration to God; and, secondly, those which define the state of holiness, as it is imperfect and perfect, or partial and entire, sanctification. In considering these, it must be observed that we have not yet to do with ethical sanctification, but with the imparted blessing of the covenant of grace : man's efforts and attainments being subordinate. Of course the corresponding duties cannot be altogether omitted ; but the distinction is important, and it must be remembered throughout our discussion of this privilege of the new covenant.

SANCTIFICATION IN PRINCIPLE AND PROCESS.

Sanctification, negatively considered, is purification from sin; considered positively, it is the consecration of love to God: both being the direct and sole work of the Holy Ghost, and their unity holiness. *Principle.*

I. Purification or cleansing from sin has in the whole Bible, but especially in the New Testament, two meanings : that of a removal of the bar which prevents the Divine acceptance of the offerer at His altar, and of the defilement which renders his offering unfit to be presented. The two meanings are in fact scarcely ever throughout the entire Scriptures disjoined. *Purification.*

1. Christians are sanctified from guilt. This may seem a strange collocation of phrases. But guilt, or the consciousness of sin as our own, is not a forensic word only : it has that meaning in court, and household, and temple. It is before the Divine altar the *conscience of sins* which would keep the offerer from approaching. *How much more shall the blood of Christ, Who through the Eternal Spirit offered Himself without spot to God, purge your conscience from dead works?* Here the term καθαρίζειν is equivalent in the temple to St. Paul's δικαιοῦν in the forum of the gospel: to be purified is to have *our hearts sprinkled from an evil conscience,* from the conscience or guilty consciousness of evil. *From guilt.* Heb. x. 2. Heb. ix. 14. Heb. x. 22.

Defile-
ment.
1 Cor. vi.
11.

Heb. ix.
13.

Ps. li 2.

Macula.

Sanctifi-
cation and
justifica-
tion.
Heb. x.
14—18.

Acts xv. 9.

1 Pet. i. 2.

Eph. v. 26.

2. They are sanctified also by the purification from their sin viewed as defilement. *But ye are washed, but ye are sanctified, but ye are justified:* here the middle term seems to unite the two others in itself. The Old-Testament illustration of this was the *purifying of the flesh,* which was the outward symbol of deliverance not from guilt but from impurity. In fact the word washing is one of the widest terms of the class : it includes all processes for the putting away of sin whether in its guilt or in its defilement, even to the uttermost ; and in this large sense the penitent Psalmist cried out for it : *wash me throughly from mine iniquity,* where iniquity stands for the defilement of which it was the cause. But guilt and defilement may be here viewed as one : since the stain or MACULA of sin is its offensiveness in the sight of God, blotted out or removed when the sinner is accepted.

3. These two are sometimes combined and shown to correspond, in the temple service of Christianity, to the blessings of justification and regeneration in the court mediatorial and the household of faith. Mark the following striking passage : *for by one offering He hath perfected for ever them that are sanctified :* made provision for their perfect pardon and holiness. *Whereof the Holy Ghost also is a witness to us : for after that He had said before, This is the covenant that I will make with them after those days, saith the Lord, I will put My laws into their hearts, and in their minds will I write them ; and their sins and iniquities will I remember no more. Now where remission of these is, there is no more offering for sin.* In these sentences we have justification, regeneration, and sanctification united : remission of sins, the new law in the heart, and both introduced to illustrate the Spirit's perfect sanctification. So in regard to the first Gentiles : *purifying their hearts by faith,* which must include the whole work of the Gospel on them and in them. Though the distinction should not be pressed, it may be said that the purification from guilt is effected by sprinkling as the more external and as it were imputative application of what in washing is more internal, the two however being really the same. We read in St. Peter : *elect . . . through sanctification of the Spirit,* which is divided into two branches : *unto obedience and sprinkling of the blood of Jesus Christ.* From the defilement and internal corruption of sin Christians are cleansed or washed : *that He might*

sanctify and cleanse it with the washing of water by the word. The washing, however, sometimes must include both, as in the doxology *unto Him that loved us and washed us from our sins in His own blood :* Rev. i. 5. here the reading λούσαντι is in some texts significantly changed into λύσαντι. Whichever reading is right, the corrector has not introduced a theological error ; for the washing is equivalent to release from guilt, the loosing and the cleansing being the same. Both ideas are found in some of the synonyms employed, such as the *putting away* or *taking away* of sin. Sanctification has Heb. x. the double meaning in another passage : *Jesus also, that He might* 4, 11. *sanctify the people with His own blood ;* and also in such as speak of Heb. xiii. Christians as *sanctified in Christ Jesus, called to be saints.* 12. 1 Cor. i. 2.

II. The positive element of sanctification is the Holy Spirit's Consecra- consecration to God of what is dedicated to God by man. In the tion. New Testament this is the love of God which *is shed abroad in our* Rom. v. *hearts by the Holy Ghost which is given unto us :* the Divine love as 5. the principle of consecration awakening our love as the principle of our personal dedication.

1. There is a lower, wider, and, as it were, improper sense of Things. the term throughout the Scriptures. (1.) What is already holy is sanctified by the acknowledgment of its holiness. *Hallowed be* Matt. vi. *Thy name ! Sanctify the Lord God in your hearts. Let him be holy* 9. *still,* signifying that the accomplished holiness of the saints is to 1 Pet. iii. be for ever ratified and accepted in heaven. The idea here is that Rev. xxii. of absolute separation from all unholiness ; and the term is always 11. ἁγιάζειν : the recognition of an existing sanctity. (2.) What is common, and in that sense unsanctified, but without connoting so far as that is possible any moral character in the object, is made holy : the opposite of κοινὸν ἡγεῖσθαι. *The temple that sanctifieth* Matt. *the gold. It is sanctified by the word of God and prayer.* (3.) The xxiii. 17. term in these last instances refers to things ; but everywhere else 1 Tim. iv. in the New Testament it is used of persons, and this personal con- 5. secration may be said to absorb into itself all other meanings. It will be useful, however, to remember the distinction when we come to consider more fully the imputative character of sanctification.

2. Consecration proper of persons is to be viewed as twofold : Persons. it is to God's possession and to God's service.

(1.) The leading, or at least the most important, idea is that of Possession

and
Fellow-
ship.

possession. All men belong to God by creation ; but the bestowment of the virtue of redemption makes them His in a special
sense ; and if they are His then all that they have becomes His :
consecration in detail follows from and is a part of the general
consecration. The believer is supposed to DEDICATE himself, and
the Spirit SANCTIFIES him to God. CONSECRATION is a term in
English synonymous with both, common therefore to the believer

Eph. v. 26,
27.

and the Spirit, as in many passages. *That He might sanctify and
cleanse it . . . that He might present it to Himself a glorious church,*
where consecration and presentation are united as the Divine act.
Here we have the sanctification following on the purification,
ἁγιάσῃ καθαρίσας, and the word dedicate or present used of Christ

Rom. xii.
1.
Rom. vi.
13.
Titus ii.
14.

Himself, even as St. Paul limits it to the believer : *that ye present
your bodies,* or *yield yourselves unto God.* Both ideas are in the
words *and purify unto Himself a peculiar people :* teaching also as
a significant addition that the consecration is to Christ as Divine ;
for none but God receives the consecrated object. The possession,
however, is the same as union and fellowship. The souls that are
dedicated and consecrated to God are not merely His ; they have

1 John i.
3, 7.

also the most intimate union with Him. *Truly our fellowship
is with the Father and with His Son Jesus Christ :* a fellowship of
sanctification dependent on our being cleansed from sin. It is the
glory of the believer's relation to God in the new covenant that it
is more than being simply His property. It is a transcendent and

John xvii.
17, 23.

mystical communion : *sanctify them through Thy truth ;* and *I in
them and Thou in Me, that they may be made perfect in one.*

Service.

(2.) Then follows consecration to the service of God. The
Divine temple and the Divine service are correlative terms. The

2 Cor. vi.
16.
1 Pet. ii. 5.
Acts xvii.
28.
1 John iv.
16.
2 Tim. ii.
21.

whole life of the Christian is spent in a sanctuary. The people
are the house of God : *ye are the temple of the living God ;* their life
is their worship : *to offer up spiritual sacrifices ;* and He is Himself
the temple in which *we live, and move, and have our being :* for
he that dwelleth in love dwelleth in God. Hence the spirit of consecration is that of entire devotion to the Divine service. Christians are vessels *unto honour, sanctified and meet for the Master's use.*

The Seal.

3. The Holy Ghost is the seal and the power of this consecration ; and these as it were in one, yet with a distinction : He is

Eph. i. 13,
14.

the SEAL of God's possession, and the POWER of dedication to

God's service. *After that ye believed—or on believing,* πιστεύσαντες— ye were sealed, ἐσφραγίσθητε, *with that Holy Spirit of promise, which is the earnest of our inheritance until the redemption of the purchased possession :* here God's possession is sealed till He finally redeems it ; and the seal that sets apart His people is the beginning of their own experience of religion, which is the possession of God as their inheritance. The mere contact with the altar sanctified the gold, but the spirit of man is sanctified by no less than the indwelling Spirit. The consciousness of the presence of the Holy Ghost within is the testimony to the Christian that he is sanctified to God : as to his pardon and adoption the Spirit as it were speaketh expressly ; but his sanctification is silently declared by His very presence and indwelling. So much for the former, the Seal ; as to the latter, the Power, the Holy Ghost is the energy of the soul's consecration to the will and service of God. The *faith which worketh by love* is the faith which is the *fruit of the Spirit.* It is the strength of all obedience, and resignation, and devotion. The Spirit whose indwelling assures of acceptance is the power of a final consecration of every faculty to God : entire sanctification—to anticipate—is this, and only this. It is the full, unhindered, unlimited, almighty energy of the power of His presence in the soul.

[margin: Eph. i. 13, 14.]

[margin: Gal. v. 6. Gal. v. 22.]

III. The unity of these is HOLINESS. Those who are purged, or sprinkled from sin, which is separation from God, and who are consecrated to Him, are holy or saints, ἅγιοι. Christ is their ἁγιασμός : the ground or principle or source of their sanctification as in process, in every sense negativing their sin. The state in which they live is that of ἁγιωσύνη, or holiness.

[margin: Holiness]

1. It is a relative sanctity : not of course forensic, but corresponding nevertheless to the imputation of righteousness. As there is a holy day, a holy church, a holy city ; and as *whatsoever toucheth the altar shall be holy,* be accounted holy, so Christians are *an holy nation.* *The holy city* was most impure when so called, in remembrance of its past, and as yet not altogether forfeited, sanctity ; and the congregation of Corinth were addressed notwithstanding their partial unholiness as *sanctified in Christ Jesus.*

[margin: Relative.]

[margin: Ex. xxix. 37. 1 Pet. ii. 9. Matt. xxvii. 53.]

[margin: 1 Cor. i. 2.]

2. But this last quotation indicates that it is also an internal holiness : not only *called saints* but *called to be saints :* the addition in the translation precisely expresses the double truth, that all

[margin: Internal.]

who are called saints are called to become such. These same Corinthians termed holy are exhorted to attain moral sanctity:

2 Cor. vii. 1. *let us cleanse ourselves from all filthiness of the flesh and spirit, perfecting holiness in the fear of God,* ἐπιτελοῦντες ἁγιωσύνην. As the soul is one and indivisible, its leading principle of consecration to God gives it its character, though that is not yet perfect.

1 John i. 7. The daily, habitual washing *cleanseth us from all sin,* καθαρίζει, as a fountain continually sending its streams over the soul.

Combined. 3. The external and internal holiness are always combined in the purpose of God. No sanctity possible to man, even at the foot of the throne, is perfect without imputation. The past sin is regarded as for ever sprinkled away: it remains as a fact of history, but a cancelled fact; as a defilement that once was, but is now effaced. But no imputation of sanctity as belonging to the church will avail without the reality. In the attainment of Christian perfection the external and the internal are one.

Terminology. 4. Many other terms are used to denote the estate of holiness under each of the two aspects of purification and consecration. It is described rather with reference to the Divine act in

1 Cor. i. 30.
1 Thess. iv. 3.
1 Pet. i. 2.
2 Cor. vi. 6.
1 John iii. 3.
Heb. i. 3.
2 Pet. i. 9.
ἁγιασμός, SANCTIFICATION. Christ is *made unto us sanctification; The will of God, even your sanctification; Chosen unto sanctification of the Spirit:* thus referring to each person of the Trinity. Purification results in PURITY: besides the more limited ἁγνεία the term ἁγνότης, *pureness,* is used. He *that hath this hope in Him purifieth himself, even as He is pure.* Καθαρισμός includes deliverance both from guilt and from pollution: objectively, *when He had by Himself purged our sins;* subjectively, *hath forgotten that he was purged from his old sins.* Though the distinction is not absolute, positive consecration to God is generally expressed by the word sanctification itself. Our Lord first spoke of His own as

John xvii. 19. *sanctified through the truth:* this, following *I sanctify Myself,* must refer to a positive consecration to God. There is no other term which in the Greek Testament expresses the positive side of dedication to God. But the consecrated state is variously viewed.

Rom. viii. 27, 28. *He maketh intercession for the saints:* the word saints here refers to the high ideal character of those who *love God,* and of whom the

1 Cor. i. 2. whole process of salvation is affirmed. *Sanctified in Christ Jesus:* Christ is the scene, and sphere, and region, the temple, and shrine,

and holiest, in which believers are consecrated and set apart. *By the which will we are sanctified through the offering of the body of Jesus Christ once for all:* here the term is ἡγιασμένοι, ideally and completely sanctified in virtue of the one perfect offering. *For by one offering He hath perfected for ever them that are sanctified:* here the word is ἁγιαζομένους, in course or process of sanctification, and ideally perfected or rendered independent of any other sacrifice. In the purpose of redemption they are the Lord's for ever.

Heb. x. 10, 14.

5. It is worthy of remark that consecration to God as a state is predicated of man's nature in all its constituent elements. *And the very God of peace sanctify you wholly; and I pray God your whole spirit and soul and body be preserved blameless.* Hence it is said, *Your body is the temple of the Holy Ghost;* and the exhortation is to *present your bodies,* that the Spirit may consecrate and sanctify them to God. This is the characteristic distinction of sanctification: it is of the whole man viewed in all the constituents of his nature. It cannot be said of justification, as the body of the justified person *is dead because of sin,* and not yet released from the executioner; nor, as yet, of adoption, which includes the whole man only at the last day, as the sons of God will be altogether such only when they become *the children of the resurrection.*

The Whole Man.

1 Thess. v. 23.

1 Cor. vi. 19.
Rom. xii. 1.

Rom. viii. 10.

Lu. xx. 36.

SANCTIFICATION PROGRESSIVE AND PERFECT.

While there is a sense in which sanctification is a permanent and unchangeable principle, it is also a process which reaches its consummation, according to the provisions of the New Covenant and the testimony of the Spirit, in the present life.

1. It is obvious that wherever the term is used to signify that in the temple which justification means in the lawcourt of Christianity it admits of no change. *The worshippers, once purged, should have had no more conscience of sins.* The term *purged* is afterwards varied into *sanctified,* κεκαθαρμένους becomes ἡγιασμένοι: *by the which will we are sanctified through the offering of the body of Jesus Christ once for all.* Like justification this sanctification is a definitive

Unchangeable.
Heb. x. 2.

Heb. x. 10.

act ; and the sanctified, like the justified, live without the consciousness of sin as an obstacle to entrance into the holiest :
Heb.x.22. having their hearts *sprinkled from an evil conscience.*

2. The positive consecration also knows no change as a principle. Whatever is on *the altar that sanctifieth the gift* is, in virtue
Matt. xxiii. 19. of being on it, the Lord's : nothing can be at one and the same time both sanctified and not sanctified. The Holy Spirit—Who is the Lord and Giver of holiness as well as of life, these two being the same—is once bestowed, and once for all, on believers
Eph. i. 13, 14. who *were sealed* as His *until the redemption of the purchased possession.* All who are born of God in the New economy enter into the privileges of the firstborn under the Old. The adopted children
Ex. xiii. 2. of the house are sanctified in the temple : *sanctify unto Me all the firstborn.* The consecrating principle of love is the first grace of the new birth. It is in all its degrees the permanent instrument of the Spirit's sanctification of the regenerate soul.

3. Holiness as a state is also in the usage of Scripture unchangeable. The New Testament speaks of that state as ideal, and as virtually perfected in all who belong to Christ. In this
Heb.ii.11. sense also, *He that sanctifieth and they who are sanctified are all of one.* They are seen by anticipation, which to God is not antici-
1 Cor. i. 2. pation, as *sanctified in Christ Jesus.* In the backward perspective
Rom. viii. 29. of St. Paul, they are already *conformed to the image of His Son,* which is once more sanctification in terms borrowed from Christian sonship.

PROGRESSIVE SANCTIFICATION.

In His administration of sanctifying grace the Holy Spirit proceeds by degrees. Terms of progress are applied to each department of that work in the saint ; or, in other words, the goal of entire sanctification is represented as the end of a process in which the Spirit requires the co-operation of the believer. This co-operation, however, is only the condition on which is suspended what is the work of Divine grace alone.

Gradual Purification.   I. The negative side of sanctification as the removal of sin is described as a process ; and in a variety of ways.

1. The most familiar is that which represents the sinning nature as under the doom of death. *Our old man is crucified with Him, that the body of sin might be destroyed, that henceforth we should not serve sin:* crucifixion is a gradual mortal process, disqualifying the body from serving any master, and as such certainly tending to death. So in the parallel to the Galatians : *they that are Christ's have crucified the flesh with the affections and lusts.* And elsewhere they are said to *put off the old man* and *put on the new man.* Moreover, in the last passage the Apostle bids us *mortify therefore your members* by killing, or weakening down to extinction, every individual tendency or disposition to evil. Not only is the old man to be destroyed by the doom of crucifixion, but every specific member of his sin is to be surrendered to atrophy : *Make not provision for the flesh, to fulfil the lusts thereof.* Crucifixion is of the whole body : mortification is of each member. Now, while all these passages refer to the earnest self-discipline of the believer, entering into the design of redemption, they represent only the submission of faith which brings into the soul the virtue of the lifegiving and deathgiving Spirit. *If we live in the Spirit, let us also walk in the Spirit:* walk in the way of sorrow, the via dolorosa, that leads to death, the death of sin. *If ye* THROUGH THE SPIRIT *do mortify the deeds of the body ye shall live.* It is the Holy Ghost who does what we do through Him.

2. From this we may deduce two principles. First, the general bias, or character of the soul, becomes positively more and more alienated from sin and set upon good ; and, proportionally, the susceptibility to temptation or the affinity with sin becomes negatively less and less evident in its consciousness. There is in the healthy progress of the Christian a constant confirmation of the will in its ultimate choice, and a constant increase of its power to do what it wills : the vanishing point of perfection in the will is to be. entirely merged in the will of God. There is also a perpetual weakening of the susceptibility to temptation : what was at first a hard contest gradually advances to the sublime triumph of the Saviour, *Get thee hence, Satan !* Every active and every passive grace steadily advances : and sin fades out of the nature. Every habit of evil is unwound from the life ; until at length the Christian can say, like his Master, *The prince of this*

Side notes:

Death.
Rom. vi. 6.

Gal. v. 24.

Col. iii.
5, 9, 10.

Rom. xiii.
14.

Gal. v. 23.

Rom. viii.
13.

Bias to
Sin.

Matt. iv.
10.

John xiv.
30.

world cometh, and hath nothing in Me. This gradual and sure depression of the sinful principle down to its zero or limit of nonentity is progressive sanctification. *He is faithful and just to forgive us our sins, and to cleanse us from all unrighteousness:* by a beautiful confusion of figures the obliquity remaining in the soul is a defilement which is in process of being entirely cleansed away. This refers to particular sins: more generally, *the blood of Jesus Christ His Son cleanseth us from all sin.*

II. The positive side—that of consecration by the Spirit of love—is also a process, a gradual process.

1. The Spirit Himself is given *by measure* to us, though not to the Incarnate Son for us. Of this great gift it holds good: *unto every one which hath shall be given.* The exhortation is to *be filled with the Spirit.* Of the first Pentecostal Christians it is said that they were *filled with the Holy Ghost;* but we afterwards find variations of gift and fluctuations in faithful use of the gift down to the lowest point of declension: *sensual, having not the Spirit.*

2. Hence the shedding abroad of the love of God by the Holy Ghost admits of increase. It is enough to cite the Apostle's prayer: *that your love may abound yet more and more.* This, in harmony with the uniform tenour of Scripture, refers to the growth of love towards God and man. It is more important to show that the love of God towards us, or, as St. John calls it, *love with us,*—where the love of God to us and our love to Him *because He first loved us,* are the same—is a progressive and ever-strengthening principle. St. John in his first Epistle proves this. Once he uses an expression which indicates that the love of God attains a perfect operation in us. Ἐν τούτῳ τετελείωται ἡ ἀγάπη μεθ᾽ ἡμῶν: *herein is our love—*or *love with us—made perfect.* St. Paul says, *the love of Christ constraineth us:* meaning that love in us which constraineth Christ Himself: *How am I straitened till it be accomplished!* The term συνέχει points to a gradually deepening pressure, and, as in the Lord Himself so in His servants, the power of love drives every impediment before it. In His servants, but not as in the Lord Himself, it gradually, surely, and effectually gathers itself within closer and closer bonds until its force becomes irresistible. And of that same love the Ephesian prayer asks: *that ye being rooted and grounded in love, may be able to comprehend*

1 John i. 9.

1 John i. 7.

Gradual Consecration.

John iii. 34.
Luke xix. 26.
Eph. v. 18.
Acts ii. 4.

Jude 19.

Phil. i. 9.

1 John iv. 17, 19.

1 John iv. 17.
2 Cor. v. 14.
Luke xii. 50.

Eph. iii. 18, 19.

with all saints what is the breadth and length and depth and height ; and to know the love of Christ which passeth knowledge.

III. Holiness as an estate is also described as progressive : first, as a goal to be attained ; to be attained, secondly, through human effort; but, lastly, only as the bestowment of the Holy Ghost, the Supreme Agent of all good.

Pro-
gressive
Holiness.

1. Once we have the expression *perfecting holiness,* ἐπιτελοῦντες, where the word indicates an end to which effort is ever converging, whether that end be fully attained or not : in any case it is a progress. Again, St. Paul prays, *The very God of peace sanctify you wholly,* where the gradual perfecting of body, soul and spirit is obviously referred to. Again, a still higher prayer, *Sanctify them through Thy truth : Thy word is truth !* truth, however, which the Lord always speaks of as gradually imparted, *He will guide you into all truth ;* and of which He says, *If ye continue in My word, then are ye My disciples indeed ; and ye shall know the truth, and the truth shall make you free.* But the clearest evidence is in the tenour of the language used on the subject, of which this is a specimen : *For both He that sanctifieth and they who are sanctified are all of one.* The brethren, whom the High Priest gradually succours and saves, are οἱ ἁγιαζομένοι, those who are *in process of sanctification :* parallel with τοὺς σωζομένους, such as were *in process of salvation.* It is important to remember the form of the present participles in these passages : in the latter it is not σεσωσμένους, such as *were effectually saved,* nor σωθησομένους, such as *should be saved ;* in the former it is not ἡγιασμένοι, such as were *once for all sanctified.*

2 Cor. vii.
1.
1 Thess. v.
17.
John xvii.
17.
John xvi.
13.
John viii.
31, 32.
Heb. ii. 11.
Acts ii. 47.

2. The sanctification administered, effected, imparted as the free gift of the Holy Ghost is also conditional on the effort of man. Here the blessing of the Christian covenant enters into the ethical region. It is exceedingly difficult to keep the two apart. Reserving for Christian Ethics the consideration of much that belongs to the subject, we note that the process of sanctification keeps pace with the fulfilment of certain conditions. A few illustrations, referring to each department, will be enough.

Con-
ditional.

(1.) We are exhorted as Christians to *cleanse ourselves from all filthiness of the flesh and spirit :* this is remarkable as being one of the few passages in which the Levitical cleansing of the Holy Ghost is actually made a human work, καθαρίσωμεν. Such

2 Cor. vii.
1.

passages, the force of which can be felt only in the original Greek, ought to be carefully studied, as shedding a rich light upon the whole doctrine of human co-operation with Divine grace. The same things are true in Him and in us. St. James says: καθα-

James iv. 8. ρίσατε, *cleanse your hands,* and ἁγνίσατε, *purify your hearts.* And St. Paul uses the strong expression *mortify therefore your members:*

Col. iii. 5, 9, 10. νεκρώσατε, a word which seems to appropriate the special office of the Holy Ghost, who alone in this sense can say, *I kill and I make*

Deut. xxxii.39. *alive.* Christians are said to *put off the old man* and to *put on the new man.* No one understands all these passages aright who does not see that they all hang upon one principle, that the Spirit's work in

2 Cor. vii. 1. us is made our own. *Having these promises* governs them all. But, on the other hand, such passages would not be found were it not the intention of the Spirit to impress on us a high estimate of our own responsibility.

Human Co-operation. (2.) Nothing is more constantly declared than that the effusion of the Spirit of consecration keeps pace with the co-operation of the believer. Whether he regards love as that of God to us, or as the response in us to Him, St. John inculcates the need of our

1 John ii. 5. compliance with conditions. *But whoso keepeth His word, in him verily is the love of God perfected: hereby know we that we are in Him.* Not by the sovereign and arbitrary despotism of grace, but as the blessing resting on earnest and universal obedience, which itself is

1 John iv. 12, 13. of God, is love made perfect. Again: *If we love one another, God dwelleth in us, and His love is perfected in us. Hereby know we that we dwell in Him and He in us, because He hath given us of His Spirit.* The Spirit of our union with God is a Spirit of consecration perfectly sanctifying those who abound in self-sacrificing devotion to

1 John iv. 16, 17. others. Once more: *God is love; and he that dwelleth in love dwelleth in God, and God in him. Herein is our love made perfect, that we may have boldness in the day of judgment: because as He is, so are we in this world.* Though the perfect copying of the Lord's example is not exactly a condition, it is a close concomitant, of the perfect effusion of the consecrating Spirit. In all three cases the indwelling of God by the Spirit is the efficient cause, while OBEDIENCE, CHARITY to man, and the IMITATION OF CHRIST are the three-one condition. Love is the channel for imparting and the instrument for producing love : FROM LOVE TO LOVE answering

here to St. Paul's *from faith to faith.* We have, however, to do Rom. i. 17.
simply with the evidence afforded, that the consecration of love
is a conditional process. The spirit of devotion to God becomes
stronger in proportion as these conditions are kept in dependence
on the Spirit who imparts that love.

(3.) As to the state of holiness it is a goal to the attainment of   Holiness
which Christian men are habitually required to bend their effort.   a grace.
It is the object of their own aspiration. This is generally and
universally true : it is the secret and strength of the command,
perfecting holiness. Here we may combine the idea of holiness   2 Cor. vii.
with those of righteousness and sonship : the three are one in the   1.
perfection which they require the Christian to keep in view. As
to righteousness : *that the righteousness of the law might be fulfilled in*   Rom. viii.
us, in whom *love is the fulfilling of the law.* The word fulfilled   4.
here must have its full force ; it refers to the gradual accomplish-   Rom. xiii.
ment of a design. But it must be carefully noted that the Divine   10.
power in this accomplishment has the pre-eminence. Indeed the
word πληρωθῇ belongs strictly only to God, for it is He who
fulfils the demands of righteousness ; while the addition *in us who
walk not after the flesh but after the Spirit* sufficiently vindicates our
use of the text : the Divine grace in our lives gradually and surely
works out the requirements of the new evangelical law interpreted
by grace. And this new law defies the criticism of man : it is *the*   Rom. iii.
righteousness of God, who is the only Lawgiver. As to sonship : The   21.
Father *did predestinate to be conformed to the image of His Son* children   Rom. viii.
who *are changed into the same image from glory to glory.* The decree   29.
that every child of God shall be like that *Holy Child,* the Eternal   2 Cor. iii. 18.
Son made flesh, is revealed in the inmost soul ; and the Spirit of   Acts iv.
adoption within us seeks the form of the Pattern in His word,   27.
and for ever contemplates it with a transforming love. As to
holiness : *Be ye holy ; for I am holy.* To all these the Saviour   1 Pet. i.
refers in the benedictions of the Sermon on the Mount. *Blessed*   16.
are they which do hunger and thirst after righteousness, for they shall be   Matt. v. 6.
filled : this is the blessing of the evangelical law. It is the benediction pronounced, as we believe, by anticipation, on the diligent
pursuit of the new righteousness of faith, the deep meaning of
which was not yet revealed. Hence the force of the future, *they
shall be filled. Blessed are the pure in heart, for they shall see God :*   Matt. v. 8.

this is the blessing of entire consecration, which is, negatively, that of the *pure* or the sanctified from sin, and, positively, that of the pure *in heart,* or those whose heart and inmost personality are

Matt. v. 9. inflamed with the love of all holiness. *Blessed are the peacemakers, for they shall be called the children of God:* this is the blessing promised to the future Christian household, one in perfect brotherly love and in the diffusion of its peace. But these and all other blessings are promised to those who by patient continuance in well-doing seek them. Christian perfection is the exceeding great reward of perseverance in the renunciation of all things for God; in the exercise of love to God, as shown in passive submission and active devotion, and in the strenuous obedience of all His commandments. The heirs of the Christian inheritance

Ps. cxliii. 10. are led and not rapt *into the land of uprightness:* there is no suspension in their case of the general law which governs all the Divine dealings with man. As there is a preliminary grace which leads to the perfect life of regeneration, so there is a preliminary regenerate grace which leads to the perfection of consecration to

Matt. xiii. 12. God. *For whosoever hath to him shall be given, and he shall have more abundance:* a word of our Lord which has a wide application throughout the entire range of Christian theology.

All of the Spirit. 3. Is then the process of sanctification ended by an attainment which rewards human endeavour simply? Assuredly not: the Holy Spirit finishes the work in His own time, and in His own way, as His own act, and in the absolute supremacy if not in the absolute sovereignty of His own gracious power.

Gal. v. 24, 25. (1.) Every act and every habit of holiness is of the Spirit. Though those who are Christ's are said themselves to *have crucified the flesh with the affections and lusts,* this is a union with the

Rom. vi. 10. mystery of the cross in the fellowship of Him *Who died unto sin once,* which only the Spirit can effect: hence it immediately follows, *If we live in the Spirit, let us also walk in the Spirit.* Whatever is done by man in the mortification of his sin is really done by the Holy Ghost in him. Self-crucifixion is abhorrent to human nature, and to human nature impossible. Approaches to it may be found in human ethics; but its inmost secret is never reached save as the mystical teaching of the Cross. When our Saviour commanded

Luke xiv. 26. His follower to hate *yea his own life also,* He first illustrated His

precept by His own self-sacrifice, and then left His Spirit to teach
the stern lesson to His people. He alone can teach it. *No man* Eph. v. 29.
ever yet hated his own flesh: applying this to his *sinful flesh*, we Rom. viii.
may say that what no man ever did by nature the grace of God 3.
can make him do. So also the highest term for the consecration
of the purified is reserved for the Spirit : while all but the highest
are given to the believer. *If a man therefore purge himself from* 2 Tim. ii.
these, he shall be a vessel unto honour, sanctified : ἐκκαθάρῃ ἑαυτὸν, his 21.
own work ; ἡγιασμένον, the Divine work in him. While the
Christian keeps his evil nature impaled on the interior cross, it is
the sword of the Spirit from on high that takes its life away ; and
when he is entirely swayed by Divine love, this is *the law of the* Rom. viii.
Spirit of life within him. 2.

(2.) There is a consummation of the Christian experience which τετέλεσται.
may be said to introduce perfection, when the Spirit cries, IT IS
FINISHED, in the believer. The moment when sin expires, known
only to God, is the Divine victory over sin in the soul : this is the
office of the Spirit alone. The moment when love becomes supreme
in its ascendency, a moment known only to God, is the Spirit's
triumph in the soul's consecration : this also is entirely His work.
And whenever that maturity of Christian experience and life is
reached which the Apostle prays for so often, it is solely through
the operation of the same Spirit. It is being *filled with all the* Eph. iii.
fulness of God, and that through being *strengthened with might by* 16—19.
His Spirit in the inner man.

(3.) While, therefore, the tenour of the New Testament represents entire sanctification as the result of a process, it is also
ascribed to the result of the constant effusion of the Holy Ghost,
crowned in one last and consummating act of His power. Of this
resurrection also we may ask, as the Apostle asked concerning
another, *Why should it be thought a thing incredible?* And with Acts xxvi.
the same emphasis : τί ; what ? a thing incredible that GOD should 8.
raise the dead ! should raise a dead soul to perfect life !

(4.) But, lastly, it must be remembered that this final and
decisive act of the Spirit is the seal set upon a previous and continuous work. The processes may be hastened and condensed
into a short space ; they must be passed through as processes.
Yea, we establish the law was the Apostle's vindication of the doc- Rom. iii.
31.

Rom. iv. 5. trine of *faith counted for righteousness ;* and the same vindication is necessary for the process of sanctification. The justified have their

Rom. vi. 22. *fruit unto holiness.* Uniting the life of justification with that of

John x. 10. sanctification our Lord said : *I am come that they might have life,* and that they might have *it* MORE : the same gift expanding unto perfection for ever. There is no new dispensation of the Spirit in any such sense as there was a new covenant superseding the old : the Spirit of entire sanctification is only the Spirit of the beginning of grace exerting an ampler power. Never do we read of a HIGHER LIFE that is other than the intensification of the lower ; never of a SECOND BLESSING that is more than the un-

Acts xix. 4. restrained outpouring of the same Spirit who gave the first. *Have ye received the Holy Ghost since ye believed?* means, Did you receive the Holy Ghost on believing ? ἐλάβετε πιστεύσαντες ? and cannot refer to a reception of the higher gift superinduced on a lower gift which was without the Spirit of entire consecration. The

Jude 19. only instance in which Christians are said to be *without the Spirit* is that one in which St. Jude describes the fallen state of men

Gal. iii. 3. who, to use St. Paul's words, *having begun in the Spirit* were now *made perfect in the flesh :* had reached the most lamentable issue of being *sensual* again. Moreover, this was said to a portion, though an ignorant portion, of the same Ephesian congregation to whom

Eph. i. 13. St. Paul wrote : *After that ye believed, ye were sealed with that Holy Spirit of promise,* πιστεύσαντες ἐσφραγίσθητε, believing ye were sealed. There is no restraint of time with the Holy Ghost. The preparations for an entire consecration to God may be long continued or they may be hastened. Whenever the seal of perfection is set on the work, whether in death or in life, it must be a critical and instantaneous act ; possibly known to God alone, or, if revealed in the trembling consciousness of the believer, a secret that he knows not how to utter. But this leads us from the Sanctuary to the Most Holy Place.

ENTIRE SANCTIFICATION.

Provision is made in the Christian covenant for the completeness of the Saviour's work as the perfect application of His atonement to the believer. This may be

viewed as the complete destruction of sin, as the entireness of consecration to God, and as the state of consummate holiness to which the character of the saint may be formed in the present life. These privileges may be regarded respectively as Entire Sanctification, Perfect Love, and Evangelical Perfection : these being one as the finished application of the Saviour's Finished Work, so far as its consummation belongs to time and to grace.

It is not meant that these three are distinct branches of Christian privilege. Each implies the other ; and neither can be treated without involving the rest. Nor are the terms exact as indicating each its particular department : for instance, sanctification is as much positive consecration to God as negative purifying from sin. But the distinction is convenient as giving opportunity for a methodical, and, if the term may be admitted, scientific view of all sides of this most important question. Controversy will be excluded as out of harmony with this most sacred subject : what polemical reference may be necessary will be reserved for the Historical Review.

PURIFICATION FROM SIN OR ENTIRE SANCTIFICATION.

The virtue of the atonement, administered by the Holy Spirit, is set forth in Scripture as effecting the entire destruction of sin. This is everywhere declared to be the design of redemption : and it is promised to the believer as his necessary preparation for the future life. The entire removal of sin from the nature is nowhere connected with any other means than the word of God received in faith and proved in experience.

I. The work of Christ has for its end the removal of sin from the nature of man : from the nature of the believer in this present life. No end is kept more constantly before us.

1. Generally viewed, this is an uncontested truth. *For this purpose the Son of God was manifested, that He might destroy the*

[margin:] Entire Sanctification.

[margin:] Abolition of Sin.

[margin:] 1 John iii. 8.

works of the devil : words which refer to evil in Christian individuals, and not only to the whole empire of sin and Satan, as the scene of active rebellion, in the history of our race. The words are introduced between two others which give them a deep and un-limited meaning. *He was manifested to take away our sins; and in Him is no sin.* Sinless Himself He makes His people sinless. *Whosoever is born of God* doth not *commit sin* in outward act; *he cannot sin because he is born of God,* in inward principle. And this is said of the final and distinguishing mark of those who are thus approved, in the highest ideal sense made real as the children of God : *in this the children of God are manifest and the children of the devil.* The manifestation is here the full and finished revelation of their internal truth of God. *He appeared to put away sin by the sacrifice of Himself :* ἀθετῆσαι, to abolish, a term which goes beyond the sacrificial terminology of the Epistle, like that of the Baptist : *Behold the Lamb of God, which taketh away the sin of the world.* Our Lord *gave Himself for us, that He might redeem us from all iniquity, and purify unto Himself a peculiar people, zealous of good works :* here is every term of sanctification applied to the design of Christ's death as it regards those who, being capable of good works, must of course be regarded as still living upon earth. Hence St. John testifies that *the blood of Jesus Christ His Son cleanseth from all sin :* both in the Levitical and in the moral sense, FROM ALL SIN, from all that is called sin, whether it be its guilt before God or its power in man. And St. Paul declares it to be the design of our crucifixion with Christ, that is of our union by faith with Christ's death to sin, *that the body of sin might be destroyed :* that sin actuating our mortal bodies, and making it its servant, might be deprived of us as its slaves, the body of our service being abolished. *He that is dead is freed* or justified *from sin ;* so the earthly instru-ment of service is destroyed that we *henceforth should not serve sin.* It is not merely that the slavery of sin is ended ; but the body that serves is to be altogether abolished. There cannot be service if there is nothing wherewith to serve. Therefore, finally, these Apostles unite in exhorting Christians to regard themselves as altogether delivered from the law of sin. St. John says : *these things write I unto you, that ye sin not.* St. Paul, yet more compre-hensively, *reckon ye also yourselves to be dead indeed unto sin :* a moral

Marginal references:
1 John iii. 5.
1 John iii. 9.
Heb. ix. 26.
John i. 29.
Titus ii. 14.
1 John i. 7.
Rom. vi. 6.
Rom. vi. 7.
1 John ii. 1.
Rom. vi. 11.

imputation in ourselves answering to God's forensic imputation. St. John evidently refers to God's purpose that the cleansing efficacy should deliver from sin; and his qualification *if any man sin* only puts the case as one not contemplated as of necessity but provided for us in mercy. St. Paul bids us make a generous use of the doctrine of imputation; and rejoice in the consciousness that we may be, and shall be, saved from all connection with evil. These several passages in their combination establish generally the whole doctrine of a purification provided for all sin.

1 John ii. 1.

2. More particularly, we have to do with Original Sin. This has two meanings here: it is the individual portion of the common heritage, and it is the common sin that infects the race of man during the whole evolution of its history in time.

Destruction of Original Sin.

(1.) As to the latter, it is not to be doubted that original sin, or sin as generic and belonging to the race in its federal constitution on earth, is not abolished till the time of which it is said, *Behold, I make all things new:* as something of the penalty remains untaken away, so also something of the peculiar concupiscence or liability to temptation or affinity with evil that besets man in this world remains. The saint delivered from personal sin is still connected with sin by his own past: the one forgiveness is regarded as perpetually renewed until the final act of mercy. *If we say that we have no sin, we deceive ourselves:* we are numbered with the transgressors in one sense still, though not reckoned with them in another. There is no man who must not join in the prayer: *Forgive us our trespasses.* Hence it is not usual to speak of original sin, absolutely, as done away in Christ. The race has its *sin that doth so easily beset,* its εὐπερίστατον ἁμαρτίαν; and we must cease to belong to the lineage of Adam before our unsinning state becomes sinlessness.

Objective.

Rev. xxi. 5.

1 John i.8.

Matt. vii. 6.

Heb. xii. 1.

Subjective.

(2.) But original sin in its quality as the *sin that dwelleth in* the Me of the soul, as the principle in man that has actual affinity with transgression, as the source and *law of sin which is in my members,* as the animating soul of *the body of this death,* and, finally, as *the flesh with the affections and lusts,* is abolished by the SPIRIT OF HOLINESS indwelling in the Christian, when His purifying grace has its perfect work.

Rom vii. 20,23,24.

Gal. v. 18.

3. And certainly the scene of our Saviour's atoning sacrifice is

On Earth.

always set forth as the scene of His redeeming power. There is only one redemption which is reserved for His second coming: *the redemption of our body.* But there is no other. The argument is complete in itself, and scarcely needs further corroboration. The counteraction of sin must needs be entire and complete in man and upon earth: the other world is the sphere of fruition and judgment. There is no hint given in the Scriptural history of redemption that the finished triumph of the Deliverer from sin is never to be known in this world. But this leads us onward.

Rom. viii. 23.

II. Full deliverance from sin is both required and promised as the preparation for final admission to the presence of God.

Sinless-ness. Required. Heb. xii. 14.

1. We are exhorted to *holiness, without which no man shall see the Lord:* with this declaration may be connected the command, remembering its solemn relation to the day of Him who *judgeth according to every man's work,* quoting from the Old Testament, *Be ye holy; for I am holy.* But both warning and command had been anticipated by the promise: *Blessed are the pure in heart, for they shall see God,* a Benediction not reserved, any more than the others which surround it, for the world to come.

1 Pet. i. 16, 17.

Matt. v.8.

2. Prayer—especially that of our Lord and His servant Paul—is used as the vehicle of teaching this. *Sanctify them through Thy truth! . . . that they all may be one, as Thou Father art in Me, and I in Thee, that they also may be one in Us.* The unity in one mystical body, and that one mystical body united to God in Christ as the Persons of the Trinity are internally united, is simply and only the perfection of Christian sanctification: in this world, for men are thence to believe *that Thou hast sent Me.* Higher than this language cannot go, but St. Paul's Prayers do not fall below it. He has in every Epistle save one a petition for the entire sanctification of those to whom he writes, and sometimes with an express reference to the presentation of this sanctity to Christ at His coming. The first of them says: *to the end He may stablish your hearts unblameable in holiness before God, even our Father, at the coming of our Lord Jesus Christ with all His saints.* And this follows a prayer for their abundance of brotherly love and universal charity. The prayers found in the Epistles to the Ephesians and to the Colossians disdain or leave far beneath them any interpretation lower than that of the attainment of perfect

Promised. John xvii. 17, 21.

1 Thess. iii.12,13.

sanctity. Purification from all sin, entire consecration to God, and a state of holiness leaving no room for imperfection, are all found in the central and supreme prayer of St. Paul : *and to know the love of Christ which passeth knowledge, that ye might be filled with all the fulness of God.* Its doxology makes this sure : *Now unto Him that is able to do exceeding abundantly above all that we ask or think.* It also shows why the doctrine is so much misapprehended : neither the ASKING nor the THINKING of the Church—especially the latter—has kept up to the high standard of Gospel privilege. *Eph. iii. 14—21.*

3. Scripture presents a sinless state as actually attained in this life. *Perfect love casteth out fear :* mark ἡ τελεία ἀγάπη, which is certainly love in the human soul ; the casting out of fear, which is the casting out of sin, the only cause of fear ; and the whole context. There is nothing plainer in the Bible than this its last testimony concerning the privilege of Christian experience. *I am crucified with Christ : nevertheless I live ; yet not I, but Christ liveth in me :* here St. Paul with the profoundest humility declares at least the possible suppression of the self of sin. Though in the contest of a later chapter *the flesh lusteth against the Spirit, and the Spirit against the flesh,* it is only *that ye might not do the things that ye would.* The victory is complete in the final echo of the same words : *by Whom the world is crucified unto Me, and I unto the world.* The triple crucifixion, to the law, to sin itself, and to the world, is unto death, perfect and absolute death. *Attained. 1 John iv. 18. Gal. ii. 20. Gal. v. 17. Gal. vi. 14.*

III. No instrumentality in the impartation of this grace is ever referred to but the Gospel and its agencies consciously received. *By the Gospel during Life.*

1. The discipline of affliction is among the instrumentalities of grace, which transforms all the sorrows of the believer in Christ into *the fellowship of His sufferings,* the *being made conformable unto His death.* But this is conscious discipline. Physical dying is not so : that death is not the putting off of the old man or the body of sin. The notion that we are not finally separated from the evil adhering to our nature until we are separated from the flesh is a subtile relic of Gnosticism. The only BODY OF SIN in Scripture is, first, the physical body as the instrument of the sinning soul, and, secondly, the figurative old man regarded as living simultaneously with the new, though only as a doomed and superfluous offender. But it is the privilege of the believer to *No other Means. Phil. iii. 10. Rom. vi. 6.*

cease from both before physical or natural dissolution. There is no virus, no substance of evil, no added element infused by it, which requires the disintegration of death for its removal. Sin is in one sense only a negation: it is the disorder of the soul which the restoration of the will to its unity with the Divine will perfectly repairs. Nor is there any Scriptural trace of a Purgatorial purification after death. Even those who believe in such an intermediate discipline, as necessary for the consummation of the work only begun on earth, do not profess to think that it is absolutely necessary in all cases.

The Present Life.
John ii. 6.

2. The only outer court of preparation is the present life. The Scripture speaks of no *waterpots after the manner of the purifying of the Jews* set at the threshold of the eternal temple, of no final baptism at the gate of heaven. We read everywhere, especially in the Apocalypse, of the final gratification of all unsatisfied hope: save that of deliverance from sin, which is never included. We hear beforehand the rejoicings of Paradise: they do not exult over this evil as at length destroyed. Among the prophecies concerning

Rev. xxii. 3.

Heb. ix. 26—28.

the final blessedness we find that *there shall be no more curse*—the penalty of sin—but not that there shall be no more sin. Christ will come at His final appearing *without sin, unto salvation :* without provision for its removal, for He hath already *put away sin, by the sacrifice of Himself,* at His first appearing. As to His visible Church His second coming will put away its indwelling evil by casting out whatsoever offends. It will not be so as to His individual saints : in each of them the indwelling sin must at that day be searched for and not found.

Entire Consecration.

ENTIRE CONSECRATION OR PERFECT LOVE.

The Spirit is imparted in His fulness for the entire consecration of the soul to the Triune God : the love of God, having its perfect work in us, is the instrument of our deliverance from indwelling sin ; and the return of our love made perfect also is the strength of our obedience unto entire holiness. This is abundantly attested as the possible and attained experience of Christians.

I. The commandment of the entire Scriptures, from beginning to end, is that of perfect consecration to God; and the spring and energy of that consecration is love. Perfect Love Commanded.

1. The love of God is the same in the Old Testament and in the New. It is not a sentiment of the mind alone, nor an affection of the sensibility alone, nor an energy of the will alone; but it is the devotion of the man, in the integrity of all these, to God as the one Object and Rest and Centre and Life of the soul. *What doth the Lord thy God require of thee, but to fear the Lord thy God, to walk in all His ways, and to love Him, and to serve the Lord thy God with all thy heart and with all thy soul?* Here perfect love stands between perfect fear and perfect service as the bond and complement of both. Our Lord has not even changed the words, which He quotes; He has not said of this: *a new commandment I give unto you.* It is *the old commandment which ye had from the beginning*, the universal law of all intelligent creatures: to make God their only Object, the Supreme End of their existence; the neighbour and all other things being objects of love only in Him, *hid with Christ in God.* This commandment is the measure of Evangelical privilege, which the believer has only to accept, and wonder at, and believe, and attain. Deut. x. 12.
John xiii. 34.
1 John ii. 7.
Col. iii. 3.

2. Its perfection is simply its soleness and supremacy. It is not in the measure of its intensity, which never ceases to increase throughout eternity until it reaches the maximum, if such there be, of creaturely strength; but, in the quality of its unique and sovereign ascendency, it has the crisis of perfection set before it as attainable. In the interpretation of heaven that love is perfect which carries with it the whole man and all that he has and is. Its perfection is negative, when no other object, that is no creature, receives it apart from God or in comparison of Him; and it is positive when the utmost strength of the faculties, in the measure and according to the degree of their possibility on earth, is set on Him. Thus interpreted no law of the Bible is more absolute than this of the perfect love of God. *Thou shalt love the Lord thy God with all thy heart, and with all thy soul, and with all thy strength, and with all thy mind.* Omitting the last, *with all thy mind*, this was the ancient law, concerning which the promise was: *The Lord thy God will circumcise thine heart, and the heart of* What is Perfect Love.
Luke x. 27.
Deut. vi. 5.
Deut.xxx. 6.

E 2

thy seed, to love the Lord thy God. The quaternion of attributes—
or the heart as the one personality, to which the understanding
and affections and will belong—as our Lord has completed it,
leaves no room for imperfection. However far this may go
beyond our theories and our hopes and our attainments, it is
and must be the standard of privilege. We are now concerned
only with the privileges of the covenant of redemption as administered by the Holy Ghost.

The Spirit of Love.

II. The Spirit of God, as the Spirit of perfect consecration, is
poured out upon the Christian Church. And He discharges His
sanctifying office as an indwelling Spirit: able perfectly to fill the
soul with love, and to awaken a perfect love in return.

1. The last document of the New Testament gives clear expres-
1 John iv. 19. sion to the former. *We love Him because He first loved us.* The
Divine love to man in redemption is revealed TO the soul for its
conversion; and it is shed abroad IN the regenerate spirit as the
1 John iv. 16. mightiest argument of its gratitude. *We have known and believed
the love that God hath to us:* this revelation received by faith was
the secret of our return to God. But St. John again and again
1 John iv. 12. speaks of this love as *perfected in us:* that is, as accomplishing its
perfect triumph over the sin and selfishness of our nature, and
its separation from God, which is the secret of all sin and self.
1 John ii. 5. *In him verily is the love of God perfected:* this ensures its being
individual, and contains the very utmost for which we plead.
The love of God, as His mightiest instrument for the sanctification
of the spirit of man, is declared to have in him its perfect work.
The Verily rebukes our unbelief and encourages our hope.

Perfected Return of Love.

2. He also speaks most expressly of the return of love to God
in us as perfected. This expression occurs but once in the Scripture in so absolutely incontestable a form. Whereas in the
previous instances the Apostle meant that the love of God is
perfected in us, in the following words he can have no other
meaning than that our own love is to be, and is—for these are the
same, in our argument—itself perfected, τετελειωμένη. It is of
course the same thing whether God's love is perfected or ours
made perfect in return; but the combination gives much force to
1 John iv. 18. the statement of privilege: *Perfect love casteth out fear. He that
feareth is not made perfect in love.* As St. John is the only writer

who says that *God is love,* so he is the only one who speaks of a
Christian's *perfect love.* This solitary text, however, gives its
meaning to a multitude. It is the last testimony that glorifies all
that has gone before.

1 John iv.
19.
1 John iv.
18.

3. The Holy Ghost uses the love of God as His instrument in
effecting an entire consecration. This is that *unction from the
Holy One* which makes us all partakers of the Saviour's consecration, Who received the Spirit not *by measure* for us. As the
Supreme Christ was perfectly consecrated in the love of God and
man, so it is the privilege of every Christian, who is by his name
an image of Christ, to be perfectly consecrated. And there is no
limitation of the Spirit's office in the reproduction of the Christly
character in us. This was the lesson of that great and notable
day of the Lord, the Pentecost. On the morning of that day the
Spirit's elect symbol was fire. First He appeared as the Shekinah
glory, without a veil, diffused over the whole Church, and then
resting *upon each.* The light which touched every forehead for
acceptance entered as fire each heart, *and they were all filled with the
Holy Ghost:* filled literally for the time being; and, if we suppose
that indwelling permanent, we have our doctrine substantiated.
That in this there may be continuance we are taught by St. Paul :
be filled with the Spirit. Lastly, as a tongue, the symbol signified
the sanctification of the outward life of devotion to God and
service to man. Hence there is no limit to the Spirit's consecrating grace. *I sanctify Myself that they also might be sanctified.*
This is the Saviour's example where it is perfectly imitable : the
methods of our sanctification, and its process in the destruction of
alien affections, find no pattern in Him; but the result shines
clearly in His example. *Beholding as in a glass the glory of the
Lord, we are changed into the same image from glory to glory, even as
by the Spirit of the Lord.* We receive unto perfection the glory
which we reflect.

Love the
Instru-
ment.
1 John ii.
20.
John iii.
34.

Acts ii. 4,
5.

Eph. v. 18.

John xvii.
19.

2 Cor. iii.
18.

III. All this may be said to be the high ideal of Christianity,
which has never been realised. But the tenour of the New
Testament forbids this theory of interpretation in every form.
An unbroken, perfect, uninterrupted concentration of all the
faculties on God is possible in itself, and it is possible on
earth.

Realised.

The
Spirit's
Honour.

1. The honour of the Spirit's office requires this. His dispensation is for man in this world; when Christ returns it ceases; and if His perfect work is accomplished it is in the present life. We hear of no operation of His grace save in this world. And Luke xxii. 37. the things concerning Him also HAVE AN END. He administers to perfection a perfect atonement. On this argument may rest with all its weight the doctrine of the entire destruction of sin from human nature and the full operation of Divine love in the heart. This also is our warrant for introducing the subject in this place. The entire sanctification of believers is deeply connected with Ethics; but it is still more inseparably bound up with the Spirit's Administration.

St. Paul's
Prayers.

2. The prayers of St. Paul invariably supplicate for Christians in the present state the most abundant outpouring of the love that consecrates. In this they only echo the Lord's own prayer for His people. But they are peculiar, and stand alone in Scripture, as a series of intercessory supplications which set no limits to the Christian privilege. They have been considered in this light already. It is sufficient now to point to the Ephesian Prayer, for instance, containing every element of our doctrine. Eph. iii. 16—21. The Spirit's strength poured *into the inner man* must needs give victory over all sin and be the energy of an entire consecration, and infuse the power of a perfect holiness. The petition that *Christ may dwell in your hearts by faith,* and that the soul, *rooted and grounded in love,* may be able to *comprehend with all saints what is the breadth and length and depth and height and to know the love of Christ which passeth knowledge,* can have no lower aim. And to be *filled with all the fulness of God* is perfect holiness. The only question is whether the Apostle prays as for an attainable blessing: a question that ought not to be asked.

Human
Nature.

3. The nature of man confirms this, and illustrates its possibility. The constitution of the human mind is made for unity, and unity is perfection. But that unity is love: that is, the Col. iii. 18. supreme aim or pursuit of the will is the love which is *the bond of perfectness.* When the faculties of the soul are withdrawn from every other distracting object, and shut up in their concentrated force to one, there remains nothing beyond. For that the Ps. lxxxvi. 10, 11. Psalmist prayed: *Unite my heart to fear Thy name!* where unity

in fear is unity in love; for its Object is the Only Being: *Thou art God alone!* The ONLY God feared and loved ALONE!

4. The example of our Lord is so presented as to assure us of the possibility of a perfect love to God and man. In the exercise of that twofold love—one in Him as in no other—He accomplished our redemption. And of this He said: *I have given you an example that ye should do as I have done to you.* The only time our love is spoken of as literally perfect, it is connected with this Supreme Pattern: *because as He is, so are we in this world.*

The Supreme Example.

John xiii. 15.

1 John iv. 17.

5. The aspiration of the renewed soul is confirmatory evidence. The argument from aspiration generally is one of the strongest that can be used to move a reasonable mind; it is valid in many departments of theology. In this case it is especially strong. As *newborn babes desire the sincere milk of the Word*, so they desire to love God supremely. No spirit touched with the love of God is content with any hope lower than a perfect love; nor can we believe that the Spirit kindles this fervour in vain. He will satisfy its desire; and that not in the future world but in this. Many of those who most unlovingly oppose this teaching have in their hearts the secret rebuke of their opposition.

Aspiration.

1 Pet. ii. 2

6. The honour put upon faith is such as to warrant the utmost expectation and sanction the highest doctrine. Thrice did our Lord speak of its unlimited power as a principle living and being developed from within like the life of the mustard-seed. As to the uprooting of sin He told His wondering disciples, who prayed for increase of faith, that they might not only overcome uncharitableness, but have its principle extirpated: *Ye might say unto this sycamine tree, Be thou plucked up by the root, and be thou planted in the sea; it should obey you!* As to the performance of supernatural duty, represented by the casting out devils, He said on another occasion: *Ye shall say unto this mountain, Remove hence to yonder place; and it shall remove; and nothing shall be impossible unto you.* Both are united in the last instance, and something is added: *Verily I say unto you, If ye have faith, and doubt not, ye shall not only do this which is done to the fig tree, but also if ye shall say unto this mountain, Be thou removed, and be thou cast into the sea; it shall be done. And all things, whatsoever ye shall ask in prayer, believing, ye shall receive.*

Faith.

Luke xvii. 6.

Matt. xvii. 20.

Matt. xxi. 21, 22.

Christian Life.

7. The recorded experience and character of the saints should have its weight : their experience ; not their testimony, which in the nature of things is not to be expected, as there is no mystery more deeply hid in God, no consciousness more unconscious of self, than that of perfect holiness and love. As to Scriptural examples the express references are few. Not biography, nor delineation of character—save that of One—is to be sought there; men are described only in their relation to the kingdom of God, and their holiness appears only in their lives of devotion. But in every dispensation some names are found to whom the Searcher of hearts bears testimony that they wholly pleased Him. In the judgment of the Christian Church many in almost every community and in every age have been saints made perfect in holiness, and self-renunciation, and charity, whose record is with God. But we are not careful to establish this argument. It is the privilege of the covenant, and not the avowal of it, with which we are here concerned.

CHRISTIAN OR EVANGELICAL PERFECTION.

The maturity of the Christian privilege is set before believers as the goal of all Evangelical aspiration. This perfection, as Evangelical and the effect of Divine grace, is estimated according to a gracious interpretation of the law fulfilled in love ; moreover, it is limited, and in all respects accommodated to a probationary condition ; while it is universal, as extending, under these conditions, to the entire relations of Christian man.

An Attainable Goal.

I. That Perfection is the goal of a possible estate is undeniable.

1. It is too common, however, to represent the Spirit as setting before Christians an ideal unattainable in the present life. On this much has been already said, and more will be said hereafter. Suffice to reiterate that no desire of holiness can be vain.

2. It is a more reasonable argument to point to passages in which the word has a less intense meaning, though, even when these are given up, there is a large and sufficient residuum of

clear testimonies. Doubtless some are incorrectly applied in the discussion: referring rather to the perfection with which Christianity begins than to that with which it ends. *Let us, therefore, as many as be perfect, be thus minded. We speak wisdom among them that are perfect.* These, and some others, refer to the perfect beginning or initiation of the soul into Christian mystery, in contrast with the preliminary knowledge of babes: *leaving the principles of the doctrine of Christ, let us go on unto perfection.* They do not touch our point: that perfection is a promised goal. Similarly *Be perfect!* καταρτίζεσθε, may refer to ecclesiastical integrity. And of this ambiguous nature are some other applications of the term in the English translation especially: for instance, *He hath perfected for ever them that are sanctified,* which refers rather to the objective perfection of the atoning provision, and is language that anticipates the eternal future.

Phil. iii. 15.
1 Cor. ii. 6.
Heb. vi. 1.
2 Cor. xiii. 11.
Heb. x. 14.

3. Injunctions to seek perfection and corresponding promises are few but very distinct. Were there no other the Redeemer's would be enough: *Be ye therefore perfect, even as your Father which is in heaven is perfect.* This, like many other words of our Lord, has a present limited signification which must be fearlessly expanded into the largest generality.

Matt. v. 48.

II. This perfection is Evangelical: that is, it is distinguished from every kind of perfection that is not of pure grace; and it bears, like everything pertaining to the estate of humanity, the impress of the condescension and lovingkindness of God. It is, however much the thought may be disapproved of men, a perfection accommodated to our fallen condition: not lowered but accommodated; a distinction this which is not without a difference. There is a consummation here as well as hereafter.

Christian or Evangelical.

1. It is not absolute perfection; nor the perfection of Adam's estate, who had not fallen; nor the perfection of sinlessness, which can never be predicated of those who will bear in them the consequences of sin until the end. Those who are unsinning in the gracious estimate of God, neither think themselves, nor desire to be thought, sinless in the utmost meaning of the word.

Not Absolute.

2. It is the perfection of that estate to which men are called by the Gospel of glad tidings: glad tidings, not only as to the remission of past sins, but also as to the acceptance of future

According to the Gospel.

service. Applying this to the threefold division of that estate, we may note: (1.) The righteousness of God, which He accepts, is regarded as a fulfilment of the law, as that is fulfilled in love: *love is the fulfilling of the law;* (2.) we are *children of God and conformed to the image of His Son,* though many infirmities are in us which could not be in Him; (3.) we are described, in the prayer of the Apostle, as sanctified *wholly* throughout spirit, and soul, and body, and *preserved blameless;* though the spirit is still beclouded with ignorance and weakness, the soul is under the influence of sensible things, and the body is on the way to dissolution. Such a threefold perfection may be traced elsewhere.

Rom. xiii. 10.
Rom. viii. 29.

1 Thess. v. 23.

3. This being understood, the doctrine is not disparaged by the use of the expression itself. The word PERFECTIONISM is sometimes applied satirically to those who hold the doctrine we here maintain: they who bear it bear in it the reproach of Christ. The term Perfection, being alone, should not be adopted without qualification; but with its guardian adjectives CHRISTIAN or EVANGELICAL it is unimpeachable. It is the vanishing point of every doctrine, exhortation, promise, and prophecy in the New Testament.

Perfectionism.

III. Christian perfection is relative and probationary, and therefore in a certain perhaps indefinable sense limited.

Relative.

1. This may be viewed with reference to the final consummation. In the hope of that last τετέλεσται all Christians unite: when HOLINESS TO THE LORD shall be the eternal law of the glorified man in his integrity. In this life, *the body is dead because of sin:* it not only perisheth itself, but, in the language of the Apocryphal Wisdom, *the corruptible body presseth down the soul, and the earthly tabernacle weigheth down the mind that museth upon many things.* Christian perfection is the estate of a spirit every whit whole, but still in a body the infirmity of which is the main part of its probation. Each has its own order. With regard to physical resurrection St. Paul says: *That was not first which is spiritual, but that which is natural.* This order is inverted as to the resurrection of the soul: first *that which is spiritual.* But when the perfection of the soul is reached, the body has still to submit to the dust: the spiritual eye sees *the King in His beauty … in the land that is very far off;* the natural eye goes down to see *corruption.* And the body on its way to dissolution impairs in ten

Zech. xiv. 20.
Rom. viii. 10.

Wisd. ix. 15.

1 Cor. xv. 46.

Isa. xxxiii. 17.
Ps. xvi. 10.

thousand ways the absoluteness of the deliverance of the spirit. Perfection under this and every aspect is relative.

2. Christian perfection at the best is that of a probationary estate. There is no reason therefore why it may not be lost again, and utterly lost, even after the fruition of the result of long years of heavenly blessing on earthly diligence. The principle of sin extinct in the soul may be kindled into life as it was kindled in Eve. There is no reason why it should not; but there is every reason why it need not and ought not. Such a second fall would be a fall indeed. It is not probable that it was ever witnessed. It is only our theory that demands the admission of its possibility. *Proba-tionary.*

3. It is that of the individual person whose relation to the race remains. Though personally in Christ, and altogether in Christ, during probation he is still under the generic doom of original sin, with a concupiscence which is not sin but the fuel of it always ready to be kindled, and generally under that law of probation which is peculiar to our race. Hence he is also a sinner among sinful men to the end of his continuance in the flesh: the inheritor of a sinful nature which, cleansed in himself, he transmits to his own children uncleansed. He does not altogether lose his connection with the line of sinful humanity. We never read of an entire severance from the first Adam as the prerogative of those who are found in the Second. The entirely sanctified believer may be, as touching his relation to Christ and in Christ, without spot and blameless; at the same time that in relation to Adam and in him he is only a sinful man. *Only Individual*

4. Once more, it is a probationary perfection inasmuch as it is always under the ethical law. Christianity is the *perfect law of liberty*: its perfection is that it is the liberty of law, the freest possible obligation and the most bounden and necessary freedom. It is a state to be guarded by watchfulness, which is subjected to an infinite variety of tests, and must be maintained by the habitual and, by Divine grace, perfect exercise of all the virtues active and passive. On the one hand it is a state of rest: *filled with the Spirit* the Christian can say, *I can do all things through Christ which strengtheneth me.* On the other it is a state in which the soul is safe only in the highest exercise of the severest virtue. *Ethical.* Jas. i. 25. Eph. v. 18. Phil. iv. 13.

To its safety its sedulity is required. In this respect it is very different from the perfection of heaven or even of paradise.

Needs the Atonement. 5. Hence this perfection needs constantly the mediatorial work of Christ: it demands His constant influence to preserve as a state what is imparted as a gift. The mediatory intercession is never so urgently needed as for those who have so priceless a treasure in earthen vessels: the higher the grace and the more finished the sanctity the more alien it is from the surrounding world, the more hateful to the tempter, and the more grace does it require for its guard. Our Lord's rehearsal of His *John xvii. 15.* abiding intercession tells us this: *I pray not that Thou shouldest take them out of the world, but that Thou shouldest keep them from the evil.*

Perfection in all Departments. 6. With all these conditions and limitations the word perfection—τελειότης, integrity—extends to all the blessings of the covenant of grace as they are provided for man in probation. In other words these several blessings are perfect in their imperfection: imperfect, when viewed in relation to the eternal requirement of the Supreme Lawgiver; perfect, when viewed in relation to the present economy of grace. (1.) In the judicial court of the *Heb.x.14.* Gospel the believer is or may be perfect in his relation to the law. *By one offering He hath perfected for ever them that are sanctified:* absolution from guilt is as complete as it could be in heaven: FOR *Rom. viii. 4.* EVER. And so is *the righteousness of the law fulfilled* that believers *1 John iv. 17.* may have *boldness in the day of judgment,* boldness that will never *1 John iii. 1.* be experienced at the awful bar unless it is carried thither. (2.) *Rom viii. 29.* As children of God their state lacks nothing: though waiting for *Phil.ii.15.* the adoption as to its final declaration and prerogative, *now are we the sons of God:* and they are *conformed to the image of His Son,* being *blameless and harmless, the sons of God without rebuke,* in the *Ps.xciii.5.* theory, and why not in the practice, of religion? (3.) And in the temple of God, of which it is said that *holiness becometh Thine house, O Lord,* the perfection of Christianity requires and reaches such a *Ps. xvii.3.* purity and simplicity as can endure the scrutiny of the Searcher *Matt.v.8.* of hearts. *Thou hast tried me, and shalt find nothing.* This is the sixth benediction, *Blessed are the pure in heart, for they shall see God.* The vision of God belongs to the consummate sanctity of the temple, whether on earth or in heaven; and the Saviour makes no such distinction as we in our unbelief are too much disposed to make.

HISTORICAL.

Though the specific doctrine thus laid down is very generally condemned among the Churches, some kind of Christian Perfection has been held in every age : held not only by the orthodox, but also by many heretical sectaries. The diverse principles which have contributed to mould opinion may be very profitably studied as shedding light upon the Scriptural doctrine. Indeed their respective views on this subject may be regarded as among the most searching tests which can be applied to the various systems. Every great theological tendency of the Christian world has had its own peculiar exhibition of it. As there is no consecutive history of the doctrine—it has no place in Histories of Doctrine generally—it may be well to adopt a method not chronological in this brief review : considering the theories of Christian Perfection which may be distinguished as the Fanatical, the Ascetic, and the Pelagian, the Mystical, the Romanist, the Imputationist, the Arminian, and finally the Methodist : this last returning to that which we shall place first in order as the continuation in the Church of the Scriptural doctrine. These, however, will be given merely in outline, and with the proviso that Christian Ethics is the more appropriate place for some of them, especially of the earlier members of the series.

Types of Doctrine.

I. The Christian Perfection taught in the Scriptures has descended as a sacred uninterrupted tradition through all Christian ages. Testimonies might be gathered from the writers of every period—a true CATENA AUREA—proving that the Spirit of finished holiness has never left Himself without witness. The essentials of the doctrine have been preserved, though with many minor differences, from the beginning, clearly discernible through all the ascetic, fanatical, ultra-mystical, semi-Pelagian veils which have obscured them.

In the Early Church.

1. The Apostolical Fathers, the common heritage of Christianity, continued the strain of the New Testament, and taught their successors not to shrink from the application of the term. So

Apostolical Fathers.

Clemens Romanus: "Those who have been perfected in love, through the grace of God, attain to the place of the godly in the fellowship of those who in all ages have served the glory of God in perfectness." Similarly, Polycarp, speaking of faith, hope, and charity, says: "If any man be in these, he has fulfilled the law of righteousness, for he that has love is far from every sin." Such words as these contain the germ of what may be called the doctrine of Christian Perfection: it is the perfection of love through grace accomplishing the righteousness of faith. The Epistles of Ignatius again and again speak of a perfect faith, of a perfect mind and intention, and of the perfect work of holiness:

Ad Smyrn. xi.

τέλειοι ὄντες, τέλεια καὶ φρονεῖτε · θέλουσι γὰρ ὑμῖν εὖ πράττειν, καὶ ὁ Θεὸς ἕτοιμος ἐστιν εἰς τὸ παρασχεῖν. With these we may connect Irenæus, who says that "God is mighty to make that perfect which the willing spirit desires," and "the Apostle calls them perfect who present body, soul, and spirit without blame before God: who not only have the Holy Spirit abiding in them, but also preserve faultless their souls and bodies, keeping their fidelity to God, and fulfilling their duties to their neighbour."

2. But it soon became evident that the high tone of New-Testament teaching was more or less lowered in Christian literature. For this three reasons may be assigned: first, the recoil from the assumptions of the Gnostics, and other fanatics; secondly, the introduction of an undue asceticism; and, thirdly, the spread of Pelagian error. The effect of these three causes respectively will be given in their order of development.

Fanaticism.

II. From the Ascetic must be distinguished the fanatical theories of Perfection which have been among the saddest developments of Christian error. The adage, Corruptio optimi pessima, has here one of its most deplorable illustrations.

Pædag. i. 6.

1. Gnosticism led the way, and found its best opponent in Clemens Alexandrinus. He lays down a high doctrine of Christian Perfection, but recoils from the pride of these Fanatics: "I cannot but sometimes wonder that some men dare to call themselves perfect and Gnostics, thinking of themselves more highly than the Apostle did." He refers here to the pride of knowledge. But elsewhere he says: "A man may be perfected, whether as godly, or as patient, or in chastity, or in labours, or as a martyr,

or in knowledge. But to be perfected in all these together I know not if this may be said of any who is yet man, save only of Him who put on humanity for us. Who therefore is the perfect man? He who professes abstinence from all evils." This negative abstinence from sin he, however, strengthens into positive fulfilment of righteousness: "It is a thing impossible that man should be perfect as God is perfect; but it is the Father's will that we, living according to the Gospel in blameless or unfailing obedience, should become perfect." This wavering language, holding fast the doctrine of Scriptural Perfection and yet shrinking from the full statement of it, may in Clement, Irenæus, and others, be fairly ascribed to a certain failure of their faith in their own principles. The Gnostics claimed to be the spiritual and perfect, as being redeemed from the bondage of matter and the flesh. The answer to them should have been that believers are, or may be, sanctified in the flesh as well as from the flesh. But this grand principle was surrendered, and Christian men were content to write as if sin was a necessary concomitant of the body.

Strom. iv.

Strom. vii.

2. Montanism in the second century was a system based on the delusion that the Holy Ghost, as the Paraclete, was not given to the Apostles but was reserved for a third dispensation. Montanus claimed to be the prophet or apostle of this new revelation, which raised the Church to a higher perfection, and made its true members the Spiritales or Pneumatici, whereas before they were only Psychici, or the Carnal. This enthusiast aimed rather at a stricter external discipline than at the establishment of any systematic doctrine of personal sanctification, and therefore his fanaticism only in an indirect way concerns our present subject. But its fundamental principle, that the Spirit may be expected to descend for a fuller and deeper baptism than on the Day of Pentecost, has from time to time reappeared in theories of the perfectibility of Christian faith and Christian experience.

Montanism.

3. Montanism was the first development of a principle which has reappeared at various times under other influences. Many of the fanatical sects of the Patristic and Middle Ages boasted of a plenary outpouring of the Spirit vouchsafed to themselves alone. Adopting the language of Scripture which speaks of the τέλειοι, or the Perfect, some of the Catharists of the twelfth and

Mediæval Fanatics.

thirteenth centuries termed themselves the PERFECTI in contra-distinction from the general body of Credentes or believers. They were wont to speak of their company as the Boni Homines or Consolati. But it has always been found that those who have perverted the term Perfect into a designation of themselves have been Antinomian in their spirit and practice. The Fraticelli, the Brethren of the Free Spirit, in the Middle Ages, the Catharist Perfecti, the Fanatics who were known during the Common-wealth as Perfectionists and more recently in America, have all been under the delusion of a principle which elevated them above the moral law. The fanatical abuse of the term has tended to bring the phrase Christian Perfection into discredit. The assumption of a claim to this perfection, and especially the use of the name, the healthy sentiment of Christianity condemns. But this should not be used in argument against the doctrine itself of a possible deliverance from sin. And the honest opponents of the doctrine ought to be cautious of branding those who hold it, but not claiming the title, with the name of Perfectionists.

Modern Tendencies. 4. There has been a tendency among some teachers of religion in modern times so to speak of Christian perfection as to seem to make it the entrance into a new order of life, one namely of higher consecration under the influence of the Holy Ghost. That this higher life is the secret of entire consecration there can be no doubt. But there is no warrant in Scripture for making it a new dispensation of the Spirit, or a Pentecostal visitation super-added to the state of conversion. *Acts xix. 2.* *Have ye received the Holy Ghost since ye believed?* means *Did ye receive the Holy Ghost when ye believed?* In other words entire consecration is the stronger energy of a Spirit already in the regenerate, not a Spirit to be sent down from on high. This kingdom of God is already within, if we would let it come in its perfection. Neither SINCE in this *Eph. i. 13.* passage, nor the AFTER in *after that ye believed,* has anything cor-responding in the original Greek. The teaching tends to diminish *Col iii. 3.* the value of regeneration, which is itself a life *hid with Christ in God;* and it undoubtedly has some affinity with the ancient prin-ciple of Montanism; just as, on the other hand, the assertors of a necessary inherence of sin until death betray a lurking and most subtle affinity with Gnosticism. But the spirit of the teachers

to whom reference is made is far from being fanatical; they have
the highest and the purest aims, and need only to guard their
doctrine more carefully.

5. A certain fanaticism of devout ignorance has in every age led
enthusiasts to mistake transient effusions of heavenly influence for
a finished work of holiness. This error, venial in one sense but
very hurtful in another, is the result of a too prevalent separation
between the sanctification of Christian privilege as a free gift and
the ethical means appointed for its attainment. Sometimes it
springs from forgetting that the present posture of the soul is a
very different thing from its abiding character. Opponents of
the Scriptural doctrine make much use of a fact which must be
admitted, that religious enthusiasm often outruns discretion. But
the fact, however lamentable, has no force as argument.

III. Asceticism is a development of the religious tendency in
man that has been almost universal and has the highest sanction. *Ascetic Perfection.*

1. Its definition is given by St. Paul in words which at once
recommend it and guard it and promise its genuine fruit: *Exercise thyself rather unto godliness.* (1.) Timothy is exhorted to make his *1 Tim. iv. 7.*
religion matter of personal thought, care, discipline: γύμναζε δὲ
σεαυτόν. Therefore the soul must not be surrendered to Divine influence with a passive quietude. Neither at the outset, nor during
the continuance, nor in the highest reaches, of the religious life
is the careful study of the arts of perfection needless. (2.)
Asceticism is guarded and protected from every error: πρὸς
εὐσεβείαν, *unto godliness. Bodily exercise profiteth little:* there are
advantages in the rules of religious life; but they must be such
as tend to godliness, which includes and indeed is the total suppression of pride, vainglory, personal sense of meritoriousness,
exultation in external religion, and morbid self-anatomy. (3.)
Godliness is the reward of this discipline, even as it must be its
end. Therefore Christian perfection, which is the perfect operation of the Holy Spirit in the heart and life, requires on its
human side a certain ἄσκησις, or personal strenuous exercise. St.
Paul said of himself, *I exercise myself to have always a conscience* *Acts xxiv. 16.*
void of offence toward God and toward men. The word is different,
αὐτὸς ἀσκῶ, but the thought is the same as in the injunction to
Timothy. In both a pure asceticism is commended.

VOL. III.   F

2. What may be called ascetical theories of Perfection are to be traced in every age. As they have expressed the most intense strivings of the Christian devotion they must be treated with respect. But in their general tendency they have declined from the spirit of the New Testament, and that in two ways :

(1.) They have laid too much stress on the human effort, thereby dishonouring the supremacy of the Holy Ghost, Who carries on His work without the instrumentality too often adopted by asceticism, and is after all the sole Agent in the spirit's sanctification. Doubtless, many of those who abstracted themselves from the world for the attainment of perfect holiness depended on the grace of the Gospel for acceptance, but many more sought by the merit of their works to win that grace. And, generally, the direct influence of the Spirit in the extinction of sin through the shedding abroad of the love of God was not the prime element in their ascetic discipline.

(2.) They have too carefully distinguished between common and elect Christians by adopting the Saviour's so-called COUNSELS OF PERFECTION as the guide to a higher life interdicted to those who do not receive these counsels. CHASTITY, POVERTY, and OBEDIENCE are the three-one estate of perfection, as exemplified by our Lord Himself, to which, it has been assumed, He called the more elect among His followers. But our Lord did not summon some men to a perfection denied to others, though He did summon some men to duties not required in all cases of others. To all His disciples the injunction came to aspire to another three-one perfection : *if any man will come after Me, let him deny himself, and take up his cross daily, and follow Me.* These three are imposed on every Christian without exception.

Luke ix. 23.

The Anchorets
3. The noblest testimonies to the grandeur of the Christian vocation are found in the writings of the early anchorets ; but the influence of an undue stress upon human effort qualifies the value of the best even of those who do most honour to the Spirit's work. The thought for ever lingers in their pages that something must remain for human vigilance to watch and keep down, without which humility would not be perfect.

Homil. x.
(1.) Macarius, of Egypt, is a typical example. One extract will show his precise relation to the question: "Such souls as

burn with ardent and inextinguishable love to the Lord are worthy of eternal life. Hence they are thought meet to be free from such motions of the mind, and to attain perfect enlightenment, and the hidden Communion of the Holy Ghost, and the mysterious fellowship of the fulness of grace." "It is the Spirit who gives him this, teaching him true prayer, true meekness, which he had long sought and laboured for ; and then he grows, and becomes perfect in God, and worthy to be an heir of the kingdom." Here the note of worthiness is a subtile fall, if not from the language yet from the spirit of Scripture. Again: "Every one of us must attain blessedness through the gift of the Holy Spirit. But he may in faith and love and the struggle of the determination of his free will reach a perfect degree of virtue, that so he may both by grace and by righteousness win eternal life. Thus not alone by the Divine grace and power, without the diligence of his own labour being added, is he counted worthy of perfect growth. Nor again only through his own diligence, as if not laying hold of the Divine hand from above, does he reach perfect freedom and purity." And what is that purity ? "Answer: the perfect cleansing from sin, and freedom from base passions, And the attainment of the highest reach of virtue, that is, the sanctification of the heart, which takes place through the indwelling of the Divine and perfect Spirit of God in perfect joy." And even this is not the highest pitch of Macarius ; but he descends again : "Never have I seen a Christian man perfect and entirely free. For though one may be resting in grace, and may attain to mysteries and revelations, and to much and deep sweetness of grace : nevertheless, he has sin within him. They think through the abounding grace and light they have that they are free and perfect : deceived by inexperience, even while they receive much grace. I have yet seen no man entirely free. I myself may have reached that point sometimes, but have learned still that no man is perfect." "In the case of a man that is sick, it may be that some members are sound ; for instance, the sight or other organs. So is it in spiritual things. For it is probable that some may have all the three members of the spirit sound, but not on that account is he perfect." It is obvious that the central idea is here wanting, that the Spirit's operation is

Homil. xix.

De Perfect.Sp. ii. 1.

ii. 2.

Homil. viii.

Homil.xv.

within the various elements of our nature, mighty in the personality itself, and that His supreme prerogative is to kill that body of sin the members of which we are to mortify. The Ascetic theory has always rested in the contest between the human spirit and the flesh : too often forgetting that the Divine Spirit is not merely the umpire and witness but the Almighty Agent also in the destruction of sin.

Nilus,
Ep. xlvii.
Ad. Eu-
nom.

(2.) Many high testimonies were borne to the Saviour's power in the inner man by Nilus, a Greek disciple or representative of Asceticism in the fifth century. "Our Lord Christ can not only scatter and make powerless the temptations which come upon us through Satan from without, but He can also restrain and still the motions and impulses which lie deep in our corrupted nature."

De Tem-
per. ch.
ii.

His teaching is, that if we give heed to purity of heart, and watch its bias, by grace "all its lusts and abominations shall be extirpated from the soul by its very roots; and joy, confidence, knowledge of ourselves and of sin be brought in, with true humility and great love to God and man." But Nilus knows

De viii
Vitiis.

nothing of a perfect destruction of sin in the heart : "When thou art assailed by evil lust, fall down before God and cry, O Son of God, help me! But do not over mightily trouble thyself, for we fight only with affections, but cannot entirely root them out."

De Tem-
per. cap.
ult.

Marcus Eremita speaks for the whole class when he says : "There may have been unspeakable heavenly glories enjoyed. It might seem that a perfect stage had been reached, and that the man was pure and free from sin itself. But afterwards that special grace was withdrawn, and the veil over the deadly evil removed, though the man still remained in a lower degree of perfection." As also

Cent.
iv. de
Chari-
tate.

Maximus : "Devotion indeed sets the will free from lusts, yet so that its nature, as will, does not fail. Think not that thou hast an entire deliverance from concupiscence, because the object is not now present : that would only be if thou shouldst remain immoveable on the remembrance or at the presence of the object. But even so thou must not be too secure, because devotion may for a long season kill the desires which yet afterwards rise again if strong devotion is suspended." This is in harmony with the uniform tendency of Ascetic writers of every age to regard concupiscence as a secret enemy in the soul left there for the discipline, humiliation, and caution of the spiritual athlete. Two sentences of the same saint may be collated : "No man may make the weakness of the flesh the patron of his sins because union with God the Word has abolished the curse, and made it inexcusable if we still, with evil concupiscence, cling to sinful objects. For the Divinity of the Word, always present by grace with the believer, makes weak the law of sin in the flesh." With this compare : "The end of godliness is the union of human weakness with Divine strength through the true wisdom. Now he who through the weakness of nature limits himself does not reach the goal of virtue, but lets his hands fall short of the strength that is afforded to our weakness. He has only his own sloth to blame that he is not better than he is." There is but a step between such views as these and the Scriptural truth that the Divine strength not only aids but is perfected in our weakness. That step, however, was never taken by the Ascetic theory.

Maximus, Cent. iii. cap. 46.

Cap. 79.

(3.) Cassian, in his Conferences on the Holy Life, gives perhaps the best examples of the dignity and the defect of the Ascetic aspiration. These must be consulted by the student himself.

IV. The most radical error of ancient times in relation to grace, in its perfection as well as in its processes, was Pelagianism. What the heresy of Arius was to Christ's Person, that of Pelagius was to His work.

Pelagian.

1. No tenet was more logically necessary to the system than that of a possible perfectibility of human nature : the strongest argument was that no reason existed to the contrary. It taught that man's free will might be educated, and had been educated in many instances, up to such a pitch of conformity with the moral law as would satisfy the merciful Governor of mankind. But the highest law was low in a theory which made forgiveness possible without expiation ; and regarded sin merely as the temporary and accidental condition of the mind, resulting from bad example, which a strong exercise of will could at any time correct. The importance of the Pelagian controversy in its bearing on this subject will justify a fuller statement of the views of the heresiarch and of his opponent St. Augustine.

(1.) The following gives the pith of the doctrine of Pelagius as to human perfectibility : "Ante omnia interrogandus est qui

Pelagius
ap.
August.
DePerf.
Justif.
c.2,3,6.

negat hominem sine peccato esse posse, quid sit quodcunque peccatum, quod vitari potest, an quod vitari non potest. Si quod vitari non potest, peccatum non est; si quod vitari potest, potest homo sine peccato esse quod vitari potest. . . . Iterum quærendum est peccatum voluntatis an necessitatis est. Si necessitatis est, peccatum non est; si voluntatis est, vitari potest. . . . Iterum quærendum est, utrumne debeat homo sine peccato esse. Procul dubio debet. Si debet, potest; si non potest, ergo nec debet; et si nec debet homo esse sine peccato, debet ergo cum peccato esse; et jam peccatum non erit, si illud debere constiterit. Aut si hoc etiam dici absurdum est, confiteri necesse est debere hominem sine peccato esse, et constat eum non aliud debere quam potest. . . . Iterum quærendum est quomodo non potest homo sine peccato esse, voluntate an natura. Si natura, peccatum non est; si voluntate, perfacile potest voluntas voluntate mutari." Here the possibility of Christian perfection is based on the broad ground of the essential power of the human will. Hence Pelagius boldly asserted that through the use of their natural faculties, and the natural means of grace, men might attain unto a state of perfect conformity with the law of God, Who prescribes nothing impossible. But his denial of original sin, and of the sanctifying power of the Holy Ghost applying the provision of the Atonement, robbed his theory of entire sanctification of any essentially Christian character.

St.Augustine.

(2.) St. Augustine's views on this subject deserve careful consideration. It will appear from the following extracts that he was not an opponent of the doctrine of entire sanctification, and that his statements on this subject were much more faithful to Scripture than those of his followers in the maintenance of what are called by them the Doctrines of Grace. He admits, in fact, that through a supernatural operation of grace the will might be so influenced as to concur with the will of God in all things. He asserts that a supreme delight in God might overcome every opposite tendency : this being the doctrine of Perfect Love which we have maintained. That St. Augustine denies the fact, or seems to deny the fact, that God has given this grace to any, does not weaken his admission; since he arbitrarily attributes the restraint to the secret wisdom of the Divine procedure, a

principle to which we shall return. "Et ideo ejus perfectionem De Spir. et Lit. n. 7, 63, 66.
etiam in hac vita esse possibilem, negare non possumus, quia
omnia possibilia sunt Deo, sive quæ facit sola sua voluntate, sive
quæ co-operantibus creaturæ suæ voluntatibus a se fieri posse con-
stituit. Ac per hoc quicquid eorum non facit, sine exemplo est
quidem in ejus operibus factis; sed apud Deum et in ejus virtute
habet causam qua fieri possit, et in ejus sapientia quare non
factum sit." Here are the two factors in entire sanctification,
plainly stated, "the power of God in accomplishing whatsoever
He has determined to do with the co-operation of His creatures'
faculties." If there is any bar to the finished holiness of the
believer, it must be found in the "wisdom of God." In the next
passage we have, in St. Augustine's striking antithetical phrases,
a luminous statement of our doctrine. It is the "revelation of
all that belongs to righteousness," and "the victory of the soul's
delight over every impediment." But here the wisdom of God's
appointment, which might forbid perfect holiness, becomes His
"judgment." "Ecce quemadmodum sine exemplo est in hominibus perfecta justitia, et tamen impossibilis non est. Fieret enim
si tanta voluntas adhiberetur quanta sufficit tantæ rei. Esset
autem tanta, si et nihil eorum quæ pertinent ad justitiam nos
lateret, et ea sic delectarent animum, ut quicquid aliud voluptatis
dolorisve impedit, delectatio illa superaret : quod ut non sit, non
ad impossibilitatem, sed ad judicium Dei pertinet." In the quotation now to be added an element is introduced which was
wanting before, the extinction of the law of sin in the members :
"Sed inveniant isti, si possunt, aliquem sub onere corruptionis
hujus viventem, cui jam non habeat Deus quod ignoscat. . . . Sane
quemquam talem, si testimonia illa divina competenter accipiant,
prorsus invenire non possunt ; nullo modo tamen dicendum, Deo
deesse possibilitatem, qua voluntas sic adjuvetur humana, ut non
solum justitia ista quæ ex fide est, omni ex parte modo perficiatur
in homine, verum etiam illa secundum quam postea in æternum
in ipsa ejus contemplatione vivendum est. Quandoquidem, si
nunc velit in quoquam etiam hoc corruptibili inducere incorrup-
tionem, atque hic inter homines morituros eum jubere vivere
minime moriturum, ut tota penitus vetustate consumpta nulla lex
in membris ejus repugnet legi mentis, Deumque ubique præsentem

ita cognoscat, sicut sancti postea cognituri sunt; quis demum audeat affirmare, non posse? Sed quare non faciat quærunt homines, nec qui quærunt se attendunt esse homines." The substance of this is, that no one should dare to say that God cannot destroy the original sin in the members, and make Himself so present to the soul that, "TOTA PENITUS VETUSTATE CONSUMPTA," the old nature being entirely abolished, a life should be lived below as life will be lived in the eternal contemplation of Him above. But then the Saint once more draws back from the legitimate conclusions of his sagacious faith, and he adds, that those who ask why it is not so do not remember that they are men. The arguments used by St. Augustine to confirm to himself the conviction which he reluctantly held, are those which have been urged by many from his time to our own. First, he repudiates the thought that perfect holiness is in man's power, and asserts "MUNUS esse Divinum," and therefore "OPUS esse Divinum:" in this all confessions agree. The doctrine we have laid down from Scripture makes entire sanctification a WORK of the Holy Ghost, whose FUNCTION is this in the administration of grace. Secondly, he refers to the consentient testimony of all saints, who in their humility confess that they are sinners. But he overthrows his argument by a certain hesitation about the Virgin Mary; and forgets, as all his followers forget, that the wholly sanctified still bear in their mind before God their sinful character by nature and practice, and confess their forgiven sins to the end. Thirdly, he insists much upon the undoubted truth that humility is part of the very perfection we speak of. " Ex hoc factum est, virtutem quæ nunc est in homine justo, perfectum hactenus nominari, ut ad ejus perfectionem pertineat etiam ipsius imperfectionis et in veritate cognitio, et in humilitate confessio. Tunc enim est secundum hanc infirmitatem pro suo modulo perfecta ista parva justitia, quando etiam quid sibi desit intelligit. Ideoque Apostolus et imperfectum et perfectum se dicit." These last words which make St. Paul confess his imperfection have nothing to do with the matter, for he spoke only of his aspiration towards his perfect consummation in soul and body, when he should in the resurrection win and apprehend Christ in all His fulness. As to the argument that a sense of imperfection is part

of entire perfection none can deny that, against Pelagianism, it
holds good for ever; but, standing alone, the assertion is not
true: the saints in heaven will have no sense of imperfection.
True it is however that human perfection is based upon humility,
and clothed with it as a garment; and that the entirely sanctified
ascribe all to the grace of God and nothing to themselves, never
professing that they are perfect, though daring to glory in the
perfecting of Divine grace in themselves. But, lastly, the strength
and the weakness of St. Augustine's argument is this, that the
will of God permits and appoints the continuance of sin for the
discipline of the soul. "Idcirco etiam sanctos et fideles suos in
aliquibus vitiis tardius sanat, ut in eos minus, quam implendæ ex
omni parte justitiæ sufficit, delectet bonum." This tremendous
plea sounds very much like continuing in sin that grace might
abound; against which the Christian sentiment protests with its
GOD FORBID! He whose will is our sanctification cannot "cure
our sin slowly so that the delight in good should be less than
sufficient for all righteousness." The argument rests upon St.
Augustine's general theory of sin, which he regards, as we have
seen elsewhere, as a defect that in the Divine scheme works a
greater good. Its force in relation to our present subject is
arrested and almost neutralised by words which follow: "nec in
eo ipso vult nos damnabiles esse sed humiles." Carried out to its
strict conclusion, this admission establishes one of the cardinal
points of our doctrine, that the infirmities of the saints, into
which their will enters not, are not counted for condemnation,
though they ensure and deepen true humility. On the whole it
will be evident that the Father of the predestinarian system of
Grace approved with his mind the highest doctrine of Christian
perfection as a privilege of the Christian covenant, but that he
was fettered by a false interpretation of certain sayings of Scripture, and by an excessive dread of Pelagianism which gave the
law to that interpretation.

(3.) Some modern tendencies, originating in America, may be   Oberlin.
alluded to, which belong partly to the Pelagian and partly to the
semi-Pelagian school. They are represented by the Oberlin doctrine of entire sanctification: "a full and perfect discharge of our
entire duty, of all existing obligations to God, and all other

beings. It is perfect obedience to the moral law." Hence on this theory the moral law is relaxed, though the expression is demurred to, in sheer justice. We cannot love God as we should have loved Him had not sin entered the world and diminished our power. But God expects from every man only the best he can do with his impaired faculties. It is obvious that on this theory Christian perfection is too much a subjective matter, and varies with every individual. Moreover, the view of original sin on which it is based is one that does not permit the thought of such an innate bias to evil as must be negatively eradicated. Its active and positive principle of perfection is that of perfect disinterested benevolence, or the ultimate choice of the welfare of all being. This, perfect at any moment, makes the man perfect. But the character profoundly impressed on the soul is not taken enough into account. And, to sum up, the essential Pelagianism of the Oberlin teaching on original sin, as exhibited in Finney's System of Theology, counteracts the good in its semi-Pelagian enforcement of the necessity of Divine grace.

Semi-Pelagian. 2. Semi-Pelagianism, the main error of which was its ascribing to human nature, notwithstanding the Fall, the power of seeking God and thus claiming Divine help by a kind of meritum de congruo, did not teach a subsequent Christian perfection attainable without special grace. Its first representatives were men who set up a very high standard of Christian perfection as attainable through the help of the Spirit. They were confused as to the relation of Divine grace to the freedom of the will in man before conversion, laying the stress rather on the power of human co-operation than upon the universal prevenient grace of the Holy Ghost, restored in virtue of redemption. That error was partially, though only partially, corrected in the Synergism of one section of Lutheran theology; it was entirely removed in later Arminian and Methodist teaching. Mediæval discussions, and the Romanist standards shaped by them, retained the confusion as it respects the first accesses of grace. That was ascribed to the remainder of good left in the Fall which ought to have been ascribed to the influence of the Holy Ghost given back to the race. If we suppose this error corrected—an error rather of phraseology than of fact—then semi-Pelagianism differs little from the truth taught by all who hold a universal redemption. And its teaching as to Christian Perfection flows into the general stream of the Mystical and Roman Catholic doctrine to which we now pass.

V. The central idea of Mysticism in all its varieties has been the entire consecration of the spirit of man to God, in absolute detachment from the creature and perfect union with the Creator. Mysticism

1. In its purest form, Mysticism proper has in every age moulded an interior circle of earnest souls, seeking the innermost mysteries of the kingdom of grace by the most strenuous ethical discipline. Its methods have been from time immemorial described as, first, the way of PURIFICATION; secondly, the way of ILLUMINATION; thirdly, the way of UNION. These may be considered as answering respectively to the Evangelical doctrines of Purification from sin, the Consecration of the Spirit, and the estate of Holiness in abstraction from self and earthly things in fellowship with God. A careful study of St. John's First Epistle will find in it laid the sure and deep foundations of this better Mysticism. It gives the three principles in their order. *The blood of Jesus Christ His Son cleanseth us from all sin:* this is the mystical Purgation. *Ye have an unction from the Holy One, and ye know all things,* that is, for the practical regulation of the life: this is the mystical Illumination. *He that dwelleth in love dwelleth in God, and God in him:* this is the perfect Union. A true Mysticism may be traced in almost every community; and, wherever found, has taught directly or indirectly the perfection to which the Spirit of God raises the spirit of man, blending in its pursuit contemplation and action: contemplation, which is faith waiting passively for the highest energy of the Holy Ghost; and action, which works out His holy will. How high its doctrine, scarcely falling below the highest, might be proved by examples taken from the leading Mystics of every type and of every community. 1 John i. 7. 1 John ii. 20. 1 John iv. 16.

2. Mediating between this highest type and its subsequent perversions is the doctrine of the Quakers, who are among the best representatives of modern Mysticism. It is thus stated by Barclay: "For though we judge so of the best works performed by man, endeavouring a conformity with the outward law by his own strength, and in his own will, yet we believe that such works Quakers. Apol. Prop. vii. 3.

as naturally proceed from this spiritual birth and formation of
Christ in us are pure and holy, even as the root from whence
they come ; and therefore God accepts them, justifies us in them,
and rewards us for them in His own free grace. . . . Wherefore
their judgment is false and against the truth who say that the
holiest works of the saints are defiled and sinful in the sight of
God. For these good works are not the works of the law excluded
by the Apostle from justification." In the following extract the
new birth is regarded as a developing process, and is not sufficiently
distinguished from the sanctification of the life that is imparted
in it. This may, however, be conformed to St. John's doctrine
of a birth of God, with which all sin is incompatible. For the

Prop. viii. rest, the true teaching of Scripture is clearly stated. "In whom
this pure and holy birth is fully brought forth, the body of death
and sin comes to be crucified and removed ; and their hearts
united and subjected to the truth ; so as not to obey any suggestions or temptations of the Evil One, and to be free from actual
sinning and transgressing of the law of God, and in that respect
perfect. Yet doth this perfection still admit of a growth ; and
there remaineth always in some part a possibility of sinning,
where the mind doth not most diligently and watchfully attend

Prop. ix. unto the Lord." "Although this gift and inward grace of God
be sufficient to work out salvation, yet in those in whom it is
resisted it both may and doth become their condemnation. Moreover, they in whose hearts it hath wrought in part to purify and
sanctify them in order to their further perfection, may by disobedience fall from it, turn to wantonness (Jude 4) ; make shipwreck
of faith (1 Tim. i. 19) ; and, after having tasted of the heavenly
gift, and been made partakers of the Holy Ghost, again fall away
(Heb. vi. 4, 5, 6). Yet such an increase and stability in the
truth may in this life be attained, from which there can be no
total apostasy." The Apologist can adduce no passage for this
last statement, which however is a venial one. Although he
nowhere expressly teaches that the evil of our nature may be
absolutely eradicated, yet his general principle leads that way ;

Prop. vii. for instance, in another place we read : "The first is the redemption performed and accomplished by *Christ for us* in His crucified
body without us ; the other is the redemption wrought by *Christ*

in us, which no less properly is called and accounted a redemption than the former. The first, then, is that whereby a man, as he stands in the Fall, is put into a capacity of salvation, and hath conveyed unto him a measure of that power, virtue, spirit, life and grace that was in Christ Jesus, which, as the free gift of God, is able to counterbalance, overcome, and root out the evil seed wherewith we are naturally, as in the Fall, leavened." This is a noble testimony, which, in its last sentence, goes beyond the general strain of Mysticism, and anticipates the doctrine we have maintained.

3. False or impure Mysticism, which came from the East through Neo-Platonism and ran into the Middle Ages, stimulated the trembling spirit to seek an uncreaturely identification with the Uncreated, after the manner of the Buddhist Nirvana; or an absorption of the finite into the Infinite Essence whose Name cannot be uttered, of Whom no attribute can be predicated, Who is beyond human thought, and of Whom our highest conception is that He is at once ALL and NOTHING. Hence the semi-Pantheism of one branch, the German; the Quietism of another, the French and Italian; the Antinomian Illuminism of a third, the Spanish. The end of perfection is such oneness with God as excludes or suppresses the consciousness of individuality and of a phenomenal universe on the way to Him; and, when that goal is reached, destroys all distinction between Him and His creature for ever. The means are abstraction and contemplation, to the exclusion of most of the processes of the Christian life.

VI. The Roman Catholic doctrine, or rather varieties of doctrine, concerning Christian Perfection, combines the results of most of the theories already referred to, and adds some elements common to it and Arminianism. Here we refer to the standards of Romanism; but it must be remembered that this most comprehensive of all theological systems includes a Jansenist teaching, which modifies the doctrine in the spirit of St. Augustine and of modern Calvinism. It may be said that in Roman Catholicism there may be found statements of the subject conformed to every one of the theories of our present sketch. But we have to do with the sanctioned dogma alone; first, in its bases of truth, and secondly, in its erroneous superstructure.

Romanist Theories.

1. The Council of Trent determined with reference to the perfection of possible obedience, that, negatively, there is no bar to an entire conformity with the law; and, positively, that a complete satisfaction of its requirements is necessary to salvation.

Sess. vi.
Cap. 11.

"Nemo temeraria illa voce uti debet, Dei præcepta homini justificato ad observandum esse impossibilia. Licet enim in hac mortali vita quantumvis sancti et justi in lævia saltem et quotidiana, que etiam venialia dicuntur, peccata quandoque cedant, non propterea desinant esse justi." But the necessity of even

Cap. 25.

venial sin is by implication denied: "Si quis in quolibet bono opere justum saltem venialiter peccare dixerit . . . anathema esto." This high doctrine of the satisfaction of the Divine law requires as its foundation that its demands are relaxed to meet the fallen estate of man: it is the law PRO HUJUS VITAE STATU that believers may and must fulfil. Hence venial sins, sins of mere infirmity or unpremeditated sin into which the will does not enter, are no deduction from the estate of perfection in the righteous estimate of God. But on this subject the Council did

Bellarm.
De Justif.
iv. 10.

not speak at length. Bellarmine expands its doctrine thus: "The defect of charity, for instance, our not performing good works with as much fervour as we shall exhibit in heaven, is indeed a defect, but not a fault, and is not sin. Whence our charity, although imperfect in comparison of the charity of the blessed, yet may absolutely be called perfect." "If the precepts of God were impossible, they would oblige no man, and therefore would not

Symbol.
sect. xxi.

be precepts." So also Möhler, a more modern expositor of Roman Catholic doctrine, says: "Either it is possible for man, strengthened and exalted by Divine aid, to observe the moral law, in its spirit, its true inward essence, or it is impossible to do so. If the former, then such observance cannot be too strongly urged; and everyone may find a proof of its possibility in the fact that, on every transgression, he accuses himself as a sinner: for every accusation of such a kind involves the supposition that its fulfilment is possible, and even, with assistance from above, not difficult. But, if the latter, then the cause must be sought only in God: either He has not framed human nature for the attainment of that moral standard which He proposes, or He does not impart those higher powers which are necessary to the pure and not merely outward compliance with His laws. . . . If it be urged that reference is had exclusively to man's fallen nature, we reply that God in Christ Jesus has raised us from the Fall; and it was justly observed by the Council of Trent that, in virtue of the power of Christ's Spirit, no precept was impracticable to man. For to the heritage of corruption a heritage of spiritual power in Christ has been opposed, and the latter can in every way be victorious over the former. Or, do we believe that the moral law was framed merely for the nature of Adam, for his brief abode in Paradise, and not for the thousands of years that humanity has to endure?"

2. But there is much error connected with the sound truth and vitiating it. The error is twofold: it undervalues the Scriptural teaching as to the extinction of sin, and it exaggerates the operation of sanctifying love. *Error.*

(1.) There is no provision for the suppression of the principle of sin in the regenerate; without which every doctrine of sanctification must be imperfect. The remains of original sin, or Concupiscence, baptismal grace does not remove; but, all condemnation being removed from the justified, God does not regard the fomes or fruit of sin to be sin itself. Here there are two things to be noted. First, the theory which so strongly protests against the forensic imputation of righteousness nevertheless resorts, though without avowing it, to a reckoning of the Divine estimate which beholds no evil in what is undoubtedly "of the nature of sin." Holding that in the regenerate this remainder of the carnal mind is not accounted for guilt, we insist that it is sin, and pardoned only through habitual faith and in prospect of its entire removal. Secondly, the inconsistency of the doctrine appears in this, that such concupiscence is a root of evil which, though not sin in itself, yet requires to be utterly removed by discipline. If removed in the present life, then the Romanist doctrine is imperfect in not making provision for this. If removed in another state, the error of purgatorial grace is introduced. Once more let Möhler be heard, who makes the best of his cause in the context: "Hence, the question recurs: how shall man be finally delivered from sin, and how shall holiness in him be restored to perfect life? Or, in case we leave this earthly world, still bearing about us some *Symbol. sect. xxiii.*

stains of sin, how shall we be purified from them? Shall it be by the mechanical deliverance from the body, whereof the Protestant Formularies speak so much? But it is not easy to discover how, when the *body* is laid aside, sin is therefore purged out from *the sinful spirit*. It is only one who rejects the principle of moral freedom in sin, or who has been seduced by Gnostic or Manichæan errors, that could look with favour on a doctrine of this kind. Or are we to imagine it to be some potent word of the Deity, or some violent mechanical process, whereby purification ensues? Some sudden, magical change the Protestant doctrine unconsciously presupposes; and this phenomenon is not strange, since it teaches that by original sin the mind had been deprived of a certain portion, and that in regeneration man is completely passive. But the Catholic, who cannot regard man other than as a free, independent agent, must also recognise this free agency in his final purification, and repudiate such a mechanical process as inconsistent with the whole moral government of the world. If God were to employ an economy of this nature then Christ came in vain. Therefore is our Church forced to maintain such a doctrine of justification in Christ, and of a moral conduct in this life regulated by it, that the Redeemer will at the day of judgment have fulfilled the claims of the law outwardly *for us*, but on that very account inwardly *in us*. The consolation, therefore, is to be found in the power of the Redeemer which effaces as well as forgives sin: yet in a twofold way. With some it consummates purification in this life: with others it perfects it only in the life to come. The latter are they who by faith, love, and a sincere penitence, have knit the bond of communion with the Lord, but only in a partial degree, and at the moment of their quitting life were not entirely pervaded by His Spirit: to them will be communicated the saving power, that at the day of judgment they also may be found pure in Christ. Thus the doctrine of a place of purifying is closely connected with the Catholic theory of justification." This is followed by a vigorous exposure of the inconsistencies of the Lutheran Formularies, in much of which we must concur. But far greater is the inconsistency of "the mechanical process" that separates sin from the nature after its departure from the body. Surely the original sin, which is the fleshly mind, cannot be the object of sanctifying grace in the pure spirit. It may be replied that it is not the principle of sin, but the stain of it, that purgatorial discipline removes. Then we fall back on the charge, that the Romanist doctrine, strong as against those who insist that death is the destruction of sin, is weak in making no provision for the suppression and extinction of concupiscence.

(2.) The love which is the strength of entire consecration in all who believe is made by the Romanist teaching a power that may more than fulfil the law. With what subtlety this erroneous principle glides into the theology of Rome may be seen in the following words of Möhler : "Some men of late have defended the old orthodox Lutheran doctrine by assuring us that the moral law proposes to men an ideal standard, which, like everything ideal, necessarily continues unattained. If such really be the case with the moral law, then he who comes not up to its requirements can as little incur responsibility as an epic poet for not equalling the Iliad." So far well ; but here follows the unevangelical notion that love may achieve Works of Supererogation, by keeping the Counsels of Perfection recommended though not imposed by our Lord ; and thus adding to the general meritoriousness of all good works the special Merits of an obedience above law. "More rational, at least, is the theory that the higher a believer stands in the scale of morality, the more exalted are the claims of the moral law upon him : so that they increase, as it were, to infinity with the internal growth of man, and leave him ever behind them. Now, when we contemplate the lives of the saints the opposite phenomenon strikes our attention. The consciousness of being in the possession of an all-sufficing, infinite power, discloses more and more the tenderer and nobler relations of man to God, and to his fellow-creatures ; so that the sanctified in Christ, filled with His Spirit, ever feels himself superior to the law. It is the nature of heavenborn love, which stands so infinitely far above the claims of the mere law, never to be content with its own doings, and ever to be more ingenious in its own devices ; so that Christians of this stamp not unfrequently seem to others of a lower grade of perfection to be enthusiasts, or men of distempered mind. Only in this way that remarkable doctrine can be satisfactorily explained,—which, like every other that

Möhler Symbol. sect. xxiii.

has for ages existed and seriously engaged the human mind, is sure
to rest on some sure foundation,—the doctrine, namely, that there
can be works which are more than sufficient (OPERA SUPERERO-
GATIONIS), the tendency and delicacy of which eluded the perception of the Reformers." If this doctrine meant only that love
in the regenerate soul aspires to a perfection which cannot be
measured by the standard of any positive precepts, it would be
unimpeachable: so stated, it would be only another form of the
Lutheran and Calvinistic assertion that the external law is abrogated in Christ, being exchanged for the internal law, by which
believers may render obedience in a higher and nobler spirit. All
that is noble in the theory of supererogatory works is maintained
by all sound Protestants; but they make it consistent with the
Evangelical covenant by declaring that no such works can be above
the requirements of the law interpreted by love, that even these
are accepted as wrought by the believer because their imperfection
is constantly forgiven for the sake of the Atonement, and that
their absolute merit is utterly excluded by our Lord when He
bids such as are supposed to have performed them call themselves unprofitable servants who have done only that which it was
their duty to do. The attempt to separate between law and love
is a hopeless one: love is said to be the fulfilling of the law, and
in maintaining that everlasting principle against their opponents
the Romanist divines had Scripture on their side; but in esta-
blishing it as a higher standard than the moral law which it only
interprets, and in linking it with special and arbitrary counsels
which are made into statutory laws binding on a particular class,
and, above all, in assigning specific merit, the merit of satisfaction,
to the acts of this Estate of Perfection, they are contradicted
both by the spirit and the letter of the entire New Testament.
But this subject carries us onward to Christian Ethics.

Imputed Sanctification.

VI. The theory of Imputation may serve to designate the doctrine of Christian Perfection as taught in the Standards of the
Reformation, both Lutheran and Reformed,. and especially in
modern Calvinism. It assumes that the Christian's entire sanctification as well as complete justification is provided for the believer,
and applied to him, as a free gift of the covenant of grace. The
three following texts may be regarded as summing up, in their

unity and their order, the essentials of this doctrine. *Ye are* Col. ii. 10.
complete in Him. By one offering He hath perfected for ever them Heb. x. 14.
that are sanctified. Who of God is made unto us wisdom, and right- 1 Cor. i. 30.
eousness, and sanctification, and redemption. These passages are not
absolutely misunderstood, but they are very partially applied.
Our Lord is not in the same sense our sanctification, with the
meaning of moral perfection, as that in which He is our righteousness. It has been seen that He is our sanctification without
any co-operation of ours, so far as sanctification is the cleansing
from guilt. But sin itself cannot be done away by imputation of
righteousness or non-imputation of guilt. Hence the Calvinist
teaching denies that it is done away; at least, in what is strictly
speaking the state of probation: in the present age it is never
abolished as a principle and power within, but vanishes by being
reckoned to the believer as non-existent, by being hidden under
the unsullied robe of the Redeemer's holiness. The people of
Christ are that Israel of whom it is said, *He hath seen no iniquity
in Jacob.* It insists that *the flesh lusteth against the Spirit, and the* Gal. v. 17, 24.
Spirit against the flesh to the end, so that *ye* CANNOT *do the things
that ye would.* But these words, soundly interpreted, say no more
than *that ye* MIGHT NOT *do the things that ye would.* The flesh itself
is *crucified* once for all, *with the affections and lusts,* not by imputation but by the act of those *that are Christ's,* who while they
wait to see the end of the body of sin, expecting till the sword
from on high smite it with the last stroke, also *mortify,* or put to
death, their *members which are upon the earth.* Col. iii. 5.

This doctrine tends to three issues in three different classes.

1. In some it leads to Antinomianism. The pursuit of an
independent perfection, such as shall crown the individual's own
character, is regarded as a superfluity, not indeed of naughtiness
but of goodness. It is thought to be the glory of Christ to defy
or negative, in the name of His own, both the condemnation and
the demands of the law. For this, however, neither Augustinianism nor Calvinism is responsible: it is *sui generis,* a heresy
apart, Antinomianism proper; and, as such, is condemned of
itself, αὐτοκατάκριτος, the object of reprobation to all true theology, and, in fact, the common enemy.

2. But even in orthodox systems which make Christ too abso-

lutely the Substitute of the believer, the thought of a perfection already belonging to His people, and ready to be revealed, must needs in some measure tend to check the ardour of desire for a personal and inwrought holiness, affording subtle encouragement to the thought that any remainders of sin serve only to feed humility and glorify the grace of God. The warnings of Scripture, and the confessions of the saints themselves, give evidence that this witness is true and that this danger is real.

3. It is in its noblest representatives a most mighty stimulant to the pursuit of personal perfection. Union with the Lord is the soul of their doctrine, and of their ethics, and of their hopes; and, where the aspiration towards fellowship with Christ has its full unhindered influence on the soul, it excites an unbounded horror of sin and thirst for holiness. It is the more Christian form of that union with God which was the goal of perfection to the more ancient Mystics.

Arminian.   VII. The early Arminians wrote much on Christian Perfection: but laid down no very determinate principles on this subject. Their statements, however, contain the germ of the doctrine which Methodism has developed. They were led by their theological convictions to the truth that such holiness as God reputes perfect may be attained in the present life. They dwelt upon a first perfection of the beginning of Christianity; a second perfection of the unimpeded progress of regenerate religion; and a third perfection of an established maturity of grace: a triple distinction which is in harmony with the teachings of the Gospels and Epistles. They did not however speak very positively about the means, the assurance and the limitations of the last stage. Episcopius says: "The commandments of God may be kept with what He regards as a perfect fulfilment, in the supreme love which the Gospel requires according to the covenant of grace, and in the utmost exertion of human strength assisted by Divine help. This consummation includes two things, (1) A perfection proportioned to the powers of each individual; (2) A pursuit of always higher perfection." Limborch describes it as "perfect, in being correspondent to the provisions and terms of the Divine covenant. It is not sinless or an absolutely perfect obedience, but such as consists in a sincere love of piety, absolutely excluding every

habit of sin. It has three degrees, that of the truly perfect being
the entire suppression of every habit of sin." The Remonstrant
divines exhibited their doctrine rather in its opposition to Romanist works of supererogation, on the one hand, and Antinomianism
on the other. They did not pursue it into its deep relation to
sin, and to love, and to Evangelical perfection. But the following
extract from Arminius himself will show their true position in
relation to this subject. "Besides those doctrines which I have
treated, there is now much discussion respecting the Perfection of
Believers in this life; and it is reported that I hold opinions
allied to those of the Pelagians, viz., that it is possible for the
regenerate perfectly to keep God's precepts. To this I reply that,
though these might have been my sentiments, yet I ought not on
this account to be considered a Pelagian, either partly or entirely,
provided I had only added that they could do this by the grace
of Christ, and by no means without it. But, while I never
asserted that a believer could perfectly keep the precepts of Christ
in this life, I never denied it, but always left it as a matter to be
decided. For I have contented myself with those sentiments
which St. Augustine has expressed on this point. He marks four
questions which claim our attention. (1) Was there ever a man
without sin, one who from the beginning of life never committed
sin? and he decides that such a person never yet lived, nor will
hereafter come into existence, with the exception of Jesus Christ.
(2) Has there ever been, is there now, or can there possibly be,
an individual who does not sin, that is, who has attained to such
a state of perfection in this life as not to commit sin, but perfectly to fulfil the law of God? and he does not think that any
man has ever reached this. (3) Is it possible for a man to exist
without sin in this life? and he thinks that this is possible by means
of the grace of God and free will. (4) If it be possible for a
man to be without sin, why has such an individual never been
found? and he answers, that man does not do what is possible to
him by the grace of Christ to perform: either because that which
is good escapes his observation, or because in it he places no part
of his delight. Besides this, the same Christian Father says,
'Let Pelagius confess that it is possible for a man to be without
sin in no other way than by the grace of Christ, and we will be

Armin.
Works,
i. 608.

Augustine
and
Pelagius.

at peace with each other.' The opinion of Pelagius appeared to St. Augustine to be this, that man could fulfil the law of God by his own proper strength and ability ; but with still greater facility by means of the grace of Christ. I have shown abundantly the great distance at which I stand from such a sentiment." But the vital question of the abolition of original sin was never, either by Arminius or his successors, decided upon. The following exposition of the general doctrine of Sanctification will put this in a clear light. It is abridged from the Private Disputations of Arminius, which contain the principles of his uncompleted system of theology : "(1) The word Sanctification denotes an act by which anything is separated from common, and is consecrated to Divine, use. (2) Common use is either according to nature itself, by which man lives a natural life ; or according to the assumption of sin, by which he obeys it in its lusts. Divine use is when a man lives unto godliness, in conformity to the holiness and righteousness in which he was created. Therefore this sanctification, with respect to the *terminum a quo,* is either from the natural use or from the use of sin ; with respect to the *terminum ad quem,* it is the supernatural and Divine use. (3) When we treat of man as a sinner, Sanctification is a gracious act of God by which he purifies man who is a sinner, and yet a believer, from ignorance, from indwelling sin with its lusts and desires, and imbues him with the spirit of knowledge, righteousness, and holiness ; that, being separated from the life of the world, and being made conformable to God, he may live the Divine life. It consists in the mortification or death of the old man, and the quickening of the new man. The Author of sanctification is God the Holy Father Himself, in His Son, who is the Holy of holies, through the Spirit of holiness. The External Instrument is the Word of God ; the Internal is faith in the Word preached. (4) The Object of sanctification is man, a sinner and yet a believer ; a sinner, because his sin has made him unfit to serve the living God ; a believer, because he is united to Christ, dies to sin and is raised in a new life. (5) The Subject is properly the soul of man : the mind, first, and then the affections of the will, which is delivered from the dominion of indwelling sin, and filled with the spirit of holiness. The body is not changed ; but, as it

Armin
Works,
ii. 408.

is a part of the man who is consecrated to God, and removed by
the sanctified soul from the purposes of sin, it is employed in the
Divine service. (6) The process lies in purification from sin,
and conformity with God in the body of Christ through the Holy
Ghost. (7) As, under the Old Dispensation, the priests, approaching the worship of God, were sprinkled with blood, so the
blood of Christ sprinkles us, His priests, to serve the living God.
In this respect, the sprinkling of the Redeemer's blood, which
principally serves for the expiation of sin, and is the cause of
justification, belongs to sanctification also. For, in justification
the sprinkling washes away the guilt of sins that have been committed ; but in sanctification it serves to sanctify those who have
received remission, that they may be enabled to offer spiritual
sacrifices to God through Christ. (8) This sanctification is not
completed in a single moment ; but sin, from whose dominion we
have been delivered through the cross and death of Christ, is
weakened more and more by daily detriments or losses, and the
inner man daily renewed more and more, while we carry about
with us in our bodies the death of Christ, and the outward man is
perishing. (9) COROLLARY. We permit this question to be made
the subject of discussion : Does the death of the body bring the
perfection and completion of sanctification ; and how is this effect
produced ?" With this unsatisfactory conclusion does the Remonstrant theology leave the question. It was the hard necessity of
its first representatives to maintain the truths committed to them
in the face of persecution and obloquy almost unparalleled.
Arminius himself transmitted only the lineaments of a system of
theology ; he was early taken away ; but his protest against ultra-
Calvinism was taken up by the Pietists of Germany, and in a
still purer form by the English Platonists, who in the exposition
and enforcement of Christian Perfection paved the way for the
Methodism of another century.

VIII. The Methodist modification of this Arminian doctrine, Methodist
and of all other congenial exhibitions of it, may be gathered from Doctrine.
the writings of John Wesley, dogmatic and defensive, from the
Methodist Hymn-book, which sings a higher strain on this subject
than any other psalmody in Christendom, ancient or modern ;
and in the commentaries and monographs which treat the ques-

tion, whether in England or in America. A clear view can be gained only by dividing between the essentials of the doctrine believed by the entire community, and certain non-essential aspects of it which appear different to different eyes.

1. The doctrine of Christian Perfection which the Wesleys taught was very early embraced, and in its main elements was consistently maintained throughout their career. It was presented to them at first in its mystical and ascetic form, as an object of ethical aspiration; it never afterwards lost this character; the grandeur and depth of Thomas à Kempis, and the best Mysticism of antiquity, are reflected in the hymns of Charles Wesley, and in all the writings of John Wesley, even the most controversial, on this subject. To this preparatory discipline the Methodist doctrine owes much: the foundations of its future highest teaching were laid before the first elements of it were clearly understood. From the very beginning it had this burden committed to it; the clear views of its Founders as to the acceptance of the believer, and his assurance of acceptance, were connected from the very outset with clear views as to his privilege of being filled with the love of God and delivered from indwelling sin, and attaining, as the result, a state of Evangelical perfection. This doctrine was not the slow result of reflection and study of the Scriptures. It was indeed confirmed by these; but it was most assuredly a truth bound up with the Methodist commission from the very first. It was simply the doctrine of former ages with one element, formerly indistinct, cleared up; that, namely, which made the entire sanctification of the believer a provision of the new covenant directly administered by the Holy Spirit to faith: to faith working by love and preparing for it, to faith making this blessing its express object, and to faith as retaining it through constant union with the risen Saviour. A few extracts from the last testimonies of John Wesley will establish all these points, and at the same time give a fair epitome of the Methodist doctrine in its relation to the work of the Spirit and the co-operation of man. They are taken from "A Plain Account of Christian Perfection, as believed and taught by the Reverend Mr. John Wesley, from the year 1725 to the year 1777," found in the eleventh volume of his works: a tract which deserves most careful study, not only as

a defence of the doctrine, but as containing one of the noblest collection of Spiritual Exercises in the English language. The selections are chosen with reference to the three points mentioned above, but they fairly exhibit the spirit of the whole.

(1.) Christian Perfection was taught by early Methodism as the seal of the Holy Ghost set upon the earnest striving of the regenerate will : "This great gift of God, the salvation of our souls, is no other than the image of God fresh stamped on our hearts. It is a 'renewal of believers in the spirit of their minds, after the likeness of Him that created them.'" From this it appears that entire sanctification was regarded as in reality the perfection of the regenerate state, a view confirmed as follows : "The more care should we take to keep the simple Scriptural account continually in our eye. Pure love reigning alone in the heart and life—this is the whole of Scriptural perfection. Q. When may a person judge himself to have attained this? A. When, after having been fully convinced of inbred sin, by a far deeper and clearer conviction than that he experienced before justification, and after having experienced a gradual mortification of it, he experiences a total death to sin, and an entire renewal in the love and image of God, so as to rejoice evermore, to pray without ceasing, and in everything to give thanks. Not that 'to feel all love and no sin' is a sufficient proof. Several have experienced this for a time, before their souls were fully renewed. None therefore ought to believe that the work is done, till there is added the testimony of the Spirit witnessing his entire sanctification as clearly as his justification. Q. But whence is it that some imagine they are thus sanctified, when in reality they are not? A. It is hence; they do not judge by all the preceding marks, but either by part of them or by others that are ambiguous. But I know no instance of a person attending to them all, and yet deceived in this matter. I believe, there can be none in the world. If a man be deeply and fully convinced, after justification, of inbred sin ; if he then experience a gradual mortification of sin, and afterwards an entire renewal in the image of God ; if to this change, immensely greater than that wrought when he was justified, he added a clear, direct witness of the renewal ; I judge it as impossible this man should be deceived herein, as that

Human Co-operation.

God should lie. And if one whom I know to be a man of veracity testify these things to me, I ought not, without some sufficient reason, to reject his testimony.

Gradual or Instantaneous.

"Q. Is this death to sin, and renewal in love, gradual or instantaneous?

"A. A man may be dying for some time; yet he does not, properly speaking, die, till the instant the soul is separated from the body; and in that instant he lives the life of eternity. In like manner, he may be dying to sin for some time; yet he is not dead to sin, till sin is separated from his soul; and in that instant he lives the full life of love. And as the change undergone, when the body dies, is of a different kind, and infinitely greater than any we had known before, yea, such as till then it is impossible to conceive; so the change wrought, when the soul dies to sin, is of a different kind, and infinitely greater than any before, and than any can conceive till he experiences it. Yet he still grows in grace, in the knowledge of Christ, in the love and image of God; and will do so, not only till death, but to all eternity. Q. How are we to wait for this change? A. Not in careless indifference, or indolent inactivity; but in vigorous, universal obedience, in a zealous keeping of all the commandments, in watchfulness and painfulness, in denying ourselves, and taking up our cross daily; as well as in earnest prayer and fasting, and a close attendance on all the ordinances of God. And if any man dream of attaining it any other way, (yea, or of keeping it when it is attained, when he has received it even in the largest measure) he deceiveth his own soul. It is true, we receive it by simple faith: but God does not, will not, give that faith, unless we seek it with all diligence, in the way which He hath ordained."

By Faith. Inbred Sin and Original Sin.

(2.) This extract has anticipated the second point: that the destruction of "inbred sin," which is to the individual what "original sin" is to the race of which he is a member, is to be made the object of faith; and therefore to be followed by assurance; and evidenced in confession. Faith, its assurance and its profession, generally go together in John Wesley's writings; but the two latter are kept in their distinct and subordinate place.

With regard to the first, a simple extract will be enough. It refers to the decisions of an early Conference as to certain points of discussion :

"Q. How much is allowed by our brethren who differ from us as to entire sanctification ? A. They grant (1) That everyone must be entirely sanctified in the article of death. (2) That till then a believer daily grows in grace, comes nearer and nearer to perfection. (3) That we ought to be continually pressing after it, and to exhort all others so to do. Q. What do we allow them ? A. We grant, (1) That many of those who have died in the faith, yea, the greater part of those we have known, were not perfected in love, till a little before their death. (2) That the term *sanctified* is continually applied by St. Paul to all who were justified. (3) That by this term alone, he rarely, if ever, means, 'saved from all sin.' (4) That, consequently, it is not proper to use it in that sense, without adding the word *wholly, entirely,* or the like. (5) That the inspired writers almost continually speak of, or to those who were justified, but very rarely of, or to those who were wholly sanctified. (6) That, consequently, it behoves us to speak almost continually of the state of justification : but more rarely, 'at least in full and explicit terms, concerning entire sanctification.' Q. What then is the point where we divide ? A. It is this : Should we expect to be saved from all sin before the article of death ? Q. Is there any clear Scriptural promise of this,—that God will save us from all sin ? A. There is : 'He shall redeem Israel from all his sins.' " Then follow a number of passages from both Testaments, containing promises and commandments which declare the believer's privilege, and indirectly make the destruction of inbred sin the object of personal faith. Indirectly : for it is never asserted that a specific promise to this effect is given. At a later time these distinct words occur : "(1) That Christian perfection is that love of God and our neighbour which implies deliverance from all sin ; (2) that this is received merely by faith ; (3) that it is given instantaneously, in one moment ; (4) that we are to expect it, not at death, but every moment ; that now is the accepted time, now is the day of salvation." But again : "As to the manner. I believe this perfection is always wrought in the soul by a simple act of faith ; consequently in an instant. But I believe a gradual work, both preceding and following that instant.

Sanctified and Entirely Sanctified.

As to the time. I believe this instant generally is the instant of death, the moment before the soul leaves the body. But I believe it may be ten, twenty, or forty years before. I believe it is usually many years after justification; but that it may be within five years or five months after it, I know no conclusive argument to the contrary. If it must be many years after justification, I would be glad to know how many. *Pretium quotus arroget annus?*" "But in some this change was not instantaneous. They did not perceive the instant when it was wrought. It is often difficult to perceive the instant when a man dies; yet there is an instant in which life ceases. And if ever sin ceases, there must be a last moment of its existence, and a first moment of our deliverance from it."

Assur-
ance.

As to the assurance following this faith Mr. Wesley's doctrine was once more a general deduction from the principle that in things pertaining to the Christian salvation perfect faith is attended by its interior evidence. The following observations are very suggestive on this subject generally. "Q. But does not sanctification shine by its own light? A. And does not the new birth too? Sometimes it does; and so does sanctification; at others it does not. In the hour of temptation Satan clouds the work of God, and injects various doubts and reasonings, especially in those who have either very weak or very strong understand-ings. At such times there is absolute need of that witness. . . . Q. But what Scripture makes mention of any such thing, or gives any reason to expect it? A. That Scripture, 'We have received, not the spirit that is of the world, but the Spirit which is of God; that we may know the things that are freely given us of God.' (1 Cor. xi. 12.) Now surely sanctification is one of 'the things which are freely given us of God.' . . . Consider likewise 1 John v. 19: 'We know that we are of God.' How? 'By the Spirit that He hath given us.' Nay, 'hereby we know that He abideth in us.' And what ground have we, either from Scripture or reason, to exclude the witness, any more than the fruit, of the Spirit from being here intended? Not that I affirm that all young men, or even fathers, have this testimony every moment. There may be intermissions of the direct testimony that they are thus born of God; but those intermissions are fewer and shorter as they grow up in Christ; and some have the testimony both of their justification and sanctification without any intermission at all; which I presume more might have, did they walk humbly and closely with God."

As to the profession of this experience the general language of Mr. Wesley was guarded: on the one hand, he was anxious to do justice to the New-Testament principle that confession is made unto salvation by all who believe; while, on the other, he was an enemy to enthusiasm, and was deeply impressed with a sense of the self-renunciation and essential humility that belong to the state of perfection. "Q. How shall we avoid setting perfection too high or too low? A. By keeping to the Bible, and setting it just as high as the Scripture does. It is nothing higher and nothing lower than this, the pure love of God and man; the loving God with all our heart and soul, and our neighbour as ourselves. It is love governing the heart and life, running through all our tempers, words, and actions. Q. Supposing one had attained to this, would you advise him to speak of it? A. At first perhaps he would scarce be able to refrain, the fire would be so hot within him: his desire to declare the lovingkindness of the Lord carrying him away like a torrent. But afterwards he might; and then it would be advisable not to speak of it to them that know not God (it is most likely it would only provoke them to contradict and blaspheme), nor to others, without some particular reason, without some good in view. And then he should have especial care to avoid all appearance of boasting; to speak with the deepest humility and reverence, giving all the glory to God.... Men do not light a candle to put it under a bushel; much less does the all-wise God. He does not raise such a monument of His power and love to hide it from mankind."

2. But the spirit of Mr. Wesley's teaching on this subject may best be discerned in the wise cautions which he threw around the profession of their experience. A few of these may be quoted, not only as showing his moderation on this point, but also as containing a noble defence of the doctrine itself, and its strict connection with faith working by love. The constant necessity of the virtue of the Atonement is strongly insisted on: "The best of men need Christ as their Priest, their Atonement, their Advocate

Profession of Attainment.

Cautions.

with the Father: not only as the continuance of their every blessing depends on His death and intercession, but on account of their coming short of the law of love. For every man living does so." " But even these souls dwell in a shattered body, and are so pressed down thereby, that they cannot exert themselves as they would, by thinking, speaking, and acting precisely right. For want of better bodily organs, they must at times think, speak, or act wrong; not indeed through a defect of love, but through a defect of knowledge. And while this is the case, notwithstanding that defect, and its consequences, they fulfil the law of love. Yet as, even in this case, there is not a full conformity to the perfect law, so the most perfect do, on this very account, need the blood of atonement, and may properly for themselves, as well as for their brethren, say, 'Forgive us our trespasses.'" Consequently, the highest state of earthly perfection is a gift that may be withdrawn: " it is amissible, capable of being lost; of which we have numerous instances. But we were not thoroughly convinced of this, till five or six years ago." There is no tolerance of the Antinomian spirit in this doctrine. " We are 'dead to the law by the body of Christ,' given for us (Rom. vii. 4): to the Adamic as well as Mosaic law. But it does not follow that we are without any law; for God has established another law in its place, even the law of faith. And we are all under this law to God and to Christ." Love is the fulfilling of every law. " The whole law under which we now are is fulfilled by love. Faith working or animated by love is all that God requires of man. He has substituted (not sincerity, but) love, in the room of angelic perfection." There is no limit to the stern cautions everywhere administered to professors of entire sanctification. " Beware of that daughter of pride, enthusiasm. O keep at the utmost distance from it! Give no place to a heated imagination. Do not hastily ascribe things to God. Do not easily suppose dreams, voices, impressions, visions, or revelations to be from God. They may be from Him. They may be from nature. They may be from the devil. Therefore 'believe not every spirit, but try the spirits whether they be of God.' Try all things by the written Word, and let all bow down before it. You are in danger of enthusiasm every hour, if you depart ever so

Warning to Professors.

little from Scripture; yea, or from the plain, literal meaning of any text, taken in connection with the context. And so you are if you despise or lightly esteem reason, knowledge, or human learning; every one of which is an excellent gift of God, and may serve the noblest purposes." "One general inlet to enthusiasm is, expecting the end without the means; the expecting knowledge, for instance, without searching the Scriptures, and consulting the children of God; the expecting spiritual strength without constant prayer, and steady watchfulness; the expecting any blessing without hearing the Word of God at every opportunity."

But everywhere, in common with the strain of the deepest theology of all ages, love is made the safeguard as it is the strength of perfection. "Another ground of these and a thousand mistakes is the not considering deeply that love is the highest gift of God: humble, gentle, patient love. The heaven of heavens is love. There is nothing higher in religion; there is, in effect, nothing else; if you look for anything but more love, you are looking wide of the mark, you are getting out of the royal way. And when you are asking others, 'Have you received this or that blessing?' if you mean anything but mere love, you mean wrong. Settle it then in your heart, that from the moment God has saved you from all sin, you are to aim at nothing more, but more of that love described in the thirteenth of the Corinthians. You can go no higher than this, till you are carried into Abraham's bosom." "Fire is the symbol of love; and the love of God is the principle and end of all our good works. But truth surpasses figure; and the fire of Divine love has this advantage over material fire, that it can reascend to its source, and raise thither with it all the good works which it produces. And by this means it prevents their being corrupted by pride, vanity, or any evil mixture. But this cannot be done otherwise than by making these good works in a spiritual manner die in God, by a deep gratitude, which plunges the soul in Him as in an abyss, with all that it is, and all the grace and works for which it is indebted to Him: a gratitude whereby the soul seems to empty itself of them, that they may return to their source, as rivers seem willing to empty themselves, when they pour themselves with all their waters into the sea. When we have received any favour from God we ought to retire,

Love.

if not into our closets, into our hearts, and say : ' I come, Lord, to restore to Thee what Thou hast given ; and I freely relinquish it, to enter again into my own nothingness. For what is the most perfect creature in heaven or earth in Thy presence, but a void capable of being filled with Thee and by Thee ; as the air which is void and dark is capable of being filled with the light of the sun, who withdraws it every day to restore it the next, there being nothing in the air that either appropriates this light or resists it ? O give me the same facility of receiving and restoring Thy grace and good works! I say THINE; for I acknowledge the root from which they spring is in Thee, and not in me."

Summary.   3. Reviewing the whole, we may conclude that, while the substance of the Methodist doctrine of Entire Sanctification is the same which has been aimed at in all the purest types of practical theology, it has some points of difference, or specific characteristics of great importance.

Love and Law.   (1.) It connects the fulfilment of the Evangelical law with the effusion of Divine love in the heart more strictly and consistently than any other system of teaching. The Mystical and Ascetic teachers of perfection have generally made love, and that the love of God, their keynote. But they seldom gave a good account of the relation of that love to the obedience which is essential to perfection. Some of them erred by making the absolute moral law the standard ; and then the highest result was a striving towards a perfection which death only could introduce. Others lost all thought of law in the contemplation of the holiness of Christ, and their perfection was the gradual transformation of the character into His image. Others rightly viewed love as the fulfilling of the law ; and supposed that its value in the sight of God was such as to obtain a meritorious acceptance beyond that of mere obedience to any law : forgetting, meanwhile, that the preciousness of love as a grace springs from its faith in the Merit and Strength of the Redeemer. Others separated between the righteousness of the law which is unattainable, and must be reckoned to the believer, and the perfection of love which he may attain in his own person : thus dividing what the Scripture joins. But the Methodist doctrine boldly declares that the righteousness of the law is fulfilled in believers, that is the righteousness of the new law of faith ; and that as faith is reckoned for righteousness, so faith working by love is reckoned for perfection.

(2.) The Methodist doctrine is the only one that has consistently and boldly maintained the possibility of the destruction of the carnal mind, or the inbred sin of our fallen nature. It is true that certain of the Mystics held, as we have seen, something almost equivalent to this doctrine ; and that the Pietists of the school of Spener included the annihilation of the old Adam among the privileges of God's children. But the utmost contemplated by them was the gradual suppression of the evil nature through the ascendency of love. Now it is undeniable that a very large portion of the Methodist teaching takes that ground. On the same principle that the shedding abroad of love is made the spring of regeneration, its perfect effusion is made the strength of entire sanctification. In many passages of Sermons and Hymns the Wesleys expressly taught this. But they failed not to look deeper into the heart than the region of its affections. They knew that life is more even than love ; and that, as the regeneration of the Spirit is the gift of a new life capable of loving God, so the perfection of that love towards God is possible only where the original death of the soul is altogether changed into life. Hence the fervour with which the Hymns appeal to the Holy Ghost for the destruction of inbred sin, and the almost equal earnestness with which the Sermons urge on believers the prayer for faith in the omnipotent power of God, not only to shed abroad His perfect love, but to finish the death of the body of sin. The combination of the two elements, the negative annihilation of the principle of sin and the positive effusion of perfect love, is, it may be said, peculiar to Methodist theology as such.

(3.) The original teaching of Methodism was peculiar also in its remarkable blending of the Divine and human elements in the process of entire sanctification. It invariably did justice both to the supreme Divine efficiency and to the co-operation of man. The charge brought against it, sometimes malevolently, sometimes thoughtlessly, that it stimulates believers to expect this supreme and most sacred blessing at any time, irrespective of their preparatory discipline, is contradicted by the whole tenour of the authoritative standards of this doctrine. Wesley's Sermon on

"The Scripture Way of Salvation" contains an elaborate discussion of this point; and it must be taken as a whole by those who would understand the subject. The sum of all is in the following sentences: "Experience shows that, together with this conviction of sin *remaining* in our hearts, and *cleaving* to all our works and actions, as well as the guilt which on account thereof we should incur were we not continually sprinkled with the atoning blood, one thing more is implied in this repentance, namely, a conviction of our helplessness." ... "But what good works are those the practice of which you affirm to be necessary to sanctification? First, all works of piety: such as public prayer, family prayer, and praying in our closet; receiving the Supper of the Lord; searching the Scriptures, by hearing, reading, meditating; and many such a measure of fasting or abstinence as our bodily health allows. Secondly, all works of mercy. ... This is the repentance, and these the 'fruits meet for repentance,' which are necessary to full sanctification. This is the way whereon God hath appointed His children to wait for complete salvation." "Yet they are not necessary either in the same sense with faith, or in the same degree. This repentance and these fruits are only *remotely* necessary, necessary in order to the continuance of his faith, as well as the increase of it, whereas faith is *immediately* and *directly* necessary to sanctification." "To this confidence, that God is both able and willing to sanctify us now, there needs to be added one thing more,—a Divine evidence and conviction that He doeth it. In that hour it is done; God says to the inmost soul, 'According to thy faith be it unto thee!' then the soul is pure from every spot of sin; it is clean 'from all unrighteousness.' The believer then experiences the deep meaning of these solemn words: 'If we walk in the light as He is in the light, we have fellowship one with another, and the blood of Jesus Christ His Son cleanseth us from all sin.'" The intense, absorbing, patient, human preparations of the heart in man are from the same Spirit who at length gives the Divine evidence of the unspeakable power of God to save from all sin. Here it is to be observed that Mr. Wesley passes from the perfect shedding abroad of love in the heart to the application of the supreme efficacy of the Atonement to take away the evil of the nature: it is "the

orks vi.
50.

moment wherein sin ceases to be." It is more, therefore, than the spirit of entire consecration to which many of those who have received his teaching limit it; it is more even than the abundant effusion of love which may fill the heart's sensibilities without purifying its hidden depths: a distinction which his own words refer to: "How clearly does this express the being perfected in love! How strongly imply the being saved from all sin!"

(4.) Finally, the doctrine which runs through the works and the whole career of the Wesleys is marked by its reasonableness and moderation as well as its sublimity. The far greater part of the definitions of it are taken up with defining what it is not. It is not absolute perfection, nor the perfection of angels, nor even that of unfallen Adam: it is a perfection which has come up from much tribulation, and bears the scars of infirmity to the end. It is not immunity from temptation, and the possibility of falling, and the remainders of ignorance and shortcoming in the presence of the perfect law the rigour of which is not applied to it in Christ. It is a perfection which is no other than a perfect self-annihilating life in Christ: a perfect union with His passion and His resurrection, and the perfect enjoyment of the value of His name of Jesus, as it is salvation from sin. It is the perfection of being nothing in self, and all in Him. It is a perfection for which the elect with one consent have longed, from the Apostles downwards: neither more nor less than the unuttered groaning desire of the children of God in every age; the common deep aspiration, with only one note more emphatic than has been always heard, though even that has not been always wanting, the destruction of the inbred sin of our nature. He who searcheth the heart hath always known the mind of the Spirit, even when its deepest desire has not been clearly uttered. And He will yet, we dare to believe, remove the last fetter from the aspirations of His saints, and give them one heart and one voice in seeking the destruction of the body of sin as well as the mortification of its members.

THE TENURE OF COVENANT BLESSINGS.

The Holy Spirit, the Administrator of Redemption, confers its blessings absolutely as the free gift of God in Christ, but not unconditionally and irreversibly. There is no fixed decree which has guaranteed all the concurrences of Providence, all the operations of grace, and all the gifts that assure an abundant entrance into heaven. The Christian covenant places man in a new and gracious PROBATION, gives ample ground of personal ASSURANCE, which as the assurance both of faith and of hope encourages to PERSEVERANCE. The present subject, therefore, requires a consideration of those three terms in their mutual relations.

There is a doctrine of Final Perseverance, which as such is only a conventional term used to signify one aspect of the covenant of grace : the irreversible bestowment of its blessings on those for whom Christ died, and for whom it is supposed He cannot have died in vain. According to the view of truth already given, perseverance is an ethical duty, and not a specific gift of the covenant. So far as provision is made for it in that covenant, it belongs to the doctrine of Assurance, which in some form occupies a large and important place in the New Testament. Omitting the term Final, which is the symbol of a peculiar dogma, Perseverance may be made an independent section, for the sake of its own importance, as also to give opportunity of controverting error on the subject, or of setting the truth underlying that error in its right point ¦of view. Thus we have three watchwords which are so correlated that they cannot well be disjoined. Perseverance is only the constant preservation of the Assurance of faith which is the conditional assurance given to a soul in Probation. The believer in Christ begins a new life in a new probation ; goes on his way with an habitual assurance ; and thus is animated to persevere to the end. This is the New-Testament economy of the Christian life, to which it is everywhere faithful.

PROBATION.

Probation is the moral trial of a free spirit, continuing for a season under conditions appointed by God, and issuing in the confirmation of an abiding and unchangeable state. The Christian scheme, as administered by the Holy Ghost, has not abolished probation, but has invested it with a new and peculiar character of grace, which, however, leaves it probation still.

I. Probation has not ceased in the economy of Redemption. The Scripture which says, *Ye are not under the law but under grace,* does not mean that we are exempted from test and predestinated to life. It is true that when Adam fell his first estate of trial ended for himself and the race in him; and, according to the analogy of the doom of evil spirits, his destiny and the destiny of manhood was then settled. But the Divine condition of human probation included the prospect of a new and different test applied to the posterity of Adam individually under very different conditions. Man's independent probation ceased for ever; and began again through a Mediator. Probation did not cease, but its conditions changed. Redemption has not interfered with the law of probationary decision which so far as we know governs the destiny of every created intelligence. Generally, every covenant of God with man implies probation; and in a certain sense all probation involves the idea of covenant. Though διαθήκη is not precisely συνθήκη—it is rather Disposition or Arrangement than Covenant proper—it is commandment with promise and condition. And these are the essentials of probation. Strictly speaking, covenant only began with the Fall: being the arrangement for salvation through a Mediator. The peculiar kind of covenant of which Scripture speaks is always propounded, ratified, and administered through the mediatorial sacrifice.

Original Proba-tion. Rom. vi. 14.

II. Probation runs through the new covenant as individual.

1. Generally, the entire economy of this dispensation of grace, in all the stages of its development on earth, is filled with the ideas and terms of test. The short history of Paradise is en-

Probation in the Gospel Covenant.

tirely governed by this principle. The Covenant of Grace—before the Law, under the Law, in the Gospel, these three being one—is not less subject to this rule. On God's part we have a long series of expressions, used to exhibit His relations to men, which are inconsistent with anything but a purpose to discipline and test character, to refuse the evil and choose the good: for instance, all such words as covenanting, testing, or temptation, striving, trial, discipline, forbearance, hardening or melting the heart, judgment, present and future, rewarding and punishing, reprobation, day of grace; which imply the Divine appointment or institute of probation, and are utterly incomprehensible on any other theory or principle of the destiny of mankind. Similarly, on man's part, we have a long series of counterpart expressions: submission, rebellion, choosing good or evil, tempting God, yielding to or vexing or grieving or quenching His Spirit, conscience, and self-judgment; all these being inexplicable on any other principle than that of a certain control over his own destiny.

Individual Probation.

2. This may, particularly, be viewed with reference to the three main elements of individual probation: its beginning, and its processes, and its end.

At the Outset.

(1.) The doctrine of Vocation has shown that the beginning of the Gospel in any heart is a test of the moral nature, as the Fall has left it, and of the preliminary and universal influences of the Spirit. *Everyone that is of the truth heareth My voice:* this must

John xviii. 37.

refer to the very commencement of a probation: the first word of God to the soul is a test, the very first thought of Christ is a

Luke xiv. 23.

revelation of the hidden fibres of the being. *Compel them to come in!* means simply the vehement appeal that through the mind and heart persuades the will; and the final mystery of acceptance or rejection, notwithstanding all the power of Divine grace, is to be found in a moral attitude of that will. The Cross attracts: *I, if I be lifted up from the earth, will draw all men unto Me:* ἑλκύσω.

John vi. 44.

No man can come to Me, except the Father which hath sent Me draw him: ἑλκύσῃ. The former is the general and the latter is the individual attraction; but both alike detect the character and confirm it. The result is always referred to as the sustaining or

2 Cor. ii. 16.

failing under a test. The preaching of the Gospel is a *savour of life unto life,* and *of death unto death.* God's co-workers beseech us to *receive not the grace of God in vain.* The Cross is a new testing tree of knowledge of good and evil : man, under the new probation, however, is commanded not to abstain but to take. The probation is now outside of Paradise, but in many of its characteristics it is precisely the same as within. It is bound up with all the issues of Christ's coming. *And Jesus said, For judgment I am come into this world :* this answers at the close to those words of the beginning, *This Child is set for the fall and rising again of many . . . that the thoughts of many hearts may be revealed.* Either through direct preaching or through indirect, in this world or beyond it, certainly before the Judgment Day, the name of Jesus will be, it must be, the touchstone of every man's will and the arbiter of his doom.

2 Cor. v. 1.

John ix. 39.

Luke ii. 34, 35.

(2.) The processes of the Christian life are all probationary. The Scriptures never address Christians as saved prospectively, only as saved retrospectively : as τοὺς σωζομένους, *such as should be saved,* or who are in process of salvation. *The manifestation of the Spirit is given to every man to profit withal :* this does not refer only to special endowments ; including these, it becomes a universal principle. The whole design of grace is disciplinary. *The grace of God that bringeth salvation to all men hath appeared, teaching us ;* παιδεύει, it puts us under training and discipline. It is to enable us to make our *calling and election sure ;* that in its strength we may *be able to withstand in the evil day, and, having done all, to stand.* On the one hand the injunction is *prove your own selves :* this is one of the few texts in which the very term probation is used ; and it signifies that we have to test, and try, and find out the secrets of our own hearts, watching ourselves under the eye of God as God watched Adam in Paradise. Another is, *that ye may prove what is that good, and acceptable, and perfect, will of God.* Reprobation is never mentioned save in regard to the Christian's failure under test : *know ye not your own selves, how that Jesus Christ is in you, except ye be reprobates,* ἀδόκιμοι. The word is unknown in the Bible save as the result of man's own act : the only reprobation is the being tried and found wanting. There is no worse self-deception than to regard personal religion as the working out of an absolute and final decree, and to it we may apply St. Paul's words : *Be not deceived ; God is not mocked : for whatsoever a man soweth, that shall he also reap.* The probation is not only decisive

Continuance.

Acts ii. 47.

1 Cor. xii. 7.

Titus ii. 11.

2 Pet. i. 10. Eph. vi. 13.

2 Cor. xiii. 5.

Rom. xii. 2.

2 Cor. xiii. 5.

Gal. vi. 7.

as to the degree of our salvation, but decisive of our salvation itself. The test is not simply to ascertain how many cities we may rule over; but whether we shall be trusted at all or rejected.

End.
Matt.xxv.
32.

(3.) At the end of all it is not said that the Judge will *separate them one from another* only, but that it will be *as a shepherd divideth his sheep from the goats:* the context shows that these words describe their several characters as the result of the probation of a life. And this declaration winds up a series of parables all of which make the eternal issues depend on watchfulness and fidelity:

Matt.xxv.
21.

Well done, thou good and faithful servant. The final judgment is the revelation of the result of a probationary course. There is a

Rev. xvii.
14.

book of life which is the record of the *called and chosen* AND FAITHFUL: this last is now at length added to complete the former. The Lord had again and again referred to the many called and few chosen; and He also indirectly spoke of the still fewer who would endure to the end. But now He combines them all.

Rev. xiii.
8.

This is *the book of life of the Lamb slain from the foundation of the world.* But the names were not indelibly written in it from the foundation of the world: had the individual names been written there, in any other sense than as foreseen to be there, it would not have been declared that the preservation of it is the reward of

Rev. iii. 5.

fidelity: *to him that overcometh,* the promise is, *I will not blot out his name out of the book of life.*

Christian
Probation.

III. Christian Probation has a specific character of grace. It ought not to be taught as a hard and rigorous doctrine, calmly leaving man to the decision of his own destiny. It is possible that, in recoiling from the former extreme which denies probation altogether, we fall into another which leaves too much in man's destiny to his own caprice. The ceasing of the first probation has introduced another presided over by grace; extending over mankind, in all their states and varieties.

The
World.
Titus iii.
4.

1. As it regards the world all men are and ever have been under a probationary constitution of mercy. *The kindness and love of God our Saviour toward* MAN *appeared* finally in the Gospel; but the same PHILANTHROPY has governed the world from the beginning. The new trial of the race as such is a profound mystery, but a mystery of mercy. Grace, like the Gospel which is its proclamation, was in the world before Christ came; and the nations

of men will be dealt with by the righteousness of Him of Whom it was said in the beginning of history, *Shall not the Judge of all the earth do right?* The probation of the world at large may be regarded under two aspects. (1.) Nationally, bodies and communities of men are dealt with by the Supreme Governor; they will be judged with strict regard to every advantage which they have enjoyed, and every disadvantage under which they have laboured. The laws by which God governs families, communities, nations, and more or less the race at large, are laws which issue from the Mediatorial Court, are administered by the Redeemer of all men. But with this we have not now to do: it has been and will be discussed in other departments. (2.) The probation of all men individually is one of grace. We can hardly tell how to reconcile this with some of the sayings of Scripture; but the duty of theology is to reconcile those sayings with this truth. The probationary discipline of vast multitudes of the human race in the present life, the hidden processes of their trial, and the apportionment of their doom hereafter, are among the reserved mysteries of faith. Not an individual of all the countless hosts of the descendants of Adam will be dealt with save on the basis of a trial that was appointed for himself as if he were the only individual in probation.

2. As it regards those who receive revealed truth Evangelical mercy yet more obviously directs probation. All things are ordered to enlist the free will on the side of God. The condemnation of original sin is removed; and its bias to evil is controlled by strong influences of grace. The power of the Holy Spirit is greater than that of evil can be. The force of Divine truth, applied by His Divine energy, and confirmed by the demonstration of Providence, is an element the strength of which must be estimated very highly in the consideration of the trial ordained for those who hear the Gospel. And as to those who hear it amidst the utmost disadvantages for its reception, we must fall back upon the mysterious internal influence which is present to every man behind and in concurrence with the earliest movements of evil.

3. In the case of the regenerate probation is peculiarly rich in the provisions of grace. (1.) Every Christian is the object of personal care and most tender solicitude to the Holy Ghost. A

Gen.xviii. 25.

Individual Probation.

The Regenerate.

comparison is sometimes made between the probation of Paradise and that of the believer in a fallen world : such a comparison can hardly be instituted to any good purpose. Whatever disabilities sin has entailed on us are more than made up by an indwelling Rom.v.20. Spirit, the Spirit of a new and higher life. *Where sin abounded grace did much more abound.* (2.) And all events are so ordered that the difficulties of religious experience tend to invigorate the spirit. As blessings temperately enjoyed increase love, so afflictions endured with resignation strengthen the inner man. Through the secret control of the Holy Ghost, not an event in life but contributes to test the character ; and under His rule every test sustained leaves that character the stronger. Hence we are Jas. i. 2. bidden to *count it all joy when ye fall into divers temptations.* The highest graces of religion, those which the passion of Jesus has invested with a supreme dignity, are the issue of stern probation encountered with patience.

Solemnity of Probation.   4. But, after all, the Christian covenant leaves men to a probation that is exceedingly solemn. Everyone is taught by the Scripture to regard himself as deciding his lot for eternity. There is very much against him, very much for him ; two worlds, of good and evil, enter into his being and contend for his soul. Under other conditions, and with differences that almost forbid the analogy, we all are undergoing the ordeal of the Garden again. The ordinary speech of mankind is true to this most affecting and impressive principle, that the present world is the scene of our trial for the eternal future. We are still in the garden of test ; but the object of the discipline of life is to win back the Paradise lost through the grace of Him whose justice cast us out. Youth is a season of probation. In another sense every critical period of life is such : especially the evil day of affliction. But time, every Gal. vi. 7. man's portion of it, is his probationary term. *Whatever a man* Eph.vi.13. *soweth that shall he also reap!* is the warning exhortation. *That ye may be able to withstand in the evil day, and, having done all, to stand :* this is the encouragement. The result closes the Bible : Rev. xxii. *he that is unjust, let him be unjust still! and he that is holy, let him* 11. *be holy still!*

HISTORICAL.

This doctrine of probation and test is itself the test of ecclesiastical systems. The history of dogma on this subject, in its wider bearing on the Divine Decrees, has already been briefly given. It is needful now only to make a few more specific allusions to some more prominent relations.

I. All systems of Fatalistic Predestinarianism are condemned by the true doctrine of human probation: whether the ancient Fatalism which renounced the idea of one supreme personal God, bringing its Pantheon under the sway of Destiny as the final authority; or the modern Pantheistic Fatalism which makes all things the necessary manifestation—material or spiritual—of one substance, God or nature. If the Deity is for ever evolving Himself in humanity, there can be no probation. The good and evil— good or evil is interdicted language—are alike God: choice, decision, probation are excluded. The tranquil confidence of many Pantheists in ancient and modern times is pure resignation to the inevitable. The triumph of Christianity is that it gives a still more perfect resignation to one who at the same time knows that every passing hour is pregnant with his eternal interest. *Fatalism.*

II. The dogma of Absolute Sovereignty in God and His government, and the decree of election flowing from it, are to a great extent inconsistent with just ideas of the probation of collective mankind, or of individual man. This may be looked at from several points of view. *Predestinarianism.*

1. The dogma of an eternal and fixed predestination to salvation and perdition cannot be made to combine with moral trial. Probation may indeed be reduced to mean the mere exhibition of the fact and the means of declaring the decree; it may also be made serviceable as tending to decide the varieties of Christian character and the degrees of final reward. But the Christian idea of a moral test is lost; for all its processes are supposed to be already predetermined.

2. The more modern Federal Theology which has been grafted on Calvinism shows this still more strikingly. According to this scheme the history of Redemption is distributed under three *Federal Theology.*

covenants : first, the Covenant of Redemption between the Father and the Son ; secondly, the Covenant of Works made with Adam, including his posterity ; and, thirdly, the Covenant of Grace, this being subdivided again into the covenant before the Law, under the Law, and under the Gospel.

The Covenant of Redemption.

(1.) With regard to the first, it almost seems to place Christ Himself under a special and peculiar probation : if not in words yet in reality. On behalf of a certain portion of the race the Son of God is supposed to have undertaken the obligation of passive and active obedience : on the condition of His fidelity, this portion of the race is assigned to Him. They are secure, at the expense of an infinite cost to their Surety. His is the stern probation, and not theirs. Though this theology would admit that He could not fail nor be discouraged, and cannot be charged with making Christ's undertaking doubtful ; yet this is a noble inconsistency on its part. In fact, with respect neither to the Surety nor to the assured, is the strict idea of probation retained. But of such a covenant with the Holy Trinity for the partition of mankind the Scripture says nothing.

Covenant of Works.

(2.) As to the second there is no such covenant of works in the record. If it is regarded as coming after that first eternal covenant it thereby loses its character as a covenant : the race of Adam is dealt with as necessarily fallen, and sin is made dangerously to rival the Atonement itself, predestined before the foundation of the world. If, on the Sublapsarian theory, the Covenant of Redemption is supposed to be based upon the Fall as a fact, then that covenant still absorbs and destroys the probation of men. The race of Adam failed in one test, and then was under trial no more. The covenant of works remains indeed as a continual remembrance of the Fall ; but its only use is to detect and condemn sin and drive men to the better Covenant of Grace ordered in all things and sure.

Covenant of Grace.

(3.) As to this third, it cannot retain the essential elements of a covenant, supposing personal probation with its contingent issues to be excluded. It may be asserted that the compact of probation ceased when it really began in Christ. To say that God took the elect out of their own hands, and saved them through a Substitute who left nothing to their own will and effort and fidelity, or to contingency, is to contradict the tenour of Scripture, however much it may seem to honour the Divine sovereignty.

3. The dogma of the express and distinct imputation of Christ's active righteousness secures the final presentation of the believer before God without spot and blameless ; hence there is no deciding test as to his ultimate state. The growth of a new character under the Redeemer's perfect robe has nothing strictly probationary in it : the Christian will not appear in the garment woven of his own righteousness save for the regulation of his reward, and even that is inconsistent with the essential principle that Christ virtually takes the place of the saint and the saint appears as Christ in the entire administration of substitutionary grace.

4. The exaggeration of the Divine sovereignty gives this dogma the character of Fatality which we have not hesitated to ascribe to it : it is no other than a Christianised Pantheistic Fatalism. Not unknown Fate or Destiny or μοίρα, but the God and Father of all absolutely disposes of the souls of men. Probation is, like all things else pertaining to their Christian estate, only imputed to them. Trial, test, and judgment and doom, are mere flatus vocis, the veils and economical disguises of a dispensation of fixed and necessitated grace.

III. There are theories of Universalism which deal with this subject, and must be tested by our principle.

Universalism.

1. That of a certain final Universal Destruction of Evil teaches that there is room enough in the universe, and time enough in the bosom of eternity, and resources enough in Divine omnipotence, for the gradual and sure annihilation or elimination of all defect, infirmity, and sin from the sum of things. This unlimited dogma maintains the idea of test in its own way : all who fail to sustain the test in this life, and in the succeeding æons, will be finally destroyed. This is Probation without one of the alternatives of confirmation, which are necessary to its definition, the fixed continuance in evil; and with a new element added, the determination of sovereign Omnipotence. It holds the Calvinistic Sovereignty with a peculiar modification of its own. Whereas Predestinarian Election has for its dark side the foreordained reprobation of the evil as doomed to a fixed estate of eternal ruin, this notion avails itself of an

Annihilationism.

eternal decree for the riddance of the universe from evil. It will plead that the idea of test includes only the detection of evil and no more ; but this is neither the philosophical nor the Scriptural meaning of the word.

2. The theory of Universal Restoration does the same, but for a different issue. It has the dogma of fixed Predestination, without the Election of Calvinism. It makes the tremendous history of human sin only an interlude that will be forgotten, or only drawn out of the recesses of oblivion as a precedent in the government of other worlds. According to such a theory of probation the Creator indeed experiments with the principle of test and fails ; finally withdrawing His creatures from this law with its responsibility, and constraining them to sanctity. Hence this scheme pleads like the former that test aims at the detection of evil alone, but only to bring out the unfathomable resources of Divine grace. In some exhibitions of this principle, the test indeed runs on after this life on principles independent of the redemption of Christ. But in them also, as in all these forms of Universalism, the strict notion of test leading to fixed confirmation is lost.

IV. The Hierarchical and Sacramentarian theories of the administration of grace, with their dogma of Merit, in their extreme forms seriously affect this doctrine.

1. The principle of a necessary conveyance of grace through Sacraments in the hand of a human mediator tends to undermine the sanctity of human probation : if not in theory certainly in practice. It may be said that the failure of that grace in the case of persons interposing the bar of mortal sin leaves the issues to the applicant : this may indeed save the system from its worst theoretical consequences, but practically it impairs the sense of personal probation, making the Church with its sevenfold hedge of Sacramental ordinances the same kind of refuge from the strain of personal responsibility which Antinomianism makes the merit of Christ. Here, as often, two opposite schools meet.

2. The specific dogma that the Counsels of Perfection test the character of believers, and stimulate them to a higher attainment, is an unscriptural one, so far as it introduces a new element in probation. It will be urged that our Lord Himself applied these as tests during His personal administration of His kingdom. But

it must be remembered that He used these tests under special circumstances; that, strictly speaking, He never applied but one of the Counsels, that of the renunciation of property; and that, in the application of this, He only laid down a principle of universal importance with a specific reference to the need of a particular case. He never used tests of probation which should distinguish one class of His disciples from another in all ages.

3. Hence the doctrine and practice of Romanism as the chief representative of the Sacramentarian system, and that of Merit resulting from obedience to Counsels, in two ways interfere with the reality of probation : first, by taking away to some extent the probationary responsibility of the believer, and, secondly, by applying a superfluous and limited test. Probation is in Christianity the same for all, and for all alike. It is not meant that these systems absolutely undermine the foundations of human trial. They retain the broad features of it, with its eternal issues; but they deeply prejudice its true Evangelical character.

V. The general principles of the doctrine here laid down will be found in the Analogy of Bishop Butler, whose chapters on the State of Trial, the Moral Government of God, and the State of Probation, should be carefully studied. A few extracts of a defensive character may appropriately close these remarks.

Anal. ch. iv.

" The general doctrine of Religion, that our present life is a state of probation for a future one, comprehends under it several particular things, distinct from each other. But the first and most common meaning of it seems to be that our future interest is now depending, and depending upon ourselves; that we have scope and opportunity here for that good and bad behaviour which God will reward and punish hereafter; together with temptations to one, as well as inducements of reason to the other. And this is, in a great measure, the same with saying that we are under the moral government of God, and to give an account of our actions to Him. For, the notion of a future account and general righteous judgment implies some sort of temptations to what is wrong: otherwise there would be no moral possibility of doing wrong, nor ground for judgment or discrimination. But there is this difference, that the word *probation* is more distinctly and particularly expressive of allurements to wrong, or difficulties in adhering uniformly to what is right, and of the dangers of miscarrying by such temptations, than the words *moral government*.

"But the thing here insisted upon is, that the state of trial, which Religion teaches us we are in, is rendered credible, by its being throughout uniform and of a piece with the general conduct of Providence towards us, in all other respects within the compass of our knowledge. Indeed if mankind, considered in their capacity as inhabitants of the world only, found themselves, from their birth to their death, in a settled state of security and happiness, without any solicitude or thought of their own : or if they were in no danger of being brought into inconveniences and distress, by carelessness, or the folly of passion, through bad example, the treachery of others, or the deceitful appearances of things : were this our natural condition, then it might seem strange, and be some presumption against the truth of Religion, that it represents our future and more general interest, as not secure of course, but as depending upon our behaviour, and requiring recollection and self-government to obtain it. For it might be alleged, 'What you say is our condition in one respect, is not in any wise of a sort with what we find, by experience, our condition is in another. Our whole present interest is secured to our hands, without any solicitude of ours ; and why should not our future interest, if we have any such, be so too ?' But since, on the contrary, thought and consideration, the voluntary denying ourselves many things which we desire, and a course of behaviour far from being always agreeable to us, are absolutely necessary to our acting even a common decent, and a common prudent part, so as to pass with any satisfaction through the present world, and be received upon any tolerable good terms in it : since this is the case, all presumption against self-denial and attention being necessary to secure our highest interest, is removed. Had we not experience it might, perhaps speciously, be urged, that it is improbable anything of hazard and danger should be put upon us by an Infinite Being when everything which is hazard and danger in our manner of conception, and will end in error, confusion, and misery, is now already certain in His foreknowledge."

ASSURANCE.

The full confidence of salvation, which the Divine Spirit works in the believer, is best studied under two aspects. First, there is objective and external ground of assurance provided in the work of redemption and the means of grace. Secondly, there is the individual assurance of faith and of hope and of understanding based upon or flowing from the former through the operation of the Holy Ghost. Having considered these, we must then review the several points in which Christian Confessions vary on these important questions.

As to the internal assurance, much has already been said in relation to the Spirit's evidence of the several blessings in the Christian covenant; and as to the external something will be added under the doctrine of the Sacraments. But a general view of the ground and nature of assurance is necessary here, as belonging to the theology of Probation.

OBJECTIVE ASSURANCE.

Objective.

The external and everlasting ground of certainty to the Christian Church that the covenant of grace is sure is the resurrection of its Surety, which is declared historically and confirmed by the Holy Ghost. This confirmation, however, is connected with certain appointed means of grace, which are standing pledges of the Divine fidelity.

I. The resurrection of our Lord is set forth throughout the New Testament as the abiding ground of Christian confidence: especially by St. Paul, who knew the Redeemer only as risen. In his First Epistle to the Corinthians, he writes: *if Christ be not risen, then is our preaching vain, and your faith is also vain.* Preaching

The Resurrection.

1 Cor. xv. 14.

in Antioch his first recorded sermon, he marks very emphatically the pledge given in Christ's resurrection. The Father receives the Son : *Thou art My Son, this day have I begotten Thee!* begotten perfectly in human nature as the finished Mediator, Priest, and Prophet, and King. Turning to us He says : *I will give you the sure mercies of David*, as the pledge of the accomplishment of all the *promise which was made unto the fathers.* To those who doubt the resurrection of Christ there is not only no assurance as to the truth of Christianity, but there is no assurance of any revelation from God ; and from this there is but a step to universal scepticism. This has been exhibited under the Mediatorial Work. It is needful only to sum up :

Acts xiii. 32, 33, 34.

1. In the resurrection of Christ, the body of believers are certified that sin is abolished as a condemnation and a power. *By one offering He hath perfected for ever them that are sanctified:* perfected their ground of assurance, whence their *boldness to enter into the holiest.* St. Paul says, on behalf of the whole company of saints : *I am crucified with Christ!* His certitude is the certitude of all who are united with the Redeemer, that His life, following on His death of expiation, declares the eternal abolition of the penalty and strength of the law.

Heb. x. 14, 19.

Gal. ii. 20.

2. His resurrection is the pledge of the presence of a living omnipotent Saviour in heaven : *He is Lord of all*, said St. Peter in his grand parenthesis : that Jesus, namely, Whom *God raised up the third day and showed Him openly.* As the Living Lord who died He Himself gives assurance in His last and most glorious manifestation on earth : *Fear not; I am the First and the Last; I am He that liveth and was dead; and behold I am alive for evermore, Amen; and have the keys of hell and of death.* The interjected AMEN is common to Christ and the Church : the mutual seal of a full assurance. This is the living pledge or Sacrament in heaven. *Him the heavens must receive until the times of restitution of all things:* the rendering given by Lutheran theology, *Who must receive the heavens*—that is, for us—is sound theology but ·unsound interpretation. Christ is, however, in heaven, and the true *Tree of life which is in the midst of the paradise of God.* Of this assurance the Church might say, IT IS ENOUGH : let this be instead of all other pledges and Sacraments.

Acts x. 36, 40.

Rev. i. 17, 18.

Acts iii. 21.

Rev. ii. 7.

II. But in the purpose of God, *willing more abundantly to show unto the heirs of promise the immutability of His counsel,* it is not enough. What the presence of Christ in heaven is as an undying pledge the means of grace are on earth. Heb. vi. 17. Means of Grace.

1. Generally, all means of grace are also seals of grace : the Word or Bible, Prayer, the House of God, the Assembly, the Christian Sabbath, are all standing ordinances which guarantee the certitude of salvation. The entire institute of external Christianity is an attestation of Divine fidelity to the covenant of grace ; an abiding memorial of the risen Lord. They are Seals.

2. Specifically, the Sacraments are silent pledges and seals as well as instruments of grace : such is Baptism at the threshold and such is the Eucharist within ; both are seals of the grace of justification, regeneration, and sanctification. Baptism for ever pledges the first and the constant washing away of sin. The Eucharist pledges the first and the constant partaking of Christ : the latter is, in this view, the continuation of the former ; and they unite to assure the certitude of the common salvation.

3. These are all external or objective pledges for assurance. The very existence of an institute of worship, the everflowing water of baptism, and the table always spread, are silent tokens that salvation is with us : we *see heaven open and the angels of God ascending and descending* on *the Son of Man.* These ordinances are midway between us and the living eternal Sacrament in heaven : they are sealing ordinances in the Church. We approach them as outward and visible pledges, VERBA VISIBILIA, which cry on earth as the resurrection of Christ does in heaven : *Be it known unto you, that through this Man is preached unto you the forgiveness of sins.* But the external becomes the internal pledge : the seal without becomes the seal within. Objective Only.

John i 51.

Acts xiii. 38.

SUBJECTIVE ASSURANCE.

Subjective.

The blessing of personal assurance is the gift of the Holy Ghost, whose office is to bear His witness TO the conscience of justification, of adoption WITH the spirit, and IN the soul of sanctification. The assurance is the assurance of faith for the present, of hope for the future, and

I 2

of understanding as underlying all. As this internal assurance is not independent of the external seals and pledges,
so it is itself verified by the testimony of the fruits of faith
in the life. The testimony of the Spirit is one, though not
one and the same, with the testimony of conscience.

THE WITNESS OF THE SPIRIT.

The
Witness
of the
Spirit.

The Holy Spirit discharges, as has been seen, two classes
of office on behalf of the Redeemer. He testifies TO the
soul the virtue of the things of Christ, and He effects
WITHIN the soul the formation of Christ Himself. There is
a sense in which both are equally within the human spirit;
but we now consider His witness as, so to speak, external.

To
Pardon.

Matt.ix.6.

1. He is not expressly said to assure of pardon. That is rather
implied and involved than stated. The Saviour declared personal
forgiveness in His own name, that men might know that *the Son
of Man hath power on earth to forgive sins.* So often did He utter
this word that we cannot doubt as to its being the universal prerogative of penitence to hear it. It may be taken for granted
that this most blessed formula was among others to be for ever
brought to remembrance by the Holy Ghost: though our Lord
has, so to speak, reserved it for Himself. If His servants were
to pronounce it in His name, it was only as the organs of the
Spirit. Jesus was exalted by God to give repentance and *forgiveness of sins,* of which there are two witnesses: first, the preachers
of the Gospel, *we are witnesses of these things;* secondly, *the Holy
Ghost Whom God hath given to them that obey Him.* It is through
the Spirit of life in Christ Jesus that we know that *there is no condemnation to them which are in Christ Jesus.* Our Lord's forgiveness, for it is His, His Agent evermore pronounces.

Acts v.
31, 32.

Rom. viii.
1, 2.

To
Adoption.
Gal. iv. 6.

2. One of His names is the *Spirit of adoption.* Though it is
our own spirit regenerate that as it were naturally says *Abba,
Father,* it is the Holy Spirit in our spirit: the distinction between
the regenerate spirit and the Holy Spirit is nearly lost in the
New Testament. *The Spirit Itself beareth witness with our spirit:*

Rom. viii.
16.

συμμαρτυρεῖ τῷ πνεύματι ἡμῶν. He mingles His life and breath with ours: we cry Father, yet not we but the Spirit in us and with us. The σὺν preserves the distinction, but it is lost again in the filial cry.

3. In the temple of Christian privilege, the Spirit is a silent seal of consecration : *ye were sealed with that Holy Spirit of promise.* This is the personal Spirit of witness, WHO is the earnest, ὅς, and concerning Whom we are exhorted, *grieve not the Holy Spirit of God.* Mark that it is the temple-epistle which alludes to the sealing, and mentions no other witness of the Spirit, though this one includes and perfects all the rest.

To Sanctity. Eph. i. 13 ; iv. 30.

ASSURANCE AND CONFIDENCE.

The certitude of the believer is constantly referred to by two terms : assurance and confidence. These may be considered first as corresponding to each other, and then as united : the former being the certitude of the inner man, the latter the expression of it in the outer life.

I. The instances wherein the former, πληροφορία, is used are three, which must be observed in their order.

Full Assurance of Faith.

1. St. Paul, in his First Epistle, speaks of the Gospel having come to the Thessalonians *in much assurance :* explained afterwards as *the Word of God, which effectually worketh also in you that believe.* This is the internal assurance of which he speaks as the being *sealed with that Holy Spirit of promise,* ἐσφραγίσθητε, *after that ye believed,* πιστεύσαντες, on their believing, and it must be observed that the term used connotes both the sealing for God and the sealing of the truth to the believer himself. The former meaning is more in harmony with other instances of its use in the New Testament, but the latter cannot be excluded ; it is indeed preferred by many expositors, who seem to confound the sealing of the truth to the mind with the sealing of the mind receiving it. Believers are assured of the Word of *Truth* of the Gospel of *salvation* on their *believing,* and this their assurance is their seal for God. They retain this confidence, and always draw near *in full assurance of faith,* having their *hearts sprinkled from an*

1 Thess. i. 5 ; ii. 13.

Eph. i. 13.

Heb x. 22.

evil conscience. This is wrought by the Spirit; it is not of the essence of faith itself but its highest prerogative; it is the general privilege of those who truly believe.

Of Hope.

2. As it respects the future faith is hope: its confidence somewhat changes its character. Absolute confidence as to the present, it may increase as it regards the future. *And we desire*

Heb. vi. 10, 11.

that every one of you do show the same diligence to the full assurance of hope unto the end: πρὸς τὴν πληροφορίαν τῆς ἐλπίδος ἄχρι τέλους. More and more full as the *work and labour of love* increases, it never outgrows hope. It becomes indeed the full assurance of hope: a subtle and most beautiful expression that experience only can comprehend: the substantiation of things hoped for.

Of Understanding.

3. Once only is the *full assurance of understanding* spoken of: St. Paul prays on behalf of the Colossians that they might add to the two other kinds of assurance an abounding and undimmed

Col. ii. 2.

confidence of the understanding, συνεσέως, in all the truths that belong to the *mystery of God,* which is *Christ.* It imports that it is the privilege of all who receive Christ to have an intellectual and experimental hold of Him, and of the whole circle of His

Eph. iv. 21.

doctrine. They know truth, as *truth is in Jesus:* that is, not only the truth but truth. They have the highest knowledge which is the knowledge of faith, they have such faith in this Object as makes it the certitude of knowledge. This is that TESTIMONIUM SPIRITUS SANCTI which the old confessions held; the seal of the Holy Ghost confirming to the believer the verity of the Christian Faith, without which all belief of the understanding is dead.

Boldness.

II. The latter, παῤῥησία, occurs in remarkable correspondence with the former.

Of Faith.

1. There is in the New Testament a παῤῥησία for each πληρο-φορία, the external profession of that internal assurance. We are

Heb. iv. 14, 16.

exhorted to *come boldly unto the throne of grace, that we may obtain mercy:* the confidence with which we ask for the mercy and seasonable help we still and always need is the confidence of uttered boldness. This is equivalent to the outward expression of inward confidence in our sympathising High Priest: *let us hold fast our profession.* The inward and outward assurance go together,

Eph. iii. 12.

or are united at the foot of the throne. We have *boldness and access with confidence by the faith of Him:* a forcible expression in which faith, its assurance, and its confident speech to God are delicately distinguished. *And this is the confidence that we have in Him,* πρὸς αὐτὸν : this πρὸς has a very wide meaning; it is the strongest preposition that could be used to signify the intimate familiarity of trust. Here then is the confident speech of the full assurance of faith. 1 John v. 14.

2. *Cast not away therefore your confidence,* τὴν παῤῥησίαν ὑμῶν : this is the confidence of hope, *for ye have need of patience;* of that hope wherein *faith is the substance of things hoped for.* Again : *And now, little children, abide in Him, that, when He shall appear, we may have confidence,* παῤῥησίαν : may not have lost it, *not be ashamed before Him at His coming.* Faith is certain now, as hope it is conditionally certain, and must persevere if it is not to be made ashamed. Here then is the confident expectation and bold expression of the full assurance of hope. Of Hope. Heb. x. 35, 36. Heb. xi. 1. 1 John ii. 28.

3. Lastly, the confidence and boldness of confession answers to the full assurance of understanding. *They that have used the office of a deacon well purchase to themselves a good degree and great boldness,* παῤῥησίαν πολλὴν, *in the faith of Christ Jesus.* The deacon's reward of fidelity is the blessing of an unfaltering confidence in the truth of what he preaches. When the Apostle says, *Seeing then that we have such hope, we use great plainness of speech,* παῤῥησία, he means that steadfast and tranquil proclamation which the sight of the unveiled Christ inspires. As the boldness of hope increases so also the confidence of the understanding. The transcendent blessing of faith and hope and understanding is one in this boldness of confession which believes and does not tremble, which believes and is raised above all shadow of doubt. Of Understanding 1 Tim. iii. 13. 2 Cor. iii. 12.

III. The Epistle to the Hebrews, which has given us so many illustrations of our doctrine, sums up its own teaching of assurance and boldness at the close, in a sentence which drops the two words but retains their meaning : just as it sums up its doctrine of the altar and temple in new terms : *We have an altar !* Ἔστι δὲ πίστις ἐλπιζομένων ὑπόστασις, πραγμάτων ἔλεγχος οὐ βλεπομένων. The great chapter of faith contains its full assurance of present acceptance, its full assurance of a conditional hope, and its full assurance of understanding as to the three supreme articles of all faith, concerning God that *He is, and that He is a rewarder of* Heb. xiii. 10. Heb. xi. 1. Heb. xi. 6, 7, 40.

them that diligently seek Him, concerning the Gospel *Righteousness which is by faith*, and concerning the better country of everlasting life in which all the saints shall be *made perfect*. As we are saved by hope, faith as hope comes first : faith gives body and substance to things unseen and future for present experience of their reality and trust in their future possession ; and its labours to make its assurance of hope perfect are the subject of the whole chapter and make the two economies of grace one. The entire strain witnesses the good confession of faith, the παῤῥησία of its πληροφορία.

THE TESTIMONY OF OUR OWN SPIRIT.

Relation of External and Internal Assurance.

The interior assurance is connected with the external ; it guards and confirms it ; and is itself guarded and confirmed by the evidence of the fruits of holiness, or the testimony of a conscience void of offence. This may be called the witness of our own spirit, though Scripture does not so term it.

1. The direct assurance or witness of the Holy Spirit rests generally upon the indirect witness of the external pledges. (1) There may be occasional departures from this law : for instance, where the Gospel vocation is independent of the Christian Church and its organisation ; where, in certain transcendent and irregular dealings of Divine grace, the soul is rapt into a region higher than the appointed ordinances. The ordinary public means of grace, including the Sacraments, may seem occasionally to be only indirectly connected with the soul's assurance. (2) But the Word of God and prayer are invariably the vehicle, instrument, and channel for His impartation of assurance : it is in answer to prayer, sometimes solitary and sometimes only ejaculatory ; and generally through the application to the soul of the promises of Rom. v. 11. the Holy Scripture. *We also joy in God through our Lord Jesus Christ, by Whom we have now received the Atonement :* the objective Atonement provided for all men in Christ must be received and internally appropriated ; and without this appropriation, through faith in the Word of reconciliation, there can be no confidence

towards God. Concerning this reception it is said that *the love of* | Rom. v. 5.
God is shed abroad in our hearts by the Holy Ghost, which is given
unto us : shed abroad in the consciousness.

2. This is the seal set by the soul itself, in its experience, to
the verity and value of the external pledges. Receiving the testimony given in the Word and Sacraments to a heavenly grace provided for man, the satisfied believer, finding in himself the Spirit's
own assurance, having *received His testimony, hath set to his seal that* | John iii.
God is true : hath added his own seal to the seal of God. Thus | 33.
the Spirit's interior seal becomes to those who believe their own
seal of the exterior Sacrament : they can say, *Now we believe, not* | John iv.
because of thy saying ; for we have heard Him ourselves. | 42.

3. The Spirit's evidence, based on the Word and Sacrament, | Witness
is guarded by the ethical and moral testimony of the life. Where- | of Our
ever the assurance of the Spirit is mentioned there is to be found | Own
hard by the appeal to the resulting and never absent evidences of | Spirit.
devotion, obedience, and charity. *For as many as are led by the* | Rom. viii.
Spirit of God, they are the sons of God. For ye have not received the | 14, 15.
Spirit of bondage again to fear ; but ye have received the Spirit of
adoption, whereby we cry, Abba, Father. The former verse gives
the test whereby we know that we are the sons of God : the test
of our submission to His Spirit. The latter gives another test :
the voice within us of the Spirit of adoption. Concerning both
and united it is said : *if any man have not the Spirit of Christ he is*
none of His. So in St. John's First Epistle the witnessing, indwelling, and renewing Spirit are one and indistinguishable.
Hereby know we that we dwell in Him—accepted in the Beloved— | 1 John iv.
and He in us—working out our holiness—*because He hath given us* | 13.
of His Spirit. God the Holy Ghost does not in His testimony
supersede conscience : He honours that ancient representative of
the Divine voice within the nature of man ; and never disjoins
His evidence from that of the subjective moral consciousness
which condemns or approves—in this case approves—according
to the standard of law written on the heart, or the conscience
objective. He is indeed *greater than our heart*—or conscience— | 1 John iii.
and knoweth all things. He knoweth the mystery of the Atonement | 20, 21.
and may silence the condemning heart. But if he assures of
pardon He commits the assurance to the conscience as its guardian ;

so that *if our heart condemn us not, then have we confidence towards God.* The same Apostle who said, *We joy in God, through our Lord Jesus Christ, by Whom we have now received the Atonement,* καυχώμενοι, said also, *For our rejoicing is this, the testimony of our conscience :* καύχησις ἡμῶν. The repetition of this expressive word deserves to be considered. The very rejoicing which the Holy Ghost inspires by shedding the *love of God* abroad in the heart reappears as the rejoicing of the regenerate soul conscious only of walking *by the grace of God, in simplicity and godly sincerity.*

Rom. v. 11.

2 Cor. i. 12. Heb. vi. 17, 18.

4. Thus, *God, willing more abundantly to show unto the heirs of promise the immutability of His counsel,* hath given seal upon seal, pledge upon pledge. The Holy Ghost, the Παράκλητος, gives us *strong consolation,* ἰσχυρὰν παράκλησιν. There are the silent pledges in which each emblem being dead yet speaketh : there is the inward personal assurance, the Sacrament in the heart; there is the confirming, attesting witness of the life; and, over all, as heaven is over all, the Risen Son of Man, the Crucified Mediator upon earth who is in the Holiest our Living Surety, Who hath entered *into heaven itself, now to appear in the presence of God for us.*

Heb. ix. 24.

HISTORICAL.

Bringing the several Confessions to this standard of doctrine, and testing them by this one article of assurance, we find many variations of more or less significance.

Sacramental.

I. The Sacramentarian doctrine of assurance contains some most important elements of truth, as has been seen, but some errors also, which may be noted in the following tendencies.

1. In Romanism and in Romanising theories it makes the evidence of salvation a concomitant of the sacrament of Penance, or of the priestly absolution; and this, when received, is fitful and occasional, and dependent on the contingency of a sufficient compliance with the conditions. It falls very much below the dignity and blessedness of a direct communication of the Eternal Spirit to the spirit of the believer in Christ.

2. The Sacramental theory in general denies rightly that to any mortal is given the assurance of final acceptance; the day of

judgment being the sealing revelation, and last assurance of safety : *looking for the mercy of our Lord Jesus Christ unto eternal life.* But it too often refuses to admit a state of present certainty as included in the provisions of the Christian covenant, at least as the common privilege of all who believe. Jude 21.

3. It has introduced a special charisma or gift of assurance of Perseverance, a sealing for the elect of the Elect : thus combining in one extraordinary privilege the assurance of faith for the present and that of hope for the future, or, in other words, adding to the witness of the Spirit a pledge of final perseverance.

4. In some forms it has sunk much below the true doctrine. As, for instance, among those who so far recoil from the fanaticism, as they term it, of the doctrine of assurance as to deny altogether the possibility of its attainment. This is sometimes an exaggeration of ascetic humility, sometimes an irrational recoil from enthusiasm, and sometimes the result of an undue preponderance given to the sterner side of probation.

II. Mysticism has always abounded in its own peculiar developments of the doctrine of probationary assurance. Mystical.

1. Its best and purest theology has generally maintained a present assurance of faith, generally though not always imparted, but without the absolute assurance as to the future. It has sometimes undervalued the objective grounds of confidence in its preference for the internal light. Mysticism has been in all ages either avowedly or virtually a reaction and protest against superstitious dependence on the external props of Christian certitude, and such exaggeration of the soleness of the inward witness was to be expected. It is seen among the Pietists of Germany, among the Friends, and occasionally among the less instructed Methodists : in fact, among all who have been suddenly aroused by strong tides of religious revival from indifference or from ceremonialism to the intense pursuit of personal salvation.

2. The extravagant Mystics of the Illuminist and Quietist types erred exceedingly : the former, forgetting the conditions of assurance, repentance, and faith ; the latter, making the perfection of religion to consist in an absolute indifference to assurance and evidence and feeling of every kind. Their doctrine of disinterested love, pressed to the extreme of the utter extinction of

desire of heaven and fear of hell, overturns the very foundation
of any theory of personal evidence of salvation.

Calvin-
istic.

III. The doctrine of Assurance, taught by what may be called
the Calvinistic system, on the one hand, falls below the standard
of Scripture, while, on the other, it goes beyond its plain
teaching. Both the defect and the excess must be studied.

Defect.

1. It falls below the calm and steadfast confidence which
the whole New Testament declares to be the privilege for the
present moment of him who believes in Christ. (1) It distinguishes too sharply between assurance and faith, and is disposed rather to overvalue the external grounds of confidence in
comparison of the internal. Certainly faith may exist without
assurance ; nor is assurance absolutely and unconditionally necessary to salvation. But, though faith itself has no reflex thought
of itself, looking only at Christ, it is in its perfect saving energy accompanied by the assurance which is indeed indistinguishable from

Gal. ii. 20.

faith in its highest exercise. He *loved me and gave Himself for me*
was the testimony of St. Paul, who, though he spoke in this style of
appropriating confidence only once, evidently intended to define
by its highest privilege the Christian's true *faith of the Son of God*
in which he lives. (2) It makes assurance a special privilege of
the few who through much discipline attain it as a gift of God ;
and, accordingly, dwells too much on the alternations and fluctuations of experience to which it pleases God for the trial of their
constancy to subject believers. (3) It confounds the assurance
of present faith with the assurance of hope : making the former
only the confidence that Jesus is what He is declared to be
generally, and the latter the confidence in personal salvation. That·
distinction is contrary to Scripture, which does not present as the
object of saving faith only Christ's Person, work, and ability, and
willingness to save us generally if we believe, but also His present
relation to us individually as a Saviour. Until faith embraces
the Lord as a personal Deliverer it is not that faith in its integrity
of which we now speak. Granted that a firm appropriating trust
in Christ, apart from the evidence of it, insures salvation, as
salvation is an objective act of God, subjective or experienced
salvation has no meaning without the knowledge of it. The
word has not its full significance and its perfect rights until the

objective and the subjective blend. This will be abundantly clear if we change the expression into justification or pardon or adoption or life from the dead. These blessings pronounced by God must be heard by man, or they are not truly his. Hence the Word of God bids those who are supposed to have the assurance of present faith to confirm continually the confidence of their hope by holy living.

2. On the other hand, it goes beyond the standard of Scripture. When once attained, the assurance is indefectible : while the essence of saving faith is regarded as the assurance that Christ generally is all that He is set forth, and will do all that He promises—a faith therefore, we repeat, independent as such of any personal appropriation—the assurance of our own personal salvation is an independent fruit of faith, and a high attainment of the spiritual life. It is the Divinely inwrought confidence of an eternal salvation, and the exhortation not to cast away its confidence is, if not superfluous, only a prudential expedient for moral discipline. But this subject belongs to our next section. Excess.

3. Both the defect and excess of the doctrine, and also its true points, are seen in the following words of the Westminster Confession : "This infallible assurance doth not so belong to the essence of faith, but that a true believer may wait long, and conflict with many difficulties, before he be partaker of it : yet, being enabled by the Spirit to know the things which are freely given him of God, he may, without extraordinary revelation, in the right use of ordinary means, attain thereunto. And therefore it is the duty of everyone to give all diligence to make his calling and election sure." Here is a certain inconsistency in making a free gift the result of diligent seeking. When it is added that "true believers may have the assurance of their salvation divers ways shaken," that is true of all assurance, though not precisely in the sense of this document.

IV. Methodism has done much to clear the Scriptural doctrine of Assurance from the misapprehensions that have obscured it. In its system of religious teaching the following points are made prominent and sharply defined. Methodism.

1. It is asserted to be the COMMON PRIVILEGE of all who believe ; being the accompaniment of every blessing of the Christian cove- Common.

nant : not, indeed, of the essence of justifying faith, but a result
of it that may be expected, and should be sought.

Works xii.
109, 110.
(1.) Mr. Wesley says on the former subject : "Is justifying
faith a sense of pardon ? *Negatur.* 1. Everyone is deeply concerned to understand this question well; but Preachers most of
all. 2. By *justifying faith* I mean that faith which whosoever
hath not is under the wrath and the curse of God. By *a sense of
pardon* I mean a distinct explicit assurance that my sins are forgiven. I allow (1) that there is an explicit assurance ; (2) that it
is the common privilege of real Christians; (3) that it is the
proper Christian Faith which 'purifieth the heart' and 'overcometh the world.' But I cannot allow that justifying faith is
such an assurance, or *necessarily* connected therewith. 3. Because
if justifying faith necessarily implies such an explicit assurance
of pardon, then everyone who has it not and everyone so long as
he has it not is under the wrath and the curse of God. But this
is a supposition contrary to Scripture as well as to experience.
Contrary to Is. l. 10, and Acts x. 34, 35. Again, the assertion
'justifying faith is a sense of pardon,' is contrary to reason : it is
flatly absurd. For how can a sense of pardon be the *condition* of
our receiving it ?"

Works v.
133.
(2.) As to the latter : "The second inference is, let none rest
in any supposed fruit of the Spirit without the witness. There
may be foretastes of joy, of peace, of love, and those not delusive,
but really from God, long before we have the witness in ourselves;
before the Spirit of God witnesses with our spirits that we have
'redemption in the blood of Jesus, even the forgiveness of sins.'
Yea, there may be a degree of longsuffering, of gentleness, of
fidelity, meekness, temperance, (not a shadow thereof, but a real
degree, by the preventing grace of God,) before we 'are accepted
in the Beloved,' and, consequently, before we have a testimony of
our acceptance : but it is by no means advisable to rest here ; it
is at the peril of our souls if we do. If we are wise, we shall be
continually crying to God, until His Spirit cry in our heart,
'Abba, Father !' This is the privilege of all the children of God,
and without this we can never be assured that we are His
children. Without this we cannot retain a steady peace, nor
avoid perplexing doubts and fears. But when we have once

received this Spirit of adoption, this 'peace, which passeth all understanding,' and which expels all painful doubt and fear, will 'keep our hearts and minds in Christ Jesus.' And when this has brought forth its genuine fruit, all inward and outward holiness, it is undoubtedly the will of Him that calleth us, to give us always what He has once given; so that there is no need that we should ever more be deprived of either the testimony of God's Spirit, or the testimony of our own, the consciousness of our walking in all righteousness and true holiness."

(3.) He also in many passages of his writings shows that the testimony of the Spirit is borne to our justification, adoption and sanctification severally and respectively. As to the two former no evidence is needed : as to the witness of sanctification he says : "To this confidence, that God is both able and willing to sanctify us now, there needs to be added one thing more,—a Divine evidence and conviction that He doeth it. In that hour it is done, God says to the inmost soul, 'According to thy faith be it unto thee!' Then the soul is pure from every spot of sin; it is clean 'from all unrighteousness.' The believer then experiences the deep meaning of those solemn words, 'If we walk in the light as He is in the light, we have fellowship one with another, and the blood of Jesus Christ His Son cleanseth us from all sin.'" Here two remarks must be made. The distinction maintained above, between the faith and its assurance, still holds good. By the "conviction that He doeth it" is meant the certainty conveyed to the soul that the work of entire sanctification is wrought. The "evidence" that is the perfection of faith itself, and the confidence that it has its object, are not always kept asunder in the Sermons. But it is undoubted that Mr. Wesley taught that the witness of finished sanctification is to be expected. Again, by "sanctify" here he means entirely sanctify : not being always careful to observe his own rule on the subject. There is no text of Scripture that directly promises the knowledge of so great an internal work; but none is necessary. It is the prerogative of the Holy Spirit to make His indwelling and work evident to the consciousness : "God 'sealeth us with the Spirit of promise' by giving us 'the full assurance of hope,' such a confidence of receiving all the promises of God, as excludes the possibility of

Threefold Testimony.

Works xi. 53.

doubting; with that Holy Spirit, by universal holiness, stamping the whole image cf God on our hearts." The subject of this last assurance will come up again. Meanwhile, it is enough to say that the Methodist doctrine of the Spirit's witness covers the whole ground of the Spirit's work. It rests upon the firm foundation of the Scripture that we *know the things that are freely given unto us of God.* The assurance in the several departments of covenant blessing may bear various characters. Given to the pardoned sinner it is a sense of unspeakable relief to the conscience; in the heart of the adopted child it is the irrepressible filial confidence; in the regenerate spirit sanctified to God it is the silent seal of a Divine indwelling, abiding in the soul as the awful sense of the Triune God within and deepening into the assurance that He fills the whole heart, or the witness of entire sanctification.

2. It is the DIRECT WITNESS of the Spirit, not independent of the objective and external grounds of assurance, but given through them, or indeed without them, directly to the soul. "The sum of all is this: The testimony of the Spirit is an inward impression on the souls of believers, whereby the Spirit of God directly testifies to their spirit, that they are children of God. And it is not questioned, whether there is a testimony of the Spirit; but whether there is any *direct* testimony; whether there is any other than that which arises from a consciousness of the fruit of the Spirit. We believe there is; because this is the plain natural meaning of the text, illustrated both by the preceding words and by the parallel passage in the Epistle to the Galatians; because, in the nature of the thing, the testimony must precede the fruit which springs from it; and, because this plain meaning of the Word of God is confirmed by the experience of innumerable children of God; yea, and by the experience of all who are convinced of sin, who can never rest till they have a direct witness; and even of the children of the world, who, not having the witness in themselves, one and all declare, none can *know* his sins forgiven." The directness or immediateness of this testimony was contended against in the early days of Methodism, as it has been opposed, more or less, in all ages. The opposition, however, was of two kinds. Some denied the possibility on the general

---

Marginal notes:

1 Cor. ii. 12.

Direct.

Works v. 132.

ground that there could be no security against enthusiasm. But the Spirit within the spirit of man is to all who know God the most real of all realities. Others insisted that there could be no such witness apart from the testimony of the consciousness of a sincere use of the external means of grace, and obedience to the commandments of God : in other words, that the testimony of the Spirit must in the nature of things be indirect if the means of grace are the objective grounds of assurance. But there are some plain passages concerning the testimony which expressly preclude the possibility that it is borne through the medium of any symbol or sacrament. Whatever voice, or word, or ordinance may be employed—each and all may be employed, and the Word in some form always—the assurance must ultimately be conveyed direct from Spirit to spirit. Mr. Wesley in his candour understates his argument again and again. He deals with an objector thus : "'But the direct witness is never referred to in the Book of God.' Vol.v.131. Not as standing alone ; not as a single witness ; but as connected with the other; as giving a *joint testimony ;* testifying *with our spirit,* that we are children of God." Strictly speaking, there is no passage which more absolutely declares the direct and sole testimony of the Holy Ghost. The συμμαρτυρεῖ is indeed a joint testimony ; but our own spirit is not supposed to bring its inferences to be confirmed ; rather the witness of the Holy Ghost to our adoption is borne through the spirit of our new regenerate life. Elsewhere Mr. Wesley says, with more precision : "the Vol.v.113. preposition σύν only denoting that He witnesses this *at the same time* that He enables us to cry Abba, Father. But I contend not ; seeing so many other texts, with the experience of all real Christians, sufficiently evince that there is in every believer both the testimony of God's Spirit, and the testimony of his own, that he is a child of God." These last words suggest the remark that the Methodist doctrine is unfairly dealt with when it is supposed to rest upon one, two, or three cardinal passages. The Sermon quoted ranges through a wide variety of Scriptural proofs ; and it does not include all. Hard by the words here and habitually quoted there are others which even yet more strongly declare the mystery of the inward assurance of the child of God : that, namely, which speaks of the Searcher of hearts hearing the voice of the interceding Spirit in the inmost consciousness of His suffering children.

Confirmed by Indirect Witness.

Vol.v.125.

3. It is always confirmed by the accompaniment of the INDIRECT WITNESS, or testimony of the conscience on the evidence of a sincere life. The latter phrase seems preferable for the reason just assigned. Though Mr. Wesley writes of it as " The Witness of our own spirit" his discourse is on the characteristics of a good conscience. "Neither is it questioned whether there is an *indirect* witness or testimony, that we are the children of God. This is nearly, if not exactly, the same with the testimony of a good conscience towards God ; and is the result of reason, or reflection on what we feel in our own souls. Strictly speaking, it is a con-clusion drawn partly from the Word of God, and partly from our own experience. The Word of God says, everyone who has the fruit of the Spirit is a child of God ; experience, or inward con-sciousness, tells me that I have the fruit of the Spirit ; and hence I naturally conclude, 'Therefore I am a child of God.'" This witness is indirect as a conclusion : but as the consciousness of experience, or of conscience, which is the moral consciousness, it is as direct as that of the Spirit Himself, who may be said to bear witness together with our conscience. The two are united ever in the perfect experience of the Christian. But both admit of variations. "Nor do we assert that there can be any real testimony of the Spirit without the fruit of the Spirit. We assert, on the contrary, that the fruit of the Spirit immediately springs from this testimony : not always indeed in the same degree, even when the testimony is first given ; and much less afterwards. Neither joy nor peace is always at one stay ; no, nor love ; as neither is the testimony itself always equally strong and clear." None of the doctrines to which Methodism gives prominence is more diligently fenced and defended from the im-putation of fanaticism than this of the direct and indirect witness of the Holy Spirit.

THE GRACE OF PERSEVERANCE.

Provision is made in the Christian covenant for the maintenance of religion in the soul to the end. The source of this grace is the effectual intercession of Christ, caring for His own. The manifestation of it is the all-sufficient power of the Holy Spirit; in its nature and operation it is superabundant and persistent; not indefectible however, but conditional on perseverance in fidelity.

The general subject belongs to the Ethics as well as to the Doctrines of Redemption. So far as it belongs to doctrine, two things must be noted. First, there is a specific GRACE OF PER-SEVERANCE provided in the Christian covenant which is too often forgotten in the ardour of controversy: this we must dwell upon briefly. Secondly, the chief stress of the treatment must needs be laid on the polemical or historical aspect of it: that is, in the confutation of the conventional dogma of FINAL PERSEVERANCE.

PERSEVERING GRACE IN ITS GROUND.

Ground.

Christ's eternal love to His own, as proved once for all in His supreme sacrifice, is the pledge of persevering grace being granted to them according to all the varieties of their need. That love shows itself in special and effectual intercession for them: intercession which is the Redeemer's expressed will, and also His prayer giving efficacy to ours.

1. There is a sense in which the Lord regards the body of believers as His own for time and for eternity. By His atonement He has secured them for Himself, and secured for them every provision for eternal salvation. They are His portion of the human race; and their continuance in grace is provided for: not only for their own sake but also for His. He waits to rejoice over them in heaven as His *purchased possession*, as His heritage or the portion that falleth to Him: *And all Mine are Thine, and*

Christ's Posses-sion.

Eph. i. 14.
John xvii. 10.

K 2

Thine are Mine. There is no more impressive and affecting representation of the bond between Christians and Christ their Head than this, that they are given Him of the Father.

Interces-
sion.
John xvii.
24.

2. For this body, as distinguished from the world, He intercedes. His will is their eternal salvation. *Father, I will that,* θέλω ἵνα, *they also, whom Thou hast given Me, be with Me where I am.* His one Divine reward for His Divine-human obedience is the salva-

John vi.
39.

tion of His own. It also takes a human form : the Father highly exalted Him and gave Him supreme dominion. He did not Himself stipulate for this ; He never even seems to glance beyond this world for His recompense ; but He does most expressly lay claim to His people as His inheritance ; satisfied with them, but with nothing less than they : *of all which He hath given Me I should lose nothing.* Death seems to appropriate part of them ; but death must relinquish its prey : I will *raise it up again at the last day.* His request or intercession also—almost as strong as His will—is

John xvii.
15.

for their grace unto perseverance. *I pray not that Thou shouldest take them out of the world, but that Thou shouldest keep them from the evil.* And in praying—ἐρωτῶ—for sufficient grace unto perseverance, our Lord included all His own to the end of time : not

John xvii.
20,

simply as His own, however, but as believers, *for them also which shall believe on Me.* They are His heritage, but as believing in Him : not one without the other.

3. Hence, nothing is more certain than the perseverance of

John x.
28.

those who continue in that body. *They shall never perish ; neither shall any pluck them out of My hand.* The Father and the Son, in eternal essence one, are united in the counsel of redemption. But there is a special emphasis upon their unity in the accom-

John x. 30.

plishment of the design of grace as to the elect : *I and My Father are One.* The members of Christ's mystical body are eternally foreknown, and grace will be found to have been sufficiently provided for their whole estate of probation. He who redeemed the world especially redeemed the Church ; and known unto Him from the beginning was the whole contest and diversified trial through which His Church must become eternally His. Therefore He added to the treasure of His redeeming merit the continual energy of His active intercession, providing grace for every time of need. The High Priest of mankind is especially the Advocate of His people : *If any man sin we have an Advocate with the Father . . . Who is the Propitiation for the sins of the world.*

1 John ii. 1.

PERSEVERING GRACE IN ITS MANIFESTATION.

Manifestation.

The grace of Perseverance is the constant impartation of the Holy Ghost: indwelling as a seal and bringing effectual succour in every time of need.

I. St. Paul, in one of those passages into which he condenses the entire substance of Gospel privilege, says : *in Whom also after that ye believed ye were sealed with that Holy Spirit of promise, Which is the earnest of our inheritance until the redemption of the purchased possession.* As to God, the Spirit is His seal on the regenerate soul. As to the believer, the Spirit is to him the earnest of a future inheritance. As to Christ, the Spirit is His representative in the soul until He redeems His possession. But it is remarkable that in the Epistle which mentions most emphatically the seal of the Spirit, of the personal Indweller, we have the most urgent exhortation, *grieve not the Holy Spirit.* Though nothing in this tranquil Epistle is said of the possibility of the seal being broken, nothing is said as to its being inviolable. *Be not ye therefore partakers with them* is an injunction which seems to refer as much to the *wrath of God* as to *these things* which caused it : have no participation with them, either in their doings or in the punishment of those doings. In another document, which teaches the same doctrine of the sealing Spirit, we read : *If any man defile the temple of God, him shall God destroy ; for the temple of God is holy, which temple ye are.*

Indwelling.
Eph. i. 13, 14.

Eph. iv. 30.

Eph. v. 6, 7.

1 Cor. iii. 17.

II. Persevering grace is imparted for every requirement of our infirmity, and that in three ways.

Imparted.

1. It is the grace of watchfulness to keep what is attained : *I have prayed for thee, that thy faith fail not.* This was said to one who failed in part: and did not wholly fail only because grace was given to him which he used. The grace he received taught him the need of watchfulness. He was bidden, when *converted, strengthen thy brethren ;* and his Epistles are specially adapted to encourage confidence in the riches of the grace of Christ, the Keeper of

To Keep.
Luke xxii. 31, 32.

Israel, at the same time that they lay very great stress upon the humility that receives and the diligence that uses His effectual grace. *Be sober, be vigilant* follows hard upon *Casting all your care upon Him; for He careth for you.* A watchful spirit is the gift of God; but its watchfulness is its own use of that gift.

1 Peter v. 7, 8.

2. It is the manifold grace which enables the soul to accomplish every duty of life. *God is able to make all grace abound toward you, that ye, always having all sufficiency in all things, may abound to every good work:* this applies not only to the duty of liberality, but to every duty. Having all-sufficiency from God we must abound in our own diligence. There is no commandment without promise: promise of reward for obedience, and promise of help to perform. But the grace which strengthens for endlessly diversified duty is pledged to those and to those only who use it. *Work out your own salvation with fear and trembling. For it is God which worketh in you both to will and to do of His good pleasure.* The good pleasure which is here the spring and the rule of the Divine working in us must become our own good pleasure. St. Paul elsewhere gives us a variation on this great saying. *We pray always for you that our God would . . . fulfil all the good pleasure of goodness, and the work of faith with power.*

To Do.
2 Cor. ix. 8.

Phil. ii. 12, 13.

2 Thess. i. 11.

3. It is the effectual grace of support that enables the believer to sustain the pressure of affliction and to endure all the will of God. The Apostle's prayer for the Colossians is, that they might be *strengthened with all might, according to His glorious power, unto all patience and longsuffering with joyfulness.* But another Apostle says that the grace which enables the soul to sustain what is a sharper test than any Satan can apply—the visitation of Providence, and the spiritual suffering which precedes the death of the body of sin in conformity with Christ who *suffered for us in the flesh*—is to be used as our own armour, not God's alone: *Arm yourselves likewise with the same mind.* Finally, however, when we have done and suffered all, and while we are doing and suffering all, persevering grace is the Divine gift: *But the God of all grace, Who hath called us unto His eternal glory by Christ Jesus, after that ye have suffered awhile, make you perfect, stablish, strengthen, settle you.*

To Suffer.

Col. i. 11.

1 Peter iv. 1.

1 Peter v. 10.

This grace is, as has been seen, strong and persistent; but mighty and enduring as it is, it is still conditional.

I. However viewed, the grace of Christ towards His own, and Persistent the power of the Holy Spirit within them, go far to secure absolutely the final salvation of the regenerate. The surpassing and unlimited love of the Redeemer, the reluctance of the Spirit to forsake the work of His hands, the plenitude of the means of grace, the growing blessedness of true religion, the might of intercessory prayer both Divine and human, the feebleness of the Lord's enemies in comparison of His lightest influence, all conspire to show that the utter relapse and final ruin of a regenerate soul is a hard possibility. If the Holy Ghost forsakes the soul for ever which He has once inhabited, such a departure, rendering the place so deeply and unalterably desolate, must be spoken of in the language of the prophet as His *strange work*, His *strange act.* Isa. xxviii. 21.

1. This blessed truth explains much in Scripture that seems to declare that the Christian heritage is absolutely secure. *If God* Rom. viii. *be for us, who can be against us?* Here is both the question of 31—39. confidence and the apostrophe of defiance. The latter is continued in the glowing words which assert that nothing, sin always excepted, *shall be able to separate us from the love of God which is in Christ Jesus our Lord.*

2. It explains the tone of assurance with which the future is looked forward to among the Christians of the New Testament. *We are not of them who draw back unto perdition; but of them* Heb. x. *that believe to the saving of the soul.* There is a drawing back; but 39. we may feel ourselves secure. Hence the strengthener of his brethren, the Apostle of perseverance, bids them *make your calling* 2 Peter i. *and election sure:* βεβαίαν ποιεῖσθαι. It may be made SURE, and 10. this is the guarantee of assurance. It must be MADE sure, and this is the pith of perseverance.

3. But it must be reconciled with the most positive testimonies that no man in the present life can go beyond the assurance of hope. *What a man seeth, why doth he yet hope for?* The solitary Rom. viii. 24.

passage in the New Testament which describes faith and hope as one and interchangeable gives the formula of the true doctrine. *Faith is the substance of things hoped for:* the present substantial realisation of what is ours only in hope. And very impressive is the fact that St. Paul in two other passages describes Christian hope as keeping pace in its measures with the increase of faith: *Now the God of hope fill you with all joy and peace in believing, that ye may abound in hope through the power of the Holy Ghost;* and in another with the increase of experience: *tribulation worketh patience, and patience experience, and experience hope.* This hope *maketh not ashamed;* but no other reason of this is given than that *the love of God is shed abroad in our hearts by the Holy Ghost.*

II. The grace of continuance is conditional, notwithstanding all that has been said. Unconditional grace may be spoken of as provided for the world as such, and for the mystical Church as such: as received by individuals it is conditional. Whether in the beginning of preliminary life, or in the mature life of the regenerate, or in the most confirmed saints, its very nature as grace is bound up with the condition that it is used by the free concurrence of him who receives it.

1. All grace of God is unconditional in its impartation to the old race in Adam, and to the new race in Christ. *The grace of God, and the gift by grace, which is by one man, Jesus Christ, hath abounded unto many.* As all mankind share the displeasure of God caused by sin, so all share the beginnings of His mercy drawing them to repentance. This preliminary grace, whether manifest through its appointed means or imperceptible in its mysterious influence on the human heart, is unconditional. So also the plenary gifts of grace, which all believers receive out *of His fulness,* are unconditionally bestowed on the mystical body of Christ, whatever and of whomsoever composed that body may be. The Church, as such, is a predestined object of our Lord's eternal complacency. Hence the language of the Scripture runs in the strain of indefectible gift of grace to the body and fellowship of believers as foreseen and predestinated from the foundation of the world.

2. But all grace, whether preliminary or saving, is as it concerns the individual, and with respect to its effectual operation, conditional. Therefore St. Paul's exhortation, beseeching us that

Heb. x'. 1.

Rom. xv. 13.

Rom. v. 3, 4, 5.

Conditional.

Rom. v. 15.

John i. 16.

we *receive not the grace of God in vain:* received freely in one sense and as irresistible, in another sense it may be received in vain. Unless εἰς κενὸν ceases to mean to no purpose, or without result, and unless it can be shown that St. Paul was addressing spurious Christians, saving grace is not irremissible. But he certainly addressed, by every token in the context, true believers in Christ, when he uttered this most impressive appeal.

2 Cor. vi. 1.

HISTORICAL AND CONTROVERSIAL.

The conventional dogma of Final Perseverance belongs to the Augustinian or Calvinistic type of doctrine. There have been sundry attempts to attach this doctrine to other systems, but they have been vain : it comports with no other theory of the economy of grace than which limits it to a definite and elect number, pre-determined in the councils of eternity. Supposing redemption to be universal, and the offer of grace free for all, and salvation possible to every man, some have also supposed that the grace of an effectual regeneration must needs be indefectible and eternal. But a more thorough examination of the Christian covenant tends to show that this generous interpretation of the doctrine of persevering grace cannot be made consistent with the freedom of will and personal responsibility which lie at the foundation of universal redemption. The arguments for the indefectibility of grace in the Elect are such as rest, first upon the nature of the Christian Covenant, and then upon misunderstood Scriptures.

THE COVENANT OF REDEMPTION.

What is called Final Perseverance, or the doctrine that grace can never be finally lost, is defended generally not so much by Scripture as by the necessary principles of the so-called Covenant of Redemption. So absolute and all-pervading in this view of the Gospel is the idea of a fixed and unalterable division of mankind that it is made a canon to which the interpretation of every passage of Scripture must conform. What seems to be wrong in these principles has been already indicated, but may be summarised once more.

1. The Absolute sovereignty of the Divine will presides over an imaginary covenant between the Father and the Son before time began ; a certain number were to be redeemed and given to the Redeemer as the fruit and reward of His atoning submission ; and fidelity to that covenant demands the immunity from possible fall of all who were included in the portion of Christ. There is no Scriptural evidence of such an unconditional covenant, though there is a catholic truth of inestimable importance underlying the error. The Redeemer has indeed His portion of mankind divided to Him ; but not by an absolutely sovereign and despotic disposal of the eternal destinies of men. He rejoices over those who were given Him of the Father; but He laments over one of them as lost. Moreover He speaks of them as being drawn to Him one by one, and promises them: *him that cometh to Me I will in no wise cast out.* Not in this style would He speak of those who were unconditionally His before time began. He prays for the Glory which He had before the foundation of the world, but not for the people who were then assigned to Him.

John vi. 37.

Imputed Righteousness.

2. The relation of Christ to those thus given Him is supposed to be such that their salvation is assured. He is their Substitute and Surety, and more than their Representative : He assumes their place at all points ; suffers for them, obeys for them, and insures them an eternal sanctity. We have seen that the Saviour's righteousness is not otherwise imputed to His people than as their sin was imputed to Him. We may conceive of an imputation of the active righteousness in the sense that we are reckoned righteous as well as forgiven ; but even of that the Scripture does not so speak. We are predestinated *elect*, St. Peter says, only *through sanctification of the Spirit.*

1 Pet. i. 2.

Irresistibility of Grace.

3. The irresistibility of Divine grace as an operation of the Spirit within the soul is necessary to the dogma of Final Perseverance. But grace, as such, is never represented as irresistible : it is free in God, and to be freely received by man. Like the will it cannot tolerate the idea of constraint, by its very name. God is irresistible ; and His will is irresistible ; but not His grace, which is only His undeserved lovingkindness moving on free intelligences. His will redeemed the world ; and that will was irresistible. The *grace which bringeth salvation unto men* was abso-

Tit. ii. 11.

lute and unconditional ; though even that grace may be received *in* | 2 Cor. vi. 1.
vain by individuals. As working within the heart it is an influence of discipline : it *teacheth us* the way of holiness, παιδεύει.

4. The distinction between the special grace that insures sal- | Common Grace.
vation and the common grace that may be, and by the terms must be, in many cases, unprofitable, is arbitrary. No grace of God should be called common : its slightest influence may lead to heaven, and is given with that intention. There is no necessity in the system more hard, no dogma in it more intolerable than that which requires us to believe in a large and most affecting expenditure of the grace of God intentionally insufficient for salvation.

5. The gift of Final Perseverance is an unreality, whether in the expression or in the thought which it expresses. Perseverance is an ethical duty. The gift, or charism, of perseverance is bestowed from moment to moment ; it is the diligent use of the grace of every hour. That it should be imparted once for all as a blessing of the Christian covenant is a contradiction in terms ; and the necessity of choosing such a phrase for the doctrine is an argument against it.

THE ARGUMENT FROM SCRIPTURE.

The testimonies of Scripture introduced into this controversy may be divided into two classes : those which the advocates of Final Perseverance use in offensive warfare, and those which they resist when alleged against them. Both classes have been already alluded to ; but the importance of the subject demands that they be more formally exhibited in their seeming contrariety.

I. Positive declarations of the Bible in favour of the necessary | Texts Pleaded for Final Perseverance.
perpetuity of grace are confessedly few. The argument most depended on is as we have seen the nature of the covenant of grace, or the compact between the Father and the Son as already explained. The few testimonies to which appeal is made may be referred to the decrees of God, to our Lord's sayings, and to the Apostolical testimonies as such.

1. *Whom He called them He also justified, and whom He justified* | Rom. viii. 29, 30.
them He also glorified. This golden chain, with others like it, only

sets forth the order of grace : not a necessary sequence, save in the case of the finally saved ; the links are beheld from eternity and not from time. It goes back to what we call the past, προέγνω, *He did foreknow ;* all whom He foreknew, προώρισε, *He also did predestinate to be conformed to the image of His Son.* Then it goes forward, as we might say, to the end : as if all were accomplished, *them He also called,* ἐκάλεσε ; *them He also justified,* ἐδικαίωσε, their adoption and sanctification being included in the *image of His Son ;* and *them He also glorified,* ἐδόξασε. This representative text stands for all those which refer to the electing and determinate purpose of God : passages which are to be interpreted as speaking in the prospect of an eternal accomplishment already decided in the Divine mind with reference to the believing heirs of grace and glory, therefore as referring not so much to the individual as to the Church viewed in its corporate mystical capacity.

2. Our Lord's declarations on this subject are few. His parable of the sheep, of whom He says that *they shall never perish, neither shall any man pluck them out of My hand,* must be interpreted in the light of that other of the Vine, whose branches are eternal, while an individual branch might be *cast forth* and be *withered.* This we shall mark hereafter : meanwhile, our Lord declares of His sheep that as such they shall never lack pasture from Him, nor shall any wrest them from Him. That they may not forsake Him He does not add ; nor could that be added by the same lips which testified, *severed from Me ye can do nothing.*

John x. 28.

John xv. 5, 6.

3. A few typical passages from the Apostles may be adduced : each represents a class, though a very small one.

Phil. i. 6—10.

(1.) St. Paul writes : *Being confident of this very thing, that He which hath begun a good work in you will perform it until the day of Jesus Christ.* The Apostle, when he speaks of the coming day of Christ, almost invariably has in view the community character of Christians : death was to the individual at least an alternative prospect : it was not so to the Church, which has only before it the coming of Christ. Hence the IN is really equivalent to AMONG you. In any case, the emphasis is in the relation between the beginning and the performing ; and the safeguard is supplied in the prayer *that ye may be sincere and without offence till the day of*

Christ. Such passages must have a generous interpretation, but not too generous. It is the will of God to accomplish fully all that He begins in love; but not all the gifts of universal mercy are without repentance: witness its vast miscarriage in those who turn *the grace of our God into lasciviousness,* the *grace that* Jude 4. *bringeth salvation to all men.* Titus ii. 11.

(2.) The only testimony of St. John that can be pressed into the service is this: *they went out from us, but they were not of us;* 1 John ii. *for, if they had been of us, they would no doubt have continued with us:* 19, 20. *but they went out that they might be made manifest that they were not all of us.* He is speaking of Antichrists, teaching without the *unction from the Holy One.* Comparison with this Apostle's own parable of the Vine will show that he could not refer to a necessary continuing or abiding in Christ, as such.

(3.) St. Peter, the Apostle who fell and rose again, whose gentle penalty was, *when thou art converted strengthen thy brethren,* is Luke xxii. naturally appealed to on this question. He has many important 32. sayings in relation to it. All Christian communions hold that doctrine of indefectible grace and final perseverance which is taught in the words: *kept by the power of God through faith unto* 1 Pet. i. 5. *salvation,* which indeed contain the whole truth in summary form. As the Atonement is set forth by the Divine counsel independently of man, but made a reality to him only through faith,—*Whom God* Rom. iii. *hath set forth to be a propitiation in His blood through faith,*—so the 25. final salvation to which it leads is *set forth* in the Divine mind for the Church, but becomes personal privilege only *through faith.* A passage, however, soon follows which has been a classical proof-text, and much relied on, so far that is as isolated texts are relied on in this controversy. It is that of the incorruptible seed. There are two kinds of life mentioned by the writer. Of the one it is said, *all flesh is as grass:* the glory and beauty of physical or temporal life perisheth. Of the other it is said: *being born again, not of* 1 Pet. i. *corruptible seed, but of incorruptible, by the Word of God which liveth* 23. *and abideth for ever.* The glory and beauty of that life of which Christ says, *I am come that they might have life, and . . . have it more* John x. *abundantly,* never passeth away. With St. Peter's text may be 10. compared St. John's, *Whosoever is born of God doth not commit sin;* 1 John iii. *for His seed remaineth in him.* The two passages are strictly 9.

parallel; but neither does St. John teach that the incorruptible seed as such makes the regenerate absolutely sinless, nor St. Peter that it absolutely insures eternal life.

II. Many passages running in an opposite direction are so clear as effectually to overturn the high theory of Final Perseverance.

Weak Arguments against Perseverance.

1. There are some, indeed, which ought not to be pressed into the controversy on either side. Such are those which refer to the falls of the saints: they might often fall, but not finally, Simon Peter being an instance, with David and Solomon, and many others. Nor should we urge the texts which enforce fidelity, diligence, and watchfulness generally as necessary to salvation. It may be fairly said that the Divine purpose includes the means with the end : the opponents of indefectible grace are glad of an analogous argument when they connect foreknowledge and election. As election is based on foreknowledge, so, might it be said, final perseverance is assured on the foreknowledge of fidelity. Nor should we use those which speak of the apostasy of Judaism or of the fall of the Israelites in the wilderness : apart, that is, from the Apostolic specific application of this latter, which does give a very solemn individual aspect to the admonition. Nor is it right to appeal to the decline and destruction of the Asiatic Churches. All these instances of a final lapse from grace may be referred to communities and not to individuals: here again we

Texts Wrested.

must allow our opponents the measure we mete with ourselves. But there is a series of declarations running through the Word of God which the advocates of the irremissibility of grace are obliged to wrest from their obvious signification, or interpret by a special canon of Hermeneutics devised for the purpose.

2. There are many sayings which are uttered by God, as it were without specific relation to the redeeming purpose, as the Moral Governor of the universe simply. *If thou forsake Him He will cast thee off for ever:* this expressed a universal principle applicable to all economies, and to all times, and to all unfaithful stewards of the Divine gifts. The unknown prophet who was raised up to rebuke Eli, speaks thus the Divine message: *I said indeed. . . . But now the Lord saith, Be it far from Me ; for them that honour Me I will honour, and they that despise Me shall be lightly*

1 Chron. xxviii. 9.

1 Sam. ii. 30.

esteemed. This is not a theocratic principle only, it is a statement of God's everlasting law. No sophistry can avail to soften the words spoken by God to the children of His people for ever : *the righteousness of the righteous shall not deliver him in the day of his transgression.* Both in the New and in the Old Testaments *God is no respecter of persons.* As a Father, He *judgeth according to every man's work. Our God*—even in the Christian covenant—*is a consuming fire:* consuming His people's sins, indeed ; but it was not to express such a meaning the word was uttered ; it was as a warning to all who, having received the grace of the earlier covenant, reject that of the later.

Ezek. xxiii. 12.

Acts x. 34. 1 Pet. i. 17. Heb. xii. 29.

3. Our Lord has left some clear sayings, recorded by the same Evangelist who has most profoundly exhibited the bond between Christ and His elect. The parable-allegory of the Vine is the pendant of that of the sheep that *never perish. Without Me*— χωρὶς ἐμοῦ—*ye can do nothing. If a man abide not in Me, he is cast forth as a branch and is withered.* This follows the great words of mystical union, *Abide in Me, and I in you ;* the warning therefore is not given to those who heard it as they were Apostles. Nor was the calling of Judas only Apostolic ; he was cast forth of the living Vine, and his loss was acknowledged as the separation of one of the elect : *those that Thou gavest Me I have kept, and none of them is lost but the son of perdition.* Three terms are used in relation to Judas which show that he had been one of the objects of the Saviour's grace in common with the other Apostles : he was given to Christ of the Father, he was chosen, and as lost he had partaken of salvation. It may be said that while the Lord was in the world, and especially during His earlier ministry, His teaching did not as yet penetrate to the strict bonds of the eternal covenant. But there is no teaching of His servants on this or any subject higher than His own. And the tone of His instruction from the beginning to the end tends to exactly the opposite of the doctrine of a necessary indefectible grace. Witness the close of the Sermon on the Mount : the last parables of the Talents and the Pounds and the Virgins ; and the final Eschatological discourses. We cannot but feel that He speaks, not of a class of persons never really Christians, but of us all. But the series of testimonies to which we here refer belongs rather to the ethics

Our Lord.

John xv. 4, 5, 6 ; comp. John x. 28.

John xvii. 12.

than to the doctrines of the covenant of grace. They are therefore not here quoted and classified.

Apostles. 4. A few of the Apostolical testimonies may be added : each the representative of a considerable class.

(1.) The last words of the first Apostolic writer : *let him know*
Jas. v. 19, *that he which converteth the sinner from the error of his way shall save*
20. *a soul from death, and shall hide a multitude of sins.* The sins thus hidden are such as cause error from the way of eternal life : St.
1 John v. John forbids the other interpretation when, as to the sin unto
16. death, he says, *I do not say that he shall pray for it.* St. James makes very emphatic the probationary character of religion : *he*
Jas. ii. 13. *shall have judgment without mercy, that hath showed no mercy.* The Apostle is speaking to Christian men, who may forget the royal law of charity ; and what in their case must mean JUDGMENT WITHOUT MERCY !

2 Pet. i. (2.) St. Peter thus exhorts : *give diligence to make your calling*
10. *and election sure, for if ye do these things ye shall never fall.* Surely this is not language used of an impossible lapse. Satan may indeed by a violent interpretation be supposed to be self-deceived in seek-
1 Pet. v. 8. ing *whom he may devour.* But the Apostle warns all not to fall
2 Pet. iii. from their *own steadfastness.*
17.
Jude 12, (3.) St. Jude, in his short Epistle, speaks of the *trees whose fruit*
19. *withereth, without fruit, twice dead ;* and of men once Christians who had become *sensual, having not the Spirit :* these had been in the spiritual family, else how could they *separate themselves ?* The tenour of the Epistle is no other than a warning against eternal
Vers.1,21. apostasy. Those who are *preserved in Jesus Christ* are bidden *keep*
Ver. 24. *yourselves in the love of God.* The doxology to *Him that is able to keep you from falling* is one that all confessions join in. These three KEEPINGS must be combined. The two former have the same Greek verb : those who are preserved in Christ must preserve themselves in God's love. The third varies the expression in two words : God is able to *guard* from falling, and He is ABLE to guard. Here is the threefold cord ; all true Christians rejoice in the combination of its strands ; but none should find in it more than the everlasting security which unites Almighty power and human fidelity.

(4.) St. Paul's view of redemption delights in the perfect sta-

bility of the eternal counsels.   He evermore sees the consummation of the Divine designs, and all the heirs of salvation as already
hid with Christ in God.   But some of his words absolutely deny   Col. iii. 3.
the indefectibility of grace.   Besides leaving on record some
other declarations which have been already referred to, he speaks
of his rigour in the care of his own soul, *lest . . . I myself should be*   1 Cor. ix.
a castaway: no believer in an inalienable salvation would have   27.
adopted such language, certainly no inspired teacher of the truth
would have spoken so unguardedly even in his deepest humility.

(5.) The Epistle to the Hebrews contains passages which cannot   The
accord with the necessary permanence of grace. Though their mean-   Epistle to
ing may be exaggerated by those who make them deny the possibility   Hebrews.
of restoration after a certain measure and degree of fall, it is no
exaggeration that they teach the possibility of an extinction of
grace in such as had *tasted of the heavenly gift, and were made*   Heb. vi.
partakers of the Holy Ghost.   This, with the previous injunction,   4, 5.
lest any man fall after the same example of unbelief, the exhortation   Heb. iv.
Cast not away therefore your confidence, which hath great recompense of   11.
reward, with the assurance that *we are made partakers of Christ if*   Heb.x.35.
Heb. iii.
we hold the beginning of our confidence stedfast unto the end, and   14.
other such passages, are thought by some simply to lay down a
desperate and impossible hypothesis, or to refer only to an
external profession without corresponding reality, or to speak of
a lapse from a presumed state of grace, the hollowness of
which is supposed to be detected.   But on such principles of
interpretation Scripture can be made to prove nothing, or rather
can be made to prove anything.

(6.) The last organ of inspiration, whose writings perfect   St. John.
the New Testament, gives his clear testimony.   St. John's First
Epistle speaks of the possibility of being *ashamed before Him at*   1 John ii.
His coming, and that to *little children,* his affectionate term for   28.
true Christians.   What he means by being ashamed a later text
shows, *that we may have boldness in the Day of Judgment :* there will   1 John iv.
be no shame at the Judgment Day but in those who experience the   17.
dread calamity threatened by our Lord Himself, again and again :
of him also shall the Son of Man be ashamed.   St. John's Gospel con-   Mark viii.
tains no teaching of his own, at least on this subject.   In the Apoca-   38.
lypse also not John but his Lord speaks : and, although the threats

against apostate Churches must not be pressed, the final words of
the Redeemer are profoundly solemn : *God shall take away his part* Rev. xxii.
out of the book of life: not refuse to write it, but take it away. 19.
Thus the Scriptures close with a testimony that is most decisive
against the doctrine of an inevitable and unconditional predestination to Final Perseverance.

III. Although they thus speak, the opponents of this doctrine Harmony.
feel that there is a peculiarity in the present controversy which
must always distinguish it from every other.

1. The instinct of the true Christian loves the dogma that he
is obliged to oppose : and the same instinct makes the true Christian who holds it act as if he held it not.   Practically all who
bear this character are one in the doctrine that Final Perseverance
is a duty and a privilege.   Those who deny that union with
Christ, once effected, is inviolable—and deny it confidently
because our Saviour Himself says, *If a man abide not in Me, he is* John xv.
cast forth as a branch—nevertheless earnestly contend that such 6.
and so sacred a union is not easily and is not often finally dissolved.
They admit that many lapses, and many grievous lapses, are
consistent with that indwelling secret grace which is of all things
the most tenacious of its hold on the heart of man.   They know
full well that there may be the residue of grace in the soul which
seems almost sealed in reprobation ; that the eye of mercy, never
more quick to discern the secrets of the heart than when seeking
for the traces of Good in the hidden depths of man's nature, may
behold life where the eye of man's judgment would see only death ;
and that Infinite Compassion may fan into flame the all but
extinguished fire which none but Himself could discern.   They
feel the full meaning of the apologetic and almost retracting
words which follow the plain warning against total apostasy :
but, beloved, we are persuaded better things of you, and things that Heb. vi. 9.
accompany salvation, though we thus speak.

2. There is a sense in which the doctrine of Perseverance is
common to all Confessions and must by all Christians be held.   To
the foreknowledge of the Omniscient not only is the mystical
body sealed, but the salvation of every member of it is fixed.
Known unto God are all His works from the beginning of the world: Acts xv.
these words of St. James have a direct reference to the subject of 18, 14.

our discussion; the God of Israel is visiting the Gentiles *to take out of them a people for His name.* The number of the saved is before Him as if the whole process were over : *an hundred and fifty and three* were reckoned in the last symbolical fishing; the exact and finished number of the eternally sealed is now present to the Supreme Eye; and each individual of those who dispute over this doctrine is either saved or not saved in that future which is to God as the present. _{John xxi. 11.}

3. But here we are on the brink of the unsearchable mystery of the union or unity between the Divine foreknowledge and the Divine predestination. What is now known to God must be to us nevertheless an issue not determined. Contemplating this truth as in the light of God's knowledge we may say that every-one finally saved must persevere. But in that light we must not contemplate it. God sees the end as an accomplished fact which man is working out as a contingency. We are all in PROBATION : each one of his descendants as certainly as Adam was. Personal ASSURANCE is given, or provision is made that it may be given, to each as the daily bread of life. And PERSEVERANCE is nothing but the holding that *full assurance of hope unto the end.* _{Heb. vi. 11.}

Christian
Ethics.

CHRISTIAN ETHICS.

By the term Ethics of Redemption, or Christian Ethics, is signified the system of moral teaching which Christ the Redeemer has introduced in connection with His atoning work and the general economy of His grace. That system may be regarded, first, in its pre-eminence and peculiarity, as CHRISTIAN Ethics; and, secondly, in the formal arrangement of its principles, as Christian ETHICS.

Eph. ii. 10. This subject seems more appropriate here than in any independent position: it belongs to the Administration of Redemption, treating as it does of the new life for which the blessings of the New Covenant prepare the regenerate, and for which the regenerate are prepared. *We are His workmanship, created in Christ Jesus unto good works, which God hath before ordained that we should walk in them.* After dwelling so long on the estate of Christian privilege we pass naturally to the obligations connected with it. The ethics flow from the life. And in our course of doctrine it is obvious that the Morals of Christianity must be viewed only or mainly as they derive a new character from the Christian revelation. This principle must be remembered throughout the present Section. In one sense it contracts the field of ethical teaching; but in another it immeasurably expands that field.

THE ETHICS OF REDEMPTION.

Jesus as Redeemer is the Supreme Legislator; and His teaching is the corrective complement of all Moral Philosophy. In the Evangelical scheme doctrine and ethics are closely connected: its revelations of truth are the foundation of its new life; its morals and its doctrine are everywhere interwoven; and, finally, the ethics of the Christian religion are the crown and consummation of its entire system.

CHRIST THE LAWGIVER.

The Law-
giver.

Our Lord is Supreme Lawgiver, whether we regard His
Person, His offices, or His manifested life.   As thus
supreme He is also the sole Teacher and Arbiter and the
highest Example of morals.

Christianity may in this department be regarded as the legislation of Christ: the NEW LAW given to the human race.   The
Saviour both began and ended His ministry by asserting His
absolute and unappealable authority: *Whosoever heareth these sayings of Mine and doeth them!*   These words close the discourse
with which the New Teacher commenced His lawgiving for all ages
and for all mankind; and it is most plain that He assumes this
universal prerogative, to be the Master of all morals and duties.
Similarly He finished His course by an equally large assertion of
His place in the world's ethics.   His disciples were to *make
disciples* (or *Christians*) *of all nations . . . Teaching them to observe all
things whatsoever I have commanded you!*   Never did human lawgiver adopt this tone.   Never did those whom God had com-
missioned thus speak.   When Moses began his function, and had
said *I commanded you at that time all the things that ye should do,* he
added the charge against the people, *ye would not go up, but rebelled
against the commandments of the Lord your God.*   And his entire
legislation is thus wound up: the people did *as the Lord commanded Moses.*   This is in strong and most decisive contrast
with the beginning and end of the new legislation.

The
New Law.

Matt. vii.
24.

Matt.
xxviii.
20.

Deut. i. 18,
26.

Deut.
xxxiv. 9.

I. It is important to remember that the Legislator in the new
economy is the Lord Jesus in His Divine-human Mediatorial
Person, both God and man in one.

The
Incarnate
Lawgiver.

1. The Divinity of the Christian Lawgiver is the first postulate
and glorious distinction of Christianity as the perfect economy.
The Creator alone can give law to His creatures: *there is One Lawgiver,* and there can be no second: νομοδιδάσκαλοι many but only
one νομοθέτης in all the Scripture.   Moses is not so called: he
gave not that law from heaven, but *was faithful in all his house, as
a servant, for a testimony of those things which were to be spoken after.*

Divine.

Jas. iv. 12.

Heb. iii.
5, 6.

obedience, and, having died for us, He still continues to be our
Master and Lord.   And to this one end and supreme unity of
His whole work give all His Apostles witness

Historical Career   III In His mediatorial history or official career the Christian
Lawgiver blended in a most mysterious and affecting manner the
Divine dignity of His Person and the Messianic humiliation.   He
learned the obedience that He taught; He exercised supreme
ethical authority even while learning it, and He presented Himself, uniting the two, as the perfect Example of His own precepts
Here, as everywhere, we find the unsearchable unity of His two
natures in one personal agency investing the whole subject

The Obedience   1. Our Lord learned obedience.   In the mystery of His Person
he united the Supreme Lawgiver above responsibility and the
human subject responsible for obedience   During His humbled

Luke ii 49   estate He began, continued, and ended with the latter   from *I*
John iv 34.   *must!* in the Temple of His early consecration, and *My meat is
to do the will of Him that sent Me!* of His mid career, down to *I*
John xvii 4   *have finished the work!* under the cross.

Heb. v 8   (1) Here there are some qualifications   The first is that the
Saviour *learned the obedience*—His proper Messianic obedience not
so much in doing as in suffering—to a law of moral obligation
His own and unshared   And, however hard it may be to our
reason, neither of that truth nor of its consequences must we
be afraid   Before He gave us a new commandment He had a
new one in a much higher sense given to Himself   Again His
obedience was necessary   The unity of His Personality shielded
Him from the possibility of sinning even as His miraculous conception introduced Him sinless into the world.   Christ is not
divided, cannot be divided, against Himself.   Sin wrapped Him
round as a garment, but never entered His soul save in its
vicarious bitterness   On the cross His seamless robe was, as it
were, in the hands of His enemies, but there lay the perfection of
the obedience to which the Incarnate was disciplined   He was
taught as a Son the mystery of unfathomable suffering for sin in
us, and of equally unfathomable suffering through temptation to
1 Cor ii 11.   impossible sin   He was not in probation   He learned *the things
of a man*, τὰ τοῦ ἀνθρώπου   *the things of God*, τὰ τοῦ Θεοῦ, He
never learned   Nor did He acquire dominion over the universal

kingdom of ethics by having been a Sojourner for a night among them. He brought down a Divine power which gave them in Him a new perfection. His supreme government in the ethical domain was not founded on His submission to human duty.

(2.) Yet the Incarnate, though a Son, learned obedience: He proved and exhibited the discharge of DUTY in all departments of life, and in this sense underwent the experience of human obligations. As a Son, as an Israelite, as a subject of Rome, as a Rabbi surrounded by disciples, as a public Instructor or Minister of the circumcision, as a member of the human commonwealth, He manifested submission to every authority. He practised obedience as an impeccable human being would practise it, or as God Himself might obey His own ordinances. This obedience was, however, VIRTUE in the meaning which it has received in Christian Ethics. It is indeed hard for us to conceive the virtue of passive endurance unallied with the active suppression of a reluctant will. It is hard to understand what virtue there can be in a submission which springs from the necessity of a will eternally one with the Divine will. But, hard as it is, it is not impossible. And only on this principle can we accept the obedience of the Incarnate Son. The sublimest holiness is the recoil from impossible wrong. Divine hatred of sin, sorrow for sinners, and endurance of the penalty of transgression, became incarnate in Jesus. The sympathy which the Creator had felt with His erring creature learned its mystery over again in the Redeemer. The New Teacher showed, beforehand, the secret of His own legislation: *love is the fulfilling of the law.* In His devotion to God and charity for man—in that love which in a sense unparalleled was in Him τετελειωμένη—He kept all the commandments: both those which were given to Him alone and strained His human endurance to the utmost, and those which He obeyed as it were unconsciously and of necessity, finding in obedience the meat and drink of life. As He took not our individual sins upon His soul for expiation, but rather our sin in its fulness and essence; so He kept and honoured not so much laws as the law. Some individual laws had nothing in Him, and He never did nor ever could learn them; but He nevertheless honoured all law generally in the principle of the perfect obedience of LOVE TO GOD AND MAN.

Christ's
Learning
of Obe-
dience.

Rom. xiii.
10.

Authority and Submission.

(3.) Our Lord exercised Divine authority at the same time that He underwent the Mediatorial discipline which His redeeming work required. The prerogative of His Godhead could not be suspended, though it might be veiled. It was by His own Divine will that He became subordinate. And, throughout His submission, there was occasionally given the most abundant proof, both of act and word, that the Supreme Lawgiver was present in Him, and that Jesus Himself Who spoke was no other than He. During His humiliation there was a veil untaken away from the face of the Greater than Moses. He does not say as yet : *Behold, I make all things new!* although He brings new commandments and new institutions. He appeals to the ancient legislation and *them of old time*, to the authority of Scripture *which cannot be broken*, and to God as the Judge of all and the ultimate appeal. But His constant reserve and general assumption of a secondary place was only a veil. The valley of His humiliation is crowned by three Mountains where the Lawgiver receives honour and glory : partly as the fruit of His submission, but still more as the revelation of what He had with God before the world was. On the first, that of the Beatitudes, He asserts His supreme, that is His Divine, authority without one single allusion to any Greater than Himself. On the second, that of the Transfiguration, His claims are confirmed by the voice of God. And, on the third, the Mountain in Galilee, after His atoning death, His words unite the subordinate and the supreme authority : the subordinate, *all power is given unto Me;* the supreme, *Lo, I am with you alway!* If in the valley we hear the voice of a man, on these mountains we hear the voice of God. But the voices are the same. After the Ascension there is no longer any concealment. The Pentecost was the festival and glorification of the New Law. Our Lord now *speaketh from heaven;* and from heaven, by common consent, none can speak but God. It was in fact the same Voice that gave the legislation of Sinai that then *shook the earth.* After being for a season lowered to human accents, it now speaks through the Spirit. Thus throughout the whole Bible there is but One Voice of moral authority. In all the New Testament, the will of God and the will of Christ are one ; and we may lawfully, when we hear our Master say, *He that hath seen Me hath seen the Father,*

Rev. xxi. 5.

Matt. v. 21.
John x. 35.

Matt. xxviii. 18, 20.

Heb. xii. 25.

John xiv. 9.

carry on His words to this further meaning: *He that hath heard Me hath heard the Father.*

2. The Lord gave a Divine-human and perfect example: the only Legislator who ever did or ever could make His own life His code of laws. He began His ministry by a perfect summary of all human duty, *But I say unto you;* He ended by declaring, *I have given you an example.* But here again the mystery of the twofold nature of the One Person of the Lawgiver suggests qualifications which cannot be too deeply pondered, or too habitually borne in mind. It is too often forgotten.

Example.

Matt. v. passim. John xiii. 15.

(1.) His example was necessarily PERFECT. This has been often questioned: the character of Jesus, as the Ideal of His own laws, has been impeached. By some its peerless perfection has been denied, by some it has been disparaged in comparison with that of other teachers, and even with that of His own disciples. But many of the reproaches cast upon it by the eyes that seeing see not are the reproaches equally of the ancient Jehovah. The God of the Old Testament wears the same moral attributes as Jesus in the New. The tones of His wrath are precisely in the same strain as we hear in the old economy; and they are mingled with the same gentleness and mercy. His anger is Divine anger; and His sternness is the same—neither more nor less rigorous—as that of the Lawgiver Who appointed Moses in all his house. But it is an offence to the censors of Jesus that He failed in the opposite sentiment: that He shrank from the endurance which He demanded of His followers, and failed, where He required them to succeed, in sovereign contempt of suffering and death. But His meekness and recoil from woe were the tribute of perfect purity to suffering unknown, and the expression of His HORROR MORTIS, or affright at death, was really His Divine-human affright at sin or HORROR PECCATI. It was because He was more than man that in meeting the infinite consequence of sin He seemed less than perfect man. None, however, who deny the mystery of the Atonement can feel the force of this. Yet even they may be challenged to prove that there was in the suffering Jesus less than the perfection of human patience and magnanimity. Even to them the *For this cause came I unto this hour* ought to explain and condone the *Let this cup pass*

Perfect.

John xii. 27. Matt. xxvi. 39.

from Me! Reverence forbids our carrying this apology further. Suffice that no clear eye and no pure heart can be in the presence of the Redeemer without yielding to the conviction that He taught no virtue which He did not exemplify; so far, that is, as a Sinless Being, who had never known nor could ever know sin, might be its exemplar.

Limitation.

(2.) Yet, as these last words suggest, His was not in all respects a perfect EXAMPLE. His Divine-human excellence is in some sense too high, we cannot attain unto it. Therefore neither does the Lord, nor do His Apostles after Him, exhibit His life as at all points the directory of ours. In some details of duty He could not set

Jas. v. 17.

Heb. v. 9.

us a pattern: for them we must go to men *subject to like passions as we are.* He became *the Author of eternal salvation,* not to those who copy Him in the process—He never passed through the process—but to *all them that obey Him.* He gives the ideal and the sum of the blessed result: the way to it we know, and He is Himself the way, but we do not see the print of His footsteps on the path from the far country back again to holiness. Whenever His example is spoken of, it is in affecting connection with humility, patience, self-sacrifice for others, and utter abandonment of the world. But He did not reach those heavenly affections as we must reach them. They were His Divine condescension brought down from above, and translated into human forms: in us they are the hardwon triumphs of His Spirit overcoming their opposites. His virtue brought Him from heaven to earth; ours must carry us from earth to heaven. We must imitate His great submission; but none of us can ever utter His vicarious

Matt.

xxvii.46.

cry, *My God, My God,* WHY HAST THOU FORSAKEN ME? For He, unlike us, had never FORSAKEN GOD.

3. Hence, to sum up, the principle of our DUTY is His obedience in love; the strength of our VIRTUE is His Spirit; and the SUMMUM BONUM of our blessedness is His Peace. In Him we see the whole Law reflected in its highest purity; by His character we interpret it, and all our obedience is the silent imitation of Himself. His excellence is Divine and human: to be adored and imitated. As God He commands, and as Man shows us how to obey. The Lawgiver gives us both the Pattern and the strength to copy.

THE GOSPEL AND ETHICS.

Christian Doctrine and Ethics. 1 Tim. vi. 3.

Christianity is a DOCTRINE ACCORDING TO GODLINESS. Christian morals are as such founded on specific Christian truth; they are taught in alliance with it; and are exhibited as the end of all its teaching.

This might seem to be the place for considering the relation of Christian Ethics to Moral Philosophy. But we must first establish the exclusive principles of these new ethics as inseparably connected with the revelation of Jesus. This is only a meet tribute to the pre-eminence of the Gospel, which has learnt nothing from the philosophy of this world that it does not hold independently of all earthly philosophy.

I. Reserving for the next Section any remarks upon the general fundamental principles of morals, we may say that the prominent doctrines first taught or fully brought to light in the Christian Revelation are the foundation of Christian Ethics. There are three great underlying truths which may be said to be at the basis of all other foundations: the Fall, or from what; the Redemption, through what; the Future, unto what; the moral discipline of Christ aims to raise mankind. These doctrines themselves are treated elsewhere. It is needful here only to indicate their essential relation to ethics. The Basis of Doctrine.

1. The Fall with its concomitant doctrine of Original Sin vitally and throughout affects Christian Morals as a system. Christianity alone reveals what was the original estate of mankind; how a perfect moral condition was lost through the misuse of freedom; what is the place freewill still holds in the formation of character; how the ethical good remaining in the elements of humanity is to be accounted for; and for what a high destiny man was created and is still reserved. It shows how entirely his nature is depraved as to the attainment of good: teaching that there is in every mortal a bias to evil irresistible save through grace; and that it is his destiny, merely as man, freely to work out that evil which has become the necessity of his freewill. It lays the foundation of its ethics amidst the ruins of our fallen The Fall.

dignity : raising a superstructure which is at once a new creation and a reconstruction, building its new temple out of the fragments of the old. It deals with the world as a deeply lapsed but not utterly ruined world ; as profoundly corrupted but not entirely dissolved. And it deals with every man as having in himself, notwithstanding his heritage from Adam, the elements of a moral nature that may be retrieved. But not retrieved through any effort of its own : the Christian legislation begins by requiring utter self-renunciation, self-distrust, or self-despair. It never allows the Fall to be forgotten, amidst all the triumphs of grace.

Redemption.

2. Redemption—objective, wrought FOR US by Christ ; subjective, wrought IN US by the Holy Ghost—does not so much follow as accompany the Fall in its relation to the ethics of Christianity.

(1.) The preliminary grace which we regard as the firstfruits of the Redeemer's intervention for the race explains the secret desire of man to be restored ; and thus lights up the whole sphere of ethics. It is that redemption before Redemption which interprets the universal condemnation of evil and approval of good recorded in the judicial court of human nature itself : so unerringly, indeed, that the word Conscience, strictly speaking the human consciousness of moral character, has been made generally to signify the human moral faculty. It is this to which the Christian Lawgiver, and those who follow His teaching, always appeal. It must never be forgotten throughout our study of the Evangelical legislation. It gives consistency to the whole sum of its moral teaching, and makes morals possible to man.

(2.) The forgiveness it seals on the conscience—which imparts to the pardoned the double consciousness, of sin on the one hand as a fact, and of guiltlessness as an imputation on the other—takes away the barrier to moral endeavour, and gives it its strongest incentive. There is unspeakable strength in the thought of having paid the penalty once for all in a Substitute who belongs to the race and to each member of it who claims Him. Vain is all teaching of morality without a preliminary forgiveness : vain the Benedictions on the Mount unless in the anticipation of an Atonement which should first have silenced the Woes in the City.

Matt. v. 3—10. Matt. xxiii. 13—33.

(3.) Redemption from the curse of the law is also deliverance from the power of evil through the supply to the secret springs of human action of the power of an indwelling God. It renders all things possible. As forgiveness, entire and constant, removes the greatest impediment to moral effort—making guilt as if it were not—so the Spirit of regeneration literally throws open to human aspiration and attainment the whole compass of ethical perfection. Nothing is impossible to one who is forgiven and renewed. Moreover, it is not too much to say that redemption as an internal experience imparts a specific character to all Christian ethics. The sense of pardon gives birth to a new order of ethical emotions and obligations, and the new life in Christ is the sphere of a new order of ethical duties and attainments and experiences of which we need not now speak more particularly.

3. Christianity has brought to light the future life, with its powers and terrors and hopes, and incorporated that also into the foundation of its ethics.

The Future.

(1.) This gives the morals of human life their probationary character; responsibility derives from it a new meaning; time becomes inestimably precious in relation to eternity; and every act, and word, and thought has a new importance through its bearing on a fixed and eternal condition. *It is appointed unto men once to die, but after this the judgment!* This was a new voice in the sphere of the world's ethical teaching: interpreting the instinct of universal conscience; lighting up the dimmer revelations of the Old Testament; and making the powers of the world to come, what they had never been so fully before, the moving forces of the world that now is, by bringing *life and immortality to light.*

Heb. ix. 27.

2 Tim. i. 10. Sanction.

(2.) It furnishes the final and deepest sanctions of moral law. Sanction is the guard thrown around a command or duty to enforce its performance: the sanction of the duty not done is the punishment of the person who fails. The only sanction of law is the displeasure of God: but that displeasure in its fullest expression is now by this doctrine, as ethical, postponed to the Great Day. The preliminary tokens of it in this world are but the beginnings of wrath: the judgment is indeed begun, and the word Eternal has entered into time; but Christianity makes the future world, with its judgment at the threshold, the issue of all its moral teaching. The penalty of eternal separation from God is the great ethical argument: Christian probation is a decision of the question whether the original doom shall be finally reversed or rendered eternal. Accordingly this gives its true character to the sin from which men are to be saved : without this its ethics are an unreality. It is ETERNAL SIN in its possibilities. There is nothing against which the sentiment or sentimentality of many thinkers so persistently rebels as this. Some so recoil as to reject the Christianity which is based upon it, while others find their refuge in recasting the doctrine of eternal retribution. To them Sin is merely a Flood of misery, and Christ only our Noah or Comforter Who will hereafter either make all men forget their sorrows in a universal restoration or put out of existence those whom He cannot restore.

Mark iii. 29.

(3.) The future is also the goal of creaturely perfection ; that Summum Bonum, or final blessedness of the soul to which the ethics of Christianity perpetually point the aspiration of its disciples : not only as the consummate fruition of the results of welldoing but as the vision of God Himself. In a lower sense the former may be said to be the final ethical argument: *My reward is with Me !* But the highest reward is the *joy of thy Lord.*

Rev. xxii. 12.
Matt.xxv. 21.

4. All this being true, we may justly speak of Redemptional Ethics. The Christian Religion knows no other. The need or problem, the method and process, the stimulant and end of all ethics are in that one truth, that we are a race delivered by the Hand of a Mediator. Redemption is the central idea : the Fall flanks it on one side, Eternity on the other. All these elements are summed up in St. Paul's last ethical compendium, which perhaps contains the largest and most comprehensive statement of the three fundamental principles of Evangelical morality, with the atoning work in the middle. The grace of redemption *hath appeared, saving to all men.* It imparts forgiveness as grace, and *teacheth,* or disciplineth to all that morality which is a realisation of the redeeming purpose. And the issue of all is the *blessed hope and glorious appearing of the Great God and our Saviour Jesus Christ Who gave Himself for us.*

Redemptional Ethics.

Tit. ii. 11—14.

II. The Christian doctrine and Christian ethics are interwoven. 1. We have not here two departments in the theology of Scripture. From Genesis to Revelation, from Sinai to Pentecost, there is no difference between the methods of exhibiting what

Doctrine and Ethics One.

man must believe and what he must practise. As in natural religion, and its almost illegible characters, conscience is at once the teaching that God is and that we are responsible to Him; so in the supernatural revelation of the Bible doctrine and duty are bound up together in their relation to the Supreme.

2. Every doctrine however has its ethical side: all truth returns in duty to Him who gave it. This may be illustrated by reference to the individual subjects that make up the sum of dogmatic theology. God is a Person and man is a person: all their common relations must be ethical. The Divine perfections are not objects of contemplation simply: so viewed they would only exhaust the mind; in ethics they mightily strengthen it, and each special attribute infers its corresponding obligation. The Trinity presides over a rich domain of ethics that have to do with the economical relations of each sacred Person to the Triune One and to every believer. The Mediatorial Work of Christ is a congregation of revealed truths, each of which, whether referring to Himself or His work, has its moral bearing. *The Life was the Light of men.* The appropriation of personal salvation introduces a series of teachings which are as much ethical as dogmatic. There is a doctrine and a practice of repentance: the doctrine of Divine conviction, the practice of confession and amendment. The influence of grace is formulated as a dogma; the activity of man is ethical. Justification by faith is a doctrine: righteousness its ethics. Sanctification is a doctrine of the Spirit's purifying consecration unto holiness: the processes of renewal unto perfection are ethical. The subject of the Church has its infinite variety of moral bearings. So also the new revelations of Christian Eschatology. Death as doctrine has its ethics of preparation. So also the Eternal Realities, and the Restoration of Christ which precedes them. But all this will appear more fully in the sequel. It may be said that no doctrine is ever taught without reference to a corresponding human duty; nor is any duty taught for which a doctrinal reason is not given. There is the utmost parsimony in the teaching: the utmost reasonableness in the requirements. We can always give a reason of our hope in the doctrine; and of our duty in the ethics.

III. Ethics are the crown and consummation of all teaching.

The Ethical Side of Each Dogma.

John i. 4.

but they are not found in is early documents, save in the ἤθη
χρηστὰ of the quotation from Menander. The terms of the New
Testament which are strictly answerable to these are only two:
GODLINESS, as a habit of soul like that of God; HOLINESS, as a
habit of soul sanctified from sin. Into these two words, at least,
all others rise, as will be hereafter seen.

But every definition of science must submit to Christian
censure and correction. Aristotle termed it ἡ περὶ τὰ ἀνθρώπινα
φιλοσοφία, THE PHILOSOPHY OF HUMAN INTERESTS, which the
Testament signifies by THE WHOLE OF MAN, and the New
ment translates into τὰ τοῦ Θεοῦ, MY FATHER'S BUSINESS, or
of GOD. In all cases that clear distinction has been
between natural and moral science, or Physics and Ethics.
has thus expressed: "Physics, the science of the
Ethics, the science of the laws of freedom." This
utterly opposed to modern Positive Philosophy—
subjects under the dominion of the same necessity
matter, though in a more refined form—is pro-
But it says what is essential to the new and
the law of freedom are under the govern-
ntham is the representative of a
He terms it "the art of directing the
as to produce the greatest
view, and, in the light of
The more Christian Paley is
which teaches men their duty
dequate in all respects; though
of its superficiality. But this
will

1 Cor. viii. 1.

su
but
in
ceas
more
accor
ledge
3. E
system
been its
of what
of the O.
the groun
dogma wh
CHRISTIAN
make no re
rather to th
worship and
and the life of

Col. i. 9.

4. The per
tends to save tl
It limits the ra
sheds a peculiar
gotten that, whil
science, the under
to their integrity.
membered, into a
phantasies, varying

is the same: for instance, conscience, obligation, or the ought and the must, law, right, good and evil, sin, judgment, reward, punishment are found with the same application in the Scriptures as outside of them. Some, however, of these words are elevated, as we shall see, into a higher meaning by the interpretation of the Spirit of liberty and love; while there are many terms of great ethical significance which are the pure mintage of Christian Ethics: such as love, purity, sanctification, peace, holiness, blessedness, godliness. A large and varied and among us most familiar branch of ethical nomenclature owes its origin to the Founder of Christianity and the Apostles whom He instructed.

2. The theories which have been and are current concerning the primary grounds and obligations of morality are not even alluded to in the Holy Scriptures. They never discuss what makes good to be good and evil to be evil, right to be right and wrong to be wrong: all such discussions are superseded and swallowed up in the testimony that *none is good save One, that is God,* and that the nature of God as the ground of obligation is His will: *I come to do Thy will, O God.* The moralists of the Bible know no eternal ground of obligation outside of or behind or independent of the Supreme. Meanwhile the interminable discussion continues. Some place it in the nature of God or in His will, some in the vague abstraction called the fitness of things; some reduce it to the subjective moral sense in man, some to the law of universal benevolence and the value of happiness; while some appeal to the idea of what is right, thus begging the question; and, others, lastly, find it in the intrinsic goodness of virtue. Christian writers join in the discussion and give their support by terms the deepest among them will admit that to man the obligation is the Divine will, while to the is the Divine nature of which As to the materialist theories God only inventions of God Himself, and all only the result of reasons not of

distinguished

1. It may be said generally that the manifold lines of revelation meet in the restoration of the Divine image in man. This is their glorious vanishing point. The various teaching of which the Fall is the centre explains the violation or loss of that image; all that is taught concerning redemption is one diversified account of the means of its renewal; and the revelations of eternity converge to its restored and perfect reflection. All the doctrine of the Bible is summed up in one word: God has become man that man might become one with God again.

2. We find a constant disparagement of mere knowledge as such: ἡ δὲ γνῶσις φυσιοῖ, ἡ δὲ ἀγάπη οἰκοδομεῖ: *Gnosis puffeth up, but charity buildeth up.* There is, however, a knowledge spoken of in Scripture which is both doctrinal and ethical. The word ceases to be only Greek, it takes a Hebrew meaning, and becomes more than mere intellectual science. It is not γνῶσις but ἐπίγνωσις: according to that great prayer, *that ye might be filled with the knowledge of His will in all wisdom and spiritual understanding.*

1 Cor. viii. 1.

Col. i. 9.

3. Hence theology is after all and in its highest form a perfect system of Ethics. In every age, and in every aspect of it, this has been its aim. Outside of revelation PHILOSOPHY was the unity of what doctrine and duty it had to teach: it was the RELIGION of the Old World, which, however ardently it aspired to unfold the grounds of morality, had but a scanty basis of theological dogma whereon to erect its teachings. When we speak of the CHRISTIAN RELIGION as well as of the CHRISTIAN FAITH, we make no real distinction; for, though the latter term belongs rather to the system of what is believed, and the former to the worship and practice resulting, both alike combine the confession and the life of the professors of Christianity.

4. The perpetual remembrance of the supremacy of Ethics tends to save theological study from its hardness and barrenness. It limits the range of that part of it which is speculative, and sheds a peculiar grace on all the residue. But it must not be forgotten that, while Ethics are the consummation of theological science, the underlying doctrines on which they rest are essential to their integrity. They degenerate, unless these are always remembered, into a subjective and sentimental reflection of human phantasies, varying with the endless variations of opinion as to

man's natural history. The moral system which is not based on a sure substratum of truth is a mere reconstruction of the broken fragments of our fallen nature, without an architect or a plan.

CHRISTIAN ETHICS AND MORAL PHILOSOPHY.

What Natural Theology is to the theology of supernatural revelation, Moral Philosophy is to Christian Ethics. They agree as to some of the main fundamentals of ethical science, but afterwards widely diverge: the Christian system of morals supplying what is essentially lacking in all moral teaching that is independent of its guidance.

It has been sufficiently shown that the morals of Christianity should be introduced into every system of dogmatic theology; and that as a distinct department, though much that belongs to redemptional ethics is anticipated in the State of Salvation. Of course there is a large region of ethical science that is only indirectly concerned with theology, the study of which leads us into the wide region of Moral Philosophy proper. This science has occupied the best thought of mankind; and the history of its development, both as apart from Christianity and as connected with it, is deeply instructive. Into that history we need not now enter. The first principles of our religion forbid us to regard Moral Philosophy as the great science of which ours is only a branch. But, if revealed theology is supreme, then Moral Philosophy loses much of its independent meaning; for, what it only seeks and speculates about, the infallible record has given us.

I. Christian Moral Philosophy—for we may adopt this compromise—accepts and enlarges, or rather corrects, the name and general definition of ethical science.

1. The terms Ethics and Morals are scarcely to be distinguished. Ethics, from ἦθος or ἔθος, has relation to the home, seat, posture, habit, or internal character of the soul; Morals, from mos, or custom, rather to the outward manifestation of that internal character. Both words have been too much limited to the region of the outer life. In themselves they are vague, and show their earthly origin. The Christian revelation does not reject them;

Defini-tions.

M 2

1 Cor. xv.
33.
but they are not found in its early documents, save in the ἤθη χρηστὰ of the quotation from Menander. The terms of the New Testament which are strictly answerable to these are only two : GODLINESS, as a habit of soul like that of God ; HOLINESS, as a habit of soul sanctified from sin. Into these two words, at least, all others rise, as will be hereafter seen.

2. But every definition of the science must submit to Christian censure and correction. Aristotle termed it ἡ περὶ τὰ ἀνθρώπινα φιλοσοφία, THE PHILOSOPHY OF HUMAN INTERESTS, which the Old Testament signifies by THE WHOLE OF MAN, and the New Testament elevates into τὰ τοῦ Θεοῦ, MY FATHER'S BUSINESS, or THE WILL OF GOD. In all ages that clear distinction has been made between natural and moral science, or Physics and Ethics, which Kant has thus expressed : "Physics, the science of the laws of nature ; Ethics, the science of the laws of freedom." This definition, so utterly opposed to modern Positive Philosophy— which lays man's acts under the dominion of the same necessity that reigns over matter, though in a more refined form—is profoundly Christian. But it omits what is essential to the new and supreme system, that the laws of freedom are under the government of the Holy Spirit. Bentham is the representative of a very different principle. He terms it "the art of directing the actions of men in such a manner as to produce the greatest happiness :" this is the Utilitarian view, and, in the light of our religion, imperfect and wrong. The more Christian Paley is not much better : "The science which teaches men their duty and the reasons of it." This is inadequate in all respects ; though it is difficult to detect the secret of its superficiality. But this will be seen when it is compared with Neander's definition : "Moral Philosophy is concerned with the development of the laws for human conduct ; Christian Ethics derives these laws from the essence of Christianity."

Eth. xii.
13.
Luke ii.
49.
Mark iii.
35.

Funda-
mental
Principles
the same.
Vocabu-
lary.'
II. The fundamental principles of Moral Philosophy as independent of revelation are accepted and confirmed by Christianity ; which, however, modifies and perfects some of those principles.

1. The words expressing moral ideas are most of them retained in their usual meaning : that which has been stamped on them by the consent of mankind. The general vocabulary

is the same: for instance, conscience, obligation, or the ought and the must, law, right, good and evil, sin, judgment, reward, punishment are found with the same application in the Scriptures as outside of them. Some, however, of these words are elevated, as we shall see, into a higher meaning by the interpretation of the Spirit of liberty and love; while there are many terms of great ethical significance which are the pure mintage of Christian Ethics: such as love, purity, sanctification, peace, holiness, blessedness, godliness. A large and sacred and among us most familiar branch of ethical nomenclature owes its origin to the Founder of Christianity and the Apostles whom He instructed.

2. The theories which have been and are current concerning the primary grounds and obligations of morality are not even alluded to in the Holy Scriptures. They never discuss what makes good to be good and evil to be evil, right to be right and wrong to be wrong: all such discussions are superseded and swallowed up in the testimony that *none is good save One, that is God,* and that the nature of God as the ground of obligation is His will: *I come to do Thy will, O God.* The moralists of the Bible know no eternal ground of obligation outside of or behind or independent of the Supreme. Meanwhile the interminable discussion continues. Some place it in the nature of God or in His will, some in the vague abstraction called the fitness of things; some reduce it to the subjective moral sense in man, some to the law of universal benevolence and the value of happiness; while some appeal to the idea of what is right, thus begging the question; and, others, lastly, find it in the intrinsic goodness of virtue. Christian thinkers join in the discussion, and give their support by terms to every theory; but the deepest among them will admit that to man as a creature the ground of obligation is the Divine will, while to man as a moral agent the ground is the Divine nature of which his own is an image or reflection. As to the materialist theories that make conscience and right and good only inventions of men's hopes and fears and calculations, like God Himself, and all ethics, in their obligation and their loveliness, only the result of unnumbered ages of social evolution, Christianity reasons not of them but beholds them and goes on its way.

3. Moral Philosophy has, in later times especially, distinguished

Grounds of Obligation.

Luke: xviii. 19.

Heb. x. 9

Moral Philosophers.

between DUTY, VIRTUE, and the SUMMUM BONUM, as regulating the processes of ethics. These terms are found in Christian ethical systems; but so much are they changed by their regeneration in Christianity that they cease to be available for their old service. They are raised into the unity of *Holiness to the Lord :* a conception known only to supernatural religion. This sacred phrase, which carries us into the inmost sanctuary of the new temple, contains the three terms: the Virtue is in the HOLINESS, which is severe separation from evil; the Duty is in TO THE LORD; and the Summum Bonum is the union with Divinity which is implied. The Chief Good of man is his blessedness in the fellowship of God: the term happiness is no longer supreme. Christ hath shown man what is good. DUTY is transfigured by its connection with redemption: *ye are not your own.* It finds its standard in Jesus; its sphere in His kingdom; and its one object in the Redeeming Triune God. And obligation is translated into love which is VIRTUE; love is the *bond of perfectness,* in the following of the Lord and the reflection of His most holy image. Love is the secret and the unity of the three.

4. Christianity, in defining the moral system founded on the New Testament, not only is willing to accept the wide extension given to the science by Moral Philosophy, but even enlarges in its turn upon that. Aristotle has been followed by most systematisers who have made it include Social Economics, Jurisprudence, and Politics: in fact, the whole sum and complex of human relations. Modern thinkers and moralists omit from it the branches that concern merely the activity of man and the education of his sense of the beautiful, or ÆSTHETICS. But they directly include, as the New Testament indirectly does, all the rest: with the addition of our relation to the Christian Church and the Future State. It has been seen already that there is a sense in which Christianity makes all its teaching on every subject whatever, throughout the whole economy of truth, *doctrine which is* ACCORDING TO GODLINESS. Its relation to God, determines the value of all knowledge.

III. Christian Ethics, while it accepts and supplements the speculative teaching of Moral Philosophy on some most important subjects, condemns many of its speculations on others.

1. It assumes willingly this favourite phrase, MORAL PHILOSOPHY,

Marginal notes:

Duty, Virtue, Summum Bonum.

Zech. xiv. 20.

1 Cor. vi. 19, 20.

Col. iii. 13.

Comprehensiveness.

1 Tim. vi. 3.

Agreement.

Philosophy.

but on the condition that its leading term be elevated into a higher meaning. Its φιλοσοφία or Philosophy does not merely seek after and love wisdom or truth, but has found it. Nor does it reject the term DEONTOLOGY rightly understood : the science of what SHOULD BE it teaches, but as the science also of what may be and in Christ is attainable and attained, practicable and practised. Truth in Jesus is positive and absolute ; and philosophy, in its elder limited meaning, is now the same anachronism that mere natural theology is. The Philosophia moralis of Cicero and Seneca was speculative inquiry : the philosophy of the ancient world, East and West, was deeply religious, but only as feeling after the Supreme. The school of seekers into the midst of which St. Paul entered was gathered round an altar to the Unknown God. But the Gospel has declared the true God of holiness to our dogmatic theology and the true holiness of God to our ethical : both in one and both in perfection.

2. Christianity, like all sound Moral Philosophy, excludes speculation as to the existence of that substratum of all ethics, the human soul. There is a philosophical system, falsely and most unworthily so called, which denies the personality and separate existence of the ethical subject. Its watchword is that all substance is one. Two schools diverge from this position : one which makes the universe only and all the universe God, Pantheism ; and another which makes all the universe only matter. In the former morals are lost, as being only the capricious and transitory developments of God's own acts, which do not mar His character only because they are passing phenomena on the way to eternal good. In the latter—which gives the present age the very dregs of philosophy—man is supposed to have slowly invented as well the ground as the form and the sanction of what he calls his morals. It may seem unjust to the Pantheism of Spinoza to link it with Materialism. But, however unjust to the founder of modern Pantheism it may be, it is no injustice to the system itself, which logically can have no morals because it leaves no room for responsibility. In fact, neither Pantheism nor Materialism—both victims of the restless pursuit of an unattainable Unity—can have any place for a Moral Philosophy ; nor can Moral Philosophy find any place for them.

Speculative Thought.

Human
Nature.

3. Christianity, in its philosophy of morals, accepts the constitution of human nature as the regulator of ethical inquiry; but it has its own clear teaching as it regards the genesis and development and tendency of that nature. It does not leave it matter of speculation whether man is rising by the law of secular evolution to perfection or is recovering a lost estate. Adopting or rather enforcing the latter theory, it guards its ethical science against the danger of reasoning too much from the elements of what is called human nature, viewed as apart from the Fall.

The
Media-
torial
Economy.

4. Its doctrine of Mediation does not alter the foundations of virtue, but introduces a God whose justice and mercy combine in a mystery of which Moral Philosophy knows nothing. Pardon assured and sealed gives birth, as we have seen, to a new department of obligations and graces. So also does regeneration and an indwelling Spirit. A new order of words is introduced—grace, graces, privileges, sanctification, union with Christ,—all unknown to human morals. In fact, it is here that Moral Philosophy and Christian Ethics separate at least, if they do not become estranged towards each other. Moral Philosophy as such takes human nature as it is, and studies it apart from the secret history of the Fall: it makes the best use of what it finds, without over-curiously investigating how its subject became what he is. It also knows nothing of the mystery of expiation: not denying it, neither does it appeal to it. Right must be vindicated, and wrong must be punished; and, according to its teaching, as such, and supposing it not to borrow from the Gospel, the Divine justice and human frailty must come to terms through some compromise that it cannot explain.

The
Future.

5. The Future in Moral Philosophy as such is either omitted, or limited to human perfectibility in the present world, or introduced as a factor of probability only into Ethics. The Christian Future sheds its light on every region, glorifies every word, and gives unity to the whole by revealing an end and consummation of which mere human systems know nothing. Nothing certainly, that is: almost every system of morals has indeed introduced the future as an element of probability. Christianity uses this factor as absolute truth; and this has always assured to it its power and pre-eminence over every other teaching whatever.

IV. Finally, it may be observed that a sound system of Christian Ethics lays the best and only sure foundation of a Moral Philosophy worthy of the name. Some of the noblest treatises on the subject have been written by professors of the Christian Faith, who have expounded the whole range of ethical questions on the principles of the New Testament.

The Science of Christian Ethics.

1. There is a sense indeed in which Christianity may be boldly said to have originated moral science as such : it has created a doctrinal system as its basis, and given ethics a distinct and definite character which it had not before. In every system which has appeared apart from the New Law there has been a marked absence of some of the first conditions of science properly so called. All was tentative, empirical, and uncertain. Ancient philosophy never pretended to include in its discussion of Ethics more than a very limited range of obligations. Why there was any obligation at all it could never clearly define. It was indeed exceedingly elaborate in its treatment of certain cardinal vices and virtues ; but there its philosophy ended. The Christian teaching may lay claim to be in the deepest sense a Moral Philosophy : it gives a full account of the moral nature of man ; it establishes the grounds of ethical obligation ; it exhibits the sanctions of law ; it gives a most comprehensive legislation, adapted to every variety of human estate ; it provides for the appeasing of conscience, and the renewal of the soul ; it sets perfection before the hope of all ; and it shows to what that perfection finally leads. The fundamental revelation on which all this is based may indeed be rejected ; and then of course the whole superstructure may be thought to fall. But it still remains that there is no other to take its place ; and that it is the only philosophy of ethics that challenges the judgment of man and appeals to his conscience and speaks to his heart. It literally has no rival, nor has ever had one.

The Only True Science.

2. What may be called Metaphysical Ethics Christianity sanctions but limits in its range. Such questions as the being of God, His relation to the personal creature, or rather the relation of the personal creature to Him, the measure and reality of our knowledge of the Supreme, the bearings of His sovereignty on freedom of will, are not left for discussion ; nor are those which have to do with the origin of evil and the immortality of the soul.

Metaphysics.

Speculative Theology is permitted to occupy its own domain; but it is not encouraged, certainly not encouraged to intrude into the region of man's ethical duties. Some very extensive systems of Christian Ethics have been deeply vitiated by the error of forcing questions of mere speculation into the region of faith.

Psychology.

3. The relation of Psychology to Ethics may be and should be most carefully studied. A thorough examination of the constituents of the human soul, and of the mutual relations and interactions of the intellect and the sensibilities and the will, throws much light upon the doctrines of the Fall and conversion and regeneration and sanctification. Especially important is it in relation to the connection between religious experience and religious obligations. It will be seen that in all the dealings of God with man the constitution of his nature is not interfered with. His ruin was ethical and psychological disorder; his recovery is the restoration of order through the ascendency of the new Spirit of life, a new relation to God which regulates without violating the laws of human nature. Christianity is a life from above, a supernatural life; but it is a life that is to be conducted according to the laws which regulate human habits and the formation of character. Reference will be made to this subject again. Meanwhile there is one principle fundamental to the sciences of Psychology and Ethics which Moral Philosophy has too much forgotten. There is one personality of the moral agent behind and beneath all the constituents of his composite nature. Neither his intellect nor his feeling nor his will is the man himself, who is the unity of these elements. His intellectual nature gives him his CONSCIENCE, which is the man morally conscious of himself: his constant knowledge of himself in relation to the standard of right and wrong lodged in his reason. His sensibilities give him another moral predominant quality, LOVE, which has the same ascendency in ethics that conscience has. His conative faculties, or his will, furnish a third moral characteristic of the whole man: the determinate bias of his INTENTION or ultimate choice. In the moral domain the man is as his intention is, as his love is, as his conscience is. These three agree in one: referring respectively to the future, the present and the past. And it is important to remember that the man himself, the person with whom the moral

law deals, is the synthesis of all these, and, more than that, is the possessor of these and responsible for them. Nor is it right to say that he has conscience as an intelligent being, love as an emotional, and will as a free agent. His whole being enters more or less into each and all. His conscience is a feeling as well as a knowledge. His love occupies equally the three elements of his nature. And His will enters into them all.

THE CHRISTIAN LAW.

There are two characteristics of the Christian moral legislation, mediating, as it were, between the principles of ethics and their application, which are so marked that they require to be studied apart. The first is the connection between liberty and law: and the second that between the law and love.

LIBERTY AND LAW.

Liberty and Law.

The Christian religion as the PERFECT LAW OF LIBERTY finds its perfection in the bestowment through the Holy Ghost of an internal freedom from the restraint of law which is quite consistent with subjection to external law as a directory of the life.

I. There is nothing more characteristic of the Christian economy of Ethics than that it sets up an internal rule : *the law of the Spirit of life in Christ Jesus* which makes us *free from the law of sin and death.* This interior rule responds to the exterior, and in a certain sense supersedes it. The external law ceases as a law of death : it has vanished with the conscience of sin removed in pardon. And as against and over the soul with its dread impossibility of fulfilment it is also gone. The Spirit of life within gives strength for all obedience ; and the law to be obeyed is set up within us, according to the promise which is the glory of the New Covenant : *I will put My laws into their mind and write them in their hearts.* This is more than the restoration of the almost effaced traces of the law engraven on the heart of universal

Internal. Rom. viii. 2.

Heb. viii. 10.

man. In Christianity this internal law is supernatural ; it is nature still, but nature restored and more than restored : a supernatural nature. This is the interior polity of holy government of which St. James speaks when he calls the Gospel the *perfect law of* *liberty :* perfect law becomes liberty from external obligation. The nearer obedience is to the uniformity of the ordinances of nature— being conscious and willing obedience, though in its perfection not conscious of its willing—the nearer it approaches the Creator's end. Law is only the rule by which the Supreme works His will. In all the economy of the physical universe His law works from within outwardly, and there is no need of any outward statute to be registered for the guidance of His unintelligent creatures. The Divine Spirit in the heart of regenerate men seeks thus to work out a perfect obedience to the law of love.

Jas. i. 25.

1. In a loose and general way this may be called the rule of conscience, to which the Apostle refers when he says, *Herein do I* *exercise myself to have a conscience void of offence :* as if the law that guided him was the decision of his own moral sense. The Scrip- ture, however, acknowledges no rule of conscience, this being rather a witness than a governor. In modern ethical science the word is made to include both functions. First, and very generally, it is made to signify the moral faculty which discerns good from evil : as men are provided with a faculty to distinguish fair from foul, and truth from error, so they have a faculty which dis- tinguishes the moral quality of things or right from wrong. This is simply, however, the Reason whereon the Creator has written those moral principles which, never altogether effaced, are re- engraven by the Holy Ghost in regeneration as the eternal standard by which men must judge themselves. Secondly, it is the estimate whether instinctive or formed by reflection as to the conformity of our own state and act to that standard. This is CONSCIENCE proper, and the only conscience of which the Scrip- ture speaks. It mysteriously suggests the due retribution of good and evil ; but this is an attribute which sin has given it. These may be distinguished as conscience objective and conscience subjective. And, uniting them, we may speak of the internal law as that of SELF-GOVERNMENT restored. The rule of God's Spirit in the spirit of the regenerate is the administration of conscience

Con- science. Acts xxiv. 13.

Self- Govern- ment.

or the renewed self according to the normal idea of the Creator. Men thus trusted—under authority to that Holy Ghost yet having their own souls under them—are in the highest and purest sense *a law unto themselves.* Yet this only as *under the law to Christ,* Who is the common Lord of all.

Rom. ii. 4. 1 Cor. ix. 21.

II. For there is still an external law, containing the Christian *commandments contained in ordinances,* which is continued by reason of the weakness of the new nature.

External. Eph. ii. 15.

1. The external standard still maintains the dignity of law, and still asserts the necessity of its permanence as an institute. Nowhere does the New Testament—even when it sounds most loudly the note of liberty—proclaim that the law is abolished. *From the law of sin and death* we are delivered, not from the law that directs to holiness and life. Written in the *fleshy tables of the heart,* the commandments are deposited also in an ark on *tables of stone* for common appeal among probationary creatures. The political and social legislation of the old economy has passed away, but not its eternal morals. They are re-enacted under other forms, and re-written in the pages of the New Testament as the standard of requirement, the condition of the charter of privileges, and a testimony against those who offend.

Rom. viii. 22. 2 Cor. iii. 3.

2. The outward enactments are still the directory of individual duty. All relations have, in the order of the providence of the moral Governor, a sense of their obligation lodged with them in the human heart, and the law serves to educate that sense in its manifold details. The best Christians need a remembrancer: they obey the law within, but are not always independent of the teaching of the law without.

3. The external is the safeguard of the internal law: against its only or its chief enemy, ANTINOMIANISM, which regards the law as abolished in Christ, or treats it as if it were so. Theoretical or theological Antinomianism is the doctrine that makes a Christian's salvation eternally independent of any other obedience than that of the Gospel offer of grace, or rather than that of the vicarious Redeemer. There is a teaching which holds that the Substitute of man has not only paid the penalty of human offence but has fulfilled the law also for the sinner: thus making the salvation of the elect secure. The believer has, in this doc-

Antinomianism.

trine, no more to do with a legal rule save as a subordinate teacher of morality. He will never to all eternity stand before any bar to be judged by the law. Now this is the very truth of the Gospel so far as concerns the demand of the law for eternal and unbroken conformity with its precepts: no one will bear that inquisition either in the court of time or in the court of eternity. But there is only a step between precious truth and perilous error here. Christ has re-enacted His law as an Evangelical institute by which all shall be tested. The Antinomian proper is one who treats the requirement of perfect holiness as met by Christ, and refuses to measure his conduct by any law whatever. To him obedience is only matter of expediency, and propriety, and it may be reward; but not matter of life and death: his disobedience may be chastised by a Father, it cannot be eternally punished by a Judge. The law is no longer a condition of salvation: obedience not being a condition of acceptance as to the past or negative salvation, neither is it a condition of acceptance as to the future, or positive salvation. There is also a still more prevalent practical Antinomianism, which uses liberty as an *occasion to the flesh.* This may be, or may not be, connected with the theoretical renunciation of law. It is found in all communities: the disgrace of all creeds and confessions. The written commandments are a safeguard against both forms of the common enemy. The noblest and best corrective is, as will be seen, *but by love serve one another.* But, besides the gentle protest of charity there is the stern protest of law with its sanctions. He who knoweth our frame has protected us, if need be, against ourselves. As the Gospel disarms the law in one sense, it arms it again in another: they are a mutual defence. *He that despised Moses' law died without mercy under two or three witnesses. Of how much sorer punishment, suppose ye, shall he be thought worthy:* but we need not fill up the quotation; suffice that it is a denunciation of those who *sin wilfully after that we have received the knowledge of the truth.* The law protects the Gospel by protecting itself. If Christian people recite their Creed to keep in memory the things they surely believe, not less necessary is it that they should recite the Commandments also to keep in memory what they must do to enter into life.

Gal. v. 13.

Heb. x. 29.

LOVE AND LAW.

Love has been seen, in the doctrine of Sanctification, to be the principle and strength and perfection of consecration to God. In Ethics we have to consider it rather as the fulfilling energy and the fulfilled compendium of law, and the unity of these two.

LOVE THE COMPLEMENT OR FULFILMENT OF LAW.

Love is the complement or filling up of all that is meant by law : the summary of all possible duty to God and man.

1. Generally, this may be said to have been our Lord's authoritative compendium. He honoured the principle as it had never been honoured before. He made it the source of all the merciful dealings of God with man. He assumed its perfection for Himself : His love and His humility being the only graces that He called His own. He made it the badge of His discipleship : the one bond of community between His people and their Lord. This thrice-honoured grace the Redeemer also made the epitome of all duty in its two branches, towards God and towards man. He was not only rebuking the Pharisaic computation of the value of precepts, but spoke for all time, when He said that *on these two commandments*—that is on the supreme love of God, and the love of the neighbour as self—*hang all the law and the prophets.* He did not enact these laws, or this twofold law, as new ; nor did He assign them a new importance in themselves. He simply declared that these were the sum of all duty, and gave them a new significance in ethical systems. In the Old Testament they seemed to be AMONG the precepts ; now they are OVER them. After the Lord had thus set the example it is not to be wondered at that every writer in the New Testament has paid his tribute to love. St. James leads the way by his νόμον βασιλικὸν, the *royal law,* limited by him however to the love of our fellows. St. Paul's great expression is that *love is the fulfilling of the law :* in both instances of its use the meaning is limited, as in St. James, to the love of the neighbour. Again and again the New Lawgiver

Fulfilment as Complement.

Matt.xxii. 40.

Jas. ii. 8.

Rom. xiii. 10.

and His Apostles sum up all duty, not as two kinds and orders of
love, but as love generally.   St. Peter makes charity or love absolute the crown of the graces introduced into the life and sustained
2 Pet. i. 7. there by faith : *Add . . . to brotherly kindness charity :* a grace therefore that is directed both to God and to man ; and, if not precisely
the sum of duty, yet the crown and consummation of all.   St.
Paul is still more express: in his hymn to charity, the noblest
ethical strain of the New Testament, ἀγαπή is evidently the substance of all personal religion ; nor is there an internal grace or
an external duty that is not regarded as an expression of love.
1 Tim. i. The same may be said of his epitome afterwards given : *Now the*
5.   *end of the commandment is charity out of a pure heart, and of a good*
conscience, and of faith unfeigned.   As the end of the law is Christ,
so the end of the commandment is charity : a declaration of large
compass.   Inverting the order of the words, pure faith leads to a
cleansed conscience and purified heart, the abode of perfect love.
But it is St. John who carries the tribute to its highest point.
He makes the ethical nature of God to be love: *God is love ;*
and the perfection of this grace the perfection of all religion, which
1 John iv. is, like him who possesses it, *made perfect in love.*
16, 18.   2. Charity in its full meaning in Christian Ethics is therefore
the substance of all obligation to God and our neighbour : it
might suffice to say to God ; for there is no real and essential obligation but to the Supreme Lawgiver.   There is no possible act of
the soul that is not an act of love, as love is the return of the
soul to its rest.   It expresses all homage and reverence to the
Divine Being, with every affection of heart that makes Him its
object ; all delight in His holy law ; all devotion to His service.
Love to man is purely ethical as it is the reflection of the Divine
love.   The neighbour is united with the self as a creature ; and
as self, literally understood, is lost in love, love views all creatures
and self included as one before God.   Hence all the variety of
our duty to our fellows is the expression of charity, aiming
supremely at the Supreme, but reflected on all men for His sake.
But we are permitted to speak of obligation to our fellows : every
Rom; xiii. obligation is summed up in charity which, negatively, *worketh no*
10.   *ill to his neighbour,* and, positively, loves *his neighbour as himself.*
Matt.xxii.
40.   3. The fulfilment of law in a perfect character may be regarded

as the formation in the soul of a holy character. Love is the πληρώμα of religion as well as of law ; the sum of all interior goodness : a life governed by this grace is necessarily holy ; for all the faculties and energies of the being are united and hallowed by charity. It expels every opposite affection ; it sanctifies and elevates every congenial desire. It regulates and keeps from affinity with sin every emotion. It rules with sovereign sway, as the royal law within, the will and intention that governs the life. Where pure charity is there can be no disobedience to Heaven and no injury to the neighbour ; there must be all obedience to God, and all bene-volence to man : therefore the whole of goodness is in the per-fection of this grace. When it thus reigns within, it diffuses its influence over the intellect and its judgments : the mind con-ducts its operations under the authority and restraint and sure intuitions of charity, and the heart is united in God.

4. The love, however, which is the ἀνακεφαλαίωσις, or summing up, of all law, is of necessity perfect love, such as neglects no injunction, forgets no prohibition, discharges every duty. It is perfect in passive as well as active obedience. It *never faileth ;* it insures the existence of every grace adapted to time or worthy of eternity. It is *the bond of perfectness.* Therefore it is that the term perfect is reserved for this grace. Patience must *have her perfect work ;* but love alone is itself perfect, while it gives perfec-tion to him who has it.

1 Cor. xiii. 8.

Col. iii. 14.
Jas. i. 14.

LOVE THE FULFILLER.

The Fulfiller.

Love is the fulfiller of law, as well as the fulfilment. This general truth, which is not so directly declared as the former, is often indirectly laid down, and is very important in many ways.

1. It is the energy of the regenerate soul which the Spirit uses : *faith which worketh by love.* When the Holy Ghost dethrones the self in the renewed spirit He makes His agent the principle that is most contrary to self, charity. Strictly speaking all men are actuated by love ; but the love by which faith worketh is turned away from self and looks outward. Hence it is the strongest power in our nature sanctified and set on its highest object.

The Soul's Strength. Gal. v. 6.

(1.) What love is cannot be defined : as we must think to know thought, and feel to know feeling, and will to know volition, so

In Man.

we must love to know the meaning of love, though even then it passeth knowledge. Something of which love in man is the highest expression is found to be as universal as life : it is as mighty in animated nature as gravitation in the world of matter. As instinct, or as merely natural affection, it achieves or seems to achieve unconsciously almost incredible wonders. But when regenerate, and made the energy of living faith, under the Holy Ghost, it is capable of the utmost task that can be laid upon it, even a full obedience to the Divine law. It is in fact the indwelling of

1 John iv. 16. Christ, the indwelling of God by the Holy Ghost : *he that dwelleth in love dwelleth in God.* Under such a condition what is impossible ? Hence it is obvious, that love as the Divine Spirit's instrument is more than that affection of human sensibility which generally bears the name. It is the bond of all the attributes and perfectness of our nature. Though it is not literally the regenerate life —any more than the essence of God is love—it is the strength of that life. It is the outgoing of the soul towards its one Supreme Object ; and this movement or energy is transmitted into every manifestation of force in the moral sphere. All that is true in the physical theories of CORRELATION of forces and CONSERVATION of energy may be transferred to the domain of Ethics : save that in the omnipotent energy of the Spirit poured into the Church, and into its individual members, there is a perpetual increase of the living power that governs the moral world of Christendom. Love in the Christian life is simply and solely seeking its way back to God : that is its centripetal force. The spirit is kept from being lost again in its Creator because of the original fiat which gave it personality : that is its centrifugal force. Hence the orbit of holy duty. Love is the very strength of the Holy Ghost in the inner personality of the regenerate. It is behind the intellect and the sensibilities and the will : ruling the man who is the possessor of these. Though it derives its name from one of the middle class of these three elements of human nature, it is exalted to be over them all. And, though it has not a new name, it has a new

1 John iv. 7. nature and a new prerogative, for *love is of God.* This is said of no one other grace as such.

Towards God. (2.) But the strength of love as a principle of obedience may be viewed in its particular relation to God. It has all the power of gratitude: *We love Him because He first loved us. If ye love Me, keep My commandments. If God so loved us, we ought also to love one another.* In these sentences, combined in this order, we have the highest tribute to the strength of gratitude, as the noblest form of love. It is worthy to be the response of the Divine charity to sinful man. To it as a sentiment of grateful devotion is committed the obedience of the regenerate life. And the manifestation of this love to those around us, in imitation of the supreme charity, gives the highest nobility to virtue. It is moreover the principle of delight in the Divine character, which inspires the desire to imitate and become like God: a desire which is capable of being intensified to unlimited strength, and may become one of the mightiest impulses of the soul in man. This is either a silent, instinctive necessity of being transformed into the image of Him Whom love adores, or an active energy that has in it the potentiality of all holiness. The law, which is a transcript of the Divine nature, becomes itself the object of love: *O how love I Thy law,* is the note of the Psalm which sings the praises of God's Word. As the Divine character and law are both embodied in the Incarnate Son, human love set upon Him is the strength of all holiness. Here our own words fail, and we take refuge in St. Peter's: *Whom having not seen, ye love; in Whom, though now ye see Him not, yet believing, ye rejoice with joy unspeakable and full of glory.*

2. Charity is the guardian of obedience: the Evangelical and better form of the Rabbinical "hedge about the law." There are two leading enemies of the righteousness of the Gospel against both and each of which it is the only and effectual safeguard. ANTINOMIANISM cannot stand in the presence of love. Its grosser and more refined forms are alike repelled. Theological dogmatic argument says: *Is therefore Christ the minister of sin? How then can I do this great wickedness, and sin against God?* The heart's best enforcement of both is, *O how love I Thy law!* PHARISAISM, whether the spirit of a vain dependence on mechanical external obedience, or in its milder form the hireling sentiment, is utterly rejected of love. Its ethical precept warns: *Thou shalt not tempt the Lord thy God.* This grace knows nothing of its *own righteousness,* never being able to forgive itself for sin against God, and all

Margin references: 1 John iv. 19. John xiv. 15. 1 John iv. 11. Ps. cxix. 97. 1 Pet. i. 8. The Guard. Gal. ii. 17. Gen. xxxix. 9. Ps. cxix. 7. Matt. iv. 7. Phil. iii. 9.

N 2

Matt. xix.
27.
Luke xvi.
5.
The Ex-
pounder.

the less because so much has been forgiven; and it at once suppresses every tendency to the question, *What shall we have therefore ?*
by another, *How much owest thou unto my lord ?*

3. Love also is the expositor of the law which it keeps and
defends. It is the scribe well instructed within the heart.

(1.) The enlightened and regenerate reason is of course the interpreter of the commandments; but love is the ever-present secretary
of the judgment, and renders the meaning of every law with an
infinite grace peculiar to itself. This heavenly Magister Senten-
tiarum explains the phraseology of ethics in its own sense; and
defines the terms of its vocabulary in its own spirit. It does not
relax the meaning of any of the most rigid of them. The Must
and Ought and Shall have their full significance; the language
of threatening and sanction is not softened; nor is the Moral
Governor of the universe reduced to a personification of mere good-
nature. But charity, without abolishing or really qualifying the
ethical ideas of the Scripture, transfigures both them and the
language that expresses them. Yet this is only by giving the commandments their deeper meaning: the spiritual interpretation, as
we call it, is really the generous interpretation of love. When
the New Lawgiver ascended the Mount and opened His mouth,
Love Incarnate then first disclosed the hidden mysteries of
ethics; and its deep interpretation pervades the whole Sermon.
Applied to the commandments generally, and to the Decalogue in
particular, it reveals a new world of morals. The precepts of the
first table, literally interpreted, seem cold and hard and limited :
but let love interpret them according to its sentiment of perfect
devotion ! So it is with the other table. Let the injunctions to
remember the Sabbath, to abstain from stealing, and murder, and
adultery, and false witness be severally expounded by perfect
charity, and how their spiritual meaning searches the heart,
quickens the pulse of duty, and inflames the desire !

(2.) Again, love supplies the omissions of every statute and code ;
being quick to discern, where the law is silent, its unexpressed
meaning and inference. Love is the fulfilling or the COMPLEMENT
of the law, and its SUPPLEMENT also. It fills up the interstices by
a running commentary, and adds an undertone of subsidiary precepts that perfect the directory of duty. It interlineates the

written code within and without, inserting its own boundless variety of unwritten commands.

(3.) It is also the Casuist which settles every difficulty. Casuistry. There are many complications in the application of ethical principles. From the beginning there has been a special department which, under the name of CASUISTRY, presides over anomalies in morals, conflicting precepts, collision of duties and seeming incompatibilities of obligation. Here Love abounds *in all judgment*, or Phil. i. 9. discrimination. It stands by the side of conscience, ever ready and seldom at a loss for the right exposition. Seldom: for there will be instances after all, Cases of Conscience, which no Casuistry will decide ; scruples and doubts which no human Ductor Dubitantium can determine ; and which perplex and embarrass even the sure instincts of love. But, generally, this interpreter keeps the honest Christian, who simply and only aims at perfection, right. This Casuist, sent by a heavenly commission into the court, lays down three general principles for the extrication of the embarrassed soul that desires to do its duty : first, the highest Object of obedience must invariably and at all costs have the pre-eminence ; secondly, the most generous interpretation of every questionable obligation is to be preferred ; and, thirdly, self as an end is always to be utterly rejected, or, so far as it is admitted subordinately as an end, it is always the self of eternity rather than the self of time. The application of these standing bye-laws is illustrated by the Supreme Sovereign Himself, much of Whose legislation had to do with collisions of duty. For instance, the disciple who says, *Suffer me first to go and bury my father*, is bidden, Luke ix. *let the dead bury their dead ; but go thou and preach the kingdom of God.* 59, 60. The voice of Christ, Who is God in His kingdom, must be supreme over every other, even the most powerful, claim. In every such case of severe collision between the pure natural instincts and the service of God, God must be first and He will hold His servant harmless. The earliest lesson from the lips of Jesus enforced this. Between what seemed His duty to His mother and His new vocation there was a collision : *Wist ye not that I* MUST *be about My* Luke ii. *Father's business?* Again, when His disciples blamed the loyal 49. woman of the alabaster box, the Redeemer taught them a lesson : on His Person, while He was yet with them, it was impossible to be too profuse in gifts, and she who seemed too lavish was shielded : *Why trouble ye the woman ?* Her large and liberal interpretation of duty, with the decision to which pure love brought her, was defended and commended to all the world. Lastly, of the third principle also He set in His own person the great example : He *pleased not Himself.* And when the greatest of all conflicts in ethics occurred, between the care of His own innocence and the salvation of guilty men, He surrendered the former : *Not My will but Thine be done ;* and suffered Himself to be *numbered with the transgressors.* In Him infinite charity expounded duty. It must do the same office in us. No other principle of exposition will carry us safe through the complications of life. Expediency, common sense, reason may err : love, armed with these principles, NEVER FAILETH.

Matt. xxvi. 16.

Rom. xv. 3.

Luke xxii. 42.

1 Cor. xiii. 8.

LOVE THE UNITY OF FULFILLER AND FULFILMENT.

Fulfilment and Fulfiller.

The perfection of the Christian system of ethics is seen in the combination of love the fulfiller and love the fulfilment of law : law and obedience to law are one in charity. To borrow terms in modern use, here is the unity of objective and subjective : a unity which impresses its various and most important influence on the whole study of New-Testament morals.

Codes.

1. It explains the fact that the Christian revelation is comparatively indifferent to legal codes and formal enactments. It does not dwell so much on the enforcement of specific obligations as on the vigorous maintenance of the principle of charity : love is the strength of the MUST, which at once prescribes obedience and gives the fulness of the commands to which obedience is due. It is obvious, therefore, that Christianity cannot have, like the old covenant, the distinction of moral and ceremonial and political law. Its legislation extends only where love can reign : that domain cannot be one of mere ceremonial observances ; nor can it be the sphere of civil government, where charity is not the vicegerent of God. The old economy, which contained indeed latently a hint of this in *Be ye holy !* and *Thou shalt love the Lord thy God !* has vanished with all its legislation. Even its DECA-LOGUE, as such, is retained only because our Lord has Himself and by His Apostles exempted it from the operation of that prin-

Lev. xx. 7.
Matt. xxii. 37.

ciple, and incorporated it in the Christian statute-book. Introduced into the legislation where charity is supreme, it is by our Lord reduced to one twofold principle, the love of God and of the neighbour. It is in other respects dealt with in a free spirit. It is rearranged, abridged, and its spirit extracted ; it undergoes also a change in the fourth commandment, a spiritualisation everywhere, and has an endless supplement added.

2. Love is an active principle, the law of the movement of the *whole of man* towards God. And, therefore, if love is both the fulfilment and fulfiller, all holiness must be no other than one concentrated and active outgoing of the strength of the whole nature of him who obeys. It does not pause to distinguish between what is forbidden and what is commanded. *I will run the way of Thy commandments, when Thou shalt enlarge my heart.* There is no mere obedience to prohibitive ordinance. The spirit that hates evil loves holiness ; and, in going to the limit of every interdict, it runs to the other side and finds the perfect opposite. It avoids sin only on its way to holiness. Its resistance to evil is the resistance of love : there is no fear in love, but there is deep wrath : an anger that sins not, but abhors that which is evil and will not be content with anything less than the abolition of the sin. Hence, further, charity, as an eternal and evergrowing activity, pursues every precept into all its ramifications. Here we have again the spiritual interpretation : charity is now the well-instructed allegorist that spiritualises every letter to infinity. It cannot ask the question : *Which is the great commandment in the law?* And it cheerfully consents to that strong word of the Moralist among the Apostles : *Whosoever shall keep the whole law, and yet offend in one point, he is guilty of all.* The ethics of love make provision everywhere *that God may be all in all*, that the very least ordinance shall be sustained by all the majesty of Heaven. *He that is faithful in that which is least is faithful also in much.* It is impatient of greater and less in duty.

3. Here we may recall the *law of liberty*, which is royal and perfect : royal and sovereign, in virtue of its being perfect. *The law was given by Moses, but grace and truth came by Jesus Christ:* the grace of the Gospel is the truth of the law ; and of those who receive it we read : *against such there is no law;* which means

Active and One. Ecc. xii. 13.

Ps. cxix. 32.

Matt.xxii. 36.

Jas. ii. 10.

1 Cor. xv. 28.

Luke xvi. 10.

Liberty. Jas. ii. 12. John i.17.

Gal. v. 23.

more than that they are uncondemned by the statute. But the
very liberty is itself law. *He taketh away the first*, the outer code, *Heb. x. 9.*
that He may establish the second, the inner. Nevertheless, the law,
as we have seen, remains for a testimony, and for conviction, and
for perpetual incentive. Its uses are thus summed up by the old
theology : its USUS POLITICUS, to regulate common life : its USUS
ELENCHTICUS, to convince of sin ; its USUS DIDACTICUS, to instruct in morals. The true Christian, however, is *not under the* *Rom. vi.*
law, but under grace. He is not indeed over law in the sense of *14.*
being independent of it. His emancipation is only so far as grace
or mercy effects it through forgiveness ; but that very grace disci-
plines or teaches him to walk according to the strictest principles
of morality. The law is neither over nor beneath the believer :
it is, like the kingdom itself of which it is the rule, within us.

4. Christianity has introduced what is sometimes called the *Perfection*
new law : it is *the law of Christ ;* or *the law of faith.* Now if all *Gal. vi. 2.*
law is love, and all fulfilment is love, it is obvious that there may *Rom. iii.*
be a *righteousness of God* attainable unto perfection : *the righteous-* *27.*
ness of the law might be fulfilled in us. Love presides over ethics *Rom. x. 3.* *Rom. viii.*
which are adapted to a disordered constitution and a lost estate. *3.*
It covers a multitude of past sins and enables the believer to
present what is accepted as a full obedience. Thus is that saying
true : *Mercy rejoiceth against judgment.* If strict justice should pro- *Jas. ii. 13.*
ceed in its inquisition according to the standard of heaven and
unfallen creatures, mercy or love cries, *Have patience with me, and* *Matt.*
I will pay thee all : these my children shall be made perfect in *xviii. 26.*
duty. Meanwhile, its perfect work is judged according to the
Evangelical standard of grace : *it is accepted according to that a* *2 Cor. viii.*
man hath, and not according to that he hath not. Whoso keepeth His *12.* *1 John ii.*
word, in him verily is the love of God perfected. *5.*

5. Lastly, this teaches that there cannot possibly be any works *Super-* *erogation.*
of Supererogation. For, as law is love, love also is law. There
can be no such thing as overpassing the limits of obligation.
The spirit of Divine charity seems to suppress the terminology of
ethics, and to change its character ; but only to revive it into
higher life. The vows of poverty, chastity, and obedience, so far
as they are Christian, are not in reality voluntary vows, but obli- *Matt. v. 3,*
gatory laws. *Blessed are the poor in spirit ! Blessed are the pure in* *6, 8.*

heart! Blessed are they which do hunger and thirst after righteousness! are benedictions pronounced upon the three severally as expressing the true Christian character. Every counsel of perfection is a commandment with promise. And, as to the whole theory on which these are founded, it may be said that Jesus the universal Lawgiver is the One DIRECTOR OF SOULS : THERE IS ONE LAWGIVER, Who is GOD-MAN, the Lord ; and His law is love, whether as to the perfect principle that keeps it, or as to the sum of the commandments which it must keep.

Jas. iv. 12.

BIBLICAL METHOD.

The New Testament, as the perfect development of the ethical teaching of progressive revelation, furnishes the rich abundance of materials from which may be constructed a systematic exhibition of applied ethics.

System.

It has been seen that the internal law which gives its character to Christianity does not supersede the external ; though it gives that law a peculiar freedom and irregularity. It remains now to consider what materials there are for the construction of anything like an ethical system ; how those materials are distributed, and on what principles they may be arranged. Here we have to do with the Lord and His Apostles alone.

I. The Supreme Lawgiver in His ethical teaching gathered up and dissolved, re-enacted in part and in part amended, the ethics of the Old Testament.

Our Lord's Method.

1. It is very observable that, though He spoke with a new and strange, because a Divine-human, authority, He did not profess to promulgate a new code of laws for His disciples. He did not directly pronounce even the ceremonial law obsolete ; in fact, He observed it Himself and connected its observance with many of His miracles. But He certainly gave sundry hints which were to be developed, after His perfect sacrifice, into an abrogation of the whole positive law of Moses. The national and political laws had lapsed in the order of Divine Providence. The purely moral law our Lord necessarily ratified. While He released His disciples from the ancient code as such, He honoured the Deca-

logue, defended it from perversion, and filled out its precepts as spiritually interpreted. A very large part of His ethical teaching was a commentary on the Ten Words of the ancient code. Moreover, He laid down some new principles or gave some new counsels which were adapted to the interval during which He in His personal presence was instead of law, being the Dictator, or Director of His disciples in an intermediate order of things. Thus many of His precepts were not of permanent obligation, but adapted to the purpose of those days. Such were some of the positive commandments, which sound like absolute precepts, to *sell all that thou hast . . . and come, follow Me*. Others, on the contrary, He laid down rather for future use, after the Spirit should have fully come. Such were those which prescribed prayer in His Name and the assembling of His people, and so forth. Again, there were innumerable indications of His will given through the medium of His miracles; and not a few precedents of morals established by Him as Supreme Judge. But it may be said generally that He taught those parts of His ethical system which were most special and characteristic— such as the virtue of humility and self-denial—by His own example. He left all these materials for His Apostles rather than leave a system of His own. His life, His words, and His works were to them and are to us a boundless accumulation of the highest ethics. His last personal question and His last personal command illustrate everything that has been said. *Lovest thou Me?* shows that love was the spring of all obedience. *Follow thou Me!* shows that imitation of His example was the supreme morality.

2. The Apostles, when His words were brought to their remembrance, followed the Master's example, and dealt with the new ethics precisely in His Spirit.

(1.) In the Acts new obligations arise, and a peculiar class of duties with them: the descent of the Holy Ghost, the formation of the new Church, the claims of devotion to the ascended Redeemer, the demands of the Gentile world, all conspired to create a new order of ethical obligations, demanding a new order of precepts. In the Epistles, however, we have the abundant exposition of the new morals of Christianity, as the Spirit brought the Master's words to the disciples' remembrance, or inspired them to make new applications of those words. It is impossible to com-

[margin notes:]
Luke xviii. 22.

John xxi. 17, 22.

The Apostles.

Acts.

pare the Gospels and the Epistles without perceiving that the Same Teacher is in both, as also that there is the same manner of teaching. In the Epistles there is more statement of doctrinal truth; but, as in the Gospels, we find that there is not a solitary revelation of truth which has not, directly or indirectly, and almost always directly, an application to practice. As in the Master's days, occasional circumstances give rise to important decisions. The precedents of the Lord's Ethical Court are many.

(2.) The Epistles teach largely by application of principles to individual cases. They open up a wide field of their own, however, in the relations between the duties and obligations of the Christian fellowship and those of personal religion: hence the new ethical word οἰκοδομή, and the inculcation of all that belongs to EDIFICATION, corporate and individual. But the ethical glory of the Epistles is to be found in three departments which are opened and consecrated to this service. First, they bring all into dependence on UNION WITH CHRIST through that indwelling of His Holy Spirit which is the unity and common bond of the Lord and His people. If we embrace this as truth and as more than mere figure, and in the light of it read the New Testament, we shall find that the entire field of ethics is illuminated by it. Again, the LAST THINGS begin to enter the field with peculiar solemnity and pathos, giving to all the Epistles in some parts, and St. Peter's throughout, a specific and indescribable tone. Finally each writer has his own constellation of GRACES AND VIRTUES, the consummate beauty as well as the ethical completeness of which cannot be exaggerated. So perfect are they that an exposition of these little compendiums of morals would furnish a system of universal Christian Ethics. Not that there is anything in the Epistles of which the Gospels contain no intimation. Every Apostle is still only *a disciple of Jesus,* ἐμαθήτευσε τῷ Ἰησοῦ, and only develops more fully the principles laid down by Him: neither in doctrine nor in morals does the stream of Apostolic teaching rise higher than the fountain in the Master.

3. Nowhere in the New Testament do we find any trace of such an outline of Ethics as should guide future systematisation. The nearest approach is the Sermon on the Mount, with which in the Epistles corresponds St. Paul's great ethical chapter in the

Epistles.

Union with Christ.

Constellations of Graces.

Matt. xxvii 57.

Rom. xii.

Romans. But our Lord's Discourse was a spiritual commentary on the Decalogue. He takes its last precept, which forbids the evil lust of the heart, and makes it the point of connection with His own new legislation. St. Paul immediately after his exposition of the graces which flow from entire consecration to God, introduces the second table of the Decalogue, and in such a way as to intimate that he acknowledged it as the compendium of Christian duty. It may be well, therefore, at this point to consider the claims of this one summary of moral obligation, and to give the reasons why it is not adopted as our basis.

THE DECALOGUE.

The Decalogue.

The DECALOGUE, ἡ δεκάλογος, sc. Βίβλος, νομοθεσία, was the central obligatory code of the Old Covenant: the most ancient as it is the most perfect of all summaries of moral duty.

Eternal.

1. Though given to a special people, and with circumstantials and appendages of limited application, it is universal and for the world. Its dignity was impressed by this, that it was given by Jehovah Himself, while Moses was the organ of the other legislation. There is a difference between the original account in Exodus and the recension in Deuteronomy; but they concur in making the commandments ten: THE TEN WORDS or THE TEN COMMANDMENTS, containing the Covenant specially so called, and therefore deposited in the Ark of Testimony in the centre of the sanctuary. The Decalogue was written on two tables of stone, inscribed on both sides; and obviously divides the precepts in the middle, five having reference to God and containing the Præcepta pietatis, and five referring to man and containing the Præcepta probitatis. Reverence to parents regards them as representative of God: even as Pietas in the old Latin combined the two.

How far the Basis of Ethics.

2. These two Tables, brought into the New Testament and expounded on the principle of the Sermon on the Mount, might be made the basis of all moral teaching. Their spiritual interpretation would furnish all the necessary principles of ethics. The Preface is a glorious announcement of the Personality and Supremacy of God: the foundation of all religion, and the ground of obligation for all that follows. To the children of

Israel He was the Jehovah who brought them out of Egypt; to
Christians the God of universal redemption; to all men everywhere the One and only Moral Governor. The first commandment enjoins the supreme homage of the One God: its Jehovah
has become the Holy Trinity; and the spiritual interpretation of
this law lays down all the principles of theological faith in the
Triune God, with the life of holy devotion and obedience which
corresponds with that faith. The second prescribes the spiritual
worship which alone the Deity will accept. Literally, it interdicts
idolatry and the use of emblems to denote the unseen Being; by
anticipation, therefore, condemning the superstitious ceremonial
and honour paid to images in degenerate Christendom. Spiritually,
it further searches the chambers of imagery and forbids every
creaturely rival of the Supreme and Only Object of the soul's
delight. The third commands the profoundest reverence of the
Divine Majesty, and forbids the irreverent use of the Holy Name
in needless oath and light swearing. Spiritually, it enjoins an
awful reverence of the Divine Presence: not only in His worship,
where it requires the most perfect and all-pervasive sincerity in
every thought, word, and act that has Him for its Object, but
also in the whole of life, which must be conducted, down to its
slightest details, in His Name which is the Name of His Son our
Lord. The fourth ordains the observance of public worship of
the One God, the ordinance for all ages of an appointed day
including the whole service of religion. This commandment
undergoes a remarkable change: while in Exodus the memorial
of the Creation is mentioned, in Deuteronomy, which looks within
and also goes forward to Christian days, deliverance from Egyptian
slavery, pointing to Greater Redemption, are alone introduced.
The spiritualisation of this precept makes the worship of God a
perpetual rest, and connects all with the final rest of heaven. The
fifth attaches an especial honour to parents: not only as parents,
however, but as representing all lawful authority; both Divine
and human. Moreover, it is the link between the Two Tables:
placed in the first, it undoubtedly belongs also to the second.
The sixth forbids murder and every passion that leads to it. The
spiritual application of this short precept is perhaps the widest of
all in its range: as to the neighbour, it includes every act that

shows an undervaluation of the worth of his life down to the slightest thought or word of hatred or violence; while, as to self, it includes every passion and practice that tends to the injury of personal life and well-being, intemperance and excess of every kind. The seventh includes in the word adultery all sins that war against the purity of the sexual relations: of its spiritual range our Lord has given us His own most suggestive illustration. The eighth protects property and forbids dishonesty in act and thought: here then will come in the whole substance of the ethics of property with its rights and obligations; and the highest spiritual interpretation, remembering that men eternally owe love to one another, will make it the basis of all the self-sacrificing ethics of the Gospel of Charity. The ninth protects the character of the neighbour, and forbids slander in every degree, and through all its stages along the whole line of its vocabulary. The last is as it were a Deuteronomical repetition on the one hand, and an advance towards the Sermon on the Mount on the other. It forbids the lust of the heart, and is again and again alluded to in the New Testament as carrying the commandments of the Second Table into the region of the hidden man where his original sin forges every species of iniquity.

Why not the Basis of Systematic Ethics.

3. But the Decalogue, as such, has not often been used as the basis of an exposition of Christian Ethics.

(1.) There has been no slight difference of view from the beginning as to the principles of its own internal order; and this contention itself has tended to prevent its adoption. Augustine, followed by the Roman Catholic Church, and in this by the Lutherans also, reduced the first two precepts to one; thus giving three commandments to the First Table. The Second Table then contains seven, the tenth being subdivided. The ancient Jews did not thus divide the tenth; but left the prohibition of all concupiscence untouched and alone. They, however, sundered the first into two, preceded by a Preface: the former of the two simply imposed belief in the Supreme and Perfect Being. Josephus and Philo, followed by the Early Christian Church, and the Greek and Reformed of modern times, adopted that order which, as in our English Bibles, is in general acceptance.

(2.) There are, however, reasons in the Code itself which make it an inadequate foundation of an ethical system : reasons which have been already more than suggested, and may here be more fully referred to. Generally, it cannot be questioned that the Decalogue as such, and as part of the Israelitish legislation, was abrogated : that is to say, it survived the passing away of the old economy because of its eternal moral principles ; principles which are reproduced, and more fully explained and based upon their true grounds by the Saviour's new legislation. While, therefore, the Ten Commandments still remain, in their Hebrew form, as a memorial of the past, and, stripped of Hebrew appendages, as binding on all nations, they are not the obligatory statement of the entire morals of Christianity. Moreover, it is obvious that the negative and limited character of some of the precepts does not fit them to be the formal expression of the perfect law of liberty : the very fact that they require so large a spiritual and positive expansion makes it embarrassing to hang on them all the precepts and aspirations of Christianity. Again, our Lord has indicated His will on this subject by summarising all our duty into the one supreme commandment of love in its two branches : including, not merely the Decalogue, but the whole compass of moral precepts : ALL *the law and the Prophets.* And, in His Sermon, which has been spoken of as a Commentary on the Decalogue, there is a large body of ethical teaching that cannot, without considerable violence, be brought into direct reference to any of its precepts. When we study morality in the Apostolical Epistles we find the same independence of the Ten Words as a formal code. In fact, very much of their ethical grandeur lies in a region beyond any commandments contained in ordinances : in the region, namely, of the experiences and aspirations and attainments of the Christian life. Hence, to sum up, while the Ten Commandments are of eternal obligation, they are not the adequate basis of Christian Ethics : they serve better for a standing witness and testimony to the conscience before God than as the programme of systematic moral theology.

Matt.xxii. 40.

SYSTEMATIC CHRISTIAN ETHICS.

Having considered Ethics in their specifically Christian principles, we shall now treat these principles as applied: first, as forming the Christian character, personal and individual; and, secondly, as regulating all external relations; one, however, which must not be observed rigidly.

Personal Ethics.

It is obvious that we adopt here the most natural and easy arrangement. There is a sense in which no such distinction as this can be justified, inasmuch as the internal character is dependent on the discharge of external obligations. But if we press this too far, we lose our systematic arrangement altogether, and the loss would be great.

PERSONAL ETHICS OF THE INDIVIDUAL LIFE.

The internal obligations of the Christian life may be presented in an endless variety of ways. The following scheme embraces all, and with some attempt at the order of their development: first come the ethics of Preliminary Grace or Conversion; then such as deal with the Ultimate Intention of the new nature; then those of the Internal Conflict; then those of Consecration to Divine service; and lastly the ethics of Devotion as expressed in the spirit and habit of worship.

Ethics of Conversion.

ETHICS OF THE PRELIMINARY GRACE OF CONVERSION.

Christian Ethics begin, in a certain sense, before the regeneration of the soul. There is a range of duties and obligations incumbent on the awakened sinner, for which sufficient grace is given. This branch of morals has been included in the general question of Preliminary Grace; and must only be touched upon here as introductory to Christian Ethics proper.

1. Generally the whole moral law is incumbent on sinners as such, from beginning to end. There is a perpetual interdict, Thou shalt not! and a perpetual injunction, Thou shalt! even though the strength to abstain and to do may as yet be wanting. These may be regarded as the ethics of a state of slavery to sin. In this case the law is set for conviction of sin, and of sinfulness its source, and of the utter impotence of the mind unrenewed, demanding always repentance with all that has been described as belonging to it. Those who yield to the influences of the restraining and prompting Spirit of conviction, and strive to *cease to do evil and learn to do well*, are in the way of duty approved by God. It is wrong to say that all sincere works done before regeneration are only splendid vices, and counted by the Judge as evil: however true it is that they are not meritorious, and can do nothing towards justification, they are in the way of preparation for Divine acceptance. It is incorrect even to affirm that there is no ethical duty possible to the unregenerate. We have seen that there is a religious life before the regenerate life, and it has its morals. There are *fruits meet for repentance*, which are also *the fruit of the Spirit*, though not yet the Spirit of regeneration.

2. The very faith that introduces the soul to salvation through union with Christ must be preceded by, or rather must include, a submission to the Mediatorial Redeemer which is an ethical law incumbent on every redeemed rebel as such. It is the duty of every living sinner who hears the proclamation of the Gospel to yield compliance to the supreme will of Christ. His conscience tells him this, and it is at his peril that he refuses. There is a doctrine indeed which removes the foundation of this ethical responsibility. But it is not the doctrine taught by the New Testament. It is unnecessary, however, to dwell on these topics, as they have been abundantly exhibited already.

3. It may be added, that, after conversion, this same repentance and faith do not cease to be ethical obligations. Penitence in sundry forms is both the grace and the duty of religion to the end: it

Repentance and Faith.

In Christian Ethics.

Isa. i. 16, 17.

Matt. iii. 8.
Gal. v. 22.
Submission to Christ.

Permanent Obligation.

may even be a profounder sorrow in the sanctified than in the unregenerate, and even when it becomes only the acknowledgment, sorrowful yet always rejoicing, of the sin which is through Divine grace entirely gone, it is repentance still.   And as to faith, or self-renouncing submission to Mediatorial authority and acceptance of the Mediator's Person, it is literally made perfect in the Christian life   But on these, and on all other topics connected with the transformations of preliminary ethics in the regenerate estate, we shall speak more fully hereafter

Ethics of Intention

ETHICS OF THE ULTIMATE INTENTION

The direction of the supreme aim of the soul is foremost in the ethics of the established regenerate life   These may classed under three general heads   first, the Glory of God, in all the forms of that highest intention; secondly, the Will of Christ, as the specific Christian end of life ; and, thirdly, the Perfection of our entire nature, as the issue of both these in their combination.

This department includes a wide range of the ethical principles of the New Testament. It may be said, indeed, to embrace them all, as there is no temper of the soul or action of the life, whether regarding self or regarding others, which is not under the government of the ultimate choice of the will   But we must strictly limit ourselves to the characteristics of holy intention as such

The Glory of God 1 Cor. x 31.

I Perhaps the final expression of the end of the Christian life is that given by St. Paul . *do all to* THE GLORY OF GOD

John xvii 4

1 The highest example and illustration of the maxim is to be found in our Lord, Who, when leaving the world, said *I have glorified Thee on the earth   I have finished the work which Thou gavest Me to do.* His whole human career as the supreme pattern had this for its supreme object · to render a perfect tribute to the glory of the Divine Name, to reflect that glory from Himself, and to bring men to render God His glory. These three combined are the highest definition we can conceive of the meaning of a phrase which has been adopted always to express the ultimate and noblest aim of creaturely life

2. But the last branch of the definition indicates that living to the glory of God has a specifically Christian meaning. It is very specially St. Paul's expression, who places it on the ground of redemption: *for ye are bought with a price; therefore glorify God in your body, and in your spirit, which are God's;* the honour of the Triune God of the Gospel salvation is now the final end of the Christian life. The Corinthian Epistle, which uses the term more than any other, begins by showing that God in Christ has taken all human glorying away, and made Himself the one Object of all glorying: *that no flesh should glory in His presence* is on one side of the Redeemer's finished work, and *he that glorieth let him glory in the Lord* on the other. When all shall be accomplished it is said that the Lord *shall come to be glorified in His saints.* In these passages we have the two ideas of rendering God His tribute and reflecting His honour from ourselves. The third idea, that of bringing others to glorify Him, that is, of so acting as to secure His honour, occurs again and again: *Whether therefore ye eat or drink, or do anything, do all to the glory of God:* where the uppermost thought is, that every action may be so ordered as not to bring dishonour upon the Author of the Gospel. The reference here is to comparatively insignificant things; but elsewhere the highest range of duty is referred to the same end: *If any man speak let him speak as the oracles of God; if any man minister let him do it as of the ability that God giveth; that God in all things may be glorified through Jesus Christ.* Thus every thought and every word and every action must in Christian Ethics aim to honour God, to reflect His grace, and to shield His name from reproach; and in these three senses Christians live TO THE GLORY OF GOD.

3. As an ethical principle this widest and most comprehensive law may assume some other forms and names.

(1.) It is the making God the one object of life: the meaning or thinking or intending the Supreme Triune, and in each Person, in all things from the least to the greatest. This is what our Lord has called the SINGLE EYE, which looks at the Divine will as the directory and end of every action. *The light of the body is the eye; if therefore thine eye be single, thy whole body shall be full of light,* on which closely follows, *Ye cannot serve God and mammon.* The full force of this precept is seen if we connect with it two

Margin notes:
Christian Meaning.

1 Cor. vi. 20.

1 Cor. i. 29—31.

2 Thess. i. 10.

1 Cor. x. 31.

1 Pet. iv. 11.

The Single Eye.

Matt. vi. 22.

Matt. vi. 24.

1 Cor. vi. 19. other passages. *Your body is the temple of the Holy Ghost ;* and His interior light shines upon the eye that gives light to the whole of that life of which the body is the organ. And, beholding God 1 Pet. iii. 15. in all things, we obey the injunction : *sanctify the Lord God in your hearts,* in the centre of your entire personality of soul and body. Thus we have the full thought of a single eye to the glory of God. Rom. xii. 8. Elsewhere this grace is called SIMPLICITY : *he that giveth let him do it with simplicity,* where our Lord's ἁπλοῦς becomes ἐν ἁπλότητι. 2 Cor. i. 12. Purity of intention and singleness of aim are united in *simplicity and godly sincerity.* These make up that UNITY of aim, as opposed to multiplicity of regards and distraction of motives, for which Ps.lxxxvi. 11. the Psalmist prayed : *I will walk in Thy truth ; unite my heart to fear Thy name.* This principle of a fixed and habitual reference of every action to the will of God pervades the Scripture, and is one of the glories of its ethical teaching.

Pleasing God.

(2.) It is presented in another form as the aim to PLEASE GOD, with its reflex, the consciousness of pleasing Him. One of the first definitions of a perfect godliness in the Bible is the word Gen.v.24. concerning Enoch that he *walked with God,* which in the New Heb. xi.5. Testament is explained that *he pleased God.* Here again we have Rom. xv. 3. the Supreme Example, that of Him who *pleased not Himself,* and Who once declared of Himself, *I do always those things that please* John viii. 29. *Him.* It was His aim to please His Father, and it must be ours : He could say I DO ALWAYS ; we in His strength must copy Him. Thus we may close as we began with our Lord's example, Who never spoke but of two aims in His life, the glory of His Father's name, and the pleasing Him in doing His will. But the honour due to God belongs to Christ Himself.

Simplicity of this Aim.

(3.) The Apostle Paul bids the Colossian servants to serve *not with eyeservice, as men-pleasers ; but in singleness of heart fearing* Col. iii. 22. *God.* This passage, with its parallel to the Ephesians, teaches that to please God, to please the Lord, is to fear Him ; and thus Ps.lxxxvi. 11. the glory of God and the pleasing Him are really one. *Unite my heart to fear Thy name* has almost its perfect echo in these words : in an undivided heart fearing the Lord. Moreover, it teaches what the whole Scripture teaches, that, as there can be only one object of fear, so there can be only One Being to be pleased. The ethical purity of this intention consists in its soleness and supremacy.

477

Do I seek to please men? for, if I yet pleased men, I should not be the servant of Christ. Gal. i. 10.

II. The Christian Lawgiver, unlike any other in the history of religion, presents Himself to His people as the Object of their final intention in all things. This truth appears in several lights.

1. It is exhibited as the bringing all life into entire DEVOTION TO THE LORD JESUS. Our Saviour is our God, and therefore He is the End of the soul as well as its Redeemer. The term end being most literally understood, the ethics of Christianity permit this application: *for to me to live is Christ.* If it signifies more generally a leading purpose in the whole tenour of probation, it is supported by St. Paul again: *whether we live, we live unto the Lord.* The Christian is thus also *under the law to Christ;* and that most absolutely, for the entire strain of the New Testament, even more than isolated texts, shows nothing in the vista of human duty and aspiration beyond the will of the Incarnate Jesus. This is a distinctively Christian end and aim in all things: and its supremacy as such is proved by the remainder of the passage already quoted: *whether we die, we die unto the Lord.* Lest, however, this should be supposed to mean only that in the Divine order Jesus of Nazareth has the destinies of men put into His hands, the Apostle says: *whether we live therefore or die we are the Lord's.* We are not now proving the Divinity of the Incarnate. Here, indeed, is absolute demonstration: for of none but the Supreme can it be said that the creature is His, and lives and dies to Him. But the specific ground of this devotion of the being to Jesus is the fact of His redeeming purpose and redeeming rights: *to this end Christ died and revived, that He might be the Lord of the dead and of the living.* As to this nothing more need be said than that the same argument is used concerning God and His Christ: *Ye are bought with a price: therefore glorify God in your body and in your spirit, which are God's.*

Consecration to Christ.

Phil. i. 21.

Rom. xiv. 8.
1 Cor. ix. 21.

Rom. xiv. 9.

1 Cor. vi. 20.

2. This is the place to dwell upon that negative end of life, which is almost the peculiarity and altogether the glory of the Christian system: the entire renunciation, or rather the entire forgetfulness of, SELF as the end of our actions: its utter extinction as the final intention of anything we think, or speak, or do. Forgetfulness, mark well: a most important truth has been aimed

Self.

at by the word negative, for if the annihilation of self-ends is made a positive end itself, the ethical grandeur of unselfishness is lost   Hence the affecting connection of this principle with the example of Christ.   *If any man will come after Me, let him deny himself, and take up His cross daily, and follow Me*.   here the following of Christ is the sum of the new life, the daily cross its constant element   the absolute renunciation of self as an end is the introductory condition   not the less an introductory condition, because the general company of the Redeemer's disciples are ever learning it, and do not come to the full knowledge of its truth, down to the last   Observe, however, that we speak only of the Ultimate Principle and scope of life   Self may still remain as a subordinate end : *Work out your own salvation !   Look not every man on his own things, but every man* ALSO *on the things of others   All seek their own, not the things which are Jesus Christ's*.   These various words follow the Apostle's exhibition of the Supreme Example of self-renunciation . *let this mind be in you which was also in Christ Jesus*   Here is the suppression of self.   They then show that the self which is lost is found again in Christ, and is an object of care combined with the neighbour, that care of self working out the will of God   The Philippian chapter contains the perfect doctrine of Self.

Luke ix 23

Phil ii 4, 5,12,21

3   This leads to the IMITATION OF CHRIST, which has been and will be alluded to   here it is also a supreme intention in life   There is no higher end than to become like Him, Who is the Perfect Good Incarnate . *There is none good but One, that is, God ;* that is, Christ, God in man   There is no higher tribute to the Supreme than to endeavour to be like Him   imitari quem colis   Our Lord, who at the beginning bade His disciples imitate the perfections of their *Father which is in heaven*, ended His teaching by commanding the emulation of Himself   His last word to an individual on earth made both the duty and the individuality of it prominent · *follow thou Me*   But here we must remember what has been already made emphatic, that our Lord has set before us an example, not so much of the means, as of the result of Christian endeavour   If He makes Himself the Pattern in the pursuit of it, it is always and only as He is the model of the renunciation of self   In that alone is He expressly proposed as an example

Imitation of Christ

Matt xix. 17

Matt v 44—48.

John xxi. 22

III   Another ultimate ethical aim is the attainment of the per-

Perfection

fection of the individual character, as the issue of personal striving after nothing less than the realisation of all the will of God, and thus by Divine grace making the result our own.

1. Generally, nothing is more certain than that this high ideal is set before the Christian. One of the first words of the New Lawgiver was : *Be ye therefore perfect, even as your Father which is in heaven is perfect.* The word τέλειοι implies the possible attainment of the τέλος, the end or moral goal, of all life. This was the new aspiration introduced into ethics by our Lord, Who made His heavenly Father the standard, reproduced upon earth by Himself, of all moral excellence, as summed up in Charity, which all His followers must aspire to reach. **Supreme Ideal.** **Matt. v. 48.**

2. That supreme standard must be aimed at by the Christian, depending on Divine grace, from the very beginning of his career of discipleship through all its processes to the end. **Beginning.**

(1.) Our Lord said to one who came to Him, *If thou wilt be perfect !* thus engaging him to the pursuit of perfection at the outset, and applying a severe test to his sincerity of intention. He was required to give the first pledge of his determination by selling all that he had for the poor. Christ made Himself the standard : *everyone that is perfect shall be as his Master.* Here the word and the application are different ; but the meaning is that those who have become His disciples must aim to share His moral perfection. **Matt. xix. 21.** **Luke vi. 40.**

(2.) The processes of the Christian life must all be conducted under the inspiration of this lofty incentive. It has been seen how the Holy Spirit administers the Atonement as a provision for making men perfect before the law, perfect as children of God, and perfect as sanctified to the Divine fellowship. It will be enough now to indicate that in these three departments Christians are taught to aspire to perfection by their own co-operant effort. *These things write I unto you, that ye sin not. He that doeth righteousness is righteous, even as He is righteous.* These words confirm St. Paul's : *that the righteousness of the law may be fulfilled in us who walk not after the flesh but after the Spirit.* And without controversy they teach that the religious walk must aim at a perfect satisfaction, through Divine grace, of every requirement of law. As the children of God we are exhorted to keep the same high aspiration before us, *that ye may be blameless and harmless, the sons of God without* **1 John ii. 1.** **1 John iii. 7.** **Rom. viii. 4.** **Phil. ii. 15.**

rebuke: tried by the highest standard, without fault, without interior stain, without reproach of God or man, being in the Divine purpose which becomes a human aim *conformed to the image of His Son.* As St. John says, *Whosoever is born of God doth not commit sin:* at least, the tenour of his aspiration is to live in a state of sacred freedom from sin and likeness to the Son of God, *Who was manifested to take away our sins, and in Him is no sin.* Thus there is a perfection of the regenerate estate which is an ideal which diligence strives to realise. So also the exhortation runs in the temple of Divine consecration: *Having therefore these promises, dearly beloved, let us cleanse ourselves from all filthiness of the flesh and spirit, perfecting holiness in the fear of God.* The end of the application of the Atonement is to *make the comers thereunto perfect. For by one offering He hath perfected for ever them that are sanctified.* The Divine τετελείωκεν expresses a design that becomes human in the Corinthian ἐπιτελοῦντες, which, as no one will deny, makes the perfection of sanctity a Christian aim. It may be added that individual graces are to be trained to their own several perfection: for instance, *let patience have her perfect work,* one grace of the *perfect man,* at least of the man who aspires to perfection, who *looketh into the perfect law of liberty, and continueth therein:* looks into it for ever with the inextinguishable ardour of determination to be a *doer of the work* in its perfection and to be *blessed in his deed.*

(3.) Finally, there is an aspiration to perfectness which is not purely ethical, though that element is not excluded. St. Paul's most intense expression of the one end of his life, *This one thing!* had reference to the final consummation of body and soul in union with Christ. *Not as though I had already attained, either were already perfected!* His view of the finished perfection of his entire nature stops not short of the resurrection. For that of course he depends on the fidelity of his Lord. But even that he makes his own aim: *I follow after, if that I may apprehend that for which also I am apprehended of Christ Jesus.* He exhorts the spiritually perfect to press on to the perfection of the last change when the perfection of earth shall put on the perfection of heaven. How far this entered into his ethical aim is obvious. It gives its sublime peculiarity to the whole passage: *This one thing!*

Rom. viii. 29.
1 John iii. 9.
1 John iii. 5.
2 Cor. vii. 1.
Heb. x. 1, 14.
Jas. i. 4.
Jas. iii. 2.
Jas. i. 25.
Phil. iii. 12, 13.
ἕν δέ.

(4.) The end of time is eternity, and the end of life is the eternal union with God. The finite may seek the Infinite. The highest aspiration of the saint must be, through life and all the varieties of probation, to see God and be one with Him for ever. This may be and must be the final intention. *I shall be satisfied when I awake with Thy likeness!* Not preparation for death, nor preparation for meeting God in judgment, but preparation to be with Him eternally! DEUS MEUS ET OMNIA!

Beatific Vision.

Ps. xvii. 15.

ETHICS OF THE SPIRITUAL CONFLICT.

Ethics of Christian Conflict.

The Christian personality is the sphere of a contest between two opposing principles which are variously described. The struggle is between the new man and the old, or the flesh and the Spirit, or the believer and Satan. The peculiarity of this conflict depends upon the doctrine of the probationary union of the regenerate with Christ the Captain of our salvation. It appears in another form in all systems of ethics, which refer to the discord between the worse and the better self; but Christianity alone gives the key to this mystery in human nature. A very large department of the moral teaching of the New Testament is occupied with the detail of virtues and duties which spring out of the spiritual warfare on which our probation depends. These topics must be taken in their order.

The doctrinal aspect of this internal discord has been already given; we deal now only with the ethical, and confining our attention to the one idea of the conflict. Many of the ethical principles and definitions are of course exhibited under other heads. It will conduce to precision if we consider the subject first in reference to the two opposite elements with their contrasted virtues and vices in particular, and then in reference to the various ethical duties and grace, arising out of their relation to each other generally, and as common to all.

The Two
Forces.

THE WARFARE IN FELLOWSHIP WITH CHRIST

Though every part of the New Testament refers to the general principles of the contest, St Paul is the only teacher who gives us a complete view of the two forces contending in the regenerate He therefore must be our main guide in this department, and his teaching as summing up the whole of Scripture, represents the ethical contest as no other than the believer's fellowship in the Redeemer's conflict and victory.   This is the profound bond
1 Tim vi
12
which unites all the various descriptions of the *good fight of faith* This entire department of Ethics is reduced to the prosecution of a contest which is in the Christian the renewal and continuation of his Master's contest and victory   Union with Christ stamps its impress on the whole doctrine of the regenerate conflict   To set this in a clear light requires only the consideration of a few passages which connect the Saviour's Headship with each department of the spiritual warfare in its two branches : first, in the struggle of the new man with the old man still remaining within him , and, secondly, as the contest of the new man with the external forces of evil , these combining in the common idea of our union with the Lord in our temptation.

The
Internal
Conflict

THE INTERNAL STRUGGLE

I It is peculiar to St Paul to describe the contest as between the old man and the new, and as between the flesh and the Spirit In the former Christ is viewed as Himself the life of the believer, raised from the dead with Him ; in the latter Christ is viewed as by His Spirit contending against the remains of the evil nature. The two are really one, but each has its distinct range

1 The doctrine of regeneration has given us all the elements of
The Old
Man and
the New
Col. iii 9,
10
distinction   In many passages St Paul speaks of *the old man* and *the new man* in seeming, though only seeming, independence of Christ The one personality of the regenerate includes a new nature and an old for a time coexisting   The residuary old man is again
Rom vi 6
regarded as having an organic body of his own, *the body of sin*   in
Col iii. 5.
this, by its *members which are upon the earth*, it performs *the deeds*

of the body. It is *the body of this death* with which the Apostle struggled before he was regenerate, and with which, though under better auspices, he struggled afterwards. In the former struggle the *inward man* is brought *into captivity to the law of sin;* in the latter, that of which we now speak, the process is inverted: *Ye have put off the old man with his deeds, and have put on the new man; knowing this, that our old man is crucified with Him, that henceforth we should not serve sin.* Sin, therefore, though remaining, is no longer the master. This is the glory of Christian ethics. Rom. viii. 13. / Rom. vii. 22—24. Col. iii. 9, 10. Rom.vi.6.

2. But again that one personality is a *man in Christ,* and the new nature is no other than Christ *formed in you,* as if His sacred μορφή, or form, were impressed on the spirit through the Holy Ghost, of Whom it is said, *he that is joined unto the Lord is one spirit.* St. Paul tells the Colossians that they *have put on the new man,* using the same word as that to the Romans, *put ye on the Lord Jesus Christ;* and the combination of the two passages shows that the new man is not so much our nature renewed as Christ in it, and also that the Christian conflict is the effort on our part to gain the ascendency of the new man over the old. This new man is the *last Adam,* a *quickening Spirit,* within the soul; and this term spirit is the link between the doctrine of the two men, or the two Adams, in the regenerate and the ethical application of it to which we now pass. 2 Cor. xii. 2. Gal. iv. 19. 1 Cor. vi. 17. Col. iii. 10. Rom. xiii. 14. / 1 Cor. xv. 45.

II. Hence the contest is not between a new nature and an old simply, but between the Holy Spirit of Christ and what is called, in this view, the Flesh. It is important to define these two opposite principles, and the nature of the conflict between them. Spirit and Flesh.

1. The Flesh is nowhere more fully described than when it is opposed to the Holy Spirit as the principle of regenerate life. There are in the New Testament abundant references to the fallen nature of man; but none which equals St. Paul's Galatian picture of its works, as they are *manifest* in the world, and by the natural conscience evidently condemned. They are *these: adultery, fornication, uncleanness, lasciviousness, idolatry, witchcraft, hatred, variance, emulations, wrath, strife, seditions, heresies, envyings, murders, drunkenness, revellings, and such like.* These are an expansion of the Lord's words concerning what proceeds *out of the heart.* St. Paul's catalogue includes the *evil thoughts, thefts, false witness, blasphemies.* The Flesh. / Gal. v. 17 —21. / Matt. xv. 19.

Col. iii. 5. To this catalogue *covetousness, which is idolatry,* is added elsewhere; and it thus includes every form of sin against God, against the neighbour, and against the self; against social, political, and ecclesiastical society. These sins are known and read of all men; Christian ethics do not require any definition of them; they are manifest. St. James in sacred satire says of them : *This wisdom descendeth not from above, but is earthly, sensual, devilish,* the middle term connecting them with St. Paul's *works of the flesh.* They are the best product of the thoughts of the *old man with his deeds.* They are the *filthiness and superfluity of naughtiness* which Christians must *lay apart.* Over against all these St. Paul sets the one *fruit of the Spirit,* which is *love, joy, peace, longsuffering, gentleness, goodness, faith, meekness, temperance :* graces which are set in peaceful array against the turbulent army of lawless vices. St. Peter sums up all in another antithesis : on the one side *the corruption that is in the world through lust,* for the works of the flesh ; and for the fruit of the Spirit, the becoming *partakers of the Divine nature,* which is in St. James *the wisdom that is from above.*

Jas. iii. 15, 17. Jas. i. 21. Gal. v.19.

Col. iii. 9.

Gal. v. 22, 23.

2 Pet. i. 4.

Jas. iii. 17.

2. The conflict between these in Christian Ethics must be carefully stated. St. Paul's leading text runs thus : *The flesh lusteth against the Spirit, and the Spirit against the flesh ; and these are contrary the one to the other, that ye may not do the things that ye would.* The same word ἐπιθυμεῖ, which expresses the not yet extirpated bias of original sin in the nature, must be referred to the Spirit's new original bias in the spirit regenerate. If decorum would suggest a different word in the latter case, we may adopt it ; but the meaning still remains, that, while the flesh would hinder us from doing what we would as regenerate, the Spirit hinders us from doing what we would as yielding to the impulse of the remainder of sin. But it must be observed that there is a difference between this contest and that described in the seventh chapter to the Romans. There the conflict is a failing one on the side of the man under conviction but not yet regenerate. It is not between the Spirit, as the *Spirit of life in Christ Jesus,* and the flesh ; but between the flesh and the *law of my mind,* or the νοῦς, under the striving of the Holy Ghost. This conflict is a fruitless struggle against a power *bringing me into captivity to the law of sin which is in my members.* In the regenerate contest the

Gal. v.17.

Rom. viii. 2. Rom. vii. 23.

watchword is : *Walk in the Spirit, and ye shall not fulfil the lust of* Gal. v. 16.
the flesh. It is the characteristic of the ethics of the Christian
warfare that the Holy Spirit of Christ in the regenerate spirit
secures the possibility of a constant victory. Still, it is a contest;
the extinction of sin, and of the flesh, is not assumed ; the Flesh
is still, as we shall see, the source of temptation for a season.

III. We may now consider the relation of this conflict to our
union with Christ and our temptation with Him.

1. St. James gives us the nearest approach to a definition of Tempta-
the process of temptation from within. *Every man is tempted,* tion from Within.
when he is drawn away of his own lust, and enticed. Temptation Jas. i. 14.
proper, in the case of a fallen creature, is strictly speaking within.
It craves the gratification that is offered from without : *then when* Jas. i. 15.
lust hath conceived, it bringeth forth sin. The contest in the regenerate man is this lust of the flesh opposing the Spirit of the new
nature ; and the Spirit continually moving the renewed spirit to
oppose its desires. In this sense our first parents were not
tempted, though in their case the temptation from without
assailed a will capable of falling and was the means of engender-
ing the concupiscence that then engendered all sin. In this sense
the entirely sanctified from sin are not tempted ; though in their
case the will that has known transgression is still liable to fall
and all the more because of the remaining effects of eradicated
evil. In this sense the glorified in heaven, after a probation
ended, will be incapable of temptation. In this sense our sinless
Redeemer was absolutely both untemptable and impeccable. He
was in all points tempted like as we are, as without sin : that is, He Heb. iv.
was tried at all points as we are tried, so far as was consistent 15.
with the entire absence of the element that could conceive sin.
In this sense, finally, *God cannot be tempted with evil, neither* Jas. i. 13.
tempteth He any man. He permits the temptation in the regenerate, but His Spirit striveth *against the flesh.* And, in that the Gal. v. 17.
renewed spirit is enabled to vanquish every temptation consists
the difference between this species of temptation and that of the
unregenerate involved as yet in the *snare of the devil, who are taken* 2 Tim. ii.
alive by him at his will. 26.

2. Hence it will be obvious that the Christian's union with his
Lord in this interior temptation must be carefully defined and

Luke
xxii. 28.
limited. Not of this inward conflict does the Saviour speak when
He says : *ye are they which have continued with Me in My temptations.*
He had no mother-lust which could conceive and bring forth sin.
In another sense, He is most intimately united with His saints in
this sacred conflict ; and the same Omnipotent Spirit Who rendered
His human nature sinless is given to redeem our nature from sin.
But there is another aspect of temptation which brings Him still
nearer to us ; and that is, the trial of the spirit from without.
This He underwent to the utmost : indeed, as much beyond the
possibility of His servants' temptation as their internal temptation was impossible to Him.   To those other and more exterior
sources of trial we must now turn our attention.

External
Conflict.

THE EXTERNAL CONFLICT.

The regenerate soul, united to Christ, but still in the flesh, is
opposed by all the elements of the present world and by the
spiritual powers of evil of which Satan is the head : these two
are closely united in the general teaching of the New Testament,
which represents the temptation of our probationary life as very
largely springing from these combined sources.

The
World.
I. The WORLD as an element of opposition to the Christian has
two distinct meanings, which must be regarded separately.

Of Sense.
1. The present world, or the state of things into which we are
naturally born, and with which we are united through the medium
of the body, is not of itself evil ; but in a multitude of ways, and
through a multitude of channels, presents the materials which the
lust of the flesh may convert into temptation.   Its innumerable
1 John ii.
16.
objects may minister to the *lust of the flesh, and the lust of the eyes,*
and the pride of life.   Its necessary occupations may be converted
Matt. xiii.
22.
into evil and become *the care of this world.*

Of Provi-
dence.
2. The world may signify the course of human life as under
the order of Providential arrangements ; and these, in their infinite diversity, are the elements of probationary-trial or temptation.   Its joy and prosperity, its adversity and sorrow, are alike
tests of the character ; making up the conflict of life.   This kind
of temptation is ordered of God Himself.   Hence the same
Apostle James who has already described the process of temptation

from within exhorts his readers to *count it all joy when ye fall into divers temptations :* they are for *the trial of your faith.* Jas. i. 2.
1 Pet. i. 7.

3. The world is the *present evil world :* the course of which is opposed to religion, and the maxims, usages, tendencies, enjoyments, and objects of which are at all points unfriendly to the cultivation of piety. Christ has appeared as the atoning Saviour to *deliver us from this present evil age,* by casting out *the prince of this world ;* but, during the process of our redemption, our existence in it is a perpetual trial of our Christian graces. The world thus defined, is thus utterly contrary to the religious life, and is under the power of the enemy of Christ's kingdom. The Evil
World. Gal. i. iv.
John xii.
31.

II. The solemn doctrine of the Scripture is that the warfare of the Christian life is not only the struggle between the flesh and the Spirit, and the new man and the evil world, but also between the believer in Christ and the vast forces of spiritual intelligences who are leagued, under Satan their head, against the Christian cause in the world. Two Ephesian texts sum up the whole revelation of the New Testament on this subject : indeed the Ephesian Epistle generally may be said to condense into its practical bearing all the teaching of Scripture as to our superhuman foes. Satan and
His
Angels.

1. From the first we learn that there is a conjunction between this class of spiritual enemies and the internal and external opposition which has been described. *Ye walked,* the Apostle says, *according to the course of this world, the spirit that now worketh in the children of disobedience.* As Jesus by His Spirit directs the course of the regenerate world, so Satan directs the course of the world that now is : whatever in it opposes the Christian life is placed under his control. Here also he is represented as the interior instigator of that other opposition of the old man and of the flesh : he worketh IN the children of disobedience. Eph. ii. 2.

2. From the other we learn not to identify these spiritual forces with either the flesh or the world. There is an opposition on the part of our unseen foes which is independent and direct. *We wrestle not against flesh and blood, but against principalities, against powers, against the rulers of the darkness of this world, against spiritual wickedness in high places.* The repeated AGAINST gives equal emphasis to the distinct antagonism of the several orders of fallen Eph. vi. 12.

spirits, as they are confederate under one head whose directing agency is referred to as *the wiles of the devil.*

Eph. i. 19, 20, 21, 22.
3. But the Epistle which thus closes has already set in its forefront the great revelation that Christ is supreme over all the forces of evil. He is set *in the heavenly places, far above all principality, and power, and might, and every name that is named, not only in this world, but also in that which is to come.* Supreme authority over the present course of things, and the supernatural order, is placed in His hands as the Incarnate *Head over all things to the Church.* And the internal conflict is conducted under His sway, according to the *exceeding greatness of His power to us-ward who believe.* Thus the proposition laid down again and again is made good, that it is in union with Christ that the universal contest is carried on by the regenerate Christian.

THE SPECIAL ETHICS OF THIS CONFLICT.

Ethics of the Conflict.

The ethics of the Christian conflict will now be viewed as comprising the duties and the graces which are strictly connected with it. These may be classified under the two general heads of Preservation, internal and external, and of Confidence in the victorious issue. Here we obviously have the defensive and offensive aspects of the whole duty of the servants and soldiers of Christ.

SELF-PRESERVATION.

Self-Preservation.

The duties and the graces of the Christian life as withstanding evil can hardly be separated even in thought. They occupy a large place in the New-Testament precepts concerning Self-discipline, and Watchfulness: these terms representing a wide variety of Christian virtues.

Self-Denial.

I. Personal interior discipline takes the lead: that discipline, namely, which negatively prepares for the future conflict, or lessens its force when it is present, or in many cases shields the soul from the conflict altogether. The duties here referred to may be summed up as belonging to the family of Self-denial: the sacred graces and duties and virtues of the Cross.

Self-Renunciation.

1. At the root of all lies Self-renunciation. This has already been considered in relation to the ultimate end of the soul. Now

it is regarded as the fundamental feeling the regenerate must entertain towards the sinful element remaining, which, as the opposite of the new man or the Christ within him, he must needs hate. It passes through many stages in the ethics of the Gospel : the hatred, in principle, with the mortification or crucifixion as the issue ; and intermediate acts of self-denial.

(1.) Our Lord has made the first emphatic ; and that in many ways. He has placed it at the very threshold of His service. *If any man will come after Me, let him deny himself, and take up his cross daily, and follow Me.* The first condition of these three is the root of the other two, and not to be confounded with them : ἀπαρνησάσθω ἑαυτὸν is the absolute renunciation of all complacency or confidence in self. This ethical principle takes different forms. Its severest is SELF-ABHORRENCE, on which all the more earnest and deeper ethical teaching of Christianity dwells so much. It is more than hating life in the sense of not loving it so much as Christ. It is the love of God turned in holy enmity against self as an enemy to God ; an enemy still so far as any evil remains ; and, even if all evil were gone, hated nevertheless in the remembrance of what it was. The Saviour's teaching allows no place for self-complacency, even when the self is sanctified : He taught His servant to say, *Not I, but Christ liveth in me!* This hatred of self sometimes assumes a morbid character in mystical theology ; but a close study of the Lord's words will show that it is hard to exaggerate : the inmost secret of religion is not found until the soul literally hates the thought of a self that is independent of God and of Christ : that is, of any SELF at all. Hence the beauty of HUMILITY, the fundamental grace of the Gospel. This virtue is many-sided : it has one aspect towards God, another towards man, and another towards self as the subject of past and present sin. This last it is here : profound consciousness of ill-desert before Heaven and impotence against evil. *I have heard of Thee by the hearing of the ear : but now mine eye seeth Thee. Wherefore I abhor myself!* This sublimest expression of humility in the Old Testament illustrates all that has been said : in the presence of the purity of God the soul, conscious of nothing but sin of its own, loathes and abhors itself. It is paralleled by Simon Peter's *Depart from me ; for I am a sinful man, O Lord!* In this self-distrust, deepened into self-contempt, is the secret of

Luke ix. 23.

Hatred of Self.

Gal. ii. 20.

Job xlii. 5, 6.

Luke v. 8.

1 Peter v. 6.

Jas. iv. 7.

Gal. v. 24.

Rom. viii. 3.

Col. iii. 5.

Rom. vi. 6.

Rom. xiii. 14.

strength. *Humble yourselves therefore under the mighty hand of God, that He may exalt you. Submit yourselves therefore to God ; Resist the devil :* each is the counterpart and also the condition of the other. SELF-CRUCIFIXION WITH CHRIST has reference to the entire sinful nature, *the flesh with the affections and lusts,* its passive susceptibility and active impulse. As our Lord *condemned sin in the flesh,* every true disciple must, in spiritual fellowship with Him, do the same. *They that are Christ's have crucified the flesh.* MORTIFICATION has reference to each individual tendency to sin. It is, on the one hand, stronger than that crucifixion : *mortify,* or kill, *your members which are upon the earth* must mean that in the strength of the Spirit the believer aims habitually at the death of, and does in fact kill, every form of the life of sin as it emerges. On the other hand, it is less than that crucifixion, which is the destruction of the whole *body of sin :* not that it is utterly destroyed in the one act of crucifixion with Christ, but it is impaled on the interior cross where it must, having no *provision* made for it, die.

Asce-
ticism.

Matt. vi. 16.

1 Tim. iv. 8.

1 Cor. ix. 27.

2 Cor. xi. 27.
1 Tim. iv. 1.

(2.) The external practices of a godly asceticism are both the expression and the instrumental aids of this internal discipline. First, and as mediating between inward and outward discipline, comes, ABSTINENCE, which is either a grace or a duty : this means in general the non-indulgence of appetite as towards things and affections as towards persons ; and may be either only internal or external also. It is the ἀπέχειν which the ancient moral philosophy so highly extolled. FASTING is then the more express and formal act, brought from the Old Testament by our Lord, Who indirectly enjoined it both by His example and by His precept : *when ye fast !* But this precept leaves the time, character, and degree of fasting to the judgment of him who practises it. *Bodily exercise profiteth little :* this regimen and sacred discipline are acknowledged to be useful. *I keep under my body and bring it into subjection* is a revelation of the Apostle's most earnest self-restraint in general, which according to his own testimony took the form of express fastings : *in fastings often.* But whatever ascetic practices are adopted must be under the restraint and regulation of one law : *Exercise thyself* RATHER UNTO GODLINESS.

Self-
Govern-
ment.

(3.) And, as godliness is the design, the warranty, and the safe-guard of asceticism, so SELF-GOVERNMENT is its best result. This has been an ethical law in most systems of moral philosophy; but the Christian differs from all others in combining the internal government of the Spirit with this government of self. St. Paul in his final ethical summary shows the combination: *The grace of God which bringeth salvation to all men hath appeared, teaching us that, denying ungodliness and worldly lusts, we should live soberly, righteously, and godly:* the παιδεύουσα is the Divine discipline; the σωφρόνως is the human; and they concur in the perfection which is the Saviour's design. The whole man is the object of this self-government; nothing is excluded, not even the will which itself governs. The law is vigorous as to THOUGHTS, which generally mean the secret motives. These are amenable to control, but not without much discipline: *Keep thy heart with all diligence.* The government of the tongue is still more emphatically pre- scribed: the tongue being generally the expression of the inward life; particularly the organ of worship to God and the instrument of usefulness to man. St. James has expounded here some of the Lord's most strict sayings: *By thy words thou shalt be justified, and by thy words thou shalt be condemned. If any man offend not in word, the same is a perfect man. So speak ye, and so do, as they that shall be judged by the law of liberty.* Here WORD AND DEED are com- bined as another Apostle combines them: *whatsoever ye do in word or deed!* Lastly, all the actions, greater or less, of life are to be ordered in all things and true. Of this St. Paul, the special teacher of self-government, has given in his own example the crowning precept, *I therefore so run, not as uncertainly:* words which, when interpreted by the whole context, show what the minute control of the entire life should be. But SELF-RESIGNA- TION to the guidance of the Spirit is the secret of all the virtues which belong to the process of the internal transformation. This grace is peculiarly Christian; and is known by many names. As the Spirit is a Teacher and Guide, it is subjection to His will, both passive and active. As He is a Friend, it is the sympathy with His design and yielding to it: *Grieve not the Holy Spirit of God. Quench not the Spirit.* While this last may refer rather to the restraint sometimes put upon His extraordinary influence, the former refers to the soul's habitual reverence and awe in the consciousness of an internal Divine monitor. The general and

Tit. ii. 11, 12.

Prov. iv. 23.

Matt. xii. 37.
Jas. iii. 1.
Jas. ii. 12.

Col. iii. 17.

1 Cor. ix. 26.

Self- Resigna- tion.

Eph. iv. 30.
1 Thess. v. 19.

Gal. v. 25. universal duty is : *If we live in the Spirit, let us also walk in the Spirit.* The interior rule of the Holy Ghost is the new secret of Christian ethics : a secret dimly felt after in heathen philosophy, promised in the Old Testament, and fully imparted in the New.

Conser-vative Graces. II. Next come the various graces of self-preservation : as they are summed up in WATCHFULNESS, which implies a perpetual consideration of danger from without ; and SOBRIETY, which is the perpetual guard over the state of the soul within. St. Peter

1 Pet. iv. 7. unites these most impressively : *Be ye therefore sober, and watch unto prayer :* here the Christian is surrounded by the snares of the passing world ; while *Be sober, be vigilant,* applies the same exhortation in the face of the spiritual adversaries of the soul. His

Matt. xxvi. 40, 41. words are only the echo of his Master's : *Watch and pray, that ye enter not into temptation : the spirit indeed is willing, but the flesh is weak.* Combining these passages of our Lord and the Apostle whose office it was to strengthen his brethren, we have the relation of Watchfulness to the flesh, the world, and the devil. We mark also that its value as a grace is not only that it prepares for temptation but that it also protects against it. And, finally, when we hear the Redeemer saying, *Could ye not watch with Me one hour ?* we learn that this virtue also is to be practised in union with Christ, in Whom alone the spirit was willing and the flesh not weak. SELF-EXAMINATION is that general watchfulness exercised at set times ; and issuing in self-knowledge and self-distrust, as opposed to careless living and presumption. This duty is enforced by the moralists of every school ; it is taught by the light of nature, according to the adage which expresses a universal instinct, KNOW THYSELF. Hence we do not find it expressly enjoined as a practice : it underlies all New-Testament ethics. Some most solemn enforcements of it are in St. Paul's writings. One has reference to the supreme question of an indwelling Saviour.

2 Cor. xiii. 5. *Examine yourselves whether ye be in the faith ; prove your own selves. Know ye not your own selves, how that Jesus Christ is in you, except ye be reprobates ?* Another aims against self-deception in the general

Gal. vi. 3, 4. business of religion : *If a man think himself to be something, when he is nothing, he deceiveth himself. But let every man prove his own work.* And yet another has reference to the preparation for

1 Cor. xi. 31. the Lord's Supper : *If we would judge ourselves, we should not be*

judged: self-judgment and the Lord's judgment are alone mentioned, and in a very remarkable conjunction. But the duty of self-examination requires itself to be guarded against morbid self-anatomy, and especially against certain perversions of it under human direction. The supreme safeguard is that it be conducted according to the standard of Scripture, and in the presence of the Searcher of hearts. *God is my witness, Whom I serve with my spirit,* is Rom. i. 9. St. Paul's example. But there is none more impressive than that of David, in his Psalm of the Omniscient. Examining his life, he could appeal in defence of his integrity to his God: but examining more deeply his heart, he would fain withdraw that appeal. The result is the affecting cry: *Search me, O God, and know my heart; try me and know my thoughts; and see if there be any wicked way in me, and lead me in the way everlasting.* To the earnest Christian who serves God in his spirit, self-examination must be more or less an habitual state of soul as well as an occasional practice.

Ps. cxxxix. 23, 24.

THE VIRTUES OF CONFIDENCE.

CONFIDENCE as to the issue of the Christian conflict gives birth to some bright graces, and is the animating principle of many noble virtues. These are some of them active, and some passive, and such as combine both characters.

Confidence.

1. What men call COURAGE the New Testament terms Virtue, or ἀρετή, which St. Peter places first among the graces that Faith inspires. But St. Paul dwells on it still more; it runs indeed through his whole ethical teaching. *Watch ye, stand fast in the faith, quit you like men, be strong.* This quaternion is one of the Apostle's unique passages. Ἀνδρίζεσθε, κραταιοῦσθε, are a reminiscence of the Old Testament; but in their Christian meaning the former is an injunction to manly and heroic energy, and the latter precept gives the reason of it in the strength which we are supposed to obtain from above. The relation of the believer to an indwelling Saviour, Whose Spirit unites His servant to Himself, gives this ethical principle a peculiarity which needs not to be here dilated on. *Be strong in the Lord, and in the power of His might,* says all that requires to be said. *I can do all things through Christ Which strengtheneth me.* There is no inbred infection of the

Virtue.

1 Cor. xvi. 13.

Eph. vi. 10. Phil. iv. 13.

flesh, no power of seduction or terror in the world, no malignity of superior beings, that should daunt the Christian man.

2. Corresponding with this is the grace of PATIENCE, which is indeed linked with it by the term FORTITUDE. It is a passive grace of the entire Christian life, though St. James gives it a Jas. i. 4. work to do : *let patience have her perfect work.* Strictly speaking this virtue has three aspects : one towards the providential appointments of God, which will be hereafter considered as SUB-MISSION ; another, towards the injuries of men, when it is rather to be called MEEKNESS ; and a third, towards the toilsome processes of the Christian life and manifold conflict. It is this we now consider, and must assign it a high place and important function. It secures against impatience with self ; and strengthens the soul to persist notwithstanding many failures. It arms the mind with fortitude in the midst of the never-ceasing assaults of the world. And it suffers with magnanimity the manifold onsets 1 Pet. v. 9. of Satan, knowing that *the same afflictions are accomplished* in the brethren everywhere. While this grace is most important, it must of course be guarded against the abuses to which its tolerance is liable : it must be combined with a vehement longing for final and eternal freedom from evil. But HOPE is everywhere in Scripture the inspiring grace of the great conflict ; being both passive and active. It is a grace that, like Patience, has many aspects. 1 Tim. i. 1. The word itself has a wide range of meanings. Christ is OUR HOPE, as the Pillar and Ground of all human expectation through Col. i. 23. the *hope of the Gospel.* Hope also is one of the theological graces, with Faith and Charity, being a blessed combination of the two others : it is Faith looking only to the future, but looking at it with the expectation of love. Undoubtedly, however, the Christian grace of Hope is most generally connected with the joyful expectation of future victory. Thus the Apostle Paul exhorts to Rom. xii. 12. a *rejoicing in hope,* the counterpart of being *patient in tribulation.* 1 John iii. 3. As we have seen it is both active and passive. *Every man that hath this hope in Him, purifieth himself :* his hope in the Supreme Fountain and Pattern of purity animates him to purify his own 1 Thess. v. 8. soul. *Putting on the breastplate of faith and love ; and for an helmet, the hope of salvation :* where the helmet is the defence, the passive defence, of the otherwise unprotected head.

3. Lastly, there is a grace which has many names in the New Testament, but not one in particular, and may be characterised as the glorying of the soul in God's work within it. St. Paul speaks much of exultation in the Lord and the riches of His grace. In one remarkable passage he strips man of all his own boasting: *that no flesh should glory in His presence.* Then after showing what Christ is made to the believer, he adds, *that, according as it is written, He that glorieth, let him glory in the Lord.* Here then we have the counterpart of that ethical principle with which this section began, the abhorrence of self. The utter contempt of self apart from God is quite consistent with religious complacency in the operation of God in edifying the new man. This tranquil and rational confidence in the new character sustained by Divine grace the Apostle means when he bids us *walk worthy of the vocation wherewith ye are called.* And the same also when he bids the Philippians think on and do *whatsoever things are honest,* or σεμνά, dignified and decorous. This precept may take the form of CONTEMPT towards sin: not only we are bidden to *abhor that which is evil,* but also to be ashamed of it, and to disdain every vice, great and small. Of some vices, indeed, the Christian moralist speaks as if the very mention of them was discreditable. The best illustration, however, of this feature in the ethical teaching of the New Testament is the way in which the Apostles refer to the several classes of virtues and vices that belong respectively to the unregenerate and to the regenerate character. They all and unanimously describe the one as the works of an evil and condemned nature, the other as the product of a Divine and heavenly Spirit. They do not speak of vices as the growth of human nature simply, but as belonging to the flesh, as from below, and as pertaining to the old man which is corrupt and condemned. It is impossible to exaggerate the importance of this ethical principle in the teaching of the New Testament. It is equally impossible to define it exactly: its force must be felt rather than learnt by definition. All the Apostles set in opposite array the virtues and vices: always with a note that the latter are products of a condemned and dying evil habit, and the former the growth of an omnipotent internal energy. St. Paul gives a cardinal instance of what is meant. He calls emphatic attention to his dictum:

1 Cor. i. 29, 30, 31.

Eph. iv. 1.

Phil. iv. 8.

Rom. xii. 9.

Gal. v. 16
—24. *This I say then, Walk in the Spirit, and ye shall not fulfil the lust of the flesh.* And then he gives the most complete catalogue of the sins which humanity abhors, and of which it is ashamed. *Now the works of the flesh are manifest, which are these : adultery, fornication, uncleanness, lasciviousness, idolatry, witchcraft, hatred, variance, emulations, wrath, strife, seditions, heresies, envyings, murders, drunkenness, revellings, and such like.* Here is a confused mass of all lawlessness, against which every law of God and man is set. The very description is, as it were, scornful and contemptuous. There is no sin against God, and the neighbour, and the self, which may not be traced here. They are all *works of the flesh.* The catalogue includes sin under every aspect, but it is significantly said that *they that are Christ's have crucified the flesh with its affections and lusts.* They are the dying product of an expiring principle. But *the fruit of the Spirit* is described as the organic result of the tree of life in the soul : *love, joy, peace, long-suffering, gentleness, goodness, faith, meekness, temperance.* While the sins enumerated are the works of the flesh, active and spontaneous though morally dead, the opposite virtues are the fruit and the work of the eternally Living Spirit. Death cannot resist life. The abominable vices that both begin and end the evil catalogue—as if the career of the flesh was rounded with lust—are opposed by the heavenly virtues of religion. Love leads the army in this war, and self-restraint brings up the rear. Christian character has here its most beautiful description as a band of militant graces, each of which is passive and tranquil. MEEKNESS is our Lord's own special grace : it is humility as passively resisting evil. JOY is a grace which becomes a virtue, and ought to be encouraged as duty. So also PEACE, which here includes the opposite of variance. LONG-SUFFERING, or tolerant bearing of wrong, rising into benignity or GENTLENESS and GOODNESS, which thinks only of getting and diffusing good, lead to general FAITH in GOD and the eternal triumph of goodness, a triumph which is assured. St. Peter gives the graces of religion which insure against falling in the contest with sin. DILIGENCE is his general preface and 2 Pet. i. 4, 5, 6. motto; FAITH is the mother grace, as the LOVE by which it works is in St. Paul; the great conflict has for its issue the escaping *the corruption that is in the world through lust* and being

partakers of the Divine nature. Here, however, the graces are seven : VIRTUE, or Divine-human energy ; KNOWLEDGE ; TEMPERANCE ; PATIENCE, or submission with hope ; GODLINESS ; BROTHERLY-KINDNESS ; CHARITY. This Apostle also aims to inspire the confidence of which we are now speaking. But no encouragement is more emphatic than that of St. James : *Wherefore* lay apart all filthiness and superfluity of naughtiness, and receive with meekness the engrafted Word : evil is something added that must be put away, leaving nature in its integrity ; yet this is not nature, but the engrafted Word. To this must be added his description of the wisdom which descendeth from heaven. As *wisdom that is from above* contrasted with that which is *earthly, sensual, devilish.*

Jas. i. 21.

Jas. iii. 15, 17.

ETHICS OF CHRISTIAN SERVICE.

The service of God bears in Christian ethics a special relation to Christ as our Lord. The duties and graces of this relation are many ; and they may be summed up under the several heads of absorbing devotion to the common Master ; self-sacrificing zeal for the good of all the objects of His charity for His sake ; fidelity to our trust and stewardship in all its branches.

Christian Service.

This extensive department of Christian ethics needs not to be entered upon very fully ; as much of it has been already and much will be hereafter introduced under other heads.

I. It has been already seen that the Christian religion has this great characteristic, that it makes Jesus, the GOD-MAN, the End of human life. It also makes Him in a special sense the Lord and Master of that life as our sphere of service to Him ; and it is with this ethical principle that we now have to do.

1. It unites all Christians in one common cause. On the eve of His passion, when our Lord gave a final summary of His will, He asserted His claim in the most affecting manner : *Ye call Me Master and Lord, and ye say well ; for so I am.* But this was not a relation of the Apostles alone : they represented the entire Christian fellowship, united to one Teacher and one Lord, through

Devotion to our Lord.

John xiii. 13.

Col. iii. 24.

1 Cor. vii. 22. all its orders down to the lowest to whom St. Paul said, *Ye serve the Lord Christ.* The slave to whom he addressed these words is now *the Lord's freeman;* and their estate of slavery, unchristian in itself, served to illustrate that absolute free bondage to Christ which is the glory and the first law of all Christian service.

2. Hence it absorbs all the actions of life. The duty of the Col. iii. 17. Christian is to *do all in the name of the Lord Jesus.* This is the new, all-pervading, sovereign and blessed law of human probation: penetrating to the minutest detail, and giving to every Col. iii. 23. act a character of reality, dignity, and cheerfulness: *Whatsoever ye do, do it heartily, as to the Lord, and not unto men.* This ethical principle of our religion needs no further illustration. It is the law, written or unwritten, that gathers Christian ethics into unity. Its sanction is clothed with all the terrors of the judgment. And its reward is the supreme approbation of the Lord Himself, Who still says to those who with perfect loyalty and unlimited John xiii. 13.

Devotion to Man. devotion call Him Lord, *Ye say well,* I AM : καλῶς λέγετε, εἰμὶ γάρ.

II. The Christian standard of devotion to the interests of our fellow-creatures is higher than it had ever entered the heart of man, until Christ came, to conceive. It requires all His followers to aspire to the charity of the Lord Himself, and to imitate His example in the self-sacrifice of their life. Outside of Christianity no such standard as this is to be found; though in many ethical systems an unconscious and undirected aspiration to it may be John xii. 24. perceived. When our Lord said, *Except a corn of wheat fall into the ground and die, it abideth alone; but if it die, it bringeth forth much fruit,* He spoke of His own glorification through perfect self-sacrifice for man. But in this the servant must be as his Lord; John xii. 26. for He added, *If any man serve Me let him follow Me.* And again, after rehearsing in the feetwashing the morrow's great self-sacrifice, He enjoined upon His followers the imitation both of John xiii. 15. His spirit and of His act: *I have given you an example, that ye should do as I have done to you.* The law of perfect service is simply and purely the law of SELF-SACRIFICE, which in union with the Redeemer and in imitation of Him makes the whole of life a ministration to mankind. But some side-lights are thrown upon this principle that bring it within the range of human possibility and show its consistency with the whole system of Christian ethics. These let us briefly consider.

1. It is the necessary consequence of union with Christ and consecration to Him. St. Paul prefaces the sublimest exhibition of the supreme self-sacrifice by the words : *Let this mind be in you which was also in Christ Jesus,* where the φρονείσθω ἐν ὑμῖν ὃ καὶ ἐν Χριστῷ Ἰησοῦ expresses very strongly the thought that the Redeemer's sentiment must needs, if not hindered, fill His servants also : let the supernatural order of grace have its course. At the same time it suggests that this is an ASPIRATION towards a lofty ideal which is not easily attained. In one remarkable passage, however, he goes far to express its attainableness. *The love of Christ constraineth us :* where the συνέχει seems like an echo of the Master's passion-words before the Passion, *how am I straitened !* πῶς συνέχομαι. It is the sublime feeling which knows *no man after the flesh,* but which yearns after the salvation of all men *in the bowels of Jesus Christ.* In New-Testament ethics this absolute self-renunciation for mankind is at least the legitimate ideal of the spirit of the Christian's service. *Phil. ii. 5.* *2 Cor. v. 14, 16.* *Luke xii. 50.* *Phil. i. 8.*

2. It is, however, an ethical standard which may be best studied in connection with the virtues and vices belonging to this domain. The Christian teaching denounces SELFISHNESS in all its forms, pursuing it as it was never pursued before through all its disguises. But here we consider it as an evil that may cling to the Lord's servant. As such it is overcome by the CHARITY which embraces every opportunity of doing good to the bodies and souls of men, and which is called BROTHERLY KINDNESS if shown towards those of the same religious household. A large part of the very last document of Scripture, St. John's First Epistle, is occupied with the enforcement of this grace, and without making careful distinction between the Christian and the non-Christian objects of it. Here HUMILITY esteems every gift as from God, and thinks soberly of self, *according as God hath dealt to every man the measure of faith.* The SOBRIETY in the spirit of the labourer for Christ may be opposed to all ENVY or jealousy of others and all over-valuation of personal importance : it being implied that the Administrator of gifts does not bestow upon any one more than a small amount. But it is certainly intended to show the neces- *Opposite Vices.* *Rom. xii. 3.*

sity of remembering always how transcendently more important the good of others, the edification of the Body, and the salvation of souls, is than the measure of any one person's contribution of effort. He who remembers the boundless work that has to be done in the world, will not *think of himself more highly than he ought to think:* the Apostle who gave the precept was too much absorbed with the grandeur of the charity in which he was engaged to think for a moment about himself at all. INSENSIBILITY to the wants of men, or apathy, or want of zeal, has no place in the Christian heart. St. Paul complains bitterly: *I have no man likeminded, who will naturally care for your state. For all seek their own, not the things that are Jesus Christ's.* The natural instinct of those who are devoted to the Lord leads them to care for all who are His, and for themselves only as included among them. In short, the ethics of the New Testament are always tending, whether they reach it or not, to the point of an entirely disinterested charity, whether as it regards the love of God Himself or the love of the neighbour for God's sake.

III. Fidelity is the watchword of another wide department of the ethics of Christian service. It is that grace in the servant which shows him to be worthy of his Master's trust. Two passages, beginning and ending the New-Testament teaching on the subject, place it in the true light. As to the servant trusted our Lord says: *Who then is that faithful and wise steward whom his lord shall make ruler over his household? Blessed is that servant!* The servant is an οἰκονόμος, and the steward is a δοῦλος. St. Paul gives the description of the faithful servant as *showing all good fidelity:* πίστιν πᾶσαν ἀγαθήν. The same word πίστις which expresses our trust in God's fidelity expresses His trust in ours. It is a grace which stands alone as having the epithet *good,* and it must pervade the whole of life. The verb which mediates between faithful and fidelity is found in St. Paul's words concerning his stewardship of the Gospel, but may be universally applied: οἰκονομίαν πεπίστευμαι, *a dispensation is committed unto me,* or *I have been trusted with a stewardship.* Here then are all the elements of our ethics: the Master commits a trust, and the trustworthy servant shows fidelity in all things. It may be added that the very faith which trusts God is the strength of the faithfulness

Marginal notes:
Rom. xii. 3.
Phil. ii. 20, 21.
Fidelity.
Luke xii. 42, 43.
Titus ii. 10.
1 Cor. ix. 17.

which God may trust. We have now to trace the applications of this principle, giving under each a few examples which represent many. No ethical principle is more pervasive.

1. Christ's servant holds his own person in trust, *For ye are bought with a price: therefore glorify God in your body, and in your spirit, which are God's.* We are specially the property of Christ: *whether we live therefore or die, we are the Lord's.* The CARE OF SELF is part of our stewardship as we are entrusted with our own persons. On this is to be based the duty of preserving health, training the body to its utmost efficiency, cultivating every faculty of the mind, and keeping the whole man in the highest possible vigour: *ready for every good work,* and *meet for the Master's use.* St. Paul inculcates on Timothy a due solicitude both for spiritual and for bodily health: as to the former, *Keep thyself pure* is a general principle; and as to the latter, *Drink no longer water* may be quoted as a significant hint. Perhaps there are few applications of the principle of fidelity which are more neglected than this. Every one of us is put in charge with his spirit, and soul, and body, to educate them to the highest pitch of service for the longest possible time, and in the most perfect possible vigour.

[margin: 1 Cor. vi. 20.]

[margin: Rom. xiv. 8.]

[margin: 1 Tim. v. 22, 23.]

2. Fidelity extends to the whole of life, with special reference to our individual vocation. Nothing is excluded from the sphere of this duty. The whole compass of life must be governed by it, and the true Christian is, what St. Paul exhorts the wives of deacons to be, *faithful in all things.* They are *the faithful,* oἱ πιστοί, as being *believers:* one word embraces both meanings. Their final seal is that of being *called, and chosen, and faithful.* But the duty is very generally connected with the special vocation. The difference here marked is shown in two parables of our Lord which are the key to all His many parables on this subject. In the one He *called His ten servants and delivered them ten pounds, and said unto them, Occupy till I come.* All His servants have one common gift of life to profit withal. In the other, *unto one He gave five talents, to another two, and to another one; to every man according to his several ability.* In both the reckoning is strict; both the equal pounds and the unequal talents are specially entrusted; they show in a certain sense that all servants have a special vocation; and yet they seem to note a difference between

[margin: Vocation.]

[margin: 1 Tim. iii. 11. Acts x.45. Rev. xvii. 14.]

[margin: Luke xix. 13.]

[margin: Matt. xxv. 15.]

what is common to all and what is proper to each.   With regard
1 Cor.iv.2.   to special ministries and vocations, St. Paul says, *it is required in*
stewards that a man be found faithful ; of himself he testifies that
1Tim.i.12.   Christ Jesus *counted me trustworthy, putting me into the ministry.* Of
Heb. iii. 1,   this fidelity our Lord Himself is the supreme pattern : *Wherefore,*
2.   *holy brethren, partakers of the heavenly vocation, consider the Apostle*
and High Priest of our profession, Christ Jesus: Who was faithful to
Him that appointed Him.   But this glorious example blends again
special vocation with the general calling of life ; for we all must be
Heb. xii.   *looking unto Jesus the Author and Finisher of the Faith,* and of fidelity
2.   to the Faith.   We reach the same conclusion when we recall how
constant is the reference to fidelity in the use of special oppor-
tunities and faculties of usefulness : especially that which the
Luke xii.   possession of earthly goods affords.   Here the virtue of PRUDENCE,
42.   or economical wisdom, is allied with fidelity : *Who then is that*
faithful and wise steward?   The parable of the Unjust Steward,
apart from its more general meaning, stamps this precept with
Luke xvi.   deep impressiveness.   *Make to yourselves friends of the mammon of*
9, 10, 13.   *unrighteousness.   He that is faithful in that which is least is faithful*
also in much.   No servant can serve two masters.   In these last
words we have the Christian Lawgiver's law of fidelity in its
highest principle and its lowest application.   It is the supreme
reference of all things to one Master and one service ; and it is
the prudent and faithful observance of that law in the most sedu-
lous and scrupulous care of the least trifles of life.

Test.   3. Fidelity, as the test applied to service, is guarded by
threatenings and stimulated by the hope of reward.   It is a duty
as well as a virtue ; nor is there any obligation in ethics which is
more closely bound up with human responsibility.

Sanctions.   (1.) It is not necessary here to dwell on the nature of the
punishment reserved for unfaithfulness : we have to do only with
the character stamped on it by our Lord.   He uses three terms
Matt.xxv.   which give this department of ethics an awful solemnity.   *Thou*
26, 30.   WICKED *and* SLOTHFUL *servant !   Cast ye the* UNPROFITABLE *servant*
into outer darkness.   Wicked in his heart, slothful in His Master's
business, and unprofitable both to himself and to his lord !   The
weeping and gnashing of teeth fearfully indicate that the penalty is
an abiding regret which is no other than hopeless remorse.   The

only mitigation is the proportion of the doom, *But he that knew* Luke xii.
not, and did commit things worthy of stripes, shall be beaten with few 48.
*stripes. For unto whomsoever much is given, of him shall be much
required.* It must never be forgotten that the far larger part of
the references to the final judgment make it the test of servant-
fidelity : at least in the case of Christian believers.

(2.) The rewards promised to Fidelity are represented in many Rewards.
lights. It brings its own recompense in the Master's approval,
who does not wait for the end to say *Well done, good and* Matt.xxv.
faithful servant! That will be the crowning blessedness of a per- 23.
sistent fidelity : *enter thou into the joy of thy Lord.* As unfaithfulness is followed by a withdrawal of the trust, so fidelity increases
it : *thou hast been faithful over a few things, I will make thee ruler* Matt.xxv.
over many things. Faithful stewardship in probation leads to a 21.
stewardship whose probation will have ceased for ever. But
another element of the reward brings it back to the present life.
Henceforth I call you not servants ; for the servant knoweth not what John xv.
his lord doeth : but I have called you friends ; for all things that I 15.
have heard of My Father I have made known unto you. They who
enter hereafter into the Lord's joy enter now into His secrets and
confidence. Their service is the service of friendship ; while their
friendship is the friendship of servants. Here is the inmost
secret of our ethics of service, which once more bases them on
union with Christ. It is this lastly which explains how the
reward is *reckoned of grace.* While we must say : *We are unprofitable* Rom.iv.4.
servants ; we have done that which was our duty to do, He, in His Luke xvii.
boundless grace, will say the opposite of this. Forgiving the 10.
neglect of our service, and not remembering in how many
instances we have not *done the things which are commanded,* He will
reckon to our own poor fidelity the virtue of His own faithfulness, 2 John 8.
and we shall *receive a full reward, μισθὸν πλήρη.*

ETHICS OF GODLINESS.

The last department of specially Christian ethics, the
issue and consummation of all the rest, pervading all
and crowning all, comprises the duties, virtues, and graces

that have GOD alone for their Object. These may be
summed up in the one word Piety or Godliness; which is
the Christian character as based upon Entire Consecration,
is expressed in the Worship of praise and prayer, and
issues in Union with God.

CONSECRATION TO GOD.

Consecration to God is the entire oblation of Self to
the Author of our being according to the terms of the
covenant of grace. This being its principle, it is evidenced
in Devotion, active and passive: devotion to the will of
His commandments and to the will of His providential
appointments; that is Obedience and Submission.

ENTIRE SELF-SURRENDER.

Self-Con-
secration.
The principles of entire self-surrender have been laid down
under the doctrine of Sanctification. It is necessary here only to
make some observations on its ethical bearing.

1. It is the beginning, the strength, and the consummation of
all religion as the human service of God. As man's act it is
negative and positive. It is the absolute renunciation of pro-
prietorship in self: *Whosoever he be of you that forsaketh not all that*
he hath, he cannot be My disciple. Know ye not that . . . . ye are not
your own? for ye are bought with a price. It is the absolute surrender
of the whole being to God: *Yield yourselves unto God.* This self-surrender is to be made in the strength of the grace of redemption,
the salvation of the Gospel being its argument and its strength:
I beseech you therefore by the mercies of God that ye present your bodies a
living sacrifice, holy, acceptable unto God, which is your reasonable service.
These words sum up the whole doctrine. Religion, or godliness,
is the habitual, conscious, never interrupted, offering up of the
spirit, soul and body, to the service of the Living God in the
entire activity of life: the self surrendering self.

2. This consecration is unto universal Submission, which is
active and passive. As active it is the devotion of the heart to the

Luke xix.
33.
1 Cor. vi.
19, 20.
Rom. vi.
13.

Rom. xii.
1.

performance of all the commandments of God as they constitute His one will: this is Obedience, the first and all-embracing duty of the creature towards the Creator as Moral Governor: an obligation expressed in many ways throughout the two Testaments, and literally absolute, being the foundation alike of the Law and of the Gospel, which is itself the announcement of the new *obedience of faith.* As passive it is the duty and grace of entire Self-abandonment to all the appointments of Divine providence as they are either afflictive or as they are inscrutable; in the former case, it is RESIGNATION; in the latter it is this conjoined with Acquiescence, or silent submission to the will of God. Obedience

Rom. xvi. 26.

Resignation.

WORSHIP.

The worship of God is the highest expression of the religious spirit, offering to God the creature's tribute in Praise, or uttering the creature's need in Prayer. These may be regarded as distinct and as united in the spirit and habit of devotion.

I. Many terms have been sanctified in the language of religious mankind to express the highest tribute of the human spirit to the Supreme. In Holy Scripture these terms are varied, expressing the sentiment of Reverence whence all worship springs; the act of Adoration which silently and Praise which audibly extols the Divine Name and Perfections; and Thanksgiving which expresses gratitude for the mercies of God. Praise.

1. REVERENCE is the supreme and eternal duty and grace of the created spirit. It is both the source and the issue of all godliness. The three passages, *Holy and reverend is His name! Hallowed be Thy Name! Sanctify the Lord Christ in your hearts!* in their combination teach us first how awful is God in Himself, then that the coming of His kingdom is the universal acknowledgment of His majesty, and finally that this reverence must be the inmost sentiment of our individual hearts. Reverence is fear tempered by love. In the Old Testament the fear predominated, in the New Testament the love; but the sentiment of reverence pervades all religion on earth and in heaven. Whether as sacred dread or loving fear, it abideth always. As the spirit formed by religion it is universal in its influence. It is the habitual sense of the Awe.

Ps. cxi. 9. Matt. vi. 9. 1 Pet. iii. 15.

Presence of God that gives dignity to life, and makes the character of him who cultivates it venerable. It extends to all Divine things as well as to the Name of God Himself: to His Word, to His ordinances, to His created temple of the world, and to all that is His. In His Presence more particularly it is AWE.

Praise.

2. PRAISE proper is in Scriptural language either Adoration or Blessing. Adoration, as the word indicates (from Os the mouth) is the prostration which as it were kisses the earth at the Divine feet. It stands for every act in which the spirit of reverence expresses itself. The Hebrew term שָׁחָה is sometimes used, like the Greek προσκυνεῖν, to indicate homage before the creature. But the closing words of the New Testament shows its highest and only true application: refusing the Apostle's lower prostration the angel said: *worship God.* But the prostrate mouth speaks in Blessing and Praise. *Hallelujah! Praise ye the Lord!* is in both Testaments the most exulting of all notes. The Hebrew בָּרַךְ, to bless, is often translated by praise. This term, however, like adoration, has a human as well as a Divine application. Moreover, it is wide in its range. *In thee shall all families of the earth be blessed :* this is the Benediction of God to man, which becomes in another passage *shall bless themselves,* or shall rejoice before God. Again, *daily shall He be blessed* (or *praised*) is the return of benediction to Heaven. But here it is observable that Christ is, in the unity of the Father, the object of this supreme praise. The term Blessed, or εὐλογητός, is used in the New Testament only of God and of Christ. The *Son of the Blessed* is Himself *God blessed for ever.* Other Scriptural terms might be mentioned, variations on these words and having reference to the forms of praise in public worship; but these we need not discuss in particular. Christian individual devotion employs a variety of expressions which are not necessarily derived from Scripture; and it is an important principle of reverence that these should be always reserved exclusively for their highest uses. To sum up all: the devout spirit offers to God the ADORATION of a creature, the HOMAGE of a subject or servant, the PRAISE of a worshipper.

Rev. xxii. 9.
Ps. cl. i.
Rev. xix. 1.

Gen. xii. 3.
Gen. xxii. 18.
Ps. lxxii. 15.

Mark xiv. 61.
Rom. ix. 5.

Thanks-giving.

3. THANKSGIVING is a duty of which GRATITUDE is the grace. This obligation of godliness is acknowledged by the universal sentiment of mankind; but as a Christian grace it has some

blessed peculiarities. It is gratitude, as for all the benefits of Divine providence, so especially for the general and personal gifts of redemption. The very term most in use shows this; it is Χάρις, which is the Grace of God in Christ, operating in the soul of the believer as a principle, and going back to Him in gratitude: *Thanks be unto God for His unspeakable gift.* The ethical gratitude of Christianity connects every good gift and every perfect gift with the Gift of Christ. Moreover, it is a thanksgiving which in the Christian economy, and in it alone, redounds to God for all things: *in everything give thanks.* This characteristic flows from the former. The rejoicing which we have in the Lord, and the everlasting consolation we possess in Him, makes every possible variety of Divine dispensation a token for good. The Christian privilege is to find reason for gratitude in all things: *for this is the will of God in Christ Jesus concerning you.* 2 Cor. ix. 15.

1 Thess. v. 18.

II. PRAYER is, like brotherly love, a duty in the obligations of which all men are, as it were, naturally θεοδίδακτοι, *taught of God.* It is the expression of man's dependence upon God for all things. Its general grounds have been discussed already, and will be considered more fully under the Means of Grace: it is here viewed only as belonging to the ethics of the Christian character, in its spirit and in its acts. Prayer.

1 Thess. iv. 9.

1. What habitual reverence is to praise, the habitual sense of dependence is to prayer. Nothing less than this is signified in the injunctions that *men ought always to pray,* and *pray without ceasing*: if the former refers rather to the importunity of request, the latter inculcates the duty of evermore, consciously or unconsciously, waiting upon God. Both are united in the words: *praying always with all prayer and supplication.* More particularly the spirit of prayer depends upon three elements: First, the inwrought habit of mentally connecting with every action of life the Supreme, for *in Him we live, and move, and have our being;* secondly, the abiding consciousness of dependence on the Mediator through whose constant advocacy our spiritual life is sustained; and, lastly, the presence of the Spirit of adoption in our hearts, Who *maketh intercession for us with groanings which cannot be uttered.* Here is the deep secret of the spirit of prayer. *He that searcheth the hearts knoweth what is the mind of the Spirit, that He maketh* Spirit of Prayer.

Lu. xviii. 1.

1 Thess. v. 17.

Eph. vi. 18.

Acts xvii. 28.

Rom. viii. 26, 27.

intercession for the saints according to God. The φρόνημα τοῦ Πνεύ-

7.

ματος is according to God what the *carnal mind,* φρόνημα τῆς σαρκός, is according to fallen nature : the habitual movement of the *unspoken* impulse. The Spirit's groaning intercession within the veil of the heart answers exactly to the intercession of the High Priest within the veil of heaven ; and both are without interval or rest. Hence the duty of PERSEVERANCE in de-

Rom. xii.
12.

votion refers to insistency in particular requests and the *continuing instant in prayer: instant* for the former, *continuing* for the latter. To combine these two is perfection.

Acts of
Prayer.

2. The formal acts of prayer are manifold, expressed by a number of terms common to both Testaments, and combining the spirit and the act. The leading word προσευχή is one of those. It is always prayer to God, and that without limitation.

Phil. iv.
6.

When St. Paul exhorts, *in everything by prayer and supplication with thanksgiving let your requests be made known unto God,* he distinguishes from this general PRAYER the δέησις, or SUPPLICATION for individual benefits. It is the difference between prayer and petition. The REQUESTS of the supplication, αἰτήματα, simply express the individuality of the prayer : the supplication noting our need (δεῖ), and the request the utterance of that need. When

John xvi.
23.

our Saviour said, *In that day ye shall ask Me nothing,* He used another term signifying, in the case of the disciples, the interrogation of perplexity : there it is ἐρωτᾶν, which is changed for αἰτεῖν in what follows : *Verily, verily, I say unto you, whatsoever ye shall ask the Father in My name, He will give it you.* The former word is used of our Lord's own prayer, never the latter : hence the former has in it more of familiarity, and is never used of human prayer. Save, indeed, in one passage, which leads us to the

Interces-
sion.
1 John v.
16.

prayer of INTERCESSION. St. John changes αἰτήσει into ἐρωτήσῃ concerning the sin unto death, *I do not say that he shall pray for it :* we may ask in confidence concerning every other sin, but concerning this we are to leave the ἐρωτᾶν to Christ. Intercessory prayer has no term to express our precise idea of it. The exhorta-

Eph. vi.
18.
1 Tim. ii.
1.

tion is generally to *supplication for all saints,* and *for all men,* after the example of the Lord's intercession. In the passage to Timothy St. Paul uses for once the word ἐντεύξεις, intercessions, which however means familiar and confident prayers, as coming from the word ἐντυγχάνειν, literally to fall in with a person and enter into familiar speech with him. In the strength of Christ's intercession we also are commanded to intercede, or to speak confidently with God on behalf of others : save indeed with the one reservation mentioned above. Intercessory prayer must blend with all our supplications ; as our Lord teaches in the solitary command which He gives concerning private prayer, *enter into thy closet,* when *the Father Which seeth in secret* is to be addressed as *Our Father!* and the individual supplication not lost in but blended with the common prayer. *When thou hast shut thy door* is the Mediator's solemn injunction of formal, habitual, regular private exercises of devotion : confirming the injunctions and examples of all Scripture. But the devout soul everywhere can shut the doors of the senses, and sink into the presence of God : there worshipping with all the effect of local seclusion, and by EJACULATORY prayer holding habitual communion with Him who makes the heart of the regenerate His temple.

Private Prayer. Matt. vi. 6, 9.

III. The perfection of these supreme offices of devotion is seen only in their combination. United they constitute Worship, as it respects God ; as it respects man, the spirit of devotion ; and in their effect upon the religious life one constantly reacts upon the other to the gradual perfection of both.

Worship.

1. Divine worship as the highest offices of religion embraces both elements : the presentation to God of His tribute, and the supplication of His benefits. In the first and only description of that worship which our Lord Himself gave, contained in His conversation with the woman of Samaria, He used again and again the one and only word προσκυνεῖν to express the whole service of God : pre-eminently adoration, but including all the σεβάσματα or *devotions* of the worshipper, as St. Paul in a solitary passage terms them. Hence the full meaning of the phrase COMMUNION WITH GOD, as both *giving and receiving.* The word *Hosanna,* which enters the New Testament from the Old, combines prayer and praise : *Hosanna (save now!) to the Son of David. Blessed is He that cometh in the name of the Lord!*

As to God.

Acts xvii. 23.

Phil. iv. 15.

Matt. xxi. 9.

2. The spirit of devotion in the worshipper is blended of praise and prayer. Those are to a great extent indistinguishable. The devotional language of Scripture strikingly illustrates this. To

Spirit of Devotion.

Lam. iii.
25.
seek the Lord in prayer and to wait upon Him in reverent silence
seem to mean the same thing. *The Lord is good unto them that
wait for Him, to the soul that seeketh Him:* the active seeking must
be accompanied and qualified by the passive waiting. Although
there are few positive precepts on the subject, it is obviously the
tendency of revealed religion from beginning to end to inculcate
a service which blends contemplation and the meditative habit
with all prayer. *Let the words of my mouth and the meditation of
my heart be acceptable in Thy sight!* MEDITATION is the silent
pondering of the soul on Divine things through the medium of
the Word, the devout consideration of some particular truth, or
revelation, or promise: as preceding, accompanying, and following all prayer it is the strength and best grace of devotion. CON-
TEMPLATION is the same posture of the devout mind, but with
some exclusive reference to God Himself. It expresses the highest
aim of the soul to behold the Supreme in anticipation of the
eternal Vision. In the devotional ethics of Mysticism the differences of the two stages of meditation and contemplation are much
dwelt upon; and the latter is regarded as the final goal of all
devotion: the state of detachment from every creature and the
pure beholding of God alone as the only Being. Nor does Scripture discourage this sacred ambition; its safeguard, however, is
this, that all contemplation be combined with prayer. The error
of false Mysticism is to believe that the soul may be raised
into a state in which every affection of the heart is stilled
and all emotion lost in the fixed and unchanging beholding of
Him in Whom all desire of personal blessedness is forgotten.

UNION WITH GOD.

As the consummation of all ethical duties is the worship of
God, so the end of all worship is union with Him. To this most
glorious issue all the revelations of Scripture converge. It is the
end of all teaching and the seal of all perfection. Our Lord's
Prayer for His people makes this the goal of Christian aspiration:
*that they all may be one; as Thou, Father, art in Me and I in Thee,
that they also may be one in Us.* But the union with God is, like
all other relations to the Supreme, attained only in and through

the Mediator : *I in them and Thou in Me, that they may be made* John xvii. 23. *perfect in one.* A few observations on this their supreme end and aim may close the department of personal ethics, whether of duties or of graces.

1. Union with God is the realisation of the one object of the redeeming economy. It is the perfect and diametrical opposite of sin, which is in its essence separation from the supreme centre of spiritual life. Sin is the violation of duty, the absence of virtue, the loss of the summum Bonum of blessedness : nothing less than union with God is the perfect restoration to duty, and the consummation of virtue, and the supremest and fullest blessedness. Any view of Christian morality which carries its vision to any point short of this is of necessity defective. Perfect Opposite of Sin.

2. An unhealthy dread of Mysticism has hindered the appreciation of this truth. Union with God has undoubtedly been the watchword of some of the sublimest systems of ethics based on erroneous doctrine. Buddhism in the East and Pantheistic Mysticism in the West are instances : so far as personal ethics are concerned Christianity can find no fault in them but that of deep defect. But their end was not as their beginning. They issued both in the deepest darkness of error : in the East it was the abyss of absolute extinction or Nirvana, and in the West the worse abyss of Antinomian indifference to moral distinctions. But the Union of which we speak is one that preserves inviolate the personal identity of him who attains it : he becomes ONE WITH GOD in thought and feeling and will : the emphasis being laid on the WILL. Error and Truth of this Union.

3. But our Lord's words dwell on that unity with the Supreme Source of life which is to be enjoyed by a corporate fellowship of saints. It cannot be too deeply pondered that the last and highest words, whether of our Lord or of His Apostles St. Paul and St. John, speak of a Body one in the fellowship of the Holy Trinity, and so one that the individual, though not lost, is never again remembered as such. This carries us forward to the next Section.

RELATIVE ETHICS.

The ethics of our relations to our fellow-creatures are inseparably bound up with the ethics of personal character. But they may also be viewed as entirely distinct; or rather as prescribing the obligations of duty in more direct relation to others. First, there are obligations arising out of the common and mutual relations of man and man. Secondly, there are those which are based upon the sacred and necessary relations of domestic society. Thirdly, there are those which are connected with the voluntary or accidental relations of men in social life, and the Divine ordinance of commerce. Fourthly, though under some reserve and restriction, we must include political ethics. Fifthly and lastly, there are the ethics of our higher relation to the society and fellowship of the kingdom of God. Upon all these Christianity pours a clear and steady and sufficient light: gathering up all former teaching, and impressing the whole with the seal of perfection.

ETHICS OF MAN AND MAN.

All men are related as fellows or neighbours. Obligations to universal man as such may be classed under five heads as the duties of Charity, of Justice, of Truth, of Purity, of Honour: each of these, with its subordinates, being marked out in Holy Scripture emphatically and distinctly. There is, however, a sense in which all are summed up in the first; again the remaining three may be regarded as one in the second: thus making Love and Justice pre-eminent in the relations of man to his fellow, as they are in his supreme relations to God.

CHARITY.

Much has been already said of CHARITY, which in the New Testament is reserved for man's widest obligation to his neighbour : it is the one term which is common to heaven and earth in this sense. It is more than the limited love of the brethren which in us answers to God's favour to His own : St. Peter, as we have seen, makes the distinction very clear, *and to brotherly kindness, charity.* This noblest of all the graces belongs by prescriptive right to all departments of ethics. As appointed to regulate the universal relations of mankind, it has a very wide family of virtues under it, which may be subdivided as in a certain sense active and passive, or, rather, positive and negative.

2 Peter i. 7.

1. It is PHILANTHROPY in the conventional use of the word to signify practical care for the wellbeing of the race which knows no limits, but extends, whether as Benevolence or Beneficence, to man as such. The word φιλανθρωπία, however, is used only of God; it is not used expressly even of the God-man, though the only passage in which it occurs attributes this sentiment to GOD OUR SAVIOUR. KINDNESS is natural regard to our kind ; therefore not employed to denote the Divine regard, for which the word is Lovingkindness, though this is extended to all the works of the Divine hand. Charity or love, as the duty which every man owes to his fellow-man, presides over a wide range of obligations, from the supreme SELF-SACRIFICE which is ready to *lay down our lives* in imitation of Him who *laid down His life for us,* down to the gentlest act of COURTESY which sheds its charm upon common life, blending love and justice into one.

Tit. iii. 4.

1 John ii. 16.

2. But its most impressive exhibitions are such as are called forth in imitation of the Divine charity. Such is MERCY : strictly speaking, God alone can be merciful ; but in the same sense as man may sin against man he is bound to be merciful to the offender, and to forgive him if need be *seven times in a day.* And more than that ; for, when reminded of His words by Peter, the Redeemer said : *I say not unto thee, Until seven times ; but, Until seventy times seven.* Longsuffering belongs to God alone : we, following the Divine example, are required to practise FORBEAR-

Luke xvii. 4.

Matt. xviii. 22.

ANCE, which is the disposition not to press to the uttermost our claims against a fellow-creature. This is by our Lord called COM-PASSION, and PITY, and FORGIVENESS. *Shouldst not thou also have had compassion on thy fellow-servant even as I had pity on thee?* All these affections towards universal man are required of those who bear the Divine image as restored in Christ. Throughout the New Testament this unlimited charity, meditating the most unbounded kindness and capable of the most unbounded forbearance, is inculcated as a grace taught of God to those who in union with Christ partake of His Spirit. Our Lord denounces the vice that seems to honour love while it robs it of its perfection as absolutely universal. *Ye have heard that it hath been said, Thou shalt love thy neighbour, and hate thine enemy. But I say unto you, Love your enemies . . . Be ye therefore perfect, even as your Father which is in heaven is perfect.* St. John, in his last Epistle, the supplement and complement of all Scripture, gives this its strongest expression. He, like all the writers of the New Testament, but more directly than any other, makes the charity of redemption the standard of universal duty. *Hereby perceive we Love, because He laid down His life for us ; and we ought to lay down our lives for the brethren.* Not for the brethren only, however : these words must be conformed to the precept of the Saviour, who commends to us the perfection of the Father's impartial love as our standard. And, if the love of God in the Atonement is made the example, it is also made the source of our strength to copy it : *If we love one another,* GOD DWELLETH IN US, AND HIS LOVE IS PERFECTED IN US. *Hereby know we that we dwell in Him, and He in us, because* HE HATH GIVEN US OF HIS SPIRIT.

Matt. xviii. 33.

Matt. v. 43, 48.

1 John iii. 16.

1 John iv. 12, 13.

JUSTICE.

Justice.

JUSTICE, as co-ordinate with Love in the ethics of man's relation to man, is the principle of respect for the rights of others. Like charity, it is a virtue of which God gives the highest standard in His acts. But here there is a difference. The retributive justice which belongs to God, Who alone can distribute rewards and punishments, may be reflected in the justice of human judicial courts where law is administered. But the virtue that honours the infinite variety of mutual human rights is righteousness in the phraseology of Scripture, which however uses both righteous and just as adjectives. It is the paying universally what we owe. St. Paul explains this, and, at the same time, shows the profound connection between love and justice, when he says; *Owe no man anything, but to love one another ; for he that loveth another hath ful- filled the law.* Here love is the eternal debt of righteousness, which justice must be for ever paying. Now Charity, as we have seen, does not suppress righteousness either in God or in man : in us it is the strength by which the debt is paid as well as the watchful registrar of the debt itself. The Christian ethics of justice are deeply affected by the supremacy of love ; as will be seen by considering the various forms of justice as they are pre- sented in the New Testament. Rom xiii. 8.

1. Justice recognises in every member of the human family cer- tain inalienable rights that belong to man as created in the image of God and redeemed by the incarnation of His Son. The precept *Honour all men* occurs in a connection which shows that the inheritor of human nature as such is to be respected. Every man is in a certain sense a brother of Jesus ; and, loved as such, must receive the tribute which is essentially his due. Closely con- nected with this is the indestructible right, subject to certain restrictions which do not touch the right itself, to the control of himself : in other words that freedom of will which is personal liberty. It is injustice to despise any man as such, to whatever degradation he may have sunk in his race : here at the one extreme, justice must give freedom to every slave, and hold slavery in abhorrence, and, at the other, must *be courteous.* The perfection of COURTESY is to give to everyone on all occa- sions his human due, as interpreted by love : while to those of high degree it is reverence, and to the lowly is condescension, it is to all alike the honour due to man as man, and especially to the weaker and more honourable sex. Like Hospitality, which is courtesy not so much in spirit and in word as in act, this is a grace too often unrecognised and unvalued. Honour to all. 1 Pet. ii. 17. 1 Pet. iii. 8.

2. There is another class of rights which are not inherent in all, but earned by the moral industry and fidelity of our neigh- bours ; those which are based upon acquired character. Every Character.

man's reputation is dear to him : whether it be his general good fame or his particular repute. Justice guards both as the right of our fellow-men ; and, reinforced by love, more than guards them. It abhors Slander, which, by backbiting, scandal-mongery, or innuendo, would rob another of his character ; and Detraction, which would rob him of his fair repute. The law of justice says : *Render therefore to all their dues.* Love had in the preceding chapter gently corrected this : *in honour preferring one another.*

Rom. xiii. 7.
Rom. xii. 10.

Property.

3. Justice respects the rights of property in general. If Christianity introduces any modification here it is not as it respects our relation to the holder of property, but the relation of the holder of property to God. He holds it only in trust, and as a steward ; and obligations arise of a personal character which have already been referred to. Relative morals, however, are independent of this ; and require that we rigidly observe the laws of what in modern language is called HONESTY.

Truth.

4. Reserving this for the ethics of commerce, we may refer to another range of application. All men have a right to our fidelity to TRUTH. Society is based on this principle. Justice, attended by love, must be SINCERE in the intention of the present moment ; must be true, in the sense of VERACIOUS, in spoken words referring to the past ; and must be FAITHFUL to every engagement concerning the future. All these virtues belong more or less, as we have seen, to personal and interior ethics ; but they enter here also. Our neighbour has no claim, no right, more imperative than that which expects truth from us. Christianity heightens the claim by showing that we belong to a corporate body, the union of which depends upon the fidelity of each to other. *Wherefore putting away lying, speak every man truth with his neighbour : for we are members one of another.* Similarly, the vice or injustice of stealing is condemned : *Let him that stole steal no more : but rather let him labour, working with his hands the thing which is good, that he may have to give to him that needeth.* Here the interpretation of love comes in. It is not enough to abstain from robbing another ; the opposite virtue must be practised, the giving to those who need instead of taking from those who have.

Eph. iv. 25, 28.

Love and Justice.

5. Finally, the law of love, blending its influence with that of justice, introduces a variety of ethical sentiments of great import-

ance. It is our obligation to respect and to our utmost ability to preserve the purity of others by a pure demeanour towards them : this duty of justice interpreted by love is elevated into a perpetual law of life. The question in Christian ethics is not, What does my neighbour expect from me? but What ought he to expect? and, What ought I to do for him whether he expects it or not? Both love and justice lie at the foundation of our Lord's precept: *All things whatsoever ye would that men should do to you, do ye even so to them ;* FOR THIS IS THE LAW AND THE PROPHETS.

Matt. vii. 12.

ETHICS OF FAMILY LIFE.

The Family relation is the ordinance of God lying at the foundation of all human society. Christian Ethics leave nothing wanting here as it respects the main elements of that ordinance : the relation of Parents and Children, that of Masters and Servants, and the regulation of the Household generally as the home of all.

MARRIAGE.

Christianity confirms, simplifies, and vindicates from abuse the original and sacred ordinance of marriage. Moreover it elevates and hallows it afresh by special benedictions.

Husband and Wife.

I. The original appointment of MONOGAMY is confirmed : *From the beginning of the creation God made them male and female. For this cause shall a man leave father and mother and shall cleave to his wife. . . . What therefore God hath joined together let not man put asunder.* Our Lord in these words gives us the sum of His decisions on this question, with all the principles the ethics of which must regulate marriage both as a religious and as a civil institution. From these principles there should be no appeal.

Monogamy. Mark x. 6—8. Matt. xix. 6.

1. Everything like Gnostic or Manichæan dishonour of this state of life is contrary to the spirit of the Christian legislation. Whatever disparagement of marriage may be found in any part of the New Testament is to be interpreted in harmony with this original ordinance of the Creator, as the Saviour, creating all things new, has confirmed it. He Himself may seem to have

Dishonour of Marriage.

occasionally set it aside, as when He spoke of those *which have made themselves eunuchs for the kingdom of heaven's sake.* The utmost that may be inferred from this is, that the ordinance was not made binding on every member of the race; and that either devotion or discretion may find it expedient to renounce or defer the marriage bond with its responsibilities. St. Paul illustrates this, both by example and by precept. He teaches the dignity and the sanctity of wedded life; and his suggestions of entire abstinence were given only *for the present distress.*

1 Cor. vii. 26.

Polygamy

2. MONOGAMY was as an institution *made for man,* like the Sabbath, and not man made for it. Although there is no express decree on the subject in the Scriptures, it may be fairly assumed that the original union of Adam and Eve was the type of the union of male and female among their descendants; especially as there is a general equality in their numbers. But no reason can be assigned why the Supreme Lawgiver might not in some cases sanction the suspension or the occasional change of the law. Hence the commanded, permitted, or uncondemned concubinage of some of the ancient servants of God. Undoubtedly, the current of the Old Testament shows that monogamy was the normal appointment; and in the New Testament our Lord has finally confirmed this. When St. Paul says that a bishop must be *the husband of one wife* he seems, but only seems, to tolerate polygamy in private Christians. We have here an alternative exposition. Either the Apostle teaches that the rule of one wife—not yet absolutely pressed upon all men, any more than the manumission of slaves—was peremptory for the bishop; or he prescribes that the bishop must never replace the wife whom he may have lost. There is something anomalous in each side of the alternative. But both interpretations are consistent with the principles that a man should be the husband of only one wife.

1 Tim. iii. 2.

Ethics.

II. In the Old Testament marriage is often used to symbolise the relation between God and His people; and in the New Testament this is more emphatically the case. St. Paul, himself not a married man and the only Apostle who has been supposed to depreciate the institution, elevates it into a standing type of the union between Christ and His people, both collective and individual. *He that loveth his wife loveth himself. For no man ever yet*

Eph. v. 28 —32.

hated his own flesh ; but nourisheth and cherisheth it, even as the Lord the Church. . . . This is a great mystery : but I speak concerning Christ and the Church. Here it is the union between the Lord and the mystical Body which is in the Old Testament *the Queen*, and in the New *the Bride* and *the Lamb's wife.* But in another passage we hear : *he that is joined unto the Lord is one Spirit :* the allusion to *one flesh* in the preceding verse makes it very plain that the personal union with Christ is in the Apostle's thoughts. Ps. xlv. 9.
Rev. i. 9.
1 Cor. vi. 17.

1. But, apart from the mystical fellowship which it illustrates, no higher tribute to marriage is conceivable than this. It carries the dignity and sanctity of the marriage relation to the highest point short of making it a sacrament. It is the most intimate and sacred union conceivable; the mutual complement necessary to the perfection of man and woman, and one which cannot be supposed to subsist with more than one person. As an institution for continuing the human race it is as pure in its own sphere as that Union between the Bridegroom and the Bride to which the spiritual increase of the Church itself is due. This sheds a strong light upon the various kinds of dishonour done to the ordinance. The violations of ethical obligation refer to the two final causes of marriage. First, in all those tempers and acts which interfere between the persons to impair the perfection of their unity, Christ's union with the Church being always in view : *Wives, submit yourselves unto your own husbands, as unto the Lord ; for the husband is the head of the wife, even as Christ is the Head of the Church. . . . Husbands love your wives, even as Christ also loved the Church.* Here there is much to ponder. The inmost grace of the wife as such is the love of submission ; the earthly reflection of that loyal homage of devotion which the man was commanded to offer : *He is thy Lord ; and worship thou Him !* The inmost grace of the husband is perfect self-sacrificing love. The two are one ; and their union is sacred. Their communion, therefore, down to the slightest offices of affection, must be pure. Thence arise interior ethics which need not to be dwelt upon ; a hint of which, however, St. Paul gives when he says : *Defraud ye not one the other, except it be with consent for a time . . . that Satan tempt you not for your incontinency.* This leads to the other class of offences : the sinful indulgence of those lusts which war against the second primary

New Testament Tribute.

Eph. v. 22, 25.

Ps. xlv. 11.

1 Cor. vii. 9.

purpose of marriage : ADULTERY, with all the train of vices that
precede, accompany, and follow it.

Indis-
soluble.

2. As it respects DIVORCE, the Christian law cannot be understood without reference to the Mosaic legislation, which it generally
comprises. Our Lord makes very express reference to the subject :
correcting ancient traditional errors on this subject, just as He corrected traditional errors on the subject of adultery. He could
not have declared more absolutely than He did that marriage is
a permanent compact, which neither the parties concerned nor
any human power can dissolve ; save on the conditions appointed
by God Himself. Whatever those conditions might have been

Matt. xix.
8.

in the days of the people's *hardness of heart* it is clear that our
New Lawgiver has decreed that one only offence, fornication,

Matt. xix.
9.

shall dissolve the marriage bond : *whosoever shall put away his wife,*

Mark x.
11, 12.

except it be for fornication, and shall marry another, committeth
adultery. Under the old law, the penalty of adultery was death ;

Divorce.

our Lord's legislation tacitly abolishes that : moreover, He gives
πορνεία the same meaning as μοιχεία, which generally signifies
the same offence committed by a married person. A remarkable
phase of the same question occurs in connection with the new
relations between married persons of differing faith. Our Lord
had intimated that the divorced might marry again. St. Paul, in
his treatment of the question as to the desertion, deliberate and
final, of an unbelieving partner, says that the forsaken one is free :

1 Cor. vii.
15.

let him depart : a brother or a sister is not under bondage in such cases.
What the extent of this freedom is Scripture does not say ; but it
has generally been held that desertion is, equally with adultery,
valid ground of divorce under the New Law.

General
Principles

3. The principles thus laid down must be inviolate, whatever
human legislation may do : rather, all human legislation must
conform to them. According to those principles marriage is not
merely a civil contract : the Scriptures make it the most sacred
relation of life ; and nothing can be imagined more contrary to
their spirit than the notion that a personal agreement, ratified in
a human court, satisfies the obligation of this ordinance. Again,
throughout the history of revelation, husband and wife are ONE

Gen. ii. 24.

FLESH, and there is no precedent in Scripture for making them
merely partners or for giving the wife independent rights. The

kindred therefore by AFFINITY, or through the marriage union, are as really related, though not so closely, as those who are kindred by CONSANGUINITY.

HISTORICAL.

Many ecclesiastical controversies have arisen in this field of ethics which it is not within our province to discuss. These have had to do with the sacramental character of marriage, the compulsory celibacy of those devoted to the service of the Church, the law and practice of divorce, the modern application of the ancient Levitical law touching prohibited degrees, and the particular question of marriage with the sister of a deceased wife. Some of these points will be considered when we reach the sacraments, and others of them must be noticed here only so far as they involve the New-Testament ethics.

Contro-versy.

1. As to the first point: there have been two extremes, as we have seen, on the subject of the religious relation of marriage. It is in the Scripture a mystery but not a sacrament. The notion of a specific sacramental grace, doing for man in the sphere of nature what the mystical fellowship with Christ does in the supernatural sphere, is an error, but a venial one in comparison of that which makes marriage a merely external union or mutual compact. The former error—to which reference will hereafter be made—has no sanction in the Word of God, and involves a certain dishonour done to the idea of a sacrament. But the latter seriously affects the very foundations of human religious society.

Sacra-ment.

2. It might be expected that the ancient churches which held the sacramental character of marriage would be rigid as to the doctrine of divorce. The Romanist doctrine of matrimony in fact allows of no separation of the parties, such as should allow them to marry again; but it multiplies causes of separation A MENSA ET THORO, and for pronouncing any marriage NULL AB INITIO. Legislation in Protestant states has varied much; but the general tendency has been to reduce the estate of Matrimony to a human arrangement under the control of human law, which by mutual consent the parties may for almost any reason dissolve. On the Continent of Europe there is scarcely any trace left, even

Divorce.

among the Evangelical communities, of the ancient high tradition , and the present English law is imitating the Continent in this laxity   much to the scandal of our Christianity

Polygamy   3 POLYGAMY, in theory and practice, has had its advocates in every age ; and in every age Divine revelation has protested against it with more or less of vigour   The Concubinage of the Old Testament may be cited in opposition to this statement   But when the instances in question are examined in the light of the New Testament, they will be found to confirm our principle   The polygamy of the patriarchs was in some cases an exceptional arrangement taken up into the scheme of Divine Providence   That of Solomon and the later kings was condemned and chastised   We have to do, however, with the New Testament, which leaves no room for doubt as to the full ratification of the original law   Where Christianity is established Monogamy must vindicate itself as the order of God , but when Christianity is in conflict with heathen practice, the same discretion should be used in the suppression of old habits as is taught in the case of slavery.   As to the Mormon revival of Polygamy it may be said that it is self-condemned

Prohi-   4 St. Paul speaks more than once of the Forbidden Degrees.
bited   When he is condemning the particular form of Corinthian incest,
Degrees   *that one should have his father's wife,* he calls it Fornication, the
1 Cor. v 1   generic term for offence against the purity of the marriage rela-
Levitical   tion   He appeals to the Levitical code as still in force, but only
Laws   as being grounded in the constitution of human nature   *None of*
Lev xviii.   *you shall approach to any that is near of kin to him   A man shall not*
6.   *take his father's wife*   This prohibition stands at the head of a
Deut.   number of interdicts, which are carried into their particulars · the
xxii 30   force of the prohibition resting upon the natural abomination of union with *the remainder of his flesh.*   The interdict does not absolutely extend to all the instances which this last expression would lead us to expect   they are taken for granted, as, for instance, the child of a brother.   It is observable that there
Lev xviii.   may be no union with the wife of a father's brother   *thou shalt*
6.   *not approach his wife· she is thine aunt.*   From this it appears that this relationship, not one of blood, was sufficient reason for the prohibition   Hence it may be presumed that the sister of a wife would be under the same interdict   How far the pro-

hibited degrees of kindred extend is, however, matter of national legislation.

PARENTS AND CHILDREN.

Ethical principles regulating this relation exhibit a considerable development when we pursue them through the whole of Scripture. Christianity has consummated that development by removing certain peculiarities of the Mosaic legislation, by confirming the original ordinances of nature, and by superadding a specific reference to the common bond between Parents and Children in the Christian household of Faith.

1. Parental obligations include necessarily the Maintenance of children, their Education in its fullest sense, their Preparation for life, and Nurture for the Lord. What Christian legislation says on this subject may be briefly summed up under the heads of Parental and Filial obligation respectively. These are all involved in the rights of children to the care of their parents as representatives of Providence. Care in things temporal is not forgotten : *If any provide not for his own, and specially for those of his own house, he hath denied the faith.* It is upon the moral discipline that the New Testament lays its chief stress, as will appear from one of St. Paul's pregnant sayings : *Ye fathers, provoke not your children to wrath ; but bring them up in the nurture and admonition of the Lord.* Here we gather that, negatively, the discipline is to be discreet, just, impartial, considerate ; positively, it must include the entire education and specific admonition of the Christian faith. *Thou shalt teach them diligently unto thy children :* this precept runs through the old economy and on into the new. Again and again it was enjoined upon the parents of the ancient dispensation that they should instruct their children in all the facts of the national history and in all the variety of symbol and type by which Divine things were taught by God. *It shall come to pass when your children shall say unto you, What mean ye by this service ? that ye shall say.* Hence the parental responsibility does not admit of transfer. The teaching of preceptors, whether in secular or in religious matters, is at best the necessary supply of the parents' duty : it must not supersede it, especially in Divine things. Claims of business, recreation, travelling, even of public worship

Parental Obligations.

1 Tim. v. 8.

Eph. vi. 4.

Deut. vi. 6, 7.

Ex. xii 26, 27.

R 2

and other services, must not interfere with this most absolute
and paramount obligation of life. With the parent is the teaching of example and ceaseless influence as with no other and
delegated authority. Catechetical and Sunday schools were never
intended in any sense to interfere with this.

Filial
Obedience
Requital.

2. The filial obligations corresponding to parental rights, are
Obedience, Reverence, and the Piety of grateful requital. In the
order of nature, as represented by St. Paul, Obedience takes the
lead: the reverence is a later expression of the filial sentiment.

Eph vi. 1.

Children, obey your parents in the Lord ; for this is right. It is right
in the essential fitness of things, and what is generally right is
specifically right in the Lord. Neither in the Old Testament nor
in the New is there any restriction to this precept : as pertaining

Col iii. 20.

simply to the parental authority it is absolute, *in all things.* Of

Luke ii.
51.

this Jesus Himself set the supreme example. *And He went down
with them, and came unto Nazareth, and was subject to them.* Both

Reverence

parents are included in this authority. Reverence grows out of
and strengthens and at the same time hallows this obedience. It
is the reflection on the parents, as representatives of God, of the

Eph. vi. 2.

honour due to Him. *Honour thy father and mother* is a commandment which belongs rather to the first table than to the
second : the word τίμα is the same which is used of the respect

John v. 23.

due to the Supreme Father and to the Son : *he that honoureth not
the Son honoureth not the Father.* Our Lord Who was subject to

John viii.
49.
1 Pet. ii.
17.

His earthly mother and Joseph said : *I honour My Father.* It
is used also of reverence for royal authority, *Honour the king;* as
of the respect due to man as in the image of God : *Honour all men.*
If it is not said that God honours all men, at least this honour

John xii.
26.

have all His saints : *If any man serve Me, him will My Father
honour.* Profound respect for parents as such is a duty which has
no restriction : not even when their character forbids its being
reverence in the strict sense of the word.

3. But this filial honour to parents as such must take the form
of recompense for their care as opportunity offers. Incidentally
St. Paul introduces a touching reference to this. Using in one
instance the term Piety, as uniting the service of religion to God

1 Tim. v.
4.

and to parents, he says : *let them learn first to show piety at home, and
to requite their parents.* The emphasis on this Christian virtue is

remarkable : *for that is good and acceptable before God.* It also has its highest example in the Supreme Pattern whose last earthly care was to provide for His ever-faithful mother : *Woman, behold thy son ! Behold thy mother !* John xix. 26, 27.

4. There are certain limitations to these rights and obligations which nature prescribes and some which Christianity adds. There is a legal majority : of that the Scripture says nothing. Though this majority releases the child from some restraints, the sanctity of the parental and filial relation remains inviolate to the limit of life. The requital of parents implies that the bond continues to the end. There is a limitation, however, which seems to be introduced by Christianity in repression of the law of nature : namely, in all instances of conflict between the express will of Heaven and parental wishes. The law of God is to be supreme in all such cases of collision : *Wist ye not that I must be about My Father's business ?* Luke ii. 49.

MASTERS AND SERVANTS.

The moral teaching of Christianity has a very marked bearing on the family bond of Masters and Servants, including every variety of relation that may subsist between the employer and the employed, which in Scripture are generally regarded as pertaining to household life.

1. The mutual rights, duties, and responsibilities of these relations are not in their widest range matter of direct statute in the Christian Scriptures : partly because they belong to the relations between man and man, and those of commerce, and those of the household; partly, because servants in the New Testament were generally, and in the Old very often, slaves. But the principles laid down by St. Paul are of permanent application, and mark the specific points in which Christian legislation affects the subject of ordinary servitude. On the employer's side there is the obligation of justice, the arbiter being the Lord : *Give unto your servants that which is just and equal; knowing that ye also have a Master in heaven.* It is obvious that the Apostle here carries the question of what is just to servants into a higher court than human, because when he wrote the servant had scarcely any legal Masters and Servants. Col. iv. 1.

rights. Justice is now regulated, so far as wages go, by human law. But in all other respects the principle of justice must be observed under the control of a feeling that before the Master in heaven all are servants alike. On the side of the servants the duties are more copiously laid down : *Exhort servants to be obedient unto their own masters, and to please them well in all things; not answering again; not purloining, but showing all good fidelity.* Here the duty of the employed is determined by a standard from which modern ideas are fast receding. Obedience, cheerful and solicitous to please ; humility, and silent acceptance of a superior will ; all negative and all positive fidelity : these are the virtues of those who serve human masters according to the Divine will. Many other matters that complicate the relation are left to the operation of a high principle that Christianity alone has introduced : the common relation of masters and servants is *in the Lord.* The exhortations to *do it heartily, as to the Lord, and not unto men ;* to *adorn the doctrine of God our Saviour in all things ;* and *not with eyeservice as menpleasers,* have their application to all servants of every degree to the end of time. And in them lie the special Christian ethics of this relation of universal family life.

Titus ii. 9, 10.

Col. iii. 23. Titus ii. 10. Eph. vi. 6.

Slaves.

2. The question of Slavery arises here. The Epistles of the New Testament undoubtedly recognise it as an extant institution which must be undermined and abolished by the operation of Christian principle and not otherwise. It had been sanctioned by the Mosaic law ; but in a form very different from that of Greece and Rome. Slaves, if Hebrews, recovered their liberty in the seventh year ; in every case they were carefully protected and had their full religious privileges, being incorporated into the Jewish household. But, like polygamy and many other anomalies, slavery was tolerated only until the fulness of time. The coming of the New Legislator cleared away from the Divine statute book many *statutes that were not good :* not good absolutely, that is, though good for a preliminary dispensation. It introduced a universal amendment as well as spiritual codification of the old laws. And with regard to slavery He abolished it in principle by His very incarnation. *If the Son therefore shall make you free !* applies to this kind of bondage also. The Apostle Paul lays down the effectual emancipatory principles. First : *There is neither Jew*

Hebrew Slavery.

Ezek. xx. 25.

John viii. 36. Christian Principles *Gal. iii. 28.*

nor Greek, there is neither bond nor free, there is neither male nor female: for ye are all one in Christ Jesus. In the presence of the Lord there is and there can be no such thing as slavery; and this is the consolation of him whom men call a slave. *But if thou mayest be made free, use it rather.* No slave is required to be absolutely contented with his position: indeed, he is virtually enjoined to use all right means for his release. *Thou owest unto me even thine own self.* The whole of the Epistle to Philemon is a specimen of the way in which the Gospel sanctifies the abuse which it will in due time destroy. The first of these passages shows that Christianity knows no slavery; the second that the slave ought to be free; the third that Christian principles alone will accomplish his freedom. _{1 Cor. vii. 21.} _{Philem. 19.}

THE HOUSEHOLD.

Over and above the obligations and duties which have been referred to, there is yet another which imposes upon the Head of the household the responsibility of its holy government as a society separate and distinct in itself and having its ramifications elsewhere. One in every family is the representative of the Supreme, and is in the Christian household the teacher, the priest, and the ruler under Christ directly responsible to Him.

1. The Household or Family occupies a prominent place throughout Scripture. It was the first form of society; and has continued to be the germ and representative of every other fellowship. In no dispensation has the family been merged in the congregation and forgotten or lost. Abraham before the Law had the church of God in his house. In his legislation Moses laid the heavy responsibility of household religion on every parent. David, rather in his Psalms than by his example, exhibits the same principle. Our Lord sanctified family religion by being the most blessed illustration of it for all His earlier years; and by governing His Apostolic company as a *Master of the House*, speaking of His disciples as *them of His household*. The Epistles generally penetrate through Churches to the families, addressing men as the heads of households, which includes more than their children. St. Paul writes, *Let the deacons be the husbands of one wife, ruling their children*

and their own houses well. Here the house includes servants and all dependants; and the passage is further remarkable as indicating a certain analogy between the house of God which is the family and the house of God which is the Church.

The Responsible Head.

2. There is only one head of the house; who is responsible for its instruction, worship, and godly discipline. That head may be of either sex, married or unmarried; consequently the household as such is independent of the married relation, and even of children. But the head is the husband, or bond of the house, in the normal state of things: though husband and wife are one, there cannot be a united head. As bound to maintain its Christian discipline, its Head is the priest of the family; and, unless incompetent to perform his duty or neglecting it, presents its worship daily to God. FAMILY WORSHIP is an institution specially prescribed and honoured in the Old Testament: tacitly or indirectly in the New. *The church in thy house* does not refer to the household of Philemon as such, but to that portion of the Christian community wont to meet there; yet it does indirectly suggest a family worship. Christians in regard to this obligation as well as that of brotherly love are θεοδίδακτοι: *ye need not that I write unto you; for ye yourselves are taught of God.* There ought to be no collision between the worship of the family and that of the congregation. No household as such can ever be a church, save under anomalous and transitional circumstances such as those already referred to; and, on the other hand, no public worship in the assembly dispenses from the family obligation to worship God. St. John, in one of his two smaller Epistles, gives the final testimony of the New Testament as to the strictness of family discipline. Respecting the duty of keeping false doctrine and corrupt teachers out of the household, he writes: *If there come any unto you, and bring not this doctrine, receive him not into your house, neither bid him God speed:* whether he come in person or by his writings, or in any way whatever. And this is made more emphatic by the fact, that the guardian of the household faith was in this case a woman. This final testimony does not receive all the attention that it demands. Issued in the name of the Saviour, and by the representative of a religion of charity, the injunction to have no domestic fellowship with an enemy of the Incarnation is of great weight.

Marginal notes:

Family Worship.

Philem. 2.

1 Thess. iv. 9.

2 John 10.

ETHICS OF SOCIAL AND COMMERCIAL RELATIONS.

Christianity sanctions the principles on which commerce is based ; enforces the rigorous principles of personal morality in the conduct of it ; and lays around it some specific safeguards of the utmost importance. It will be needful only to dwell upon these last; as our consideration of Christian Ethics is mainly limited to the specifically Christian characteristics of it.

I. Commerce stands here for all that industry and activity   Commerce which develops the resources of the earth, creates property, and advances culture. The Religion of Jesus sanctions all its funda-   Principles mental principles, though for the most part only in an indirect way. It teaches that Property is of God, whose will has ordained that His creatures should have exclusive possession of certain things which they may call their own. Our Lord came not to destroy the ordinances of nature and the original charter on which mankind inherited the earth. He has confirmed that primary con- stitution of things according to which man was ordained to *replenish*   Gen. i. 28. *the earth and subdue it*, and extract from it its resources. The same natural law that declares it wrong to take from another his pos- session requires the deeper principle that he has a possession which may be taken : the prohibition, *thou shalt not steal*, implies   Ex. xx. 15. the personal right to something of one's own. The question how such property is acquired now, or was acquired originally, and by what tenure it is held in its various forms, does not here enter into consideration. It is enough that the Divine order for the development of man individually and collectively requires the idea of personal possessions, and their use and multiplication in commerce. It is lawful to possess and accumulate the substance which commerce makes its Capital and from which it derives Interest. This is a fundamental principle which the Bible no- where contradicts ; in it all the laws of honest merchandise have the fullest sanction. In fact, every other theory is opposed by the tenour of Scripture. In its pages might is nowhere the foundation of rights ; the possession of property is never made dependent upon the caprices of popular will, or social compact. There is no sanction of Communism. The Community of Goods in the Acts was extraordinary, and the result of a special influence of the Spirit; voluntary, and binding on none; transitory, and soon gave way again to the common order of life; and prophetic of a far distant future.

Ethics.　　II. The ethics of commerce, as they are affected by Christian teaching, are of more importance. They are both direct and indirect; partly general principles, and partly safeguards.

Principles　　1. It is a primary law of the New-Testament legislation that the principles which regulate personal holiness must be carried

Ex.xx.15. into the commerce of life. For instance, *Thou shalt not steal;* the precept which forbids all injury to the property of another, must carry its sanction into trade: condemning fraud of every kind, whether by false representation, by adulteration, by overreaching, or by any other of those numberless methods of advancing one's own interest at the expense of others which are the disgrace of modern trading. But the positive virtues which belong to

Rom. xii. 11. ordinary life must be carried into commerce. *Not slothful in business* is a general precept which may bear this special application: it is true that τῇ σπουδῇ μὴ ὀκνηροὶ has no such reference to business in the modern sense of the word as many suppose; but that which is a virtue in the whole course of life is a virtue in

Prov.x. 4. commerce, and the secret of success. *The hand of the diligent maketh rich:* the blessing of God rests upon the operation of a natural

Eph. iv. 28. law. *Let him that stole steal no more* is followed by: *but rather let him labour, working with his hands the thing which is good, that he*

2 Thess. iii. 10. *may have to give to him that needeth. We commanded you, that if any would not work neither should he eat.*

Safe-
guards.　　2. While the Christian legislation sanctions all kinds of industry and all enterprises of civilisation, it throws around the whole many safeguards which may be said to constitute a large part of

Col iii.17. its commercial ethics. For instance, the precept, *Whatsoever ye do in word or deed, do all in the name of the Lord Jesus* forbids the engaging in any occupation which cannot be sanctified in all its details by that Name. This injunction would cut off very much of the speculative enterprise of commerce, though by no means

Col. iii. 2. all of it. The indirect precept contained in the injunction, *Set your affection on things above, not on things on the earth,* with others

1 Cor. vii. 29—31. like it, such as this, *It remaineth . . . that they that use this world as*

not abusing it, affects these ethics profoundly, inasmuch as they forbid all accumulating for the sake of hoarding riches. It is possible though difficult, and it is necessary, to make a distinction between the commercial possession of substance, or the possession of it as a steward, and the personal complacency and delight in it. Substance may be and must be increased in order to prosperous commerce, and many of the Divine promises expressly sanction and sanctify this. But there is no teaching either in the Gospels or in the Epistles which permits the accumulation of earthly treasure for self. *Lay not up for yourselves treasures upon earth* is a precept for every spiritual man in Christ, who must in the ground of his nature be poor in spirit. The design to acquire the means of usefulness sanctifies thrift; but there is no department of probation which requires more watchfulness and discretion.

Matt. vi. 19.

POLITICAL ETHICS.

Divine revelation has from the beginning been bound up with government, and the social and political affairs of the world. Its history shows the sanctification of every form of developing rule among men; from the primitive household and family, its simplest and typical form, to the most violent form of imperial despotism. We have now to do with the final teaching of the New Testament, about which there is little room for doubt. Its general principles are very plain, both as to the rulers and as to the ruled.

I. The institution of government is Divine: not founded on any compact or agreement among men, as the modern figment is. The more carefully we examine the basis of tribal and national distinctions among men—in other words what goes to constitute a distinct people—the more clearly shall we perceive that it is conditional by a certain relation to God Whose worship was the original bond of unity to every race, and Whose representative the earthly ruler was. Government was made for man and man was also made for it. The form of that government is not prescribed rigidly and definitively: certainly not in the Christian legislation. Every form of valid authority is sanctified in the Old Testament. The New Testament introduces a universal Monarchy in the

Government.

Rev. xi. 15.

Rom. xiii. 1. Representing God.

Rom. xiii. 4.

Rom. xiii. 6.

spiritual economy of things; and only in a very subordinate way deals with *the kingdoms of this world.* But the foundations of civil and political society for earth were laid in heaven : *the powers that be are ordained of God.* Human magistrates represent the Supreme Judge : being in the state His deputies. *He is the minister of God to thee for good :* for the protection and peace of the law-abiding. *He is the minister of God, a revenger to execute wrath :* for the administration of the Divine justice on transgressors. These principles are indisputable. The same term is used concerning the representation of ecclesiastical authority in the church and in the world : they are both διακόνοι and λειτουργοί, or ministers.

Obedience

Matt. xxii. 21.

II. Obedience to magistrates and the government of the land is made part of the Christian law : expressly included in His ethics by our Lord on the broad ground of the duty to *render therefore unto Cæsar the things which are Cæsar's,* though the Cæsar of that day held the land in bondage. St. Paul recognised in his own person, and commands all men to recognise, what was at best a despotic and cruel authority.

Rom. xiii. 2.

Dan. vi. 5.

1. The duty of submission is, first, in a certain sense, passive. *Whosoever, therefore, resisteth the power, resisteth the ordinance of God; and they that resist shall receive to themselves damnation.* This forbids, negatively, personal insurrection and resistance. How far submission is to be carried, at what point resistance is permitted—not to the individual as such, but to a people—is a question which our present ethics do not contemplate. Inter arma leges silent. The obligation comes in, however, before the arms are taken up. No individual Christian may resist without betraying his trust, and losing the meekness of his wisdom. When the question is *concerning the law of his God,* the servant of Jehovah must resist, but not until submission has had its perfect work.

Tribute.

Rom. xiii. 5, 6, 7.

2. Positively, obedience to the government requires that diligence be given to uphold the honour of the law at all points, and that *for conscience sake.* Much emphasis is laid both by our Lord and by His Apostles on paying *tribute to whom tribute is due:* a principle which involves very important issues. *For this cause pay ye tribute also.* Let it be observed that St. Paul's ethics of submission to government follow and are, as it were, incorporated

with his sublimest and most comprehensive doctrine of Christian morality.

3. The Bible, from beginning to end, inculcates and honours PATRIOTISM. It has been sometimes said that neither the sentiment of love to country nor that of personal friendship finds a place in Christian ethics. It is true that the supreme devotion to a kingdom which is *not of this world* everywhere has the preeminence; and that the individual sympathies of friendship are merged in brotherly love. But both these sentiments are really inculcated and encouraged. There is no profane history that surpasses or equals its annals in examples of both, and Christianity must have the benefit of the old religion of which it is in a certain sense a continuation. Patriotism John xviii. 36.

ETHICS OF THE CHRISTIAN FELLOWSHIP.

Christian Fellow-ship.

This is a department of Ethics which Christianity has to a great extent created. As the Christian Society sprang out of a religious community established by God, it inherited the general principles of its ecclesiastical economy of duties. But the bond of fellowship has changed, as also its relation to the world; and with these changes corresponding duties and responsibilities have arisen. Our ethical system will not be complete without some remarks on the general principles of Christian duty as connected with Christian communion, under the three heads of the external organisation, the internal fellowship, and the common mission, of the Christian Society as laws are prescribed for it in the New Testament. The next section, that of the Church, will open up this subject more fully. Here it will be viewed only in its general principles as regulating one specific branch of Christian Morals. It must be remembered that the question concerns only those who belong to the community of Christ; the preliminary duty of the Church to offer its privileges to all, and of every man to accept these privileges, is not here discussed. It has been considered already and will arise again.

I. Membership in the external Church confers rights and imposes obligations. Here we have to regard the religious Membership.

Society founded by our Lord as being the depository and representative of His will, and the trustee of His commandments.

Acts ii. 47.   1. It is His law, that every believer should be *added to the church* by the rite of baptism : this is not left optional, either to the adult believer himself, or, as we shall see, to the parent of Christian children, who must be baptised. The Eucharist also

Luke xxii. 19. 1 Cor. xi. 25.   imposes a duty whilst it confers a privilege : *This do in remembrance of Me. This do ye, as oft as ye drink it.*

  2. Submission to the authority of those whom He sets as pastors and rulers over His people is a Christian duty, to which corresponds the obligation of the same pastors and rulers to watch for the people's souls and instruct them in the truths of

Heb. xiii. 17.   religion : *obey them that have the rule over you.* The sanctions of the commandments binding upon the Society in its external constitution are manifold : the extreme is what became afterwards known as separation from the Church, or excommunication.

Worship.   3. The ethics of ecclesiastical worship are distinct from those of devotion generally. They involve some matters of great importance, which, however, will be more fully considered when the Church is the subject. Public worship, the sanctification of the Lord's Day, and attendance on services prescribed by due

Heb. x. 25.   authority, belong to this class of *positive duties. Forsake not the assembling of yourselves together, as the manner of some is.* Modern Christianity brings into prominence some ethical questions as to the obligation of submitting to ordinances of Christian fellowship and worship which the several communities appoint, without express authority of the Word of God. In other words, every community has the nature of a Society as well as of a Church ; and every one who binds himself to the usages of the Society is bound by them. On the other hand, the Society must so regulate its legislation as to pay deference to the Scriptural and superior enactments for the universal Church as such. Those Societies within Catholic Christendom have prospered most which have wisely adapted their bye-laws, and skilfully subordinated them to the laws of the Church as laid down by the Saviour and His Apostles. But the further consideration of this whole question belongs to the next section, that of the Church.

Internal Ethics.   II. The internal fellowship of the Christian Society involves a large body of ethics that may here be alluded to in a preliminary way. They fall under two branches: such as refer to the obligations of brotherly love and mutual kindness among the members themselves, and such as govern the relations of the fellowship to the outer world *or them that are without.*

1. The specific form of charity which is BROTHERLY KINDNESS: shown in mutual watchfulness, practical *admonishing one another,* bearing *one another's burdens,* mutual edification and sympathy and help. The foundation of all these ethics is given in our Lord's words: *All ye are brethren.* They prescribe the most self-denying and careful and persevering attention to the claims of the sick and sorrowful and needy of the flock; and the support, according to every man's ability, of all the institutions of charity that the Society contains.

2. One of the most important branches of the ethical obligations we now consider is that which regulates the bearing of the Christian Society on the world without. Here there are two distinct and seemingly opposite aspects of the subject.

(1.) There is a sense in which the Christian Fellowship is bound to maintain its absolute separation from the world. It is a community which is passing through the present scene of things as a band of pilgrims. Much of our Lord's directory of duty, as well of His Apostles', regards the present constitution of things as passing away, tolerated only by the Christian discipleship, and permitting usages which are to be conformed to only under protest or by way of accommodation to national laws. Of this character is the legislation concerning Oaths and some other matters which will be considered elsewhere. It may be said that a keen solicitude to maintain the honour of the religious community as the kingdom of heaven is inculcated. *But it shall not be so among you!* This principle involves many difficulties especially in regard to social relations: and this therefore is a very difficult branch of conventional ethics. There is a separation from the world which is rigorously demanded of the Christian fellowship as such: *Come out from among them and be ye separate!* By five distinct terms St. Paul marks the contrariety between the world and the Church. *What fellowship,* μετοχὴ, *hath righteousness with unrighteousness? And what communion,* κοινωνία, *hath light with darkness? And what*

Marginal references:

1 Cor. v. 13.

2 Peter i. 7.
Col. iii. 16.
Col. vi. 2.
Matt. xxiii. 8.

Those Without.

Separation.

Matt. xx. 26.

2 Cor. vi. 14—18.

concord, συμφώνησις, hath Christ with Belial? or what part, μέρις, hath he that believeth with an infidel? and what agreement, συνκατά-θεσις, hath the temple of God with idols? for ye are the temple of the living God, as God hath said, I will dwell in them. The Epistles constantly make the dignity of the Christian fellowship an argu-

Phil. ii. 14—16.
ment for high propriety: *Do all things without murmurings and disputings; that ye may be blameless and harmless, the sons of God, without rebuke, in the midst of a crooked and perverse nation, among whom ye shine as lights in the world, holding forth the word of life.*

Influence.
(2.) But this passage carries our thought to another aspect of these ethics. The Christian Society must penetrate the world

Matt. v. 13, 14.
around with a holy influence. *Ye are the light of the world! Ye are the salt of the earth!* The duty of our Lord's disciples is to carry with them an influence which shall pervade social life; and while, with regard to it—its festivities, recreations, diversions—the Christian law strictly demands that all should be so ordered as

Jas. ii. 7.
not to dishonour *that Worthy Name by the which ye are called*, it demands also that in the midst of the world, or of that kind of semi-religious life which often comes near to what the New Testament calls the world, a pure and holy example should be set by those who are spiritual.

Recon-ciliation.
(3.) There is great difficulty in reconciling these two aspects of our ethics. But they must be harmonised. The passage quoted above from the Philippian Epistle is chiefly of a negative character: it shows what the sons of God must be in contrast with others. There is another passage in the same Epistle which is

Phil. iv. 8, 9.
more full and complete in its bearing on this subject. *Finally, brethren, whatsoever things are true, whatsoever things are reverend, whatsoever things are just, whatsoever things are pure, whatsoever things are lovely, whatsoever things are of good report; if there be any virtue, and if there be any praise, think on these things. Those things which ye have both learned, and received, and heard, and seen in me, do: and the God of peace shall be with you.* This perfect compendium of Christian morals regards the Brethren as setting their thought —their rightly estimating, studious and pondering, affectionate and ardent, practical and energetic, peaceful and triumphant— thought on all the obligations of morality in its highest perfection. But some of the elements of the description show that it

is an excellence which must be known and seen and read of all men. The Church is before the world's bar.

III. The ethics of the Church's mission next claim attention. Hitherto we have considered the obligations arising from the common fellowship as within; but there is a duty incumbent on every Christian to co-operate with his fellows for the spread of the kingdom of Christ around and to the ends of the earth.

The Church's Mission.

1. Here is the corporate obligation of universal Christendom to preserve the Faith, to diffuse it, to wield its truth in the contest with all error, to demand from men submission to the Gospel, and to put forth every effort to evangelise the world. The Catholic Body as such has this for its first and great command, which briefly comprehends every other.

2. This corporate obligation rests upon the several Evangelical branches of Christendom: it may be an unreality to speak of its resting upon the universal Church as such; since it has been long the demonstrated will of the Spirit that the various sections of the Christian Commonwealth should carry on the work of discipling all nations. Hence it is the duty of every religious community, either alone or in combination with other similar bodies, to engage in the common effort to spread the Gospel: an obligation never enough remembered until the present century.

Individual Churches.

3. The most solemn and binding of all personal responsibilities are those which require every individual member of the body to make its universal work his own. This is the peculiarity and also the perfection of Christian ethics, that every duty which it enjoins and every grace which it commends has some reference, more or less direct, to the Church of God which is the kingdom of Christ. The relation of the individual to the fellowship of the saints pervades the New Testament. There can be, strictly speaking, no isolated religion: every Christian man belongs to the visible household of faith, and is partaker of all its privileges and responsibilities. In virtue of the universal priesthood of believers—of which more hereafter—all who name the name of Christ are regarded as under an obligation to preach His Gospel, and promote His glory in the Church, and make the salvation of souls their business for His sake. The Christian is born into a new world; and his relations to the new economy do not permit

Individual Christians.

him to regard himself for a moment as an independent unit. After St. Paul had spoken of the ministries of the appointed and ordained agents of the Spirit, he goes on to speak of the growing up of the entire community into *the Head, even Christ; from Whom the whole body fitly joined together and compacted by that which every joint supplieth, according to the effectual working in the measure of every part, maketh increase of the body unto the edifying of itself in love.* This great word, read in the light of the hymn to charity, is the final expression of ecclesiastical ethics. *None of us liveth to himself.* Every joint supplieth strength; every part effectually worketh; and the growth of the whole body in love is the contribution of all the members in particular. The Christian ceases from self not only in Christ but in His body the Church: it is no longer to him an independent principle and end of action; no longer an end at all as distinct from a higher end. This is the doctrine of that Philippian chapter which shows how Self is lost in Jesus, and then found again in the care of our own and of others' souls. *Let this mind be in you which was also in Christ Jesus:* here is the supreme example of self-renunciation. *For all seek their own things, not the things which are Jesus Christ's:* here is the perfect opposite. *Work out your own salvation with fear and trembling:* this shows that solicitude for self is not to be utterly abolished. *Look not every man on his own* things, *but also on the things of others:* here is the unity of care for self and care for our neighbour in the common self-surrender to the Lord and His service.

Eph. iv. 15, 16

1 Cor. xiii. Rom. xiv. 7.

Phil. ii. 5, 21, 13, 4.

THE CHRISTIAN CHURCH.

The Christian Church is the sphere as well as the organ of the Spirit's administration of redemption. As a corporate body it was founded by our Lord Jesus Christ; is invested with certain attributes and notes as the representative of His agency among men; discharges its functions as an institute of worship and depository of the Faith; has definite obligations to the world as an instrument for its conversion; and, lastly, bears special relations in its temporal form to the eternal Kingdom of Christ.

These several branches of the one subject must be considered in relation to Biblical, Dogmatic, and Historical Theology : from the Word of God we gather the materials for the true doctrinal statement; and make this the standard by which to test the various ecclesiastical phenomena of the Christian world. That this whole question belongs generally to the Administration of Redemption has been already shown at the outset, where the special relations of the Holy Spirit to the work of the Redeemer was the subject. It may be added that many topics connected with this department of theology must needs be distributed over several sections, especially those of the Three Offices of Christ and the consummation of the Kingdom in Eschatology.

THE HISTORICAL FOUNDATION OF THE CHURCH.   Foundation.

A large portion of the New Testament is occupied with the details of its establishment of the Church as His own new institution : more particularly, this is a prominent subject down to the beginning of the Acts. We may embrace the whole under two heads: the preparations made by our Lord in the Gospels, and its actual foundation on the Day of Pentecost.

THE PREPARATIONS IN THE GOSPELS.

Gospel
Prepara-
tions

The
Kingdom
Matt. iv.
17
Mark i 15
Matt
xxiv 14
Acts i 2,
3

Matt xiii
52.
Rev xi 15
Rev i 9.

Acts i 3.

1 Our Lord proclaimed the advent in His own person of the *kingdom of heaven*, or *the kingdom of God*. His new revelation to mankind was the *Gospel of the Kingdom*. the Baptist preached its coming, as the forerunner both of Christ and of the Apostles, and the Saviour made it the subject of His teaching *until the day in which He was taken up* By this term He linked His own government with the ancient Theocracy · but not with its earthly form, for His was the kingdom of *heaven*, as such predicted, though not by that name, throughout the prophets. The new kingdom, however, was a *mystery* revealed and the main secret of that mystery lay in the fact that, while it was still the kingdom *of God*, it was also the Messiah's, the kingdom *of our Lord and of His Christ*, the *kingdom of Jesus* the Son Incarnate. The phrase pervades the Lord's teaching, down to the last He was *speaking of the things pertaining to the kingdom of God* It was not however His purpose that it should be retained as the denomination of His new community. The company of His people is the sphere of His reign to the end of time, but the name and character of the dominion is held in abeyance until the consummation of all, until its final manifestation as the one kingdom of heaven and earth, of God and man, of Christ and His saints. it was of that the Incarnate Redeemer spoke, when, at the close of His ministry,

Luke xxii
30.

Matt vi
10

throwing off all reserve, He termed it *My kingdom* As our study here begins with this name, so it will revolve back to it at the close, and meanwhile the first prayer of Christendom is, *Thy kingdom come* a prayer that will end only when all prayer shall cease.

The
Church
Matt xvi
18, xviii
17

Mark xi.
17

2 At a memorable crisis in His history our Lord gave His institution its new name: MY CHURCH Twice, and twice only, He used it, and on two occasions closely connected both instances, be it observed, occurring in the very midst of St Matthew's special collection of parables and discourses concerning the kingdom In the former, it seems to be the great temple or *house of prayer for all nations*, in all ages, and for the worship of eternity; in the latter, the visible assembly of Christian people, gathered together in one place for the administration of His laws. Putting

the two passages together, we have a summary of the Saviour's will concerning His future congregation. He gave it then a name that we need not yet further expound : the word ἐκκλησία has from that day had the pre-eminence over every other by which the fellowship of Christians may be described. No one who considers this origin of the term will consent to allow it to be displaced by any other. The abuses of it should not bring it into contempt.

3. It is observable that our Lord, having given this new name, and thrown a brief but effectual ray of light upon first the invisible and then the visible congregation of the future, did not again mention the word : leaving it for future use. His parables and discourses flowed on in their former channel, keeping the kingdom of God in view. But the last discourses including the last prayer give some elements of teaching concerning the future Church which are of the deepest interest. These will only be alluded to now : the fuller exposition of their meaning must be reserved for the future. Provision was made for the permanent memorial of redemption in the Holy Supper : the sacrament of His people's corporate unity with Himself and with each other as the heirs of a new covenant. Baptism, the sacramental rite of initiation, was also substituted for the ancient rite of circumcision, now virtually abolished. The new congregation or church was, as it were, formally consecrated to God by its Head in what may be called the High-priestly Prayer : the first Prayer in *His own house.* In it He refers to the company of believers as given Him of the Father : the suffering obedience which nevertheless purchased the gift is kept back or dimly alluded to ; as kept from the world, or, as one afterwards said who heard the words, *preserved in Jesus Christ ;* and to be made perfect in one, in that spiritual and eternal unity of perfection of which the highest type is to be sought though it can never be found in the interior relations of the Trinity. But it is observable that the Saviour speaks of this new community, describes it, and prays for it, as future. Even after His passion, when the resurrection had put all power in His hands, and He appeared in the midst of His disciples as their glorified Head, the New Fellowship was yet in the future. He spent forty days in speaking about its history or destiny, and His Apostles' duty in the coming days ; doubtless

Our Lord's Teaching.

Heb. iii. 6.
John xvii.

Jude 1.

Acts i. 3, 4.

gave many instructions that have not been recorded ; but always His Church was yet to come.

4. While it is true that the Church, in the strict sense of the word, and as a corporate institute, was not founded while the Lord was upon earth, in another sense He was laying its foundation during the whole of His ministry. He left a large body of instruction concerning it which waited only for the Day of Pentecost to disclose its fulness of meaning. The germs and principles of all that is to follow in this branch of theology are to be found in the Gospels : indeed, we may be more bold, and say that nothing on this subject, or any subject, can go beyond the meaning of the Lord's own words. He spoke of the Comforter as the future Divine Presence in the congregation ; but His office was only to glorify, expound, and expand the sayings of the Redeemer Himself. We shall find that this holds true in a very remarkable degree concerning the doctrine of the new Church or Kingdom. A large part of the Saviour's teaching in the four Gospels treats of its nature, of the methods of its spread, of the character of its subjects, of its relations to the world, and of the principles of His own government in it. The development of this teaching will appear in all that the subject brings before us.

THE PENTECOSTAL FOUNDATION.

Foundation of Church.

The Day of Pentecost was the epoch of the foundation of the Christian Church. The prepared disciples of Christ were assembled, and upon them the Holy Ghost came down, making them the New Temple of the Triune God. Those were added whose faith received the preaching of the Finished Gospel ; and the disciples were constituted into an organised and visible fellowship, to continue for ever during this dispensation under the government of the Spirit as the representative of Jesus its Head.

The Day of Pentecost.

1. The institute of the Feast of Weeks, representing the presentation of the Jewish harvest firstfruits, typified the oblation of

the firstfruits of the Christian ingathering. It also, though not by Divine enactment, commemorated the giving of the Law, and had its antitype in the full revelation of the New Law of Faith. The Risen Lord appointed a meeting of His disciples in Galilee for the proclamation of His Kingdom; but bade them wait in Jerusalem for the founding of His Church. There they received, as representatives of the Saviour's old discipleship and the germ of the future body, that baptism of the Spirit which was to them, as their special dignity, instead of the baptism of water. But the Holy Ghost represented the Triune God, now fully revealed, who took possession of this consecrated body, and made them the new Temple or Church. The Shekinah, which was the symbol of the union of God with man, appeared for the last time, and was resolved into the Personal Spirit, the Presence of God in the midst of His people, and resting upon every person present from the Apostles downwards. *And it sate upon each of them.*

Trinity.

Acts ii. 4.

2. After the *wonderful works of God* had been proclaimed by the many new tongues of the worshipping assembly, the one new tongue of the preaching brotherhood began the everlasting Gospel. The new Law was the proclamation of the finished work of Christ. The day of the foundation thus gives the first and perhaps the most complete exhibition of the process by which the Church is to be formed to the end of time. The ἐκκλησία is the company called out from the mass by the preaching of the completed redemption of the Incarnate Mediator. It is the CHURCH as gathered from the world; it is the CONGREGATION as assembled together; it is the FELLOWSHIP as replenished with common gifts. And these three ought to be one.

Preaching
Acts ii.
11.

3. This Day also began the organisation of the community: that is, if we include the final words of the chapter as belonging to its history. The elements of order, prepared in the Gospels, now take their instant and permanent form. Pentecost is the typical day of the future of Christendom: in the morning the worshipping assembly, glorifying God for the accomplishment of all His purposes; in its noon the full Evangelical preaching; the rest of it given to organisation and fellowship. Amidst such shaking of heaven and earth as was never known before, whilst the Christian company was in its first ecstasy of worship, and

Organisation.

the crowd in the strong excitement of conviction, the water of
Baptism begins to flow as the symbol of order and of introduction
to the new fellowship.   And, as the rite of initiation was remembered in honour of the Lord's final command, so the community
was immediately organised within.   Here first indeed we have

Acts ii.
47, 42.

the ἐκκλησία, or church, mentioned as an historical fact : *the Lord
added to the church daily such as were in course of salvation.*   And

Matt. xvi.
18.

what was the course or process of salvation ?   *The Apostles' doctrine :* that is, the Great Confession of an earlier day expanded by
the Apostles ; their *fellowship,* that is, the submission to all the
obligations of the society life that day begun, and the enjoyment
of the blessings of the Christian covenant under Apostolical
sanction ; the *breaking of bread,* the Lord's Supper this, not the
Apostles' ; and, as embracing, and pervading, and sanctifying all,
the *prayers* ordered by the new Spirit of adoption.

Epistles.

4. The later New Testament—the Acts and the Epistles being
interwoven into one history of the beginnings of the perfected
fellowship—shows us the gradual consolidation of the economy of
the Church, under the guidance of the Apostles, who were for a

John xx.
21.

season all in all as Christ had been.   *As My Father hath sent Me,
even so send I you.*   We see the formation of a pastoral ministry
in its elements afterwards to be developed.   We see the growth
of the community from without by the preaching of the Word,
from within by the incorporation of the children of believers.
Meanwhile, orderly arrangement never fails.   The new brotherhood
was not moulded by an esoteric influence, acting like a philosophy :
the leaven leavened a lump which the Holy Spirit shaped into a
body as fully and exactly organised as any known to men.
Simple as are the elements of this primitive ecclesiastical polity,
it is very sharply defined.   The visible Jesus, surrounded by His
disciples, was not more isolated and apart from the mass of the
people around, than His Church is, under the influence of His
Spirit, marked off and isolated from the world.   And that
organisation, thus perfectly sketched, remains as the standard of
order in the congregation for ever.

The Holy
Ghost.

5. This Day placed the Christian community under the jurisdiction and government of the Holy Ghost.   What the presence
of Christ was in the Gospels, the Head without a corporate body,

the presence of the Spirit is, representing the Invisible Head of a body now visible. This doctrine is vital in many ways. It overturns the delusion of any earthly vicar of Christ. *There is one body and one Spirit.* What the great hierarchical theory gives to the Pontiff is taken only by usurpation. The delegated headship of the Holy Ghost is the security of the infallibility and indefectibility of the Christian Body in the conservation of the truth. *The Spirit of life* is strong against every enemy of the Church : *the gates of Hades shall not prevail against it.* For He is the Giver of life : of all ecclesiastical life, as well organic as individual. He moulds its elements and fashions them as He will : being τὸ Κύριον, τὸ ζωοποιόν, as defined in the Nicene Creed. There are crises in the history of Christianity when new forms are given to the outward organisation, and He makes those a people who *were not a people.* This truth may be and has been perverted ; but the Spirit Himself vindicates it in His own way, and the history of Christendom cannot be understood without it. More generally He is the Source of all energy and strength to the body of Christ upon earth : He is the *breath of lives,* of many lives, inbreathed into it, and Himself the Inbreather. Lastly, the Spirit is the Representative of the Lord, Whose Headship abideth ever. He acts for Christ in His one Person. As the whole Trinity generally is represented by the Spirit, and not the Father alone, so it is the whole Christ and not the Eternal Son alone. But, as the Lord's Vicegerent in His Church, He does not exclude the Lord Himself. When the Saviour declared the necessity of His going in order that the Spirit might come, He so spake as to reserve His own dignity as that of One who would be never absent. *I will come to you. He shall take of Mine.* It is not as in the case of that other Forerunner : *He must increase, but I must decrease.* The Lord Christ Himself, and not the Spirit, is *Head over all things to the church.* We know that the presence of our Intercessor is behind the veil, we know also that in the Holy Ghost He is here also : *at hand* as well as *afar off.* One name is common to the heavenly and the earthly Head : that of Παράκλητος or Advocate. He who pleads FOR the people, our *Advocate with the Father* in words unheard, pleads IN them by the Spirit Who *maketh intercession for us with groanings not spoken.*

Eph. iv. 4.

Rom. viii. 2.
Matt. xvi. 18.

1 Peter ii. 10.

Gen. ii. 7.

John xiv. 18; xvi. 15.
John iii. 30.
Eph. i. 22.

Jer. xxiii. 23.

1 John ii. 1.
Rom. viii. 26.

It is true that the phraseology of the Acts introduces a great change in the Divine personality : the I is that of a Third Voice not heard before. As, passing from the Old Testament into the Gospels, we have a new Divine Speaker, so it is in the Acts.

Acts xiii. 2.

Separate Me! is the command of the Holy Ghost. But, as the Father sometimes is heard during the earthly dispensation of the Son, and is never absent, so the Lord Jesus in the Acts is never absent, and sometimes speaks in His own name. He is King in His kingdom : He has that universal kingship which He will surrender at the last day ; He has that special kingship over His redeemed which will not really begin or be consummated till the last day. But He is in Apostolical language the Head over His Church, the Head of the Church, rather than its King. This indicates, if possible, a yet nearer and closer relation. The Incarnate Person has a union with His Body unshared and pre-

Acts xx. 28. Matt. xvi. 18.

eminently His own. *It is the Church of God—or the Lord—which He hath purchased with His own blood.* We return to His own first word : MY CHURCH !

ATTRIBUTES AND NOTES OF THE CHURCH.

The Church in the later New Testament is represented passively as the Temple of God, actively as the Body or organ of Christ's manifestation : the former, as the sphere of Divine worship and holy influence; the latter, as the instrument of Christ's manifold operations on earth. To both, in their unity, there are certain attributes assigned in Scripture, the study of which brings before us the whole subject in the most complete way. These qualities are Unity, Sanctity, Invisibility, Catholicity, Apostolicity, Indefectibility, Glory. But we also find by the side of these, which generally describe the Body in its higher and ideal character, qualities in some measure their counterparts or opposites : such as Diversity, Imperfection, Visibility, Localisation, Confessionalism. Mutability, and Militant Weakness. Hence we gather that the true church of Christ is a body in which these opposite attributes unite.

1. These correlative qualities of the one Church of Christ One Personality. suggest a certain analogy with the Person of its Head in Whom Divine perfections and human attributes meet. It also is one organised body with two natures or modes of presentations. The concept church is not that of a Divine body and a human ; but of one reality under two exhibitions, as in the case of our Incarnate Lord. But the analogy must not be pressed too far. Here there is the same reserve and the same protection that was found necessary in the higher doctrine. As the Son of God uses human nature as His body or flesh, He is the same with humanity. As He occupies it as a temple He is distinct from it. The church is the temple of Christ : it is inhabited by Him. It is His body : the complement or fulness of Himself. The higher and Divine church is in the visible and human as a temple : distinct from it. It acts and works in the human as a body : inseparable from it. We have to speak of all its attributes—higher and lower, Divine and human, temporal and eternal—as belonging to the one church. And the habit of doing this saves from much confusion.

2. These attributes are in Historical Theology transformed Notes of the Church. into Notes, by which, as tests, the true Church is supposed to be known. In the Apostles' and Nicene Creeds, as united, those are specified as four : One, Holy, Catholic, Apostolic. The controversial theology of Rome has multiplied these Notes very abundantly. We shall adopt the method of connecting each attribute with its seeming counterpart as the ideal community is realised in the world. There will, of course, be less to be said on each series of opposites as we proceed, because each more or less anticipates those that follow. Moreover, these Attributes and Notes do not exhaust the subject, being dwelt upon only as introductory to what follows.

ONE AND MANIFOLD.

Unity and Variety are both and alike essential to the idea of the Christian Church ; and their sound combination is a test that may be applied to all ecclesiastical systems.

The Scriptural doctrine on this subject will be most fully exhibited by considering, first, the universal Body of Christ of which the Christian Church is the last earthly form; secondly, the Christian Fellowship proper as an institution. As to the first, the note of manifoldness is most conspicuous; as to the second, oneness and multiplicity unite.

Universal
Law.

I. Taking the largest view of the Church of Christ as the fellowship of the people of God in every age, we may affirm that unity in manifoldness has been its law of existence and development. Its oneness from the beginning is recognised throughout the Scripture as founded upon the common redemption, whether revealed or unrevealed. The Holy Company of all ages has been one in the unity of many forms and varieties of manifestation.

Rev. xxi.
24.
Rev. v. 9.
Acts x.35.

It is the company of *the nations of them which are saved :* the Church of the Redeemed *out of every kindred and tongue and people and nation ;* the unseen unity of all those of whom it is said *in every nation he that feareth Him and worketh righteousness is accepted with

John xi.
52.

Him ; the children of God that were scattered abroad,* and gathered together in Christ. Hence it binds together the several economies ; the Patriarchal Church, the Jewish and the Christian : one as the

Mark i.15.

kingdom of God, or the Civitas Dei running its course through all ages. In this large sense it unites all the forms of the Church to which we shall refer : the Church as universal, or as in a province, or as in a city, or as in a building, or a house.

Christian
Church.

II. But the Christian Church as an institution founded by Jesus is one and manifold ; its unity in the Spirit of its Head being the blending of many believers in one common confession, and their participation in one common grace. The teaching of the New Testament may be viewed, first, as to the essentials of oneness and then as to the breaches of that oneness. From these we may gather the true doctrine of Scripture.

One
Ground of
Unity.

1. The unity of the Church has but one ground, that of a common union with Christ; nor is there any positive reference to it which does not make that prominent. The first word on the subject is that of the High Priest, whose Unction is the bond of

His people's union with Himself and with each other : *that they all* John xvii. 21.
may be one : as Thou, Father, art in Me, and I in Thee, that they also
may be one in Us : that the world may believe that Thou hast sent Me.
The former part refers to a unity never to be seen or understood
of men ; the latter to such a spiritual manifestation of that holy
fellowship as may suggest to all who witness its effects the secret
of its bond. It was reserved for St. Paul to expound these words
of our Lord, in the Epistle which comes nearest to the idea of a
treatise on the Church. He speaks of unity nine times in one Eph. iv. 3—6.
paragraph, and in five applications. There is *one God and Father*
of all ; and there is *one Lord*, the common Revealer of that Father
and Redeemer of men ; and in Him there is *one faith*, one baptismal confession of doctrine. Again, there is *one body and one*
Spirit : the mystical body visible in the world as the organ of its
invisible Head, the oneness of which, let it be observed, is *the*
unity of the Spirit in the bond of peace : the oneness of all who
receive the reconciliation with the Father through the Son, and
its seal in the communication of the Holy Ghost. Lastly, there
is *one hope of your calling :* the unity of that heavenly aspiration
which makes the pilgrim companies one in the hope of eternal
blessedness. This is the fundamental, and almost the only, text
on the subject, and it gives all the elements of the direct and
positive Evangelical teaching concerning the unity of the Church.

2. If we turn to the negative or indirect teaching, we find
much that is instructive on this subject. First, the omissions are Omissions
remarkable. There is no prescription of a necessary uniformity
according to any supposed theory : external oneness is never
directly even alluded to as existing beyond an individual congregation, while, on the other hand, a certain measure of external
differences and mutual independence must be assumed in order
to give reality to the exhortations to unity. Secondly, the constant tone of Apostolic doctrine points to the maintenance rather
of a spiritual than of a visible oneness. This appears in the
figurative language used to describe the Christian fellowship, Figures.
which always shows that the only unity directly aimed at in
Scripture is the mystical. It is that of *His body, the fulness of* Eph. i. 23.
Him that filleth all in all : the πλήρωμα of Christ, whatever the
precise meaning of the word may be, must signify one pure and

perfect spiritual complement of this Divine-human Person, one in His unity, or in Himself. Now that is said of *the Church ;* and that body is never spoken of as one in any external John xv. 1. sense. In our Lord's allegory it is *the Vine* from the unity of which dead branches are cut off : that unity is in Christ Himself and belongs to a tree of life ; which strictly speaking has none but living branches. The same remarks hold good of the figure which describes the universal Church as a Temple, or House. In the final sayings of the New Testament, when external organisa- tion must have been nearly complete, we read only of spiritual 1 John i.3. oneness, not of outward uniformity. Christian *fellowship is with* 1 John iii. *the Father and with His Son,* and that through *the Spirit which He* 24. *hath given us.* The violations of that fellowship are doctrinal and 1 John iv. practical : he *that confesseth not that Jesus Christ is come in the flesh,* 3. and *he that committeth sin.* The former is said to have *gone out* 1 John iii. 8. *from us.* There is not a word in this final document of the unity 1 John ii. of the outward body. In the Apocalypse the seven churches are 19. one in the central Lord who holds them in His *right hand ;* nor Rev. i. 20. among their offences is their violation of external unity mentioned. Schism. The divisions condemned in the New Testament as schisms are always factious or doctrinal divisions within particular churches. The overt acts of separation, according to the modern notion of heresy and schism, are not contemplated in the New Testament. The breaches of unity are breaches rather of the spirit than of the form : of the latter there are but few traces.

Dogmatic or Visible Unity. 3. Hence we may gather up these Scriptural elements into the statement that the One Church is the unity of all the congrega- tions of believers in Christ in which the pure Gospel is preached, the sacraments duly administered, and the discipline of the Chris- tian fellowship maintained in its purity.

Basis. (1.) The basis of this unity is the common property of a sound Col. ii. 19. confession of faith in Jesus. This is called *holding the Head,* or 1 Cor. iii. building on the one *foundation.* With this must be conjoined the 12. unity of worship offered to the Holy Trinity through the Mediator, the Christian sacraments as the seals of admission and continuance in the Church, and the maintenance of sacred discipline.

Expres- sion. (2.) As to the expression of this oneness it is regarded in the New Testament as seen of God, and of Him only. He beholds the one great assembly and hears the secret harmony of what may seem to result from many discordant voices. As to man it is the object not of sight but of faith: "I believe in one holy, catholic church,"—not faith IN it, but faith that it exists—is the later expression of the Scriptural principle. This admits of its exhibiting the reality of oneness by manifestation in many ways: by an essential agreement in faith, worship, and discipline, witnessed of all men; by methods of combination for the express purpose of declaring union, and that not only by admissions of individual brotherhood, but also by acknowledgment of ecclesiastical relations; and by intercommunion and fellowship in all holy enterprises of Catholic Christian charity.

(3.) The Scriptural ground of this unity is the general supervision of the Holy Spirit: *The Lord knoweth them that are His* in the *great house;* and this is the inscription on the seal of its security, the obverse being only this, *Let every one that nameth the name of Christ depart from iniquity.* During Apostolic days the presence of the Lord's inspired representatives was the bond of union among the churches; but we find no express provision for that bond after their departure. In every individual church unity is maintained by discipline, committed to the hands of responsible pastors. 2 Tim. ii. 19, 20.

ECCLESIASTICAL.

Differences as to this attribute or note of the Church are bound up with its best and worst developments. The subject belongs strictly to ecclesiastical history; but a few hints may be noted here, having relation both to doctrine and ethics.

1. It has been seen that within the Scripture there is a unity observable which is quite different from uniformity. In Israel there was indeed only one temple: no breach of unity was permitted, and the separation of the kingdoms was not sanctioned by God. The Romanist theory, false now, was true then: the High Priest was the bond of absolute unity to the covenant people. But after the Captivity, another temple was built in Egypt; synagogues organised local centres of worship; and sects arose. Our Lord sanctioned none of the sects as such, neither did He condemn them as such: the Monachism of the Jews and Scriptural Unity.

the ascetic isolation of the Essenes He did not once refer to. He certainly condemned by implication the worship of Samaria, not as a violation of unity, however, but as false : *ye worship ye know not what.* For *salvation is of the Jews.* We naturally study with great interest all the hints of the Master's will on this most important subject ; and certainly gather from some indications that it was not His purpose to bind His people in the bonds of a very rigorous uniformity. The disciples rebuked on one occasion those who followed not them ; but they in turn were rebuked by their Lord. The Apostles were a bond of unity after their Master's departure. But there is no hint of a continuance of their authority as uniting the whole Church ; and the council of Jerusalem was not repeated.

John iv. 22.

Ecclesiastical History.

2. Leaving the Scriptures, we find at once the tendency that has made the unity of the Church a prominent question. During the ante-Nicene and Patristic ages generally the foundations were laid of a doctrine of absolute uniformity. The growth of heresies and schisms was the first occasion of this very early idea of a mechanical unity : these two words becoming very soon fixed in their meaning as follows. HERESY is the self-willed choice of some particular error and consequent departure from the Christian Confession. Every church which renounces the fundamental doctrines of Christianity is out of the unity of Christendom : not that it must necessarily be at once cut off ; the tribunal is an invisible one ; and the excision is from on high. As to the outward expression of unity the violation is SCHISM : strife within the community itself, separation from it, whether by voluntary act or as cast out. In the latter case there may be a justification which shall clear the apparent break of its sinfulness. But in the Patristic age there was no thought of a justifiable schism. Three representative men may be cited as the leading exponents of these views, and of the different ways in which they were maintained. Ignatius, an Apostolical Father of the first century, laid down the principle that the one episcopate was the only bond of union : meaning, however, only that in every church the chief minister was the guarantee of order as against schism and of sound doctrine as against heresy. Irenæus in the second century made the One Church, as the congregation of all churches under

Heresy.

Schism.

this episcopal government, the only organ of the Holy Ghost: where we have a singular combination of visible and invisible unity. Cyprian of the third century (250), in his work De Unitate, pointed to Rome as the centre of unity, though rejecting Roman jurisdiction : a position which was very generally assumed.

3. The further development of the principle that internal unity must be expressed by external uniformity belongs to Ecclesiastical History. By degrees the Roman bishop of bishops assumed to be to the whole church what each bishop was to the individual church. The ecclesiastical was conformed to the civil order, the Cæsar of a temporal universal empire must have for his counterpart the spiritual Cæsar, or the Vicar of Christ as the centre of unity and final appeal. The spirit of protest against this began in the East, which resented both the FILIOQUE added to the Nicene Creed and the authority by which it was added. The breach between Eastern and Western Christendom has never been healed : it remains as a standing protest against the erroneous doctrine of unity. While Rome denounces the Protestant communities as out of the pale of the one body of Christ, the Orthodox Greek Church denounces Rome as the first of all Protestant dissenters, heretics, and schismatics. In the West the Protestant Reformation utterly rejected the theory of an external unity as held by both communities, whether Catholic or Orthodox.

Unity and Uniformity.

4. A few remarks may be made upon modern tendencies in the interpretation of the note of unity since the Reformation.

(1.) It is generally conceded to be impracticable to aim at oneness in the visible church save in the fundamentals of faith, worship, and discipline. It must be obvious to every dispassionate mind that there has never been since the times of the Apostles any other unity than that which God alone can discern. Eastern and Western Christendom would agree that there has been none such since the seventh century : and each despairs of the restoration of union save on terms which the other cannot accept. Among Protestant communities only one judgment ought to prevail here. There are found, however, certain Hierarchical or High-Church enthusiasts who dream of a unity which a lineal Apostolical succession of orders gives to Eastern and Western Episcopal communions. But this is the most unreal of unrealities.

Erroneous Theories.

A compromise is attempted by those who, whether Anglican with episcopacy, or Lutheran without it, give up the hope of a universal unity, but cling to that expressed by national churches in every land. This is the religious unity of race or nation or territory. But it can never be proved that the Head of the Church divided His kingdom, or intended that it should be divided, territorially. The Congregational theory which admits only of voluntary aggregation of churches, and neither has nor desires any guarantee for more than that, goes to an extreme but in the right direction.

Heresy
and
Schism. (2.) But this tends to the modern correction of the notions of Heresy and Schism.   There are some important principles which are now generally accepted.   These two violations of unity generally go together : the αἵρεσις or heresy being self-willed choice of private interpretation in opposition to Scripture, and the σχίσμα the following of a party. Few schisms can be named which have not been the result of doctrinal error : few leading heresies which have not issued in schisms.   Here, however, there is a distinction. Heresy can never be perpetuated ; but the result of schisms may.   Ecclesiastical schism may be taken up by Divine wisdom into the development of the kingdom of Christ : having been in fact not schism in the sight of God, or soon losing the taint. Apparent schism may be the only cure of heresy. Many minor heresies may co-exist with holding the Head.   But where, on the one hand, there is such infidel subtraction from the faith, or, on the other, such superstitious addition to it, as neutralise the fundamentals, separation may be inevitable and lawful. Discipline may be so relaxed or perverted as to necessitate separations which are not schismatical : Dissent and Nonconformity are not necessarily and as such sinful. Schism may be the sin of the community left as well as of the community leaving.   But all this rises to the higher principle that the Holy Spirit is the Giver of life corporate as well as individual.   He quickeneth whom He will.   The body is more than its raiment : any such act of the sovereign Spirit must aim at the more effectual growth of the Church. He thus prevents unity from degenerating into stagnant uniformity. He calls them His people that were not a people, in order to provoke others to jealousy. Lastly, whenever the Spirit thus goes out of His way to divide existing churches, He never fails to authenticate His own act: as Paul among the Apostles was able to authenticate his vocation and work. As to heresy or self-willed and needless schism it is still one of the *works of the flesh*: condemned of itself. Gal. v. 19.

(3.) There are two opposite errors on the whole subject which, always observable, are very prominent in modern times. One is the overvaluation of the importance of unity, as uniformity. This is rebuked by reason, Scripture, and the evidence of the fact that the Holy Ghost does administer the work of Christ by sects and divisions. Much of the progress of the Gospel, and many of its most glorious achievements, at home and abroad, may be traced to the labours of Christian Societies to a great extent independent of each other. But undervaluation of it is equally wrong. Though variety is ordained of God, the nearer to uniformity, or at least to thorough mutual recognition, the estate of Christendom can be made the better will it be for its peace and dignity and prosperity. In due time Christ Who at His first coming *made both one*, uniting Jews and Gentiles, will blend all communions into unity, and His Church shall by His presence be in all its multitude of branches *made perfect in one*. Safe-
guards.

Eph. ii.
14.
John xvii.
23.

SANCTITY AND IMPERFECTION. Sanctity.

The Church, as the organ of the Holy Ghost, is necessarily holy. But its holiness as imputed is consistent with much imperfection; and as real and internal is only by degrees carried onwards to a perfection which will not be reached in this world.

I. The meaning of ἅγια, sancta, as applied to the Body of Christ, is the same which the term has been seen to bear as applied to individuals: with regard to both it signifies simply that which is set apart from the world and consecrated to God.

1. The Church is spoken of as holy in the Divine purpose: the end proposed by the Creator. *Let Us make man in Our image, after Our likeness*, must be referred to redeemed mankind also. In this the Three Persons concur. *He hath chosen us in Him before the foundation of the world. Who gave Himself for us, that He might redeem us from all iniquity, and purify unto Himself a peculiar people.* This final aim—to gather out of the world a people for His name—is ever kept in view by *the Holy Spirit of God, whereby* Triune
Purpose.
Gen. i. 26.

Eph. i. 4.
Tit. ii. 14.

Eph. iv.
30.

T 2

ye are sealed unto the day of redemption. The common design of the Holy Trinity was the new creation of a perfect humanity or body of mankind : as THE CALLED, κλητοί, from the world or mass of the unregenerate into THE CHURCH, ἐκκλησία.

Means.

2. This design is accomplished through all the means of grace. The process is spiritual and in union with Christ, Who as the Head can have only members like Himself. Hence their vocation is *an holy calling.* Of them the Lord says, *I have chosen you out of the world,* and of the Father they are *accepted in the Beloved.* The *temple of the living God,* and the *temple of the Holy Ghost* dwelling in it, the Church is sacred : its holiness is real, though its sanctification is a process at best : *that He might sanctify and cleanse it with the washing of water by the Word.* The building, *fitly framed together,* formed by holy members and at the same time forming them, *groweth unto an holy temple in the Lord.*

2 Tim. i.9.
John xv. 19.
Eph. i. 6.
2 Cor. vi. 16.
1 Cor. vi. 19.
Eph. v.26.
Eph. ii. 21.

3. This design is supposed by anticipation and in prophecy to be accomplished. Always over the visible and imperfect church hovers the image of a sanctified Ideal already *in heavenly places in Christ Jesus.* Thus in the design of redemption, in the process on earth, and in the glorious result, already the congregation of Christ is before the mind and in the purpose of God holy.

Eph. ii. 6.

Sanctity, External and Internal.

II. More particularly, the holiness of the one church is that of an external imputation ; of an internal process ; and of the gradual approach of these to coincidence, never perfect in this world, but to be perfected at the coming of Christ.

Imputed Holiness.
Zech. xiv. 20.
Matt. xxi. 13.

1. There is a relative and imputed sanctity. As *holiness unto the Lord* was stamped on the *bells of the horses,* so all in what our Lord called *My house* is impressed with a certain character of holiness down to its very dust. Hence all that pertains to the outward and visible community—the assembly and the building itself in which they gather, the Divine service, the table, the sacraments—are all among τὰ ὅσια, the *holy things.* This is not affected by the unholiness that lingers still in the external fellowship. The Epistles are written to the companies of *saints,* among whom, however, are many whose unholiness is rebuked. Our Lord's own Catholic Epistles are written to *the churches* which are His and yet needed much amendment : until He removes the *candlestick out of his place,* it shines upon a holy company. Jerusalem

Acts xiii. 34.

1 Cor. i. 2.

Rev. ii. 5, 7.

at the worst was still the *holy city.* But this is only a relative sanctity, and avails not of itself, being alone. Matt. xxvii. 53.

2. There is an internal and real sanctity, which inheres in the body, being derived from the sanctity of the individual members of the mystical fellowship, never wanting in any community that holds the Head. Their life, aim, and communion are holy; the sanctity of the Church is really their sanctity; and of them the Creed says: I believe in the communion of saints. This holiness is matter of faith; it is also imperfect necessarily: for whatever perfection of sanctity individual members may reach cannot be imputed to the whole body unless all shared it alike. Real Holiness.

3. The internal and external are gradually becoming one, in the whole Church as in the individual Christian. Within the universal community, reckoned holy, there is going on the silent, ceaseless operation of a sanctifying grace: by love, by discipline, by melting, and by burning, the Church as a whole, and every branch and congregation, is brought gradually towards perfect purity. Hence the importance during the interval of process that we should remember St. Paul's twofold seal. *The Lord knoweth them that are His:* whatever the anomalies, while the candlestick remains, we may have perfect confidence in the Divine discrimination of His own. *Let everyone that nameth the name of Christ depart from iniquity:* he that in the visible fellowship puts away sin, and lives in holiness, may also have rejoicing in himself when oppressed by the errors in doctrine and variations in practice observable in the GREAT HOUSE we have this double watchword to fall back on. One inscription on the seal bids us remember that God discerns His own from all others. The obverse inscription tells us that we must insure our own salvation: according to our Lord's principle, *What is that to thee? Follow thou Me!* But St. Paul's large and tolerant watchword must be somewhat limited in the case of any one community. In the individual church the case is different. It is not said of this, *let both grow together until the harvest.* On the contrary, an effectual discipline is appointed: pastoral oversight must see to it that disorderly members be reproved, and, if persisting in evil, put away; while the injunction is laid upon Christians, *withdraw yourselves from every brother that walketh disorderly.* Coincide. 2 Tim. ii. 19. John xxi. 22. Matt. xiii. 30. 2 Thess. iii. 6.

III. This leads to the consideration of two currents of error Historical.

which this Note of the Church detects : the exaggeration of the relative and of the absolute sanctity respectively.

Exaggeration of External Sanctity.

1. As to the former, many circumstances have had the effect of limiting the sanctity of the body to its outward fellowship. The notion of an inherent virtue in the sacraments, especially when these sacraments were multiplied so as to hedge in all life, tended to externalise the idea of religion generally, and of the ordinances of Christian fellowship in particular. So also the early and unregulated alliance of Christianity with the State had the same effect, as the perversion of what was in itself not necessarily evil. Whether the developed Roman theory, that the Church is invested with the supreme authority over the world, or the Erastian, that it is only an organ of the State, or the Latitudinarian, that the Church and State are several aspects of the same thing, the evidence of fact, multiplied into endless instances, goes to prove that the union, as it has been generally seen in Christendom, has always had this evil issue. Neglect of discipline, one of the worst results of bringing into too close relations the world and the Church, has tended the same way. The Lord's *Take these things hence!* gave a law and established a precedent too soon forgotten. The illustrations of this are endless, but they carry us too deeply for our present purpose into ecclesiastical history.

John ii. 16.

Of the Internal.

2. The internal sanctity has sometimes been undervalued. Some schisms in the early Church—Montanism in Phrygia, Novatianism in Rome, Donatism in Africa—were the result of undue rigour in rooting out the tares : the extremest fanaticism was the consequence. In more recent times Puritanism, whether on the Continent or in England, has pushed its high principle too far. Hence Modern Congregationalism, its lineal descendant and representative in this country, counts no sanctity of the external Church as valid to establish a Christian character or availing for membership without the profession of conscious faith. The Baptists go further, and refuse to admit that the dedication of children to God in baptism confers on them any even external relation to the Church as holy. This at least is their principle when carried to its issues.

Medium.

3. The true theory seems to be that which aims at the medium.

(1.) All who approve themselves believers in Christ, and who, whether as adults or as children, are baptized, belong to the external

body, and are entitled to all its privileges. Due respect to the outward and visible church requires the recognition of all baptized
and consistent members of it, without demanding personal testimony of conscious experience. But the internal sanctity of the
fellowship has its rights. The Sacrament of the Lord's Supper,
the seal of the communion of saints, and their note of profession
among men, must be guarded with care, its approaches being fenced
in every possible way suggested by pastoral vigilance and mutual
watchfulness. In some manner communicants ought to be examined and approved one by one.

(2.) The method of accomplishing this has varied with every
age and almost with every community. By many of the later
national churches it has been too often entirely neglected : public
warnings and confessions being only to a slight degree reinforced
by private investigation. The CLASS-MEETING among the Methodists is their method of meeting one of the greatest difficulties of
the times. It does not profess to impose a new condition of
membership in the Christian Church. It is only one out of many
forms—certainly the most widespread and permanent—which the
Ecclesiola in Ecclesiâ, or the society within the Church, has
assumed. No religious community has long maintained its vigour
and purity without some such expedient. This one in particular
honours the Church's note of external sanctity by admitting freely
every anxious applicant on the sole condition that he as a baptized
member of the Church of Christ is desirous to flee from the
wrath to come and to find salvation in the name of Jesus. It
brings everyone under pastoral supervision, direct or indirect :
indirect, as the leaders of these classes are themselves part of the
minister's flock, and direct, inasmuch as these little companies
are under the discipline of a quarterly visitation. This institution
provides the means of mutual social edification, in addition to the
general means of grace, and thus does much to promote both the
external and the internal sanctity of the community : the external,
because it tends to give more reality and dignity to the outward
fellowship of the Christian Church ; the internal, because it brings
all the members under the influence of an edifying mutual exhortation and prayer. Apart from its modern name, this form of
fellowship may be traced almost up to the times of the Apostles.

Class
Meeting.

These attributes of the organic fellowship of Christ have played a prominent part in ecclesiastical controversy. But there are none which are clearer in their elementary principles.

Invisible.　　I. The Church is, as the Redeemer's mystical body, animated by His Spirit, essentially invisible. In its deepest and most comprehensive sense it is a spiritual and unseen reality ; and therefore an ideal or the mystical fellowship. But, in its manifestation as the kingdom upon earth it is no other than the invisible Church taking visible form. Lastly, in its eternal consummation the invisible and the visible will be one.

John xviii. 36.　　1. *My kingdom is not of this world:* this declared to Pilate as the representative of those outside the spiritual and super-terrestrial character of the community ; afterwards, within the circle of His disciples, the Lord dwelt upon the same aspect of His fellowship. The entire strain of the Final Prayer presents before God a mystical and invisible body, with hardly an allusion to any other than that. This, in the language of St. Paul to the Ephesians, is

Eph. iv. 12; i. 23.　　*the body of Christ,* and *the fulness of Him that filleth all in all.* It is as an organic body spiritually organised and is invisible as its

Col. iii. 3.　　Head Himself is, like every faithful member, *hid with Christ in God.*

2. But this language concerning the mystical fellowship is addressed to a visible community as concerning itself. St. Paul does not speak of the *Saints which are at Ephesus* as distinct from

Eph. i. 1.　　the *Faithful in Christ Jesus,* though the whole question of visible and invisible lies in that distinction. The entire New Testament goes on to the assumption that every extant community is the earthly embodiment of the kingdom of heaven. In this the servants are faithful to the teaching of their Master, Who taught the unity, though not identity, of the visible and the invisible communions. The only two recorded instances of our Lord's use

Matt. xvi. 18.　　of the word illustrate the unity and the difference of the two. *Upon this rock I will build My church, and the gates of hell shall not prevail against it:* here is the foundation of the invisible Church which is the temple built by Christ spiritual and eternal, yet built up by human fellow-labourers with Himself: here the mystical idea is prominent though not exclusive of the other. That same Church is also shut in and the offender is in the midst, and discipline enforced, before the spiritual presence of Jesus who says : *Where two or three are gathered together in My name, there am I in the midst :* here the visible and concrete reality is prominent. But the two churches are one. So also the High-priestly prayer, which consecrates the spiritual temple, is uttered over a body that had just been bound together in visible sacramental unity. To return, however, from our Lord to His Apostles, St. Paul dilates upon the administration of gifts in a visible ministry, and then glides into the increase of the invisible body. So the *great house* is a visible one, but it has an eternal, invisible foundation ; as its *seal* testifies, *the Lord knoweth them that are His :* and the Lord alone.

Matt. xviii.20.

2 Tim. ii. 19, 20.

3. The Apocalypse gives us a clear vision of the visible and invisible reduced to final and eternal unity: mystical still, but eternally visible as one glorified organic whole, the Church is a distinct spiritual counterpart of the Lord Himself. Moreover He is the Bridegroom, and His Church the *Bride adorned for her husband,* in the last exhibition of both which the Scriptures contain.

Rev. xxi. 2.

II. The application of this double Note in historical theology concerns only the relative importance of the two ideas of visible and invisible. No confession has ever denied the reality of either. The differences between them have concerned only the results flowing from the undue preponderance of one or the other.

Historical

1. Romanism exalts the visibility almost to the suppression of the invisibility: not, however, denying the latter. It teaches that there is "one Ruler of the church invisible, Christ; and one Ruler of the visible, the successor of St. Peter." The spiritual body has a place in its interior theology, but is not, by any means, a governing idea : its theory is constructed in entire independence of the mystical reality, which is acknowledged indeed to be its crown and glory, but only in another state and to the eye of faith. Hence, it makes one of the many notes of the true church —of which a large number is sometimes reckoned—Exclusiveness : there is no salvation beyond the pale of the one visible institution.

Rome.

2. The Protestant idea strives to unite the two attributes : but giving always the priority and pre-eminence to the invisibility. The Roman Dogma will have nothing to do with an invisible church apart from the visible : the Protestant rejects the thought

Protestantism.

of a visible which is not created by the invisible to be its organ. The Reformed Confessions differed from the Lutheran only so far as their doctrine of election obliged them to differ. In the former the elect are the true fellowship; but the visible church is a holy institution "to depart from which," in Calvin's words, "is to deny Christ." Calvin says, further: "God substitutes the judgment of charity, in which we acknowledge those to be true members of the Church who confess the same God with us in profession of faith, in goodness of life, and in participation of sacraments." The Lutheran and the Reformed were agreed at the outset as to the close connection between the congregation visible and the body politic; but the close alliance of Church and State is not so generally accepted by their modern representatives.

Modern Efforts and Theories.

3. Much of the differences between the modern communions results from variations in theory as to the possibility of bringing the visible and the invisible into coincidence or unity. Here are two opposite extremes, and a middle way between them. The Broad-Church theory holds that the distinction should never be made, except in extreme cases of apostasy and excommunication: the whole world, waiting for baptism, is as it were the visible church, and the invisible must be left with God. The stricter Congregationalist theories strive to limit it as much as possible to authenticated professors, and aim very closely at making the visible the measure of the invisible in every society. This has introduced the modern distinction between the church and the congregation. Lastly, there has been a compromise, adopted under various forms among various communities: that of the Society within the church, which is not a theory of the mystical within the visible body, but the attempt to save the general fellowship from some of the evils which are inseparable from the constitution and working of the visible fellowship as the Apostles left it: an attempt that in some form or other has been made in almost every earnest and faithful communion.

Catholic and Local.

CATHOLIC AND LOCAL.

The ascription of catholicity to the Christian body dates from a very early time. The term catholic means universal; and when local is added, as its counterpart, the two expressions signify that the one church of the Redeemer, His body on earth, has such a universality in its design and destiny as is consistent with the local independence of individual churches. Nothing more is meant than this; but we shall find that the word catholic has a very different application in ecclesiastical history.

1. The testimony of Scripture on this subject is very simple. The ancient church, Hebrew and Jewish, was strictly local and national. All who might enter it from other lands must submit to what was a Jewish rite: retaining their own nationality as men, they must as worshippers become Jews. But the ancient Scriptures predicted a future religious fellowship which should embrace all nations, and be independent of everything national. The New Testament explains what in this matter the old predictions left indistinct. In the Gospels almost all the discourses and parables bearing on this subject dwell much on this enlargement of the kingdom : it is in fact hardly ever left out down to the last commission. In the later New Testament the theory is that of a church which is to be diffused through all nations; and the labours of the Apostles are directed accordingly. But, while thus catholic, the local community meets us everywhere. We read of *the church*, that is, of Jerusalem, and *the churches of Galatia*. The last time the word is mentioned, it is in connection with distinct and independent branches of the one universal Fellowship : *the seven churches which are in Asia* being a sevenfold unity.

2. The earliest use of the term Catholic, in the middle of the second century, probably introduced into it a meaning which the Scriptures do not refer to. The word was used to distinguish the one universal and faithful body from the fragmentary companies of heretics and schismatics which were therefore not parts of the catholic body. That meaning the word has never lost: the Great Majority. But, since the division between East and West, and the plain fact that the majority of professing Christians is on the side of the dissentients from the see of St. Peter, the term has been conventionally used by Rome to signify simply the one and only church, outside of which there is no salvation. The Eastern communities do not so much affect the term, preferring that of Orthodox and Apostolic.

3. The Christian Church may be regarded as CATHOLIC:

Margin notes:

Scriptural

Acts ii. 47.
Gal. i. 2.

Rev. i. 4.

Historical.

How Catholic.

designed and adapted for universal diffusion ; and embracing the
totality of those communions which maintain the great truths in
which the essence of Christianity lies.   The term, therefore,
ought never to be used of any particular community.   The Church

Local.

is also LOCAL or Particular : it exists in independent and even
isolated forms, whether as it respects individual, or connexional,
or national bodies ; and it may, holding the catholic verities,
maintain in its Confession truths that are not catholic, and adopt
un-catholic usages, without impairing its catholicity.   For the
one church of Christ is at once adapted for every variety of
mankind, and influenced in its turn by every variety of human
life.   It is not more certainly Universal than it is Particular.

APOSTOLIC AND CONFESSIONAL.

The New Testament to some extent sanctions the attribute
of Apostolicity.   After our Lord had chosen the Twelve—dis-

Matt. x. 1,
2.

tinguished by this number whether as *disciples* or as *Apostles,*—
He declared that upon them, represented by St. Peter, and pro-
claiming a sound confession, He would build His church.   To
these He entrusted the keys, gave His commission, and promised
the special effusion of His Spirit.   St. Peter, the representative
Apostle, was the instrument of laying the foundation of the new
community both among the Jews and among the Gentiles.   From

Acts ii.
42.

the Day of Pentecost the disciples *continued steadfastly in the Apostles'
doctrine and fellowship.*   When St. Paul was added to the company,
he became, as they were, an absolute authority under the Lord ;
and it is he who says that the members of Christ's body are

Eph. ii. 20.

built upon the foundation of the Apostles and Prophets.   The same
pre-eminence is given to them in the Apocalypse.   Leaving the
New Testament, we soon find the term Apostolic used as a note of
the visible Christian body.

Primacy
and
Prelacy.

I. At first the application of it was sound : the true church
traced its institution, under God, to the Apostolical foundation,
and maintained the Apostolical faith and traditions as yet un-
corrupted.   But gradually the theory arose which merged the
authority of the Twelve in that of Peter, and the Church was
regarded as Apostolic so far as it was one with the see of Rome.
But the primacy of Peter, only representative in the New Testa-

ment, ceased altogether when he departed; and thus this application of the note is convicted of being unscriptural.

2. The Apostolic note is applied, altogether independently of Rome, by many churches in the form of Apostolical succession. That there is an uninterrupted succession of ministers which the Divine eye can trace up to the Apostles' times, there can be no doubt. But it is utterly impossible to prove that in any part of the world there is a ministry that can trace its orders up through episcopal hands to the Apostles. This theory of the transmission of the Apostolic authority is closely connected with a wider theory of sacramental grace, which is elsewhere examined. As belonging to the Apostolic note, the doctrine of succession has no place in sound theology: at least in its modern conventional sense. *Apostolical Succession*

3. Another error—based on a theory curiously opposite to the last—interprets the Note thus: that the true church is one in which the Spirit, after the long pretermission of ages, has restored the Apostolate, with the original gifts and prerogatives of speaking with tongues and other miraculous endowments. But the Scripture does not make the existence of the Christian fellowship dependent on the permanence of the Apostolic office : on the contrary, St. Paul and St. John write as contemplating a state of things in which they and their prerogative would be absent. *Irvingism.*

4. During the last few centuries all Evangelical communions, not in bondage to the theory of succession, have held that the Apostolical doctrine and discipline may be maintained in common by communities which on minor points, not absolutely determined by the Apostles, differ according to their various standards of confession. Hence we may lay down our dogma : the Church is Apostolic, as being still ruled by the Apostolical authority living in the writings of the Apostles, that authority being the standard of appeal in all the Confessions that HOLD THE HEAD.

INDEFECTIBLE AND MUTABLE.

Both these attributes are clearly given to the one church in Holy Scripture. They refer to the perpetuity of the Christian community and of the Christian faith delivered to it. *Indefectible. Scriptural*

1. As to the former, it is enough to quote our Lord's words on *As to the Church.*

two occasions : when He first spoke of His church, and when He
Matt. xvi. last spoke of it. *The gates of hell shall not prevail against it.* He
18.
saw in the great futurity the anti-church—the kingdom of false-
hood, vanity, and death, the power of Hades—striving from age
to age to dissolve His kingdom, but in vain. It cannot fall;
Matt. vii. for, like the faith of every true member of it, it is *founded upon a*
25.
Rock. In His own Epistles in the Apocalypse, however, He
Rev. ii. 5. expressly threatens Ephesus to *remove thy candlestick out of his place :*
that is, to extinguish the light, and quench the existence, of an
individual church. His prophecy was fulfilled. Thus we have
His authority for believing that the Christian Church shall never
fail, but that Christian churches may pass away.

As to the   2. As to the latter, the perpetuity of the Faith, it needs no
Faith.
Matt.   special evidence beyond the assurance *I am with you alway.* Our
xxviii.20.   Lord is *the Truth ;* the Faith is one with Him ; and He is to be
John xiv.   glorified by the Spirit in the Church showing the things of Christ
6.
John xvi.   and guiding the Apostles into *all truth.* We need no further
13.   witnesses. On the other hand, that churches may corrupt the
faith, in part and in whole, and become apostate, is proved by a
catena of evidence going up to the Apostolical foundations which
did so corrupt it. These testimonies of Scripture establish our
dogma : that the Christian Church, in its unity, is at once and
while it is extant below both indefectible and mutable.

MILITANT AND TRIUMPHANT.

Militant
and
Trium-   1. There is no necessity for any illustration, either from history
phant.   or Scripture, of these last correlative attributes. Here at length
Scriptural
all exposition, all confessions, all communions agree. The same
one body which is waging war with principalities and powers,
slowly winning and hardly maintaining its conquests, is at the
same time triumphant, rejoicing in Paradise with its Head in
anticipation of that deeper joy, that joy of their Lord, into which
all shall at once enter in the end of the days. . The Church
militant expects its most severe conflicts yet in the future ; but
the apocalyptic agonies shall at the set time be swallowed up in
the song of eternal triumph. These two attributes are the most
comprehensive as they are the last. And, as they belong to the

one church, so in a certain sense they are themselves one. We hear the Apostles say : *Now thanks be unto God, which always causeth us to triumph in Christ!* The warfare and the victory go on together, as we hear in the Apocalypse, where the toiling assembly below hears the doxology of the general assembly above, and all but joins in it : like the prophet Isaiah in the typical vision of the mystical temple.

2 Cor. ii. 14.

Isa. vi.

2. The measure of the sympathy between the militant and the triumphant fellowship is clearly defined in Scripture ; but the early Church soon began to chafe at its restrictions. From Origen onward may be traced an ever-widening current of doctrine, the issue of which was the creation of a new intermediate estate of the Christian company, not precisely militant and not yet triumphant, that of Purgatory. Connected with this was the enlargement of the article on the Communion of Saints, so as to include the good offices of prayer between the living and the departed : intercession for the dead in Purgatory on the part of saints on earth ; on the part of saints in heaven, intercession both for the dead in Purgatory and the militant living. This department of theology is simply an addition to Scripture, the teaching of which, as we have seen, and shall see again, altogether repudiates it.

Historical.

THE CHURCH AS AN INSTITUTE FOR WORSHIP.

The Church of Christ is not only His representative Body on earth, it is also the Temple of Divine service, continuing and perfecting the worship of the past. This service may be studied under two aspects, as it includes offering presented to God, and blessing received from Him. The former embraces the entire ordinance of worship, with its nature, reasons, and observances ; the latter embraces the means of grace, Common Prayer, the Word, and Sacraments. These, however, are really one, and their relations to each other as one are of great importance. Both require for their realisation the institution of the Evangelical ministry. We have then now before us the Divine worship, the Means of Grace, and the Christian Ministry.

As to the unity of worship and the means of grace, it must be remembered that both are taken in their widest meaning. Worship includes all that belongs to the service offered by men to God as He is the Object of adoration and the Source of blessing: including praise and prayer in all their forms. Communion with Him, therefore, is the channel of all benediction; and we may speak generally of waiting upon God in the means of grace. But this latter term (Media Gratiæ) has also its technical signification, as designating the appointed and specific channels through which the Divine Spirit pours His influences into the Church. Into the Church: for, while all doxology and all benediction is individual, we are now regarding them as ordinances of the congregation. Their congregational character is represented by the ministry, which must be regarded as an institution for the corporate body, affecting individuals only as being members in particular.

DIVINE WORSHIP.

The worship of the Christian Church may be regarded in its Divine principles and in its human arrangements. As to the former, its object is the revealed Trinity; its form is Mediatorial, through the Son Incarnate, by the Holy Spirit; its attributes are spirituality, simplicity, purity, and reverent decorum; its seasons are the Christian Sabbath pre-eminently, and all times of holy assembly. As to the latter, it is left to the congregation itself to determine the minor details, according to the pattern shown in the Scripture: this latitude extending to the order of worship, its set times, its forms, liturgical or otherwise, and its decent ceremonial generally.

THE DIVINE ORDER.

Divine Principles   The Divine and permanent laws of the perfect economy of public worship prescribe the following general principles.

1. That always and everywhere the TRIUNE GOD be its object,   Object.
as now fully revealed in the Christian dispensation. All homage
or adoration or gratitude must, virtually or actually, pay its
tribute to the Three-One Name; and whatever acts of worship
are offered to One Divine Person must be offered to That One in
the unity of the Other Two. The God of the Christian temple is
the Same Who in the ancient temple received the threefold Doxology and bestowed the threefold Benediction.

2. That the stated form of all worship, whether of praise or   Media-
prayer, must be, either informally or avowedly, MEDIATORIAL.   torial
God the Father, the Representative of the Trinity, is to be   Form.
addressed only through the mediation of the Incarnate Son, Whose
intercessory office, based on His one sacrifice, has special reference
to our privilege of *boldness to enter into the holiest.* And *through*   Heb. x. 19.
Him we both have access by one Spirit unto the Father. That *Spirit*   Eph. ii. 18.
of grace and of supplications alone inspires the energy of intelligent   Zech. xii.
and acceptable worship; and His influence is equally present in   10.
every assembly from the least to the greatest. These are the full
mediatorial preparations, in heaven and upon earth,—there
through the High Priest and here through His Spirit,—for the
perfect devotions of the Church below. We find this Divine
order observed in all the prayers and praises of the later New
Testament. In harmony with this law we arrange all our
liturgical worship. And, though we do not presume to add the
formula of mediatorial words to the Lord's Prayer, we silently
present it through the name of Him Who gave it to us.

3. *The preparations of the heart in man,* also, are *from the Lord.*   Nature.
It is the first condition of Divine worship that it be SPIRITUAL.   Prov. xvi.
God is a Spirit: and they that worship Him must worship Him in   1.
spirit and in truth. This law of Christ is the law of all the Scrip-   John iv.
ture; but He thus solemnly re-enacted it, as He re-enacted the   24.
law of love, to show its supreme importance: it demands the
heart of man as the shrine of worship, *sanctify the Lord God in*   1 Pet. iii.
your hearts; it forbids all representations of the Supreme save   15.
those which He has appointed and are spiritual in their
meaning; and it reduces all externals of service to their true
place. PURITY also is an essential of this worship: the *pure in*   Matt. v. 8.
heart in His temple *see God,* and none really approach Him,

though found in the congregation, whose motives are not sincere ;

1 Tim. ii. 8. .
1 Cor. xiv. 33, 40.
without wrath and doubting. ORDER is another Divine law of worship : *God is not the author of confusion,* ἀκαταστασίας. And His will is that *all things be done decently and in order,* εὐσχημόνως καὶ κατὰ τάξιν. In the presence of God a sacred decorum is the rule as well of nature as of grace. Again, worship must be COMPLETE in its tribute to the Supreme : in the adoration of His name which is Praise ; in the remembrance of His mercies, which is Thanksgiving ; in the acknowledgment of unworthiness, which is Confession ; in the expression of dependence, which is Prayer ; in the oblation of Charity, which is Intercession. Lastly, worship must be INDIVIDUAL. There is in Christianity, as our Lord teaches it, no representative worship but His own ; and in that we are united with Him. The devotion is the Church's devotion, but its harmony is the blending of the melodies of all its individual members not one of whom is forgotten.

Seasons.
The
Sabbath.
4. Amongst the permanent Divine ordinances of worship must be reckoned THE SABBATH as its chief and representative season. This institution was an appointment of God from the beginning of time to that end. Rest from labour was a physical design subserved in connection with a spiritual design : that man might cease from every other occupation in order to hold communion with his Creator. This was the supreme purpose of the day ; and as such bound up with all the Old-Testament regulations of religious service. Christianity has retained the institution as belonging to Divine worship ; but, by the same authority which gave the original law, has modified it. Its connection with the Jewish sabbatical cycle ended, and therefore its place as a covenant sign between Jehovah and the peculiar people. Its original purpose to commemorate the creation and bear witness to the government of the One God was retained ; but, as the new creation of mankind in Christ Jesus had more fully revealed the Triune God, the day of our Lord's resurrection, the first day of the week, became the Christian Sabbath, or Lord's Day. The special relation of the day to the worship of the Church, apart from its place in the Moral Law, is to be found in the opportunity it affords of full public assembly, generally impossible at any other time, with which the continuance of religion in the world

is vitally connected. To sum up, the Lord's Day in the Christian Church is the great season of worship and of assembling to worship; it retains its original design of commemorating creation, it adds the festival of redemption, and it periodically suspends this world's labour to anticipate the worship of heaven. Some points in this general statement require expansion.

(1.) It has been doubted whether the account in Genesis asserts the institution of the Sabbath at that time: *God blessed the seventh day, and sanctified it* may, it is said, be proleptical. But the obvious intention of the narrative is historical; there are also indications of the hebdomadal division of time throughout the early books; and our Lord's testimony is that *the Sabbath was made for man.* Hence we find the institution referred to as one that had been familiarly known before the Mosaic law was given on Sinai: *Remember the Sabbath day, to keep it holy.* Gen. ii. 3.

Gen. viii. 10, 11; xxix. 27, 28. Mark ii. 27. Ex. xx. 8. Ex. xvi. 23, 26. Abolished

(2.) So far as the Sabbath was introduced into the ceremonial law, and was made the basis of a Sabbatic cycle of days; so far as it became a sacrament of the old law, commemorating the redemption from Egypt, *a sign between Me and you throughout your generations; that ye may know that I am the Lord that doth sanctify you,* and fenced about by severe enactments;—it is abolished in Christianity. *Let no man therefore judge you in meat, or in drink, or in respect of an holy day, or of the new moon, or of the sabbath days.* Ex. xxxi. 13. Jer. xvii. 20—27. Col. ii. 16.

(3.) The new ordinance of the Sabbath in the Gospel was given by Christ Himself, the *Lord also of the Sabbath.* Before His passion He dealt with it as with all His institutions, by preliminary indications of His future will. He condemned false interpretations, while He included it in the law which He did not *come to destroy.* By His example and precept He relaxed its severity. With His resurrection began His formal appointment of the First day, and with the Pentecost He finally ratified it. In the interim we may suppose that He enacted by word what in His majesty He had sanctioned by act. Hence we find the first day, as the Lord's Day, hallowed throughout the New Testament: the last tribute uniting the Resurrection and the Pentecost: *I was in the Spirit on the Lord's day.* To use St. Paul's word on another occasion, the law of the Christian sabbath is *not of men, neither by man,* not of the Church nor by the Church, *but by Jesus Christ.* Renewed. Mark ii. 28. Matt. v. 17. Rev. i. 10. Gal. i. 1.

υ 2

Sacra-
ment of
Time.

(4.) It is, so to speak, the sacrament of holy time in the Evangelical economy. The first day of the week sanctifies all the days
which follow, but it retains its symbolical meaning. It is the day
of holy convocation, concerning which it is said, pre-eminently
Heb. x. 25. though not solely, *not forsaking the assembling of ourselves together.*
As Baptism is a sign of the severance between the world of the
unregenerate and the church of the renewed, and as the Eucharist
1 Cor. xi. is a standing memorial of the redeeming Atonement, and both *till*
26. *He come,* so the Holy Day is an abiding memorial of the permanent obligation of congregational worship. Hence it is one of
the three Dominical institutes: the LORD'S HOUSE, the LORD'S
SUPPER, the LORD'S DAY, ἡ Κυριακὴ ἡμέρα.

(5.) Lastly, this general view of the Sabbath in relation to
worship connects it with the Church, though it is scarcely right
to number it among the INSTITUTIONS OF CHRISTIANITY. It is
an institution of the Christianity that is as old as the Creation.
But this connects it with the Moral Law, where, as a positive
enactment, it is of perpetual obligation in the Ethics, not of the
Church only, but of all religion. The Sabbath as an ordinance
for worship is the day which assembles the congregation; but in
that worship itself the injunction of the Sabbath is read as one of
the precepts of the eternal code of morality. What its spiritual
interpretation is as a permanent law for mankind is a question of
ethics, and has already been considered as such. At present we
have considered it in its relation to Divine service.

THE HUMAN FORMS.

Human
Ordi-
nances.

Public worship is left, as to its form, to the discretion of the
congregation, subject, however, to the authority of the Divine
laws, and guided by the usage of Scripture. The questions that
here arise are not strictly included in dogmatic theology: they
therefore need only slight indication.

Times and
Seasons.

1. The rights of the laws already laid down being reserved,
the Church may appoint times and seasons and places of religious
service. There is no restriction: the Lord's Supper itself is not
limited to any certain day. There is no hour that may not be

set apart. Daily service, and canonical hours, are not in themselves evil, save in connection with superstitions, and as tending to absorb family and private worship. Days of Thanksgiving and of Fasting have the plenary sanction of Scripture. But Saints' days have not that authority; and, although much may be said in favour of making the names of our Lord's inspired servants prominent in the service, it is expedient to abstain. There is but a step, as the history of the corruptions of Christianity shows, between this and the Invocation of Saints. As to places, there is no Temple or Sanctuary : this word is reserved for the spiritual community or body of the Church, and the regenerate spirit of the Christian. In a certain sense there is a House of God, but wherever the congregation may meet there is, in the truest sense, the House of Prayer : *Whose house are we.* Heb. iii. 6.

2. As to the arrangements of Divine service, there is the same latitude. The law of Decency and Order requires that the worship be regulated, and that no room be left for caprice. The relations of worship, and sacrament, and preaching must be arranged by the community. As to the much-vexed question of LITURGICAL PRAYER, it may, at least, be said that its use is within the prerogative of the congregation. The Saviour gave the germ of it in His sacred pattern, in His sanction of the Temple and Synagogue service and hymns, and in His sacramental institutes. It has been one of the most universal usages of Christendom ; its abuses do not discredit its use ; it approves its value in experience, both as insuring the completeness of worship and by aiding tranquil devotion ; virtually it enters into all extant services ; and, as supplementing while not superseding spontaneous or rather unliturgical prayers, it may with assurance be both practised and defended. Arrangements. Liturgical Worship.

3. As to the superadded ceremonials of public worship, there is hardly the same latitude. The jurisdiction of the Church here, or its power to ordain ceremonies, is attended with great difficulty. We have not now to decide between the hard requirement that forgets everything but the purely spiritual nature of the worshipper and the opposite extreme that panders to all his senses. Neither of these can be right. There is a spirit in worshipping man, or he could not worship the Invisible ; and he is also flesh and blood, or he Ceremonies.

could not worship in public assemblies. There is a simple æsthetical vesture of Divine service without which it ought not to appear before God, without which it cannot commend itself to man. But what is now conventionally called Ritualism must be entirely condemned; that is to say, the introduction of symbols not ordained by the Head of the Church: symbols in the architecture of the building, in the dress of the officiating minister, and especially in the conduct of the worship itself. It tends to dishonour Holy Scripture, by making ceremonials teach doctrines that the Word of God alone should teach: in fact, Ritualism is another form of the Oral Tradition which is made co-ordinate with Scripture as the teaching authority. It endangers the dignity of the Sacraments, which, as the sole elements of ritual given us in a religion that closed the ritual temple, should be rigidly guarded in their simplicity as the Saviour left them: whereas the ritual superadded to them in later times teaches principles and applications never contemplated by the Founder of Christianity. And what is called the ritualistic spirit dishonours the Spirit of devotion by such numberless and ever-varying appeals to the senses as distract the soul from its one function. Concerning such additions of men's will-worship the Lord of the Temple says still: *Take these things hence!*

John ii. 16.

THE MEANS OF GRACE.

As an institute of worship the Church of Christ has its ordinary channels for the communication of the influences of the Holy Ghost to the souls of men. These are the Media Gratiæ, or MEANS OF GRACE. Though the Spirit is not bound to these, they are "generally necessary to salvation." They are not, however, equally and in the same sense necessary. The Word of God and Prayer are unitedly and severally what may be called the absolute and universal means: as such they may be first discussed. The sacraments are economical means, distinct from the former, yet entirely dependent upon them for their virtue.

THE SUPREME MEANS: THE WORD AND PRAYER

These are the supreme means as they are the basis of
all: they give their virtue to the ordinances of the Church,
including the sacraments. They are united: the Word
gives the warrant to prayer and all its objects; Prayer is
the instrument which makes the Word effectual. But as
means of grace they may be regarded separately.

THE WORD

The Word of God in the Scriptures contains the whole **The Word**
compass of that spiritual truth which the Holy Spirit uses
as His instrument for the communication of every influence on which the salvation of man depends. As the
revelation of God's law He uses it for conviction; as the
Gospel promise He uses it for salvation; as the depository
of ethical truth He uses it for sanctification through
all morality and the discipline of holy life.

Let us view this in the light of Scripture itself, and then
glance at ancient and current divergences
I. The doctrine of the Word concerning itself is that it is the **Testimony to itself**
universal channel of grace; that it is not this of itself, through
any inherent efficacy, but as the organ of the Holy Ghost, and
that its efficacy is nevertheless in a certain sense inherent, as the
Spirit's instrument, though it may be resisted These topics have
been discussed, in their application, under the Administration of
Redemption Their bearing on the Word as chief among the
means of grace may, however, be briefly considered
1 The sufficiency of Scripture is declared throughout both
Testaments The praises of the law of the Lord abound in the Old
Testament, especially in the Psalms One of them expatiates on
the subject by taking all the ten names given to the Law and **Ps. cxix.**
applying them to every phase of human need and religious

experience. In the New Testament we have not one passage only, but a pervasive testimony. What St. Paul says of the Scriptures generally, that they make *wise unto salvation*, and are profitable for every function of grace, *for doctrine, for reproof, for correction, for instruction in righteousness*, must be true of the supreme Scripture, the words of Christ, which are and comprise in themselves *All the truth*. He therefore prays, *Sanctify them through Thy truth: Thy Word is truth.*

2. The fallen estate of man forbids the thought that the mere presentation of truth should save him. He has an organ or faculty to receive it, for it is as much adapted to his soul's need as bread is to the need of his body; but the organ or faculty itself needs quickening. Hence the inherent power of the Word requires the influence of the Spirit to make it effectual. The Apostle Paul declares that his preaching was *in demonstration of the Spirit and of power* generally; but he also declares that *the natural man receiveth not the things of the Spirit of God; for they are foolishness unto him; neither can he know them, because they are spiritually discerned.* The language or alphabet of the doctrine of the Holy Ghost must be taught to him who shall understand His consecutive and general teaching. He appeals, as the Lord appealed: *why do ye not understand My speech* (λαλιὰν)? *even because ye cannot hear My word* (λόγον). A man must submit to the doctrine of sin generally, which is hearing Christ's word or testimony concerning Himself and the sinner's relation to Him, before he can receive the full exposition of that doctrine as it is salvation.

3. But there is an inherent efficacy in Scripture, as applied by the Spirit. It is the universal means of grace, though men may resist it. The Word of God is as efficacious as it is universal and sufficient. It is its inherent efficacy that detects unbelief and convicts it: it is not only effectual in saving, but in condemning also. It is the same Gospel power of God which is a *savour of death unto death*, and a *savour of life unto life*. The Scriptural doctrine of the Divine Word as the means of grace will not allow it ever to be made *of none effect*. It is an instrument that never fails. Regarded as the Word spoken to mankind, it cannot be without its power. The Spirit is never absent from the Word: in it He lives and moves, and through it He sheds an infinite

Margin notes:
2 Tim. iii. 15, 16.
John xvi. 13.
John xvii. 17.
The Word.
1 Cor. ii. 4.
1 Cor. ii. 14.
John viii. 43.
Word and Spirit.
2 Cor. ii. 16.
Matt. xv. 6.

variety of influences on all who either reject or receive it. Regarded as the means of grace within the Church, it has a sacred, specific, and always present grace accompanying every truth and every promise   The Spirit is in the Truth, as the virtue was and is in Christ · ready for impartation to every touch of faith   The self-evidencing energy of the Bible is its sure credential   No living man can say that it has utterly failed to find him out, and move his inmost being, and work upon his deepest convictions.

II It will be enough to indicate some more or less prevalent errors belonging to two entirely opposite types   **Errors.**

1 There has never been wanting a tendency to make the Scriptures sufficient of themselves, without any supernatural accompanying influence, to effect the salvation of men   The ancient Pelagians and semi-Pelagians regarded the Word of God as the intellectual and moral discipline which best suits the spiritual nature of man, its honest use leading sincere inquirers to perfection   As human nature retains its original elements unimpaired, its natural powers are supposed to be sufficient under the influence of truth to guide to salvation   Modern Rationalism has the same general estimate of the Word of God   not regarding it as in any specific sense the means of grace, but only as one among many instruments of moral discipline.   **Pelagian-ism**

2 The highest mysticism of every age seeks through means to rise above means and become dead to them   To the more Scriptural mystics of every communion the Word is to be valued by its substance of truth ; which exerts its influence upon the mind, but only in order to raise it to the higher intuition of God   Meditation on the principles and truths of the Word leads to Contemplation which leaves all words, thoughts, and images behind   This is the line beyond which mysticism becomes unsafe   **Mysticism**

3 The doctrine which makes the Divine sovereignty its supreme principle holds the Word to be the means of an absolute and irresistible grace.   Whatever effect it produces is produced by the effectual operation of One who cannot be resisted.   The Holy Ghost, as a personal Spirit, free in all His acts, and applying redemption only to those whose names are already written in the Book of Life, uses the Word to accomplish His purposes, or accomplishes them without it, as seemeth good to Him   When   **Predesti-narianism**

the Word is used, it is literally His CHANNEL of grace to the souls predestined to salvation.

Scriptural　　4. The doctrine which we hold combines all that is good in them, and rejects the evil. It gives a high, indeed the highest, place to the Scripture as the instrument of all grace. It pays its tribute to the Spirit Who alone makes it such. But it regards the Spirit's operation as operating not simply and alone THROUGH the Word, but also IN it and WITH it, for salvation.

Prayer.

PRAYER.

Prayer, or communion with God, is not generally reckoned among the Means of Grace, technically so called. It is regarded rather as the concomitant of the others. But, while it is undeniably true that Prayer is a condition of the efficacy of other means, it is itself and alone a means of grace. In many respects, it is the highest, simplest, most universal, most comprehensive, and most effectual of these means.

1. It is the most universal. Wherever the creature is found, *Ask and it shall be given you* is the law that governs its relations to the Creator. The mediation of Christ, which embraces or wraps round the history of all mankind, has established this never-failing medium of communion between the Supreme and every human being. The constitution of nature is framed with reference to this law, and all the acts of Providence suppose it. No philosophical speculations can avail to disturb the original ordinance, though none can avail to explain it. In the whole compass of the Word of God the question never rises as to the difficulty of adjusting the fixed economy of things to this everlasting interference with it: in fact, this everlasting interference is part of the fixed economy. However much the question may be argued, here is the very last word on the subject. The Personal God is the Hearer and Answerer of prayer: as His existence is always postulated and never proved, so His regulation of all things on earth according to the Pre-established Harmony of peti-

Matt. vii. 7.

tion and supply is taken for granted throughout   Prayer is the
eternal medium of grace, as grace is distinguished from gifts that
are bestowed independently of the creature's will   though, strictly
speaking, much of that grace is independent also

2. It is all-pervading   The Word by which man lives is made   All-per-
the channel of blessing when its promises are pleaded in prayer.   vading
Sacraments derive from this their efficacy.   And it is adapted to
all conditions of life , private, social, and common prayer open
and keep open their several channels into the individual soul, the
family, and the congregation   But, while prayer pervades all
other means, it extends beyond them all   There is no moment
of life, there is no occupation, nor can the petitioning spirit be
found in any place, where the turning of the soul to God may not
be attended by the full virtue of this everlasting ordinance.

3. Hence we see the importance of uniting the Word and
Prayer most closely as the abiding, pre-eminent, and essential
means of grace.   They do not disparage the other means ; but
must not by them be superseded   This will, however, appear
more fully in the consideration of what follows

THE SACRAMENTS AS THE ECONOMICAL OR COVENANT MEANS OF GRACE

The Saviour, who came not to destroy but to fulfil the
law, has retained under new forms those two of the
ancient ritual observances which were the specific badges
of the old covenant as such   Circumcision, the rite by
which the covenant was entered, has become Baptism ;
and the Passover, the rite by which it was annually
confirmed, has become the Lord's Supper.   These have
been instituted for the perpetual observance of the
Christian Church, and placed among its means of grace.
As means of grace they have elements of difference, and
elements in common with the other means.   Their difference is that they are Federal Transactions : signs and
seals of the covenant of redemption.   As signs, they

represent in action and by symbols the great blessings of the covenant; as seals they are standing pledges of the Divine fidelity in bestowing them on certain conditions, being the Spirit's instrument in aiding and strengthening the faith which they require, and in assuring to that faith the present bestowment of its object. Thus they are, on the one hand, objective institutions which assure the continuance of the Spirit's administration of redemption in the Church, and, on the other, subjective confirmations to each believing recipient of his own present interest in the covenant. Moreover, as the covenant is NOT OF ONE, but implies the condescension of God in entering into covenant relations with His people, the signs and seals are mutual: they are emblematic ordinances by which the Divine fidelity is pledged, and they are on our part the outward and visible token by which our faith gives its pledges to God of a cordial acceptance of His terms : both, however, by the Holy Ghost. These federal transactions as belonging to the means of grace have also their elements in common with other means. They are based upon the mediation of Him who is the supreme Means of Grace ; they are appointed by the same authority ; like other means, they are external notes and badges of Christian profession ; and, finally, they depend for their efficacy on the Holy Spirit's power working in and through human faith. These ordinances have been from the beginning termed SACRAMENTS. Their nature, and efficacy, and number, and general relation to the means of grace are questions which have been much controverted, and given rise to some of the most important differences among the Christian Confessions.

What more this topic requires will be best given in a brief view of the history of the sacramental principle in general.

1 In the New Testament no designation is given to these Scripture
symbols All types, or prophecies in act, ended with Christ the
universal Antitype, and all symbols, or visible prophetic representations of invisible realities, ended with the Tongues of fire on
the Day of Pentecost, and therefore with the Holy Ghost, the
universal spiritual reality So far as they are prophetic types
and symbols they must cease with their fulfilment This gives
deep emphasis to the fact that two symbols were retained, or
rather instituted anew, for permanent observance They are
closely connected with the blessings they signify they are also
distinctly separated from them , and by plain command, which
we see always obeyed throughout the New Testament, they are
made perpetual This will appear more fully in the discussion of
the several Sacraments themselves

2. Very early two names were given to the sacramental insti- Mystery
tution In the Greek Church the term Μυστήριον was used
mystery, not in the more general Pauline meaning of a secret Rev 1 20
disclosed, but in that of the profound significance of some per-
ceptible emblem · hence it is preserved as a remembrancer of the
past in the English Communion Service, ' these holy mysteries."
By the Western Church the corresponding word SACRAMENTUM
was employed . in Roman usage the term had a wide variety of
meanings, all however based on the idea of a sacred obligation. It
was the oath, particularly that by which the soldier was bound
to fidelity obtemperaturus sum et facturus quicquid mandabitur
ab imperatoribus juxta vires The two ordinances were in the
early Church regarded as the rites of religion through which
Christians came under the most solemn obligation to do their
part in complying with the conditions of grace Baptism, however,
had more of the sacramental character, the Eucharist more that
of mystery In ecclesiastical Latin the word sacramentum came
to signify anything consecrated ; in the Vulgate it was adopted
as the translation of μυστήριον , and, as the sign of a sacred
thing, became the conventional name of the institute Later
diversities may be referred to the several topics of the Sign, and Varieties
the Seal, and the Divine appointment. of
Opinion

SIGNS.

As to their significatory character there has been no real differ- Signs ence from the beginning among those who have held fast the Sacraments as belonging to the permanent economy of the Gospel. Augustine's "aliud videtur, aliud intelligitur" or "verba visibilia," Visible Words; and Chrysostom's ἕτερα ὁρῶμεν ἕτερα πιστεύομεν, "one thing we see, another we believe," have been accepted by all Christians alike as rightly indicating the meaning of the emblems, whether of the old covenant or of the new. Here there is no discussion. It has pleased God in every age to Heb. i. 1. include among His *divers manners* the method of teaching by symbol. The Saviour Himself so taught: witness His records in the Gospels, from the scourge of cords down to the Feetwashing. Nor is there a word spoken in the New Testament that formally abolishes symbols generally, though the institution of the two sacraments may be fairly considered as implying that they were to stand alone in the worship of the Christian congregation.

Seals.
SEALS.

Their character as seals has been the subject of much discussion and of wide discrepancy. The various theories which have predominated may be studied to great advantage in their historical order.

1. In the Early Church we find the germs of every later teaching. But to one who studies attentively there can be no question that a strong tendency betrayed itself almost as soon as the Apostles departed to dwell more on the Mysterium than on the Sacramentum, and to make the whole of religion depend as it were on these two sacramental rites.

Tridentine.
2. This exaggerated estimate of the ceremonial ordinances took its final form in the Tridentine teaching, which makes the sacraments, not seals of a covenant, but depositories of grace flowing through them of necessity and through them alone: their intrinsic efficacy being supposed always to accompany the priestly administration; if performed, that is, with intention according to the mind of the Church, and on recipients who do not interpose the obstacle of mortal sin. The Council of Trent has this canon: Si quis dixerit per ipsa novæ legis sacramenta ex opere operato non conferri gratiam sed solam fidem divinæ promissionis ad gratiam consequendam sufficere, anathema sit. This dictum is capable of two constructions. As in the case of Justification it may be said

that the faith ALONE is all that is condemned; but the common
instinct of Protestantism has seen in it the foundation of the error
of a necessary impartation of grace lodged only in the sacraments.
This very ancient and wide-spread error, though not held by the
Greek Church, has three characteristics. It elevate sunduly the
means, which are supposed to contain and as it were mechanically
or magically discharge their grace. It makes too much depend
upon the mind and purpose of the administrant. And its negative
condition, the not interposing an obstacle, or the OBICEM of mortal
sin, tends to the dishonour of Evangelical faith, and complicates
the subject by involving with it the definitions of mortal and
venial sin. The direct influence of the Holy Spirit is also omitted.

3. The Lutheran and Reformed types of doctrine concerning
the sacramental idea condemn the EX OPERE OPERATO, or that
which makes the sacramental act efficacious per se or without
reference to the faith of the recipient; but they in some other
respects differ. Lutheranism lodges the virtue in the sacraments,
makes it inherent in them by the ordination of Christ, but saving
only to the believer: it approaches the Romanist theory as to
their being the appointed and generally the only channels of
salvation. Adopting St. Augustine's maxim, accedit verbum et fit
sacramentum,—the Divine word added makes it a sacrament—it
regards that consecrating word as conveying into the elements a
grace which they must needs impart, to the evil for condemnation
and to believers for their good. It makes the sacraments necessary means of grace : not merely the first, and generally necessary;
but, as to the specific grace they represent, the only means. A
participation in these institutes is held essential to a participation in
the things they signify. Hence the sacraments are made in a
certain sense the centre of the plan of salvation. This must be
remembered in every estimate of Lutheranism as such.

Lutheran and Re-formed.

4. The Reformed doctrine lays more stress on the concurrence
of the Holy Ghost : virtus Spiritus sancti extrinsecus accedens.
Not the Word, as in St. Augustine's maxim, but the Spirit, makes
the sacrament a channel of grace; and, as that Spirit is not bound
to forms, He can dispense His grace without the sacraments,
before them or after them. Still, though not absolutely necessary,
sine quâ non, they are preceptively necessary; and, as the

Reformed.

appointed seals and pledges of the administration of redeeming grace, they must be observed. The early Socinians went beyond the Swiss Zwingli in making sacraments only signs of Christian profession, and emblems intended to exert a moral influence on the mind : a view which is extensively prevalent among the lesser sections of Christendom both on the Continent and in England.

Arminian.　　5. The early Arminian doctrine is sometimes classed with the system to which these last-named views belong. But let us hear the words of the Remonstrant Confession : Sacramenta cum dicimus, externas Ecclesiæ cæremonias seu ritus illos sacros ac solennes intelligimus, quibus veluti fœderalibus signis ac sigillis visibilibus Deus gratiosa beneficia sua in fœdere præsertim evangelico promissa non modo nobis repræsentat et adumbrat, sed et certo modo exhibet atque obsignat, nosque vicissim palam publiceque declaramus ac testamur, nos promissiones omnes divinas vera, firma atque obsequiosa fide amplecti et beneficia ipsius jugi et grata semper memoria celebrare velle. These words should be carefully studied in their connection, and translated ; as presenting, beyond those of any other Symbol, all the elements necessary to make up the true sacramental idea. The definition lays stress on their being Federal signs and seals : not only adumbrating the evangelical blessings of the Christian covenant, but exhibiting and applying them ; while they express also our public faith, and grateful remembrance. This testimony includes all that is included in our great British Confessions ; and, if it adds anything, the addition is an improvement. The Westminster Confession says : "Sacraments are holy signs and seals of the covenant of grace. There is in every sacrament a spiritual relation, or sacramental union between the sign and the thing signified ; whence it comes to pass that the names and effects of the one are attributed to the other." And in the Shorter Catechism the Presbyterian standard thus speaks : "A sacrament is a holy ordinance instituted by Christ ; wherein, by sensible signs, Christ and the benefits of the New Covenant are represented, sealed, and applied to believers." Here the last expression gives additional strength to the idea of the seal : not only are blessings pledged, but they are then and there imparted. So the Article of the Church of England : "Sacraments ordained of Christ be not only badges or tokens of Christian men's profession, but rather they be certain sure witnesses and effectual signs of grace, and God's goodwill towards us, by the which He doth work invisibly in us, and doth not only quicken, but also strengthen and confirm our faith in Him." With these symbols —Arminian, Reformed, Anglican—our general Proposition agrees.

DIVINE INSTITUTION.

As to the Divine institution of the sacraments there have been two leading errors. One, represented by some of the more pantheistic Mystics in earlier ages, and by the Quakers in modern times, denies the permanent obligation of these ordinances. According to the latter baptism was intended only for the first introduction of Gentiles into the new community; the Eucharist was only the sanctification of the common nourishment of life; and, generally, the Christian economy has and can have in it no ritual. The other error has gone to the opposite extreme, and multiplied the sacramental institutions of Christianity.

ADDITIONS TO THE SACRAMENTS.

1. The origin of this multiplication of sacraments may be traced to the indefinite use of the term in early phraseology: it was applied to almost every mystery of the Christian Faith and almost every religious symbol. Thus Augustine, while allowing their supremacy to the Two, speaks in an uncertain and wavering manner concerning some other rites of a sacramental nature. Bernard was disposed to add the Feet-washing, and many writers before and after him mention other symbolical acts of Christ among the sacraments. The Seven Sacraments were first defined by Otto of Bamberg, A.D. 1124; these received ecclesiastical sanction at Florence, A.D. 1439, and were confirmed at the Council of Trent. They were variously illustrated and defended by the Scholastics. It was supposed that each was symbolised by or symbolised one of the seven cardinal virtues, Faith, Love, Hope, Wisdom, Temperance, Courage, Righteousness; they were explained by the analogy of the spiritual life with the physical, as to Birth, Growth into adult age, Nourishment, Healing, Reproduction, Instruction, Death; and so forth. The final definition at Trent admits the pre-eminence of the Eucharist:

Multiplication.

The Seven.

Sess. xiii. 3.

Cat. Rom. ii. 1, 22.

Sanctitate longe cæteris antecellit. Baptism, Confirmation, Orders were held to have an indelible character, never effaceable, and never to be repeated. The anathema is pronounced upon those who deny that the Seven were all, if not equally, instituted by Christ: admitting therefore that the appointment of our Lord is the only and final test of a true sacrament.

Greek and Roman Communions.

2. It is remarkable that the Greek and the Roman communions, differing in so much besides, agree in accepting seven sacraments. Both base their acceptance on the authority of the Church as interpreting the will of Christ, and vindicate them as enfolding and hedging round, and sanctifying the whole of life at its several stages: Baptism is the sanctification of birth, Confirmation of adult life, Penance of the life of daily sin, the Eucharist of life itself, Orders of legitimate authority, Matrimony of the Church's law of continuance and increase, and Unction of the departure hence. Other communions have attempted, and are attempting, to introduce the distinction between sacramental ordinances which are not sacraments and sacraments proper, but the test of our Lord's own institution absolutely forbids any addition to His two covenant institutes. "A sacrament is an outward and visible sign of an inward and spiritual grace, ordained by Christ Himself as a means whereby we receive the same, and a pledge to assure us thereof." Our Lord has chosen and hallowed two, only two; and it is vain to elevate acts which are rather benedictory or only symbolical than sacramental into sacraments proper.

Reformation.

3. The Apology for the Augsburg Confession allowed Penance to be one of the Saviour's sacramental institutes, and Melanchthon was disposed to admit into the number Ordination. These were not retained, however, in the churches of the Reformation, although the Lutherans preserved Confession as a wholesome part of the rejected Orders. The definition in the English Article strikes the true note: the Five added by Rome "are not to be counted sacraments of the Gospel, being such as have grown partly of the corrupt following of the Apostles, partly are states of life allowed in the Scriptures; but yet have not like nature of sacraments with Baptism and the Lord's Supper, for that they have not any visible sign or ceremony ordained of God." To this, however, may be added that they have no connection with the

covenant character of the Gospel of Christ. Having this test to apply, we may consider the additional sacraments in their order.

THE FIVE ADDED SACRAMENTS.

1. The supposed sacrament of CONFIRMATION sprang out of a rite anciently known as CHRISM or THE SEAL, which was thought to add the positive gift of the Spirit to the baptismal removal of guilt : thus early binding up with its error a certain truth. It was administered not before the seventh year, and only by a bishop, as succeeding to the Apostolical prerogative of imposition of hands. In its final development in the Middle Ages the imposition and anointing constitute the matter of the sacrament ; and the form : Signo te signo crucis et confirmo te chrismate salutis in nomine, etc. The Scriptural ground for this fails before strict examination. Our Lord's baptism with the Holy Ghost has of course no relation to the question. Nor are the instances in which Apostles imparted the Holy Ghost to the Samaritans : this was a special recognition of Samaritan Christianity by peculiar and almost Pentecostal tokens. The baptism and anointing of John's disciples at Ephesus were simultaneous : they had not before received Christian baptism. Another passage commonly adduced is that in which St. Paul says that after they believed the Ephesians were sealed : here the Greek requires, *when ye believed ye were sealed*. The reception of the young by formal profession of faith into the congregation has been a laudable usage in most communions. But there is no sacramental institute for that purpose. *[margin: Confirmation.]* *[margin: Acts viii.]* *[margin: Acts xix. 4.]* *[margin: Eph. i. 13.]*

2. The system of PENANCE elaborated in the early Church was based upon the supposed necessity of making satisfaction to God for sin committed after baptism. As finally elevated into a sacrament, its Matter—to use the scholastic phrase—is Contritio cordis, Confessio oris, Satisfactio operis. The form is the judicial act and word of absolution. The Contrition of heart is not required to be absolutely perfect, Attrition, or a sincere desire to repent, may be enough ; the Confession is auricular, including omnia et singula peccata mortalia, and at least once in the year. The satisfaction supposes that the priest is a judge who, in the name of God, imposes penances as the condition of the remission of temporal punishments of the sin, which, as to the reatus culpæ and its *[margin: Penance]*

X 2

eternal consequences, is forgiven for Christ's merits' sake. These temporal penalties may be exacted in this life or in the intermediate state : both being temporal. They may be commuted for satisfactions of various kinds, fasting, prayer, alms ; which, however, were connected often with the most unevangelical forms of self-discipline. On this sacrament of Penance hangs the doctrine of Purgatory, the scene where the supreme satisfaction of Christ is supplemented : as also Indulgences, based on the fund of merit stored in the Church, and granted, avowedly for the remission of temporal penalty, often, in popular acceptation, for the remission of all sin whatever. This most important institute is not based upon the Word of God : the Scriptural Absolution is the declaration of the terms of forgiveness, its Confession is not auricular and enforced, its only Satisfaction is the perfect obedience of Christ, and its only Judge and Confessor the Lord Himself.

Orders.

3. The sacrament of ORDERS or consecration to the priesthood is closely connected with the last : quo tribuitur potestas consecrandi corpus et sanguinem Domini, nec non remittendi et retinendi peccata. As the baptised were endued with grace by imposition of episcopal hands, so episcopal hands alone could confer the specific grace of the priesthood. But there is nothing either in our Lord's appointment of His ministers or in the Apostolical confirmation of it, that sustains such an investiture with such tremendous privileges and responsibilities. Of this more will be said in the appropriate place.

Matrimony.
Eph. v. 32.

4. MATRIMONY was elevated to the dignity of a sacrament mainly on the ground of the Apostle's words: *This is a great mystery : but I speak concerning Christ and the church.* As a sacrament the ordinance of marriage is treated most elaborately in the Roman and in the Eastern Theology. It has really, however, the slenderest title of all the usurpers of the sacramental character ; being only a natural relation sanctified, and honoured as signifying the Saviour's union with His Church. In strange contradiction to this high character of the ordinance was its undervaluation in the celibate life, whether in or out of the priesthood.

Unction.
Jas. v. 14, 15.

5. EXTREME UNCTION rests mainly on the anointing in St. James, where, however, the rite had no reference to death. Its sacramental institution by Christ is supposed to be found in the re-

ference to the same subject in St. Mark's Gospel, concerning which Mark vi. 13. the same remark may be made. It is a comprehensive sacrament, the Viaticum, useful for the soul and, if God will, for the body too : effectus est mentis sanatio et, in quantum autem expedit, ipsius etiam corporis (Conc. Flor. 1439).

UNDERVALUATION OF SACRAMENTS.

The opposite error, that of those who deny the authoritative institution of sacramental means of grace, in the sense in which we understand the term, that is, ordinances which pledge or seal, as well as symbolise, to those who worthily receive them the grace of redemption, should be carefully avoided.

Denial of Sacraments.

1. There are those, as we have seen, who would honour the spiritual character of the religion of Christ by dispensing with His own express appointments. But they are surely on the way to the same error who regard our Lord as having placed in His Church two rites, which are only rites, only symbols teaching the eye, whether of the assistants or the spectators, and thus make Him the Founder of a purely ritual and symbolical service. Had that been His design, we should have accepted it with reverence. But it was not His design. There is nothing ordained by Him for the permanent observance of His people which is not accompanied by the Holy Ghost, and made the channel of its own appropriate grace. The rites of Christianity have their concomitant benedictions ; and are never without them, save to such as bring no preparation of faith, the absence of which makes all religion a mere ceremonial. The true doctrine is between two extremes. It avoids the delusive over-statement that connects specific blessings, regeneration, and the sustenance of Christ's life, with the sacraments as their sole conductors to the soul : these are only the covenant pledges of a gift that is with and through them imparted, but not necessarily with and through them alone. And it avoids the delusive under-statement that makes sacramental ordinances mere signs that æsthetically act on the minds of those who wait upon them. This, it may be repeated, is to abolish the distinction between those symbolical actions of our Lord—such as His setting a child in the midst, blighting the fig-tree, washing His disciples' feet, breathing forth

the Holy Ghost—which were actions that taught their lesson by symbol first, and were afterwards interpreted by His words, and those permanent ceremonies which He ordained to be Means as well as signs of His grace to the believer.

2. There is, however, an undervaluation of the sacraments which springs from no theological opposition or scruple, but is the result of indifference or ignorance. There are many unbaptised children whose parents are responsible for the neglect of the Saviour's command, a neglect which will not be visited on the children themselves. But the neglect is, perhaps, more striking in the case of the other sacrament. It is not that it is treated with irreverence; but, for want of adequate instruction, there are many who regard the Lord's Supper as a religious solemnity, in some way or other connected with the acceptance of religious responsibilities, and dependent for its blessing upon the vigour of faith and expectation in the communicant, but without any distinct perception of its peculiar and distinct place in the Evangelical economy. The recoil from one extreme has carried many too far in the opposite direction. It ought to be matter of solicitude on the part of Christian ministers to teach their people the right doctrine of the sacraments: especially that which lays emphasis upon their relation to the new covenant, its benefits and obligations.

BAPTISM.

Baptism is an ordinance appointed by our Lord to be the rite of initiation into the new covenant of grace and fellowship of its kingdom; being the sign and seal of the blessings of that covenant conferred upon those who thereby avow their acceptance of the one condition of faith in Jesus Christ with its obligations. It is the sacrament of union with Christ, of pardon and renewal through His Gospel, and of membership in His Church: being the outward and visible sign of the sealing of the Holy Ghost, who [is the interior Bond of Communion between the believer and the Lord; the Agent in imparting that forgiveness and regeneration of which the washing of water is the sign; and the Sanctifier of the people of God. The nature, mode of administration and subjects of this rite are clearly set forth in the New Testament; but have been variously interpreted in ecclesiastical doctrine and practice. It will be expedient, therefore, to examine the authoritative Scripture first, and afterwards briefly to view the subject in the light of controversy.

THE DOCTRINE AND PRACTICE OF BAPTISM IN SCRIPTURE.   Scripture.

The Word of God furnishes a preliminary history of this rite as linked with the Old Covenant, through usages which are changed in the New; it gives a clear account of its institution and observance; and defines its meaning and relation to the economy of grace. These topics correspond to the teaching of the Old Testament, of the Gospels and Acts, and of the Epistles respectively.

I. Many rites, ceremonies, types, symbols, and predictions pointed forward to baptism and found in this simple ordinance their fulfilment. Its special Old-Testament representative was   Old Testament. the covenant rite of circumcision: the type of baptism as it was the rite of admission into the old covenant of grace, established first with Abraham for all nations in his Seed the Christ, and renewed through Moses with the same People now more distinguished from the rest of mankind   As given to Abraham it was the *seal of the righteousness of the faith which he had yet being uncircumcised: that he might be the father of all them that believe, though they be not circumcised*   It was as it were the baptism of the father of the faithful, and in its very origin predicted its own future abolition. As limited in Moses, it was the symbol of the sanctification of physical life and natural increase, and the seal of participation in external and limited privileges.   In both respects it was ordained only *till the Seed should come to Whom the Promise was made.*   Baptism took its place as the sign of the sanctification of the whole of life both of man and woman, of a spiritual birth and increase ; as the seal also of internal, universal, and unending privileges. Of another order were the two great historical types, the Deluge, and salvation by its waters, and the passage of the Red Sea. Each of these is alluded to in a very significant way.   St. Paul says that the circumcised people *were all baptised unto Moses in the cloud and in the sea .* a solitary instance of the term baptism being carried back to the Old Testament.   St. Peter gives an equally unique instance of the use of the word Antitype : speaking of the Deluge he says, *the like figure (ἀντίτυπον) whereunto, even baptism, doth also now save us*   Passing by the ritual types, such as the ceremonial washings of the old law, we find a wider field in the Prophets who predicted the effusion of the Holy Ghost, of which Christian baptism was to be the symbol, under the similitude of cleansing waters   poured out, for ever flowing, and sprinkled upon the soul   The ancient baptism of proselytes from heathenism —ancient as to us, modern as to the Hebrews—probably had no foundation in the Old Testament beyond the general practice of washing before sacrificing to God.   But it seems indisputable, from Rabbinical authorities, that after the captivity every proselyte was circumcised and baptised , moreover, that this baptism included the women and children of his house   This accounts for the general familiarity with the rite assumed in the Gospels   It sheds light upon the institute of John the Baptist and our Lord's baptism of His disciples   It must be borne in mind in our inter-

Rom iv. 11.

Gal iii 19

1 Cor x. 2

1 Pet iii 21

Zech xiii. 1.
Ezek. xxxvi.25.

pretation of St. Peter's words on the Day of Pentecost : there can be no doubt how his hearers would understand, *The promise is unto you, and to your children.* Acts ii. 39.

II. The institution of Christian Baptism has its gradual history. We have the Gospel preliminary baptisms ; the Saviour's express and formal New-Testament appointment : and the occasional observance of the rite as described in the first records of the early New-Testament Church. New Testament.

1. The Baptism of John has a distinct significance and stands alone : τὸ Ἰωάννου βάπτισμα. It was the baptism of repentance as the preparation for Christ and the New Covenant ; even as it was the rite of transition from the Old Testament to the New. As it belonged to the Old, Jesus Himself, *made under the law,* submitted to it ; as it belonged to the New, He received it not : His New-Testament baptism was the effusion of the Holy Spirit upon His human nature, restoring to MAN in Him the Spirit forfeited by the Fall. Our Lord's preliminary act of baptising, as administered by His disciples, was partly a continuation of the Baptist's, even as He preached over again John's repentance ; partly an accommodation to the later Jewish usage of baptising proselytes ; and partly a preparation for His own final ordinance. Neither of His two sacraments was absolutely new : both were rather the sanctification of a certain remainder of past observances which linked them with the old economy. John's Baptism.

Acts xix. 3.

Gal. iv. 4.

2. The Christian institute itself was enacted in one clear and definite injunction. It had been prepared for in act, as we have seen ; doubtless also in word during the Forty Days : hence the formula was understood when finally given : *in the name of the Father, and of the Son, and of the Holy Ghost.* The baptised were to be dedicated by man, and consecrated by the Spirit, to the possession and service and redeeming grace of the Mediatorial Trinity. Both sacraments were appointed by Christ, to be fully interpreted by the Holy Ghost. The Supper preceded the death of which it was the commemoration ; Baptism preceded the Pentecost which was its fulfilment. That day declared its meaning : the One Triune Name, and the various blessings of the Persons in that name ; its substitution in place of circumcision as appointed for all nations ; its covenant character, as sealing the Christian Institution.

Matt. xxviii. 19.

benefits of the Christian charter of privileges to all who on their part believe and observe the commandments.

Acts.

3. From the Day of Pentecost onward the rite is observed as an indispensable ordinance. There is no instance of conversion Acts viii. with which it is not connected : *they were baptised, both men and* 12. *women.* But the full formula does not occur : baptism was *in the* Acts ii.38; *name of Christ* or *of the Lord* (ἐπι and ἐν as well as εἰς), representing x. 48. Rom. vi. 3. the Trinity. Once, in the case of Samaria, the sacrament was Acts viii. 17. supplemented by the imposition of Apostolic hands and the gift Acts x. 47. of the Holy Ghost ; once, in the case of Cornelius, it followed Acts viii. that gift ; once it was a fruitless ceremony, in the case of Simon 13. Magus. Always it was administered by the officers of the church : those who preached thus admitted their converts into the community. St. Paul was a high exception, but he gives the reason of his satisfaction at having baptised so few in Corinth : partly, his jealousy for the name of Christ, partly his higher obligation Acts xvi. to preach the Gospel. The households of believing persons were 15. 1 Cor. i. thus consecrated : including obviously their children, whose 16. baptism is not mentioned because implied in the Lord's benediction of them. That they received it, however, needs no other proof than that baptism superseded circumcision, and that children Eph. vi. 1. are already addressed as members of the Christian Church.

Apo- III. The later Apostolic teaching on this subject remains to be stolical considered : it will be found abundantly full and clear.
Teaching.
Baptism 1. The new ordinance is everywhere regarded as having superand Cir- seded circumcision as a sign and seal of the Christian covenant.
cumcision. Nothing can be plainer than that the old rite was done away with. If admitted in any case, it was for reasons of expediency ; if not practised as the rite of an imperfect covenant, but only as a national usage slowly given up, it was a thing indifferent. But circumcision, as the initiatory rite of the preparatory dispensation, was lost in baptism. Negatively and positively St. Paul says : Col. ii. 10 *Ye are complete in Him,* which *is the Head of all principality and* —12. *power . . . in Whom also ye are circumcised with the circumcision made without hands, in putting off the body of the sins of the flesh by the circumcision of Christ : buried with Him in baptism.* Let us note the points here. There is no longer any circumcision save that which is WITHOUT HANDS ; but this rite, which, like the Passover, had

its last observance in our Lord, revives in another ceremony: baptism is the circumcision of Jesus, and teaches the old lesson in another way. The same death of the sinful flesh which the ancient rite signified is signified also by the new one. But it was done away by being transfigured, and baptism is the sign and seal of the better covenant.

2. We may view this more generally and more particularly.

(1.) All the blessings of the Christian covenant are represented as summed up in the Promise made to Abraham; that Promise was Christ, *the Seed*, and *the blessing of Abraham*, the Holy Spirit. *As many of you as have been baptised into Christ have put on Christ:* Gal.iii.27. here is the relation of baptism to the reception of Christ and union with Him. *Be baptised, and ye shall receive the gift of the* Acts ii. *Holy Ghost:* here is its relation to the bestowment of the Spirit. 38. These connect it with the two branches of the covenant Promise.

(2.) But this is general: we may find many references to the specific blessings which are exhibited and pledged to the believer in his baptism. Foremost is justification or the forgiveness of sins: St. Peter cries, *Repent, and be baptised every one of you in the* Acts ii. *name of Jesus Christ for the remission of sins;* and Ananias to Paul, 38. *Be baptised, and wash away thy sins.* Christian Sonship, both as Acts xxii. adoption and as regeneration, is sealed in baptism: *Ye are all the* 16. *children of God by faith in Christ Jesus. For as many of you as have* Gal. iii. *been baptised into Christ have put on Christ.* Naturally, however, 26, 27. the relation of baptism to circumcision would suggest its more frequent connection with regeneration than with adoption. After having spoken of the symbolical design of circumcision, the putting off the body of the sins of the flesh, the Apostle goes on: *Buried with Him in baptism, wherein also ye are risen with Him* Col. ii. 12. *through the faith of the operation of God, Who hath raised Him from the dead.* This passage makes baptism represent the dying to sin and rising to holiness: one part of the ceremony, the immersion, signifying the conformity to our Lord's death; the other, the rising out of the water, conformity with His resurrection. With this may be connected the parallel to the Romans. It was our Rom. vi. 3. Lord Who first connected baptism with the new birth, *Except a* John iii. *man be born of water and of the Spirit;* and St. Paul winds up the 5. long strain of Christian teaching in his words to Titus concerning

Tit. iii. 5. *the laver of regeneration.* Less directly baptism is sometimes con-
1 Cor. xii. nected with sanctification. *For by one Spirit are we all baptised*
13. *into one body:* where the Church is referred to as the Lord's
Eph. v. 26. sanctified body, of which it is said, *that He might sanctify and*
cleanse it with the washing of water by the Word. St. Peter calls
the Christian baptism the antitype of the typical salvation of the
1 Pet. iii. ark *wherein few, that is, eight souls, were saved by water; which, in*
21. *its antitype, baptism, now saveth you also (not the putting away of the*
filth of the flesh, but the inquiry of a good conscience after God); where
justification and sanctification unite, though neither of the terms
is used. In the Epistle to the Hebrews, as in St. Peter's First,
1 Pet. i. 2. we cannot but feel that the inward *sprinkling of the blood of Jesus*
Christ corresponds with the outward sprinkling of water, its sign.
So also in St. John's mysterious words, *This is He Who came by*
1 John v. *water and blood, even Jesus Christ, not by water only, but by water and*
6. *blood.* While the primary allusion is to the Lord's ministerial work
as begun at the Jordan, and ended on the cross, there is also a
reference to the external washing of baptism and internal washing
of the Atonement of which that is the sign.

Covenant 3. Now, in all these passages the sacrament of baptism is, as it
Sign were, identified with the blessings which it signifies; and in such
and Seal. a way as will not allow us to think for a moment of its being a
Eph. iv. 5. mere ritual sign. St. Paul speaks of *one Lord, one faith, one bap-*
tism: this gives the last of the three a very prominent place; as
it not only makes it the badge of Christian profession, but also
seems to embrace in one word all the blessings of Christianity, not
otherwise mentioned. In fact, the privileges of the covenant are
supposed to be sealed, obsignated, imparted to true believers in
connection with their baptism. This ordinance is never made
the sole instrument on the part of God, nor ever the sole condition
on the part of man; but it is invariably the seal of the transaction
between God and the believer as in the presence of the Church.
Blessings may be bestowed before the sealing transaction; and
still larger blessings follow it; but in any case they are all, according to the rule certainly, sealed over and pledged to the baptised
believer as one of the congregation. However looked at—
whether as affusion, sprinkling, immersion,—it is a SIGN of the
descent of the Spirit, and the washing away of sin. And it is a

SEAL once for all given of the bestowment of the blessings of the Spirit upon the believer continuing to believe. But it must ever be remembered that, in every reference to this symbolical ordinance, we find it flanked on the one hand by the absolute condition of faith as a condition, and on the other by the sole efficiency of the Spirit as the Agent of all good.

4. It must not be forgotten that the initiatory sacrament has in the Epistles a universal character, as extending and enlarging the meaning of the former rite, and adapting it to a more catholic economy. The cardinal passage has been already quoted in part: *For as many of you as have been baptised into Christ have put on Christ. There is neither Jew nor Greek, there is neither bond nor free, there is neither male nor female: for ye are all one in Christ Jesus. And if ye be Christ's, then are ye Abraham's seed, and heirs according to the promise.* Circumcision here vanishes in the very nature of the case, as we need not further explain. Our Lord's sign must be on every one that is His; and baptism for all, for men and women, for adults and children, takes its place. Water everywhere flows for all the world: *See, here is water.* By this the God of the Christian covenant should *sprinkle many nations:* in a figurative view of the passage. Nothing that circumcision either signed or sealed under the old economy can be lost under the new: therefore children have their privileges in the Christian covenant sealed to them in their baptism. Accordingly, they are addressed as members of the church in every Epistle. If it be asked, What is the blessing sealed to them? the answer is, all that they are capable of receiving. As children of a race under condemnation they are *justified freely by His grace through the redemption that is in Christ Jesus.* Children of wrath as belonging to the lineage of the first Adam, they are grafted into the Second: their baptism is the seal of their present adoption, and the pledge of their regeneration when they are capable of it. Unholy by nature, they are sanctified through baptismal consecration to God: Christ has blessed them, their unholiness is gone, and *now are your children holy.* In the case of adults personal faith, and conscious acceptance of the terms of the covenant, are essential. Of this infants are incapable; but the Lord is their everlasting Sponsor; and when He said, *of such is the kingdom of heaven,* He

Catholicity of the Rite.

Gal. iii. 27—29.

Acts viii. 36.
Isa. lii. 15.

Rom. iii. 24.

1 Cor. vii. 14.

Matt. xix. 14.

admitted them to all the privileges of His covenant, including the gift of the Spirit, to take from them the doom of the race, and to afford them all the preliminary influences of His salvation. The baptism of the children of believing parents is, therefore, a sign of the washing away of original guilt, and a seal of their adoption into the family of God; a sign of the regeneration which their nature needs, and a seal of its impartation in God's good time.

BAPTISM IN HISTORICAL THEOLOGY.

Early Church.

The development of doctrine concerning this ordinance or sacrament needs to be exhibited only in broad and general outline.

I. The primitive Church attached to it a very high importance as the SACRAMENT OF THE NEW LIFE. It was in the East usually termed the φωτισμός, or Illumination; and hyperbolical language abounds in the description of its virtues and privileges. The ritual of the ordinance soon began to reflect this teaching.

1. Very early it was regarded as the instrument of the conveyance rather than as the sign and seal of Christian blessings; but the forgiveness it conveyed was only of past sins. Hence arose by degrees the necessity of a new Sacrament of Penance. The absolute necessity of baptism was expressed in unqualified terms; though in the case of its accidental absence only contempt was ground of condemnation. Martyrdom with its baptism of blood was supposed to supersede it or condone its absence. The Eastern Church has always preferred dipping, the Western sprinkling.

Catechumenate.

2. The Catechumenate as an institution sprang out of this sacrament by an internal necessity, at first preceding adult baptism and afterwards following that of infants. With its Catechists, Catechumens, and Catechisms, it has always in some form existed in Christendom: though its early character has never been fully maintained in later years, much to the loss of the Christian cause. In the third century the catechumens were divided, with reference to their final initiation into the mystery of the Supper, into Audientes or outside hearers of doctrine, Genuflectentes or those who prayed with the Church, and Competentes or candidates for full and determinate admission to all the privileges of Christianity.

3. The ceremonial of baptism soon became elaborate: so

elaborate as to form, equally with the ceremonial of the Eucharist, a perfect contrast to the simplicity of our Lord's institution. In the fourth century the water was consecrated; and Epiphany, Easter, Pentecost were the seasons of the year preferred for its celebration. Tertullian mentions the Sponsors, the Confession, and the Creed. Three immersions were usual in some parts, and a triple sprinkling, both with reference to the Trinity. Exorcism and the renunciation of Satan occupied in the rite an important place, which both in East and West they have retained. The particulars of the ritualistic development must be elsewhere studied.

4. INFANT BAPTISM gradually, and of necessity, rose into ascendency. The objection of Tertullian establishes the fact of the practice: he urged against precipitancy in performing the ceremony that its blessing once forfeited never could be retrieved or fully restored. As early as Cyprian (Conc. Carth. 253) early baptism was decreed: the third day, though the eighth was admissible. From that time it was an uncontested usage of Christendom, and that on the ground of its being an Apostolical usage. On this latter point Origen is express, and he is but one of a large consensus of authors. For instance, in the Pelagian controversy it was used as an argument in defence of Original Sin.

Infant Baptism.

5. In the third century heretical baptism was matter of earnest controversy. Cyprian denied its validity, on ecclesiastical principles, but the authority of the Church at Rome prevailed: resting its plea on the ground of the objective value of the rite, by whomsoever performed in the name of the Holy Trinity.

Baptism of Heretics.

II. The Romanist doctrine confirmed at Trent the doctrinal decisions and the symbolical ritual which had long been current in the mediæval Church. It ordained that Baptism must be supplemented by Confirmation. It decreed that in Baptism "that is taken away which has the character of sin: it is not merely cut down or not imputed." Concupiscence not in itself sinful, either in Adam or in us, remains as the fomes or fuel of possible sin, and for the matter of our virtue and reward through its constant suppression. In fact all the benefits of redemption are applied to the soul. Nothing, however, so clearly exhibits the doctrine as the variety of ritual: from the blessing of the water, through exorcism, the chrism, the white garment, to the giving of the name.

Trent.

Lutheran and Reformed.

III. Lutheranism, in harmony with its high theory of the sacraments, makes baptism ordinarily necessary to salvation, conveying by Divine appointment the blessings of remission of sins and regeneration. Without faith, however, the adult receives no benefit; and the Spirit works in infants the receptivity of faith, about which, it need not be added, there have been endless discussions. Repentance after baptism is, as it were, a "regressus ad baptismum," a return to the baptismal position. The Reformed Churches generally make the internal effect concur with the external act in the case of the believing elect. Infants are presumed to be elect, and the benefit in their case is only seminal and prospective. The Anglican Formularies are, taken as a whole, a combination of the Lutheran and the Reformed. They distinctly teach regeneration to be the secret virtue of baptism, in adults believing and in all infants. But there are two views of the doctrine which have always had their supporters: first, that which is more Lutheran and sacramentarian and supposes a renewal of the soul of the infant or a certain infusion of a new life: and, secondly, that which regards the new birth as in infants a change of relation only, by which they are translated into the kingdom of grace: thus confounding regeneration with adoption.

Baptists.

IV. The doctrine of the Baptist Communities differs from that of Christendom at large in two points: they insist that baptism was appointed to be an expression of adult faith in Christ, denying the right and duty of infant baptism; and they maintain that the only valid baptism is that of immersion in water. Agreeing with them in what they hold, the majority of Churches differ from them in what they deny; but not attributing so much importance to the points of difference as they do.

Infant Baptism.

1. It is important to establish the validity of infant baptism, inasmuch as by degrees that becomes, in established Christian communities which admit infants to the rite, the only baptism. Moreover, the settlement of this question is bound up with the wider question of what constitutes membership. in the external body or fellowship of Christendom.

Continuation.

(1.) The Christian Fellowship is the continuation of a community in which children had always been reckoned members. The Church of God in Christ has been one through all ages: the

ancients believed in *the Seed* that *should come to Whom the promise* Gal. iii. 19.
was made, and were circumcised, they and their children; we
believe in the Christ who has come, and are baptized, we and our
children. The Gentiles were *graffed into* the old, the *good olive-* Rom. xi.
tree, which olive-tree is really the True Vine. The covenant with 24.
Abraham was for *all the families of the earth* in due time ; and, mean- Gen. xii.
while, the sign and seal of that covenant was impressed on children 3.
not as subjects of the Hebrew commonwealth merely, but as members of the Hebrew Church. Not a word in the New Testament
indicates any change : *the promise* of the Spirit is *unto you, and to* Acts ii. 39.
your children ; households were baptized and the family still sanctified ; and even the very silence of the New Testament forbids that
we should take from children a birthright they had enjoyed from
the beginning. From this argument there is no appeal.

(2.) The theory of the Church held by those who reject infant Theory of
baptism is not a sound one. It is simply this, that none are to the
be admitted to membership who do not give credible evidence to Church.
the congregation of being regenerate. This principle, as adopted
by the Congregationalists, allows all such professors to communicate and to bring their children to baptism for their training
towards the full privileges of the new covenant. As adopted by
the Baptists, it allows of no membership at all until a credible profession of living faith is made and sealed in the sacrament. These
views are altogether too narrow for the spirit of the catholic
Gospel. It is impossible to limit the Church, or admission to its
ordinances, to the regenerate as approved by men. All who profess
faith in the doctrines of Christ, who are seeking salvation, whose
lives do not contradict their profession or impeach their sincerity,
may be accepted to baptism ; and their children with them. To
such all the ordinances of religion are open ; according to their
faith they are dealt with, and *the Lord knoweth them that are His.* 2 Tim. ii.
The Baptist theory denies to children, who cannot consciously 19.
believe and intelligently profess the faith, a place in the congregation of the regenerate. We deny that the visible Church is limited
to the regenerate. Children belong to the Christian fellowship as
an institute for making men perfect Christians : they are adopted
into the family of God and the household of faith ; they are to be
trained *in the nurture and admonition of the Lord ;* they are members Eph. vi. 4.

before they finally ratify their vows; and the gentle supposition of Christianity is that the influences of the Spirit upon them will bless their instruction amidst Evangelical ordinances to their full participation in all the blessings of both the visible and invisible fold. Meanwhile, the Lord still says, *Of such is the kingdom of God.*

Mark x. 14.

Mode.

2. The mode of baptism might seem to be a less important matter in a religion which is not ritualistic. But the Baptist community thinks otherwise. In dealing with this subject we have only to show that the three kinds of baptism—by immersion, by affusion, and by sprinkling—are equally valid according to the appointment of Christ; but that the weight of the evidence is in favour of the last, or of the two latter, which in this argument may be regarded as one and the same.

Sprinkling or Affusion.

(1.) The equal admissibility of the two kinds, pouring or sprinkling and immersing, is proved by three considerations. First, the influences of the Spirit, of which baptism is the outward and visible sign, are described throughout Scripture in language

Joel ii. 28.

Ezek. xxxvi. 25.

Tit. ii. 6.

which aptly represents both. *I will pour out My Spirit;* and *then will I sprinkle clean water upon you.* These begin the series; it is ended by *the washing of regeneration.* Secondly, the word baptize in the original Greek, whether in its classic or in its Scriptural

2 Kings v. 14.

Mark vii. 4.

Num. xix. 13.

Ecclus. xxxiv. 30.

Rev. xix. 13.

Isa. lxiii. 3.

use, is capable of both significations: *then went he down, and dipped himself seven times in Jordan* (ἐβαπτίσατο). *Except they wash* (βαπτίσωνται) *they eat not.* The defiled person was *sprinkled* from his uncleanness, which in the Apocrypha is βαπτιζόμενος ἀπὸ νεκροῦ, baptized from a dead body; and in the Revelation βεβαμμένον αἵματι describes the Saviour's vesture stained in blood, according to the prophet, *Their blood shall be sprinkled upon My garments.* In fact, the word in all its forms refers to the contact of water without prescribing the manner. Thirdly, the practice of the Christian Church from the beginning has allowed both, as we have seen, and this should have its weight.

Sprinkling.

(2.) But there are many considerations which lead us to regard affusion or sprinkling as the ordained form of the rite. The catholic design of the Gospel suggests that the simplest and most universally practicable ordinance would be appointed. Again, the most important realities of which baptism is only the sign are such as sprinkling or affusion indicates: the blood of atonement was sprinkled on the people and on the mercy-seat; and the gifts of the Holy Ghost are generally illustrated by the pouring of water and the anointing. Moreover, the multitudinous baptisms of the New Testament forbid the possibility of immersion : especially when it is remembered that whole families were baptized, and individuals sometimes, where large quantities of water cannot be supposed to have been accessible. As to the passages which describe this sacrament as burial with Christ and resurrection with Him, they must be interpreted by the analogy of those which describe it as dying with Christ and putting Him on. . It may be said, further, that there are words which obviously would have been employed instead of baptism if the practice of immersion had been deemed essential. This last argument is of great force when we remember how carefully the institution of the two sacraments has been guarded in the revelation of the New Testament. As it respects the Lord's Supper, there is no room for misapprehension : every departure from the simplicity of the ordinance is self-convicted. Now, if it had been the Saviour's will that every convert and every infant throughout all ages should be immersed in the baptismal flood He would have told us so in language that could not be mistaken. But the vast majority of the Christian world has understood by baptism the pouring or sprinkling of water. It may be said that this only shows our Lord's intention to have been to allow a large latitude of observance. Be it so : of this none can complain. But it may be inferred that if the more cumbrous and difficult rite was not ordained, the simpler one would everywhere be understood to be more in harmony with His will.

V. We may sum up with a few concluding remarks on the Extremes. two extremes in relation to the doctrine of baptism between which the truth is surely to be found. On the one hand lies the notion that it is merely a sign or badge of Christian profession, as held by Unitarians and Rationalist professors of all kinds. This is improved upon by those who make it moreover an impressive ritualistic emblem of the blessings of the new covenant. Both views are correct, but they fall short of the truth. On the other hand, there is the notion of those who make it the sole ordinary appointed method of communicating the virtue of the Atonement in the remission of sins, and the impartation of the new life.

Y 2

This notion, common to all high sacramentarian theology, Romanist, Oriental, Lutheran, and Anglican, dishonours the supremacy of the Spirit and the Word. Its watchword is Baptismal Regeneration, which, as ordinarily accepted, unevangelically links the sign and the thing signified. The true doctrine includes the first theory and stops short of the last. It makes baptism the initiatory sign of a covenant the blessings of which it most aptly symbolises: the sprinkled blood and the Spirit poured out. It makes it also the seal of a covenant which pledges these blessings to all who believe and dedicate their children to Christ; a seal therefore of an impartation which is quite distinct from the seal, though it may accompany it, as it may have preceded it, and may also, as in part it must do to unconscious infancy, follow the seal. Its importance therefore is great in its own order. To the adult, who has received it in infancy, it remains a perpetual memory of a most solemn obligation; and to him who receives it as an adult it is a present encouragement to faith, and a pledge to his faith of present union with the Lord. To our children it is, when they come to know its responsibilities, a memorial of blessings provided for them before they were born. And on the congregation administering it by its appointed ministers to infants it enforces the necessity of taking all spiritual care of its little ones.

THE EUCHARIST.

The Lord's Supper is a rite ordained by our Lord for perpetual observance in His Church, as a sacramental feast in which bread and wine are signs of His sacred body and blood offered in one oblation on the cross, and seals of the present and constant impartation to the believer of all the benefits of His passion. In this supper the Church joyfully and thankfully celebrates before the world the sacrifice once presented in the past, until He come again without sin unto salvation. Moreover, the Lord's people partake of the elements as the symbol of a common Christian life and sustentation, as the mutual pledge of union and brotherly fellowship, with all its enjoyments and obligations. Thus this ordinance is the Sacrament, as it signifies and seals the mystical nourishment of Christ; the Eucharist, as commemorating the sacrifice of redemption; and the Communion, as the badge of united Christian profession. While most Christian people agree as to this last, there have been many and great divisions both as it respects the blessings conveyed in the Sacrament, and the nature of the Eucharistical commemoration. We shall find it useful, as in the case of the other Sacrament, to examine the testimony of Scripture, and then consider the controversies of dogma.

SCRIPTURAL DOCTRINE.

The statements of the New Testament are few, but exceedingly distinct. They describe the institution of a new rite instead of the Passover, and connect it especially with the ratification of the new covenant. St. Paul adds the account that he received by special revelation, and in it a few additional points of doctrine.

Besides these four records of the institution, there are sundry incidental allusions tending to complete our view of the circumstantials of the rite itself. We must glance at the doctrine and the ritual of the second sacrament, which was instituted in connection with the Passover, and to supersede it for ever.

Passover and Commemoration.

1. Now the ancient rite was an annual commemoration of the typical redemption of the Hebrew people; and the Lord's Supper is the solemn act of the Church's commemoration of the redeeming death of the Saviour of the world. St. Paul's account, the last and fullest authentic statement of the institution, stamps great

1 Cor. xi. 23—26.

prominence on this. He adds *In remembrance of Me* to the giving of the bread, as well as to the giving of the cup; and, with reference to both, says, *Ye do show forth the Lord's death till He come.*

Matt. xxvi. 26. Luke xxii. 19.

Our Saviour *blessed* the elements and *gave thanks:* offering the praise of His own atonement which His people continue for ever. Hence the rite is the great expression of the Church's gratitude for the gift of Christ, and especially for His atoning death. It is the feast of thanksgiving within the Christian assembly, and it is

1 Cor. xi. 26.

the feast of testimony before the world, *showing forth* His death. And the first word used, εὐχαριστήσας, gives the ordinance a name:

Eucharist.

it is a thankful and glorying commemoration, or the EUCHARIST.

Passover and Sacramental Ratification.

2. The ancient Passover was also the annual ratification of the covenant between God and His people. As such it was itself a sacrifice both of expiation and thanksgiving; and summed up or represented all other covenant sacrifices. When our Lord substituted His Supper, He used language that included all, and specially referred to the solemn covenant transaction in which

Ex. xxiv. 6—8. Heb. ix. 19.

Moses divided the blood of atonement into two parts: *half of the blood he sprinkled on the altar,* to denote the propitiation of God; with the remainder he *sprinkled all the people,* to signify to them the Divine favour, and the *book of the covenant* also, to signify the ratification of the covenant of which that book was the record:

Heb. ix. 20.

This is the blood of the testament which God hath enjoined unto you. These words of Moses our Lord connects with the new passover

Matt. xxvi. 27, 28.

of His new covenant: *Drink ye all of it; for this is My blood of the new testament which is shed for many for the remission of sins.* Obviously, the blessings of the better covenant, symbolised by the bread and wine, deliverance from guilt and life in Christ, are pledged and sealed to all who receive these tokens in faith. He who spiritually *discerns the Lord's sacrificial body* in the emblems, *examines and judges himself* as to his submission to the terms of the covenant, and *thus eateth and drinketh not unworthily,* has his faith confirmed by this sacred pledge even to the assurance that all the blessings of redemption are his always and his while he thus receives the seal of the covenant. The Holy Spirit uses the sacramental ordinance for the assurance of faith : hence the meaning of the term SACRAMENT as applied to this solemnity.

1 Cor. xi. 28, 29.

Sacrament.

3. But the ancient Passover was the rite that kept in annual remembrance the birth of the people as such and their community life in the bond of the covenant. When our Lord ordained His Supper, He distributed to each and laid emphasis on the ALL. So St. Paul makes this the external bond of unity : *For we being many are one bread and one body; for we are all partakers of that one bread.* And this follows the declaration that the cup is *the communion of the blood of Christ,* and the bread *the communion of the body of Christ.* The Supper is the sacrament of union with Jesus the True Vine ; and of union with one another in Him : hence it might seem that the elements represent not only the sacrificed body of Christ, but the spiritual body itself saved by that sacrifice and made part of Himself. The real bond of union, however, is not the bread and wine ; it is the common participation of life in Christ by the Spirit. But the sacramental eating and drinking together is the outward and visible sign of that union. The Supper therefore is the perfect badge of common discipleship : the mutual pledge of all the offices of brotherly love. It is guarded by the most solemn sanctions. All who profess faith in Christ's atonement, who desire His salvation, and are willing to keep His laws, are invited to come, forbidden to remain absent. But God is the Judge. He was *provoked to jealousy* by those who partook of both *the Lord's table* and *the table of devils.* He smote with *condemnation* those who did eat and drink *unworthily.* The Church also must watch over the ordinance of its holy fellowship, and the individual must judge himself. After all vigilance is used the Lord's Supper in this world will never be without its Judas : it is the typical and imperfect feast of a fellowship that will one day be perfect. Meanwhile, as the sacra-

Passover and Community Life.

1 Cor. x. 16, 17.

1 Cor. x. 21.

1 Cor. xi. 27.

Com-
munion.
· Ritual
in New
Testa-
ment.
1 Cor. x.
15—17.
Acts ii.42.

ment of unity in Christ and with Christ, it is termed by us, with
Apostolical sanction, the COMMUNION.

4. The notices scattered through the New Testament give us
plain indications of the ritual of this ordinance. The elements,
or constituents, are bread and wine: common bread and un-
adulterated wine. These elements were consecrated; the bread
was solemnly broken, and the cup was blessed. The ordinance
was called the *breaking of bread*, as if the distribution to each
from one common loaf was preserved symbolically. The consecration was the setting apart to the most sacred possible use;
the express thanksgiving for redemption commemorated by the
bread and wine; and invocation of the grace signified. Each
element was received separately, and by the act of each recipient.

Acts ii.46.
The communion was frequent: at first daily, certainly every
Lord's Day. It is obvious that there is no precept on this subject,
though there are two extremes which the language of the New
Testament shuts out. Annual, or very occasional, celebration
1 Cor. xi.
26.
does not comport with the words *As often as ye eat this bread,*
interpreted as they are by the signs of frequent communion in the
1 Cor. xi.
20.
early part of the Acts. On the other hand, St. Paul says, *when ye*
come together into one place, or the congregation; which implies a
formal assembly that could not be of daily recurrence. The cere-
1 Cor. xi.
20—34.
monial was simple: not for eating and drinking simply, but sacramental and symbolical. It was indeed connected sometimes with a
preceding feast, the abuses of which are noted in the Epistle to the
Corinthians. It was celebrated by the minister as Christ's representative: *the bread which we break, the cup which we bless.* But
there was nothing priestly in the ministerial act, nor was the
1 Cor. xi.
20.
Acts ii.42.
Lord's Supper, the Κυριακὸν δεῖπνον, in any sense the one central
act of worship: *they continued steadfastly in the Apostles' doctrine*
and fellowship, and in breaking of bread and in prayers. Lastly, it
was observed as an ordinance perpetually binding: the Corinthian
community was no exception to a general rule.

THE EUCHARIST IN HISTORICAL THEOLOGY.

The history of doctrine on this subject may be broadly viewed
as falling under four heads: first, the Patristic period, when

germs of error are seen growing up in teaching and ritual; secondly, the controversies which issued in the Tridentine doctrine of Rome; thirdly, the different formularies of the Reformation; and, lastly, the present aspect of the question throughout Christendom generally and especially in English theology.

I. In the Patristic age, down to the first great controversy on the subject in the ninth century, we mark in every school of doctrine the signs of coming development. That development took two forms which afterwards united: respecting the sacramental presence in the Communion, and the sacrificial offering in the Eucharist. Patristic.

1. As to the former, there was always much difference in expression. The earliest Fathers, while using very ambiguous language, never went beyond the figurative presence. So even Cyprian alludes to the Calix, quo sanguis Christi ostenditur. They speak of the Eucharist as being the body of Christ, and the heavenly food, but only as they speak of the Gospel and faith being the same. Down to Chrysostom there is no hint of the conversion of the substance, though Ignatius and Justin use the term $\mu\epsilon\tau\alpha\beta o\lambda\acute{\eta}$. But both Ambrose and Chrysostom strike the note of future transubstantiation, though generally using the language of a purer faith: the latter declares that the priest held in his hand what was the most adorable in heaven, and the former, Hoc quod conficimus corpus ex virgine est. Sacrament.

2. The sacrificial idea was added to the Eucharist in the third century, though it entered furtively. At first it was an oblation of gratitude for the gifts of God in life as crowned in redemption: the people brought the bread and wine themselves: part was consecrated for the Eucharist proper, the remainder was left for the lovefeast and the use of the ministry. This resemblance to the ancient oblations soon went further. Even Tertullian speaks of sacrifices for the dead; and Cyprian of the priest as offering in the place of Christ, Sacerdos vice Christi vere fungitur. Then the Greek Fathers refer to the unbloody sacrifice, and even the sacrifice of propitiation. Cyprian and Augustine are content with the Sacrificii peracti memoria; but Chrysostom and others delight in representing the Eucharist as a repetition of the great oblation, though in such terms as only suggest the error of the future: suggesting it however in the plainest manner. Sacrifice.

Mediæval.

II. During the Middle Ages this sacrament had the concentrated attention of the Schoolmen fixed upon it. There were two crises of controversy, and then the dogmatic construction of Mediæval materials went steadily onwards towards Trent.

1. In the middle of the ninth century Paschasius Radbertus wrote a treatise in which the idea of Transubstantiation was first expressed : " that the earthly substance of the bread and wine, sacrificed by the virtue and consecration of the Spirit, are converted into the selfsame body and blood which the Blessed Virgin by the virtue of the same Spirit conceived and brought forth : only the corporeal appearance and taste remain for the exercise of faith." Ratramnus opposed him, asserting only the symbolical and denying the actual change and use of the elements.

2. Precisely two hundred years later (1030) Berengarius wrote a treatise asserting the spiritual participation of the whole Christ, and the logical contradiction of the other theory. His protest was vain, and Gregory VII. compelled him to recant.

Transubstantiation.

3. Ecclesiastical sanction was given to the theory of TRANSUBSTANTIATION, as elaborated by Thomas Aquinas and Hildebert, by the fourth Lateran Council, under Innocent III., 1215. But the dogma took various forms. Aquinas supposed that the Divine power retained the accidents without any substance behind : thus the substance was not so much changed as annihilated, or there was a simple substitution instead of change ; others adopted the notion of what is called IMPANATION : the unity of Divine and human, following the analogy of the Incarnation. The consequences rapidly followed : the dogma of CONCOMITANCE, as laid down by Aquinas, was made the ground for withdrawing the cup from the laity, the blood being in the body and the bread sufficient ; the sacrilege of which had been protested against from Leo the Great downwards. The feast of the Adoration of the Host, Hostia, or sacrifice, was established in 1264. The Mass—probably from the " Ite missa est " of the Western Liturgy—was decreed as the bloodless repetition of the one sacrifice for the benefit of quick and dead, at the same time with Transubstantiation, in 1215.

Trent.

4. The Council of Trent fixed the Roman dogma : it boldly affirms that the substance is gone and the accidents only remain, in the emblems ; it teaches that the presentation to God of the elements is

a propitiatory offering, and includes the body, soul, and Divinity of the Redeemer, though the transubstantiation itself is only of the bread and wine into the body and blood. Moreover, masses were sanctioned for the living and the dead, and for particular individuals, their effect being to remove the temporal consequences of sin ; and the private masses of the priests were permitted. The connection between Transubstantiation and the Sacrifice of the Mass governs all the sacramental acts : the Elevation, the Adoration, the Reservation, the Circumgestation or procession which presents the Adorable Presence to the worship of all beholders.

5. The Greek Church differed in some points : retaining Transubstantiation it imposed unleavened bread, gave the cup to the laity, and always administered to children, which last peculiarity the Western Church had gradually abandoned. *Greek Church.*

III. Protestantism was mainly a revolt against this teaching : first against its abuses and then against its fundamental principles. We must glance at the forms it assumed after the Reformation. *Protestantism.*

1. Lutheran Protestantism abolished—that is in its final form and standard, for the abolition was very gradual—the Sacrifice of the Mass, with its concomitants. It retained the Sacramental Presence of the body and blood of Christ, but not in the form of Transubstantiation : the sacramental union was the basis, and expressed by sub, in, and cum pane, under, in, and with the elements. Hence the term Consubstantiation, which required the doctrine of Ubiquity, or the presence everywhere of the glorified body of Christ, after a Divine and celestial manner. The reception of the elements is by all who partake the receiving of the corporeity of Christ : but to the advantage of believers only, as the sign and seal of remission of sins ; to the unbeliever for condemnation. The impartation of Christ's glorified humanity is therefore for the benefit of the whole nature of man : for the nourishment of his soul and for the sustentation of the germ of the resurrection in the body. This view of the Lutheran doctrine is much developed in its later theology. The basis of the whole system is the assumption that the words of institution must be taken literally, not figuratively : *This* IS *My Body ; this* IS *My blood.* And the Lutheran formularies elevate the sacrament to the very highest point as a means of grace : for the impartation *Lutheranism.* *Matt. xxvi. 26.*

of the forgiveness of sins ; the strengthening of faith ; union with Christ and each other ; and all other benefits of the Passion. But the real distinction in the doctrine is its element of Consubstantiation ; the very presence of the glorified body and blood of the Lord in, with, and under the elements, these still remaining only elements however, received by the communicants.

Reformed. 2. Reformed Protestantism diverged widely from the doctrine of Luther. It altogether gave up the Lutheran manducatio oralis, and substituted the manducatio realis sed spiritualis ; it gave up therefore the hyperphysical or physical presence. It insisted that Matt. *This* is *My body* meant *This* SIGNIFIES *My body ;* and that the xxvi.26. sacrament was the sign and pledge of a spiritual union with the Head of the Church. But there were certain decided differences among the Reformed communions themselves.

Zwingli. (1.) Zwingli represented the view that tended towards the merely commemorative design ; but his doctrine went beyond that : Christ to the contemplation of faith is not only subjectively but objectively present ; and that spiritual eating of His heavenly body which is the appropriation of His atoning grace is a sacramental eating or receiving of the signs and seals of a present Saviour. He rejected the "IN pane et vino," but would retain the "CUM pane et vino," and with this a specific sacramental blessing.

Calvin. (2.) Calvin went much nearer to Lutheranism. What the elements symbolised was to him the Person of the Redeemer as well as His atoning work ; and His body as part of His person. This is received spiritually, but not the less on that account really : the communicant is lifted up by faith to heaven, and his soul is as surely invigorated by the spiritual body of Christ as his body by the emblems. With these views perhaps the Presbyterian Confession and certainly the Anglican substantially agree.

Armi- (3.) The Remonstrant Arminians leaned rather to Zwingli nians. than to Calvin ; and perhaps laid more stress than either upon the commemorative design of the ordinance. But that they ought not to be classed with the Socinians and their descendants, who make the sacrament only a memorial of the death of Christ, whatever value that death may have, will appear from these words of the Remonstrant Confession : " The holy supper is the second sacred rite of the New Testament, instituted on the night of His betrayal, to celebrate the eucharistical and solemn com-memoration of His death ; in which believers, after they have duly examined themselves and tested their true faith, eat the holy bread publicly broken in the congregation, and at the same time drink the holy wine publicly poured out, to show forth with solemn thanksgivings the bloody death of Christ undergone for us (by which, as our bodies are sustained with meat and drink, or bread and wine, so our souls are nourished up into the hope of eternal life), and to testify publicly before God and His Church their own vivifying and spiritual fellowship with the crucified body and shed blood of Christ (or with Jesus Christ Himself crucified and dead for us), and with all the benefits obtained through the sacrifice of the Redeemer, as well as their mutual charity towards each other." It is true that the covenant seal is omitted ; but we must remember what has been already adduced as to the Arminian doctrine of the sacraments generally.

IV. It remains that we refer to certain modern tendencies.

1. Protestantism has renounced altogether the perversion of the Eucharist into a propitiatory sacrifice or mass ; as also the perversion of the mystery of the spiritual presence into the sacrament of the impartation of the whole Christ through material elements that are only the accidents, or bread and wine without the substance. The Tridentine dogma is a fundamental violation of the symbolical and covenant character of the ordi-nance, and is refuted in its two main elements by all that has been shown to be the New-Testament doctrine.

2. But the doctrine of the REAL PRESENCE—not the reality of His presence, accepted by all, but His PRESENTIA REALIS— is held by the Lutheran Church : which, however it may guard the doctrine by limiting the corporeal presence of our Lord to the elements in their use only, and denying any local circumscription of that presence, still errs against the truth of Scripture, that the Sacred Body is in heaven, and that the whole Christ, and not His glorified flesh only, is imparted spiritually through a sacramental union with Him by the Holy Spirit.

3. The Anglican Church retains in her formularies nothing that favours the Romish error ; but many of the elements of Lutheran, Calvinistic, and Zwinglian doctrine are combined. The Twenty-

Modern Tenden-cies.

Real Presence.

Anglican.

eighth Article, however, ought to be decisive, that " the body of Christ is given, taken, and eaten in the Supper only after a heavenly and spiritual manner: and the means whereby the body of Christ is received and eaten in the Supper is faith." The modern theory of comprehension in the English Church allows all types of doctrine to be held: but by no just interpretation can the article of the Real Presence be attributed to that Church as represented by her authoritative formularies. The Presbyterian teaching of the Westminster Confession is substantially the same, and conformed to the Scripture. But the notion that the sacrament is only a commemorative and representative rite is held by many of the religious communities of England.

4. The true doctrine generally is that which bears in mind the design of the ordinance to be a sign to the believing Church of all the blessings purchased by the oblation of the one sacrifice for sins, and a seal to the believer of his constant and present interest in those blessings. Whatever other ends it subserves, as a perpetual memorial of the life and death of Christ, as a badge of union among Christian people, and as a sacred service in which all holy affections and purposes are quickened, it is also the abiding exhibition to the eye, in sensible emblems, of the blood of atonement and the bread of life, and also a pledge to those who accept the propitiation, as it is offered to penitent and believing faith, of their present, and constant, and eternal heritage of life in Jesus. Each of the terms SIGN and SEAL must have its full meaning preserved, while they are made one to the eye and hand and experience of living faith. That which the sign represents and the seal pledges is a benefit proceeding from Christ which must not be separated from Christ Himself. It is not the Holy Spirit save as He is the Spirit of Jesus.

THE CHRISTIAN MINISTRY.

For the discharge of the offices of worship towards God, and for the administration of the means of grace, an order has been set apart: men called to this function by the Holy Ghost, approved of the Church by its representatives, and ordained to office by their brethren in the same order. The history of this institution in the New Testament is very simple, and may be thus summed in its results. First, the ancient ministry of the Temple and priesthood was entirely abolished. Secondly, an irregular vocation appeared in ministerial gifts and functions which were transitional, adapted to the days of the foundation, yet patterns also for future extraordinary vocations according to the Spirit's wisdom and the exigencies of the Christian society. Finally, the established constitution takes its permanent and final form as a Presbyterial body described not so much by name as by office, and in some respect conformed to the model of the Synagogue: its function being ministerial, in the Divine service; pastoral, in the spiritual case of the flock; and ruling, in the government of the Church. But, simple as the Scriptural arrangements are, they assume in historical theology the widest variety of developments.

THE UNIVERSAL PRIESTHOOD.

The ancient Temple, with its typical offerings, having been done away in Christ, an entire change takes place in the ministry of the congregation. There is one High Priest, who hath passed into the heavens; the whole Church is a spiritual temple; and all its living members are a sacrificing priesthood. Whatever the New Testament says concerning sacrifice in the new worship either has reference to the priestly character of all true believers, or is figuratively applied to the functions of the ministry. The universal priesthood of Christianity is, however, only the New-Testament fulfilment of the typical priesthood of the entire congregation of Israel. Its fundamental principle is most important, as teaching the true dignity and essential equality of individual Christians, and the corporate sanctity of the Church whose inalienable prerogatives are represented by its ministry. But it has been perverted to the undermining of a distinct ministerial order, and therefore requires qualifications and guards.

Ex. xix.
6.

Ye shall be unto Me a kingdom of priests, and an holy nation : this word spoken to the ancient people is the foundation of what may be called the doctrine of the universal priesthood. Israel after the flesh was separated from the rest of the world as much as the sons of Levi were separated from the rest of the Israelites. So the spiritual Israel in union with Christ are unitedly and singly taken out of the world ; and it is in them that the type has its perfect accomplishment. All the Apostles rejoice in this truth, the influence of which pervades their language. St. John feels it

1 John ii.
20.
Jas. i. 26,
27.
Rom. xii.
1.
1 Pet. ii.
5.
Guards.

when he says : *Ye have an unction,* χρῖσμα, *from the Holy One.* St. James also when he calls religion a θρησκεία, which alludes to a ceremonial service. St. Paul and St. Peter call upon believers to present their *bodies living holy, acceptable sacrifices,* and to regard their whole life as spent in a *spiritual house,* where they *offer up spiritual sacrifices acceptable to God through Jesus Christ :* their devotions and almsdeeds and good works being their priestly oblations. The doctrine thus established guards against one abuse, and must itself be guarded from another almost equally perilous.

No Priesthood.

1 Pet. ii.
5.

1. There is no separated order of priesthood in the new service : one is our Priest even Christ, and all we are priests through fellowship with Him, presenting through Him as our Representative our *spiritual sacrifice.* The sacerdotal theory of the Christian

ministry is a dishonour to our Lord, and is specially condemned by the tenour of the Epistle to the Hebrews. *We have an altar:* but that altar is the Cross, which He hath consecrated that it may sanctify all our gifts. We all have it and surround it and may habitually minister before it.

Heb. xiii. 10.

2. Yet there is a separated ministry in the New Testament representing the universal priesthood. While the offices of religious worship are more or less common to all, in private and social and public assemblies, there is provision made for the responsible presentation of the Church's religious acts of service and discharge of the Church's teaching function. After St. Paul and St. Peter have bidden all believers to present their *living sacrifices,* they go on both of them, and in the same passage, to speak of the ministries of prophecy, and teaching, and eldership. The Epistle to the Philippians illustrates the whole subject of the Apostolic use of sacerdotal language. At its close the pecuniary offering of that people is said to be a priestly *sacrifice acceptable, well pleasing to God;* in the beginning the *bishops and deacons* are representatives of the people; and in the middle St. Paul speaks of the Apostolic devotion of his own life as a priestly libation *upon the sacrifice* of their faith. The ancient Levitical service supplied figures for the new ministry; but the new ministry was an ordained function equally defined with that of the old priesthood which it superseded.

No Priesthood but yet an Order of Ministers.

Rom. xii. 1. seq. 1 Pet. ii. 5. seq.

Phil. iv. 18. Phil. i. 1.

Phil. ii. 17.

OFFICES EXTRAORDINARY AND TRANSITIONAL.

Extraordinary.

Christianity was founded by the instrumentality of an extraordinary body of agents, pre-eminently endowed and authenticated. Their ministry was transitional; and, as such, continued for a season the various extraordinary administrations of the Holy Ghost under the old economy, not one of which passed away without being consummated and glorified in the service of the New Faith. While their function was designed to be transitory, it was at the same time to exhibit the types of an irregular vocation for special service according to the will of the Free Spirit in all ages wisely guiding the destinies of Christendom.

References to all these extraordinary agents are dispersed through the Acts and the Epistles; but there are certain passages in which St. Paul enumerates and describes them. Comparing his words to the Ephesians with those to the Corinthians we gather that God *set*, that Christ *gave* as the fruit of His ascension, and that the Spirit *divided to each*, these several functions. We find the whole in an inverted order in these words: *Now there are diversities of gifts, but the same Spirit; and there are differences of administrations, but the same Lord; and there are diversities of operations, but it is the same God which worketh all in all.* While all are the ἐνεργήματα of the One Triune God, they are the διακονίαι, or ministries of the Lord Jesus, and the χαρίσματα of the Holy Ghost. They are distinguished also as gifts of individual knowledge and faith; gifts of devotional utterance in new tongues; gifts of miraculous acts of healing; and gifts of administration in office. It is with these last, as including the others and yet surpassing them, that we have to do; and we must consider them first severally, and then in their common transitional character.

I. There are three orders of this original and extraordinary service: Apostles, Prophets, and Evangelists.

1. The APOSTOLIC office was pre-eminently a ministry ordained of the Lord Himself. *He chose twelve, whom also He named Apostles.* St. John, who never mentions the Apostles as such, save symbolically in the Apocalypse, gives nevertheless—as in regard to the sacraments, and the Ascension, and some other matters—the best definition of what he omits. *As the Father hath sent Me, even so send I you:* the idea of mission or embassage, which has its highest meaning in Christ and in the Holy Ghost, is attached to the Apostolate, but descends no lower. Apostles were ambassadors to the world; their credentials were a direct mission from the Lord in person, confirmed by miraculous powers. Their office was to preach the Gospel to all men, in the name of the Risen Lord, whose resurrection they proclaimed; and everywhere to lay the foundation of churches, or to sanction the foundation laid by others, to be the models for all the future. As the Spirit was the invisible representative of the Lord, so the Apostles were the visible. Their absolute authority is indicated in two ways: first, as teachers of Christianity, by word and writing, they had the

Eph. iv. 11.

1 Cor. xii. 11.

1 Cor. xii. 4, 5, 6.

Apostles.

Luke vi. 13.

John xx. 21.

Heb. iii. 1.

gift of inspiration; and, secondly, as founders of the Church, they had the power of the keys, of binding and loosing, that is, of uttering the unchangeable decrees of ecclesiastical government. Their sway everywhere is seen to be uncontrolled, and from their word there is no appeal. They had, and could have, no successors: they form a body of men chosen to lay the foundation of the universal Church, *built upon the foundation of the Apostles and Pro-* Eph. ii. 20. *phets,* and to commit to it the final documents of Scripture. A succession of such men would not have been in harmony with the known will of Christ, which we may interpret as purposing to leave a Fellowship with a settled organisation, and a finished doctrine, and a natural development under the supreme guidance of the Holy Ghost. But being dead they yet speak in their writings, which are the only representatives of the Apostolical company in the visible community. It is from St. Paul, the one Apostle of the Gentiles, that we gather our fullest information concerning the Apostolical prerogative.

2. The PROPHETS occupy a large place in the New-Testament Prophets. history. They spoke, like the Apostles, under the direct inspiration of the Holy Ghost: not necessarily, or chiefly, predictions, but always utterances distinguished from ordinary teaching. Their function was a fulfilment of the Pentecostal promise: *And* Acts ii. 14 *on My servants and on My handmaidens I will pour out in those days* —18. *of My Spirit; and they shall prophesy.* These words teach us to expect an abundant effusion of this gift; and we find it accordingly. The Epistle to the Corinthians shows that it was common to men and women, that it was occasional and not the special 1 Cor. xiv. endowment of an order, and that it sometimes pervaded the 3, 24, service of the congregation. But when St. Paul tells the 25, 31. Ephesians that they were *built upon the foundation of the Apostles* Eph. ii. *and Prophets,* he allows us to infer that there was a well-known 20. body of men whose ordination was directly from the Spirit; to whom, though not as a permanent class uttering revelations which were to be preserved, the truth was immediately revealed. This high prerogative of the new order is confirmed by the remarkable words of the same Epistle: *As it is now revealed unto* Eph. iii. 5. *His holy Apostles and Prophets by the Spirit.*

3. The link between Prophets and EVANGELISTS is given in the Evangelists.

account of Timothy's ordination : *According to the prophecies which went before on thee ;* and, *Neglect not the gift that is in thee, which was given thee by prophecy.* Timothy is the type of this third order : the last charge to him of St. Paul, his superior, is : *Do the work of an Evangelist,* εὐαγγελιστοῦ, *make full proof of thy ministry,* διακονίαν. That ministry was the performance, in subordination to the Apostles, of the Apostolic offices of preaching everywhere the Gospel and founding churches. It was strictly subordinate, as is testified in the Acts by the Apostles' confirmation of their work through the bestowment of the Spirit, and by the plenary instructions given to Timothy and Titus by the Apostle who appointed them. It was an office that vanished with the apostolate on which it depended. In due time the name was given to the writers of the Gospels which the first Evangelists preached : Eusebius seems to have been the first to give it this application, and it has been accepted by the consent of Christendom.

II. The transitional character of these offices suggests their connection both with the past and with the future.

1. By them the Old Testament was linked with the New. The human instruments in the foundation of both economies are men extraordinarily appointed and supernaturally endowed. The Apostles in the New Law answer to Moses in the Old ; the Prophets have risen again, having begun at the advent of Christ and not ceased until the foundations of His kingdom were laid ; and the Evangelists correspond with those great men who anciently combined the legislative and prophetic functions. But there is the difference which the universal mission of the Gospel introduced : the publishers of the Evangelical glad tidings were only predicted in the Old Testament.

2. In their relation to the future, these offices have, in the strictest sense, passed away. The Apostles have no successors. Their number was sealed : Twelve to represent the tribes of Israel, Matthias having been most solemnly added to complete their body when Judas fell from it ; and One supernumerary introduced to represent the Gentile world. If others, such as Barnabas, seem to bear the name, a careful examination of the texts will show that they receive it only in an accommodated sense, or as appendages of the true Apostles. The prophetic office also has

Marginal notes:

1 Tim. i. 18.
1 Tim. iv. 14.

2 Tim. iv. 5.

Acts viii. 14, 15.

Transitional.

As to the Past.

As to the Future.

been withdrawn. And in the full meaning of the office there are no longer Evangelists, or men endowed with a delegated apostolical authority. But, though they passed away, their relations to early Christianity cannot be studied without leaving the impression that the same Spirit Who set them in the Church may reproduce their extraordinary influence without their names and without their miraculous endowments. We need no other Apostles, for the Apostolic body rules over us still; we need no Prophets, for the prophecy is sealed; but Evangelists, in the spirit and power of Apostles and Prophets, though not in their Spirit, —that is, not with their vocation—will always be needed while the earth is anywhere covered with the darkness of heathenism.

THE REGULAR MINISTRY.

Regular.

The New Testament, especially in its latest documents, makes it certain that a regular and uniform ministerial constitution was appointed for the service of the Church after Apostolical supervision should be with drawn. This ministry was divided into two offices: one, having more particularly the care of the spiritual interests of the flock, and the other more particularly that of its temporal or quasi-temporal affairs. The former is the Pastorate, the latter the Diaconate; and these two have been generally retained, though with different names and varying functions, by most bodies of Christian people.

The term Ministry, διακονία, is the most comprehensive that can be used. It is sanctified by its application to the Lord Himself, Who announced that He came *to minister*, and was once called a *Minister of the circumcision ;* it is used by St. Paul of the ministry generally; while it descends to the lowest office, *to serve tables.* The origin of the word is obscure; most probably it is to be derived from an obsolete διάκω or διήκω, to run, connected with διώκω, to hasten after. Conventionally it is limited in modern times to the pastoral office, or the ministry of the Word; which is only one of many instances illustrating the remarkable freedom with

The Term.

Matt. xx. 28.
Rom. xv. 8.
Acts vi. 2.

which the original terminology of ecclesiastical government has been dealt with in later ages. Generally it may be said that no one function as described in the New Testament finds its precise and unvaried representative in the modern Churches: a fact which should tend to lessen the confidence and mitigate the asperity of controversy concerning ecclesiastical principles.

THE PASTORAL OFFICE.

The terms employed to denote the ordinary spiritual office-bearers of the Christian community are in their English equivalents Presbyters or Elders, and Bishops or Overseers or Superintendents. These, however, constitute one order in the New Testament. The functions assigned to them are those of ministering the Word, and watching over the flock, and ruling the churches: they are accordingly called Teachers or Preachers, Pastors, and Rulers.

Names.

NAMES.

The only official names of a permanent character are πρεσβύτεροι and ἐπίσκοποι: the former being far the more common.

Identity of Bishops and Elders.

1. The New Testament uses these terms interchangeably for one and the same order of spiritual officers. The passages which prove this will also throw light upon the functions of this undivided order. St. Paul *sent to Ephesus, and called the elders of the* *Acts xx. 17, 28.* *church,* τοὺς πρεσβυτέρους, and at the close of his charge bids them take heed to the flock over which the Holy Ghost had made them *overseers* or bishops, ἐπισκόπους. In the Pastoral Epistles also the two names signify one order. Titus was left in Crete for this *Titus i. 5, 7.* among other obvious and undeniable reasons, to *ordain elders* *in every city;* and as the first qualification of these elders his Superior says, *A bishop must be blameless.* So St. Peter affirms *1 Pet. v. 1, 2.* that the duty of the elders is to feed the flock, ἐπισκοποῦντες, or *Phil. i. 1.* *taking the oversight.* Hence, writing to the Philippians, the Apostle *1 Tim. iii. 1, 8.* mentions only two orders of spiritual officers, the *bishops and* *deacons,* as also in his former Pastoral Epistle to Timothy.

2. The differences between the terms are obvious. That of Elder had reference to age or dignity, and was derived from Judaism, that of Bishop to office, and was derived from the Greeks There is therefore no office of eldership as such, but there is of course an ἐπισκοπή this is mentioned once in a sad connection, and once as an object of desire It is remarkable, however, that no Episcopate is alluded to, in the sense of a collective body of bishops, but once at least we read of a Christian Presbytery, as having ordained Timothy, after the pattern of the Jewish πᾶν τὸ Πρεσβυτέριον, *all the estate of the elders*, literally THE WHOLE PRESBYTERY The Elders of Judaism were seniors in age, chosen as assessors in the Sanhedrim with high priests and scribes The Elders of Christianity formed a body, generally but not always seniors in age, who presided over the Christian community as the only directing and governing authority. The term Presbytery, therefore, runs up to the most reverend antiquity, and is invested with a dignity quite unique.

Difference.

Acts i 20
1 Tim. iii. 1
1 Tim iv. 13

Acts xxii 5.

3 There are some traces of a pre-eminence given to one member of the Presbyterial body During the New-Testament age the Apostles themselves were absolute in all churches and over all their affairs the Evangelists representing their authority where it was delegated But every corporate governing body must have a head, at least as Primus inter pares ; and in the Apocalypse that one representative of the presbytery seems to be pointed out in the ANGEL who is addressed in each of the Epistles to the Seven Churches The term Angel is symbolical, probably like Stars, though in another sense *The seven stars are the angels of the seven churches.* It may be said that this would be making the stars symbols of symbols, that the angels therefore must represent something more real than an ideal guardian of the flock. Allowing this, there are those who say that it symbolises the ministry collectively, which is exceedingly probable, but even then the individual term Angel, though not the name of an office, suggests the Divine sanction of an arch-presbyter within a single limited pastoral charge But there is no clear and distinct indication of the appointment of any such authority as pertaining to a distinct order, such as we have seen revived in the present century, and certainly not as bearing the name of Bishop

Primus inter Pares.

Rev i 20

FUNCTIONS.

Functions   The three functions of dispensing the Word of doctrine, watching over the flock, and ruling in the congregation, are distinctly laid down especially in St. Paul's Pastoral Epistles, to which in this connection it may be sufficient to refer as containing the sum and substance of New-Testament teaching on the subject.

Minister.   1. The ministration in Divine service includes the ordering of worship, administering the sacraments, and preaching the Word. Here the term Minister is specially appropriate : as angels are ministering spirits, so pastors are ministering men : but both as offering their liturgic service first to God and then from God. The responsibility of the due celebration of worship rests with the Ministry : the service, that is, whether of prayer or praise, which has been already described. As the representatives of the Divine will to the congregation, the duty of these spiritual officers is to administer the Sacraments, to preach the Gospel for conversion, and to teach the souls by their instrumentality converted. All this is in their commission, and for all this they must seek every Divine and human qualification. In the Gospels and Pastoral Epistles these endowments are, as might be expected, amply described.

Pastor.   2. The responsibility of the pastoral care springs out of the former. The feeding of the flock is the instruction of its members, old and young ; but it is also the vigilant distributive attention to all its interests in the whole economy of life. The

John x. 3.   under-shepherds must imitate the Ἀρχιποίμην, Who *calleth his own sheep by name.* For the general and particular care of the church the elders are responsible. But in this, as in the dispensation of the Word, and indeed in all their functions, they have the ministries of the whole congregation at their disposal, and cannot dispense with them. Among the gifts bestowed on the

1 Cor. xii. 28.   Church were the *helps* or ἀντιλήψεις ; and the New Testament exhibits Christians of all classes as being employed in the services of prayer, preaching, and care of the sick. But in all and over all the Presbytery have the supreme responsibility.

Ruler.   3. This pastoral relation passes naturally into what we have Scriptural authority for calling the spiritual government of the Church.

Its ministers are called ἡγουμένοι, *rulers* or προεστῶτες, *presidents,* and all its members are bidden to *obey them that have the rule.* This authority may be viewed under two aspects: first, as committed to them by the Chief Shepherd, to Whom alone they are finally responsible as representing Himself; and, secondly, as representing the authority of the congregation committed by its own formal delegation to its representatives. Heb. xiii. 7.

(1.) Such rule as they have is ordained of Christ, and the solemn sanctions of their responsibility are connected with the great day when they must give account to Him who now *walketh in the midst of the seven golden candlesticks* and holdeth their *seven stars in His right hand.* The extent and objects of this authority are to be measured by the degree in which the Presbytery are the representatives of the ordinary ministerial authority of the Apostles, in governing the Church by maintaining and guarding the doctrines and laws of Christianity, by exercising discipline as to receiving and excluding the members of its fellowship, and by the general regulation of its affairs. That government of the body which was committed to the Apostles, they committed through Evangelists to *faithful men,* who should discharge their ordinary ministerial function when the guidance of inspiration ceased. Representing Christ. Rev. ii. 1.

2 Tim. ii. 2.

(2.) Their jurisdiction may be said also to be representative of that of the congregation itself. Though *there is no power but of God,* and the government of the ministry is included as *ordained of God,* there is a sense in which it is only the authority of the whole Church delegated to its ministers. The three Mediatorial offices are committed to the entire body of His people who are said to have received an *unction from the Holy One,* that is, the Christly anointing from the Christ: they have the doctrine of truth and *know all things* and can *try the spirits;* they are invested with the priestly function, so far as they *have an altar* and *offer up spiritual sacrifices;* and they are kings, a *royal priesthood.* But all that the Church has received as a corporate body from its Head it lodges again in a certain sense with its ministers: all, literally and without deduction. The body of the people have resigned to them the right to teach; they have deputed their elders to that office. As a congregation their priestly functions are in the hands of their ministers; though in discharging them these are no longer priests. And the Representing the Church. Rom. xiii. 1.

1 John ii. 20. 1 John iv. 1. Heb. xiii. 10. 1 Pet. ii. 5, 9.

rule of the flock they have given over by the Lord's will to their ministerial superintendents.

Teaching and Ruling one Office.

4. This Presbyterial government is one and not divided. Distinctions between a Teaching and a Pastoral or Ruling Eldership have been established in various communities, as will be hereafter seen ; but the Scripture does not sanction them, for it generally speaks of ministerial teaching as a necessary part of pastoral duty. *Remember them which have the rule over you, who*

Heb. xiii. 7.

have spoken unto you the word of God. That a bishop be διδακτικός,

1 Tim. iii. 2.

didactic, or *apt to teach,* was spoken of by St. Paul as indispensable.

1 Tim. v. 17.

Afterwards the Apostle says : *let the elders that rule* WELL *be counted worthy of double honour, especially they who labour in the word and doctrine.* Very earnest elders must be doubly honoured, with a doubtful side-glance at their ample sustenance : doubly if their excellence is in ruling, and still more so if it is teaching.

United Churches.

5. Lastly, these offices of the Presbytery have relation not only to individual churches but to congregations of churches. Neither in the Old Testament nor in the New is there anything to favour the supposition that a congregation was ever regarded as isolated and independent in its government. The unity of the churches as representing the one Church appears everywhere : whether in our

Matt. xvi. 18.

Lord's use of the term—first, *My church* universal, then, *tell it unto the church* local—or in the Acts or in the Epistles or in the Revela-

Matt. xviii. 17.

tion, where *the seven churches which are in Asia* refer to variety in unity.

Rev. i. 11.

Everywhere we find Apostles representing the church, then pastors and teachers representing the congregation. The Ecclesiastical government of the future was sketched in the New Testament. We do not find the exact pattern shown us, but sufficient to indicate that there was in every region a bond of unity among the churches, and that, supposing the Apostles withdrawn, that bond was the Presbytery. In the Acts we have the first council at Jerusalem, and the assembly of elders at Miletus. With respect

Acts xvi. 4.

to the former we read : *as they went through the cities, they delivered them the decrees for to keep, that were ordained of the Apostles and Elders which were at Jerusalem. And so were the churches established.*

Acts xx. 17, 18.

With respect to the latter, St. Paul *sent to Ephesus, and called the elders of the church.* When they had come he proceeded to speak to them as representatives of Asia : *Ye know, from the first day that I came into Asia.* An entirely isolated or independent Christian community is unknown in the New Testament.

THE DIACONATE.

Diaconate

The first officers whose appointment is mentioned after Pentecost were set apart as helpers of the Apostles in the service of tables: the feasts and charities of the Church. The Seven originally designated were in all respects an extraordinary creation; but in due time a distinct order is mentioned by the name of Deacons, whose vocation was, first, to assist the Presbyters in their several offices generally, and, secondly, as their assistants, to take charge of the sick and the poor. To the Deacons corresponded a much less prominent order of Deaconesses.

1. The Seven were to the subsequent deacons what, as we have seen, the extraordinary ministers were to the ordinary. Their appointment was one of the results of the transitory community of goods; a temporary expedient out of which a permanent institution grew. An outpouring of love altogether new and peculiar to the Christian fellowship demanded a service of which the ancient economy, temple or synagogue, had no type. Hence the men appointed to assist the Apostles were scarcely below them in spiritual endowments; and indeed added to these new functions the offices of preachers and evangelists and prophets. Certainly nothing in their duties corresponded with the *Minister*, ὑπηρέτης, of the Synagogue, or חַזָּן. As we read often of THE TWELVE, and more than once of THE SEVENTY, so once we read of THE SEVEN.

2. The later New Testament mentions the office and qualifications for the office in such a manner as to show that it was mainly though not exclusively secular: the deacon is not required to be *apt to teach,* and the *good degree* he is said to purchase is simply the higher more distinctively pastoral office to which the lower ministries sometimes led. They were an order common to all. Their first care was for the sick and poor; they dispersed the

Origin.

Luke iv.
20.

Acts xxi.
8.
Pastoral
Epistles.

1 Tim. iii.
13.

348 THE ADMINISTRATION OF REDEMPTION.

Acts xi. 30.

alms of which the Presbyters were the treasurers: *and sent it to the elders by the hands of Barnabas and Saul.* They were employed

Acts vi. 2.

to serve tables: that is, to take order for the lovefeasts which at first were daily connected with the Lord's Supper. This, however, became gradually a less onerous service, and allowed more time for private and public instruction; so that they were by degrees intermediaries between the elders and the people, just as the elders were intermediaries between the individual church and the churches elsewhere. St. Paul describes their duties in the vivid sketch he gives of their qualifications, among which are

1 Tim. iii. 8, 9.

that they be *grave, not double tongued,* and *holding the mystery of the faith in a pure conscience,* these pointing to the offices of private instruction in smaller assemblies or classes and local preaching as connected with the function of the deacon. The service is often

Deaconesses.

in modern times rendered without the name.

3. The deaconesses constituted a distinct order, originating in the necessity of the female portion of the congregation, especially among the Greeks. The office was strictly like that of the deacons so far as concerned the care of the poor and private instruction: it allowed women to minister in countless ways to the good of the saints under the direction of the elders. These seem to be

1 Tim. v. 9, 10.

referred to when St. Paul says: *let not a widow be taken into the number*—καταλεγέσθω, be enrolled—*under threescore years old,* though this limitation of age was not regarded as imperative and was afterwards relaxed. The other qualifications show how important was the office in the Apostle's judgment; and generally how extreme was the care taken as to the character of the women who discharged any functions in the congregation. But the deaconesses were more limited

1 Cor. xiv. 34, 35.

than the deacons as to public teaching. *Let your women keep silence in the churches; for it is not permitted unto them to speak,* λαλεῖν. There is nothing more severe in St. Paul's writings than what follows: *it is a shame, αἰσχρὸν, for women to speak in the church.* Natural decorum was the ground of his interdict, which would apply, however, only to the more public assembly.

Orders.

VOCATION AND ORDINATION.

To this ministry there is a Divine vocation, of the Spirit; and a human, of the Church. And this vocation is, in the

New Testament, generally sealed by Ordination, through laying on of the hands of the Presbytery.

VOCATION, OR THE CALL.

To every service in the Christian fellowship there is a vocation : the ministerial, whether pastoral or more administrative, is connected with a special call, more emphatically marked than any other on account of its greater spiritual importance. Vocation.

1. The Divine call is supposed throughout the New Testament. As in the old economy *no man taketh this honour unto himself but he that is called of God,* so in the new our Lord chose the Twelve and the Seventy; He also gave His special sanction to the twelfth Apostle Matthias, and the thirteenth Paul. Of the ordinary elders it is said, *all the flock, over the which the Holy Ghost hath made you overseers.* The Scripture gives no specific indication of the way in which the secret vocation of the Spirit shows itself ; save that the person called must be one who has a spiritual experience of the Christian religion, must have the requisite gifts for the office to which he is called, and must purchase to himself his degree by the usefulness of his preparatory service, these being the fruits meet for his candidature. GRACE, first : *hath reconciled us to Himself by Jesus Christ, and hath given to us the ministry of reconciliation ;* GIFTS, secondly : the elder must be *apt to teach ;* FRUIT, lastly : he must have used the office of a deacon well, or, literally, have *ministered well.* Divine.
Heb. v. 4.

Acts xx.
28.

2 Cor. v.
18.
1 Tim. iii.
2—13.

2. The vocation on the part of the church is much more expressly dwelt upon. Generally, the body of elders or ministers pronounces the call of the congregation : the Apostles set apart the deacons ; the *prophets and teachers* announced their specific call to Paul and Barnabas ; Timothy and Titus evidently had the same function as the representatives of the Apostles and of the Church. Obviously, this implies the consent and ratification of the people, though not their initiative : in the case of the deacons, the judgment of the congregation was naturally more relied on and had more weight than in the case of the elders. But in neither case was the approval of the community omitted ; though we are without the means of judging how in many instances their suffrages were obtained or their consent shown. Human.

Acts xiii.
1.

ORDINATION.

Ordination.

What is now called ordination took place generally by imposition of the hands of the Presbytery. This ceremony was borrowed from Judaism, being the symbol and medium of the appointment to office, and the pledge of all requisite grace for its discharge.

Designation.

1. It was the designation to the sacred business of their lives. They on whom hands were laid were set apart as the act of the congregation representatively performed. Hence it was the pledge on the part of the Church of the maintenance of those

1 Cor. ix. 14.
1 Pet. v. 2.
1 Tim. iii. 2.

thus enrolled. *Even so hath the Lord ordained that they which preach the gospel should live of the gospel:* an appointment of Christ which explains the Apostolic injunction to elders, that they feed the flock *not for filthy lucre* and that they must be *given to hospitality.*

Admission into an Order.
1 Tim. iv. 14.
1 Tim. v. 22.

2. On the part of the body of elders it was the formal admission of the ordained into their own number: *With the laying on of the hands of the presbytery.* Over this body Timothy himself presided when others were ordained : *lay hands suddenly on no man.* In this case Timothy, like Titus, was the representative of the Apostle, who, however, seems himself to have presided over

2 Tim. i. 6.

the Presbytery which ordained Timothy : *stir up the gift of God, which is in thee by the putting on of my hands.* From which it follows that in this function the Apostle was only the chief or President of the body, and did not supersede them.

Pledge of Gifts.

3. On the part of the Spirit it was the pledge of His bestowment of grace for the discharge of the duties of the office : that gift, namely, which St. Paul speaks of as latent or inherent in Timothy. The laying on of the hands of the Apostles was never without a specific blessing : specific as to the blessing, specific also as to the Apostolic hands. But in every subsequent age the ministerial GIFT is imparted : not as a present mysterious virtue, or grace, or sacramental gift, but as the pledge in the soul of all needful strength and guidance for every emerging duty.

HISTORICAL.

The development of ecclesiastical opinion as to the function and authority of the Ministry, or the Power of the Keys, has been bound up inseparably with the development of the idea of the Church itself. A few leading points only will require attention here: much of the subject belongs to Ecclesiastical history.

I. The ante-Nicene distinction between Clergy and Laity contained the germ of the latter Hierarchy, with most of its accompanying errors, but with some striking peculiarities. **Ante-Nicene.**

1. The Apostolical Fathers began the development very early. The first of them, Clement of Rome, speaks of the λαϊκὸς ἄνθρωπος, the LAYMAN. Another, Ignatius, distinguishes bishop, presbytery, and deacon; and makes the bishop the centre of catholic unity. In the third century the ministry were called the CLERUS or CLERICI: both as the lot or portion of God, after the analogy of the Levitical tribe, and as the elect guides of the people. Their rank was an ORDO SACERDOTALIS or ECCLESIASTICUS; and here we have the origin of Clergy and Ecclesiastics. There were in this order two departments: the Ordines Majores, comprising the diaconate, the presbyterate and the episcopate, of Divine institution; the Ordines Minores, comprising all the lower functions from the sub-deacon to the door-keeper. During that period celibacy was optional. The consent of the people to the appointment of their pastors or bishops was required. Laymen were permitted to teach, though not in the presence of the clergy or without their consent. The episcopal institute as that of a distinct order sprang from ecclesiastical custom, based upon the necessity of continuing the Apostolic bond of unity. It became universal in the middle of the second century: but Irenæus and Cyprian did much in the third to exalt the office to its highest dignity. The hierarchical idea, with its full complement of gradation in its train, was only by slow degrees fully developed. The Chorepiscopi, or country-bishops, were the lowest in episcopal rank. The Metropolitans were the bishops of the leading cities: Antioch being the see for all Syria; Alexandria for Egypt; Rome for Italy and the West. In the fourth century the term Patriarch was attached to these, and to Constantinople and Jerusalem: the five ecclesiastical and political centres of the Roman Empire. To this system the East has adhered. The West has passed on to the Pontificate: the unity and consummation of all lower spiritual orders.

Apostolical Fathers.

Clergy and Laity.

Episcopacy.

2. These beginnings of error are to be traced in another direction. **Judaism**

tion. Almost every doctrinal deviation from the faith as a whole had its specific influence on the theory of the Christian ministry and its relation to the sacrifice of Christ. So far as Judaizing prevailed it brought back the sacrifice and the sacrificing priest-hood with the sacrificial altar. The notion of a necessary external unity pointed to the supremacy of the bishop as the bond of union in the individual church, according to Ignatius ; and of the supremacy of one bishop to secure the unity of all the churches. Even the wholesome doctrine of Catholicity, in opposition to schisms and heresy, tended the same way. The Power of the Keys, which originally guarded the purity of the fellowship, became to the clergy a great temptation ; and tended, together with the exaggerated notion of the mysteries of which they had the keys, to invest their character with an unevangelical prerogative. In the second century two views predominated on this subject : one which made the binding and loosing identical with retaining and forgiving sin ; and another which made it refer more generally to all ecclesiastical authority. Both, however, took a high stand on this subject. Cyprian asserted that the power of the keys was entrusted first to Peter and then to the other Apostles : making that difference between the two on which so great a superstructure has since been raised. The prescriptions of penance for Peccata Mortalia, or sins which threatened spiritual life, with the excom-munication and reconciliation or reception into the Church again by absolution, did not before the time of Augustine give the priest more than the authority of intercession as the representative of the congregation. Leo the Great did much to exalt the priestly independent power as his own official prerogative. Confession was not as yet made to the priests under obligation ; and, while the binding and loosing had some reference to Divine forgiveness, it had more to certain ecclesiastical privileges. Public expulsions from the church on Ash-Wednesday, and public receptions after-wards on the Ascension Thursday, were usages of Rome in the fifth century. These gave place during the Middle Ages to private penance and private absolution.

II. From the time of Constantine to the Reformation—twelve hundred years—there was a steady development of the germs of error observable in the first centuries. The main points only

Marginal notes:
Power of the Keys.

Germs of Error.

Mediæval.

need be here noted : to follow them out into their details belongs rather to ecclesiastical history.

1. Though some of the highest authorities—Jerome, Chrysostom, Theodoret—asserted the original identity of bishops and presbyters, the episcopal order came to be regarded as representative of Christ and the Apostles, the special organs and instruments of the Holy Ghost. The bishops assumed the sole right to ordain, and in the West to confirm : their hands alone being supposed to communicate the sealing grace of the Gospel. The Episcopate.

2. When Christianity was made the religion of the empire the ministry of the Church became in the strictest sense a HIERARCHY. After A.D. 395, the Empire being divided into East and West, this Hierarchy had two heads : the Patriarchs of Rome and Constantinople. These long contended for the mastery ; but Rome finally gained the victory. ROMA LOCUTA EST became the standard of judgment. The bishop of Rome claimed to be PAPA, POPE or PRIMATE of the whole Church, and to possess a dignity beyond that of all other bishops, though in order still only a bishop. Rome was the only Sedes Apostolica in the West, and was therefore the Latin Patriarchate. But the patriarchal system was oligarchical, not monarchical ; and the four Œcumenical Councils,—of Nicæa, Constantinople, Ephesus, and Chalcedon—made the bishop of Rome only PRIMUS INTER PARES among the patriarchs and bishops, just as every bishop was only Primus inter Pares among the presbyters. The separation of the Greek Church from the Latin is proof that the claim was never conceded. But it was reserved for the Reformation to bring the only good argument—that of Scripture—against the Hierarchical system, which as such seemed naturally to require a head. It is historical fact that Leo I., called the Great, who died A.D. 461, laid the firm foundations of the modern Papacy ; and that Gregory I., who died A.D. 604, consolidated the system which culminated with Gregory VII. and Innocent III. in the Middle Ages. The Roman Pontiff.

3. The Jewish priesthood and worship had gradually become the model of the Christian service. Ordination was accompanied with oil : this being to the special priesthood what baptism was to the universal priesthood, and, like baptism, having a Character Indelibilis. By slow degrees every trace of popular election and Jewish Sacerdotalism.

confirmation passed away; and the clergy virtually became the church. Their sole administration of the sacraments, the number of which gradually increased, gave them more than the ancient Jewish priestly ascendency. The central service of the Unbloody Sacrifice was waited on by priests clothed in vestments surpassing those of the Temple service in variety of symbolical meaning, and concentrated on them all the confidence and awe which the Levitical priesthood inspired.

Schools of Clergy.

4. Seminaries of ministerial instruction—of which the Catechetical School at Alexandria was the model—abounded in the East from the fourth century. In the West there were many such schools privately set up by the bishops: such as the Monasterium Clericorum of Augustine. But the majority of the clergy were found to be profoundly ignorant as ages rolled on; although their ignorance was not so universal as is sometimes represented.

Monasticism.

5. The history of Monasticism is only indirectly connected with that of the ministry. Asceticism marked the private life of many of the clergy from the beginning; in the fourth century this became Anchoretism, or hermit life separated from the world (ἀναχωρέω to retire, ἐρεμία a desert); thence came the cœnobite or cloister life, or monasticism proper, the ascetic life organised (κοινὸς βίος, vita communis, common life); and in the middle ages the monastic orders were the climax. The vows of poverty, chastity, and obedience undertaken by them all were not of themselves ministerial. The monks were Religiosi but not therefore necessarily Clerici until the tenth century.

Mediæval.

6. The Mediæval doctrine of the Keys underwent much development; and was finally completed by Thomas Aquinas. He distinguished between the Potestas (and the Clavis) Ordinis and the Potestas (and the Clavis) Jurisdictionis: the former opening heaven directly, the latter through the excommunication and absolution dispensed in the ecclesiastical forum. The sacramental power of the Keys became the centre of the sacrament of penance. Absolution, according to the final doctrine, procures forgiveness of sins. The opus operans of the penitent's repentance is followed by a pardon ex opere operato. But as judge in foro Dei, the priest can give absolution only as passing judgment on the

reality of the penitence. This must after all, even in this doctrine of the Keys, be left conditional and with God alone.

7. The full Roman Catholic doctrine places the administration of grace in the hands of an Ordo Sacerdotalis; an ecclesiastical hierarchy jure divino—with its Clerus Minor rising to the Clerus Major—which in its stricter sense the bishops really form, culminating in one visible Head, the successor of St. Peter and the representative of Christ on earth. The Church is represented by general councils, consisting of the collective episcopate summoned and presided over by the Pope, who has the Suprematus Jurisdictionis over all bishops. By the same Divine right the Church—the authority of which the Vatican Council of 1870 has really vested in its Head—has the Potestas Ordinis, magisterii and ministerii, the ordering of all doctrine and worship; the Potestas Jurisdictionis, that is the Potestas Clavium or Power of the Keys, the authority to dispose of all the treasures of the grace of Christ; the Potestas Regiminis, or religious authority over the world, which however is an authority always, to a greater or less extent, in conflict with the Potestas Sæcularis. Tridentine Doctrine.

III. The general principle introduced by the Reformation was this, that the living church is the subject and source and centre of all power: that the Potestas Clavium, or Power of the Keys, was committed by Christ to the Apostles as His representatives, and through them to the universal body. The ministerial function or office is of Divine appointment; but its various forms and names are of human arrangement. As human and Divine at once, the ministry is representative of the whole Church, acting through it and in it and devolving upon it its rights. The Reformation.

1. The Lutheran doctrine was higher than that of the Reformed. It connected the ministerial office more expressly with the KEYS. Its Ministerium Verbi et Sacramentorum assigns to the pastor authority to preach the Gospel and remit sins. The following sentences from the Formularies will further explain: "Wherever the (true) Church is there is the right of administering the Gospel. Whence it is needful that the Church retain the right of calling, choosing, and ordaining ministers." "No one ought to teach in the Church or administer sacraments unless duly called." The connection between the Divine and human call is left indefinite: Lutheran. The Keys.

but "by Divine right bishops and rulers in the Church are to be obeyed. But if they teach or ordain contrary to the Word of God the Divine command forbids obedience." The Power of the Keys was regarded as consisting in preaching the Gospel or the terms of forgiveness; but both Luther and the Lutheran Standards and doctors left much room for confession and personal absolution of the minister.

Reformed.   2. The Reformed type of doctrine was more rigorous. It laid more stress on ecclesiastical discipline, which it reckoned among the notes of the true Church; and rejected private confession and absolution altogether. It introduced a more stringent theory of the equality of pastors. By the side of the Ministri Docentes it placed the Ministri Ministrantes or Lay-elders who represented the Church in another sense and in matters of economy and discipline: set apart, and generally ordained, but not to teach.

Anglican.   3. The Anglican doctrine of the Ministry, established at the Reformation, differed in some respects from both these. It retained Episcopacy with the name of Bishop and its special prerogatives: which Lutheranism disguised under the name of Superintendents and reduced it to a mere human expedient. It retained the Hierarchy, as adapted to a territorial and national religion. It went further than the other bodies in its interpretation of the Power of the Keys: using language as to the private absolution of the minister which at least in some of its services is more than merely declarative and significative. The presbyter is also styled priest by an equivocal abbreviation of the word. And, lastly, the Anglican doctrine assumes a special gift and influence of the Holy Spirit in ordination: though the strictly sacramental character of orders is denied, it lays much stress, and rightly so, on the express provision of grace provided for every ministerial function.

Modern Theories.   IV. It will suffice to indicate the theological points involved in these several tendencies: as they affect, that is, doctrine concerning the Christian Ministry.

Papal Infallibility.   1. The Hierarchical tendency has reached its natural consummation in the dogmatic definition of Papal Infallibility in 1870. The Pontiff, or Bishop of Rome, or Pope, speaking ex cathedrâ, that is, avowedly pronouncing the mind of the Church, or of the Spirit in the Church, is the infallible oracle of truth. Thus the long controversy as to the meaning of the Keys being given to St. Peter before they were given to the Apostolic company, seems to be settled, though in a manner inconsistent with other parts of the New Testament. It is forgotten that the special authority given to Peter, that of first opening the kingdom of heaven to Jews and Gentiles, and decreeing what was binding on the Church, and declaring the terms of forgiveness,—the Power of the Keys— was never arrogated by him for himself alone, or even as superior to the rest; and that he declared only that God *made choice among*   Acts xv. 7. *us that the Gentiles by my mouth should hear the word of the gospel,* but no more. Moreover, Simon Peter is the only Apostle whose fallibility is expressly afterwards declared : *he was to be blamed ;*   Gal. ii. 11. and not a word is said of his primacy among the living Apostles being transmitted in any way whatever.

2. From the time of the Reformation there has been a reaction   Reaction against the Hierarchy which has in some communities gone to   against extremes. The QUAKERS, as a branch of the mystical family,   Separated Ministry. swept away the ministry with the church and the sacraments :   Friends. substituting, however, a secret and distinct influence of the Holy Ghost on His own selected organs for the benefit of the assembly. Thus the ministry in their teaching is a perpetual creation instead of a separated order. Their ecclesiastical government is simply the government of a society on principles of human expediency. More recently the PLYMOUTH BRETHREN, or BRETHREN, have   Brethren. arisen as the English branch of a community the principles of which are found in other lands and have never been unrepresented in the Church. This sect denounces the denominations of Christianity, falls back upon the Word of God, retains the sacraments, but rejects the separated pastorship, whether as a body or represented by an individual. The order of the ministry is renounced; and the teaching of the Brotherhood is left to the Spirit's supply of gifts or charismata of teaching. This system utterly lacks the consistency of that of the Quakers. Both these Brethren and those Friends, however, are condemned by the Pastoral Epistles.

3. The Catholic Apostolic Church strives to combine almost all   Irvingites. the theories already alluded to. Its ministry is one of charismata, or gifts, restored according to the pattern in the Corinthian Epistles, and the Epistles of the Revelation. Its Power of the

Keys is very similar to that of the Romanists. Its priestly service seeks to go back to the early ages ; but halts midway.

Laity.

4. The importance of the Laity or general body of the congregation has been in modern times steadily more and more acknowledged. The abuse of terms which made the church and the clergy synonymous has passed away to a great extent ; though its effect is not nor is it likely to be entirely removed. It is

Vindication.

more and more generally acknowledged that laymen may act as Evangelists towards the world, and even as teachers within the church ; that they may be employed in instruction of children, or as catechists ; that they may read the Scriptures, publicly and privately ; that they may sustain manifold offices more or less spiritual ; that they may mainly direct the financial affairs of the community ; and that they ought to be representatives in many ecclesiastical courts of the economics of the Church. There are

Excess.

excesses in this direction, which go to the extreme opposite of the hierarchical excesses. Such is the lay power which is retained by the constitution of the established church as a final appeal. Such is the lay-representation in the Presbyterian government proper : ruling elders, chosen for life, in the presbyteries, synods, and general assemblies. These presbyters—laymen in all other respects, and representatives of the lay element—have a voice in matters which affect the ministerial jurisdiction as such. This applies also to several of the minor Methodist bodies not professedly Presbyterian. In the congregational system the power of the Pastor as such is reduced to a very slight element in comparison with that of the body of the laity.

Methodism.

5. Methodism is in regard to its doctrine and practice on this subject eminently high at once and free. It is Presbyterian as to the basis of its theory : its ministers are of one order only, its Conference being composed of representatives of the Presbytery of the body of Societies or Churches forming the Connexion. It is episcopal, after the earliest type. Augustine says (de Civ. xix. 19) : Episcopatus nomen est operis, non honoris. Græcum est enim, atque inde ductum vocabulum, quod ille qui præficitur eis, quibus præficitur, superintendit, curam eorum, scilicet gerens, ἐπὶ quippe super, σκοπὸς intentio est : ergo ἐπισκοπεῖν latine SUPERINTENDERE possumus dicere. Hence the Superintendent in English Method-

ism occupies precisely the position of early episcopacy and of episcopacy in some parts of Lutheranism. The name Bishop is retained in America. Methodism employs the laity in every diaconal function; though it does not retain the name deacon. It has its Leaders, Local Preachers, Poor Stewards, and Society Stewards, generally of the laity, male and female. It uses the service of women in private ministries, as catechists or teachers in Sunday-schools and leaders. It more carefully than most other religious bodies distinguishes the functions of the pastorate and of the laity: reserving for the final ministerial jurisdiction all questions that affect the Power of the Keys as left by Christ in His Church. The Methodist doctrine is that our Lord left the Keys—the general government of His body, the special binding and loosing of authoritative decrees, and the reception and expulsion of its members—to the Church itself, as represented, however, by the men whom the Spirit would raise up with concurrence of the congregation to represent its authority.

THE CHURCH IN ITS RELATION TO THE WORLD.

Church and World.

The Church of Christ, at once visible and invisible, exists to continue and perfect the work which He began. It is His organ for the preparation of His final kingdom. As such it has a twofold relation to those without: first, to maintain itself, in the midst of the world, as the depositary and witness of saving truth; secondly, to win the world to the obedience of Christ, as a Missionary Institute.

Some of the topics here indicated have been already more or less fully discussed. Some of them must be reserved for Eschatology. But the view or the Administration of Redemption would not be complete without some general remarks here on the three branches of this subject.

THE WITNESS OF TRUTH.

Witness.

The Church, as an organisation in the world but not of it, is the depositary and guardian and witness of the truth.

The truth which it has received is the standard of its faith and discipline ; as it respects both individual Churches and union of Churches on whatever principles united.

Rom. iii. 2.

Tim. iii. 15, 16.

1. One of the chief prerogatives of the ancient people was that *unto them were committed the oracles of God.* The last declaration of St. Paul was that the house of God was *the pillar and ground of the truth :* a final testimony of the Apostle which, taken in all its large context, gives a most impressive view of the prerogative, responsibility, and dignity of the visible Church. These words go back to our Lord's which declare that the Spirit of the truth should abide with His people : the promise was not, by the very terms, limited to the Apostles. In this, as in all, they were representatives of the whole community for ever ; representatives also of its permanent Ministry as a whole ; besides being as Apostles a unique and pre-eminent class. The Church universal is the guardian of Scripture. There was a company of disciples prepared by the Word SPOKEN to receive the Word WRITTEN. To show that the cause of God was not absolutely dependent on the complete Canon, that canon took centuries for its determination. But it was completed for the long future ; and no individual church is faithful which either adds to or takes from the collection of the sacred oracles. Hence it is also the guardian of the truth which is derived from Scripture. One end of its existence is contradiction of error as it arises : hence the variations of dogmatic definition in Creeds and Formularies. The THREE CREEDS were, until the Reformation, a protest against all the errors of the world and of the Church itself. Since then it has pleased the Spirit that various communities should have their various STANDARDS, ARTICLES, or CONFESSIONS OF FAITH.

2. The individual churches have been raised up to bear witness to sundry and several neglected elements of the truth : it being manifestly the mind of the Spirit that the denominations should act as mutual restraints and excitements. It was not His will that there should be uniformity in the Confessions of Christendom : when that uniformity existed for a season corruption was at the door. He administers the Work of Christ by unity in essentials, and mutual antagonism in things of less moment.

3. But it is also the doctrine of Scripture that even the truth as it is in Jesus is not in this world to be revealed in all its fulness. *For we know in part.* A perfect church on earth is not one of the promises or predictions of Scripture. Nor is a finished and rounded scheme of Christian Theology to be expected. Before the exact text of Scripture shall have been determined, and all errors eliminated out of the confessions, and a perfect system of doctrine unfolded, He will have come who is Himself the truth, and will not give His honour to another.

1 Cor. xiii. 9.

THE MISSIONARY INSTITUTE.

Missions.

The Church of Christ exists for the sake of the spread of the Gospel through the world: it is in virtue of its original commission a missionary body. Its obligation rests upon all individual Societies and all their members. With the fulfilment of this commission the functions of the Church will cease: the kingdom of Christ will more and more fully be revealed; until by His coming it will be translated from a kingdom of grace to a kingdom of glory.

The doctrine of Vocation has brought out the distinction of the Christian Church that it has received a commission for all nations: partly, in contradistinction to the limitation of the Theocracy; partly as the term and goal of its own mission.

Scripture.

1. Hence the preaching of the Gospel was the *revelation of the mystery* that the Gentiles should be called. And it is declared by our Lord that the Gospel is to be preached for a *witness unto all nations*, before He Himself should come: only for a testimony, however; for *shall He find faith on the earth?* It is true that in the history of the New Testament we find both principles only by degrees established. The admission of the Gentiles was very slowly acknowledged: not Jerusalem but Antioch was the missionary centre. The universal preaching of the Gospel was too soon assumed to have prepared for Christ's return.

Rom. xvi. 25.
Matt. xxiv. 14.
Luke xviii. 8.

2. No truth concerning the mission of Christianity has

Historical.

been so unfaithfully dealt with by the Church itself. Until the Roman Empire became Christian, missions, the record of which are lost, were vigorously conducted. But from that time down to the Reformation they were affected by two evils, which however did not hinder the spread of Christianity. The faith was propagated to a great extent by the agency of the civil power; it was diffused in its corrupt form, and sometimes by heretics; but the foundations were everywhere laid on which a better superstructure was afterwards upreared. The Reformation was not mindful enough of the missionary obligation: the English Church organised her missions only for the sake of her colonies in the seventeenth century; the Lutheran Church made energetic beginnings in the Danish mission; but it was the Romish Propaganda that showed most vigour.

3. With this century began the Missionary era proper, after the preparations of the last century. It is now acknowledged by most Christian communities that the churches exist as such in order to the preparation and diffusion of the kingdom of Christ among men. MISSIONARY SOCIETIES have everywhere sprung

Mission-
ary
Societies.

up, and are the glory of the present age. In strange contrast with this is the fact that there are some communities, and many individuals in other communities, who believe that the diffusion of the Gospel is a subordinate matter; and that the destruction of His enemies and the establishment of His kingdom must be effected by the visible reappearance of Christ, who will for a thousand years before the end reign upon earth. But the uniform tenour of the New Testament declares that this Gospel is to be preached in all the earth, to every creature, and that Christ's presence with His missionary Church will continue always to the end of the world. This subject will return in the last section, that of Eschatology.

Church
and
Kingdom.

THE CHURCH AND THE KINGDOM.

The New Testament ends as it began, with the Kingdom of God and of Christ. That kingdom is the kingdom of heaven, as being in its origin not of this world. It is the kingdom of heaven on earth, as the spiritual authority that is already pervading human society. It is the kingdom of heaven also as the final form into which all the individual Churches of Christ upon earth shall melt. It is the kingdom absolutely as it is the one manifestation of Christ's mediatorial rule, which had its earlier Old-Testament stage of preparation in Israel, its New-Testament fulfilment among Israel and the Gentiles, and will have its glorious consummation at the Coming of the Lord.

1. The one βασιλεία, or Kingdom, was established in Israel and as a THEOCRACY, which was really a CHRISTOCRACY in disguise, as the rulers in the ancient economy were types and representatives of Christ, Who in all ages and in all economics has ruled virtually or actually in the house of God. The One Kingdom.

2. The kingdom of grace coincides with the Church, as it has been exhibited in its united visibility and invisibility, good and evil combined. The kingdom, during the interval until the coming of the Lord, is, however, mainly regarded as invisible. Our Lord speaks of it as already come : *behold, the kingdom of God is within you ;* ἐντὸς ὑμῶν, among you invisibly. *He that is least in the kingdom of God is greater than he,* John the Baptist. *And from the days of John the Baptist until now the kingdom of heaven suffereth violence*—or is gotten by violence—*and the violent take it by force.* Concerning this, and some other similar passages, it is to be remembered that our Lord speaks by anticipation, as well as with reference to the present, and that His words are of prospective and abiding significance. *Verily, I say unto you, that there be some of them that stand here which shall not taste of death, till they have seen the kingdom of God come with power.* This does not refer to the final Parousia, or the Redeemer's visible coming in His kingdom, but to the invisible coming in the kingdom of grace. This was the outpouring of the Spirit, the founding of the Church, and the revolution which laid waste the old Theocracy and its holy city. In this period of grace the Redeemer is KING OF RIGHTEOUSNESS, KING OF PEACE : His metropolis being Jerusalem, the city of the vision of peace. Church and Kingdom.
Luke xvii. 21.
Luke vii. 28.
Matt. ix. 12.
Mark ix. 1.
Heb. vii. 2.

3. The kingdom even now has in some respects the pre- The Kingdom.

eminence. It is the subject of most of our Lord's parables. Many of the prerogatives and privileges which are too often assigned to the Church really belong to the Kingdom. It is, for instance, the supreme good which must be sought and purchased, at the cost of all that we have: the *treasure hid in a field*, and the *one pearl of great price*. Whatever differences are here, the kingdom stands for Him who is the inestimable treasure in it: *unto you therefore which believe He is precious.* The Benedictions of our Lord's commencement are the enjoyments of this kingdom; they begin and end with it: *Blessed are the poor in spirit: for theirs is the kingdom of heaven. Blessed are they which are persecuted for righteousness' sake: for theirs is the kingdom of heaven.* It is not said of the Church that it is *righteousness and peace, and joy in the Holy Ghost.* The Evangelical proclamation is *this gospel of the kingdom:* one of the largest and most comprehensive sayings in the New Testament. Whatever glorious things are said of the Church, it after all carries with it a reference to the evil world whence it came: *a glorious church, not having spot or wrinkle, or any such thing.* The kingdom is also mixed, for *they shall gather out of His kingdom all things that offend;* but the predominant idea in it is that of the sphere of Christ's supreme sovereign manifestation.

4. It is this kingdom that is *an everlasting kingdom.* It is now not yet revealed; and of it St. John, after having spoken of his apostleship to the Churches, says: *I, John, who also am your brother and companion in tribulation, and in the kingdom and patience of Jesus Christ.* We are all fellows in the patience of the kingdom in Jesus: ἐν τῇ βασιλείᾳ καὶ ὑπομονῇ ἐν Ἰησοῦ.

Margin references: Matt. xiii. 44, 46. — 1 Pet. ii. 7. — Matt. v. 3, 10. — Rom. xiv. 17. — Matt. xxiv. 14. — Eph. v. 27. — Matt. xiii. 41. — Dan. vii. 27. — Rev. i. 9.

ESCHATOLOGY, OR THE LAST THINGS.

DEATH AND THE INTERMEDIATE STATE.

THE COMING OF CHRIST: RESURRECTION AND
JUDGMENT.

THE CONSUMMATION.

THE LAST THINGS.

It has been seen, as we have proceeded, that all the facts, doctrines and ethics of theology point forward to one great Consummation. The things concerning Christ and His kingdom HAVE AN END. To exhibit that End, whether as universal or as individual, in one connected whole is the province of Eschatology, or the doctrine of the Last Things. It is obvious that all the lines here converge to one event, the Return of the Redeemer, which is the supreme Hope of His people : His Coming, however, cannot be disconnected from the Resurrection of all men and the universal Judgment. Before that final event of time, however, the destinies of Christ's cause belong to the other world as well as to this, and we have a profoundly interesting department of theology in Death and the Kingdom of the Dead : here time is strangely blended with eternity, though it is time still. After that final event, when time shall be no more, we have only the Consummation of all Divine designs and human destiny.

GENERAL CHARACTERISTICS.

Before entering on these topics in detail a few observations may be made on the general characteristics of this branch of theology, as it is specifically the prophetic part of the perfected revelation of Christianity.

1. As such it is almost if not altogether shut up to the predictions of Christ and His Apostles. Of the future of mankind, whether in this world or in the next, we can from other sources know nothing. Men may speculate as to the destinies of the race, and argue as to what is to be by an induction of what has been, but all this adds nothing to knowledge. But the very same authority which gives us our theology of the past and of the present gives us also our theology of the future. If we examine the New Testament carefully we find that a very large portion of it is occupied with THINGS TO COME. Our Lord Himself spoke very much of the future of His kingdom and Church. What He predicted in the hearing of His Apostles was to be brought to their remembrance. Moreover, He said of the Holy Ghost, *He will show you things to come.* One remarkable form of the accomplishment of this prophecy was His own disclosure of the future to His Church by the Spirit through the last Evangelist : *The revelation of Jesus which God gave unto Him to show unto His servants things which must shortly come to pass.*

John xvi. 13.

Rev. i. 1.

2. There is an analogy between the Old-Testament prophecies of what were then the Last Things and those of the New Testament. In ancient times the prophets enquired and *searched diligently . . . searching what or what manner of time the Spirit of Christ which was in them did signify.* The same may be said of their successors the Apostles. There is throughout evidence that the law of disciplinary reserve which governs the prophetic part of Divine revelation rules with scarcely any relaxation. What the First Coming of the Messiah was to the ancient saints His Second Coming is to us : we have the same certain but indefinite future ; very much more clearly outlined as to its great events, but equally undefined as to times and seasons, and vanishing into equal if not deeper mystery. It might have been expected that it would be otherwise ; and that the coming of the Object of all prophecy would have introduced a new order of prediction, leaving no room for uncertainty or error as to the future. But it is far otherwise. A few words, here and there spoken, might have precluded a thousand controversies. But they are unspoken. As the Master of Wisdom saw in the olden and more immature economy *it is the glory of God to conceal a*

1 Peter i. 10, 11.

Prov. xxv. 2.

thing, the glory of His wisdom; so still *the honour of kings is to* Limitation.
search out a matter, and all the Lord's people have this royal prerogative. From beginning to end the law of revelation is probationary: man's original sin of penetrating to forbidden knowledge seems to be remembered in the Divine economy of discipline.
While on all points that concern probation the teaching is distinct
and sufficient, nothing is disclosed for the gratification of curiosity.
From the Apostles' first question, *Lord, wilt Thou at this time* Acts i. 6.
restore again the kingdom to Israel? there has been constant
evidence of the error of the Church to speculate unduly: sometimes in fanciful, sometimes in tragic, sometimes in sentimental
outlines the future of Christianity has been sketched with more
or less of confident temerity. The Saviour's answer, *It is not for* Acts i. 7.
you to know the times or the seasons, which the Father hath put in His
own power, is of wide and unlimited application. We are taught
that we must be content to leave some portions of the unknown
future in their obscurity; and to muse without definitions before
the unlifted veil: remembering that for us it may be lifted even
while we are musing. This is a severe discipline, especially to
the theologian, who delights in a clear confession of faith, and is
sorely tempted to aim at the same formal analysis of the Last
Things as he has been able to give of the work of Christ finished
on earth and of the present administration of the Holy Spirit. He
would fain weave into a system the scattered hints of prophecy.
But nothing is more certain than that the Holy Ghost does not
encourage this desire: prophetic theology can hardly be dogmatic.

3. Meanwhile, it is equally certain that there is a peculiar Encouragement.
blessing attached to the humble, patient, and earnest study of the
dread realities of the future. Eschatology, or the doctrine of the
Last Things, appeals to certain principles and instincts of our
nature which it alone has power to touch. There are elements in
the constitution of man the cultivation of which is of great importance to religious discipline; and their education is almost
entirely dependent on this branch of subjects. These have also an
irresistible attraction to all classes, especially in times of sorrow
and in advancing life; and their very indefiniteness and obscurity
and unsearchable mystery enhance that attraction. Moreover, a
considerable range of the ethics of Christianity grows out of the

contemplation of future destiny and preparation for it. Hence there is the amplest encouragement to the study of these things, though there is no encouragement to the systematic, or, as it were, scientific arrangement of them. It is left on record as

Rev. i. 3.   a general principle that *Blessed is he that readeth, and they that hear the words of this prophecy:* not blessed because either reader or hearer will ever know the times and the seasons which symbolically expand before the vision; but blessed because this kind of meditation tends to withdraw his mind from all lower interests and will keep him at the Saviour's feet in the attitude of adoring expectation, humility, and trust.

Methods.   4. The methods of analysis that may be adopted are many, and will be shaped variously according to the bias and prepossessions of the theologian: especially his bias on the subject of the Millennial future glory of the Church and the second coming of the Lord. Some are so prejudiced against the perversions of Millenarianism that they place the Lord's return generally under His judicial office and thus rob Eschatology of its keystone. Others are so bewitched by that one theme that they virtually divide redemption into two sections: the first and the second Coming of Christ. Certainly, the return of its Head as such is the undying hope of the militant body on earth. It is the vanishing point of all Christian expectation. It commands the great futurity; but in theological order Death and Hades belong to the preparations for His advent; the Coming itself precedes the resurrection and judgment; and beyond it, though still suffused with its glory, opens out the consummation of all things.

DEATH AND THE KINGDOM OF THE DEAD.

Death is a word of large meaning in theology. There is a sense in which it does not belong to the Last Things, being one of the first facts in the religious history of mankind. As the penalty of sin it has already been considered. Here it must be viewed chiefly, though not exclusively, as the last event in the probation of man translated by it into the region of the dead, which in its relation to the coming of Christ and the final consummation may be called an Intermediate State.

DEATH AND IMMORTALITY.

Death spiritual and eternal will reappear at a later stage in Eschatology. Its physical aspect is here more directly concerned; and it must be regarded, first, as in a certain sense abolished by the death of Christ, but, secondly, as nevertheless continued in the discipline of the Gospel and made the minister of the Divine purpose. All is summed up in one word, that Christianity has taught us what death is as the result of sin under the economy of grace.

DEATH.

It is said by St Paul that Jesus Christ *hath abolished death, and hath brought life and immortality to light through the Gospel.* Death is in fact abolished by being also brought under the light by the same revelation. that is, Christianity has finally and fully explained what death is, and under what conditions the human race is subjected to it notwithstanding the great redemption.

B B 2

Death and Immortality.

1. Death in the new dispensation never means the opposite of existence : were it such, it could not be said to be annihilated, unless indeed the Saviour's intervention as the Second Adam gave back to mankind an existence that would otherwise have been forfeited. But it is never said that existence was forfeited by sin : the threatening of death that took effect when disobedience entered was the separation of the soul or spirit from the body. The body began at once to sink towards the earth whence it came ; and the spirit began to know those preliminary infirmities that issue in the agony of the final severance, the most violent and unnatural experience to which in this life transgression has made man subject : the physical type of the separation of the soul from God.

The Sentence of Death.

2. This is the only death that can befall the soul, so far at least as the sentence pronounced upon the sinner is concerned. The immortality or continued conscious existence of man's spirit is everywhere assumed in Scripture and nowhere proved. And, so far as the doctrine of death is before us, continued existence and immortality are one. The absolute immortality of the human spirit is not in question as yet. Absolute immortality, indeed, can never be matter of argument. God *only hath immortality ;* if He has given it to man as such it must be as something that is made inherent in man's reflection of God's likeness. The Christian doctrine of death leaves untouched the natural immortality of mankind. The arguments in its favour, in their variety and their various degrees of strength, belong to the subject of the Divine Image in man. Those which rest upon the immateriality of the soul and its indivisibility, upon its high aspirations, upon its universal instincts, are valid pleas against the materialist ; but all subordinate to the original testimony given to the stamp of the Creator's own nature impressed upon it. Apart from that no argument demonstrates the immortality of the soul, even as there is none that proves the being of God. But we have only now to make emphatic the fact that the Christian doctrine of death implies that immortality : first, because nothing is said to the contrary when the separation of soul and body is spoken of ; and, secondly, because death is said to be in its widest meaning done away in Christ.

1 Tim. vi. 16.

DEATH ABOLISHED.

Death as a penalty, whether physically or spiritually considered, is abolished in the Gospel of our redemption. Death Abolished

1. In the widest possible sense it is negatived or done away. There is no restriction in the words used to signify the Saviour's endurance of death in the stead of the human race. He underwent in dying the curse of the law, received the wages of sin not due to Himself, and all mankind are delivered as one whole from the original sentence For the entire family of Adam it is virtually and provisionally abolished. Our Lord tasted death *for every man,* ὑπὲρ παντὸς. He removed this specific condemnation from the race; and if annihilation were, in any sense whatever, the meaning of the sentence, the Substitute of man, the Second Adam, abolished it. But we have no hint in Scripture that annihilation was the import of the original sentence It was rather the separation of the soul from the body and of both from God ; and that as an absolute sentence upon mankind was reversed and abolished For the Race. Heb. ii. 9

2. It is really abolished to all who are found in Christ. *He that believeth on the Son hath everlasting life:* the opposite of that *wrath of God* which *abideth* on the unbeliever *He that hath the Son hath life* It is true that the abolition is conditional, and gradually revealed both in the soul and in the body , even as the full revelation of the death from which we are saved is gradual. *We are saved by hope ·* this law runs through the Christian economy , we receive only the firstfruits, every blessing and every deliverance being at best given in its earnest alone *until the redemption of the purchased possession.* But the day will come when every trace of this sentence shall be effaced *The last enemy that shall be destroyed is death.* It was also the first enemy destroyed. For the Individual John iii. 36. 1 John v 12. Rom. viii 24. Eph i. 14. 1 Cor. xv 26

DEATH A PERMANENT DISPENSATION.

Death, in its more limited sense as physical, is taken up into the Evangelical economy . continued as an ordinance for the human race, and as a discipline for every believer. It is this death which specifically belongs to Eschatology Death Continued

As to the
Race.

Heb. ix.
27.

1. The continuance of death is bound up with the Divine purposes touching the development and the destiny of mankind. What that development would have been without sin we know not : all that we know of the eternal counsel concerning the human species deals with it as a race continued through a succession of dying generations. *It is appointed unto men once to die* in their federal relation with the first Adam, that they may rise again with the Last. The economy of redemption which was established before the gates of Paradise opened on human history retains death as a law in the government of the world. This is all that can be affirmed ; and speculation beyond these limits finds no encouragement. It may be said that this was, in a certain sense, letting the original tendency go on, inasmuch as physical death had reigned upon the earth before Adam was created ; and further that the earth was adapted to the condition of man as living and dying. Such a view requires us to believe that without sin man would have risen above the general law : the tree of life being a sign of what might have been a sinless immortality. But this, like the question whether or not the Son would have become incarnate had the Fall not taken place, is left in profound silence in the holy record. Suffice it that when the history of the world has reached its last term death shall cease. Mankind waits till the Deliverer comes for its emancipation. Then will He prove Himself the Lord and Abolisher of death by superseding and displacing it ; and the last undying generation will give evidence that this firstborn of sin was only assumed into the Divine counsel for human development within the limits of time.

Christian
Death.

2. Christian death is abundantly and most impressively brought to light as not abolished absolutely ; but as taken up into the Divine plan for the individual just as it is for the race.

Fellowship with
Christ.
2 Tim. ii.
11.

(1.) It enters into the probationary discipline of believers. Hence it is hallowed and dignified as part of the fellowship of their lot with Christ. *If we be dead with Him, we shall also live with Him :* here the suffering of death physical must be included ; the awful graces of our Lord's dying experience must be reflected in the dying of His saints. That unknown element in His suffering which negatived the sinner's eternal death is of necessity unshared, but His physical surrender to death admits us to a fellowship with it. Hence it is the last sacrifice of Christian obedience; according to the Apostle's word, *I am now ready to be offered.* This refers to less or to more than martyrdom, specifically so called: in a sense all death is a martyrdom, by which the servants of Christ testify of redemption and *glorify God.* There is no grace of Christian life which is not made perfect in death: not that death is the minister of the Spirit to destroy sin, but the last earthly act and oblation of the sinless spirit in which the sacrifice of all becomes perfect in one. Therefore it is the appointed end of human probation. Other methods of placing a limit to the probationary career, especially in relation to the unfallen creature, may be imagined: this is the appointed end since sin and redemption began. The very execution of doom is made the goal of destiny, in which the sentence is finally reversed. And thus in a certain sense death is the preliminary and decisive judgment for every individual on earth who knows the connection between sin and deliverance.

2 Tim. iv. 6.

John xxi. 19.

(2.) Finally, Christian death is transfigured into a departure from this life to another. Every former name is retained in the dispensation of the Gospel; no new one, strictly speaking, is added; but all are sanctified to a higher character and put on their perfection. It is Dissolution, but not as limited to the idea of going down to the dust of death: it is the separation of spirit and body; the body being also dissolved into its component elements in the earth, and the spirit, no longer a soul, gathered to the fathers and to Christ, returning to God who gave it, but not dissolved into the abyss of Deity. The Christian thought of being *unclothed* is an advance upon any former revelation: the body is only the clothing which, folded in the grave, will be hereafter re-fashioned for the naked spirit. Death is *rest*, as of old: but rest in the ceaseless service of the Lord. It is sleep; but it is *sleep in Jesus.* It is still the penalty of sin; but no longer only a penalty. For to those who believe in Jesus death is no more death: not only is its sting gone, but itself is already as to its terror—which is its shadow following it, the Second Death—annihilated; *whosoever liveth and believeth in Me shall never die.* Finally, it is more than the Old-Testament *going the way of all the earth:* it is a Departure or Decease, for these two words are one. Such it was in the case of our Lord: Moses and Elias spoke of

Names of Christian Death.

2 Cor. v. 4.

2 Thess. i. 7.

1 Thess. iv. 14.

John xi. 26.
Josh. xxiii. 14.

the *Decease*, τὴν ἔξοδον, *which He should accomplish at Jerusalem.*
And among the last allusions to death in the New Testament it
is regarded as only a removal to another sphere : *the time of my
departure is at hand ;* which is the simplest and sublimest description
of it given to our faith and our hope.

Luke ix.
31.
2 Tim. iv.
6.

THE INTERMEDIATE STATE.

Throughout the Scriptures, from Genesis to Revelation,
the departed souls of men are represented as congregating
in one vast receptacle, the interior conditions of which
differ much in the Two Testaments and vary in each
respectively. There is, however, a steady increase of light
as revelation proceeds, though even its final disclosures
leave much obscurity which only the Lord's coming will
remove. It is, however, made certain that the intermediate state is under the special control of the Redeemer
as the Lord of all the dead who have ever passed from the
world; that those who have departed in unbelief are in a
condition of imprisonment waiting for the final judgment,
while those who have died in the faith are in Paradise, or
rather with Christ, waiting for their consummation ; and
that the universal resurrection will put an end both to
death and to the state of the disembodied dead. Some few
hints which the New Testament gives as to the conscious
personality of the subjects of the Lord's kingdom in Hades
have been made the basis of doctrinal determinations and
ecclesiastical institutions and speculative theories which
belong to the department of historical theology.

OLD TESTAMENT.

The
Under-
World.

1. In the earlier revelation the collective inhabitants of the
earth pass through death into a state or place which is to the
spirit what the grave is to the body. This has one invariable

name: SHEOL, שְׁאוֹל, the *house appointed for all living* This
word was derived from a root signifying to be hollow, or from
one denoting a chasm or abyss, or from a third, meaning to ask,
in reference to its insatiable demand for souls. It is to be distinguished from the grave, which is often used in the English
translation   For instance, when Jacob says, *I will go down into*
the grave unto my son mourning, the word is שְׁאֹלָה, *unto Sheol*
Joseph was supposed not to be in any grave   The patriarchs
went to their forefathers: Abraham, as afterwards Aaron, was
gathered unto his people, they were gathered to their people, but in
the great majority of cases were not buried with them   From the
beginning the hollow place in which the body was deposited had
neither more nor less reality than the Sheol or under-world supposed
to be local and within the earth, into which all souls descended,
retaining their conscious personality   They are never called souls,
however, or spirits, but, in writings later than those of Moses,
REPHAIM, רְפָאִים, signifying languid, or nerveless, or shadowy
beings   different therefore from the giants of the Pentateuch

2 It is moreover in the earlier books, and indeed throughout
the canonical Old Testament, one indistinguishable receptacle of
all the dead, generally a place of terror and gloom cut off from
God, not without conscious and continued existence, but with
only a feeble hold of life; brightened to the righteous by hope,
but by fluctuating hope. The testimonies of Job and of Hezekiah
represent the darkest aspect of Sheol   *Are not my days few?*
Cease then, and let me alone that I may take comfort a little, before I
go whence I shall not return, even to the land of darkness and the
shadow of death; a land of darkness, as darkness itself, and of the
shadow of death, without any order, and where the light is as darkness.
We hear his own answer to his desponding question, *If a man*
die, shall he live again? that his sons come to honour, and he knoweth
it not, .. but his flesh upon him shall have pain, and his soul within
him shall mourn. Hezekiah's forecast is as gloomy as Job's:
The grave cannot praise Thee, death cannot celebrate Thee   Job's
anticipation, *yet in my flesh shall I see God*, finds no permanent and
satisfying comfort this side of the resurrection

3 There are hints, though only hints, of distinct allotments of
doom   While the Old Testament everywhere assigns to the

Marginal notes:
Job xxx. 23.

Gen xxxvii 35.

Gen xxv. 8.
Numb. xx. 24

Sheol.

Job. x. 20—22.

Job xiv. 14, 21, 22

Isa xxxviii 18.
Job xix. 26

Retri- bution.

departed a continued existence — immortality, therefore, as making the spirit survive bodily death—it preserves a silence almost unbroken as to retribution after the probation of life. But the one Pit, בּוֹר, into which all alike descend has its lower depths. The servants of God, faithful to His covenant, have in Him their portion, and therefore He is their God, *not the God of the*

Matt.xxii. 32. *dead but of the living;* but in the mystery of gradual revelation the secret of the prison is reserved for the coming of Christ. Of

Gen.v.24. Enoch it is not said that HE DIED; *he was not, for God took him;* but this was only a standing testimony, that death is not essential

Numb. xxiii. 10. to the development of man. Balaam's wish, to *die the death of the righteous,* is indefinite, and did not necessarily refer to anything beyond this world. But many of the prayers of the Psalmists

Ps. xxviii. 3. more than hint at a difference hereafter: *draw me not away with the wicked, and with the workers of iniquity.* The speculations of the Preacher point to the same difference; as one, however, that

Eccl. xi. 9. the day of judgment will bring to light: *for all these things God will bring thee into judgment.*

New Testament.

NEW TESTAMENT.

In the New Testament there is a resumption and very remarkable development of doctrine concerning the state of the dead in the interval preceding the final resurrection.

The Gospels. 1. Before His own resurrection our Lord adopted the ancient description of the unseen world, using the term Ἅιδης, which the Septuagint had invariably employed as the Greek representative

Hades. Luke xvi. 22, 23. of the Hebrew SHEOL. But He subdivided it into two departments: the place of Lazarus He called, with the Jews, *Abraham's bosom;* but He does not place the rich man in Gehenna, which had also become the Rabbinical term for the place of final woe. *In Hades he lift up his eyes, being in torments;* but in the same Hades he could see Lazarus though afar off. Our Lord this once uses the word in the Old-Testament meaning of the general receptacle of departed souls. But elsewhere He employs it to signify the empire of ruin and desolation and subversion of human life:

Matt. xvi. 18. in this sense He said of His Church, *The gates of Hades shall not*

Matt. xi. 23. *prevail against it;* and of the doomed city of Galilee, *thou shalt be brought down to Hades.* In the Apocalypse the Lord returns to

the old idea of one vast disembodied realm *I have the keys of* Rev. i. 18.
Hades and of death, though, as in the Dives-parable, with a predominant reference to the condemned prison-house in it. This
last the Lord calls Gehenna again and again, as in that ever-
memorable word concerning *the fire* of hell, *that never shall be* Mark ix.
quenched, and in that solemn denunciation of the Pharisees which 43.
seems to make this hell a state, like eternal life, which may be
the present characteristic of the soul . *twofold more the child of hell,* Matt
or *Gehenna, than yourselves.*   Before His departure our Lord gave xxiii. 15
a new designation to the realm of the blessed in Hades · *To-day* Luke
shalt thou be with Me in Paradise. xxiii 43.

2 What had been the descent of the Redeemer into Hades has The
been elsewhere considered   it introduced, not only a new state of Lord's
things in the under-world, but a new terminology for the inter- Descent.
mediate state   The Paradise and Gehenna of the Gospels—
figurative names, one taken from the original Garden, and the
other from the Valley of Hinnom where the perpetual fire burnt
up the refuse—reappear, with Hades including both , but neither
of them emphatically, nor with certain reference to the intermediate condition of souls   The place is not described so much
as the state or character and employments of its occupants.   The
Lord's victory over death and glorious descent has changed the
whole scene   The saints who are in life and death united to Him
are spoken of as those who *sleep in Jesus*   He is their κοιμητήριον, 1 Thess.
or Cemetery, where sleep is life while life is sleep   The current iv 14.
language of the Epistles refers to their death as departure *to be* Phil. i. 23
with Christ, the entering *an house not made with hands, eternal in the* 2 Cor v.
heavens, and the attainment of an almost consummate state in *the* Heb xii
general assembly and church of the firstborn which are written in heaven, 23.
where are *the spirits of just men made perfect.*   All this seems
inconsistent with a locality in any sense corresponding to the
under-world of Sheol . in fact the term Hades would be all but
lost, save in the symbolical Apocalypse, were it not for the
explicit declaration that in the resurrection its victory will be
taken away   *O Hades, where is thy victory !* With the Lord's 1 Cor xv.
resurrection Paradise seems to have risen also into a lower 55
heaven · as it were the *third heaven* if not the seventh   Of the 2 Cor. xii
elevation of Paradise some hint was given when *many bodies of* 2.

Matt. xxvii. 52, 53.

the saints which slept arose, and came out of the graves after His resurrection: these may have been the mysterious symbolical first-fruits, whose spirits reunited to their bodies *appeared unto many on their way with Christ from Paradise to heaven.* The dis-embodied ungodly are never spoken of save as being generally or

Rev. xx. 14.

by implication in Hades. It is said in the Apocalypse that *death and hades were cast into the lake of fire. This is the second death.* As symbols they vanish for ever; and the real persons they

Mark ix. 43.

represent know the second death in the *lake of fire,* which is the same as the *Gehenna of fire* in the Gospel. In the language of Christendom these terms have been exchanged for HELL, which is moreover often regarded, contrary to Scripture, as existing for the lost before the judgment. St. Peter uses yet another word,

1 Peter iii. 19, 20.

when he speaks of the *spirits in prison* to whom the Saviour preached or announced the accomplishment of redemption.

History.

HISTORICAL.

Historical theology has here a wide domain, especially if we include, as we ought, the entire range of the opinions and practices of mankind beyond the pale of revelation.

EXTRA-BIBLICAL BELIEFS.

Comparative Theology gives ample evidence that all, or almost all, the religious systems of antiquity have had their Region of the Dead. From east and west and north and south all travel thither in their various systems of belief. In the east, however, what we call the intermediate state was distorted into an ever-recurring series of transmigrations until the final heaven of souls was reached in a state of absorption into God. In all the mythologies with which revelation came into contact there is an estate and a place and a government of the lower world. So was it in Egyptian eschatology. So also in the classical. Hades or Plutus, and Persephone or Proserpine received the dead, the Inferi, into Hades or Tartarus below it, and into the Elysian fields: their jurisdiction being that of strict retribution. The speculations of mythology were far more definite than those of the Old Testament in one sense; but had not in them the distant Messianic hope that lightened the gloom of the Hebrew Sheol. And, when the True Light appeared, the dim and distorted shadows projected upon the future all vanished : giving place to a clear and definite doctrine of Hades, as linked with the probationary past still, but now declared to be the threshold only of the resurrection and eternity, neither of which were in distinct human conception until the Gospel brought them out of darkness into light.

CHRISTIAN BELIEF AND SPECULATION.

Many and various speculations of Christian Theology, which have not been confined to any particular age, may be noticed

1 That of the SLEEP OF THE SOUL in the Intermediate state very early prevailed : strictly speaking, it was the sleep of the whole man reduced for a season to nonentity, to be called into existence by a new creation linking the personality to its former self This notion regards the spirit as only soul and having no existence apart from the body forgetting the tripartite distinction of body and soul and spirit, according to which the immaterial principle in man is soul as using a corporeal organisation and spirit as independent of the bodily organ The article in the Creed "He descended into Hades" expressed the early condemnation of this hypothesis In the third century Origen opposed the same belief as held by the THNETOPSYCHITÆ. In the Middle Ages and at the Reformation the speculation was revived ; and again and again condemned under the name of PSYCHOPAN-NYCHIA, or the spirit's intermediate night The idea has exercised a strong fascination on many who, like Luther occasionally, have found it hard to believe in a continuance of consciousness without the corporeal organism , and they have sought support in the fact that the dead *sleep in Jesus* · a figurative expression which by no means favours the view It has seemed to many that the subject is relieved of much difficulty if we assume that in the consciousness of the soul the moment of death is literally the moment of resurrection, the long interval being in that consciousness less than a moment. But both the Lord's parable of Dives and the whole scenery of the Apocalypse present the intermediate state as a scene of life. The Apostle says that

Specula-
tive
Theories
Sleep of
the Soul.

1 Thess.
iv. 14.

2 Cor. v. 8.

to be absent from the body is to be *present with the Lord;* and the tenour of the New Testament runs that way. This hypothesis, however, has found and still finds many supporters in modern times.

No Resurrection.

2 Tim. ii. 18.

2. The basis or tendency of that theory is materialistic; but there has never been wanting a current of anti-materialist speculation, which, asserting *that the resurrection is past already,* equally annihilates the intermediate state though in a different way. Those who early represented this notion, condemned by St. Paul, held the Gnostic error that redemption wrought its final triumph in the deliverance of the spirit from its bodily prison. They

Heb. xii. 23.

supposed the dead to have already come to *the spirits of just men made perfect;* misunderstanding that perfection as the release from matter of all creaturely existence. This error, like the former, is inconsistent with the uniform doctrine of Scripture that the dead are assembled in an antechamber of eternity, a waiting-place for final decision; and that the consummation of the individual, whether for weal or woe, is that of his triple nature: death being a violent dissolution of elements never intended to be disjoined, and the resurrection being the raising of the whole man in his integrity in order to his appearance in the body of his former probation before the bar of God.

Mediæval Divisions of Hades.

3. The dogma of Purgatorial discipline in the great Interval has been already alluded to when the sacraments were studied. It must be noticed here in its connection with a vast system of formulated doctrine, concerning the souls of the departed, which has been erected especially by the Western Church. The older mediæval theology taught that there were five regions: Heaven and Hell, on the extreme frontiers of Hades, if not beyond; the Limbus Infantum, where the unbaptised infants wait, without suffering but without the vision of God, for their higher beatification; the Limbus Patrum, where in the same negative state of mere pœna damni the Old-Testament fathers long expected Christ's

Purgatory

coming and finally welcomed Him; and Purgatory, where the mass of imperfect Christians are fitted for heaven, aided in the process, whether that of literal or of spiritual fire, by the suffrages of their friends on earth. This dogmatic addition to the Faith was confirmed at the Council of Trent. But it does not profess to find its foundation in Scripture. It is true that it appeared early among the tendencies of Christian speculation. We find traces of it in Tertullian, Cyprian, and Augustine; it was largely developed by Gregory the Great—the last of the Fathers proper, and the first of the Pontifical Fathers—about the beginning of the seventh century; and it was laid down as dogma by the Council of Florence in 1439. But it is not the unforced teaching of any passage in the sacred Canon. And the superstitions based on it in the current Roman theology, with the abuses to which it has ministered, are its sufficient condemnation : if any other argument is needed than its too close affinity with heathenism, and the dishonour it puts on the perfect satisfaction of the Atonement.

4. Modern views of the continued application of the Redeemer's work in the other world do not lie open to the same objections; though they also are beset with much difficulty and equal danger. They have taken a variety of forms, some having a slight Scriptural support, others only defended by sentiment. It has already been seen in connection with the Mediatorial History of the Redeemer that His Descent into Hades was accompanied by a proclamation of His Gospel. Sound exegesis requires this; but sound theology will be careful to found no dogmatic teaching upon a revelation which is strictly limited to our Lord's own personal assumption of the *keys of Hades.* He is declared to be the *Lord of the dead ;* but it is not said of Him or of His servants that they preach to the dead. Nothing is more plainly revealed, for all who hear the Gospel, than this : *Behold, now is the accepted time ; behold, now is the day of salvation.* There is no branch of theology the study of which requires more self-restraint and strict submission to the Word of God. Nor is there one in which there is more need of avoiding opposite extremes. It is hard to conceive that the spirit which we trace only as developed in strict harmony with a bodily organism can exist in full consciousness without it; but we must hold that mystery of a resurrection before the resurrection—a resurrection of the spirit from its body —until the time of the revelation of all solvable mysteries shall come. It is equally hard to understand that the *spirits of just men made perfect* with Christ are only in a state of comparative consummation, and wait for a fuller disclosure of what is to them almost as full of mystery as it is to us. Yet it is so, and we

The Gospel in Hades.

Rev. i. 18.
Rom. xiv. 9.
2 Cor. vi. 2.
Results.

Heb. xii. 23.

Jas. i. 4.

must submit to regard the intermediate state as one in which the grace of patient waiting will *have her perfect work:* the grace which pre-eminently belongs to time, and in time almost shares the supremacy of love, but cannot exist in eternity. The reaction from the dogma of purgatory has tended of late to efface the distinction between what is after all the kingdom of the dead and what has yet to be revealed as the kingdom of the living beyond. The extremes of assuming a perfect unchangeable fixedness of condition, on the one hand, and of assigning to Paradise the full work of probation, on the other, must be avoided. The permanent and unalterable destiny of mankind is always associated with the day of judgment and its issues. We must not antedate those issues; nor ought we, with regard either to the saved or the lost, to decide that the eternal state as such precedes the crisis for

Rev. x. 6, 7.

which the angelic oath gives a watchword, *that there should be time no longer,* χρόνος οὐκέτι ἔσται. Not until then may either exegesis or speculation insist that *the mystery of God should be finished.*

Rev. xiv. 4.

5. The Apocalypse shows that the disembodied spirits of the saints *follow the Lamb whithersoever He goeth.* Remembering all that this phrase means in the Gospels, we conclude that they enjoy the blessed discipline of communion with Him. Moreover,

Rev. vii. 14, 15, 17.

we are told that having *washed their robes, and made them white in the blood of the Lamb,* they still *serve Him day and night in His temple;* that *the Lamb Which is in the midst of the throne shall feed*

Rev. vi. 11.

them; that, with us *their fellow-servants also and their brethren,* while

Rev. i. 9.
Rev. vi. 10.

they *reign on the earth,* they are still companions *in the kingdom and patience of Jesus Christ,* crying: *How long, O Lord?* All this indicates a progress in blessedness and in the development of moral energy during the disembodied state. They have the discipline of hope; and of hope as not yet eternal in the heavens, though no longer probationary. They wait for the consummation, their Lord's and their own. And their progress in the spiritual life is not simply that which after the judgment will go on for ever, but an advance from stage to stage peculiar to the intermediate state. Time is behind them; time is also before them; the day of eternity is not yet fully come.

6. As to the locality and the bodily investiture of this state we know only that we know nothing. In proportion to the

scantiness of revealed doctrine has been the abundance of speculation By some it has been supposed that the spirit is naked and absolutely bodiless an idea which our physical training on earth renders inconceivable, but which is not on that account to be rejected. Others suppose that the descriptions of the Apocalypse are not entirely figurative, but that the separated spirit will as it were create for itself, or have provided for it, an ethereal vehicle answering to the soul once animating the body. But this intermediate corporeity, this Prima Stola, which has found large acceptance among modern theologians, and has received its highest poetical expression in Dante, has no countenance in Scripture The *white robes* of the Apocalypse are by the Apocalypse explained *they washed their robes in the blood of the Lamb* The notion is inconsistent with the Scriptural idea of death, as well as with the description of the departed as πνεύματα or spirits, and it is a peculiar version of the first resurrection which unscripturally anticipates the resurrection proper. No subject has been more fantastically dealt with, but speculation is here misplaced Suffice that all who die in the Lord are united to Him in His glorified incarnate nature; and His heavenly body is their home.

Rev iii 5.
Rev vii. 14
Heb. vii. 23

7. This leads us back once more to the awful subject of the estate of the ungodly departed, already hinted at in another connection Whatever the progress of the disembodied spirit of the saint may be from glory to glory, there is nothing in Scripture to sanction the hope of any influences in the intermediate state that shall tend to translate from their dishonour the disembodied rejecters of Christ. In the present day the word of God is most keenly scrutinised for any the faintest gleam of encouragement But none is found upon which hope may be surely founded Certainly as to the despisers of the atonement no language can be more explicit than the testimony of our Lord and His Apostles. And as to those who have not deliberately rejected Him of Whom they never heard, the silence of revelation should be our silence There is no distinct announcement as to the publication of the glad tidings of redemption in the other state to those who never heard them on earth This, like many other secrets of that state, is kept hidden in the Divine counsel. *Son, remember !* may seem to imply that until the Day of Judgment

Luke xvi 25

warning counsel is given for profit; but those words were spoken to one whose condition could not be changed: *There is a great gulf fixed.* And, what is more, the definitive separation is not only ordained of God, but it is also declared to rest upon an internal disability: *If they hear not Moses and the Prophets, neither will they be persuaded, though one rose from the dead.* The Saviour certainly speaks of one kind of sin which is to be forgiven *neither in this world, neither in the world to come;* and it might appear that there is pardon to be offered at least for all other sins. But it is undeniable that the entire phrase was current in the sense of NEVER. Moreover, the words might mean that the sin against the Holy Ghost would be committed as well in the coming dispensation of the Messianic kingdom after Pentecost as in His own preliminary dispensation. Certainly no doctrine can be based on such designedly mysterious words. Undoubtedly the whole tenor of the New Testament teaches us that, as *there is none other Name under heaven given among men, whereby we must be saved,* all who are not saved must reject that Name directly proposed to them. From this conclusion neither Scripture nor human charity permits us to decline. But how that light is to irradiate the awful future we know not, and it is presumptuous even for charity too curiously to inquire: this and many other mysteries must be left to the infinite love and the infinite wisdom of the Holy Trinity. *Shall not the Judge of all the earth do right?*

Margin references:
Luke xvi. 26.
Luke xvi. 32.
Matt. xii. 32.
Acts iv. 12.
Gen. xviii. 25.

THE DAY OF CHRIST· RESURRECTION AND JUDGMENT.

The second coming of our Lord is the one all-commanding event of prophecy and the future itself supreme, it is always associated with the universal resurrection, the judgment of mankind, and the consummation of all things. Though these epochs and crises are in the style of prophecy presented together in foreshortened perspective, they are widely distinct. But while we treat them as distinct, we must be careful to remember their common relation to the Day of the Lord ; which is a fixed and determinate period, foreshadowed in many lesser periods to which the same term is applied, but the issue and consummation of them all.

THE SECOND COMING OF CHRIST

Throughout the ancient economy a future period called the day of Jehovah appears as the one perspective of all prophecy. In the New Testament this day is declared to have come , all the purposes of the Divine mercy and judgment are regarded as accomplished in the advent of Christ, which is the last time or the end of the world. But the day resolves itself into days . and what Old-Testament prediction beheld as one undistinguished whole is now divided into times and seasons, which all however converge to one decisive and fixed event, the return of Jesus from the invisible world. There is a rich and steady light thrown upon the Christian day of Jehovah, which is variously described in relation to the final manifestation of the Person of Christ, and the final consummation of His work. As it regards the latter, there are some historical theories of very considerable importance which must be examined.

As to His Person.

This event cannot be studied to advantage apart from the work of the Redeemer. But a few observations on the final manifestation of His Person will pave the way; besides being a fit tribute to the Lord Himself. The great crisis is connected with Him as His final Mission, His second Coming, and in both His Day. In this order we have a certain ascending progression, terminating in the Divine-human dignity of the Lord Whose day is always associated with His highest glory. The first expression suggests that even in heaven the Incarnate is still subordinate and will be

Sent.

Acts iii. 20, 21.

SENT of the Father, this being the end of His mediatorial estate of humiliation. *He shall send Jesus Christ, Which before was preached unto you: Whom the heaven must receive until the times of restitution of all things.* In harmony with this the New Testament

Rev. i. 1.

ends with the *Revelation of Jesus Christ which God gave unto Him.* But in that revelation He foreannounces Himself as waiting for the hour when in His majesty He will return to the earth with no trace of His humbled estate. He will, as the glorified Divine-

Coming.

John xiv. 3.

Acts i. 11.

Rev. i. 7.

human Person, COME. So had He promised His disciples: *I will come again. This same Jesus, Which is taken up from you into heaven, shall so come in like manner,* said the angels of the Ascension omitting the Again. *Behold, He cometh with clouds,* is the corresponding human testimony of the last Apostle when in prophetic vision he beheld His glory and spoke of Him. Thus it is the coming, in one sense, in another, it is the second coming, or the coming again of the Lord. Hence, also, the Scripture rises

The Day.

Luke xvii. 24.

2 Tim. i. 18.

Phil. i. 6.

1 Thess. v. 2.

above both these phrases, and speaks of that future event as *His Day,* or *that day,* or *the day of Jesus Christ,* which is in the new economy all that the day of Jehovah was in the old. *The day of the Lord* is the horizon of the entire New Testament: the period of His most decisive manifestation in a glorious revelation of Himself which could not be, and is never, predicated of any but a Divine Person. And this may be regarded as the most emphatic word used concerning the great Future.

THE CONSUMMATION OF HIS WORK.

Consummation.

The Second Coming of our Lord is His final and definitive appearance for the consummation of all things pertaining to His work of redemption.

1 The terms used to describe it are such as refer both to His Person and to His office They must be taken in their combination as including both. The most prominent is Παρουσία, indicating that when He comes He will always be present . the time of His absence shall have passed for ever It may not mean the blessed paradox that present always by His Spirit He will then be always present in person . but the word simply signifies His Presence, which will then be so different from what it is now that the change from one to the other is no less than a coming again. Hence it is Ἀποκάλυψις, the disclosure or manifestation of Himself from heaven which has received Him. It is the Ἐπιφάνεια, His manifestation in a glory which His people will share · *When Christ, Who is our life, shall appear,* or be made manifest, *then shall ye also appear with Him in glory* At His first coming, when He became incarnate, *the saving grace appeared,* ἐπεφάνη, and we still look for *the glorious appearing of the Great God and our Saviour.* These several terms must be united. They are found all together in one classical passage *When the Lord Jesus shall be revealed from heaven,* ἐν τῇ ἀποκαλύψει τοῦ Κυρίου Ἰησοῦ, *that Wicked,* also to be *revealed,* He shall *destroy with the brightness of His coming,* τῇ ἐπιφανείᾳ τῆς παρουσίας αὐτοῦ. Thus it follows from the combination of all, that, while He is always present by His Spirit, He will yet be revealed from the other world, *from whence also we look for the Saviour ,* and His glorious power and perfections will attend Him for the rejoicing of His saints, and the confusion of His foes.

Terms Used.

Col. iii.4.

Titus ii 11—13.

2 Thess. i 7.

2 Thess ii 8

Phil. iii 20.

2 It is very important to note that this great event is always connected with a complete end and consummation of that work which the Lord began in His first appearance . which, indeed, had been commenced with the beginning of human history, but which more truly commenced in the fulness of time With regard to His atonement it is said that He will *appear the second time without sin unto salvation:* that is, without any redeeming relation to the sin which He will still find, and for the complete and bodily

The End of His Work.

Heb ix. 28.

salvation of those whom He has already saved in spirit. This is
a cardinal text, and the variation in the phraseology, chosen with
great precision, must be observed. In this verse the word is

Heb. ix. 24, 26, 28.

ὀφθήσεται, while in another which says that *He appeared to put
away sin* it was πεφανέρωται. His manifestation between these
two, *now to appear in the presence of God for us,* is ἐμφανισθῆναι,
which indicates the most visible exhibition of Himself as King
in the judicial form of His kingly office. He vindicates His atonement as against all who have despised it. Sin will be finally

2 Thess. i. 7.

punished as the rejection of Himself and His redemption. *The
Lord Jesus shall be revealed from heaven with His mighty angels, in
flaming fire taking vengeance on them that know not God, and that obey
not the Gospel of our Lord Jesus Christ:* upon all hearers of that
Gospel who shall then be found without Evangelical knowledge of
God: of which more hereafter.

The Ex-
pectation.

3. Hence the Παρουσία is the object of expectation only to the
Church as such, as a collation of the passages in which it is used
will prove. The word literally means the Lord's PRESENCE with
His people for ever, answering to the שְׁכִינָה of the Old Testament,

Rev. xxi. 3.

and *the tabernacle of God is with men* in the New. It is applied in
Scripture, and in current theology, to the beginning of that presence by a common metonomy; the Coming being made to stand
for what follows the coming. The individual Christian has his share

John ix. 4.
Rom. xiii. 12.

in the hope; but not as expecting necessarily to see it. To him *the
night cometh when no man can work.* As to the corporate body *the
night is far spent, the day is at hand.* The Church never dies nor
thinks of death, though she buries her dead. But throughout the
New Testament the two prospects are always in view, and referred
to in the same style. As the individual must remember that death
is at hand, though with every probability of surviving many years,
so the Church must remember the coming of the Lord, though it
may probably be ages in the distance.

The
Time.

THE TIME OF THE LORD'S APPEARING.

The period of the Second Coming is perpetually referred to in
the New Testament; but in such a way as to demand the utmost
caution in the interpreter. The historical review of the question

will bring it again into consideration, meanwhile the following hints are of importance.

1 It is evident that the Day of the Lord is one definite season or καίρος, preceded by times or χρόνοι But it is evident also that the several terms are applied to other events which foreshadow its coming The whole space of the Christian dispensation is described as *these last days* of which it is said that *the darkness is past, and the True Light now shineth*. It is this of which the Lord said, *Your father Abraham rejoiced to see My day and he saw it, and was glad* He also spoke of events anterior to the final consummation as His coming. For instance, when He declared, *There be some standing here, which shall not taste of death, till they see the Son of man coming in His kingdom,* He referred to the destruction of the Jewish polity, and to the Pentecostal glory of His kingdom assumed in the Ascension To that great event, immediately impending over the generation to which the Lord was a Prophet, may be referred many of the predictions which are sometimes referred to the final catastrophe Moreover, it is undoubted that every special intervention for judgment, whether in the case of a church or even of an individual, is spoken of as a coming of the Lord It is, indeed, sometimes very difficult to decide when the prophecy leaves behind all lesser accomplishments and points to the supreme consummation But, allowing all this, there is a constant and clear allusion to one definite day which marks the second coming, or the return of Jesus to the earth which He has left

2 Again, it is obvious that the Supreme Prophet of His own dispensation has made it a law of His kingdom that its final consummation shall for ever be uncertain as to its date. Even after His resurrection He said *It is not for you to know the times and the seasons, which the Father hath put in His own power* During His humbled estate He condescended to be a partaker in His human faculties of that ignorance *But of that day and that hour knoweth no man, no, not the angels which are in heaven, neither the Son, but the Father* Hence in His eschatological discourses He answered the disciples' double question, *Tell us, when shall these things be?* in such a manner as to prevent them attempting to define either the date of the nearer *end of the world*, the destruction of Judaism, or that of the more distant end of all things He gave, after the

Marginal notes:

καίρος and χρόνοι

Heb. i 1
1 John ii 8
John viii. 56.
Matt xvi 28.

Unknown Date

Acts i. 7

Mark xiii. 32

Matt. xxiv 3.

manner of ancient prophecy, an answer that embraced all the future in one sublime series of predictions : giving the prominence to that more immediate catastrophe which concerned the present generation ; so much so that He did not hesitate to say : *Verily, I say unto you, This generation shall not pass, till all these things be fulfilled.* The final consummation, however, was present to His thoughts, and nothing short of it, when He added, *Heaven and earth shall pass away, but My words shall not pass away.* In His eschatological revelations in the Apocalypse the order is inverted. First, it is said, *Behold, He cometh with clouds ; and every eye shall see Him, and they also which pierced Him ; and all kindreds of the earth shall wail because of Him ;* and then follows a series of sub-ordinate comings before the end, *Behold I come quickly,* which returns to the beginning again. This is one key to all the escha-tological notes of the New Testament. St. Peter, speaking of the great event, says, *One day is with the Lord as a thousand years, and a thousand years as one day,* in order to suppress the spirit of rest-less impatience. Nor is there a single passage in all the Apostolical writings which lends any help to an exact chronological deter-mination.

Matt. xxiv. 34, 35.

Rev. i. 7.

Rev. xxi. 12.

2 Peter iii. 8.

New Testa-ment Per-spective. The Fulness of the Gentiles. Matt. xxiv. 14. Rom. xi. 25.

3. In harmony with this truth, it must also be maintained that the New Testament gives some hints of an historical development in its eschatology. There are some events which are predicted as to take place before the return of Jesus.

(1.) Our Lord Himself has given one clear note. *And this Gospel of the kingdom shall be preached in all the world for a witness unto all nations, and then shall the end come.* He does not say that all nations will receive it, though St. Paul prophesies that *the ful-ness of the Gentiles,* τὸ πλήρωμα τῶν ἐθνῶν, will enter into Christen-dom, by a general conversion which leaves the question of the personal conversion of all individuals untouched. Of course, it is understood that these nations are literally the entire congregation of the tribes of heathenism scattered over the whole earth. Let this be connected with the commission given to the Christian company as represented by the Apostles ; and it will be manifest that the *times of the Gentiles* stretch over the whole stadium of the present missionary work of Christendom. The final and proper coming of the Lord cannot take place until the whole world has been, in

Luke xxi. 24.

the New-Testament sense of the word, evangelised. The Lord will never again preach His own Gospel in person, though He will be always with those who preach it *unto the end of the world*

Matt. xxviii.20

(2) The calling of the Gentiles implied, in a sense, the diminishing of Israel's prerogative, but *if the casting away of them be the reconciling of the world, what shall the receiving of them be but life from the dead?* The conversion of Israel is to follow the ingathering of the heathen, and issue in a virtual resurrection of Christendom The whole tenor of Scripture points to a restoration of the Jewish nation through its acceptance of the Messiah; and that as taking place before the final return. St Paul here also is the interpreter of prophecy, as well as a prophet himself At the close of the Epistle to the Romans he gives its rightful prominence to the *revelation of the* MYSTERY which was now at length *made known to all nations for the obedience of faith ,* but on his way to the close he had alluded to the same secret of heaven as affecting the Jews *I would not, brethren, that ye should be ignorant of this* MYSTERY, *lest ye should be blind in your own conceits , that blindness in part is happened to Israel, until the fulness of the Gentiles be come in.* The hardness of heart that has fallen upon the rejecters of Jesus is to continue—not through any determinate counsel of God, but in the order of their own probationary course; as the same Apostle preached, *Seeing ye put it from you, and judge yourselves unworthy of everlasting life, lo, we turn to the Gentiles*—until the great mass of the heathen nations is at least nominally converted But their hour will come *As touching the election, they are beloved for the fathers' sakes.* The descendants of Abraham must, sooner or later, enjoy the fulfilment of a thousand promises, and enjoy them as a people, for *the gifts and calling of God are without repentance* There will be to them *times of refreshing* prepared for by penitent faith But this involves no restoration to their own land , nor any distinction between them and the rest of mankind: the calling and gifts of the Gentiles also are not repented of; they also may say *We are the circumcision , and the children of the promise are counted for the seed The middle wall of partition is broken down* for ever. And all the predictions of the Gospel which introduce the entire scenery of the Law and the

The Jews brought in.
Rom. xi 15

Rom xvi. 24—26.

Rom. xi 25

Acts xiii. 46.

Rom xi 28

Rom xi. 29
Acts iii. 19—21

Phil iii 3
Rom. ix 8
Eph. ii 14

Temple are to be understood as figurative representations of the Christian Church.

Millennial Life from the Dead. Rom. xi. 15. Rom. xi. 25.

(3.) What this *life from the dead* may mean is part of the MYS-TERY of the great change in the relative position of Israel and the Gentiles which will take place. It is not the literal resurrection; for the Lord has not yet come. It is doubtless the great result to the Catholic Church; and we may make it the foundation of the largest millennial hopes that ever gladdened the hearts of Christ's suffering people. There is in prospect a resurrection state of His cause in comparison of which all previous life has been death. Though the first resurrection has long begun, and multitudes of souls have heard the voice of the Son of God and lived, yet the future age has in store the more abundant life, of which we enjoy at the utmost only the firstfruits.

Apostasy.

(4.) Yet the coming of the Lord will not even then be literally at hand. A great Apostasy, or a series of apostasies, governed by one spirit of Antichrist, and issuing in one mysterious develop-ment, is in the unrolled history of the Church before the Lord's Day. This enemy of the Faith is described as having two cha-racteristics : it is a political power, and a gigantic spiritual delusion, separate and combined. But these will be finally concentred in

2 Thess. i. 8.

one personality, the ἄνομος, *that Wicked One*, who is sometimes called the Antichrist pre-eminently. This Antichrist, if that is his name, no man knows. Previous manifestations, as St. John teaches, have never been wanting. The Roman power or the Beast has been broken, but other forces, political and intellectual, have always been opposing, and will reach a height as yet un-paralleled. Spiritual and ecclesiastical corruption in a carnal church has overshadowed Christendom for ages; but it has a career yet to be run, before it will vanish away. Prophetical theology has its many hypotheses for the explanation of the symbols of Daniel and the Apocalypse, and the plain words of St. Paul. But there has not yet been found on earth the power or the being to whom all St. Paul's terms are applicable. Before the end he will be made manifest. Of the tribulation thence resulting, when Satan, hitherto bound, is for a little season let

Matt. xxiv. 21.

loose, our Saviour said that it will be *such as was not since the beginning of the world to this time, no, nor ever shall be.* For it will be the last : the longsuffering of Jesus will be exhausted. When His Church shall be oppressed to the uttermost He will suddenly appear, *taking vengeance on them that know not God*, but *to be glorified in His saints* 2 Thess i 8—10.

HISTORICAL.

On the subject of our Lord's Return, Christian speculation has from the beginning found matter of deep and inexhaustible interest Errors have abounded , and all the more as the standard of appeal is the prophetic, and therefore the obscurer part of Scripture The history of opinion may be traced with ease so far as concerns the leading idea—that of the Millennial Kingdom—which has been its centre. There have been no sects based solely upon opinions on this topic , but almost all Christian communions have been more or less infected by them It will be sufficient to note the critical stages of thought in the ante-Nicene age , the aspect of the question during the Mediæval times down to the Reformation , and its development in more modern theology

1 But first it must be observed that the New Testament itself contains the germs of all subsequent speculation on this subject Beginning with the Apostles, we find the restless spirit of inquiry as to the future dates of the Divine dispensations at once repressed by our Lord in an interdict which was never afterwards removed. He who well weighs the words of Jesus will never feel any disposition to calculate the times and the seasons · not even when the Apocalypse earnestly enjoins their study generally. The Thessalonians were disposed to err on this subject ; and the Apostle simply declares that the coming of the Lord must not be regarded as instantly impending he does in fact intimate that all thought on this subject must take account of intermediate events The visions of the Apocalypse described, for the then present community, scenes which were shortly to come to pass, for the encouragement of the suffering Church , but those who first read them were not taught precisely when to expect the downfall of the persecuting emperor, and the events that followed And, on the whole, the tone of New-Testament teaching regards the Day of the Lord, His coming and His eternal reign, as at hand always. Neither the Apostles nor the Churches knew when He would come. Nor

(margin:) Apostolical Age.

can we without presumption suppose that any study of the prophecies will give us a knowledge denied to them.

Ante-
Nicene. 2. There was an early CHILIASM, or MILLENARIANISM—the Greek and Latin forms respectively of the thousand years of our Lord's supposed reign on earth—which was predominant in early times especially among the Jewish or Judaising Christians: part of the residue of their carnal Messianic expectation so tenaciously held. In the second century this doctrine was largely held by orthodox Christians, and was adopted by the heretical Montanists. It was undoubtedly the faith of some of the Fathers, such as Papias, Justin, Irenæus, Cyprian, Tertullian, and Lactantius; but by no means at any time the faith of the Church, as is proved by its absence from all the early Creeds. It may be said, further, that as a general belief Chiliasm vanished from Christendom with the fourth century. It was resolutely opposed by those—such as Caius of Rome and Dionysius of Alexandria—who denied the apostolicity of the Apocalypse, on the twentieth chapter of which the notion of a pre-millennial advent is mainly based. The Alexandrian theology, always spiritualistic and allegorical, condemned it on account of its grossly carnal conception of the earthly reign of Christ with the saints. Clement and Origen strongly argued against it in every form. With the accession of the empire, under Constantine, to Christianity the main inducement to cherish the hope of a speedy visible return of a victorious Redeemer passed away. Augustine and other teachers introduced an interpretation of the First Resurrection and the Millennial Reign which referred both to the present estate of Christianity; and this has been in subsequent times the prevalent catholic interpretation. Hence the doctrine of a pre-millennial Coming of Christ was excluded from every form of the Early Creeds, the keynote of all these being, FROM THENCE HE SHALL COME TO JUDGE THE QUICK AND THE DEAD.

Mediæval. 3. Mediæval Chiliasm was generally the badge of fanatical and heretical sects. At the close of the tenth century Christendom was deeply disturbed by an undefined expectation that, the thousand years—dating from the first Advent—having elapsed, the end of the world would come. When that fear was suppressed the notion again deeply slumbered. But after the Reformation, the

Anabaptists in Germany preached a carnal reign of Christ upon earth, as the Fifth Monarchy Men in England afterwards did, and with frightful consequences to life and morals   Hence the Lutheran Symbols were emphatic in condemning it   The leading Confession conjoins in its condemnation the idea of a personal Reign and of the final restoration of all souls   "Damnant Ana-   Augs. baptistas, qui sentiunt hominibus damnatis ac diabolis finem pœnarum futurum esse   Damnant et alios, qui spargunt Judaicos opiniones, quod ante resurrectionem mortuorum pii regnum mundi occupaturi sint, ubique oppressis impiis"   Similarly the earlier English Articles, or Confession of Edward   I   The Reformed Churches were equally strenuous. The Belgi Confession assigns the date of Christ's Coming as that in which the number of the elect shall be complete   "Credimus Dominum nostrum Jesum Christum, quando tempus a Deo præstitum, quod omnibus creaturis est ignotum, advenerit, et numerus electorum completus fuerit, e cœlo rursus venturum"   The Articles and Formularies of the Anglican Church are not in favour of Pre-Millenarianism. "Christ Art iv ascended into heaven, and there sitteth until He return to judge all men at the last day"   It may be safely affirmed that the Con-fessions of the Reformation, as well as its leading divines, were opposed to the doctrine of two resurrections, and of a personal reign of Christ on earth intervening between them

THE PRE-MILLENNIAL ADVENT.

Pre-
Millennial
Advent

No Church having incorporated the doctrine into its profession of faith, it has been in modern times confined to schools of thought within the several communions, influenced, for the most part, and led by individual students of prophecy   Modern hypotheses for the solution of the mystery of a double resurrection are far too numerous and far too diversified to be sketched even in outline. They spread into a great variety of schemes, almost every holder of the general idea having his own interpretation   From Mede, perhaps its earliest and ablest supporter in England, and Bengel in Germany, a century later, through a multitude of students of prophecy in nearly all religious communities, there has been an always in-creasing number of believers in the intermediate coming of the

Lord. Widely differing on a thousand subordinate points they agree in this one, and all their speculations may be said to be variations on the theme of a Pre-Millennial Advent. This belief has, during the present century, been incorporated into many systems, being almost the leading characteristic of some. Still it is generally speaking held only by individuals and private schools of interpretation : inconsistently by divines of the Lutheran, Anglican, Westminster, and some other Confessions ; consistently by those alone who in other respects deny the analogy of the faith as expressed in the ancient creeds and the formularies of the Reformation and the general consent of the Catholic Church, being limited by no Confession.

Rev. xx.
1—9.

1. The main foundation of the system is the Apocalyptic passage which is thought to predict the binding of Satan a thousand years, the first resurrection of martyrs and other elect saints who reign with Christ upon earth, the subsequent loosing of Satan for a season, a final apostasy, and the coming of the Redeemer to vindicate Himself and His Church. Now we have seen that our

John v.
28, 29.

Lord expressly speaks in one and the same discourse of a first resurrection, understood spiritually, and of a second resurrection understood physically. If we apply the same principle here, this much contested symbolical prophecy is made perfectly harmonious with the rest of Scripture, and the most substantial ground of the pre-millennial advent is taken away.

Various
Hypo-
theses.

2. Those who understand both resurrections literally build so many and such contradictory systems on this passage that it is impossible to reach any consistent dogmatic result. Some, like Mede, admit a glorious presence of Christ, but not a personal visible reign. Others think, following Bengel, that there will be two periods of a thousand years. Some again hold that the reign of Christ will be visible, at Jerusalem, and in the midst of His risen and glorified saints ; that the Temple at Jerusalem will be rebuilt, the ancient sacrifices restored, though only as commemorative ; and that the end of the Christian economy, as it precedes the final consummation, will be little other than another glorified Jewish dispensation. Rejecting this, many think that the Lord will reign from heaven amidst His risen saints : He and they alike being only occasionally visible, after the analogy of the Forty Days'

Interval between the visible and the invisible Christ before the Ascension. A still more moderate class allow that there are certain events in the programme of prophecy which must previously take place, and patiently wait for them; though the endeavour to insert these events before the Return really undermines their doctrine. Baffled in this endeavour, the majority are content to live in daily expectation of a Saviour, Whose coming will vanquish all opposition, and begin a new, better, more effectual, and more glorious dispensation of the Gospel though this requires them to suppose that the residuary processes of the mediatorial work will be miraculously condensed or foreshortened in a way for which the Scriptures allow no encouragement. Finally, in despair of any other solution, not a few blend all theories into one indiscriminate confusion, and profess to believe that the return of Jesus will accomplish all prophecies in a manner of which no theory ever devised gives a hint: that He will carry on a judgment for an indefinite period, and gradually glorify the earth into a meet residence for a generation of the holy which will be propagated, as some of them think, throughout eternity.

3. The inconsistency of this hypothesis with the Scriptural representations of the work of Christ is its sufficient refutation. There is but one visible appearance of Christ set before the expectation of His people. We have seen the several terms which describe this appearance; but it is observable that one, not yet mentioned, is reserved by St John for his final document. He speaks of the Lord's manifestation to *take away our sins*, ἐφανερώθη, he speaks of only one other manifestation *when He shall appear*, ὅταν φανερωθῇ. Here is the clear and sufficient final testimony of the Bible. Again, the testimony of Jesus declares that the coming of the Lord will bring deliverance to the labouring Church *lift up your heads, for your redemption draweth nigh*. This is inconsistent with such a Millennium as modern theories paint, in it the earth is transformed as the scene of a reign in which only an election of the saints are concerned, in which, moreover, the redemption from sin and from sorrow has not taken place not till afterwards *there shall be no more death, neither sorrow*. And the notion of such a personal reign after His glorious coming is encumbered with hopeless difficulties. A church, made perfect in

[margin notes:]
Inconsistency with Scripture

1 John iii 5
1 John ii 28

Luke xxi 8.

Rev. xxi. 4.

spirit and body, glorified with the Glorified Christ, in the midst of a world still in sin and death, cannot be reconciled with sober interpretation of Scripture. A rebellion of the world against such a rule would be a thing incredible : the lapse of such a Christendom would be death from life, a second and profounder FALL OF MAN. But yet such a lapse must be assumed on this theory. Again, where would be place for the judgment, awaiting all alike ? There must be another resurrection of those, who, during the Millennium, had been converted, and a second coming of the Lord to raise them, and to conduct the more general judgment. Finally, the intercession of Christ is represented as continuing ever, even as His spiritual presence in His missionary Church endures to the end of the world ; but both of these are inconsistent with the Millennial hypothesis in any form which subtilty may give it.

The Catholic Faith.

4. It cannot be denied that there are many difficulties in any view of the subject, and in ours. There are wide differences of opinion among expositors who hold fast the general principle that there is only one Second Coming answering to the First. Some suppose, with Hengstenberg, that the Millennium dates from the establishment of the Germanic Empire, about 800 A.D., and that it is now behind us, with the end close approaching. Others, and they are the majority, assume that the thousand years indefinitely describe a future triumphant state of the Church that will be followed by a temporary lapse, after which the Lord will suddenly appear for the destruction of the yet unrevealed leader of the final opposition. Others fall back upon the interpretation which may be called the catholic one, since it ruled the mind of the Church from the time of Augustine. It is content to understand figuratively the glowing representations of the ancient prophecies as applying to the present Christian Church. It takes the Apocalypse as a book of symbols, which does not give consecutive history, but continually reverts to the beginning, and exhibits in varying visions the same one great final truth. Satan was bound,

John xii. 31.

or *cast out*, when the Saviour ascended : he has never since been the god and seducer of the nations as he was before, and as he will for a season be permitted to be again. The saints, martyrs,

Rev. i. 6.

Rev. v. 10.

and others—the martyrs pre-eminently—now rule with Christ: *and hath made us a kingdom !* they themselves sing ; *and they reign upon*

earth. The Apostles, and all saints, have part in *the first resurrec-* Rev xx 6
tion, and in the present Regeneration reign with Christ, though
the future Regeneration shall be yet more abundant The unani-
mous strain of prophecy concerning the glory of the Messiah's
kingdom is to be interpreted as partly fulfilled in the spiritual
reign of Christ in this world which is not yet fully manifested as
it will be, and partly as the earthly figure of a heavenly reality
hereafter   There can be little doubt that the principle is correct
which makes this great vision a recapitulation of the whole contest Luke xi.
of our Lord with Satan the *strong man* who was *bound* by the 21, 22
Stronger than he. The Angel is He Who was manifested *that He* Matt. xii.
might destroy the works of the devil, and Who gave His people the 1 John iii
pledge of victory *over all the power of the enemy* Luke x
19.

THE RESURRECTION.

Resurrec-
tion

   The resurrection of the dead, as the immediate effect of
our Lord's coming, will be the first or preliminary act of
the consummation of His redeeming work. It will be to
the entire family of Adam the restoration of their bodies
to the spirits from which death had severed them, but it
is the specific rising again of the saints in union with their
Head of which the New Testament especially speaks. The
prominent notion given us is that man recovers his integrity, his flesh being adapted to a new sphere, and
resumed in order to its final glorification.

CHRIST AND THE RESURRECTION.

   In its relation to the Redeemer the resurrection is of essential, In Rela-
fundamental, and universal importance It gives Him one of tion to
His pre-eminent names I AM THE RESURRECTION And there Christ.
is no function of His Messianic office which is more habitually John xi.
and more exclusively referred to Himself As the Prophet He 25
first revealed it fully, not as a new doctrine but as one that had
been in obscurity, as the Priest He procured it by His atonement,
which was the ransom of the whole nature of man; and the word

of His authority as King will effect it. Without following this specific arrangement we may with advantage trace through the New Testament the connection between the Saviour's work and the resurrection of all men.

Christian Revelation.

I. Our Lord has confirmed and perfected the imperfect revelation of the Old Testament : this was part of that life and immortality on which He shed His light.

Old Testament.

1. He expressly declares that the resurrection was everywhere in the old economy presupposed. The rebuke of the Sadducees

Luke xx. 37, 36.

was very explicit. *Now that the dead are raised, even Moses showed at the Bush, when he calleth the Lord the God of Abraham, and the God of Isaac, and the God of Jacob.* As the *children of God,* so called in the Saviour's new terminology, are *the children of the resurrection,* so the ancient fathers were, and are, and will ever be His in their integrity : His now in their spirit, hereafter in spirit and body. The key thus put into our hands by the Master His Apostles have instructed us to use freely. Concerning Abraham we hear again

Heb. xi. 19.

that he offered up Isaac, *accounting that God was able to raise him up, even from the dead ; from whence also he received him in a figure :* this FIGURE of the future resurrection of Jesus and of the general resurrection in other forms runs through the Old Testament. It

Heb. xi. 16.
Heb. xi. 22.

was with this confidence that the patriarchs desired *a better country, that is, an heavenly,* not without allusion to which Joseph *gave commandment concerning his bones.* The Psalms often rise to the hope of a redemption from Hades generally, and in such language as implies a restoration of all that death *shall consume in the grave :*

Ps. xlix. 14, 15.

but God will redeem my soul from the power of the grave, the object of the redemption being the psychical soul, animating a body, as well as the spiritual soul kept in prison. And to that hope God responds

Hos. xiii. 14.

in Hosea : *I will ransom them from the power of the grave,* where there is the remarkable addition that a figurative is based upon a literal truth. The same may be said of many passages which refer in the like figurative way to the resurrection ; such as the

Isa. xxvi. 19.

wonderful prophecy, *Thy dead men shall live, together with my dead body shall they arise,* and the vision of the dry bones in Ezekiel. The translation of Enoch and Elijah shed more or less brightness on all the conceptions of subsequent ages. It may be said generally that the literal restoration of the body was but dimly alluded to, and that with special reference to the saints   In Daniel, however, the literal resurrection is proclaimed, and that as universal, and as linked with judgment . *And many of them that sleep in the dust of* Dan. xii. *the earth shall awake, some to everlasting life, and some to shame and* 2. *everlasting contempt*   In this, as in some other points of revelation, the prophecy of Daniel seems to take a large step towards the New Testament : this is specially observable in the combination of resurrection and judgment

2. But St Paul speaks of *the appearing of our Saviour Jesus*   New *Christ, Who hath abolished death, and hath brought life and immor-* Testa- *tality to light through the Gospel.*   Though the distinction between 2 Tim 1. Pharisees and Sadducees proves that the resurrection was accepted   10 and believed by many, and our Lord appeals to Martha's latent faith in it, yet He always speaks, as His disciples do, of the resurrection as a truth which only in the Gospel is fully announced and confirmed   The proclamation of the glad tidings counteracts death in all its manifestations   Taking up that last prediction of Daniel the lifegiving Redeemer sums up His great gift as consum- mated in two stages   After having said that the believer *is passed* John v. *from death unto life* He speaks of the hour that is *coming, and* NOW   24—29 IS, *when the dead shall hear the voice of the Son of God, and they that hear shall live ;* and then He speaks of the hour that *is coming—* and not now is—*in the which all that are in the graves shall hear His voice, and shall come forth , they that have done good unto the resurrection of life , and they that have done evil unto the resurrection of damnation.*   The fuller revelation of immortality and eternal life includes, therefore, the foreannouncement of a resurrection of the whole man, and of the whole race of man, to an endless existence. When, accordingly, we hear the Saviour uniting the life of His own people with their resurrection—*that everyone which seeth the Son,* John vi. *and believeth on Him, may have everlasting life · and I will raise him*   40. *up at the last day*—we must remember that this limitation, like that of St Paul and St John afterwards, presupposes the back- ground of that earlier passage.

II As to the relation of the Redeemer's person and work to   Christ's this event, the testimony of the New Testament is full and ex-   Person plicit : the Lord's own words here leading the way.   and Work

1 He calls Himself and is called generally *the Life ,* and this

largest name is on one solemn occasion limited to the bodily resurrection, with the sublime 'Εγώ εἰμι appended : I AM THE RESUR-
RECTION AND THE LIFE. The Redeemer's testimony here is the
grandest and most comprehensive we have on the subject : the
I AM includes a source of life and power deeper than the mediatorial : *For, as the Father hath life in Himself ; so hath He given to
the Son to have life in Himself.* But the order of the words indicates that life, as it concerns us, is bound up with the resurrection.
Man is appointed to pass through a rising again, in order to final
and unchangeable life : he must know the power of a first resurrection for the soul, and a second for the body. Both these are
described in the words that follow, presenting the Lord's relation
to us. Here, however, we have to do with the body. And the
importance of its resurrection the Saviour exhibits by the fact
of His progressive miracles in the three acts of resurrection : to
show that the Son of Man had power on earth, as to forgive sins,
so also to raise the dead, He restored the spirit of the daughter
of Jairus, which had scarcely left the body ; He arrested Death on
the way to the sepulchre with his prey, in the miracle at Nain ;
and He made him give up Lazarus after some days in the grave.

2. But it is difficult here to separate the Person from the work.
The universal resurrection is, like everything in the process of
human development, the fruit of the Atonement ; though this is
not clearly stated, save in connection with the universal judgment, it necessarily flows from the mediation of the God-man.
Because He is the Son of Man He hath authority both to raise and
to judge all men. This will be the last function of the mediatorial
lordship : requiring Divine power in the hands of a Man. It
will be like the Lord's own resurrection, the sum and consummation of all miracle : rather as it were a second creation, the formation of ALL human bodies out of the dust as at first Adam was
formed, but in a resurrection which shall preserve their identity
for ever. The new creation shall be a reconstruction also.

III. With special reference to His people, the risen Lord is the
Pledge and the Pattern and the Source of their resurrection life.

1. He is Himself, as the PLEDGE, called the *Firstfruits of them
that slept,* and the *Firstbegotten of the dead :* in this sense also the
Πρωτότοκος, besides being such as the Son *before every creature,* and

Margin notes:
John xiv. 6.
John xi. 25, 26.

John v. 26.

His Work

John v. 27.

Pledge.
1 Cor. xv. 20.
Rev. i. 5.
Col. i. 15.

as the Incarnate brought *into the world.* In no relation more
emphatically than in this He and His saved people are one : the
resurrection is of the righteous and unto life; it is ἐξανάστασις.
When St Paul uses this term, he indicates that those who rise
not to eternal glory remain, as it were, dead, or rise only to die
again. Their resurrection is only to *the second death* As there is
a *better resurrection,* in comparison of the resurrection back to the
present life, so there is also a better or a true resurrection in comparison of the *resurrection of damnation* And of that specific
rising from the dead Christ is the pledge.

2. The glorified body of the Redeemer is the PATTERN after
which the bodies of His saints will be raised   Speaking of our
spiritual conversation in heaven, with which, therefore, the body
has nothing to do, the Apostle says *From whence also we look for
the Saviour, the Lord Jesus Christ, Who shall change our vile body,
that it may be fashioned like unto His glorious body* There are two
words here of great importance the σύμμορφον suggests the same
idea as that above in *conformable unto His death* · the body is to
be subject to the blessed law of our predestination to be *conformed
to the image of His Son.* This word CHANGE is not the same as in
the Corinthian chapter, here it is μετασχηματίσει, which refers
only to the new fashion of the risen body, there it is ἀλλαγησό-
μεθα, *we shall all be changed,* which refers to the entire transformation of the already existing bodies   Now it is of this latter only
that our Saviour was the pattern. He *saw no corruption,* and
consequently could not be a perfect example at all points of our
restoration from death, any more than He is the pattern at all
points of our redemption from the final penalty of sin   There is
an analogy here with His example of holiness . He leads not the
way in the process of attainment, but is the consummate exemplar
only of what we are to attain. We shall live in glorified bodies
like His, but in our redemption from the dust He has no part
with us

3. And the risen Jesus is the SOURCE of that life, as the common life of man in body and soul. Union with Him is the ground
and condition and secret of the resurrection of believers   It may
not be possible to establish that here lies the secret of the emphasis
laid upon the ἐξανάστασις, the resurrection within the resurrection.

Heb i. 6.

Rev. xx 6, 14.
Heb xi. 35
John v 29.

Pattern

Phil iii 20, 21

Phil iii 10
Rom viii. 29.

1 Cor xv 51.

Acts xiii 37

Union with Christ

But it is certain that the passages which dwell most copiously
upon this event refer only to the rising of the saints. *If Christ be
in you, the body is dead because of sin ; but the spirit is life because of
righteousness. But if the Spirit of Him that raised up Jesus from the
dead dwell in you, He that raised up Christ from the dead shall also
quicken your mortal bodies by (*rather, *on account of) His Spirit that
dwelleth in you.* Hence, the great resurrection-chapter is, as it were,
an expansion of the Lord's own word, *Because I live, ye shall live
also.*

Rom. viii. 10, 11.

John xiv. 19.

THE RESURRECTION OF THE BODY.

Its Object. The Object of the resurrection, as the active exertion of the Divine-
human power, is the Body. But this formula must be understood
in a wide latitude of meaning. It must include the perfect or
undivided integrity of the Man raised up ; the actual sameness or
unity of the body as the organ of the spirit ; and the change that
adapts it to its new state when raised. Hence three terms are
the watchwords of our doctrine : the Integrity, the Identity, the
Glorification of the flesh raised in the last day.

Integrity of Man. I. The main, or at least the most important, teaching of Scripture is that of the return of the whole man to existence : to existence, that is, in the integrity of the nature which in the idea of
the Creator was that of a spiritual being using a bodily organisation. Man suffers in death the penalty of a dissolution which
will then be repaired. He is perfect only as spirit, soul and body.
Of physical death it is said, *then shall the dust return to the earth as
it was ;* the psychical soul, the spirit as using material organisation,
in that sense of necessity vanishes with it. *The spirit shall return
unto God who gave it :* not into His essence, but into His keeping,
for final issues which it was not given the ancient Preacher to
know. *Behold, all souls are Mine,* Jehovah said once, in vindication of His righteousness as determining the destiny of every
individual of the race involved in hereditary guilt : and we hear
again and again, the same vindication with reference to their
bodies. The man in his integrity is the man before his Maker,
both now and hereafter. Hence the resurrection is the goal of all
redeeming acts. We have, says the Apostle, *the firstfruits of the*

Ecc. xii. 7.

Eccles. xii. 7.

Ezek. xviii. 4.

Rom. viii. 23.

Spirit, but that is not the realisation of all our hope; we still *groan within ourselves* The resurrection is the finished redemption of the man ; *waiting for the adoption, to wit, the redemption of our body* We now groan, being burdened, for rest we shall after death groan, being *unclothed*, to be *clothed upon.* Everywhere throughout Scripture it is the person who is said to rise again No criticism can rob us of Job's ancient testimony *Though after my skin worms destroy this body, yet in my flesh shall I see God* The fathers died and were gathered each *to his people* Though all *live unto Him*, God waits for their resurrection that He may fully appear to be *the God of Abraham and the God of Isaac and the God of Jacob* As He is *not ashamed to be called their God , for He hath prepared for them a city*, so will He not be ashamed of them as its inhabitants Speaking of that city in which we have our πολίτευμα, our citizenship, St Paul says, *He shall change our vile body that it may be fashioned like unto His glorious body.* We are enrolled in our present integrity, and in that shall we take possession. This general view of the resurrection is of great importance

Rom viii. 23

2 Cor v. 2—4.

Job xix. 26

Luke xx 38.

Gen xxv. 8

Heb xi. 16.

Phil iii 21

II The specific resurrection is of the flesh , and the express revelation of Scripture is, that the same bodies shall rise from the graves But the identity of the body is not the identity of the man nor is the identity of the body dependent upon the continuation of the particles in their union which were deposited in the grave A brief reference to Scripture examples and testimonies is sufficient to obviate misconception on this subject

Identity of Body

1 If appeal is made to our Lord's resurrection body, it must be remembered that there is no analogy We have seen that death never finished its work of dissolution on Him : His bodily organisation was inviolate. The only permissible argument is that, as His glorification took place upon a physical frame, so also will ours. But it is not said that we shall be raised as He was, in order to be afterwards glorified . *it is raised a spiritual body ,* raised immediately as such Nor have other instances of resurrection to which allusion is sometimes made any bearing on the question of identity. Some few were restored to earthly life by our Saviour Himself, which, however, are not spoken of as patterns or illustrations of the general resurrection , nor do we

Analogy with Risen Lord

1 Cor xv 44.

know even that Lazarus—save in Martha's supposition—was permitted to decay.

St. Paul.

2. The only express reference to the subject is in St. Paul's resurrection chapter. The Apostle rebukes the folly of the doubter; and uses the argument of analogy, not to solve what he leaves a mystery, but to obviate objection. The present world furnishes abundant analogies but no resemblances of the future resurrection. Nothing in the buried flesh germinates as the life in a seedcorn:

1 Cor. xv. 38.

the new life is a direct creation. *God giveth it a body as it hath pleased Him.* He does not mean that the disembodied spirit will form for itself a new vehicle; but that in the resurrection the spirit will have a spiritual-psychical organism given to it, which, in the wonder of Divine power, will be to it the same organ it had in time.

Glorification.

III. The change wrought will fit the body for new conditions of spiritual and psychical existence.

Rev. xxi. 1.

1. There will be *new heavens and a new earth,* to which the new inhabitants will be fitted. *The children of the resurrection* will be

Luke xx. 36.

ἰσάγγελοι, *they neither marry nor are given in marriage;* and, as

Matt. xxii. 30.

reproduction will cease, so also nutrition : *God shall destroy both it*

1 Cor. vi. 13.

and them, ἡ κοιλία τοῖς βρώμασιν. Though the relations of sex will not be entirely destroyed—for that would destroy individuality —they will be glorified. The soul will be so renewed as to be a new creation, and the body will be more than a mere restoration : a new creation also. A strictly carnal resurrection was part of a system of Judaizing error which affected expectations connected with the second coming of Christ, even as it had perverted the doctrine of His first coming and His relation to the law. St. Paul contends against that. But a still higher view is given by him

Phil. iii. 21.

when he is not opposing heresy : *Who shall change our vile body—* the body of our humiliation—*that it may be fashioned like unto His*

Rev. i. 13—16.

glorious body, according to the working whereby He is able even to subdue all things unto Himself. What that glorious body is to be, the last revelation of Jesus to St. John in Patmos tells us : but that only dazzles our imagination while it enkindles our hope. Those who

1 Cor. xv. 51.

never see physical death will be *changed.* This is a very strong word, and illustrates that glowing series of counterparts which St. Paul dilates upon : *corruption* and *incorruption; dishonour* and *glory, weakness* and *power*, *a natural body* and *a spiritual body*, all consummated in *this mortal*, having *put on immortality.* 1 Cor xv 42, 44, 53.

2 There is one express prophetic passage, which a few incidental allusions are thought to confirm, seeming to predict a first resurrection of martyrs and saints before the Millennial appearance and reign of the Lord The prophet being supposed to signify a literal resurrection, St Paul is further supposed to have referred to this when he said *Christ the Firstfruits, afterwards they that are Christ's at His coming, then cometh the end* But everything is here kept out of view save the order of relation between the resurrection of the Head and that of His members. There is no distinction or interval hinted at between their rising and the rising of all men. Again, St Paul is thought to have alluded to this when he spoke of his hoping to *attain unto the resurrection of the dead,* τὴν ἐξανάστασιν τὴν ἐκ νεκρῶν. Even if τὴν ἐκ is admitted into the reading, this is no argument that the Apostle aspired to the distinction of sharing in a first resurrection before *the rest of the dead* Ἐξανάστασις and ἀνάστασις are, as may be seen, used interchangeably And the sequel of the chapter already quoted proves that St Paul, like the other writers of the New Testament, knows no resurrection which is into the physical conditions of this life. There is no passage that can be made without pressure to serve the theory of a twofold resurrection that in the symbolical vision of the Apocalypse being excepted. As to this doubtful text more will be said in the sequel Meanwhile, it is enough now to affirm that such a principle of interpretation must be applied as shall bring it into conformity with the universal strain of the New Testament, which speaks of one common resurrection to one common judgment. And that principle is a spiritual sense put upon the first resurrection in that passage.

Two Resurrections

1 Cor. xv 23, 24.

Phil iii 11.

Rev. xx 5

1 Cor. xv. 44.

HISTORICAL.

Historical

1 The resurrection is pre-eminently a doctrine of Christianity. The germs of it, as of all other truths, are found in the Old Testament, but its full development, as one branch of the life and immortality brought to light by Jesus Christ, was reserved for the final Revealer. In the New Testament its development begins

afresh. Before His own resurrection our Lord announced it generally as a truth, partly in connection with His ultimate judicial office, and partly as a protest against error; but the Apostles, and especially St. Paul, have given us the full positive basis of our expectation. And, in the form stamped upon it by them, it is a doctrine new to the world, of which ancient Hindoo, Zoroastrian, Egyptian, and other speculations scarcely gave a hint. It is as a doctrine, whether of Anthropology or of Eschatology, a new and distinctive Christian revelation.

Early Church.

2. Every recension of the Apostles' Creed contained this article: chiefly εἰς σάρκος ἀνάστασιν, sometimes ἀνάστασιν νεκρῶν. The early Fathers discussed the subject with great fullness, either in pure exposition or in opposition to the Greeks, who denied, and the Gnostics, who refined away, this truth. The Gnostic sects, in their abhorrence of matter, and misinterpreting the first spiritual resurrec-

2 Tim. ii. 18.
1 Cor. xv. 44.

tion, affirmed that *the resurrection is past already.* The Alexandrian school, with Origen at their head, laid stress on the *spiritual body* of St. Paul; and upon the difference between νεκρῶν and σάρκος as connected with ἀνάστασις: their Christian philosophy was infected by Platonism, which in some cases, though not in this, elevated their conceptions. But they were opposed by a very literal theory, which went to the opposite extreme: Irenæus and Tertullian accepted a first resurrection, after the analogy of the Lord's body during the Forty Days, to be followed by a final and fuller spiritualisation. These two opposite views—the spiritual and the carnal—alternated, until Augustine struck out a middle course: Erit spiritui subdita caro spiritualis, sed tamen caro, non spiritus; sicut carni subditus fuit spiritus ipse carnalis, sed tamen spiritus, non caro. He, moreover, thought that all would rise at the age of thirty years, the standard of perfection which Christ made the normal one. The Mediæval Schoolmen took the two opposite sides, but mostly adhered to Augustine. Those who went to the extremes were exceedingly fanciful: some of them taught that the same bodies would rise again; the same, even to the hair and nails.

Protestant Confessions.

3. The Protestant doctrine was generally faithful to the ancient Creeds: the Apostles' Credo carnis resurrectionem; the Nicene, Exspecto resurrectionem mortuorum; and the Athanasian, Ad

cujus adventum omnes homines resurgere habent cum corporibus suis   Subsequent Confessions conform to these with a remarkable unanimity   The Lutheran divines very copiously dilated on this topic. They taught that the new body would be the same sub- J. Ger-stance, but clothed with new qualities   differunt non ratione sub- hard, stantiæ, sed quoad qualitates et dona (corpora gloriosa, potentia, xix 26, spiritualia, cœlestia)   Impiorum corpora sunt vasa ad ignominiam xx. 416. et contumeliam   Their high sacramental doctrine was thus ex-pressed   "Our bodies were framed in Adam for immortality, by the incarnation of the Son of God they were taken into affinity with Him ; in His resurrection they began to be glorified, they were washed from sin in the laver of regeneration, by faith they became members of Christ in His mystical body, the temples of the Spirit, and fed and sanctified by the body and blood of Christ unto eternal life "

4 Modern speculations are too various to be examined at Modern length · they are, for the most part, modifications of errors held Specula- in early times   There are a few which should be mentioned, as tions a sound theology must oppose them.   Some literalists would re-store the earthly body absolutely, while others, erring on the opposite side, teach that a new spiritual body will be created without any point of union with the old, or supposing that in the restitution the human form or εἶδος will be retained without the human substance   Not a few think that there is a germ of a higher corporeity which remains in the body dissolved, and will form for itself in some inexplicable manner a new frame · thus in fact making the BODY the principle of resurrection.   While others, like the ancient Greek fathers, teach that anima corpus suum creat, and that the SOUL will, by the miraculous power of God, form its own vehicle out of the transfigured matter around it   There is a well-known hypothesis, that the Holy Spirit invests the dis-embodied with an ethereal vehicle which will be the nucleus of the resurrection body.   But in this matter we must be content to 1 John iii wait   *it doth not yet appear what we shall be*   The new creation at 2 the end will after all have some analogy with that at the first, Rev xxi. when God created the body.   *Behold, I make all things new*   a 5. second time *Let us make man* Gen i 26

Judgment

THE JUDGMENT.

The judgment is emphatically the final revelation of the Judge: as such the consummation of a judicial work that has ever been going on in the world. It will be executed by Christ as God-man, in strict connection with His coming to raise the dead; and its range will be universal and individual. The principles of the judgment will be the application of sundry and just tests, which will reveal the characters of all, to be followed by a final and eternal distinction or severance. In the case of the ungodly this judgment will be condemnation in various degrees but eternal; and in the case of the godly their everlasting confirmation in glory and the rewards of heaven.

The
Judge.

THE JUDGE.

The JUDGE is our Lord Jesus Christ in His indivisible Person as the God-man; but His person may be regarded both as Divine and as human. The office requires both, and each, and together.

God.
Heb. xii.
23.

1. Assuredly God is *the Judge of all*, even in the Christian dispensation. And Christ is God. None but the Creator can appoint the destiny of His creatures, and bring to His bar all subjects of His dominion; but our Lord Jesus hath power to

Phil. iii.
21.
Dan. v.
23.
Acts i. 24.

subdue all things unto Himself. The Judge must of necessity be the Searcher of all hearts: *in Whose hands thy breath is, and Whose are all thy ways.* Our Lord is appealed to as *Thou, Lord, Which knowest the hearts of all men.* There could be no delegation to the creature of universal judgment, even as there could be no delega-

Isa. xliv.
8.

tion of universal and absolute miraculous power. *Is there a God beside Me? . . . I know not any!* If the Redeemer were appointed Judge as simply man, according to the notions of some, His function would be only the visible accomplishment of the judgment and sentence of the invisible God; but that is not the style of Scripture. Our cause is altogether and only in His hands.

Man.

2. But in the economy of redemption the Father *hath given Him*

authority to execute judgment also, because He is the Son of man   And   John v
He will judge the world in righteousness by that man whom He hath   27.
ordained   In relation to no part of His office is the manhood of   Acts xvii.
Christ more necessary to our failing hearts, and of no office there-   31.
fore is it more expressly declared   He is not of like passions with
us, but He is of like flesh and blood, *He knoweth our frame, He*   Ps ciii 14
remembereth that we are dust   His experience of temptation—notwithstanding His necessary sinlessness—makes Him a sympathising High-priest and a merciful Judge, in whose Divine-human
soul, now and ever, to the last extreme of what is consistent with
immutable holiness and law, *mercy rejoiceth against judgment.*   Jas. ii 13

3. Our Lord Himself declares that the *Father judgeth no man, but*   The
hath committed all judgment unto the Son, that all men should honour   God-Man
the Son   In other words the judgment, as the last mediatorial   John v
act, is committed by the most Holy Trinity to the Second Person   22—27.
as incarnate, because He is the Mediator of God and men, Jesus
Christ, Man; and the exercise of that function must redound to
His honour   Hence it will be the final vindication of His own
dignity   He who, at His first coming, was *meek and lowly of*   Matt xi.
heart, never speaks of His second coming but in language of the   29
most lofty self-assertion.   Here only He is *the King, on the*   Matt xxv
throne of His glory   His Divine-human majesty will receive its   31—34
rights in the judgment   In that day He will Himself be DIS   1 Cor. xi.
CERNED, or rightly judged of, and seen as He is   *then shall all the*   29.
tribes of the earth mourn because of the dishonour done to Him by   Matt.
the human race   Accordingly, it will be the overthrow of His   xxiv 30
enemies, then emphatically His own foes   *those Mine enemies*   Luke xix
Whether it be the one enemy, or those who hold with him, the   27.
vengeance of Christ awaits them all alike   Sin will be reduced
to its essence as unbelief in Jesus, and its punishment is decreed
as the act of Christ's own vindication of Himself   And it will be
the final display of His saving attributes towards His saints   The
most profound secrets of the Saviour's grace towards His people
can never be known till then.   *Ye cannot bear them now*   words   John xvi.
which were as applicable to the blessings of the Christian covenant   12
as they were to its mysteries   In this sense also that day will be
the day of the revelation of Christ   And, lastly. our Lord will
then vindicate His moral government, exercised through all ages

of His mediatorial history. He Himself was the most signal instance of the anomaly that perfect goodness should be encountered by perfect wrong. He will then vindicate Himself as the Administrator of moral government from the beginning. The deep, strong argument for a final judgment is the necessity for such a final rectification. He will prove that this instinct of human nature has not been implanted in vain.

The Judged.

THE JUDGED.

The JUDGED are the Race of mankind, in all its generations, and specifically every individual member of the race.

The Race. 1. Throughout the whole economy of human things the unity of the race is maintained. Though all men will not literally undergo the penalty, *it is appointed unto men once to die;* and still more absolutely *after this the judgment:* other things, even death, are contingent; judgment like sin is certain. *He cometh to judge the earth;* which in Daniel is more fully set forth : *The judgment was set, and the books were opened,* when *the Ancient of days did sit.* In the New Testament the doctrine of *eternal judgment* has become one of the *principles* of the new faith. *Before Him shall be gathered all nations :* these words of the judicial Gospel are very explicit. They are confirmed in the Acts, *He will judge the world in righteousness;* and in the passage which, taking it as a whole, gives perhaps the largest and most solemn, and at the same time most gracious, view of the judgment : *in the day when God shall judge the secrets of men by Jesus Christ, according to my Gospel.* The vision presented of the vast congregation of the human race, *the quick and the dead,* is the most wonderful that the human mind has ever been required to conceive : no finite thought can do it justice. Among the last sayings of the Word of God on this subject there are two points to be specially noted : the congregation of the nations are *the quick and the dead* and *small and great :* many who never died shall be judged, and all our Saviour's little ones who have *not sinned after the similitude of Adam's transgression* in any sense. The judgment, therefore, must be conceived as part of a final administration generally, of which the inquisition of iniquity and its requital will be only a part.

The Individual. 2. The individuality of the judgment is implied in all the

Margin references:
Heb. ix. 27.
Ps. xcvi. 13.
Dan. vii. 9, 10.
Heb. vi. 1.
Matt. xxv. 32.
Acts xvii. 31.
Rom. ii. 16.
2 Tim. iv. 1.
Acts x. 42.
1 Pet. iv. 5
Rev. xx. 12.
Rom. v. 14.

passages already adduced, and it is the most solemn secret of
man's own instinct *It is appointed unto men once to die, but after
this the judgment*, even as *He hath appointed a day* and the Judge.
The only thing absolutely both universal and individual is the
judgment not even sin and sorrow can compare with it in this.
In the Old Testament, we read *God will bring thee into judgment*,
and in the New, *Who will render to every man according to his deeds*.
This obviates every false presumption as to judgment by class,
whatever form the notion may take A theory, never shaped
into words, but which is sometimes called MULTITUDINISM, silently
infects many speculations It is hard to reconcile the infinite
detail with Divine dignity; but not harder to receive a special
judgment than a special providence Moreover, there is no common conscience · the conscience of every living man is the sure
pledge and earnest of an individual judgment And it precludes
the thought that believers will escape the final ordeal *For we
must all appear before the judgment-seat of Christ; that everyone may
receive the things done in his body, according to that he hath done,
whether it be good or bad.* Here there might be some doubt, as it
is only said to *receive the things* But in another passage the contrary must have been stated, if true *So then everyone of us shall
give account of himself to God*, to the Lord Christ God must be
justified at the last day, as well as now, in absolving the sinner
now, by the Atonement, then, by the form and reality of judgment,
as declaring the finished result of grace, and allotting to the saints
their several rewards However, it must be observed that there
is a difference put between the judgment of the good and that of
the evil *Judgment must begin at the house of God* both now and
hereafter . but it will not be true hereafter that the righteous
scarcely be saved The ordeal will not be then a doubtful one , its
peculiar strictness and severity are confined to the present life

3 The universality at once and the individuality of the judgment form one of the most powerful arguments that can be used
in dealing with men St Paul's application in the case of Felix is
an instance in relation to the unconverted *And as he reasoned of
righteousness, temperance, and judgment to come, Felix trembled* As
to the believer he makes a most solemn use of it in another
passage *Knowing therefore the terror of the Lord, we persuade men*

Heb. ix
27
Acts xvii
31.

Eccl vi 9
Rom ii 6

Christians
Included
2 Cor v
10

Rom. xiv.
12

1 Pet. iv
17

Argument

Acts xxiv
25

2 Cor. v.
11

And, again, with special rebuke to the spirit of human judgment
and censoriousness: *But why dost thou judge thy brother? or why*
dost thou set at nought thy brother? for we shall all stand before the
judgment-seat of Christ.   And here we may refer to the awful
descriptions of the scenery of the great day, which are found in
both the Old Testament and the New: some literal, such as the
ministry of *all the holy angels,* and especially the *voice of the arch-*
angel and *the trump of God;* some figurative, such as the *books were*
opened; but all being the translation into human language of the
most tremendous realities that the mind of man can conceive.
It may be said that without these adjuncts of dread the great
day is scarcely ever mentioned.

[margin: Rom. xiv. 10.]
[margin: Matt.xxv. 31. 1 Thess iv. 16. Rev. xx. 12.]

PRINCIPLES OF THE JUDGMENT.

[margin: The Judgment]

The principles of the Judgment may be exhibited and summed
up in the following five watchwords: the Test applied according
to various measures of probationary privilege; the Revelation of
character; the Separation of classes; the Execution of the condemning sentence; and the Confirmation or ratification of the
acceptance of the saved.   All these will be combined in one result.
The omniscient Lord will justly apply His unerring tests.

THE STANDARD OF PRIVILEGE.

[margin: Test of Conscience.]

1. The universality of the law of conscience is the first, and in one
sense the most comprehensive test, as preceding or underlying all
others.   Faith or unbelief in Christ will be thus witnessed; though
this standard is not generally referred to in that case.   But the
moral consciousness of all men who have not heard the Gospel
will be appealed to: *accusing or else excusing* in the present life
according to the standard *of the work of the law written in their*
hearts; so, says St. Paul, it will be *in the day when God shall judge*
the secrets of men by Jesus Christ according to my Gospel.   Hence
this test, that of the internal judge and deputy, will be the only
one for a large number of mankind.   Emphatically the Apostle
speaks of the *revelation of God, Who will render to every man accord-*
ing to his deeds; and that with reference *to the Jew first, and also to*
the Gentile; for there is no respect of persons with God.   How that

[margin: Rom. ii. 15, 16.]
[margin: Rom. ii. 5, 6. Rom. ii. 10, 11.]

test will be applied to individual men and vast nations that never
heard, or could hear the Gospel, we must leave to *God the Judge* | Heb. xii.
of all There is no word in the Bible, we may be sure, that pro- | 23
claims the perdition of the Gentiles as such. How *the Only Wise* | Jude 25.
God our Saviour will reconcile this righteous judgment with the
truth that *there is none other Name under heaven given among men,* | Acts iv
whereby we must be saved than that of Jesus is a mystery, but not | 12.
an unsearchable one St Peter perceived that, as St Paul taught,
God is no respecter of persons; but in every nation He that feareth | Acts x.
Him and worketh righteousness is accepted with Him, and many have | 34, 35.
been bold to suppose that a like preparation for Christ will hereafter both be accepted of Him and accept Himself. But this is
beyond the limits of dogmatic theology.

2. The measure of revealed truth granted will be another test | Revela-
or standard of judgment With reference to this very subject our | tion
Lord said of the Jews, *They have Moses and the prophets,* and the | Luke xvi
Old Testament ends with its prediction of judgment thus: *Re-* | 29
member ye the law of Moses Our Lord's own words will be the | Mal. iv. 4
standard, specifically, to His own generation: *it shall be more* | Matt xi.
tolerable for the land of Sodom in the day of judgment than for thee ! | 24.
More generally, this will be the test for all who have heard the
Gospel *The word that I have spoken, the same shall judge him in the* | John xii
last day. And the measure of religious knowledge of the Gospel | 48.
imparted to peoples and individuals will, according to our Lord's
own repeated exposition of the principle of judgment, constitute
a subordinate test. *To whomsoever much is given, of him shall be* | Luke xii.
much required There are varieties of light and manifestation, | 48.
within Christendom itself, almost as distinct as the line which
divides the best heathenism from Christianity.

3 The several tests of Faith and Works, distinctly and com- | Faith and
bined, are represented as constituting the standard applied only | Works.
to Christians, but to them both these will be applied.

(1) Now, in relation to the judgment and its final decision, | One
faith and works are really one. The *work of faith* is the sum and | 1 Thess i
substance of the whole life Works will be the test and faith | 3.
the test, but these will be one and the same: faith the principle
and works the expression of a Christian life in Christ We are
justified now not by faith and by works, but by faith without

the merit of works, and with the evidence of works. So will it be at the supreme vindication of the righteousness of faith.

Works.　(2.) That the works are, throughout the New Testament, made so prominent as the judicial test has many reasons. It is the standing and most solemn rebuke of all Antinomianism. It has also reference to that final and full manifestation of the Divine righteousness, against all who might impugn it, which is made so prominent everywhere. And, finally, as will be seen hereafter, the works will be the standard by which the allotment of the various degrees of reward will be determined. Gradations will be as manifold then as now: these will not be decided by faith but by works. *My reward is with Me, to give every man according as his work shall be:* this is our Lord's last testimony.

Rev. xxii. 12.

SELF-REVELATION.

Manifestation.　Both in the Old Testament and in the New the day of judgment is represented as the final manifestation of all secrets: of all secrets, whether as such unknown fully to man, or as known only to himself, or as designedly kept hidden by him and known only to God. The depths, whether of the Satanic or of the human spirit, are penetrated only by the Searcher of hearts. But nothing is more constantly impressed than that all secrets shall then be made manifest. Only in two applications is the term SECRETS used: to the mysteries of God's Providence on earth, and the mysteries of the human heart and life. But as to both the true meaning of the word mystery is preserved: what is hidden in the present world will be made known in the world to come.

Self-judgment.　1. Hence all the judged will be in a certain sense their own judges. Our Lord lays stress upon this in the parables of the Talents and the Pounds: *out of thine own mouth will I judge thee, thou wicked servant.* The Holy Ghost is in this life the Representative of Christ's judicial function; and He makes the sinner condemn himself in the conviction of sin which is the voluntary acceptance of the justice of the sentence. We may refer also to St. Paul's memorable words: *If we would judge ourselves, we should not be judged.* This principle, applied to the Lord's Supper, is of general application: *we may have boldness in the day of judgment.*

Luke xix. 22.

1 Cor. xi. 31.
1 John iv. 17.

2. The righteousness of the Judge will thus be vindicated : *That Thou mightest be justified in Thy sayings, and mightest overcome when Thou art judged.* The future Judge will, by the perfect correspondence between the books of His own unerring remembrance and the books of the human consciousness read in the light of that day by every man for himself, approve His own righteousness both in justice and in mercy. And the present Judge keeps this now in our remembrance : *If I had not come and spoken unto them, they had not had sin ; but now they have no cloke for their sin.*

3. And thus the Redeemer will maintain His unshared glory. The last exercise of judgment will be the last exercise of mercy. *Mercy rejoiceth against judgment.* The revelation of the holiest saints to themselves will prove that only infinite mercy saved them : therefore the revelation of their own hearts to them also. But that revelation will not be suffered to produce shame in those who are judged : if a miracle is needed to efface this element from the memory of sin it will be wrought ; for nothing may interrupt the continuity of paradise and heaven.

SEPARATION.

The idea of Separation or discrimination inheres in the Greek term κρίσις, and in all the disclosures of the judgment.

1. It will be the final separation or sifting of the world. Judgment is even now continually and indeed decisively proceeding. The Saviour said : *If any man hear My words, and believe not, I judge him not.* This must be understood as meaning that His own pre-eminent work was salvation ; and that final judgment was reserved for the last day. Elsewhere He said : *For judgment I am come into this world, that they which see not might see ; and that they which see might be made blind.* As our Lord in His own person for a season, so now by the preaching of the Gospel the Spirit evermore, executes the offices of Judge. But no judgment in the economy of grace, and within the bounds of temporal probation, is irreversible : there is a *great gulf* between characters, but it is not *fixed ;* but the *judgment to come* will be final, absolute, and unchangeable. Hence it is the LAST or ETERNAL JUDGMENT.

2. This separation, again, will be in two senses twofold : a broad separation between two classes ; and also a discrimination within

The Judge Vindicated.
Rom. iii. 4.

John xv. 22.

Glory to God Alone.
Jas. ii. 13.

Separation.

Final Distinction.

John xii. 47.

John ix. 39.

Luke xvi. 26.
Acts xxiv. 25.

Heb. vi. 2.
Two Classes.

Matt.xxv.
33.
Matt. xiii.
49.
2 Thess. i.
8.

those classes themselves. As to the former, the distinction will be between *the sheep* and *the goats; the wicked* and *the just ;* the *saints* and those who *obey not the Gospel*. Everywhere this division into two vast masses is maintained: acceptance or rejection of Christ being the alternative. But within these great masses the same process of sifting discrimination and decision goes on. For every man there will be a distinct judgment, succeeding or included in the former, by which his position and degree either in salvation or perdition will be determined.

Condem-
nation.

CONDEMNATION.

There can be no doubt that the term judgment is most frequently connected with condemnation : this, in fact, is the more common meaning of κρίσις. Judgment determining the sentence, condemnation pronouncing it, and execution administering it, are almost synonymous terms with regard to the wicked : in Scripture, as in the common language of human justice.

Punish-
ment.

Heb. xii.
6, 9.

1. This requires the strictest meaning of the term punishment. It is not a Father's chastisement the testimony speaks of : that is expressed by παιδεία ; as when we read, in three forms of this word, of the Lord Who *scourgeth every son whom He receiveth.* Of that discipline it is said, *Shall we not much rather be in subjection unto the Father of spirits,* AND LIVE ? But this sentence is always unto death. There is not one hint throughout the Scriptures of a discipline to which the great day commits the rebellious that they may be purified and amended. Surely, if it had been so, no economy of reserve would have kept back the revelation.

Loss or
Damna-
tion.

Matt.xxv.
41.

Matt.
xxv. 34.

2. As to the nature of the condemnation it is, negatively, loss, or the pœna damni or damnation : the quality and essence of sin being separation from God, and its direct penalty separation from the soul's life and centre and rest. Sin is no other than the severance of the will from the Divine will. Our merciful Lord never pronounced, nor ever will pronounce, a sentence more terrible than this : to be without God in eternity is Hell. *Depart from Me, ye cursed :* cursed supremely in that departure itself. Here we have one instance of that series of correlatives running through all the revelations of this awful doctrine which no subtilty of exposition can soften away. *Come, ye blessed of My Father !*

Depart from Me, ye cursed! Men in their integrity come, men in their integrity depart. But, positively also, the condemnation of judgment is to punishment internal and external: the departure is not only from Christ but into everlasting punishment, κόλασιν αἰώνιον. The internal mourning *because of Him* is always con- Rev i 7. nected in the figurative language of Scripture with external suffering, and that inflicted by the *wrath of the Lamb.* But what Rev vi. the dread figures mean it is not possible to define. We know 16. that no material emblems can describe, certainly they cannot enhance, the blessedness of the vision of God; and we know also that no material emblems can describe the misery of the conscious eternal exclusion from that vision. And the penalty will be eternal *These shall go away into everlasting punishment.* Here Matt. there is no room for a timeless abstraction in the interpretation of xxv. 46. the term αἰώνιος. Whatever it means to the righteous it means also to the wicked, *who shall be punished with everlasting destruc-* 2 Thess. 1. *tion from the presence of the Lord* The word punishment implies 9 the abiding continuance of him upon whom *the wrath of God* John iii *abideth* 36.

3. The judgment on the lost is regarded in Scripture as con- Fruit of demnation to bear the fruit of his own doings *Whatsoever a man* Men's own *soweth, that shall he also reap.* There is the sinner from whom the Doings neglected talent is withdrawn, leaving the spirit officeless, un- Gal vi. 7. honoured, and shut out *take from him the pound* And there are Luke xix. the enemies of whom it is said · *bring hither and slay them before* 24—27 *Me.* But always the dreadful burden is laid upon the sinner himself. He is viewed as the author of his own character, and as responsible for his own ruin. In the integrity of his body and soul he reaps the fruit of his own devices: part of his sin was the sensual misuse of the body, part of his sin was the turning away of his spirit from God, in the reunion of body and soul he suffers the result And from this it follows that the final condemnation is that of a nature now fitted for it the harvest is the character formed by the seedtime. There lies the most awful aspect of this awful subject It is not that the Judge assigns eternal punishment for temporal sin, but that sin is taken confirmed into eternity Non cessante peccato nequit cessare poena It is not because man has sinned only, but because his nature is turned away from God,

Accepted
of all.

John viii.
24.

and he sins still: one of our Lord's most solemn words of threatening prediction was this, *Ye shall die in your sins.*

4. That judgment will be accepted and submitted to by all throughout the universe. No profounder mystery is in the Apocalypse than the hallelujahs which are uttered over the demonstrations of the Divine wrath as they proceed from judgment to judgment in their direful procession. Our Lord gives hints of some kind of remonstrance at the last. He interprets beforehand the thoughts of many hearts as they receive from Him recompense for deeds done, or not done, to Him in the persons of men, His representatives: as if, in His own absence as a revealed Saviour, human faith working by love might find in His needy ones Himself in another form. But He says nothing of a thought remaining in any created spirit suspecting or censuring a miscarriage of justice. On this, however, we dare not dwell.

CONFIRMATION OF PAST SENTENCE.

Confirmation.

It is part of the dignity of the saints that the judgment in their case will be only the ratification of a previous decree in their favour and already known to themselves.

Judged
but not
con-
demned.
John v.
24.

1. Though judged, in the more general sense of that administrative word, they *shall not come into condemnation.* Death was really the judgment to them; men have often personified it in their instinctive hope as the Great Revealer. Through it they pass into the presence of Christ Who receives them as a Judge and Divider. Moreover, some descriptions of the resurrection, and notably the great one of St. Paul, describe it as in its dis-

Acts xxiv.
25.

crimination a preliminary decision. This may be harmonised with the fact of a judgment, even in their case a *judgment to come.*

Rank in
the Future.

Dan. xii.
2.
Dan. xii.
13.
Phil. iii. 9.
1 Cor. vi.
2.

2. Their Place and order in the State of salvation has yet to be determined. *Shame and everlasting contempt* are only for the ungodly; but Daniel himself must *stand in his lot at the end of the days:* in the degree purchased by a life of duty. And this suggests a wonderful paradox, that believers are in Christ even while standing before Him, and they hope, like St. Paul, to be *found in Him.* And still another passage finds here its solution *Do ye not know that the saints shall judge the world?* which is St.

Paul's version of our Lord's *Judging the twelve tribes of Israel.* Every individual saint will be confirmed in the state and position for which his Christian character fitted him   He will have his own particular one among the many mansions , his own specific jurisdiction, whether over the ten or the five cities; his own degree of the Vision of God

Matt. xix. 28.

3. It may be said finally that the last Judgment will, in the case of believers, introduce a new economy of service in the universal kingdom of the Triune God, no longer the kingdom of the Mediator.   The infinite variety of employments which the Saviour always in His parables suggests to our expectation and hope will occupy the talents and individual gifts of the redeemed for ever.   But in that new world they are not, nor can again be, in probation   Their state is confirmed, and will admit only of a necessary development of good   Hence there is not, nor can be, any Second Day of Judgment.

In heaven no judgment to come.

THE CONSUMMATION.

The Consummation.

The final issues of our Lord's return may be said to be the consummation of all things. This, with reference to the Redeemer, will be the end of His mediatorial kingdom as such, while as it respects Man it will be the finished redemption of the race, and its restoration to the Divine ideal and primary purpose of the Creator. In regard to the scene of redemption, the world, it will bring in its renewal or transformation; and, as to the Church of Christ collectively and individually, it will seal its perfection in the eternal vision of God and blessedness of the heavenly state.

End and New Beginning.
1 Cor. xv. 24.
Luke xxii. 37.

Rev. xxi. 5.

Generally, there is a close of all things which is only a new beginning of all. The supreme τέλος is the point, the vanishing point, to which all the rays of revelation converge: *Then cometh the end.* With reference to this, as well as to all subordinate processes of His work, our Lord said: *The things concerning Me have an end.* As every part of the Bible, and the whole volume of the Book, is finished with its Amen, so the great and boundless scheme which it records waits for its close, when the entire universe shall respond with its own Amen. But with this there is always conjoined the idea of a new beginning. *Behold, I make all things new.* The re-established order will be so new that the old things shall hardly come to remembrance; but the relation between the new and the old is in many points a mystery reserved. Meanwhile, the combination of these is the only notion of CONSUMMATION, an end opening to a new beginning. The end of human development, combined of sin and redemption, is but a contribution from one little section of what is to us an unlimited universe presided over by a Being Whose infinite resources prepare our feeble minds for wonders which we cannot sketch, even in outline, to our imagination. Human science has taught us much of the amazing consummation which the physical universe has reached;

the science of faith knows no limits to its hope. There is a third τετελέσται of the Divine economy, the fullness of time in the fullest sense, which we expect The first was when the world was finished as the scene of redemption ; the second was when the Lord's cry declared the new creation finished   We must reverently look at the dim reflection of the last as it is thrown upon us only from the Word of God. The contemplation ought to be one of wonder and of joy. As Abraham rejoiced to see the day of Christ in the distance, so may all the children of faithful Abraham rejoice to see in the future the day for which all other days were made.

THE MEDIATORIAL KINGDOM.

There will be an end and beginning of the Redeemer's Kingdom, as it is a kingdom of grace translated into glory. *As to Christ.*

1 The mediatorial economy will cease in its relation to the Triune God : the redemptional Trinity which introduced the economy of subordination in the Two Persons will be again the absolute Trinity. The Son Incarnate will cease to mediate, as Incarnate He will be for ever subordinate, but there will be nothing to declare His subordination no mediatorial rule over enemies, no mediatorial service or worship of His people. The Triune God will be seen by all mankind in the *face of Jesus Christ ;* and the mediation of grace will become the mediation of glory. The Intercessor will pray for us no more, but will reveal the Father openly for ever. *A mediator is not a mediator of one ,* but the prayer of our Lord will then have been fulfilled *that they also may be one in Us.* Man taken up into the US of the Triune God will need a mediator no more *End of Mediatorship* *2 Cor. iv. 6.* *Gal iii 20.* *John xvii. 21.*

2 The kingdom will cease because its ends will have been attained. *Then cometh the end when He shall have delivered up the kingdom to God, even the Father* to the Father as the Representative of the Trinity ; *when He shall have put down all rule and all authority and power.* The process of His victories is described in the Apocalypse · first and last, the Antichrist, which is a spirit of infidelity, *ἀντὶ,* AGAINST CHRIST, having many forms, such as the Beast and the Man of Sin, and also a final personal manifestation ; every description of heathenism to the ends of the earth , the *End of Kingdom. 1 Cor. xv. 24.*

corruptions of Christianity, exhibited in Babylon and the Second Beast and the Harlot; and finally Death, the last enemy that shall be destroyed. In all these conflicts the Church is the fellowship of companions *in tribulation and in the kingdom and patience of Jesus Christ.* We are one with our Lord, and He is one with us, in this progressive warfare and final victory. It is as *Head over all things to the Church* that the Redeemer exercises now and will end then His rule; nor is any other suppression of authority alluded to than that which opposed the designs of His mediatorial kingdom. Moreover, there is nothing said of the destruction, only of the putting down, of all hostile authority and power.

Rev. i. 9.

Eph. i. 22.

3. The kingdom will have a new beginning: new as the kingdom of the *new heavens and a new earth* made one. The Spirit of Christ will be the immanent bond between Him and us, between us and the Holy Trinity: *He that is joined unto the Lord is one Spirit.* The Incarnate Person will be glorified then as never before: His personality as Divine will be no more veiled or obscured by any humiliation, nor will it be intermittently revealed. GOD shall BE ALL IN ALL: first in the Holy Trinity, and then through Christ in us.

New Kingdom.
2 Pet. iii. 13.
1 Cor. vi. 17.

1 Cor. xv. 28.

ERRORS.

On this subject some errors, chiefly ancient, may be noted.

1. Amongst early struggles to reconcile the absolute unity of God with the economical Trinity, we find traces of the Noëtian and Sabellian heresy that with the consummation of Christ's work the triune essence of Deity will be dissolved: the Holy Ghost ceasing to be the name of the operative manifestation of God, and the Son surrendering His office and sinking into the Deity, so that in this sense God shall be all in all. But the relation of the Son to the Father is distinctly personal at the close as throughout: the word which describes to us the very last agency of Him Who has done so much as the Mediator of God and men defines the last act of the Son in His very relation of Sonship; for the kingdom is delivered up to *God, even the Father.* The sanctified host of mankind is one with Christ; and thus the sanctifying work of the Spirit is ended. The Trinitarian economy has ceased; and God the Holy Trinity is all in all.

His-torical.

Patristic.

1 Cor. xv. 24.

2 It has been thought that the Son, having accomplished the
object for which He assumed our nature, would renounce that
nature and give it up also to the Father. But neither can we
give up our Head nor will the Head give up His members. His
human nature is a vesture that He will not lay aside, indeed it
is more than His vesture, it is part of His eternal Self. There is
no independent human personality to be renounced

The Son
One with
Man for
Ever.

3 A subtle notion sometimes slumbering and sometimes
waking in theology may now and then be detected, that another
government will be finally set up, wider, deeper, more catholic
and more effectual than the old, and that among the all things
new will be new expedients connecting the deficiencies and
anomalies of the superseded economy   Shrinking from the plain
assertion that the failure of the Son incarnate will be repaired by
some new and better dispensation, this nevertheless they perpetually hint at. In fact, every speculation that insists upon
finding a basis for the hope of a universal restoration of all
creatures to God really proceeds from such a thought

A New
and Un-
known
Economy.

MANKIND SAVED AS A RACE.

Man.

In the consummation Mankind as such and as a race will be
saved   The Divine purpose in the creation of man in His own
image will be accomplished. through the atoning mediation of
Him Who came to *destroy the works of the devil* among men   The
whole history of the race has been the carrying out of one design ·
one design in the attainment of which many others have been
subsumed, and the attainment of which may open out many others.
Here it is important to remember that the purpose of our Lord's
coming is always regarded as being accomplished   He came as the
predestined and necessary Saviour   The Old-Testament prophetic
triumph was, *He shall not fail nor be discouraged;* the New-Testament response is, *He must reign till He hath put all enemies under His
feet*, and the song of all the Scripture is that *His right hand and
His holy arm hath gotten Him the victory.* The redeeming purpose
of Christ as to the family of Adam must be accomplished, and has
been accomplished : not merely in the gathering of an elect residue
from the generations, but in the salvation of humanity   But how

The Race
Saved.

1 John iii.
8

Isa xlii. 4.
1 Cor. xv.
25.
Ps xcviii.
1.

can this be said to be the case? There are two answers: the race in its vast majority, the race as such, is actually saved; and as to the residue, it will be cast out not only from God but from mankind, and not accounted of.

The Race Saved.

Rom. xiv. 9.

Luke ii. 14.

Matt. xxv. 37.
Isa. ix. 7.

Luke xviii. 8.

1. The majority of the objects of redemption are either already or certainly will be the Lord's for ever; He is not only *Lord of the dead* by prerogative, but also by actual possession. All infants whose development has been cut off on earth pass by prescriptive right to Him. And we may believe, without being able to state positively the grounds of our assurance, that many of the *men of goodwill* who never heard the angelic *peace on earth* will nevertheless sing *glory to God in the highest.* This we seem to hear in the proleptic description given by the King of those who will marvel at their deliverance and their Deliverer: *When saw we Thee?* Of the *increase of His government* apart from the direct preaching of His Gospel we know little, but we may hope much. And as that increase runs on into the best ages of the Millennium, the flow of the nations into the city will abound more and more. Although there will be a great falling away, and the Son of Man leaves with us His question *Shall He find faith?* that defection will be only for a short season.

Rom. xi. 26.

Jer. xxiii. 28.
Matt. xxv. 41.
Dan. xii. 2.
1 John ii. 19.
Isa. liii. 11.

2. In the same sense that it is said, *All Israel shall be saved,* it may be said that Mankind is saved. The lost will not mar the unity of the race: disowned of God they are disavowed of men: *What is the chaff to the wheat?* They are supposed to leave the communion of humanity and go into the fellowship of the *devil and his angels,* into *shame and everlasting contempt;* and of them also we may say, *They went out from us, but they were not of us.* But our best argument and assurance is that He who knows the price of His own life and death *shall be satisfied.*

ERRONEOUS HYPOTHESES.

His-
torical.

There are two opposite theories respecting the Redemption of the Race which differ from the one given in the Scripture: that of those who maintain the doctrine of a final restoration of all moral intelligences, and of men in particular; and that of those who think that the reprobate members of the race will be annihilated.

Some intermediate speculations retain the doctrine of an eternal continuance of the lost, but endeavour in various ways to extenuate the idea of its punishment, or mitigate its horror.

UNIVERSALISM.

The belief or the hope that the consummation of all things will be the restoration of all intelligent beings to the image and favour of God has found advocates in every age This hope has always sought its best support in what may be called à priori arguments; it claims also some passages of Scripture as maintaining its principle; but it has never been accepted by the Christian Church generally from the beginning, nor in any of its branches until its recent development, chiefly in America.

I. Its general principles, however plausible, admit in every case of a sufficient answer

1 If it is said that punishment is in the nature of things only remedial, that assertion cannot be maintained. Reformation is the design of chastisement, and the amendment of the offender is necessarily bound up with our notion of corrective discipline; but the idea of penalty that underlies all human thinking on this subject has in it no other element than that of retribution. If appeal is made from human jurisprudence to Divine, then we have only to say that the Scripture at least carefully distinguishes between pure chastisement, which aims to amend the offender and deter others from like offence, and the vindication of law While prevention, reformation, and retribution co-exist in the judicial principles in human jurisprudence,—none can deny this,—they co-exist also in the Divine economy. As the last extreme in the former is the infliction of pure penalty, so it is in the latter : there is a sin unto death in the court of man's justice, and there is also in that of Divine. As an argument for necessary restoration this fails also when the test of experience is applied to it. There is no connection between suffering the penalty of transgression and amendment of life. If the latter follows the former, it is through the operation of something besides the penalty. Although we are not supposed to be yet on Scriptural ground, we cannot but point to the perpetual strain of its warning against neglect of

the purposes of discipline, the issue of which is said to be a state of reprobation that cannot be amended. What the Bible describes we see in human life : that men rebelling against chastisements and the Spirit of grace that inflicts them, go on to more and more ungodliness, hardened by their calamities. And if the penalty remains, without the grace of probation, what rational judgment can make the design of punishment an argument for necessary restoration to God ? The natural religion of mankind has, with a true instinct, regulated its conceptions of the future by the principle of a final and strict retribution as such. And in the revealed religion of the Bible we find such a testimony as this : *Vengeance is Mine, I will repay, saith the Lord.* Earlier in the same Epistle, St. Paul asks : *Is God unrighteous Who taketh vengeance ? (I speak as a man) God forbid, for then how shall God judge the world ?* If the two sentences are weighed, ἐμοὶ ἐκδίκησις and ὁ ἐπίφερων τὴν ὀργήν, and the emphasis of the last, *the wrath*, observed, it will be impossible to doubt that there is a coming manifestation of the Divine indignation against sin with which the amendment of the sufferer has nothing to do. This is felt by all who regard the threatened death as an extinction of the condemned spirit, of whom we shall speak more hereafter.

Rom. xii. 19.

Rom. iii. 5, 6.

Tendency to Perfection.

2. The argument against a final condemnation of any intelligent creature is often urged on the general ground of the tendency of all the works of God towards perfection. It is assumed as a principle that, if a Supreme Controller of all development exists, He must make all His works issue well in the end. It is hard to resist this argument : it seems logically unanswerable. This is the strong plea of Optimism ; what we call evil is made the necessary stage to ultimate good. An analogy is sometimes drawn with the phenomena of the physical universe ; but this is an unfortunate analogy, for the perfect development sacrifices many individuals on the way. It would be only answering the argument according to its folly to say that the perfectibility of the race is consistent with the final loss of many individuals from it. · But the fact is, that any such perfectibility, apart from the leaven of the Gospel, does not seem a reasonable theory. The progression of the race, intellectually, socially, and æsthetically, may be granted ; on the whole it is advancing steadily. That progress is, on the one

Optimism.

hand, much due to the Gospel, and, on the other, it is by no means synonymous with moral improvement High culture and conformity to perfect law do not necessarily go together. As to the individual we often see a manifest progression in all that is evil down to the last, in unhappy connection with a steady progression in all that is intellectually good Moreover, the argument, as a whole, proves too much · if it is insisted that all God's works must reach a standard of perfection, we are obliged to invert the application, and ask why they were imperfect at any stage. This and many other pleas of the Universalist must be reduced to silence by the plain fact that evil exists.

II. The argument from Scripture is more strictly within the reach of our faculties, and this must to us be the final arbiter. Here we find the general representations of the Divine character appealed to, then the special design of the Atonement, and lastly express declarations of the New Testament as to the issue of the whole work of Christ. *Scripture.*

1. The strength of the first plea is simply this · that if the Divine Being is infinite in love, infinite in power, and infinite in wisdom, it is impossible that any creature of His hands should be shut out from His presence eternally. There is something in this plea that almost disarms resistance; until we call to mind that both the revelation of nature, which knows the terrors of the Lord and persuades men, and that of revelation, conspire to exhibit to us a Being who contradicts the argument. The love of God as an attribute is always carefully qualified in such a way as to guard it from perversion. *Herein is love, not that we loved God, but that He loved us, and sent His Son to be the propitiation for our sins* · it requires an ἱλασμός, provides it for the world, and mourns over its rejection by many. There are necessary limits to the exertion of the Divine power, if not to the power itself; and the relation of a Moral Governor to free intelligences gives one of those necessary limitations, at least in the doctrine of Scripture And in Scripture it is literally the Wisdom of God that predicts its own failure. *because I have called and ye refused !* This style of argument leads to Atheism, or Manicheeism, as the case may be; but not legitimately to Universalism Whatever force it has on this subject must issue to the advantage of the annihilationist argument. *Divine Character.* 1 John iv. 10. Prov i 24.

But the fact is, however strange the assertion may seem, that, with the Bible in our hands, we must make no appeal to the nature of God in the abstract. It would, if pressed to the utmost, render the awful Atonement a superfluous exhibition of resources against evil; nay more, it would pursue the difficulty farther back, and ask why evil was permitted at all. Both the beginning and the continuance of sin are inscrutable; but the one not more than the other.

Design of the Atonement.

2. The argument from the design of the Atonement is still more easily answered. We must, of course, accept the statements of the New Testament on this subject, as there is no room here for abstract discussion of what we might conceive the Atonement

Heb. ix. 26.

should be. It is said that Christ came to *put away sin*, ἀθετῆσαι, which indeed is very strong, but does not involve the idea of universal abolition, as the context shows. Nor does the passage

1 John iii. 8.

which says that Christ *was manifested* to *destroy the works of the devil*, λῦσαι. There is not a single allusion to the Atonement which makes its object the annihilation of moral evil. The Atonement has provided for the effectual destruction of sin in those who receive it; and we maintain, with Scripture, that it availed for many who nevertheless perish, whatever that word may mean.

Eph. i. 10.

St. Paul's words are urged, that *He might gather together in one all things in Christ, both which are in heaven and which are on earth ;*

Col. i. 20.

with which must be connected : *by Him to reconcile all things unto Himself.* The context shows that these passages mainly refer to the redemption of mankind as the bringing back of the race to its unity with the other orders of the universe. We must remember here the fundamental canon of the analogy of Scripture. It is

Heb. ii. 16.

declared of the same Redeemer that *He taketh not hold of angels ;* and, whatever the mysterious reconciliation between man and the other orders of intelligence may mean, it cannot signify that the Saviour has reconciled the devil and his angels to God. He was

Heb. ii. 9.

made a little lower than the angels *that He, by the grace of God, should taste death for every man.* This is a flexible text. The Predestinarian understands ὑπὲρ παντός of the whole mass of the actually redeemed : all for whom the Lord died are saved. The Universalist takes the word in its widest extension : he may follow Origen, who interpreted ὑπὲρ παντός not *for every man*, but *for everything*, and read not χάριτι Θεοῦ, *by the grace of God*, but χώρις Θεοῦ, *outside of God ·* thus bringing all sinners, from the greatest to the least, within the sphere of redemption We maintain that the context limits it to man; and that the entire New Testament speaks of two designs in the Atonement one extending to the whole race, and the other limited to its actual beneficiaries. Thus it is said that *the free gift came upon all men unto justification of life.* But it speaks of God, *the Saviour of all men,* as the Saviour *specially of those that believe.* Rom. v. 18
1 Tim iv 10.

3 It is said that a few allusions to the final consummation expressly foreannounce a restoration of all things to God. That they are few is no argument against them the express assertions of everlasting penalty are also few. Nor is it a refutation that they seem to contradict others, for there are on many subjects seemingly antithetical statements, the reconciliation of which must be deferred to eternity But the passages quoted in the Restoration service have no direct reference to the question those which are quoted against it were spoken expressly on this subject and no other. St Paul in the sayings of the resurrection chapter, so often pleaded, obviously refers only to the design of Christ's death as accomplished in His saints the keynote of the whole is *Christ the first-fruits, afterward they that are Christ's at His coming* These are the ALL of whom it is said that. as they died in Adam, in Christ they shall be made alive it will be true that the whole race of the dead will live again, but not *in Christ.* The Lord will *put down all rule and all authority and power* Both of these and of death the verb καταργεῖν is used, which does not include the idea of literal destruction; and when it is added that *God may be All in all,* we must understand that GOD is all, as distinguished from the mediatorial and intermediate government through man's Representative, and God *in all* the saved, who alone are mentioned. To the enemies *under His feet* are elsewhere opposed the possession whom He hath redeemed and purified *unto Himself* here are the opposite poles throughout eternity. Passages of Scripture.

1 Cor xv. 23

Ver 24.

Ver. 28.

Ver 27.

Tit. ii 14.

III. There has been a steadfast opposition to this doctrine in the catholic Church of Christ from the beginning; although many influential individuals in early times held it, and some more modern sects have striven to bring it into vogue Origen some- Historical

Origen.

times more boldly, sometimes more timorously, advocated the
idea of a universal restitution : not Restoration as of man merely,
but UNIVERSALISM, including Satan and his angels.   Destrui
novissimus inimicus ita intelligendus est, non ut substantia ejus,
quæ a Deo est, pereat sed ut voluntas inimica, quæ non a Deo sed
ab ipso processit, intereat.   Destruetur ergo non ut non sit, sed
ut inimicus non sit et mors.   Nihil enim Omnipotenti impossibile
est, NEC INSANABILE EST aliquid Factori suo. . . . Quæ quidem a
nobis etiam cum magno metu et cautela dicuntur, discutientibus
magis quam pro certo et definito statuentibus.   Origen was written
against and formally condemned.   He had few followers, though
Diodorus of Tarsus, Gregory of Nyssa, Theodore, and a few others
followed hesitatingly in his track.   The early Creeds note the
progress of the catholic doctrine.   The Apostles' and the Nicene
speak only of the life everlasting.   The Athanasian adds : Ad
cujus adventum omnes homines resurgere habent cum corporibus
suis, et redituri sunt de factis propriis rationem, et qui bona
egerunt ibunt in vitam æternam, qui mala in ignem æternum.
In the Middle Ages the Pantheistic mystics favoured alternately
the extinction of evil and its transformation into good.   Some of
the sectaries that troubled the age of the Reformation revived
the notion of universal restoration, and were specifically condemned by the Lutheran Confessions.   In modern times a large
number of sects have arisen, especially in America, who hold this
doctrine ; some of them deriving their name from it.   But it has
never been taught in any Confession of Christendom ; however
largely it may enter into the private speculations and hopes of
individual thinkers.

Origen de Princ. iii. 6, 5. i. 6, 1.

ANNIHILATION.

Annihilation.

The end that Universalism reaches in one way is in another
way reached by the hypothesis of ANNIHILATION, which saves the
race as a whole at the expense of the very existence of the unsaved
part of it.   As in the alternative hypothesis, we have to consider
some fundamental principles ; then the direct testimonies of Scripture ; and lastly its historical relations to the creed of the Church.

Principles

I. The principles underlying this view may be regarded as

opposite aspects of the one fundamental argument, that man has no immortality apart from the gift of Christ, and that this immortality is the one blessing of His redemption.

1 The question of man's natural immortality is not allowed to be absolutely decisive ; and perhaps more has been made to depend on this in the controversy than it will bear Those who maintain that in the image of God, impressed upon man, there was a reflection in the creature of His eternity, and that this natural image was not destroyed by the Fall, are in possession of an argument which settles the subject at once.   That is undoubtedly the view of Scripture, which nowhere asserts or proves the deathlessness of the human spirit any more than it asserts or proves the being of God   To us, therefore, the question is determined at the outset. But our conviction has no force against those who maintain that the gift of immortality was forfeited when man sinned

Natural Immortality.

2 The question, therefore, must revert to the other aspect of it.   Was the benefit of redemption the restoration of immortality, or a new gift of it, to the fellowship of those found in Christ? This is asserted by the advocates of Annihilation, whose manifold arguments may be met in manifold ways

Life in Christ

(1) First, there are two aspects of Christ's redeeming intervention, one absolutely universal and one particular As to the former, in whatsoever sense the race of man died in Adam it lives again in Christ.   The universal resurrection is the proof of this , and on the ground of it all men are dealt with, not as on probation for eternal existence, but as on probation for their destiny in that eternal existence.   The reconciliation of God to man, or to the whole world, implies that all men are by their very birthright members of a race saved from extinction   This we believe, because we believe in universal redemption   Annihilationists do not believe it   They limit the benefit of our Lord's relation to the race to the offer of living for ever.   They teach the end of Predestinarianism in a way of their own . Predestinarianism consigns the unredeemed to eternal reprobation, the annihilationist theory to eternal extinction   Both deny to the race as a race the reality of a redemption in Christ, and make it matter of individual experience.

Redemption of the Race as such.

(2) A special and individual redemption there undoubtedly is ;

Life in the Christian System

F F 2

it does not, however, consist in the negative immortality, but in the positive life, which is in the Christian system never existence merely nor continuing to exist. On this the Lord's own words are decisive : *I am come that they might have life, and that they might have it more abundantly.* Life is a gift that a man may have or not have now : *he that believeth on the Son hath everlasting life; and he that believeth not the Son shall not see life; but the wrath of God abideth on him.* Surely οὐκ ὄψεται ζωὴν is not a phrase that could signify extinction : it is not that he shall see death but that he *shall not see life.* And St. John's Epistle makes this, if possible, more plain : *he that hath not the Son of God hath not life.* Life is in Christ; life is Christ; and Christ is a possession which a man may have or not have, either in time or to eternity. It has nothing whatever to do with continued existence as such. The only passage that even seems to hint at the contrary is in the same Epistle : *he that doeth the will of God abideth for ever.* But there the contrast is with the world and its passing lusts, in comparison of which religion and its fruits are permanent; just as in another passage the life of regeneration is contrasted with the perishable things of time : *being born again, not of corruptible seed but of incorruptible, by the word of God which liveth and abideth for ever. For all flesh is as grass, and all the glory of man as the flower of grass. The grass withereth, and the flower thereof falleth away; but the word of the Lord endureth for ever.* In these passages there is no thought of extinction in any sense. The world does not perish save in its fashions. The phenomenal universe will in some form abide for ever. But pure and perfect existence, clothed with all the blessedness of the life of God, will be revealed only when the phenomena as such have disappeared.

3. The Annihilationist hypothesis meets the Universalist on common ground with respect to certain fundamental or à priori principles; while, on some others, they are singularly at variance.

(1.) It is common to the two systems to dilate on the impossibility of reconciling the eternal misery of a punished soul with the attributes of God as He is depicted in Scripture. But there is no sound argument in this : at least what strength it has must lie on the Universalist side. That God should destroy a soul that He had created is as inconsistent with some of His attributes, His

John x. 10.

John iii. 36.

1 John v. 12.

1 John ii. 17.

1 Pet. i. 23, 24.

Two Opposite Hypotheses.

What in Common.

power for instance, taken alone, as the eternal punishment is inconsistent with His love, taken alone In fact, this system of thought does not relieve the difficulty, save in appearance How could the power of an omnipotent being suffer rebellion to begin ? Having suffered it to begin, how could it be baffled finally, and for ever, in the attempt to save the sinner ? The abiding continuance of sin and its necessary doom is, in some sense, a more conceivable, a more tolerable, idea than its origination. These improvements on the theology of Scripture do seem to unite in ridding the universe of every trace that sin has existed, in restoring God to His supremacy, and thus in delivering our minds from one of the heaviest burdens they can bear. But they cannot blot out the fact that evil has been permitted, and wrestled with, and severely punished for generations uncounted, both in this and other worlds. They reconstruct our God , but the God they give us needs still to be reconstructed if certain human notions of Him are to prevail. Certainly the Divine Being never thus vindicates Himself He does not speak of it as a strange thing that the universe should pay everlasting tribute to His holy justice. But this is, after all, speaking foolishly. All theories alike are confounded before this awful subject

(2.) Another argument, common to the two, is that the punishment of offences committed in time must needs have a temporal limit But the analogy of the temporal penalties themselves is strong against measuring the consequences of the sin by its seeming importance ; persistent sin against God is beyond all finite reckoning , and, lastly, there is no eternal punishment but of eternal sinning . the eternal state of separation from God is both sin and its punishment It may be added that annihilation is to all intents and purposes an eternal punishment of sin committed in time the Universalist escapes this difficulty , but only to plunge into another, that of making the Supreme the Author of a threatening of eternal doom which shall prevent its own execution But we vainly talk about the relations of time to eternity. And certain it is that the price set on the Atonement, and the penalty for rejecting it, are represented in the New Testament in a very different style from that adopted by this theory The despiser of the Cross hath *no more sacrifice for sins :* his sin remains without

Temporal Punishment of Temporal Sin.

Heb. x. 26

a covering, and *the wrath of God abideth on him*   Sinners rise again in a *resurrection of condemnation*   they are *condemned already*, but then their condemnation will be to *everlasting punishment*.   Does the Scripture tell us that they are called up into their perfect existence in spirit and soul and body—created as it were anew—to perish as finding their misery in the consciousness of their loss? Then the *fearful looking for of judgment and fiery indignation* has no meaning; for whatever the penalty of Hades may be annihilation must be in comparison a blessing and only a blessing   Moreover the second death is not annihilation   Of the beast and the false prophet it is said that *these both were cast alive into a lake of fire.* Of the devil it is said that he was *cast into the lake of fire and brimstone, where the beast and the false prophet are, and shall be tormented day and night for ever and ever* . . THIS IS THE SECOND DEATH: corresponding to the second and better life in life : that which is *more abundantly* given.

II The argument in support of the final annihilation of the unsaved portion of mankind lays much stress on the terms of the Biblical vocabulary concerning life and death, and the meaning of everlasting as the predicate of both.   Life is made synonymous with existence, and death with ceasing to exist, and everlasting is a term which is made to suit the theory of each respectively . applied to life it has its full significance of unending duration, applied to death its significance is reduced to absolute or perfect. Appeal is made to the sense in which these words, with their various correlatives of destruction, perishing, and so forth, are used in classical Greek

1. With regard to this last argument it is enough to say that the whole phraseology of revelation, especially New-Testament revelation, has undergone a great and momentous change.   Scarcely one of the religious and ethical terms of classical Greek but has been raised to a higher meaning   No writer would have protested more earnestly than Plato against his terms for destruction being applied to the final destiny of what he thought the immortal spirit of man   It may be said, further, that the New Testament did not take these words directly from classical Greek, but from the Septuagint.   The Septuagint will speak for itself.   Very many passages might be cited in which the strongest terms that express

Margin notes:
John iii. 36
John v. 29.
John iii 18.
Matt xxv. 46
Heb x. 27.
Rev. xix. 20, xx 10—14.
John x. 10.
Biblical Terms.
Greek Testament Phraseology.

destruction are used without involving anything like the idea of Septua-
gint.
extinction. Let us take one passage, for instance, which singularly
unites some of the strongest of all: it must be cited in full.
Ποιμένες πολλοὶ διέφθειραν τὸν ἀμπελῶνά μου, ἐμόλυναν τὴν Jer. xii.
10—12.
μερίδα μου, ἔδωκαν τὴν μερίδα μου ἐπιθυμητὴν εἰς ἔρημον ἄβατον.
ἐτέθη εἰς ἀφανισμὸν ἀπωλείας· δι᾽ ἐμὲ ἀφανισμῷ ἠφανίσθη πᾶσα
ἡ γῆ, ὅτι οὐκ ἔστιν ἀνὴρ τιθέμενος ἐν καρδίᾳ·   Here is a constellation of the entire terminology.   But was the pleasant
land of Jehovah abolished, or annihilated?   The answer is
given by Jehovah Himself.   In the sublime words that follow
we read: *They have sown wheat, but shall reap thorns; they have put* Jer. xii.
13.
themselves to pain, but shall not profit; and they shall be ashamed of
your revenues because of the fierce anger of the Lord.   The application
of these words to our present subject is obvious: *no flesh shall have* Ver. 12.
peace, and that *because no man layeth it to heart.*   But they are Ver. 11
quoted to show how little truth there is in the sweeping assertions
that the inspired terminology of destruction is the terminology of
annihilation.   The student will do well in this matter, and in the
interpretation of the New Testament generally, to track every
word through the Concordance of Trommius.

2. A careful examination of the leading terms Life and Death Life and
Death.
as used in the New Testament will show that, as they are applied
to the spirit of man, they mean something superadded to mere
existence, either as a blessing, or the opposite of blessing.   Life
is evermore the communication of the *Spirit of life in Christ Jesus;* Rom. viii.
2.
it is the correlative of salvation, blessedness and union with God.
It is the opposite of condemnation, of misery, of the Divine displeasure; never the antithesis of annihilation, not even in relation
to the bodily existence, and much less in relation to the existence
of the spirit.   Death is the correlative of the sentence of condemnation, of the withdrawal of the Spirit, and of a state of
alienation from God: those who have not *passed from death unto life* John v.
24.
are said to be *dead in trespasses and sins;* and we may enlarge the Eph. ii.
1.
application of St. Paul's word concerning one *dead while she liveth.* 1 Tim.v.6.
Anyone who traces it through the New Testament must come to
the conclusion that it expresses the exact opposite of the new life,
the life eternal, which is imparted by Christ.   Hence the advocates
of the theory we now consider are obliged to resort to a proleptic

sense : sinners are counted dead by anticipation. But it might as well be said that the saints have not, but only shall have, everlasting life Similarly, the synonyms which vary the idea of death, or rather which describe the way in which it is inflicted, do not carry the notion of absolute suppression of existence. The strongest term that is ever used is applied by our Lord to the state from which the prodigal was rescued . he *was lost* or *was destroyed*, ἀπωλωλὼς ἦν, *and is found*. By that one word our Lord for ever rescued this verb from the misapplication forced upon it the loss of the soul is a state the opposite of its being found again. The prodigal lost in the far country came to himself first, and then came to his father, but he had been destroyed, or had destroyed himself If the Restorationists, using this passage against that doctrine of annihilation which none more forcibly argue against than they, appeal to it as confirming the hope that those who are lost in the other world will be found again, they are met by another most peremptory word of Christ : *good were it for that man if he had never been born*, for that man who was the son of perdition, the υἱὸς τῆς ἀπωλείας, a prodigal who was not found for, had there been a certainty of his coming back from his far country, eternal life would have made his birth a blessing notwithstanding all intermediate woes. A member of the same family of terms is used by St Paul when he says that at the appearing of Christ those who are found not having obeyed the Gospel shall *be punished with everlasting destruction from the presence of the Lord*, ὄλεθρον αἰώνιον The construction of this passage is such, at all points, as to be a warning to theorists on this solemn subject. The addition of αἰώνιον would be needless if the ὄλεθρον meant what they suppose it to mean ∙ absolute extinction of being. As eternal life is the confirmation for ever of a life that now is in Christ, so eternity is added to the word which St Paul elsewhere uses to express a present penalty of hurtful lusts, which *drown men in destruction and perdition* men ἐμπίπτουσιν εἰς *temptation and a snare*, and these βυθίζουσιν εἰς destruction This everlasting destruction is to take place *when He shall come* it is not therefore before the judgment, nor is it after the judgment It is *from the presence of the Lord*, ἀπὸ προσώπου τοῦ Κυρίου, for the meaning of which let the Septuagint vouch, which so translates in Genesis .

Luke xv. 32.

Mark xiv 21.

John xvii 12

2 Thess i 9.

1 Tim vi. 9.

2 Thess i 10.

They *hid themselves from the presence of the Lord* as the first effect Gen. iii. 8. of sin, and *Cain went out from the presence of the Lord* as the second Gen. iv. 16. and still worse effect, our text being the third and worst of all. Finally, as to the αἰώνιον, Daniel's εἰς αἰσχυνὴν αἰώνιον is quite sufficient: what is *everlasting contempt?* But St. Paul himself gives Dan. xii. 2. the law for his use of this word in this relation when he says, *the things which are seen are temporal, but the things which are not seen* 2 Cor. iv. 18. *are eternal:* phenomenal or passing things, and abiding or eternal things, are the only correlatives.

III. The history of this phase of Christian speculation lends it History. no substantial help.

1. Most of the earliest Fathers believed in the absolute eternity Ante-Nicene. Clemens. of the punishment of the reprobate. The first testimony after inspiration ceased is that of Clemens Romanus : μετὰ γὰρ τὸ ἐξελθεῖν Eph. ii. 8. ἡμᾶς ἐκ τοῦ κόσμου οὐκ ἔτι δυνάμεθα ἐκεῖ ἐξομολογήσασθαι ἢ μετανοεῖν. Just. Mar. Justin Martyr asserts this, in opposition to Plato's teaching that Apol. i. 8. they would last a thousand years; but some passages in his writings are thought to hesitate : for instance, when he says to Trypho, ἔστ' ἂν αὐτὰς καὶ εἶναι καὶ κολάζεσθαι ὁ θεὸς θέλῃ, which, however, is a truth that all must admit. Sentences may be gleaned from the ante-Nicene writers which lean in almost every direction ; but the idea of a total cessation of being, or of its gradual extinction, cannot be traced save perhaps in a few isolated passages of Hermas, Irenæus, and the Alexandrian Clement. The question, however, of these sporadic opinions is of very little importance ; save as showing that the seeds of almost every subsequent speculation were early sown.

2. Arnobius, at a later time, gave expression to the idea of a Arnobius. gradual cessation of sufferings, ending in the annihilation of the individual : "A corporalibus vinculis exsolutos expectat mors sæva, non repentinam adferens extinctionem, sed per tractum temporis cruciabilis pœnæ acerbitate consumens." This strange inversion of the dogma of purgatory was maintained here and there by many of the Fathers. Didymus of Alexandria, Gregory of Nyssa, perhaps Theodore of Mopsuestia, and Gregory of Nazianzum, inclined to this as φιλανθρωπότερον καὶ τοῦ κολάζοντος ἐπαξίως, more charitable and more worthy of the Divine Punisher. But it is admitted that the strong, full, and scarcely checked stream of

doctrine after Arnobius set the other way · neither turning aside
to the Restitution of Origen nor to the Annihilation of Arnobius
During the Middle Ages a Pantheistic view of the absorption of
all good and all evil too in God moulded much thought, but it
generally, though not always, took the form of the Apocatastasis.

Modern   3 In modern times the tenet of an eventual annihilation of the
perishing soul has been argued out with great ability by individual men, who have offered it to their fellow-Christians as a
refuge from the awful doctrine which the Church of God in every
age has found in the Bible   The notion has been elaborated with
many diversities of hypothesis, and with an enthusiastic determination to make all things bend to it. It is not possible, nor is
it necessary, to systematise the shapes which the central idea is
in process of assuming   the witnesses to it do not agree, and we
must wait till there is at least more semblance of agreement.
Meanwhile, a few closing remarks may be made.

Some
Sound
Principles
    (1) It must be admitted that the theologians of this new school
have steadfastly asserted some fundamental principles   They hold
fast the doctrine of the eternal punishment of sin; and that of
the absolute and inherent claims of the Divine righteousness. They
do justice, in their manner, to the terrors of the Lord, and vindicate the reality of Divine wrath against unrepenting and obdurate
transgressors   They are among the most determined opponents of
the Restitution theory in all its forms   regarding it as their most
formidable rival for the suffrages of human mercy and hope. Both
these hypotheses set out with the foregone conclusion that every
trace of evil must be swept out of the universe   each waiving the
consideration that it has existed, and that the same awful Will
which permitted it to be, may, in His eternal wisdom, suffer it to
continue under new conditions   But they are mutually intolerant .
each on its own side of the cross of redemption thinks the other
a despiser of that cross   The two hypotheses of extinction and
universalism meet with no such thorough refutation as in the
writings of their advocates respectively.   The annihilationists,
however, pay a tribute to the Divine holiness, and the freedom of
the human will, and the essential evil of sin, which their opponents
at the other extreme fail to pay

Unsound.   (2) But this is all that can be said. Their dogma is inconsistent with the Spirit's testimony concerning sin and righteousness and judgment, as these three are illustrated by the gift of Christ to the race. Sin is estimated in the New Testament by the price of its expiation; it is the act of man, generic and individual, possessed of a nature capable of offending an infinite Being. Before it was committed, that same nature was in the eternal counsel assumed by the Son of God to retrieve its consequences on behalf of the whole race: whatever objection may be urged against this high and catholic view, it must be maintained that the infinite value of the offering implied an infinite offence. According to this new view, man at the time of his transgression was only a living soul, not having yet the quickening Spirit, and therefore utterly incapable of such an offence. Christ comes not to save an immortal sinner; but to give a mortal sinner, who had sinned, the offer of immortality. Such a sin of such an Adam as this doctrine has invented is not matter for such an intervention. Nor does this doctrine comport with the Redeemer's finished and accepted righteousness. That was wrought out for the race; and restored as a free gift all that sin had forfeited. Now man, we repeat, did not forfeit the possibility of living for ever, he forfeited that life itself. If death were annihilation, that was reversed for the nature of man by Him who assumed it; if death were the forfeiture of eternal life in God, that was given back to all who should believe. *The free gift came upon all men unto justification of life.* Rom. v. 18. Hence the judgment, with all its preliminaries, accessories, and results, is equally misapprehended. The resurrection belongs to all men as the fruit of the Atonement, because all men are by the Incarnation vivified by a Head common to all. The mystery of the union between Christ and His Church is based upon a yet deeper, though, alas! not more blessed, mystery, that of His union with mankind. It is the Son of man Who comes in His glory, not the Head of the Church; and in the final separation those who are not His He has LOST. The judgment will make the eternal distinction. Here our new dogma is uncertain and faltering. Some of its advocates, holding that death is the dissolution of an integer which does not exist, save as an integer, make the sinner a nonentity until he is recreated to be marred for ever. Others, maintaining the survival of part of the man, make that part of him pay the full penalty of retribution before the resurrection: on the one hand, denying that in the body the deeds done in the body are punished, while, on the other, they think they pay honour to the instant execution of judgment by making the resurrection the crisis of the despatching stroke, justice being at length satisfied. Some, however, protract the ages of suffering indefinitely, until, by some process of disintegration, of which neither Scripture nor philosophy knows anything, their sin has brought forth in eternity the death which it conceived in time. Meanwhile, the dreadful harmony, though not, alas! the melody, of Scripture, is set to the note that there will be a division of the one race of Adam: the innumerable company of the saved entering into the city brought down to the renewed earth, and the lost, with no mention of their number, WITHOUT the walls, with the devil and his angels.

Other objections.

(3.) Many other objections to this hypothesis of annihilation might be mentioned, which do not affect theology so much as isolated interpretations of Scripture, and the psychological or physiological theories of human nature which it forces or tempts those who accept it to adopt. The student must be constantly on his guard as to both these points; otherwise he will be bewildered by the variety of plausible arguments with which both the heavier and the lighter literature on this subject abound. But, after all, it cannot be too habitually remembered that this solemn question does not depend upon isolated texts, nor upon speculations as to the nature of personality and consciousness. It is connected with the great principles and steadfast tendency of all the teaching of revelation, which everywhere speaks to man as an immortal being, having an eternal destiny, the issues of which are bound up with his use of the means provided of God for his salvation in this probationary state.

Intermediate Theories.

INTERMEDIATE AND MITIGATING HYPOTHESES.

There always have been, and still are, certain opinions held on this subject which can hardly be called intermediate, since they deny both the views already discussed, but which nevertheless aim to abate the extreme rigour of the Scriptural doctrine of eternal separation from God. They refuse to allow that any moral agent will ever perish out of existence; or that evil will be banished as such from the universe; but they introduce certain mitigations which must stand or fall on their own merits.

1. It has been held by some that while the state of the lost is one of hopeless separation from the vision of the Blessed One, it will be also one of absolute submission to and even adoring contemplation of Divine justice. In other words, the final penalty of sin will be an everlasting pœna damni, or sense of irreparable loss unrelieved by hope and accepted in despair. Certain indications of that feeling in the description of Dives and Lazarus are continued beyond Hades into the state beyond; and emotions made eternal which prove that the active rebellion of the sinning will is for ever over. This theory does justice to the undeniable truth that the empire of sin will be subverted and every created will brought into subjection. To suppose that lawless rebellion and defiance may continue eternally offends as much against the kingly authority of Christ as universal restoration offends against His priestly work. But it is hard to distinguish between the sentiment of submission to the Divine authority, and the germ of holiness: as it has been sometimes described it is utterly inconsistent with eternal punishment. One of the most solemn words towards the close of Scripture says that *fear hath torment*, ὁ φόβος κόλασιν ἔχει. Fear is not torment in itself, but it hath torment; hath it in the germ, and what the full development is our Saviour tells us: *these shall go away into everlasting punishment*, or κόλασιν αἰώνιον.

Universal Submission to the Pœna Damni.

1 John iv. 18.

Matt. xxv 46.

2. But, apart from this, the sentiments ascribed to the rich man by our Lord, and the word of Abraham to him, *Son, remember!* have been fondly dwelt upon, as implying a possible benefit of reflection which must be taken into account so far as Hades, or the Intermediate State, is concerned. A generous interpretation of our Lord's words has been suggested by many most eminent divines, who connect them with those other words concerning a possible forgiveness of all sins save one in the other world. They put the whole strength of a possible repentance in the Remember; and suppose that the rich man's regard for his brethren shows the first stage of it. The step from this is an easy one to converting processes that shall finally reduce the number of the irreparably lost. Others limit much of the severer language of punishment to

Repentance in Hades.

Luke xvi. 25.

that intermediate state, leaving for the eternal condition a penalty adapted to a degraded, lowered, and comparatively unconscious existence. This singularly inverts the order of Scripture : assigning the sensuous woe to the state in which the body has no part, and forgetting the express reference to the punishment in the body of deeds done in the body.

Gradation of punishment.

3. In ancient and in modern times much stress has been laid upon the infinite diversity in punishment and reward, as constituting an important element in our judgment on this solemn subject. It is observed that our Lord Himself, Who has uttered the most clear words of Scripture as to the eternal separation of two classes, has again and again referred to gradations in this eternal estate. There is no more definite prophetic teaching than that which speaks of the *few stripes* and the *many stripes.* And the charity of the Christian heart is perfectly justified in deducing from them the utmost possible legitimate inferences. But they must be legitimate : the words give no sanction to the idea that heaven and hell will shade off into each other by imperceptible degrees, or that the few stripes are disciplinary for salvation in opposition to the many stripes which are eternally punitive. Had this meaning been in our Lord's thoughts He might most easily have made that meaning clear. Collating such words, however, with others, we are bound to assume that, though the great gulf is fixed now in Hades, the judgment day will prove that the lost estate of some of the lost is *more tolerable* than that of others.

Luke xii. 48, 47.

Matt. x. 15.

Eternal Love and Power.

4. But all palliative hypotheses and reasonings have, by a natural necessity, revolved back to the power and goodness of the Redeemer Himself, the last only hope of mortal distress : what reserves of infinite resource may be in Him ! In the mystical contemplations of Augustine and other Fathers, and of multitudes since, may be heard occasionally the sublime but very bold idea of an Intercession that may avail to bring back the prodigals whose lost estate is described as an ἀπολέσις, even as the prodigal in time *was lost* and was *found.* How easy is it to form the conception of an effort put forth by the Great Restorer, urged by His own mercy, by the memory of His passion, and the compassionate appeals of His saints glorified, to create at least a place and a state, neither heaven nor hell, for the spoil of eternal justice ! But He

Luke xv. 24.

Who is the Sole Intercessor form an leaves no assurance of such an intercession : indeed He has done all that in Him lay to preclude the thought of any such possible intervention when the mystery of His kingdom is finished.

NEW HEAVENS AND EARTH.

Not only in psalm and figurative prophecy, but in plain teaching also, the new beginning and consummation of man's universe, of an actual heaven and earth, is taught in Scripture.

New Heavens and Earth

1. Generally, there will be a regeneration of all things, as if there were a certain analogy with the salvation of the individual man : the earth, being justified or released from its condemnation, renewed and regenerate, and sanctified to God and man for ever. The original sentence will be repealed, and *there shall be no more curse.* The earth will be in the fullest sense sanctified ; and then it will be said pre-eminently : *every creature of God is good.* So our Lord speaks of the general παλιγγενεσία, or new birth, in a designedly indeterminate way : *in the regeneration when the Son of man shall sit in the throne of His glory.* That is first in the present time : He now sits on that throne, and the Apostles now judge *the twelve tribes of Israel.* But it is also in the future. The same may be said of *the times of restitution of all things.* As man is to rise again, so in a certain sense will the scene of his history. When the heavens and earth are said to pass away and *there was found no place for them,* this must not only be harmonised with other words, *as a vesture shalt Thou fold them up, and they shall be changed,* but also with the Apocalyptic scenes that follow, which expressly declare : *and I saw a new heaven and a new earth ; for the first heaven and the first earth were passed away ; and there was no more sea.* This is evidently the new Genesis, with express reference to the former, no longer, as the prophet Isaiah predicted, to be *remembered, nor come into mind.*

All Things New.

Rev. xxii. 3.

1 Tim. iv. 4.

Matt. xix 28.

Acts iii. 21.

Rev. xx. 11.

Heb. i. 12.

Rev. xxi. 1.

Isa. lxv. 17.

2. *Behold, I create new heavens and a new earth.* If this prediction refers to the physical world, the glowing descriptions that follow must also depict in earthly strains the consummate transformations of the final kingdom. St. Peter says : *We, according to His promise, look for new heavens and a new earth, wherein*

New Heavens and Earth. 2 Pet. iii. 13.

dwelleth righteousness. In the Apocalypse heaven and earth are

Rev. xxi.
1.

made one : *I John saw the holy city, new Jerusalem, coming down from God out of heaven.* Hence what the present heaven and earth

Rev. xxi.
2.

are to our probationary estate the future will be to our eternal and fixed state : not heaven to be ascended to from earth ; but the Lord will make BOTH ONE. The highest heaven, like eternity, will be for ever unknown to man. God alone inhabiteth both.

Rev. xxi.
3.

Our heaven will be our earth, and our earth heaven : *the tabernacle of God is with men*, the Incarnate Son dwelling in redeemed mankind as a temple, and redeemed mankind dwelling in Him ; but both in a transfigured earth.

The
Creature.

3. This is all that we learn from Scripture. It is supposed by many that St. Paul introduces into the heart of his most theological Epistle, into one of the most didactic portions of the New Testament, a poetical reference to the entire κτίσις as longing for and finally

Rom. viii.
21.

sharing in the *glorious liberty of the children of God* at the Adoption. And this would seem to imply, what the Scripture never asserts, that the irrational creature was subjected through man's sin to death, and will share in his redemption. But, unless it can be proved that the κτίσις here is not groaning man as a creature, or heathenism subjected to vanity, this passage has no dogmatic force. Nor is such an extension of the great expectation

Rev. xxi.
1.
Rev. xx.
11.

necessary. When the Apocalypse says that *there was no more sea*, and that for the present phenomenal heaven and earth *there was found no place*, it teaches us to interpret the whole as meaning no more than that the scene and sphere of human development will undergo a corresponding change. As man's body will be fashioned after our Lord's glorious body, so the earth will be fashioned after the similitude of heaven. Men will not therefore be in every sense ἰσάγγελοι.

The Fire.

4. All this will take place through the power of Christ, by the agency of fire. But whatever agency the material fire may exert, the change upon our earth will not be effected by material fire alone. The result will be as utterly beyond any conception we now have as the spiritual body of Christ exalted in heaven. Withal it must be remembered that it is only the earth as the scene of redemption that will undergo this change. It is the earth that

2 Pet. iii.
12.

being overflowed with water perished which is *reserved unto fire.* In the awful greatness of the realms of God and His Christ we and our whole economy are but as the mote in the sunbeam; and it is an error to involve the entire universe in this consummation. Science may trace a connection between every atom of matter and the whole compass of material nature, and refuse to admit the possibility of the abstraction of our world from the sum of things. But we are now in a region in which physical knowledge is inarticulate or without authority; and, moreover, its own theories have nothing to say against the possible extinction of worlds. However, as the declaration, *He made the stars also,* at the beginning, refers only to the phenomenal relation of the universe to our earth, so, at the close, *there was found no place for them* refers only to the sphere of human redemption. Gen. i. 16. Rev. xx. 11.

5. As to the renovation of the earth two opposite errors are to be observed, with many variations on them. One is that of a too spiritual view, which makes the material universe, like the idols, nothing in the world, and man's ethereal vehicle literally a spiritual body. But we have no reason to think that anything made by God is destroyed: in this sense also *The gifts and calling of God are without repentance.* Worlds are known to be undergoing changes which to us are equivalent to disappearance; and creation and glorification may be henceforward an everlasting law. But the opposite is that of a too literal restoration. This way tends much Lutheran speculation, that makes corporeity the law and end of existence: the Gospel is supposed literally to be preached *to every creature;* the Eucharist to be the sustentation of both body and soul; the Holy Ghost as much the physical as the spiritual Lifegiver; and the redemption of Christ a restoration of all created nature, in this the exact opposite of ancient Gnosticism. From this the transition is easy to a literal resurrection of all animated existence. Modern, like ancient, Millenarianism adopts this theory, so far as concerns the intermediate kingdom of Christ; and this is one of its many extreme difficulties. Renovation. Rom. xi. 29. Mark xvi. 15.

ETERNAL LIFE.

The consummation of all consummations as it respects the human race is the entrance of the redeemed into eternal life. Eternal Life.

Viewed as to God this is the realisation of His purpose with regard to mankind in the Incarnate Son. As to Christ it is His presentation of Himself, one with His own, to the eternal Father. Regarded with reference to the heavenly world it is the reconciliation of all the inhabitants of heaven and the race of man : the fellowship being now eternal and complete. As to the whole Church it is the sealing ratification of its oneness with its Head, for His possession and His service. As to the individuals of that Church it is the perfection of their own nature in itself and in that union with the Triune God which is eternal blessedness.

Divine Idea Realised.

Gen. vi. 6.

Jude 24.

Eph. iii. 15.

I. What in human terms we call the Divine idea of humanity we must also in human terms speak of as not having been realised ; precisely in the same sense, and in no other, as that in which it is said : *It repented the Lord that He had made man on the earth.* But the idea not fulfilled in the first Adam has been realised in the Second Adam. He, therefore, the spiritual Father and Head of the new humanity, will represent the new creation unto God, and present this new and better mankind *faultless before the presence of His glory with exceeding joy.* The Adam of Paradise will not be the father of this race, but only the first among many brethren, sons of God through Christ. The human family will be added to the vast multitude of other aggregate families : with the distinction of a relation to God—*of Whom every race in heaven and earth is named*—in the Eternal Son unshared by any other.

All Orders of Creation.

II. Hence, there are some indications that the end of human history will be the restoration of harmony to the universe ; as if man will then at length, perfectly redeemed, join with the other orders of intelligent creatures in the worshipping service of the eternal temple : their harmony, without human voices, not being counted perfect. But this does not sanction the speculative notion that the number of the saved from the earth will precisely fill up the vacancy caused by the fall of those who kept not their first estate. This speculation of the Middle Ages introduces a predestinarian element into the final consummation which the Scripture does not warrant. Nor does the testimony of Jesus by the Spirit of prophecy sanction the thought that the consummation will unite all spirits with all men in the blessedness of union in God. Discord will be suppressed, but not in that way. The reconciliation of which St. Paul speaks is of heaven and earth: it does not couple hell. And the union is effected as the result of the Atonement by the sacrifice of Jesus, which was offered in human nature and in human nature alone.

III. The consummation will be the perfection of the mystical body, the company of the *Preserved in Jesus Christ.* This Church of the redeemed will be, in eternal union with Christ, one with the Holy Trinity. *Behold, the tabernacle of God is with men,* and He will dwell with them, and they shall be His people. But what is this tabernacle? *I John saw the holy city, new Jerusalem, coming down from God out of heaven, prepared as a bride adorned for her husband.* Reserving this last symbol, we must fix our thought upon the former; the glorified Church is the Tabernacle or Temple of God: *the fulness of Him that filleth all in all.* But it will be specially one with Emmanuel, God with us. The last words concerning it drop the name church, inasmuch as that carries with it a suggestion of a larger mass out of which it is called. When the process is over, the Church, or ἐκκλησία, shall lose its name. It will be the Bride of Christ: a term often prepared for in earlier Scripture, but reserved for the last revelation, to intimate the unity of the corporate body of the elect, its everlasting and most intimate union with Christ, and the perfect love which He will bestow on it for ever. It will be His Kingdom also: we *shall reign for ever and ever.* This intimates, not that the Saviour will rule over His Church, or through His Church rule over the universe of other worlds, but that the fellowship of the redeemed and glorified will be His servants to serve Him for ever. That holy company will be a priesthood also: to present eternal worship, not through Christ, but in Him and with Him. Priests eternally as worshippers, they will be kings for ever as servants. Their service will be no longer limited and partial. It will have the universe as its sphere; and in its eternal activity, and infinite variety, will surpass every conception that can be formed of it here. Without the *tribulation,* and without the *patience,* of the *kingdom in Jesus*—save peradventure in sympathy with other worlds where patience may still share with love the honour of being the royal law—they will be for ever its ministering servants.

IV. The consummation will not, however, merge the individual

The Church. Jude 1. Temple of Trinity. Rev. xxi. 2, 3.

Eph. i. 23. In Christ.

The Bride.

The Kingdom. Rev. xxii. 5.

Rev. i. 9.

Individual Saints.

G G 2

in the body corporate, any more than the body corporate will be merged in God   Eternal blessedness will be the portion of every soul in the innumerable company of the redeemed . that individual blessedness will be the perfection of the created nature of man, which, implying its deliverance from all evil. rests not short of its union with God, the Beatific Vision, and the fullness of the spirit's satisfaction in the creaturely reflection of the Divine image.

Negative

1. Negatively, eternal life will be in its final issues the absolute and perfect removal of every evil : that is to say, of the results of sin and the possibility of sinning   Every trace of this sojourner for a night will be effaced from body and soul and spirit   a consummation reserved for the heavenly state   And this negative fruition of rest and deliverance is itself the positive perfection of man according to the primitive constitution of human nature. From the moment when the dust of the earth yielded to the Finger of God the material for the creation of its most perfect product, the human personality has never yet, save in Jesus, seen its highest estate : nor in Jesus upon earth. It will remain for heaven to blot out the last remembrances of the Fall   On the earth the sanctified carry with them the results of past transgressions to the grave , in the intermediate world, though they *see the King in His beauty* with the eyes of the disembodied spirit, their bodily eyes *see corruption*. Only on admission into heaven will the Redeemer save the whole man : at His second coming *shall He appear the second time without sin*. UNTO SALVATION . unto that residuary salvation which will change *the firstfruits of the Spirit* into full redemption   The temporal state with all its restrictions and infirmities will give place to an eternal from which these shall have vanished for ever   But salvation at the best is a negative term   We are lost, and it is our dignity to be capable of being conscious that we are lost, in the thought of our entering into an eternal state.   The finite will be received into the bosom of infinity ; time will be taken up into the bosom of eternity   The most blessed negative result of this will be that change or progression will be only and absolutely upward and forward   Development will continue, but without the possibility of lapse into evil · separation from God, which is sin, will be impossible for ever.

Isa xxxiii.17

Ps xlix 9

Heb ix 28

Rom viii 23

Positive.

2   But all this is only negative   There are some positive terms

by which hope is taught to define without definition its conception
of eternal life. They rise in a sacred gradation from the vision of
God to union with Him and the perfect reflection of His image
in Christ Jesus for ever. This gradation marks the stages of the
religious life on earth ; but it will be perfected in the eternal
state.

(1.) The glorified saint will be admitted to the direct, intuitive
VISION OF GOD, of the Triune God as revealed in Christ, the
eternal Mediator of that vision. In this life we have the same
vision, but yet *We walk by faith, not by sight :* these words describe
the present estate of Christians, as opposed to that in which we
shall *be present with the Lord.* St. John also tells us, when despair-
ing of any other thing to say, that *we shall be like Him, for we shall
see Him as He is.* What the glorified Redeemer is now we know
not : for in this world we *see through a glass darkly.* St. Paul makes
himself a representative of every saint in probation, even the most
privileged, when he says : *Now I know in part : but then shall I know
even as also I am known.* The vision of Christ is vouchsafed to faith
now ; but faith sees Him only as in a mirror : *beholding as in a
glass the glory of the Lord.* With His own face unveiled, and to
the direct intuition of our unveiled faces, He cannot reveal Himself : that will be the prerogative of heaven. He is pleased indeed
to use the same word to express our vision of Him here, ἐμφανίσω
αὐτῷ ἐμαυτόν, and the vision of Him in heaven ἐμφανισθῆναι τῷ
προσώπῳ τοῦ θεοῦ ; but the same vision will be seen by very different eyes. Whatever meaning the promise has for the present, its
fullest meaning is for the future : *Blessed are the pure in heart, for
they shall see God.* This is the BEATIFIC VISION of the Father in
the Son of God in Christ, which the contemplation of faith now
prepares for and longs for : no other than the fulfilment of the
Saviour's request : *that they may behold My glory.*

(2.) This vision implies a distinct personality, which will never
be lost in God. But in a certain sense it must be lost in God,
for the Saviour's last prayer, which was really His last promise,
was *that they all may be one ; as Thou Father art in Me, and I in Thee,
that they also may be one in Us.* Not content with this, He proceeded and said : *I in them, and Thou in Me, that they may be made
perfect in One.* This union with God is, as we read, begun on

The
Vision of
God.

2 Cor. v.
7, 8.

1 John iii.
2.

1 Cor. xiii.
12.

2 Cor. iii.
18.

John xiv.
21.
Heb. ix.
24.

Matt. v. 8.

John xvii.
24.
Union.

John xvii.
21.

John xvii.
23.

earth *that the world may know that Thou hast sent Me, and hast loved them, as Thou hast loved Me* Of such union as this there is no analogy on earth, nor among created things · it has its type in the Holy Trinity itself

Blessed-
ness

(3.) This is Eternal BLESSEDNESS · the term which Christian theology uses to express the utmost bliss of which the created spirit is capable in the vision and enjoyment of God, and in the pure, undimmed reflection of His image. Perfectly reflecting the image of the Eternal Image of the Father, we shall have reached our truest and fullest personal consummation εἶτα τὸ τέλος, the spirit of man finds its rest in Him who is the principle and beginning of its life, being now the glorified realisation of what Adam was in Paradise, with such a superadded union with the Son of God as Adam had not Here is the final issue of the Redeemer's work of God in the soul of man His own purity. the vision of God in Him, and perfect blessedness Once more, this is but the consummation of what is begun on earth In the spiritual vision

1 John iii
3
2 Cor iii
18.

of Himself, He enables us to purify ourselves *even as He is pure,* for we *are changed into the same image, from glory to glory* And all who are thus transformed by grace shall be translated into the glory beyond. In our glorified bodies our glorified spirits will see God, and in that vision enjoy the eternal benediction of the pure in heart. we shall know that absolute blessedness, to bestow which was the final end of the whole work of the Redeemer on

Acts iii
26

earth *God, having raised up His Son Jesus. sent Him to bless you, in turning away every one of you from his iniquities*

Rom xvi
27

TO GOD ONLY WISE, BE GLORY THROUGH JESUS CHRIST FOR EVER. AMEN

GENERAL INDEX

COMPILED BY

THE REV. G. A. BENNETTS, B.A.

GENERAL INDEX.

A.

A POSTERIORI arguments for the existence of God. i. 238.

A Priori arguments for the existence of God, i. 237. 238.

Abelard (A.D. 1141), his theory of inspiration, i. 180 ; chief opponent of Anselm's doctrine of the Atonement, ii. 305, 306 : theory of the relation of knowledge to faith, Intellige ut credas, 377.

Absolute, the doctrine of an impersonal, i. 306 ; the Absolute and morality, 326—329.

Access to God one of the privileges of sonship, iii. 16, 17.

Adam, the natural and federal head of the human race, i. 428—430.

Administration of Redemption (see Table of Contents, vols. ii. and iii.), harmony of holiness. righteousness and love in, i. 352, 353.

Adonai אֲדֹנָי, i. 251.

Adoptianism, a heresy concerning the Person of Christ condemned by the Council of Frankfort (A.D. 794), ii. 138, 139 ; a revival of Nestorianism, 190.

Adoption, relation of, to sanctification and righteousness. ii. 393. 394 : its relation to regeneration and sonship, iii. 3, 4, 14 ; υἱοθεσία, iii. 4. 14 : passages in which it is united with regeneration, 4, 5 ; more generally ascribed to the Son than regeneration, 5 ; a branch of sonship, 13—16 ; the terms (adoptio, arrogatio, υἱοθεσία). 14 : relation of, to the Trinity, 14, 15 ; administered to faith, 14, 15 : as received by man. not the sonship of creation, nor of likeness, but of restored prodigals, 15, 16 ; its relation to justification,

17, 19 ; baptismal, 23 : relation of baptism to, 315.

Adoration, a branch of the ethics of godliness, iii. 226.

Adultery, iii. 239, 240.

Æsthetics, iii. 166.

Agnosticism, a disguised form of Atheism, i. 389.

Ahriman (see Zoroaster).

Alcuin, an opposer of adoptianism, ii. 138, 139, 190.

Alexander of Hales, his doctrine of the Atonement, ii. 307.

Ambrose. his doctrine of sin, ii. 74 ; his application of the term " satisfaction " to the Atonement, 304 ; his doctrine of grace and free-will, 386 ; his doctrine of transubstantiation, iii. 329.

Ammonius Saccas, his system of philosophy, i. 280.

Amphilochius, the first to apply the term Canon to the Scriptures (about A.D. 380), i. 193.

Amyraut, his doctrine of hypothetical redemption (A.D. 1664), ii. 99, 353.

Anabaptists, iii. 397.

Analogy, the argument from. i. 147.

Anchorets, their doctrine of perfection, iii. 66—69 ; origin of anchoretism. 354.

Angel of the covenant, i. 263, 413 ; Old Testament name for the Mediator. ii. 95, 123, 184, 256.

Angel, the, of the churches, iii. 343.

Angelology. i. 8. 408—416.

Angels, i. 411—414 : superstitions with respect to, 414. 415 ; their place in theology, 416 ; evil. enemies of the Christian, iii. 207, 208.

Anglican Church, its theory of inspiration. i. 181 ; its views on the canon, 202 ; its doctrine of baptismal regeneration, iii. 22 ; its theory of the unity of a national Church, 274 ;

its doctrine of the nature of sacraments, 304, 305 ; its doctrine of the sacrament of the Lord's Supper. 333, 334 ; its doctrine of the Christian ministry, 356 ; not millenarian, 397.

Annihilationism, its relation to the doctrine of probation, iii. 109, 110 ; treated of. 434—444.

Anointing, symbol of consecration. ii. 197 : oil. the emblem of the Holy Ghost. 197 ; oil used for the consecration of priests. prophets, and rulers, 197—199. 219, 220 ; the anointing of Christ with the Holy Ghost in the Incarnation. 202—204 ; Christ's unction at His baptism, 204 —207.

Anselm, the first of the schoolmen. i. 21 ; advocate of traducianism. ii. 76 ; his doctrine of the Atonement—Cur Deus Homo ?—304, 305 ; his theory of the relations of faith and knowledge, Crede ut intelligas. 377 : his doctrine of justification, 425, 426.

Anthropology, i. 6, 421.

Anthropomorphism, i. 8, 246. 247.

Anthropopathy, i. 8. 328, 329.

Antichrist. the, iii. 394, 395.

Antinomianism, its theories of perfection, iii. 64, 83 ; the external law a safeguard against. 173. 174 ; love, the guard of obedience against, 179, 180.

Antitheism. i. 389, 390.

Apocrypha, the, i. 195. 200—202.

Apollinarianism. Apollinaris, Bishop of Laodiæa (A.D. 362). his denial that Christ had a human spirit, condemned at the Council of Constantinople (A.D. 381), ii. 135, 136 ; modern tendencies to, 194.

Apologetics, i. 15.

Apostasy. the great, iii. 394, 395.

Apostolate, an extraordinary and transitional office of the primitive Church, iii. 338, 339.

Apostolic. use of the term by the Eastern Church, iii. 283 : one of the notes of the Church, 284, 285.

Apostolical succession, iii. 273, 274, 285.

Aquinas, his theory of inspiration, i. 180 ; advocate of traducianism. ii. 76 ; his doctrine of the Atonement, holding only its relative necessity, superabundans satisfactio, 306, 307 ; his doctrine of free-will and grace,

meritum de congruo, de condigno, 388, 389; his doctrine of transubstantiation, iii. 330 ; his doctrine of the keys, 354, 355.

Arausio, Synod of, its condemnation of the doctrine of a predestination to evil, ii. 99.

Archæology of the Bible, i. 220, 221.

Archangels, i. 413.

Arianism (ὁμοούσιος and ὁμοιούσιος), i. 274, 275 ; ii. 134, 135.

Aristotle, on ethics, iii. 166.

Arminian theology, general remarks concerning i. 19, 20 ; its theory of inspiration, 181, 182 : its views on the canon, 202 : subordinationism of, 283, 284 ; its doctrine of sin, ii. 78, 79 ; compared with the Methodist doctrine, 79—81: doctrine of universal redemption, 100 : its doctrine of atonement. a mediation between the doctrine of a satisfaction which is the commercial equivalent and the Socinian rejection of substitution, something like acceptilatio of Scotus, difference between Grotius and Arminius, Grotius limiting the satisfaction to the dignity of law, universal, 312—314 ; remonstrance against predestinarianism, 356, 357; its doctrine of justification, 442—448 : remonstrant doctrine of justification, errors of later Arminians. akin to the Romish doctrine of fides formata charitate, sometimes called neonomianism, 442—445 ; its doctrine of human agency in regeneration, iii. 24 : its theories of Christian perfection. 84—87 ; its doctrine of the nature of sacraments, 304, 305.

Arminius. his doctrine of the Atonement, how differing from that of Grotius, ii. 312—314 ; his doctrine of justification, 442, 443 ; his doctrine of Christian perfection, iii. 85—87.

Arndt, his views on inspiration. i. 182.

Arnobius, his doctrine of annihilation, iii. 441, 442.

Artemon (A.D. 189), his denial of the Divinity of Christ, ii. 134.

Aryans, the Aryan mythology, i. 375—379.

Ascension, the, of Christ, ii. 178—183 ; preliminaries, 178, 179 : its relation to the past, 179, 180 ; the witnesses,

180 ; its relation to the future, commencement of His priestly intercession and mediatorial reign, its relation to His second coming, 180, 181 ; its result, the session, the descent of the Holy Ghost, 181—183 (*see* Session) ; Lutheran doctrine of, 192.

Asceticism, ascetic theories of Christian perfection, iii. 65—69 ; its relation to Scriptural perfection, 65 : true, a branch of the ethics of the external conflict, 210.

Assurance of salvation, relation of, to faith—πληροφορία πίστεως, ii. 382, 383 : the reflex act of faith, 415 ; Tridentine doctrine of, 437, 438 : doctrine of, iii. 113—130 (*see* Table of Contents) : πληροφορία, 117, 118 ; παῤῥησία, 118, 119.

Athanasian Creed, the, i. 18, 276, 277.

Athanasius, his testimony to the canon, i. 201 ; his doctrine of the Atonement, ii. 302.

Atheism, i. 51, 55, 235, 387, 390, 392.

Athenagoras, his doctrine of the Trinity, i. 271.

Atonement, relation of, to the judicial righteousness of God, i. 339 ; its relation to the attributes of holiness and love, 348—351 : pre-eminence of love in, 351: doctrine of the Fall modified by, ii. 19 ; guilt modified by, 41, 42 : doctrine of sin modified by, 46 ; its relation to original sin, 55—61, 63 ; foretold, 92, 93 ; preparations for, 93 ; in the Divine purpose, 90—100, 102 ; relation of the Incarnation to, 143—145 : sealed by the resurrection of Christ, 172, 173 ; idea of, in the Levitical sacrifices (לְכַפֵּר), 222, 223, 273 ; idea of, in Abel's sacrifice, 225 : idea of, in the burnt-offering (עֹלָה), 225, 226 ; especially foreshadowed by the sin-offerings and trespass-offerings, 226—230 ; day of (*see* Atonement, Day of): its relation to the intercession of Christ, 236—242 ; relation of the priestly benediction to, 243 ; belonging particularly to the high priestly function of Christ, 248, 249 ; the finished Atonement (*see* Table of Contents), 263—316 ; meaning of the term "finished Atonement," 263, 264 ; obedience and sacrifice, their unity and difference seen by referring them to the mediatorial court and temple, 265—267 ; its merit, not for Himself, offered by a Man, Divine, 267—269 : vicarious, for the race (ἀντί, ὑπέρ), ἀντίλυτρον ὑπὲρ πάντων, 269, 270 ; for Christ's people, the ideas of representation and mystical union modifying the doctrine of substitution, 270, 271 : Scriptural phraseology, two families of terms represented by ἱλασμός and καταλλαγή, 271, 273 ; atonement, Ἱλασμός, Ἱλαστήριον, reconciliation, καταλλαγή, 272; theological modifications, satisfaction (כִּפֶּר), expiation and propitiation distinguished, change in the meaning of atonement, 273—275 ; revelation of the Trinity, 276, 277 : the Divine attributes glorified in, 277—279 ; the Divine government vindicated in three views of the Atonement, a mystery transacted in the Divine mind before its manifestation in time, a demonstration of God's love to man, a vindication of God's government, 279—282 ; God, the reconciler and the reconciled, the atonement before the Atonement, 282—284 ; the reconciled world, the reconciliation is the making peace, mankind reconciled, personal reconciliation, 284—287; terminology, 288 ; from the bondage of sin, both as a condemnation and a power, from the power of Satan and death, 289, 290 ; the price : the life of Christ, the blood of Christ, Christ Himself, 290 ; connection between the price and the salvation : a satisfaction to justice, purchase for the Redeemer, various terms, 290—292 ; redemption, a Divine transaction in its origin, methods, and results, 293 ; errors examined : no discord in the Divine nature, not offered to Satan, not an experiment, all of grace, 293, 294 ; universality of redemption : à priori arguments from the instinct of man, the nature of God, the dignity of the Redeemer, positive declarations of Scripture, 294—296 ; special redemption, 296, 297 ; early Church : ante-Nicene age, no controversy on this subject, 297—299 ; Gnostic controversy in second and third centuries, 299, 300 ; summary of the patristic doctrine. Satan's place exaggerated, errors of Origen, 300—302 ; from the Nicene age to Anselm : Greek Church, Athanasius and Gregory of Nazianzum, &c., orthodox, more precise in definition, Western Church, no advance beyond the early Fathers, 302—304 ; Anselm, Cur Deus Homo ? 304, 305 ; mediæval controversy : Abelard, nothing in the Divine nature requiring satisfaction. Peter Lombard, Christ's penal sufferings deliver from the temporal consequences of evil, Duns Scotus. theory of acceptilatio : refinements upon Anselm's teaching by Bonaventura, Aquinas, and others : mediation between Anselm's theory and Abelard's, 305—307 : Tridentine (see Tridentine); Reformation : Luther more rigid as to the absolute necessity of the Atonement than Calvin ; distinction between Christ's obedience and passion, 308, 309 ; Reformed doctrine, limited, 309 ; Socinian: denial of Divine sovereignty of mercy, denial of substitution, sacrificial language figurative, repentance and obedience the ground of forgiveness, 309—312 ; Unitarian, 312 ; Arminius and Grotius, agreement and difference, 312—314 ; three ideas united in the Biblical doctrine : the atonement in God a necessity in the Divine attributes, the reconciliation on earth vindicating to the universe the rectoral justice of God, and the exhibition of the redemption moving the heart of man : thus uniting the Substitutionary, the Governmental, and the Moral Influence theories, 314 ; errors arising from a Pantheistic undervaluing of the personality of man. 314, 315 ; errors arising from under-estimating the evil of sin, 315 ; errors arising from ascribing a wrong place to love among the Divine attributes, 315, 316 ; Scriptural and theological phraseology, 316 ; Atonement received, the epitome of all the Gospel blessings, 393 ; its relation to the

legislation of Christ, iii. 150—152 ; its relation to Christian ethics, 158, 159, 168 ; relation of the second coming of Christ to, 389, 390.

Atonement, Day of, effecting reconciliation between God and the people, distinction between the type and the antitype, the scapegoat (לַעֲזָאזֵל), entrance of the high priest into the holiest, ii. 233, 234 ; combined with the passover, 234—236.

Attributes of God, exhibition of, in revelation, i. 61—99 ; treated of (see Table of Contents), 287—358 ; essential to the definition of God, 289 ; natural and moral, absolute and relative, positive and negative, communicable and incommunicable, 290 ; theology founded upon, 353, 354 ; importance of the harmony of, 354 ; to be contemplated in Christ, 356, 357 ; in creation, 363, 364 ; in providence, 443—446 ; ascribed to Christ, ii. 111, 112 ; glorified in the Atonement, 277—279.

Augsburg Confession, general remarks concerning, i. 19 ; its doctrine of inspiration, 181 ; penance allowed to be a sacrament by the Apology for, iii. 306.

Augustine, argument of his De Civitate against heathenism, i. 145 ; his theory of inspiration, 179, his statement of the cosmological argument for the existence of God, 238 ; his doctrine of the Trinity, 277, 278 : his views respecting the Divine foreknowledge. 318; his theory of the origin of sin, ii. 23; his doctrine of man's relation to the sin of Adam. 76 ; his view of the eternal purpose of God with regard to redemption, 98, 99 ; his doctrine of the Atonement, the first to limit it, 303, 304 : his doctrine of predestination in relation to grace, 349—351 ; doctrine of common grace, his doctrine of original sin, grace efficacious, immediate grace, 387, 388 ; his doctrine of justification. introduction of the doctrine of good works as the ground of forgiveness after the loss of baptismal grace, 420—423 : his doctrine of Christian perfection. iii. 70—73 : his doctrine of the sacraments, 302,

303. 305 ; on episcopacy, 358 ; germs of the doctrine of purgatory, 383 ; his interpretation of the pre-millennial reign, 396 : his doctrine of the resurrection, 410.

Awe, a branch of the ethics of godliness, iii. 226.

B.

Baptism, doctrine of Trinity in the formula of. i. 259, 260. 262 ; of Christ. ii. 204—207 ; sacrament of, its relation to regeneration, iii. 13, 21—23 ; doctrine of baptismal regeneration probably one of the results of Jewish influence, 21 ; its position among the seven sacraments of the Greek and Roman Churches, 306 ; fully treated of, 311—324 (*see* Table of Contents) ; among the Jews, 312 ; by John and the disciples of Christ, 313 ; its relation to Pentecost, 313 ; in the name of Christ or of the Lord (ἐπὶ and ἐν as well as εἰς), 314 ; justification, adoption, regeneration, and sanctification, exhibited and pledged by. 315, 316 ; blessings sealed to infants in. 317.

Baptist, John, the, his baptism of Christ. ii. 205 ; significance of his baptism, iii. 313.

Baptists, their high theory of the internal sanctity of the Church, iii. 278.

Barclay, his views on inspiration, i. 182 ; his doctrine of the pretemporal humanity of Christ. ii. 194 ; his view of justification. 450. 451 ; his doctrine of Christian perfection, iii. 75, 76.

Barnabas, writings ascribed to. i. 200.

Baxter, his modification of predestinarianism, ii. 353.

Behmen, a leading mystic, i. 22 ; his doctrine of the pretemporal humanity of Christ, ii. 194.

Bellarmine, his exposition of the Tridentine doctrine of justification. ii. 433. 434 ; his exposition of the Tridentine doctrine of Christian perfection, iii. 78.

Benediction of Christ in His priestly office, ii. 242—244 ; relation of. to the Atonement, 243 ; deliverance from sin and impartation of all spiritual blessings, 243, 244 ; imparted through the Holy Ghost, 244.

Bengel, his views on inspiration, i. 182 ; his millenarian doctrines, iii. 397, 398.

Bentham, his definition of ethics, iii. 164.

Berengarius, his doctrine of the Lord's Supper (A.D. 1030), iii. 330.

Bernard, his doctrine of grace and free-will, ii. 84 ; his doctrine of the Atonement, 307 : his doctrine of justification, 426, 427 ; his view with respect to the feet-washing, iii. 305.

Bible (*see* Scriptures).

Biblical theology, i. 26, 27, 229, 230.

Birth, the new, iii. 7 (*see* Sonship).

Bishops, ἐπίσκοποι, identity of presbyters with, iii. 342 ; difference between the term and presbyter, 343 : distinguished from presbyters by Ignatius, 351 ; the Methodist Superintendent, 358.

Blessedness, an attribute of God, i. 302.

Blessing, a branch of the ethics of godliness, iii. 226.

Body (*see* Resurrection), identity of, in the resurrection, iii. 407, 408 ; glorification of, in the resurrection, 408, 409.

Bonaventura, his doctrine of the Atonement, ii. 306, 307.

Bradwardine, Thomas, Archbishop of Canterbury (A.D. 1349), a predestinarian, ii. 99.

Brahmanism, i. 57, 141 ; relation of its teachings to the doctrine of the Trinity, i. 279 : its errors with regard to creation, 367, 368.

Brethren of the Free Spirit, a body of mediæval fanatics, their doctrine of perfection, iii. 64.

Brethren, the Plymouth, iii. 357

Brotherly-kindness one of the graces of the external conflict, iii. 217 ; a branch of the ethics of Christian service, 219 ; a branch of the ethics of Christian fellowship, 255.

Buddhism, general remarks on, i. 57 : Buddha without any profession of miracles wrought by himself, 66 ; spread of, compared with that of Christianity, 141 : relation of its teachings to the doctrine of the Trinity, 279 : doctrine of sin, ii. 72 : view of final perfection, or nirvâna, iii. 231.

Bunting, Dr., his doctrine of justification, ii. 445.
Butler, Bishop, his doctrine of probation, iii. 111, 112.
Buxtorf, his theory of inspiration, i. 181.

C.

Caius of Rome, his opposition to millenarianism, iii. 396.
Calixtus,his theory of inspiration,i. 181.
Call (*see* Vocation) to the Christian ministry, iii. 349.
Calvin, his doctrine of inspiration, i. 181 ; his view of the decrees, supralapsarian, ii. 99 ; his doctrine of the Atonement, 308, 309 ; his doctrine of predestination, unconditioned and unconditional sovereignty, 351, 352 ; his doctrine of justification, 441 ; his teaching respecting the visibility of the Church, iii. 282 ; his doctrine of the sacrament of the Lord's Supper, 332.
Calvinism, its doctrine of sin, ii. 78 ; compared with the Methodist doctrine, 84, 85 ; supralapsarianism, infralapsarianism, hypothetical redemption, 99 ; predestination ; Calvin's view, view of the reformed confessions, views of Amyraldus and Baxter, 351—354 ; its doctrine of justification, 440, 441 ; its doctrine of human agency in regeneration, iii. 23, 24 ; regeneration put first in the order of the bestowment of Gospel privileges by, 25 ; its doctrine of sanctification, 82—84 ; its doctrine of probation, 107—109 ; its doctrine of assurance, 124, 125 ; its doctrine of final perseverance, 137—147 ; its view of the Word of God as a means of grace, 297, 298.
Canon, the, i. 193—230 (*see* Table of Contents), etymology and meaning of the term (κανών), 193 ; objective, 194—205 ; testimony of Josephus to, 195 ; testimony of Christ to, 195, 196 ; tests applied for the determination of the canon of the New Testament, 199 ; homologoumena and antilegomena, 199, 200 ; Deutero-canonical books, 200 ; decisions of synods with regard to, 200 —202 ; testimony of the Holy Ghost to, 204, 205.

Care, providential, i. 449—451.
Carthage, Third Council of (A.D. 397), decision of, with respect to the canon, i. 201.
Cassian, his doctrine of free-will and grace, ii. 388 ; his doctrine of perfection, iii. 69.
Casuistry, love the casuist, iii. 181, 182.
Catechetical Theology, i. 15.
Catechumenate, iii. 318.
Catharists, a body of mediæval fanatics, their theory of perfection, iii. 63, 64.
Catholic, one of the notes of the, Church, iii. 282—284.
Causality, i. 311, 312.
Cause, First, i. 439, 440.
Causes, final, i. 320 ; second, 439, 440 ; relation of miracle to second, 440.
Celibacy of the clergy optional in the time of the Apostolic Fathers, iii. 351.
Cerinthus, a Docetic, ii. 134.
Chalcedon, council of (A.D.451), its condemnation of Eutychianism (ἀσυγχύτως, ἀτρέπτως) and Nestorianism (ἀχωρίστως, ἀδιαιρέτως), ii. 137.
Charity (*see* Love), a branch of the ethics of man and man, iii. 233, 234.
Cherubim, i. 412.
Chiercy, synod of (A.D. 853), its condemnation of the doctrine of a predestination to evil, ii. 99.
Chiliasm (*see* Millenarianism).
Chinese religions, the, i. 380.
Chrism, an ancient rite from which confirmation sprang, iii. 307.
Christ, the Centre and Teacher of Christian Theology, i. 10—14 ; the Great Revealer, and the sum of all revelation, 38, 39 ; testimony of, to the Scriptures, 39, 40, 159—163, 192, 195, 196 ; the supreme subject of prophecy, 80, 81 ; character of Christ a credential of Christianity, 99—125 ; His testimony to Himself, 100 ; soleness of His person, 101 ; the claim of, a response to the anticipations of the race, 102 ; His personal character a justification of His claim, 102, 103 ; His incarnate mission conducted in a way consistent with His twofold nature, 103, 104 ; His style of teaching in harmony with His claim, 104, 105 ; the truth of His claim exhibited most clearly in

the consummation of His work, 105—108; His claim confirmed by His predictions as to His kingdom, 108, 109: His provision for the future a confirmation of His claim. 109, 110; contrasts in, 110, 111; the influence of. 111—113; hypotheses explaining the manifestation of. 113—125; the personal character of, 114—117: Divine attributes to be contemplated in, 356, 357; Second Adam. ii. 55—61, 117; His sinlessness and impeccability. 64; Divinity of, proved. 108—113 (*see* Christ, person of); incarnation of (*see* Incarnation); estates of (*see* Estates); descent of into Hades, 167 —169; resurrection of (*see* Resurrection); His resurrection ascribed to His own power, 170; His resurrection the great proof of His Messiahship, 173. 174; offices of (*see* Offices); the Christ of prophecy, 197 —202; the Christ of fulfilment, 202—207; baptism of, 204—207; personal ministry of, 207—213; Lawgiver and Preacher. 210—213, iii. 149—156; the Supreme Revealer, Himself the truth (נָבִיא and רָאָה)

ii. 213, 214: our Passover. 231, 232; the Antitype of the Temple, 246. 247; names of, 254—262; pretemporal names, God, Son of God, &c., 254; names indicating the Person: Immanuel. the Branch, the Son, the Son of Man, Man, Mediator, 255; theological phrases denoting the Person: God-man, the Incarnate, the Divine-human Person, Theanthropic Person, 255; official names, those connecting Him with the creation generally: Prince ('Αρχηγός). Prince of Life. the Life. Prince (or Captain) of Salvation. Prince (or Author) of the Faith. Prince and a Saviour. 256; those belonging to the prophetic preparation: the Angel of Jehovah. the Messenger of the Covenant, the Servant of the Lord (New Testament παῖς. Minister), Wonderful. Counsellor. the Mighty God, Prince of Peace, Shiloh, the Seed, 256; Names belonging to the redeeming work: Jesus, Prince of Salvation. Messiah, Christ, Holy One, Redeemer, Light of

the Gentiles. Glory of Israel. Desire of Nations. Salvation, the Lord our Righteousness, Sanctifier, Surety, Testator. Finisher of the Faith. the Life. the Eternal Life. 256—258; Names belonging to the separate offices: Prophetic—Rabbi. Master, Teacher. Minister of the Circumcision. Apostle, Wisdom of God, Light of the World. Truth, True Light, 258; names belonging to the priestly office of: High Priest. Priest, Propitiatory, the Lamb. Paraclete. Propitiation, 258, 259; names belonging to the kingly office of: Lord of All. King of Kings, Lord of Lords, King's Son. Judge. 259, iii. 412 — 414; combinations of names: Our Lord Jesus Christ, Great God and our Saviour Jesus Christ, The Only Wise God our Saviour, Shepherd and Bishop. our Lord and Saviour Jesus Christ, Alpha and Omega, the Beginning and the Ending. is, was, is to come. the Almighty, &c., ii. 259, 260; Names denoting His relations to His people: Rock. Foundation. Chief Corner Stone, Good Shepherd, Head, Way, Friend of Sinners. Bridegroom, Brother, Fountain. Bread of Life, Water of Life. Physician, All in All, 260, 261; the object of saving faith. 379. 380, 414, 415; Gospel blessings *one* in union with, 394 —397; our righteousness, 403, 404; the ἁγιασμός. iii. 33, 34, 35; dependence of ethics upon union with, 187; submission to, a branch of the ethics of conversion. 193; devotion to, a branch of the ethics of intention. 197: imitation of, a branch of the ethics of intention, 198; devotion to. a branch of the ethics of Christian service. 217, 218: the day of, 387; the second coming of, 387; terms used to describe the second coming of (παρουσία, ἐπιφάνεια, ἀποκάλυψις), 389: the time of the second coming of (καιρός, χρόνοι), 390—395: relation of. to the resurrection. 401— 406: the pledge, pattern, and source of the resurrection life of His people. 404—406; theory of "Life in," 434—444.

Christ, the Person of, the Doctrine

of. ii. 106—139 (*see* Table of Contents) ; the Divine Personality, 107—113 ; passages in which He is called God, 108 ; passages in which He is called Lord (= Jehovah), 108, 109 ; passage (John xx. 28) in which He is called Jehovah and God, 109, 110 ; Antithesis of Divine and human natures, 110, 111 ; St. Paul—Flesh and Spirit, 110 ; Flesh and God, 111 ; St. Paul and St. John— Son of God and Flesh, 111 ; Divine attributes ascribed to Him, 111, 112 ; Divine worship and honour paid to Him, 111—113 ; personality that of the Son, 113— 116 ; perfect manhood, Son of Man, Second Adam, 116—118 ; the Divine-human person, hypostatic union, 118—122 ; predicates taken from both natures, 119, 120 ; one mediatorial work, 120, 121 ; two natures unconfused, 121, 122 ; Scriptural development of the doctrine, 122—132 ; in Old Testament the Seed, Angel of Jehovah ; Psalms, Prophets—Angel-servant, Servant-son, 122—125 ; testimony of Himself—Son of God, Son of Man, the Son, 125—127 ; testimony from heaven, 127 ; testimony of evangelists and apostles, 127— 132 ; παῖς, 128 ; ἰδίου υἱοῦ (Rom. viii. 3, 32), πατέρα ἴδιον (John v. 18), 129 ; Logos, 131, 132 ; historical, 133—139, 188—196 (*see* Table of Contents) ; relation of resurrection to, 169—172 ; as effected by His own power, proving His Divinity, 170 ; as effected by God the Father, the reward of His suffering and testimony to His incarnate dignity, 170, 171 ; names denoting Immanuel ; the Branch, the Son, the Son of Man, Man, Mediator, 255 ; theological names denoting God-man ; the Incarnate, the Divine-human Person, the Theanthropic Person, 255 ; the Person of, His office of lawgiver bound up with the doctrine of, iii. 149, 150.

Christianity (*see* Faith, the Christian), the influence of, a credential of revelation, i. 126—150 ; the avowed aim of, 126—130 ; its claim sustained, 130—134 ; influence of, upon personal character, 134—137 ; slow development of, 138, 139 ;

persistence of, 139, 140 ; the early spread of, 140, 141 ; the conflict of, with Judaism, 142—144 ; conflict of, with heathenism, 144—146 ; conflict of, with natural religions, 146, 147 ; conflict of, with false science, 147—150.

Christology (*see* Christ, Person of), meaning of the term, i. 10.

Chronology, Biblical, i. 219, 220 ; of the antiquity of man, 434, 435.

Chrysostom, his doctrine of inspiration, i. 179 ; his doctrine of justification, ii. 420 ; his doctrine of the sacraments, iii. 302 ; his doctrine of transubstantiation, 329 ; his representation of the Eucharist as a repetition of Christ's sacrifice, 329 ; his assertion of the identity of bishops and presbyters, 353.

Church, the (*see* Table of Contents, iii.), theology developed in, i. 14—24 ; an evidence of the resurrection of Christ, ii. 177, 178 ; the antitype of the Temple, 247, 248 ; distinguished from the kingdom, 252 ; formed by the Spirit (ἐκκλησία), the organ of the Spirit, 330, 331 ; the work of preaching the Gospel committed to, 342—344 ; ethics of, iii. 253—258 ; term only used twice by Christ (ἐκκλησία), 260, 261 ; Eph. iv. 3—6, principal text for the unity of, 269 ; and State, influence of false theories of the relation of, on the doctrine of the external sanctity of the Church, 278 ; reformed and Lutheran theories of the relations of State and, 282 ; a Society distinguished from, 282 ; the Sabbath in, 290—292 ; human forms of worship in, 292—294 ; in the consummation, 451.

Cicero, his etymology of the term "religion," i. 7 ; on divination, 176 ; his views of creation, 368, 369 ; definition of sin, ii. 30 ; moral philosophy of, iii. 167.

Circumcision, its connection with the doctrine of sin, ii. 52 ; of Christ, its relation to His humiliation, 156 ; Christ, the minister of the, 207—213 ; regeneration described as, iii. 8, 9 ; baptism substituted for, 311—316.

Class-meeting, the Methodist institution of, a guard of the internal sanctity of the Church, iii. 279.

Clemens Alexandrinus, his doctrine of the Trinity, i. 273 ; his statement concerning the narrative of the Fall, ii. 10 ; his doctrine of justification, 420 ; his doctrine of Christian perfection. iii. 62, 63 : his opposition to Millenarianism, 396 ; his views on eternal punishment, 441.

Clemens Romanus. his doctrine of inspiration, i. 178 ; his writings. 200 ; his doctrine of the Atonement, ii. 298 ; his doctrine of justification, addition of δι' ἀγάπης. 419 ; doctrine of Christian perfection. iii. 62 ; λαϊκὸς ἄνθρωπος. 351 ; his doctrine of eternal punishment, 441.

Clergy, ante-Nicene distinction between laity and, iii. 351, 352.

Cœlestius, follower of Pelagius (*see* Pelagianism).

Coleridge, his theory of inspiration, i. 183, 186.

Commerce, ethics of, iii. 249—251.

Communion, the term distinguished from eucharist and sacrament, iii. 325—328 ; the bread and wine not the bond. but the outward and visible sign of, 327.

Communism, iii. 249, 250.

Compassion, as belonging to the moral attributes of God. i. 347.

Comte. Auguste. his account of the universe, i. 392—395.

Conception. Immaculate. Papal dogma of, i. 19 ; ii. 76.

Concomitance, theory of. iii. 330.

Concord, Formula of. i. 19.

Concursus, theory of, i. 440, 447.

Condemnation removed from the human race by the Atonement. ii. 59 ; in the judgment (παιδεία, κόλασις), iii. 420, 421.

Confession, its place in worship. iii. 290 ; auricular. 307.

Confessional, theology. i. 16—21 : in relation to the notes of the Church, iii. 284, 285.

Confidence, the virtues of. a branch of the ethics of the external conflict, iii. 213—217.

Confirmation, one of the seven sacraments of the Greek and Roman Churches, iii. 306, 307.

Conflict. ethics of the spiritual. iii. 201—217 ; the internal, 202—206 : the external, 206—217 ; graces of

preservation and confidence (*see* under these words).

Confucius, without any profession of miracles. i. 66.

Congregationalists, their high theory of the internal sanctity of the Church, iii. 278 : their teaching with respect to the visibility of the Church, 282.

Conscience, what? ii. 34, 35, iii. 172, 173 ; St. Paul. συνείδησις : St. John, καρδία. ii. 34 ; enlightened by the Holy Ghost. 60 : and the intellect, iii. 170 ; objective and subjective, 172, 173 ; a test in the Judgment, 416.

Consecration. anointing the symbol of. ii. 197 ; expressed in the burning of the Levitical sacrifice, 223—226 : treated of, iii. 31—33 ; of things. 31 : of persons, 31—33 : to God's possession, 31. 32 ; distinguished from dedication. 32 ; to the fellowship of God, 32 ; to the service of God, 32 ; the Holy Ghost the seal and the power of. 32, 33 : the term sanctification used to express, 34 : predicated of all the elements of human nature, 35 ; progressive. 38. 39 ; entire. 50—56 ; to God. a branch of the ethics of godliness. 224—231.

Conservation. providential, of the universe, i. 446—449.

Constantinople, Second Œcumenical Council of (A.D. 381), its condemnation of Apollinarianism, its assertion of the Divinity of the Holy Spirit. i. 275, 276, ii. 135, 136 : Synod of (A.D. 544). its condemnation of Origen's errors. 301 ; Sixth Œcumenical Council of (A.D. 680), its condemnation of the Monothelite heresy. 138.

Consubstantiation, Lutheran doctrine of, iii. 331, 332.

Consummation, the (*see* Table of Contents), iii. 424—454.

Contemplation, a branch of the ethics of godliness, iii. 230.

Conversion. ii. 367—371 ; definition of, narrower and wider sense, explanation of the term. 367, 368 ; strictly belonging to preliminary grace. co-operation of Divine and human agency, 368, 369 : relation of, to repentance and faith, sudden and gradual. 369—371 ; the ethics of, iii. 192—194.

Cosmogony (*see* Table of Contents), i. 395—408.

Cosmological argument for the existence of God, i. 238.

Counsels of perfection, iii. 66, 81, 82, 110, 111. 184. 185.

Courage, one of the virtues of confidence in the ethics of the external conflict (ἀρετή), iii. 213. 214, 217.

Court Mediatorial, the (*see* Righteousness), righteousness the supreme attribute in, i. 352 ; term obedience referred to. ii. 267.

Courtesy, iii. 233, 235.

Covenant, of works (so called), ii. 8. 13, iii. 108 ; of grace, ii. 60, 61, iii. 101, 102. 108 ; with man in Adam and in Christ, ii. 62, 63, 78, בְּרִית, διαθήκη explained, 93, 94 ; angel of, 95 ; various covenants : Patriarchal, Mosaic, Christian, 95 : theory of a pretemporal covenant of redemption discussed, 102 ; iii. 108, 137, 138 : the idea involved in probation (συνθήκη and διαθήκη distinguished) iii. 101 : the sacraments, the covenant means of grace, 299—334 ; the five so-called sacraments added by the Greek and Roman Churches no connection with the covenant character of the Gospel, 306, 307 : the Lord's Supper, the ratification of. 326, 327.

Creation, the Trinity in, i. 362 : the Divine attributes in, 363, 364 ; proper, 364—367 ; theories contradicting, 367—395 (*see* Table of Contents) : speculations with regard to eternal, 366, 367 ; secondary, or cosmogony, 395—408 ; theory of, continuous, 447 : terms denoting, used to describe regeneration, iii. 6, 7.

Creationism, i. 429, ii. 76.

Creator (*see* Table of Contents). i. 361—408.

Creature, the attributes of God related to the (*see* Table of Contents), i. 307—325 ; the law of God right as to, 336, 337 ; God and the (*see* Table of Contents), 359—456.

Credentials of the Christian revelation, i. 46—155 (*see* Table of Contents) : and evidences, 49 ; of Christ's prophetic office : miracles, His own Person, ii. 215.

Creeds, the three, i. 17, 18, 276, 277.

Criticism, Biblical, i. 213—217.

Crucifixion, the date of, ii. 160 : its relation to the Passion, 160—163.

Cyprian, his doctrine of the unity of the Church, iii. 273 ; his doctrine of the Lord's Supper, 329 ; his mention of the priest as sacrificing in the place of Christ in the Eucharist, 329 ; his teaching with respect to the episcopate, 351 ; his teaching with regard to the power of the Keys, 352; germs of the doctrine of purgatory, 383 ; his millenarian views, 396.

Cyril of Alexandria (died A.D. 444), chief opponent of Nestorius, ii. 136 ; doctrine of the Atonement, 303.

Cyril of Jerusalem (A.D. 386), his doctrine of the Atonement, ii. 303.

D.

Damian, his tetratheism, i. 279.

Day of Christ, the, iii. 387—401 (*see* Table of Contents).

Deaconesses, iii. 348.

Death, punishment of sin, ii. 36—42 ; spiritual, 37, 38 ; physical, 38, 39 ; not extinction, 39 ; eternal, 39—42 ; hereditary, 48—51 : redemption from bondage of, 289 ; in eschatology, iii. 371—376 ; abolished, 373 ; of believers, part of their fellowship with Christ, 374, 375 ; names of Christian death, 375, 376 ; not annihilation, 439—441.

Decalogue, iii. 182, 183, 185, 186, 188—191.

Dedication, meaning of the term, iii. 32.

Deism, i. 13, 51. 52, 147, its views on inspiration, 185.

Deontology, iii. 167.

Dependence, theory of absolute, i. 447, 448.

Depotentiation, theory of, ii. 190, 193, 194.

Depravity, hereditary, ii. 51—55.

Design, the theory of immanent, in creation, i. 369..

Destruction not annihilation, iii. 438—441 ; ὄλεθρον αἰώνιον, 440.

Development, Romish theory of, i. 212 : scientific theory of, 396—399 (*see* Evolution).

Diaconate, the, iii. 347, 348.

Dichotomy, theory of, i. 435, 436.
Didymus of Alexandria, his views on eternal punishment, iii. 441.
Diligence, one of the graces of the external conflict, iii. 216.
Diodorus of Tarsus, his views on restoration. iii. 434.
Diognetus. Epistle to, its doctrine of the Atonement, ii. 299.
Dionysius of Alexandria. his opposition to millenarianism, iii. 396.
Dispensation or economy (οἰκονομία), Patriarchal, Mosaic, Christian, ii. 95, 96 ; of the Spirit, not an absolutely new dispensation, but one with that of the finished Atonement, 325, 326.
Divorce, iii. 240, 241.
Docetics (name from δοκέω), their denial of the reality of Christ's manhood, ii. 134.
Doctrine, different types of, within New Testament, i. 16, 17 ; different creeds and confessions of the Church, 17—24 ; Christian doctrine a credential of Christianity, 130—134 ; relation of, to Christian ethics, iii. 157—163.
Dogmatic theology. i. 16, 27.
Donatism, its theory of the internal sanctity of the Church, iii. 278.
Dort, synod of (A.D. 1618), doctrine of sin. ii. 79 ; predestinarianism, 352, 353.
Doubt, i. 48.
Dualism, Divine protest against. i. 256, 257 ; its views of creation, 381—385 ; its relation to the doctrine of sin. ii. 72 (*see* Zoroaster, Parsism, Gnostics).
Duns Scotus, Pantheistic doctrine of the Incarnation, ii. 191 ; his doctrine of the Atonement, 306.
Duty, the discharge of, by Christ, iii. 153 ; the principle of our, 156 ; what in Christian ethics, 166.
Dynamical theory of inspiration, i. 171, 182, 183.

E.

Ebionites, their doctrine of the Person of Christ, ii. 133.
Economics, social, a branch of ethics, iii. 166.
Economy (οἰκονομία), (*see* Dispensation).

Eldership. no Scriptural sanction for distinguishing between a teaching and ruling eldership, iii. 346.
Election. in Old Testament, of a people to receive the direct call, ii. 338—340 ; the result of accepting the Gospel call, 345, 346 : blessings of, may be forfeited, 347 ; historical, 348—357 : one of the privileges of sonship, iii. 17, 18.
Elipandus, Bishop of Toledo, one of the founders of Adoptianism, ii. 138.
Elohim (אֱלֹהִים), i. 250—254.

Encyclopædists, French. their hypothesis of the manifestation of Christ, i. 115.
Ephesus, Council of (A.D. 431), its condemnation of Nestorianism, ii. 136.
Epicurus, his views of the universe, i. 386, 387 ; the relation of his teaching to the doctrine of Providence, 438, 439.
Episcopius. subordinationism of, i. 283, 284 ; his doctrine of Christian perfection, iii. 84.
Erastian theory of Church and State, iii. 278.
Erigena, Scotus, a mystic, i. 22 ; his Pantheistic view of the universe, 369, 370.
Eschatology, its relation to Christian ethics, iii. 159, 160, 168, 187 ; treated of, 367—454 (*see* Table of Contents).
Essence, the Divine, i. 248, 249, 277, 286 ; the essential names of God, 249—286 ; the relation of the attributes of God to, 287—289 ; attributes of, 291—307 ; love in. 344, 345.
Estates of Christ (*see* Table of Contents), ii. 151 — 196 ; the estate of humiliation, 152—166 ; humiliation in respect to His Person, 152—155 ; the humble development of His human nature, 152, 153 ; the obscuration of His Divinity, 153—155 ; His Godhead immutable, 154 ; the humiliation in respect to His redeeming work, 155—163 ; His humiliation in order that He might become the Representative of sinful man, 155—157 ; His obedience as the Servant of God, as making reparation to the Divine law, His active and passive righteousness,

158, 159 ; His passion and death, 159—163 : reconciliation of apparent discrepancies as to the time of the crucifixion, 160 ; limits of the humiliation, 163 ; the humiliation in respect to His Person and work one, the redeeming work giving its reality to the humiliation, and the Divine dignity of the Redeemer giving its glory to the submission, 163—166 : manifestations of Christ's glory in His humbled condition, the three testimonies from heaven, His own assertion of His dignity, 164—166 ; the estate of exaltation, 166—183 ; the descent into Hades, reasons for fixing the commencement of the exaltation at the descent into Hades. 167—169 ; His resurrection (see Resurrection), His ascension and session (see Ascension), Scriptural development of, 184—188 ; exinanition, 184. 185. 187 ; ecclesiastical development, 188—196.

Eternal (see Death, Life).

Eternity of God, an attribute of the absolute essence of God. i. 296—300.

Ethics, Christ as Lawgiver presides over. ii. 211, iii. 149—156 ; treated of, 148—258 (see Table of Contents) : distinction between morals and. 163, 164 ; Kant's definition of, 164 ; attitude of Christian, towards metaphysics and psychology, 169, 170 : their dependence upon union with Christ. 187 : objections against the, of the Bible, 190, 191.

Eucharist. one of the seven sacraments of the Roman and Greek Churches. iii. 306 : full treatment of (see Table of Contents). 325—334 ; the term distinguished from sacrament and communion. 325 ; the commemoration of Christ's death, 326 ; sacrificial idea added to. in the third century. 329.

Euripides, his doctrine of sin, ii. 73.

Eutychianism, Eutyches, heresy concerning the two natures in the Person of Christ, condemned by the Council of Chalcedon (A.D. 451). ii. 136, 137 ; Monophysitism and Monothelitism. later forms of, 138, 189 ; modern French and German school of, 139 : tendencies to in Lutheranism, 193, 194.

Evangelists, an extraordinary and transitional order in the New Testament, iii. 339, 340.

Evidences distinguished from apologetics, i. 15, 16 (see Credentials); credentials and, 49 ; presumptive, 50 ; of miracles, 68—76 ; of the canon, 202—205.

Evil, relation of Divine goodness to the existence of. i. 322 ; not good disguised, 322, 323 ; not ordained for the glory of God, 323 ; controlled by Divine goodness, 323, 324.

Evolution. theory of. i. 402—405, 431, 432 (see Table of Contents).

Exaltation, the. of Christ (see Estates).

Example, the. of Christ, iii. 155, 156.

Exinanition, the, of Christ, His own testimony to, voluntary subordination, ii. 184. 185 ; a mystery, 185 ; Apostolic testimony to, 187.

Exorcism, iii. 319.

Expiation (see Atonement) : punishment of sin modified by, ii. 41, 42 ; connoted by the sin-offering, 227 ; connoted by the passover, 231 ; distinguished from propitiation, 274, 275 : its relation to other terms, 316 : its relation to the legislation of Christ, iii. 150—152.

Expository theology, i. 15.

F.

Faith, its relation to theological science, i. 29 ; the instrument by which revelation is accepted, 42—46 ; a primary faculty of human nature, 43, 44 : relations of reason and, 43, 45, 46 ; relation of, to our knowledge of God. 246 : relation of conversion to, ii. 369—371 ; its place in the preliminaries of salvation, 376—383 : definition of, 376 ; belief of man Divinely directed, relation of knowledge to, 377, 378 ; saving, trust (πιστεύειν, הֶאֱמִין), the object,

Christ, πιστεύειν used with εἰς, ἐπί, ἐν, active and passive, the act of the whole man under the influence of the Holy Spirit, connection of, with regeneration, 378—382 ; assurance objective, 382, 383 ; relation of, to repentance, repentance after regeneration, 384, 385 ; justifying,

411—418 : without works. 412—415 ; the condition of justification, renouncing every other dependence than the Atonement. counted for righteousness, two meanings of imputation (λογίζεσθαι, ἰλλογεῖν), of the operation of the Holy Ghost. 412—414 ; the instrument of justification, apprehending Christ (διὰ or ἐκ πίστεως, not διὰ πίστιν), not assurance, which is its reflex act, produced by the Spirit, 414. 415 : and works. made righteous as well as reckoned righteous. faith justified by works, 415—418 : historical. 418—451 ; errors of the Fathers : love and good works conjoined with faith as the ground of justification, 419—423 ; fides informis, fides formata charitate. 424 ; adoption administered to, iii. 14. 15 : in relation to perfect love, 55 : "full assurance" (πληροφορία) of. 117, 118 ; a branch of the ethics of conversion, 193 ; one of the graces of the external conflict. 216 ; and works a test in the Judgment, 417, 418.

Faith, the Christian. i. 42—155 (*see* Table of Contents) ; meaning of the term, 45.

Faithfulness, one of the moral attributes of God, i. 342—344.

Fall, origin of term, ii. 17 ; of angels, 4—6 ; of man, 6—19 ; narrative of. 7—13 ; mythical and allegorical theories of narrative, 9, 10 ; symbolism in narrative, 10—13 ; narrative. in sacramental terms. 10, 11 : narrative. in terms of coming redemption. 11 ; narrative. in terms of later knowledge, 11—13 ; the original probation, 13—15 ; internal and external. 15—17 : active and passive, 17—19 ; viewed in the light of the Atonement. 19 ; relation of. to Christian ethics, iii. 157, 158, 168.

Family, ethics of. marriage, parents and children, masters and servants, the household, iii. 237—248.

Fanatical theories of Christian perfection, iii. 62—65.

Fanaticism, attempt to account for Christianity on the ground of. i. 118, 119.

Fasting. iii. 210.

Fatalism, Calvinism related to, ii.

352. iii. 109 ; its relation to the doctrine of probation, iii. 107.

Father, God the Father, in creation, i. 362, 363 ; in providence, 440, 441 ; His relation to redemption, ii. 103, 104 : His relation to the Incarnation, 150 ; resurrection of Christ ascribed to, 170, 171 ; agent in regeneration, iii. 5.

Federal theology (*see* Covenant). ii. 78. iii. 107—109.

Felix. Bishop of Urgella, one of the founders of adoptianism, ii. 138.

Fellowship, iii. 263, 264.

Fetichism, i. 375.

Fidelity, a branch of the ethics of Christian service, iii. 220—223.

Fifth Monarchy Men. iii. 397.

Finney, his Pelagianism, iii. 74.

Fitness, the, of things. i. 338, 339.

Flacius, his doctrine of original sin, ii. 78.

Flesh (σάρξ)opposed to spirit (πνεῦμα). ii. 25, 65 ; contrasted with the Spirit (σαρκικός, πνευματικός), 26, 65 ; denoting human frailty, 26, 27, 66 ; dominion of, spiritual death, 37, 38 ; St. John's use of, iii. 6, 53 ; St. Paul's use of. 54 ; σάρκινος. 65 : applied to the human nature of Christ, 110, 111. 121 : contest between flesh and the Spirit, 202—206.

Fletcher, his doctrine of original sin. ii. 81.

Florence, Council of (A.D. 1439), decision of. respecting the canon, i. 201 : sanction of the seven sacraments. iii. 305 ; doctrine of purgatory, 383.

Foreknowledge, of God. the, i. 317—319 : relation of, to providence, 438, 454, 456.

Fortitude. one of the graces of the external conflict, iii. 214.

Frankfurt. Synod of (A.D. 794), its condemnation of adoptianism, ii. 138, 139, 190.

Fraticelli. a body of mediæval fanatics, their theory of perfection, iii. 64.

Fredegisus, of Tours (A.D. 804), his theory of inspiration, i. 180.

Freedom, one of the relative attributes of God, i. 308—311 ; of God, its relation to His moral government, 309, 310 ; the Divine, a freedom of righteousness, 310 : the relation of the freedom of God to pantheism, 310, 311 ; formal cause of sin, the abuse of, ii. 27, 28 ; one of the privileges of sonship. iii. 17 ; relation of. to the Fall and Christian ethics, 157, 158.

G.

Gehenna, iii. 378—380.

Generation, terms denoting, used to describe regeneration, iii. 6.

Gentleness, one of the graces of the external conflict. iii. 216.

Geography of the Bible. i. 220.

Geology, its evidence with regard to the antiquity of man. i. 433, 434.

Ghost, the Holy (see Spirit).

Gibbon, his objections to the argument from the rapid spread of Christianity, i. 141.

Glory, i. 287. 288.

Gnostics. influence of heathen philosophy in Gnosticism, i. 145 ; dualism of, 256, 382—385 ; their theory with regard to the spirit in man, 435; their doctrine of the origin of sin. ii. 20, 21, 24 : their doctrine of the Person of Christ, as Æon, the humanity only a semblance, 134: their doctrine of the Atonement, 299, 300 ; their doctrine of necessity. 386 ; their views of perfection. iii. 62, 63 ; their doctrine with regard to the Resurrection. 410.

God, sense of, in humanity. i. 50—52 ; exhibition of the attributes of. in revelation. 61—99 ; doctrine of, 231 —358 (see Table of Contents) : moral argument for the existence of, 236, 237 ; ontological argument for the existence of. 237, 238 ; à priori argument for the existence of, 237, 238 ; cosmological argument for the existence of. 238 : teleological argument for the existence of. 238. 239; the theory of. a merely regulative knowledge of. 244, 245 ; Elohim and Jehovah. 250—254 ; Shaddai, Adonai, 251 : polytheism, 252 ; unity of. 255—259 : Trinity of. 259—286 ; attributes of, 287—358 ; the attributes essential to the definition of. 289 ; morality in, 326—328 ; God not responsible, 327, 328 ; passions and emotions in, 328, 329 ; the standard of all holiness, 333 ; love in the

essence of, 344. 345 ; reconciliation of holiness and love in, 348, 349 ; harmony of the representations of, in the Scriptures, 357, 358 ; and the creature (see Table of Contents). 359 —456 ; image of, in man, 423—428 ; of providence (see Table of Contents), 437—446 ; transcendence of, over, and immanence of, in, the creation. 437—440 ; title applied to Christ, ii. 108—110 Resurrection of Christ ascribed to, 171, 172 ; the glory of, a branch of the ethics of intention, iii. 194—197 ; self-surrender to, a branch of the ethics of godliness, 224, 225 ; union with, 230, 231 : "ALL IN ALL" in the consummation, 426, 433 ; the beatific vision of. 452—454.

Godhead (Θεότης), meaning of the term, i. 277.

Godliness, one of the graces of the external conflict, iii. 217 ; the ethics of, based upon entire consecration. expressed in worship, and issuing in union with God, 223—231.

Goodness, one of the relative attributes of God, i. 321—324 ; relation of, to the existence of evil, 322 ; one of the graces of the external conflict. iii. 216.

Goodwin, his view of the imputation of Christ's righteousness, ii. 447.

Göschel, his doctrine of the pretemporal humanity of Christ, ii. 194.

Gottschalk (9th century), a predestinarian, ii. 99, 351.

Government, moral. of God, the, relation of the Divine freedom to, i. 309, 310 ; providential, 452—455.

Grace, one of the moral attributes of God, i. 346, 347 : Calvin's doctrine of "Common Grace," ii. 352. 387: preliminary. 358—390 (see Table of Contents), iii. 158 ; nature of, inability of man. is from God (χάρις), 359—361 ; Scriptural descriptions of prevenient. 361, 362 ; co-operation of free will and prevenient, 365, 366 ; the Holy Spirit pre-eminent in. 366, 367 : conversion (see Conversion) : efficacious. immediate, Massa Perditionis, 387, 388 ; continuity of. 390 ; standing for all the blessings of the Gospel, 392 ; means of. absolute and economical, iii. 294 —334.

Gratitude, a branch of the ethics of godliness, iii. 226, 227.

Greek Church, general remarks on the theology of. i. 18 ; canon of, 202 ; its doctrine of universal redemption. ii. 99 ; its doctrine of baptismal regeneration. iii. 22 ; its doctrine of the nature of the sacraments, 303 ; its doctrine and ritual of the sacrament of the Lord's Supper, 331.

Gregory of Ariminum, Child-tormentor. ii. 76.

Gregory of Nyssa. his views on restoration, iii. 434 ; his views on annihilation. 441.

Gregory of Nazianzum (A.D. 390), his doctrine of the Atonement. ii. 302 ; his views on eternal punishment, iii. 441.

Gregory the Great (A.D. 604). the first Pontiff, his doctrine of inspiration. i. 179 ; his doctrine of the Atonement. ii. 304 : his doctrine of purgatory. iii. 383.

Grotius, his theory of inspiration. i. 181 ; founder of the governmental theory of the Atonement, difference between his view and that of Arminius, ii. 312—314.

Guilt. consciousness of. ii. 32—35 ; guilt as fault. 35. 36 ; Αἰτία. 35 ; guilt as punishment (culpa reatus), 36—42(*see* Death, Punishment); modified by the Atonement, 41, 42 ; hereditary. 48—51 ; τέκνα φύσει ὀργῆς, 50 ; sanctification from, iii. 29—31. 35, 36 ; entire sanctification from. 60.

Guilt-offering (*see* Trespass-offering).

H.

Hades or Sheol. the descent of Christ into, ii. 167—169 ; treated of, iii. 378—380.

Hagiographa. i. 194.

Hamartiology. ii. 3.

Hannah. Dr.. his doctrine of justification, ii. 446.

Heart, meaning of. in Scripture. ii. 53.

Heathenism. Christianity a correction of the errors of, i. 52—58 : conflict of Christianity with, 144—146 ; doctrine of inspiration in, 176.

Heavens, new, iii. 447—449.

Hegel, his views concerning the knowledge of God, i. 243 ; his views respecting the Trinity, 280 : his pantheistic doctrine of the Incarnation, ii. 191.

Heidelberg Catechism, the (A.D. 1563), i. 19.

Heirship, one of the privileges of sonship. iii. 19, 20.

Hell, iii. 380.

Helvetic Confession (A.D. 1564), i. 19.

Hengstenberg, his view of the Millennium, iii. 400.

Henotheism, i. 376. 377.

Heresy used by opponents as an objection against Christianity, i. 133, 134 ; definition of. iii. 272—275.

Hermas, writings of, i. 200 : his views on eternal punishment. iii. 441.

Hermeneutics, i. 223—228.

Hierarchy, iii. 351, 353.

Hilary, his doctrine of the Trinity. i. 285 ; his application of the term "satisfaction" to the Atonement, ii. 305.

Hildebert, doctrine of transubstantiation, iii. 330.

Hinckmar, opponent of Gottschalk's predestinarianism. ii. 351.

Hippo. Council of (A.D. 393). decision of. with regard to the Canon, i. 201.

History. Biblical, i. 219—222.

Holiness and love the fundamental moral attributes of God. i. 329. 331 ; one of the moral attributes of God, 331—344 ; meaning of the term, 332—344 ; God the standard of all. 333 ; of God—the condemnation of all sin. 333. 334 ; communicative, 334 : relation of, to justice, 335 ; and love as combined in redemption, 348—351 ; real distinction between love and, 349—351 ; harmony of love, righteousness and. in the administration of redemption, 352, 353 ; of God glorified in the Atonement, ii. 278 : holiness—the unity of purification and consecration, iii. 33—35 : ἅγιοι, ἁγιασμός, ἁγιωσύνη, *ibid.* relative. 33, 275. 276 ; internal. 33. 34. 275—277 : relative and internal combined, 34. 277 ; progressive (ἁγιαζόμενοι), 39—44 ; human agency in. 39—42 ; agency of the Holy Ghost in. 42—44 : one of the notes of the Church, 275—279 (*see* Sanctity).

Hollaz, his doctrine of justification. ii. 441.

Holy (*see* Spirit). one of the notes of the Church (*see* Sanctity).

Homage, a branch of the ethics of godliness. iii. 226.

Honesty. iii. 236.

Hooker, his doctrine of justification. ii. 438.

Hope, full assurance (πληροφορία) of. iii. 118 ; one of the graces of the external conflict. 214.

Horace, his doctrine of sin. ii. 73.

Host, the adoration of, established in A.D. 1264. iii. 330.

House, mediatorial (*see* Sonship). love the supreme attribute in. i. 352, 353.

Humiliation of Christ (*see* Estates).

Humility. iii. 209, 210, 219.

Hylozoism, i. 368, 369.

Hypostasis (ὑπόστασις). meaning of the term, i. 277, 286.

Hypostatic union, ii. 118—122.

I.

Idealism, i. 418, 419.

ἰδιότης, meaning of the term. i. 277.

Idolatry, an element of spiritual death, ii. 38.

Ignatius, his doctrine of justification. ii. 419, 420 ; his doctrine of Christian perfection, iii. 62 : his doctrine of the unity of Church. 272 ; use of the term μεταβολή in reference to the sacrament of the Lord's Supper. 329 : his distinction between bishop, presbytery, and deacon. 351.

Illuminism, its views on inspiration. i. 185 ; its view of assurance. iii. 123.

Image of God in man. i. 423—428 : concreated, 426, 427 : of the eternal Son in man. 427 : relation of the Holy Ghost to. 427, 428.

Immensity, an attribute of the absolute essence of God. i. 295, 296 : relation of, to the omnipresence of God. 295.

Immortality of the soul always assumed in Scripture, iii. 372.

Immutability an attribute of the absolute essence of God, i. 302—304.

Impanation. iii. 330.

Imperfection, one of the notes of the Church, iii. 275—279.

Imputation, of sin as hereditary guilt, ii. 50 ; the three imputations, 62 : mediate, immediate, 78 ; of righteousness to the believer, non-imputation of transgression, 408, 409 : two senses of. 413 ; Methodist doctrine of, 446—448 ; of sanctity, iii. 33 ; imputationist theories of Christian perfection, 82 — 84 ; of Christ's active righteousness in relation to the doctrine of probation, 109 : of Christ's active righteousness in relation to the doctrine of perseverance. 138.

Incarnation, the, considered in its relation to the entire work of Christ, ii. 141—151 : a permanent condescension, 141, 142 ; fundamental basis of the redeeming work, 143—145 : the virtual accomplishment of the purpose of salvation, 143 ; the purpose of, that He might make reconciliation, 143—145 ; not the first step in an experiment, nor itself the bestowment of salvation, 144 ; must not have an undue preponderance. 144, 145 ; in Scripture, 145—151 ; in Old Testament predictions, theophanies, 146 ; traditions of the nations. 147 : narratives of Matthew and Luke, 147, 148 ; subsequent silence considered, 149, 150 ; relations of, to the Three Persons of the Holy Trinity, 150, 151 ; perfected in the resurrection, 170, 171 : pantheistic, 191 ; office of the Holy Ghost in, 202—204, 323.

Incense, type of the intercession of Christ, ii. 236, 237.

Indefectibility, one of the notes of the Church. iii. 285, 286.

Indulgences, ii. 308, 439 ; iii. 308.

Infallibility, Papal, i. 19, 212 ; iii. 356, 357.

Infants, baptism of, blessings sealed in. iii. 317 ; in the early Church. 319.

Infinity, an attribute of the absolute essence of God, i. 293—295.

Infralapsarianism. ii. 99.

Inspiration, that supernatural intervention of the Divine wisdom by which the miracle of prophecy is made permanent in the organic unity of Scripture. i. 62, 63 ; a credential of revelation. 92—99 ; πᾶσα γραφὴ θεόπνευστος (2 Tim. iii.

16), 92, 93 : summary of argument from prophecy, miracle, and. 98. 99 ; treated of, 156—192 (*see* Table of Contents) ; distinguished from revelation, 156, 157 ; testimony of the Scripture to its own, 157—168 ; testimony of Christ to the inspiration of the Scriptures, 159—163, 192 ; the testimony of the Apostles to. 163—168 ; dogmatic. 168—192 ; definition of, 168 ; the Holy Spirit of, 168—170 ; the organs of. 170—173 ; dynamical theory of. 171, 182, 183 ; verbal, 171, 172, 182, 189, 190 ; the Scriptures of, 173—175 ; shadow of, in heathenism, 176 ; Jewish views of, 176—178 ; Tertullian the inventor of the term "inspiratio," 178 ; plenary, 183.

Intention, relation of, to the will. iii. 170 ; the ethics of, 194—201 ; the glory of God, a branch of the ethics of, 194—197.

Interactio, meaning of the term, i. 277, 278.

Intercession, its place in worship, iii. 290.

Intercession. the. of Christ. commencing at His ascension, ii. 180. 181 ; treated of, 236—242 ; typified by incense, 236, 237 ; the presentation of *Himself*, 237, 238 ; direct supplication (παράκλητος), 238, 239 ; the objects of, the world, the Church, individuals, 239—241 ; relation of the intercession of the Holy Spirit within our hearts to, 240 ; its relation to the grace of perseverance, iii. 132.

Intercommunio, meaning of the term, i. 277, 278.

Interexistentia. meaning of the term, i. 277, 278.

Intermediate state, the, iii. 376—386 ; in the Old Testament. שְׁאוֹל, בּוֹר, 376—378 : in the New Testament. Ἅδης. 378—380 ; heathen beliefs, 380, 381 ; sleep of the soul. 381. 382 ; the theory that the resurrection is past, 382 ; mediæval divisions of Hades, 382. 383 ; modern errors concerning the Gospel in, 383—386.

Invisibility, one of the notes of the Church, iii. 280—282.

Irenæus, protest against the invoca-

tion of angels, i. 414 : his doctrine of the Atonement. ii. 299 ; his doctrine of justification, 420 ; his doctrine of Christian perfection, iii. 62 : his doctrine of the unity of the Church. 272, 273 ; his teaching with respect to the episcopate, 351 ; his millenarian views. 396 ; his doctrine of the resurrection. 410.

Irvingism. its doctrine of the Apostolate. iii. 285 ; its teaching with regard to the Christian ministry. 357, 358.

J.

Jansenism. ii. 356, 435—439 ; its view of Christian perfection. iii. 77.

Jehovah (יְהֹוָה), i. 250—254.

Jerome. his assertion of the identity of presbyters and bishops, iii. 353.

Jerusalem. decrees of the Synod of (A.D. 1672), i. 18.

Jesuit theory of Postspiratio, i. 182.

John of Damascus (A.D. 759), his doctrine of the Atonement. ii. 303.

Josephus. testimony of, to the canon, i. 195.

Joy. one of the graces of the external conflict. iii. 216.

Judaism. conflict of Christianity with, i. 142—144 ; after Old Testament. expectation of the Messiah. interpretation of prophecies concerning the Messiah, ii. 199—202.

Judge. God, the. i. 337—342 ; Christ, the. ii. 253. iii. 412—414.

Judgment, part of Christ's kingly office, ii. 253 : the (*see* Table of Contents), iii. 412—423 ; the universality and individuality of, 414—416 ; theory of Multitudinism with respect to, 415 ; conscience a test in the. 416 ; measure of revelation a test in the. 417 ; faith and works a test in the. 417, 418.

Judicial righteousness. the. of God. i. 337—342 : relation of Atonement to. 339 : final manifestation of. rewards and punishments, 339—342.

Julian. follower of Pelagius (*see* Pelagianism). the Apostate. his attempt to revive heathenism. i. 144.

Jurisprudence, a branch of ethics, iii. 166.

Justice, one of the moral attributes

of God (*see* Righteousness). i. 335—342 ; Justitia interna. 335, 336 ; distributive. the, of God. 337—342 ; retributive. the, of God. 340, 341 ; in rewards. 341, 342 : a branch of the ethics of man and man, iii. 234—237.

Justification. relation of original sin to, ii. 64 : its relation to sonship and sanctification. 393, 394 ; iii. 4, 10. 11. 17, 19, 29, 30, 35, 36 ; by faith (δικαιοσύνη), ii. 407—418 : God, the justifier, the act (δικαίωσις), 407. 408 ; man justified, pardon or remission. righteousness imputed, transgression not imputed, faith counted for righteousness. 408, 409 ; justify. meaning of the word—*to reckon just* (הצדיק). 409

—411 : justifying faith (*see* Faith); historical, 418—451 (for complete analysis of the history of the doctrine *see* Table of Contents) ; errors of the Fathers, justification often taken to mean the making righteous. love associated with faith as a ground of justification. introduction of the doctrine of good works as a ground of justification after the loss of baptismal grace, 419—423 ; mediæval errors respecting, meritum de congruo, de condigno, righteousness infused, supererogation. counsels of perfection. sacrifice of the mass, 423—425 : Methodist doctrine, laying stress upon pardon but not forgetting the absolute side of the blessing, its protest against the Calvinistic doctrine of the imputation of the active obedience of Christ. 445—448 ; its relation to Christian ethics. iii. 158, 168 ; relation of baptism to, 315.

Justin Martyr. his doctrine of inspiration, i. 178 : his subordinationist doctrine, 273 : his doctrine of the Atonement, ii. 299, 300 : his use of the term μεταβολή in relation to the Sacrament of the Lord's Supper, iii. 329 ; his millenarian views, 396 ; his views concerning eternal punishment, 411.

K.

Kant, his pantheistic doctrine of the Incarnation. ii. 191 ; his definition of ethics and physics, iii. 164.

Kathenotheism, i. 376, 377.

Kenotism, a phase of Lutheran doctrine concerning the humiliation of Christ, ii. 193.

Keys, the power of, iii. 350—359.

Kingdom. Christ's claim confirmed by His predictions as to His Kingdom, i. 108, 109 ; the, of Christ, distinguished from the Church. ii. 252 ; Christ's teaching respecting, in its relation to the Church. iii. 260—262 ; its relation to the Church. 362—364 ; its relation to the consummation, 425—427. 451.

Kingly Office of Christ (*see* Offices), commencing with His ascension. ii. 180. 181 : connection of, with His session, 182 : treated of. 249—253 ; predicted, proclaimed by our Lord, His judicial and moral right to, 248—251 ; the reward of His self-renunciation. 251 : assumption of, 251 : Divine-human only, 251 ; in the Church, distinction between the kingdom and the Church, 252 ; within the heart, 252, 253 : providence. 253 ; judgment, 253. iii. 412—414 ; the end. ii. 253 ; names of Christ belonging to, Lord of all, King of kings, Lord of lords, Judge, 259 ; in relation to His legislation, iii. 150—152.

Knowledge. one of the graces of the external conflict, iii. 217.

Kryptism, a phase of Lutheran doctrine concerning the humiliation of Christ, ii. 193.

L.

Lactantius. his etymology of the term " religion." i. 7 : his doctrine of sin, ii. 74 ; his millenarian views, iii. 396.

Laity, distinction between clergy and, made early (λαϊκὸς ἄνθρωπος). iii. 351. 352 ; modern views with regard to, 358 ; position of, in Methodism, 359.

Lateran Council, fourth (A.D. 1215). its condemnation of nihilianism, ii. 190;

its confirmation of the doctrine of transubstantiation. iii. 330.

Latitudinarianism. its view of regeneration, iii. 25 : its theory of the relation of Church and State, 278 ; its teaching with respect to the visibility of the Church, 282.

Law, the righteousness of the Divine, i. 336, 337 ; Christ the fulfilment of all, ii. 210 ; the relation of Christ to the Jewish, 210, 211 ; the moral, re-enacted by Christ, 211 ; relation of repentance to. 375, 376 ; Christianity the new, iii. 149 ; the Christian, 171—185 ; liberty and, 171—174 ; the external, a guard against antinomianism, 173, 174 ; love the fulfilment and fulfiller of, 175—185.

Legendary hypothesis of Christianity, i. 119, 120.

Leibnitz, his doctrine of the Monad, i. 23 ; his optimism. 407 ; his theory of the origin of sin, ii. 23.

Liberty, and law, iii. 171—174.

Life, regeneration described as sharing the life of Christ, iii. 9 : in Christ, the unity of the Gospel blessings, 11. 12 ; theory of "Life in Christ," 434—444 ; eternal, 449—454.

Limborch, his subordinationism, i. 284 ; his doctrine of grace and free-will, ii. 79 ; his doctrine of justification, 443 ; his doctrine of Christian perfection, iii. 84, 85.

Limbus, infantum, patrum, iii. 382.

Liturgy, iii. 293.

Local, one of the notes of the Church, iii. 282—284.

Logos. ii. 131, 132 ; the Logos Spermaticus, i. 136.

Lombard, Peter (A.D. 1164), advocate of the theory of creationism. ii. 76 ; his doctrine of grace, 77 ; his doctrine of the Atonement. 306.

Long-suffering, one of the moral attributes of God. i. 347 : one of the graces of the external conflict, iii. 216.

Lord, applied to Christ (= Jehovah), ii. 108—110.

Love (*see* Charity). and holiness, the fundamental moral attributes of God. i. 329, 330 : one of the moral attributes of God. 344—353 ; in the Divine essence, 344, 345 : reserved for redemption, 345, 346 ; relation of, to Grace, 346, 347 and holiness as combined in redemption, 348—351 ; real distinction between holiness and, 349—351 ; pre-eminence of, in the Atonement, 351 ; harmony of holiness, righteousness and. in the administration of redemption, 352, 353 ; of God, the origin of redemption, ii. 91 ; of God, glorified in the Atonement, 278 ; erroneous views of the Atonement arising from assigning a wrong place to. among the Divine attributes. 315, 316 : to God, its place in the doctrine of sanctification, iii. 28, and *seq.*; progressive, 38, 39 ; bestowal of the Spirit of. conditional. 40, 41 ; perfect. 50—56 ; perfect love commanded, 51, 52 ; nature of perfect, 51, 52 ; inwrought by the Holy Ghost, 52, 53 ; perfect, attainable in this life, 53—56 ; relation of faith to perfect, 55 ; relation of, to entire sanctification, 95, 96 ; the perfection of, in Christ, 153 ; its relation to duty, virtue, and the summum bonum. 166 : and the sensibilities, 170 ; the fulfilment and fulfiller of law, 175—185 : the guardian of obedience against antinomianism and pharisaism, 179, 180 ; the casuist. 181, 182 ; one of the graces of the external conflict. 216 : a branch of the ethics of Christian service, 219.

Lucretius, his view of the universe. i. 386, 387.

Luther, general remarks concerning his theology, i. 19 : his theory of inspiration, 179, 181 ; his views on the canon, 202 ; at first a predestinarian, subsequent modification of his views, ii. 354 ; his doctrine of justification. 439.

Lutheran theology. general remarks concerning, i. 19; its theory of grades of inspiration. 181, 182 : its doctrine of the Trinity, 280, 281 ; its views respecting the Divine foreknowledge. 318, 319 ; synergism. ii. 75, 76, 389, 390 ; iii. 24, 74 ; its doctrine of sin. ii. 77, 78 : its doctrine of universal redemption, 100 ; its doctrine of the Person of Christ, communio naturarum, or communicatio idiomatum, 191—194 ; ubiquity of Christ's human nature taught by, 192 ; Kryptists, Kenotists, 193 ; its teaching with regard to predestination various, 354—356; its doctrine of justification, 441, 442; its doctrine of baptismal regeneration, iii. 22; its doctrine of sanctification, 82—84; its theory of the unity of a national church, 274, 282; its teaching respecting the visibility of the Church, 282; its doctrine of the nature of the sacraments, 303; its doctrine of baptism, 320; its doctrine of the sacrament of the Lord's Supper, 331, 332; its doctrine of the Keys, 355, 356; its condemnation of the Anabaptists, 397; its doctrine of the resurrection, 411; its condemnation of universalism, 434; speculations of, concerning the renovation of all things, 449.

M.

Macarius of Egypt, his doctrine of perfection, iii. 66, 67.
Macedonius, one of the Pneumatomachoi, i. 275.
Maimonides, on inspiration, i. 178; his doctrine concerning the narrative of the Fall, ii. 10; on proselytes, iii. 21.
Mainz, Synod of (A.D. 848), its rejection of the predestinarianism of Gottschalk, ii. 351.
Majesty, an attribute of God, i. 302.
Man, Christian theology for, i. 5—9; the object and subject of theology, 6, 7; sense of God in, 50—52, 234—236; his place in the created universe (*see* Table of Contents), 421—436; creation of, 422, 423; God's providential care over, 450, 451; integrity of, in the resurrection, iii. 406, 407; judgment of the individual, 414, 415; mankind saved in the consummation (*see* Table of Contents), 427—447; image of God in (*see* Image).
Manes (*see* Manichæism).
Manhood of Christ, ii. 116—118.
Manichæism, influence of heathen philosophy in, i. 145; a development of the dualistic idea, 256; ii. 20; its relation to the doctrine of original sin, 63; its doctrine of necessity, 386.
Manuscripts of the Bible, i. 214, 215.

Marcus Eremita, his doctrine of perfection, iii. 68.
Marriage, the ethics of, iii. 237—243; not a sacrament, 241, 306, 308.
Martensen, his theory of inspiration, i. 184.
Mass, the sacrifice of, unscriptural, ii. 238; decreed in A.D. 1215, iii. 330.
Materialism, i. 417—419; conflict of Christianity with, 150; its relation to the arguments for the existence of God, 240, 241; its views of creation (*see* Table of Contents), 385—395; its theory of the origin of man, 431, 432; relation of, to ethics, iii. 167.
Matrimony, one of the seven sacraments of the Greek and Roman Churches, iii. 306, 308.
Matter, i. 417—419.
Maurice, his theory of inspiration, i. 183, 184.
Maximus, his doctrine of perfection, iii. 68, 69.
Means of grace, pledges of assurance, iii. 115; treated of, 294—334; the supreme, the Word of God and prayer, 295—299; the economical means: the sacraments, 299—334.
Mede, his millenarian doctrines, iii. 397, 398.
Mediator (*see* Mediatorial Ministry); surety, ii. 94; in Old Testament, "Angel of the Covenant," 95; Christ the Mediator in the Incarnation, 203; one Mediator, 203; its relation to other terms, 316.
Mediatorial ministry (*see* Table of Contents, vol. ii.); relation of, to Christian ethics (*see* Redemption).
Meditation, a branch of the ethics of godliness, iii. 230.
Meekness, an aspect of patience, iii. 214; one of the graces of the external conflict, 216.
Melanchthon, one of the principal expositors of the Lutheran theology, i. 19; at first a predestinarian, subsequent modification of his views, ii. 354; his doctrine of synergism, 389; his doctrine of justification, 439; his disposition to admit orders to be a sacrament, iii. 306.
Mercy, one of the moral attributes of God, i. 347.
Meritum, condigni et congrui, ii. 76, 388, 389, 423, 430.
Messiah (*see* Christ).

Metaphysics. its relation to Christian ethics. iii. 169, 170.

Methodist theology, general remarks concerning, i. 20, 21 ; its views on the canon, 202 : its doctrine of sin, ii. 79—86 ; compared with the Arminian doctrine, 79—82 ; compared with the Tridentine doctrine, 82—84 : compared with the Calvinistic doctrine, 84, 85 : its doctrine of universal redemption, 100 : its doctrine of Christian perfection, iii. 87—99 ; its doctrine of assurance, 125—130 ; its institution of the Class-meeting, 279 ; its doctrine of the Christian ministry, 358, 359.

Militant. one of the notes of the Church. iii. 286, 287.

Millenarianism, iii. 396, 397 ; Premillenarianism, 397 : theory of. with respect to the new heavens and the new earth, 449.

Ministry, the Christian (*see* Table of Contents), iii. 335—359 ; the term διακονία, 341, 342.

Miracles. the intervention of the Supreme Power in the ordinary course of nature. i. 62 : the credential of, 63—76 : works of God (ἔργα), 64, 65 ; signs (σημεῖον, אוֹת). 65—68 ; evidences and test of, 68—76 ; prophecy and. 91, 92 ; summary of argument from prophecy. inspiration and. 98, 99 ; the relation of to second causes, 410 : credentials of Christ's prophetic office. ii. 215.

Missionary institute, the. iii. 361, 362.

Modalism, Sabellian theory of, i. 272, 273.

Moehler, his exposition of the Tridentine doctrine of justification, ii. 435 —437 ; his exposition of the Tridentine doctrine of Christian perfection, iii. 78—82.

Mogila, Peter, confession of (A.D. 1643), i. 18.

Mohammedanism, a perversion of revealed religion. i. 13 ; Mohammed without any profession of working miracles. 66 : spread of, compared with that of Christianity, 141.

Monarchianism. i. 272.

Monasticism, iii. 354.

Monism, i. 381.

Monogamy, iii. 237—243.

Monophysites, their doctrine that there is only "one nature" in Christ, ii.

138 : their doctrine that Christ's humiliation was a renunciation of His Divine nature, 189.

Monotheism, tendencies toward, in polytheism, i. 375—381.

Monothelites. their doctrine of "one will" in Christ, condemned by the 6th Œcumenical Council at Constantinople (A.D. 680)—μία θεανδρικὴ ἐνεργεία—ii. 138 : their doctrine that Christ's humiliation was a renunciation of His Divine nature, 189, 190.

Montanism. its doctrine of inspiration, i. 179 ; its theory of perfection, iii. 63 : its theory of the internal sanctity of the Church, 278.

Moral argument for the existence of God, i. 236, 237 : attributes of God (*see* Table of Contents), 325—353.

Morals (*see* Ethics), distinguished from ethics. iii. 163, 164.

Morell. his theory of inspiration, i. 183.

Mormonism, iii. 242.

Müller, Max, his exposition of the Aryan religions, i. 375—379.

Multitudinism, theory of, with respect to the Judgment, iii. 415.

Mutability. one of the notes of the Church, iii. 285, 286.

Mystery (μυστήριον), its relation to theological science, i. 29, 30 ; of the delay of revelation, 59, 60 : urged by enemies of Christianity as an objection against it, 131—133 : a term early applied to the sacraments. iii. 301, 302.

Mysticism, general remarks concerning. i. 22, 23 ; pantheistic, influence of heathen philosophy in, 145 ; its views on inspiration, 180—182 : its doctrine of the pretemporal humanity of Christ, ii. 194, 195 ; mediæval, its doctrine of justification, 428 ; its view of justification, 450, 451 ; its theories of Christian perfection. iii. 75—77 ; its doctrine of assurance. 123, 124 : its ethics of devotion, 230 : its view of union with God. 231 ; its views of the Word of God as a means of grace, 297 ; views of mediæval, concerning the consummation. 434.

Mythical theory of the origin of Christianity. i. 120, 121.

Mythology, i. 12.

N.

Natural history, Biblical. i. 221. 222.

Nature, Divine, i. 248, 249 ; of man. 421—423 ; human, the elements of (trichotomy). 435. 436 ; meaning of term. 286 ; ii. 64 ; human, fallen, 64—71 ; human, how affected by regeneration. iii. 26, 27 ; argument for the attainability of entire consecration in this life derived from the constitution of human, 54, 55 ; human, in relation to ethics, 170, 171.

Nazarenes. sect of, their doctrine of the person of Christ. ii. 133.

Nenæus, his views on eternal punishment, iii. 441.

Neonomianism, a name sometimes given to Arminianism, ii. 444, 445.

Neo-Platonism, relation of, to the doctrine of the Trinity. i. 279, 280 ; its pantheistic view of the universe, 369, 370 ; the origin of false views of Christian perfection, iii. 77.

Nescience. i. 240, 241, 244, 245, 253.

Nestorianism, Nestorius. patriarch of Constantinople (A.D. 428), condemnation of its doctrine of the dual personality of Christ, by the Council of Ephesus (A.D. 431), ii. 136 ; and by the Council of Chalcedon (A.D. 451), 137 : adoptianism, a later form of, 138, 139 ; its view of redemption as an experiment, 294.

Newton, Sir Isaac, his statement of the teleological argument for the existence of God, i. 238. 239.

Nicæa, Council of (A.D. 325), Nicene Creed. i. 18, 179, 276 ; doctrine of the Nicene Creed with respect to angels, 411 ; its condemnation of Arianism. 275, 276 : ii. 135 ; protest of the East against " Filioque," iii. 273 ; Seventh Œcumenical Council at (A.D. 787), concession of προσκύνησις to angels, i. 414.

Nihilianism. its doctrine that the Son underwent no change through the assumption of flesh. condemned by the Lateran Council of A.D. 1215, ii. 190.

Nilus, fifth century, his doctrine of perfection. iii. 68.

Noëtianism, iii. 426.

Nominalism, its relation to the doctrine of the Trinity, i. 278, 279 ; its teaching with regard to the attributes of God, 288.

Notes of the Church, iii. 266—287.

Novatianism, its theory of the internal sanctity of the Church, iii. 278.

O.

Obedience of Christ, relation of, to the Atonement, ii. 265—267 ; its relation to other terms, 316 ; in relation to Christian ethics, iii. 152—155.

Obedience, a branch of the ethics of godliness, iii. 225 ; of children to their parents, 244 ; of servants to their masters. 245, 246 : to magistrates, 252, 253 ; to church authority, 254.

Oberlin school of theology. its doctrine of Christian perfection, iii. 73, 74.

Obligation, grounds of moral, iii. 165.

Oetinger, his doctrine of the pretemporal humanity of Christ. ii. 194.

Offices, the, of Christ, Christ justified in by His resurrection. ii. 172. 173 : fully treated of, 196—253 (*see* Table of Contents) ; His Divinity underlying all. 203 ; when assumed, 206, 207 ; Prophetic office, 207—216 (*see* Prophetic) : Priestly office. 216—249 (*see* Priestly) ; Regal office (*see* Kingly), Calvinistic view of, 309 ; His legislation bound up with, iii. 150—152.

Omnipotence, one of the relative attributes of God, i. 311 — 313 ; limitation of, 312 ; conditions of (potestas absoluta and ordinata), 313.

Omnipresence of God, relation of immensity to. i. 295, 314 : a relative attribute of God, 314, 315.

Omniscience, one of the relative attributes of God, i. 315 — 319 ; opposed to pantheism. 317 : foreknowledge and fore-ordination, 317 —319 ; scientia media. 318, 319.

Ontological argument for the being of God. i. 237—238.

Optimism, i. 407 ; iii. 430.

Orange, Synod of (A.D. 528). its condemnation of the doctrine of reprobation, ii. 351.

Orders. one of the seven sacraments of the Greek and Roman Churches, iii. 306, 308 ; Ordines Majores et Minores. 351.

Ordination to the Christian ministry, iii. 350.

Origen, his doctrine of inspiration. i. 179 ; his doctrine of the Trinity, 272. 273 : his definition of Divine justice, 341 ; his doctrine concerning the narrative of the Fall. ii. 10 : his doctrine of the fall of the soul in a pre-existent state, 75. 301 : his errors respecting the Atonement,300, 301 : his doctrine of free will and grace, 386 : his doctrine of justification. 420: his errors concerning the Counsels of the Gospels, and in the fundamental idea of justification, 420, 421 ; his doctrine of the intermediate state. iii. 287 ; opponent of the Thnetopsychitæ, 381 : his opposition to millenarianism, 396 ; his doctrine of the resurrection, 410 ; his doctrine of restoration (ὑπὲρ παντός and χωρὶς Θεοῦ.), 432—434.

Original sin (*see* Table of Contents, vol. ii.). doctrine of. its relation to the origin of evil. ii. 25—27 : its relation to the first Adam. 47—55 : hereditary guilt. 48—51 ; hereditary depravity, 51—55 ; Old Testament proofs of. 51, 52 ; New Testament proofs of. 53—55 ; its relation to the Second Adam, 55—61 : χάρις and δωρεά, 55—61 ; modified by the Atonement. the "Free Gift," the Spirit restored, human nature preserved from sinking below the possibility of redemption, condemnation removed from the race. sin and grace. 56—61 ; its general theological relations, 61—63 ; theodicy, statement of St. Paul's vindication and of the imputationist view of St. Paul's method, 61—63 ; relation to God's government of nations, 63 ; its relation to Christian doctrine, to the Atonement. to regeneration, to justification, and to sanctification, 63. 64 ; its relation to the constitution of man's nature. examination of the term "human nature," human nature in bondage. σάρξ, σάρκινος, σαρκικός, πνευματικός, this bondage considered in relation to the spirit of man, bondage of the will, objec-

tions against this view considered, 64—68 ; its relation to the development of sin. sin habitual and actual, mortal and venial (a false distinction), of omission and commission, voluntary and involuntary, unpardonable. sin in the regenerate, 68—71 : history of the doctrine, 72—86 ; profane. 72, 73 ; Jewish : in the Old Testament. and in Rabbinical Judaism. 73, 74 ; Patristic : Vitium Originis, 74, 75 ; Pelagian controversy, fifth century, 75. 76 ; Scholastic ; transitional, creationism and traducianism, immaculate conception. 76, 77 : Tridentine : combination of Augustinian realism and semi-pelagianism, 77 ; Lutheran : formularies constructed in the Augustinian spirit. Synergism, Flacianism, 77. 78 ; Reformed : mediate and immediate imputation, federal theology, 78 ; Arminian, 78, 79 ; Methodist : compared with Arminian, its connection of the universality of grace with that of redemption, extracts from Wesley. Fletcher. and Watson ; compared with the Tridentine doctrine, sin in the character ; compared with Calvinism ; agreement of the Methodist doctrine with St. John's First Epistle, comparison between St. John's First Epistle and Rom. v., the destruction of sin accomplished in the perfectly regenerate, 79—86 ; Rationalistic: its denial of the doctrine, 86 ; Augustine's doctrine of, 349 ; relation of. to free-will, 364 ; in what sense abolished in the entirely sanctified. iii. 47 ; Finney's doctrine of. 74 ; relation of, to Christian ethics, 157, 158.

Ormuzd (*see* Zoroaster).

Orthodox, use of the term by the Eastern Church. iii. 283.

Osiander, his doctrine of the Mediator, ii. 203 ; his doctrine of justification, 440.

Otto of Bamberg, the first to define the seven sacraments (A.D. 1124), iii. 305.

P.

Paganism, origin of the name. i. 144.
Paley. his definition of ethics, iii. 164.
Pantheism, conflict of Christianity

with. i. 147—150; its views on inspiration, 185, 186; its views respecting the knowledge of God,
243, 244; its views respecting the
essence of God, 248, 249, 252, 253;
Divine protest against, 257; its
views of the Trinity, 279, 280; its
views of the spirituality of God,
293; relation of the freedom of
God to, 310, 311; opposition of the
omniscience of God to, 317; its
errors with regard to creation, 367—
372; polytheism a perversion of,
372—375; its relation to the doctrine of providence, 438; its relation to the doctrine of sin, ii. 22,
72; its doctrine of the Incarnation, 191; its doctrine of the
Person of Christ, 194; certain views
of the Atonement tinged with, 314,
315; Calvinism related to, 352;
pantheistic fatalism in relation to
the doctrine of, probation, iii. 107;
relation of, to ethics, 167.

Papias, his millenarian views, iii. 396.

Paraclete (Παράκλητος), name common to Christ and the Holy Ghost,
iii. 265, 266.

Paradise, iii. 378—380.

Parousia, iii. 389, 390.

Parsism (see Zoroaster).

Passion of Christ, part of His humiliation, ii. 159, 160; its relation to
His crucifixion, the death predestined, the cross foreknown, the
crucifixion the fulfilment of prophecy, the act of the world, the
cross His altar, the symbol of the
curse, 160—163.

Passover, the, a sacrifice for sin, and
a peace-offering, origin of, Christ
our, ii. 231, 232; combined with
the day of atonement, 235, 236;
relation of, to the Lord's Supper,
iii. 325—328.

Pastor, iii. 344.

Patience, one of the graces of the external conflict, iii. 214, 217.

Patriotism, iii. 253.

Patripassians, i. 272.

Patristic theology (see under history
of the various doctrines), general
remarks on, i. 17, 18, 21.

Paul of Samosata (A.D. 261), his doctrine of the Person of Christ, ii. 134.

Peace, one of the graces of the external conflict, iii. 216.

Pearson, Bishop, his doctrine of the
Trinity, i. 285.

Pelagianism, its doctrine of sin, ii. 75,
76; its view of God's eternal purpose
of redemption, 98, 99; Semi-Pelagian
tendency in the Ante-Nicene age,
386; its doctrine of free-will, 386,
387; Semi-Pelagianism, its doctrine
of will and grace, 388, 389; its doctrine of human agency in regeneration, iii. 24; its theories of Christian
perfection, 69—73; Semi-Pelagian
views of Christian perfection, 74,
75; its errors respecting the Word
of God as a means of grace, 297.

Penance, Romish sacrament of, its
relation to the doctrine of assurance, iii. 122; its nature, 306—
308; admitted by the apology for
the Augsburg Confession, 306; its
relation to the doctrine of the
Christian ministry, 352; relation of,
to the doctrine of the Keys, 354.

Pentecost, relation of the gift of the
Holy Ghost to Christ's ascension
and session, ii. 182, 183; commencement of the dispensation of the
Holy Spirit, 324—326; relation of,
to the new law, iii. 154; relation of,
to the foundation of the Church,
262—266; relation of baptism to,
313.

Perfection, an attribute of the absolute essence of God, i. 304, 305;
Christian, iii. 56—99 (see Table
of Contents); attainable in this
life, 56, 57; passages in which the
word has a less intense meaning,
56, 57; importance of the qualifying term Christian or Evangelical,
58; relative, 58, 59; probationary,
59; only individual, 59; under
ethical law, 59, 60; needing the
Atonement, 60; in the court, house,
and temple, 60, 61; counsels of (see
Counsels); a branch of the ethics
of intention, 198—201.

Perfections of God, the (see Attributes), meaning of term, i. 288.

Perfectionists, iii. 64.

Περιχώρησις, meaning of the term,
i. 277, 278; Lutheran use of, 280.

Perrone, his doctrine of inspiration,
i. 182.

Perseverance, iii. 131—147 (see Table
of Contents); the doctrine of Final,
examined, 137—147.

Person (Persona), i. 277, 286.

Personality, its connection with freedom, ii. 28, 363. 364 : in relation to conscience, love, and will, iii. 170, 171.

Petersen, his doctrine of the pretemporal humanity of Christ, ii. 194.

Pfaff, his theory of inspiration, i. 181.

Pharisaism, love the guard of obedience against, iii. 179, 180.

Philanthropy, iii. 233.

Philaret, Catechism of (A.D. 1839), i. 18.

Philo, his doctrine concerning the narrative of the Fall, ii. 10 : and his influence upon Christian thought, i. 280.

Philology of the Bible, i. 222, 223.

Philosophy, its relation to religion, i. 12, 13 ; errors of Greek, with regard to creation, 368, 369 : the religion of the old world, iii. 162.

Philosophy, moral, relation of Christian ethics to, 163—171 : influence of Christianity upon the vocabulary of, 164, 165 ; grounds of moral obligation, 165.

Physics, Kant's definition of, iii. 164.

Pietists, their views on inspiration, i. 182 : their view of Christian perfection, iii. 87, 97 ; their doctrine of assurance, 123.

Pity, one of the moral attributes of God, i. 347.

Placæus, his doctrine of sin, ii. 78.

Plato, his definition of God, i. 246 ; relation of his teaching to the doctrine of the Trinity, 279, 280 ; his theory of trichotomy, 435.

Platonists, the English, their view of Christian perfection, iii. 87.

Plenary Inspiration, theory of. i. 183.

Plotinus, his pantheistic view of the universe, i. 369.

Pneumatomachoi, the, i. 275.

Pœna, damni and sensus, ii. 76.

Poiret, his doctrine of the pretemporal humanity of Christ, ii. 194.

Polemics, i. 16.

Politics, a branch of ethics, iii. 166 ; ethics of, 251—253.

Polycarp, his doctrine of inspiration, i. 178 ; his doctrine of the Trinity, 271 ; his doctrine of Christian perfection, iii. 62.

Polygamy, iii. 242.

Polytheism, i. 252 ; its views of creation. 373—381 : origin of, 373—375 : tendencies towards the doctrine of one God in, 375—381.

Ponerology, ii. 3, the etymology of πονηρία, 31.

Pontificate, the Romish, iii. 353.

Porphyry, his pantheistic view of the universe, i. 369.

Positivism, conflict of, with Christianity, i. 150 ; its relation to the argument for the existence of God, 241 ; its account of the universe, 392—395 ; the necessitarianism of, iii. 164.

Possession, demoniacal, i. 415, 416.

Postspiratio, Jesuit theory of, i. 182.

Praise, a branch of the ethics of godliness, iii. 225—227 ; its place in worship, 290.

Praxeas (A.D. 160—180), his Patripassian doctrine, i. 272.

Prayer, a branch of the ethics of godliness, iii. 227—229 ; distinction between προσευχή, δέησις, αἴτημα, ἐρωτάω, ἔντευξις, 228, 229 : its place in worship, iii. 290 ; one of the supreme means of grace, 298, 299.

Predestination, its relation to omniscience, i. 317—319 ; (*see* Augustine, Calvinism), (*see* Vocation, Election), ii. 348—357 ; in relation to the doctrine of probation, iii. 107—109.

Prelacy, iii. 284.

Presbyters (πρεσβύτεροι), the identity of, and bishops in the New Testament, iii. 342 : difference between the term and " bishop," 343.

Presbytery (πρεσβυτέριον), iii. 343 (Acts xxii. 5) ; related not to individual churches but to congregations of churches, 346, 347 ; distinguished from bishop and deacon by Ignatius, 351.

Presence, the Real, doctrine of, iii. 333.

Preservation, the graces of, a branch of the ethics of the external conflict, iii. 208—213.

Priesthood, priests anointed with holy oil, ii. 198.

Priesthood, universal, of believers, iii. 335—337 ; the Romish, 353, 354.

Priestly Office of Christ (*see* Offices) ; His intercession commencing with His ascension, ii. 180, 181 ; treated of, 216—249 (*see* Table of Contents) ; when assumed, 217, 218 ;

the high priest, vocation, consecration, and functions, 218—221 ;
general priestly functions. 221—
236 ; rites of sacrifice. 221—230 (see
Sacrifice) ; intercession and benediction (see under these words) ; the
Jewish and the Christian temple,
244—249 ; the type, the altar, the
tabernacle, the temple, 244—246;
the antitype, Christ, the Church.
heaven and earth. 247, 248 ; atonement belonging especially to, 248,
249; names belonging to.High Priest,
Priest.Propitiatory,Lamb. Paraclete.
Propitiation. 259 ; Socinian view of.
311 ; in relation to His legislation,
iii. 150—155.
Primacy, Romish errors concerning,
iii. 284. 285.
Probation, of Adam and Eve, ii. 13—
15 ; Christian, iii. 101—112 (see
Table of Contents) ; idea of a
covenant involved in (διαθήκη and
συνθήκη distinguished). 101.
Procession, the, of the Holy Ghost,
i. 266.
Proclus, his pantheistic view of the
universe. i. 369.
Propaganda. the Romish. iii. 362.
Properties of God. the, i. 288.
Prophecy, the intervention of the
supreme knowledge. imparted to
man independently of the ordinary
laws of knowing, i. 62 ; one of the
credentials of revelation. 76—91 ;
רָאָה נָבִיא, 76 ; laws of, 79—85 ;
Christ the supreme subject of, 80,
81 ; double sense of, 80 ; progression in, 81, 82 : reserve in, 82—84 ;
a sign to every generation, 84, 85 ;
tests of, 85—91 ; and miracle. 91,
92 ; cumulative. 91, 92 ; summary
of the argument from miracle,
inspiration. and, 98, 99.
Prophetic Office, of Christ (see Offices);
Christ the supreme Revealer. i.
38, 39 : treated of, ii. 207—216 ;
personal ministry of Christ, minister of the circumcision, 207—213 ;
a continuation of the ancient prophetic economy, 208 ; characteristics of His teaching, 209, 210 ;
Prophet for the world, 210 : Lawgiver and Preacher, 210—213 ; the
preaching of the Gospel prophetic
of the kingdom, 212 ; prophecies of

Christ through His Apostles, 212,
213 ; universal ministry of Christ,
Himself the Truth. and the Prophet (נָבִיא and רָאָה), credentials
of His office, Christ's revelation the
final and abiding one, 213—216 ;
names belonging to, Rabbi, Master,
Teacher, Minister of the Circumcision. Wisdom of God, Light of
the World. the Truth, True Light,
258 ; in relation to His legislation,
iii. 150—152.
Prophets, consecrated with holy oil,
ii. 198 : an extraordinary and transitional order in the New Testament,
iii. 339.
Propitiation (see Atonement), Christ
the, ii. 238, 242, 259 ; distinguished
from expiation, 274, 275 ; its relation to other terms. 316.
Proselytes, Jewish, iii. 21.
Πρόσωπον, meaning of the term, i. 277.
Protestant, general remarks on Protestant theology, i. 18, 19 ; doctrine
of justification, ii. 439—442 ; doctrine of the visibility of the Church,
iii. 281, 282 ; doctrine of the sacrament of the Lord's Supper, 331—
333 ; doctrine of the Keys, 355, 356.
Protevangelium, ii. 92.
Providence (see Table of Contents),
i. 437—456 ; general and special,
444—446 ; relation of, to sin, 453 ;
relation of. to redemption, 453,
454 ; principles of Theodicy, 455 ;
relation of the terms πρόνοια,
πρόθεσις, πρόγνωσις, 438, 453, 454,
456.
Prudence, a branch of the ethics of
Christian service, iii. 222.
Psychology, its relation to Christian
ethics, iii. 170, 171.
Psychopannychia, iii. 381.
Punishment (of sin). final, relation of,
to the judicial righteousness of God,
i. 340, 341 : death, ii. 36—42 ; death
spiritual, 37, 38 ; death physical,
38, 39 ; death eternal, 39 — 42 ;
nature of, iii. 429, 430 : doctrine of
eternal (see Consummation, Universalism, Annihilationism, &c.).
Purgatory, iii. 287, 308, 382, 383.
Puritanism, its high theory of the
internal sanctity of the Church, iii.
278.

Q

Quakers, their views on inspiration, i 182 , their doctrine of Christian perfection, iii 75, 76, their doctrine of assurance. 123, their abolition of the Christian ministry. 357

Quietists, their view of Christian perfection, iii 77, their view of assurance, 123, 124

R

Rabbinical Judaism a perversion of revealed religion i 13, its doctrine of sin, ii 74 , the doctrine of baptismal regeneration probably a result of, iii 21

Racovian Catechism its theory of inspiration, i 182, its doctrine of the Atonement, ii 311

Radbertus, Paschasius, the first to express the doctrine of transubstantiation iii 330.

Rationalist theology. general remarks on, i 23, its views on the Canon, 209—211, its doctrine of sin. ii. 86, its watchword, Intellige ut credas, 377, its view of justification 149 150 its errors respecting the Word of God as a means of grace iii 297

Ratramnus his support of Gottschalk in his predestinarianism, ii 351, his opposition to Radbertus' doctrine of transubstantiation, iii 330

Realism its relation to the doctrine of the Trinity, i 278 279, its teaching with regard to the attributes of God 288, 289, philosophical theory of, as opposed to idealism 417—419.

Reason. relations of, to faith i 43—46, 209—211.

Reconciliation (καταλλαγή), ii 271—273 282—287, God, the Reconciler and the Reconciled, 282—284, the world reconciled personal reconciliation, 284—287, its relation to other terms, 316

Rectoral righteousness of God, the, i. 336, 337

Redemption, relation of Providence to, i 453 454, sin and, ii 13—46 (*see* Atonement), in the eternal purpose of God, 90—100, foretold, 92, 93, prepared for, 93, gradual unfolding

of the covenant of grace. 93—96, accomplishment of, 96—98, Augustine s view of the eternal purpose of God 98, 99, hypothetical. doctrine of. 99 Redemptional Trinity. 101—103, theory of a pretemporal covenant of, discussed 102 sealed by the resurrection of Christ 172 173, treated of particularly, 287—297, terminology (λύτρον, ἀγοράζειν, λύειν, ῥύεσθαι). redemption by price and by power 288, from the bondage of sin as a condemnation and as a power, from the bondage of Satan, and from the bondage of death 289 290 the Price the Life, Blood and Self of Christ, 290 connection between the price and the salvation satisfaction to justice. purchase of the redeemed for the Redeemer paying of a debt, cancelling a bond, 290—292 , a Divine transaction in its origin, methods, and results, 293 errors examined, no discord in the Divine nature not paid to Satan, not an experiment, all of grace, 293 294, universality of, à priori arguments for, from the instinct of man, the nature of God, the dignity of the Redeemer positive assertions of Scripture 294—296 special 296 297, its relation to other terms, 316 , administration of (*see* Table of Contents, vols ii and iii), application of, objection to the term, 319, appropriation of, objection to the term 319, relation of to Christian ethics, iii 158, 159, 168

Reformed theology, general remarks concerning, i 19, its theory of inspiration, 181, its views on the Canon 202 its doctrine of sin. ii. 78 its doctrine of predestination,99, ii 352,353, its doctrine of the person of Christ as opposed to the Lutheran. ii 191, 192 its doctrine of the Atonement, 309 its doctrine of the visibility of the Church iii 282, its theory respecting Church and State 282, its doctrine of the nature of the sacraments, 303, 304 its doctrine of the sacrament of the Lord's Supper 332, 333, its doctrine of the Christian ministry 356

Regal, the, Office of Christ (*see* Kingly)

Regeneration, relation of original sin to, ii. 64; connection of, with preliminary faith, 382; its relation to sonship and sanctification, 394; its relation to adoption and sonship, iii. 3, 4, 14; παλιγγενεσία, τέκνα, iii. 4; passages in which it is united with adoption, 4, 5: branch of sonship, 5—13 (see Table of Contents); generation, terms used to describe, 6; described as creation, renewal (νέος, καινός, and their compounds), 6, 7; described as new birth, 7; described as resurrection, 7—9; described as circumcision, 8, 9; described as introduction into a new world, 9; described as illumination, 9; described as sharing the life of Christ, 9; described as a new law within, 9, 10; described as renewal into the Divine image, 10, 11: the central blessing of the Christian covenant, 11, 12; relation of the means of grace to, 12, 13; baptismal, 21—23; put first in the order of bestowment of Gospel privileges by Calvinism, 25; sanctification from defilement corresponding to, 29, 30; relation of, to Christian ethics, 158, 159, 168; relation of baptism to, 315.

Relative attributes of God, the (see Table of Contents). i. 307—353.

Religion, the meaning of the term. i. 7: the art of which theology is the science, 25; religiousness of man, 52—58; science of religions, 55—58, 379—381.

Remission, idea of, in the Levitical sacrifices, ii. 230.

Remonstrant Confession, general remarks concerning. i. 19, 20; Apology for, its doctrine of sin. ii. 79 (see Arminian), its definition of sacraments, iii. 304; its doctrine of the sacrament of the Lord's Supper, 332, 333.

Renewal, regeneration described as—νέος, καινός, and their compounds, iii. 6, 7; into the Divine image, 10, 11.

Repentance incapable of expiating sin, ii. 44, 45; relation of conversion to, 369—371; definition of. 371, 372; Divine in its origin, 372, 373; human evidences of, contrition, submission, amendment, 373, 374; relation of,

to law, 375, 376; relation to faith, after regeneration, 384, 385: a branch of the ethics of conversion, iii. 193.

Reprobation, not the result of a decree, ἀδόκιμοί, ii. 346, 347; failure under test, iii. 102—104.

Resignation, a branch of the ethics of godliness, iii. 225.

Restorationism, its relation to the doctrine of probation, iii. 110 (see Universalism).

Resurrection, regeneration described as, iii. 7—9; of man (see Table of Contents), 401—411; testimony of the Old Testament to the, of man, 402, 403: testimony of the New Testament to the, of man, 403; relation of, to Christ's Person and work, 403, 404; Christ the Pledge, Pattern, and Source of the, of His people, 404—406; ἐξανάστασις, 405, 406, 409; the identity of the body in, 407, 408; two resurrections, 409; the doctrine of, distinctive of Christianity, 409, 410.

Resurrection, the, of Christ, a step in His exaltation. ii. 169—178: in its dogmatic relations, 169—173; its relation to His Person, proving His Divinity and the perfection of His Divine-human Person, 169—172; its relation to His redeeming work, viewed under the offices of Prophet, Priest, and King, 172, 173; evidences of, 173—178: the great evidence of His Messiahship, 173, 174; the forty days, 174—176; time of, 175; assaults upon, considered, 176, 177; the Holy Ghost, the supreme witness, 177, 178: the Church an evidence of, 177, 178; evidence in the hearts and lives of believers, 178: relation of, to the regeneration of believers, iii. 8; the ground of objective assurance, 113, 114.

Revelation, i. 35—155 (see Table of Contents); meaning of the term (ἀποκάλυψις), 36—38; other terms, φωτίζειν, φανεροῦν, οὐκ ἀμάρτυρον, 36, 37; general and special, 37; external and internal, 37, 38; the complete revelation in Christ, contained in the Scriptures, 38—40; Christ, the substance of all, 38, 39; as received by man, the Christian

Faith, 42—155 , addressed to faith, the relations of faith to reason in the acceptance of, 42—46 , a response to the religious expectation of mankind, 49—61 , Christianity the perfecting of former revelations 58—60 , mystery of the delay of, 59 60 ; exhibition of the attributes of God in, 61—99 , distinguished from inspiration 156 157 , the measure of, a test in the Judgment, III 117.

Reverence, a branch of the ethics of godliness III 225. 226

Rewards, final, relation of, to the judicial righteousness of God, I 341, 342 ; of fidelity in the ethics of Christian service. III 223

Righteousness one of the moral attributes of God, I 335—342 , the essential, of God, 335, 336 , communicated, 335, 336 , rectoral, of God, 336, 337 , judicial, of God, 337—342 , the judicial, of God under an economy of grace, 339 , final manifestation of the judicial, of God, rewards and punishments, 339—342 , relation of, to holiness and love in the Atonement, 349—351 ; harmony of holiness love, and, in the administration of redemption 352 353 , of Christ, active and passive, II 158, 159 ; put for all the Gospel blessings, 392 , its relation to sanctification and sonship 393 394 , III 41, 42 imputed and inwrought, II 397 , regarding the Gospel as administered in the court, 399, 400 Christian privilege of 402—451 (*see* Table of Contents) , objective the righteousness of God, 402—407 , in Christ Our Righteousness, a vindication of Divine justice just honour put upon the merit of Christ, 403, 404 , in the Gospel ($\delta\iota\kappa\alpha\iota\sigma\sigma\acute{\nu}\nu\eta$) connected with faith the Divine method of justifying the ungodly 404—407 , subjective. applied to man, 407—418 (*see* Justification) , imputed, 408, 409 , historical, 418—451 Christian perfection in relation to, III 58, 60, 199

Ritualism, III 293 294

Romanism, differences between the Greek Church and, I 15 (*see* Tridentine)

Rothe, his theory of inspiration, I 184.

Rule of faith, I 33—230 (*see* Table of Contents).

S

Sabbath, the, III 290—292

Sabellianism, I 272, 273, 281—283, III. 426

Sabellius (A D 250), his doctrine of the Trinity, I 272, 273.

Sacraments (*see* Baptism , Supper, the Lord's), their relation to regeneration, III 23 , Sacramentalism in relation to probation, 110, 111 , pledges of assurance, 115 , sacramentarian views of assurance, 122, 123 , their place in the ethics of Christian fellowship, 254 , influence of a false doctrine of in producing an exaggeration of the doctrine of the external sanctity of the Church, 278 , the dignity of, endangered by Ritualism, 294 the economical means of grace (*see* Table of Contents). 299—334 , the term Sacramentum, 301 , the seven, of the Greek and Roman Churches 305—309 , the term distinguished from Communion and Eucharist. 325—328.

Sacrifice, Levitical rites of a type of Christ, II 221—236 presentation of the victim, and the laying on of hands 221, 222 , slaughtering and sprinkling of the blood 222, 223 , burning of the offering and the sacrificial meal, 223, 224 , various offerings, 224—230 origin of, 224 225 burnt-offering (עוֹלָה), its twofold meaning of expiation and self-surrender, 225, 226 , peace-offerings 226 , sin-offerings and trespass-offerings, חַטָאת and אָשָׁם 226—229 distinction between sin and guilt offerings, 227. 228 , sin-offerings for individuals and for the people, 228. 229 purifications, 229 unity of all sacrifices, 229 230 sacrificial seasons, 231—236 (*see* Passover) . (*see* Atonement, day of) . of Christ 265—267 , idea of added to the Eucharist in the third century, III 329

Salvation preliminaries of state of (*see* Table of Contents, vols II and III) , unity of Gospel privileges, ii. 391—401 ; general terms—related to God, GRACE : related to man. SALVATION, LIFE, KINGDOM OF GOD, EARNEST OF THE SPIRIT, the ATONEMENT received, PROMISE IN CHRIST BY THE GOSPEL, 392, 393 : all the blessings administered by the Holy Ghost as the special application of the Atonement. the communion of the Holy Ghost. He revealing and attesting justification and adoption, and sanctifying the believer, order of thought demanding a distinction between the blessings, 393, 394 ; Gospel blessings, one in union with Christ, 394—397 ; errors concerning union with Christ, some making it to be union with the Church, others a privilege of the elect to whom it has been eternally decreed, 396, 397 : each Gospel blessing perfect, perfection in the law court, in the house, in the temple, terminology ; blessings either absolute or relative, external or internal, declaratory or imparted, imputed and inwrought, forensic or moral, ideal or actual (realised), unconditional to the Church, or conditional to individuals, 397—399 ; diversity in unity of the Gospel privileges, righteousness regarding the Gospel as administered in the mediatorial court, sonship as in the house, sanctification as in the temple, 399—401 : righteousness (see Righteousness).

Sanctification, relation of original sin to, ii. 64 ; put for all the Gospel blessings, 392 : its relation to sonship and righteousness, 393, 394, iii. 41, 42 : external and internal, ii. 397 : regarding the Gospel as administered in the TEMPLE, 401 : its relation to sonship, iii. 4 : its relation to regeneration, 11, 12 : doctrine of, treated, 28—99 (see Table of Contents), (see also under Consecration, Holiness), relative, 33 : internal, 33, 34 ; relative and internal combined, 34 ; ἁγιασμός, 33, 34 ; the Divine act of, 34 ; ἁγνεία and ἁγνότης, 34 ; καθαρίζω and its compounds, 29, 34, 39, 40 : term used to express consecration, 34 : predicated of all the elements of human nature, 35 ; ἁγιαζόμενοι, 39 ; human agency

in, 39—42 : effected by the Holy Ghost, 42—44 ; "higher life," "second blessing," terms not warranted by Scripture, 44, 64, 65 ; relation of faith to entire, 55 ; entire sanctification the ethical aim of the Christian, 200 ; relation of baptism to, 316.

Sanction, of moral law, iii. 159, 160 ; of fidelity in the ethics of Christian service, 222, 223.

Sanctity, one of the notes of the Church, iii. 275—279 ; external and internal, 275—277.

Satan, the prince of the evil spirits, i. 411 : personality of, 415 ; the original sinner, ii. 4, 5 : names of, in Scripture, 6 : not redeemed, 46 : redemption from bondage to, 289 ; one of the enemies of the Christian, iii. 207, 208.

Satisfaction, connoted by the trespass-offering, ii. 227 ; in the court what expiation is in the temple, 274 ; first applied to the Atonement by Hilary and Ambrose, revived by Anselm, 304, 305 ; its relation to other terms, 316.

Scapegoat (לַעֲזָאזֵל), its relation to Christ, ii. 233, 234.

Scepticism, i. 48.

Schism, meaning of the term in New Testament, iii. 270 ; Patristic view of, 272, 273 ; modern view of, 274, 275.

Schleiermacher, his theory of inspiration, i. 183, 185, 186 ; his views respecting the Trinity, 282, 283 : his classification of the attributes of God, 291 : his doctrine of sin, ii. 25.

Scholastic theology, general remarks concerning, i. 21, 22 ; its doctrine of sin, ii. 76, 77 (see under history of the various doctrines).

Science, theology a, i. 24—32 : theology scientific in its aim, 25 : theology scientific in its methods, 25, 26 ; peculiarities of theological science, 28—32 : of religions, 55—58 : conflict of Christianity with false, 147 —150 : objections against the, of the Bible, 190, 191.

Scotists, the followers of Duns Scotus, their doctrine of the Atonement, ii. 307.

Scriptures, contain the perfect revelation, i. 39—41 ; identity of, with the

Christian faith, 41 the inspiration of, a credential of revelation 92—99, worthy of Divine authorship, 93, 94. Divine-human, 94, supremacy of, 94, 95, unity of. 95, 96, development in, 96 97 the argument from the presence of the Divine Hand in the construction of Scripture analogical. 97, 98, the inspiration of (*see* Table of Contents) 156—192, the testimony of, to their own inspiration 157—168; testimony of Christ to 159—163 192, testimony of the Apostles to, 163—168, the, of inspiration, 173—175, internal difficulties and discrepancies of, 186—192, autographs not preserved, 187 — 189 objections against the science and ethics of, 190, 191, probationary character of, 191,192, the Canon of (*see* Canon), the fabric of 217, 218, Biblical history, 219—222 chronology of, 219 220, geography, archæology, and natural history of 220—222, philology of 222, 223, hermeneutics of, 223—228 the exegesis of 229,230.

Seals the sacraments iii 302—305, baptism a seal, 316,317, the Lord's Supper a seal, 326 327

Self selfishness first manifestation of sin, ii 30,31; ascendency of spiritual death 37 renunciation of, a branch of the ethics of intention, iii 197 198, renunciation of, a branch of the ethics of the external conflict. 208—212, self-examination, 212 213, self-sacrifice for the good of others, 218—220, surrender of a branch of the ethics of godliness, 224, 225

Self-sufficiency (αὐτάρκεια) of God, one of the attributes of the absolute essence of God i 300—302

Seneca moral philosophy of, iii 167

Separation, in the judgment (κρίσις), iii 419 420.

Seraphim, i 412

Serpent, the tempter ii 8 9

Servant of Jehovah a title applied to Christ (παῖς), ii 124, 125, 128, 146, 184, 256

Service, ethics of Christian, iii 217—223; devotion to Christ, 217, 218; zeal for the good of others 218—220, fidelity to our trust, 220—223

Session, the, of Christ (*see* Ascension)

subject of prophecy ii 181 dwelt upon throughout New Testament, 181, 182 connection of Kingly office with 182

Shaddai (שַׁדַּי) i 251

Sheol (שְׁאוֹל), iii 376—378

Signs, Scripture name for miracles (σημεῖον, אוֹת), i 65—68 the sacraments, iii 301 302 baptism a sign 316 317 the Lord's Supper, a sign 326 327

Simplicity, iii 196

Sin, not good disguised i 322 323 not ordained for the Divine glory, 323, the evil of, controlled by the Divine goodness, 323, 324, relation of, to Providence, 453, origin of the word "sin," ii 34, doctrine of (*see* Table of Contents) 1—86 Scripture terms for, 3, 29—32 41 origin of i 1—19 origin of, in the universe. 4—6, original sinner 4, 5, origin of in the world, 6—19, Fall (*see* Fall) the original probation 13—15, origin of, a mystery, 15, 27, principle of. what? 15, first sin spiritual and sensuous 15, 16, effects of 16 17; modified by the Atonement 19, 41, 42 46 theories of origin of, 20—28, theory of necessary principle of evil, 20—22, theory which accounts for the origin of sin by the limitation of finite nature 22—24 theory which accounts for the origin of sin by the sensuous nature of man 24—27, doctrine of original sin in relation to the origin of evil 25—27, "body of sin" law of sin 25 26 theory of the abuse of freedom, 27 28; nature of sin. 29—42, self-separation from God 29—32 guilt (*see* Guilt) punishment of (*see* Guilt), (*see* also Punishment), development of 38, an accident of the nature 38, sin and redemption, 43—46 God's nature opposed to 43 man unable to expiate 43, 44, repentance cannot atone for, 44 45 original sin, 47—71 (*see* Original Sin), habitual and actual 68 69 mortal and venial, 69 iii 303 of omission and commission, voluntary and involuntary, unpardonable, ii 69, 70, history of doctrine, 72—

86 : sin-offering (*see* Sin-offering) ; redemption from bondage of, ii. 289, 290 ; erroneous doctrines concerning the Atonement arising from light views of. 315 ; relation of free-will to the bondage of, 364 ; sanctification from guilt and defilement of, iii. 29—35 ; sanctification from, progressive, 35 — 38 ; sanctification from. entire. 44—50 ; eternal, the sanction of moral law, 160.

Sinlessness of Christ, i. 114, 115, ii. 117. 118.

Sin-offering (חַטָּאת), ii. 226—229 ;

distinguished from guilt-offerings, 227, 228 ; connoting the idea of expiation, 227 : for individuals and for the people, 228, 229.

Slavery. iii. 246, 247.

Sleep of the soul, iii. 381, 382.

Smalkald articles, Lutheran formulary, their doctrine of sin. ii. 77, 78 ; doctrine of justification (*see* History of the Doctrine of Justification).

Sobriety, one of the graces of preservation, iii. 212 : a branch of the ethics of Christian service, 219.

Society. distinguished from Church, iii. 282.

Socinian theology. general remarks concerning, i. 20 ; its views on inspiration, i. 182 ; its denial of God's foreknowledge of contingencies. 319 ; its doctrine of sin, ii. 86 ; Socinian doctrine of the Person of Christ compared with the Unitarian, 133 ; denial of the Atonement. Divine sovereignty of mercy, denial of the possibility of substitution, sacrificial language figurative, priesthood in heaven only. repentance and obedience the ground of forgiveness, 309—312 : its view of justification, 448, 449 ; its doctrine of the nature of the sacraments, iii. 304.

Socrates, his theory of creation, i. 368.

Son. God the, in the Old Testament, i. 262—264 ; in the New Testament, 264—267 : in creation, 362, 363 ; in providence, 441, 442 ; His subordination in the work of redemption. ii. 104, 105 ; His incarnation. 113—116 : relation of, to the Incarnation. 150 : Agent in regeneration. iii. 5 : adoption more generally ascribed to Him than

regeneration, 5 ; relation of adoption to. 14.

Sonship. the Christian privilege of. put for all the Gospel blessings, ii. 392 ; its relation to sanctification and righteousness, 393, 394 : declaratory and imparted, 397 ; regarding the Gospel as administered in the house, 400 ; iii. 4 ; branch of the state of salvation, 3—27 (*see* Table of Contents) ; adoption external, regeneration internal, 3 ; relation of, to the Trinity, 4 ; its relation to justification and sanctification, 4, 41, 42 ; passages in which regeneration and adoption are united, 4. 5 : privileges of, 16—20 ; Christian perfection of, 58, 60, 199, 200 ; relation of baptism to, 315, 316.

Sonship, the eternal. of Christ, doctrine of, i. 264, 265 ; the ground of His incarnation,. ii. 103 ; relation of Christ's Sonship to our sonship, 116 : iii. 4.

Sophocles, his doctrine of sin, ii. 73.

Soteriology, ii. 319 : objective and subjective, 320.

Soul, the, of man, renewed (ψυχή), iii. 11, 26.

Sovereignty. of God. the ordinary meaning of this term unscriptural, i. 354, 355; absolute. ii. 62, 351—354 ; its relation to the doctrine of probation, iii. 107—109.

Spener, his views on inspiration. i. 182 ; doctrine of Christian perfection, iii. 97.

Spinoza, his doctrine of the one eternal substance, i. 23, 24 ; his views on inspiration, 185, 186 ; his views on the Divine essence, 253 ; his pantheistic view of the universe, 370, 371 ; relation of his pantheism to ethics, iii. 167.

Spirit, God the Holy, i. 292, 293 ; His office in producing a conviction of the truth of revelation. 44, 45 ; a credential of revelation, 150—155 ; in inspiration, 157, 168 —170 : testimony of. to the canon, 204, 205 ; His relation to the hermeneutics of the Bible, 228 ; in the Old Testament, 262—264 ; in the New Testament, 264—267 : personality of, 266 : procession of, 266 ; in creation. 362, 363 ; relation of, to the image of God in man, 427, 428 ;

in providence, 442 πνευματικός ii
26 , " Free Gift," 59—61 , His relation to redemption, 104 · assertion of
the Divinity of by the Council of
Constantinople (A D 381), 135, 136,
relation of, to the Incarnation 150,
151, 202—204 , gift of, depending on
the resurrection of Christ, 173 . His
witness to the resurrection of Christ,
177 , gift of, the proof of Christ's
ascension, and demonstration of His
authority, 182 183 , anointing oil
the emblem of. 197 , descent of,
upon Christ at His baptism, 204—
207 , relation of His intercession
within us to the intercession of
Christ, 240 benediction of Christ
in His priestly office imparted
through, 244 , His office in the
administration of redemption, 321
—334 ; in the Old Testament, the
Giver of Life, in the Prophets,
322 323 , in the Gospels, His office
in the Incarnation, in the Redeemer's work, promises of 323,
324 , after Pentecost, 324—334 ;
economy of the Spirit the dispensation of the finished Atonement
and of the Spirit, one , still in a
sense Pentecost the introduction of
a new economy 325, 326 , Representative of the Saviour, 326—329 ,
the Paraclete. 328 ; the Agent in
personal salvation, external and
internal functions, 329 , in the
Church the Spirit forming the
Church (ἐκκλησία), in which He is
supreme as the representative of
its Head, the Church the organ of
the Spirit, 330, 331 · a personal
Divine agent a gift (τὸ πνεῦμα τὸ
ἅγιον and πνεῦμα ἅγιον). 331 — 334 ;
the Gospel call made by, 341 , of
grace, 359, 362 pre-eminent in the
co-operation of grace and free-will,
366, 367 , faith of the operation of,
382 , unity of Gospel privileges as
seen in the fact that they are all
administered by the Holy Spirit as
the special application of the Atonement, 393, 394 , justifying faith, of
the operation of, 413, 414, 415 ,
agent in regeneration, iii 5, 6
(τὸ πνεῦμα το ζωοποιόν); adoption declared and attested by. 14. 15: the
guidance of, one of the privileges
of sonship, 18, 19 , the earnest of

our inheritance, 20 ; sanctification
effected by 28, 31—33, 36, 38, 39,
42—44 ; effusion of the Spirit of
sanctification conditional, 40 , perfect love inwrought by 52, 53 ,
dishonoured by ascetic theories of
perfection, 60 , witness of, 115—
117 , witness of, historical, 122—
130 , the constant impartation of,
the grace of perseverance 133,
134 ; the strength of our virtue,
156 ; contest between flesh and,
202—206 ; self-resignation to, one
of the graces of preservation, 211—
212 , relation of, to the foundation
of the Church, 262—266 , unity of
the Church maintained by, 271 ,
makes the Word of God effectual
as a means of grace, 296, 298.
Spirit of man, creation of, i 422, 423 ;
dichotomy and trichotomy, 423,
435 436 , πνεῦμα opposed to σάρξ,
ii 25 , denoting the Divine nature
of Christ, 110—112 , renewed, iii.
11. 26 , witness of our own, 120—
122
Spirits i 409—411 ; probation and
fall of, 410 ministering, 412—414
Spirituality, an attribute of the absolute essence of God, i 292, 293 ,
relation of, to worship, 293
State, Church and iii 278 ; reformed
and Lutheran theories respecting
Church and State, 282
Stancarus his doctrine of justification
ii 440
Staupitz, his doctrine of justification,
ii 428, 429
Stœudlin, his view of justification, ii
449.
Sublapsarianism iii 108
Submission, an aspect of patience, iii
214 a branch of the ethics of godliness, 224 225 to those in authority in the Church 254
Subordinationism, i. 273, 274, 278,
283, 284 285
Subsistences, meaning of the term,
i. 286.
Substance, meaning of the term as
applied to God (οὐσία), i 248, 249,
277 286
Substitution, the idea of, the basis of
atonement, unqualified for the race
(ἀντί, ὑπέρ ἀντίλυτρον ὑπὲρ πάντων),
for Christ's people modified by the
ideas of representation and mystical

union, ii. 269—271 ; denied by the Socinians, 310, 311.

Suetonius, his testimony to the expectation of a Messiah, ii. 201.

Summum bonum, iii. 156, 160, 166.

Supererogation, works of, iii. 81, 82, 184, 185.

Superintendent, the Methodist, iii. 358, 359.

Supernatural, revelation supernatural, i. 61—63 ; the supernatural order, 75, 76.

Supper, the Lord's, relation of, to regeneration, iii. 23 : the sacrament of, fully treated, 325—334 (see Table of Contents) ; relation of the Passover to, 325—328 ; the ratification of the covenant, 326, 327 ; the ritual of, 328 ; the Patristic doctrine of, 329 ; the mediæval doctrine of, 330, 331 ; the Protestant doctrine of, 331—333 ; modern views of, 333, 334.

Supralapsarianism, ii. 99, 351, 352.

Swedenborg, his views respecting the Trinity, i. 281, 282 ; his doctrine of the Person of Christ, ii. 195.

Sympathy of Christ with His people, ii. 240, 241.

Synergism, Lutheran doctrine of, a form of Semi-Pelagianism, ii. 77, 78, 389, 390 ; iii. 24, 25, 74.

T.

Tabernacle, the, ii. 245, 246.

Tacitus, his doctrine of sin, ii. 73 ; his testimony to the expectation of a Messiah, 201.

Talmudism, a perversion of revealed religion, i. 13.

Teleological argument for the existence of God, i. 238, 239.

Temperance, one of the graces of the external conflict, iii. 217.

Temple, the, ii. 244—249 ; Christ the antitypical, 246, 247 ; the Church the antitypical, 247 ; heaven and earth the antitypical, 247, 248 ; mediatorial, holiness the supreme attribute in, i. 332, 333, 352 ; term " sacrifice " referred to, ii. 267 ; sanctification terms referred to, 399 —401, iii. 28 ; perfection in, 60.

Temptation from within, iii. 205.

Tendency, theory of the origin of Christianity, i. 121—123.

Tenure of covenant blessings, iii. 100 —147 (see Table of Contents).

Tertullian, " animus naturaliter Christianus," i. 53; inventor of the term " inspiratio," 178, 179; his doctrine of the Trinity, 272 ; his doctrine of sin, ii. 74 ; his doctrine of the Atonement, 299 ; his references to the ceremony of baptism, iii. 319 ; his mention of sacrifices for the dead, 329 ; germs of the doctrine of purgatory, 383 ; his millenarian views, 396.

Tetratheism, its relation to the doctrine of the Trinity, i. 278, 279.

Thanksgiving, a branch of the ethics of godliness, iii. 226, 227 ; its place in worship, 290.

Theism, i. 13.

Theodicy, i. 191, 445, 446, 453—455.

Theodore of Mopsuestia, his theory of inspiration, i. 179 ; real founder of Nestorianism, ii. 136 ; his views on restoration, iii. 434 ; his views on annihilation, 441.

Theodoret, his doctrine of justification, ii. 420 ; his assertion of the identity of bishops and presbyters, iii. 353.

Theodotus (A.D. 180), his denial of the divinity of Christ, ii. 134.

Theology, definitions, i. 3, 4 ; for man, 5—9 ; Christian, 10—14 ; natural, confirmed and supplemented by Christian, 10, 11, 52—58 ; perversions of natural and revealed religion, 12, 13 ; in the Church, 14— 24 ; the Word of God the sole source of, 14, 15 ; laws of its development within the Church, 15—24 ; expository, catechetical, Biblical, apologetic, dogmatic, historical, polemical, and systematic, 15, 16, 26, 27, 229, 230 ; confessional, 16—24 ; difference between Eastern and Western, 18 : a science, 24—32 ; its aim scientific, 25 ; its methods scientific, 25 ; the peculiarities of the science of, 28—32 ; analysis of the system of, 27, 28 ; unity of, 28 ; conventional terms of, 30, 31 ; theologia viatorum and theologia beatorum, 248 ; the Divine attributes the foundation of, 353, 354 ; natural, and science, 399 ; the place of angels in, 416.

Theopaschitism another name for monophysitism ii 189

Theophanies, relation of to the Incarnation ii 146 147

Theophilus of Antioch, his doctrine of the Trinity (Τριάς), i 271

Thnetopsychitæ, iii 381.

Thomists followers of Thomas Aquinas their doctrine of the Atonement ii 307

Thucydides, his doctrine of sin, ii 73

Toledo Synod of (A D 594) its addition of 'Filioque' to the Nicene Creed, i 275

Tradition, Romish doctrine of, i 13, 180, 211—213

Traducianism, i 429 ii 76

Transcendentalism, its doctrine of incarnation, ii 191, its doctrine of the Trinity, 193 194

Transgression, ii 30 (see Sin) 68

Transmigration of souls, iii 380, 381

Tree of knowledge ii 7—13

Tree of life, ii 7—13, 39

Trent, Council of (see Tridentine)

Trespass-offering (אָשָׁם), really guilt-offering, ii 33 treated of 226—229; connoting the idea of satisfaction, 227

Trichotomy, theory of, i 435 436

Tridentine theology, general remarks concerning i 19, its doctrine of the authority of tradition 180, decision of the Council of Trent respecting the canon, 201, its doctrine with respect to angels, 414, its doctrine of sin, ii 24, 25 76, its doctrine of sin compared with that of Methodism 82—84 its doctrine of universal redemption its doctrine of the Atonement, satisfaction to Divine justice fully recognised meritum superabundans, not availing for the sins committed after baptism, not the sole meritorious ground of justification 307, 308, its doctrine of grace and free-will, meritum de congruo meritum de condigno (see Meritum), its doctrine of justification, 429—439 its doctrine of baptismal regeneration, iii. 22 its theories of Christian perfection, 77—82, its doctrine of probation, 110, 111 its doctrine of assurance 122 123, its view of marriage, 241, 242, its

doctrine of an earthly vicar of Christ, 265 266, its teaching with respect to Church and State 278, its exaltation of visibility as a note of the Church, 281; its use of the term Catholic, 283, primacy 284; its doctrine of purgatory (see Purgatory) its doctrine of the nature of sacraments, 302 303 its doctrine of the seven sacraments iii 305—309 doctrine of transubstantiation 330,331; its doctrine of the Keys, 335

Trinity, the, i. 259—286 (see Table of Contents); the attributes of the Divine essence applied to, 306 307 in creation, 362, 363 in providence 440—443, independent of the work of Christ, ii 103, transcendental doctrine of, 193 194 in the priestly benediction, 242, 243 revealed in the Atonement, 276, 277; relation of, to sonship iii 4, Persons of, Agents in regeneration, 5, 6, relation of adoption to, 14 15 relation of to Pentecost, 263, the Object of worship, 289 relation of to the consummation, 425—427

Trinity redemptional or economical in creation, i 362, 363 treated of, ii 101—105 unity of the Triune purpose of redemption, 101, relations of, to redemption, 102—105 its relation to Christian worship, iii 289

Triumphant, one of the notes of the Church, iii 286, 287

Triune name, the i 255—286 (see Table of Contents)

Triunity of God the, i 270

Truth, one of the moral attributes of God i. 342—344, a branch of the ethics of man and man iii 236

Tubingen tendency theory of the origin of Christianity, i 121—123

U

Ubiquity of God, relation of immensity to i 295, of Christ's human nature, a doctrine of Lutheranism, ii 192; iii 331,332

Unbelief i 48

Uncials i 214, 215

Unction (see Anointing), Extreme, one of the seven sacraments of the

Greek and Roman Churches, iii. 306—309.

Understanding, full assurance (πληροφορία) of, iii. 118.

Union with Christ, regeneration described as, iii. 9; ground of the unity of the Church, 268, 269.

Union with God, a branch of the ethics of godliness, iii. 230, 231.

Unitarian theology, general remarks concerning, i. 19; its doctrine of sin, ii. 86; its doctrine of the Person of Christ compared with the Socinian, ii. 133; its view of the Atonement, 312; its view of justification, 448, 449.

Unity, the, of God, i. 255—259.

Unity, one of the notes of the Church, iii. 267—275; the ground of union with Christ, 268, 269; basis of, 270; maintained by the Holy Ghost, 271; not uniformity, 271, 272, 273.

Universalism, its relation to the doctrine of probation, iii. 109, 110, treated of, 429—434.

Universality of redemption, à priori arguments for, from the instinct of man, the nature of God, the dignity of the Redeemer, ii. 294, 295; assertions of Scripture direct and indirect, 295, 296; its relation to vocation, 336, 337.

Universe, created, the (see Table of Contents), i. 408—436; terms describing (πάντα, τά πάντα, ἡ κτίσις, ὁ κόσμος, οἱ αἰῶνες), i. 408.

Utilitarianism, its definition of ethics, iii. 161.

V.

Valence, Synod of (A.D. 855), its adoption of the predestinarianism of Gottschalk, ii. 351.

Variety, one of the notes of the Church, iii. 267—275.

Vedas, i. 375—379; the cosmogony of, 401.

erbal inspiration, i. 171, 172, 182, 189, 190.

Virtue, Christ's obedience was, iii. 153; the strength of our, 156; what, in Christian ethics? 166.

Visibility, one of the notes of the Church, iii. 280—282.

Vision, beatific, the, iii. 452—454.

Vocation (καλεῖν, κλῆσις, κλητός), ii. 335—357; Vocation and universal redemption, 336, 337; historical process, 337—340; the indirect or universal, 337, 338; direct, through the Word, in Old Testament to the people first elected, then called; in New Testament to all men, first called, then elected, 338—340; nature of, 340—347; the proclamation of salvation, the offer of its blessings, the command to submit to Christ, 340, 341; in the Church through the Word by the Spirit, 341—344; the Divine intention in, 344, 345; calling and election, no vocatio interna as distinguished from vocatio externa, election the result of accepting the call, 345, 346; contingency, the call may be resisted, blessings of election may be forfeited, reprobation (ἀδόκιμοί) not the result of a Divine decree, 346, 347; historical, 348—357; its relation to probation, iii. 102, 103; to the Christian ministry, 349.

W.

Watchfulness, one of the graces of preservation, iii. 212, 213.

Watson, Richard, his doctrine of original sin, ii. 81, 82; on imputation, 447.

Watts, Isaac, his doctrine of the Person of Christ, ii. 195, 196.

Wegscheider, his view of justification, ii. 449.

Wesley, his doctrine of original sin, ii. 80, 81; his doctrine of justification, 445—447; his doctrine of entire sanctification, iii. 87—99; his doctrine of assurance, 126—130.

Wessel, his doctrine of the Atonement, ii. 307.

Westminster Confession (A.D. 1643—1648), i. 19; its theory of inspiration, 181; its predestinarian doctrines, ii. 353; its doctrine with regard to baptismal regeneration, iii. 22; its doctrine of assurance, 125; its definition of sacraments, 304.

Will, in God, i. 308, 309; relation of, to sin, ii. 38; bondage of, in fallen man, 67; free-will, Limborch's doctrine of, 79; St. Bernard's doctrine of, 84, 85, sin in the character not merely in the will, 83, 84, free treated of 363—367, psychology of free-will, relationship to the personality and conscience, relation to the bondage of sin 363, 364, relation of grace to free, 364—367; history of the doctrine of the relation of free-will to grace, 386—390, Ante-Nicene age controversy against the necessitarianism of the Gnostics, the Greeks exaggerating the function of will the Latins making much of grace tendency Semi-Pelagian 385, Pelagian doctrine of free-will, 386 387 Augustine's doctrine of the will and grace, common grace, efficacious grace, immediate grace, massa perditionis, 387 388 intermediate theories between Pelagianism and Augustinianism Semi-Pelagianism Synergism, Arminianism 388—390, Romanist meritum de congruo, meritum de condigno, 388 389 Methodist, prevenient grace bestowed upon all men continuity of grace, 390, and intention, iii 170

Wisdom one of the relative attributes of God, i 319—321, of God compared with that of man, 320; in the Gospel, 321

Witness of the Spirit, of our own spirit (*see* Assurance)

Witsius theory of inspiration i 182.

Wolfenbuttel Fragments, hypothesis of the manifestation of Christ, i 115

Word (*see* Logos) the, of God, the Gospel call through, ii 341 342, the instrument in regeneration, iii 12, 13, one of the supreme means of grace, 295—298 (*see* Scriptures).

Works, a Scriptural name of miracles (ἔργα), i 64, 65, the evidence of justifying faith, ii 415—418 and faith a test in the judgment, iii 417, 418.

World, the, as opposed to the Christian, iii 206, 207, duty of the Church to 255—258

Worship, relation of spirituality of God to, i 293; a branch of the ethics of godliness, iii 225—230 the ethics of public, 254, the Church as an institute for 287—364; the Divine order of 288—292 human forms of, 292—294, ritualism in. 293, 294, means of grace, the Word of God prayer and the sacraments, 294—334

Wyclif, a predestinarian, ii 99

Z.

Zoroaster, his views concerning creation i 382 : his cosmogony, 401, relation of his teachings to the doctrine of sin, ii 20, 21, 22

Zwingle one of the principal expositors of the Reformed theology i 19 his doctrine of predestination, ii. 351, his doctrine of the nature of the sacraments, iii 304 his doctrine of the sacrament of the Lord s Supper, 332

LONDON
PRINTED BY BEVERIDGE AND CO.,
HOLBORN PRINTING WORKS FULWOOD'S RENTS, W.C.